Gewidmet allen Partnern, Mitarbeitern und Bauherren,
durch die dieses Buch erst entstehen konnte.

Dedicated to all the partners, co-workers and owners
who made this book possible.

© Prestel Verlag,
München · Berlin · London · New York 2007
und
von Gerkan, Marg und Partner, Hamburg

Die Deutsche Bibliothek verzeichnet diese Publikation
in der Deutschen Nationalbibliografie;
detaillierte bibliografische Daten sind im Internet über
http://dnb.ddb.de abrufbar.
The Deutsche Bibliothek holds a record for this
publication in the Deutsche Nationalbibliografie;
detailed bibliographical data can be found under:
http//dnb.ddb.de

Library of Congress Control Number: 2006939121

British Library Cataloguing-in-Publication Data
A catalogue record for this book is available from the
British Library.

Prestel Verlag
Königinstraße 9
D-80539 München
Tel. +49 (89) 38 17 09-0
Fax +49 (89) 38 17 09-35
www.prestel.de
info@prestel.de

Prestel Publishing Ltd.
4, Bloomsbury Place
London WC1A 2QA
Tel. +44 (0)20 7323 5004
Fax +44 (0)20 7636 8004

Prestel Publishing
900 Broadway, Suite 603
New York, N.Y. 10003
Tel. +1 (212) 995 2720
Fax +1 (212) 995 2733
www.prestel.com

www.gmp-architekten.de

Herausgeber Editors
Meinhard von Gerkan, Volkwin Marg

Redaktion Editing
Bernd Pastuschka, Gonni Engel, Bettina Ahrens

Verlagslektorat Copyediting
Claudia Stäuble, Danko Szabó

Übersetzung Translation
Murphy Translation Office

Grafische Gestaltung und Satz
Graphic Design and Typesetting
Birgit Meyer;
Tom Wibberenz, ON Grafik

Bildrecherche und digitale Bildbearbeitung
Picture Research and Digital Picture Editing
Beatrix Hansen, Dominic Daubenberger

Reproduktion Origination
Satz und Bild, Altenburg

Druck und Bindung Printing and Binding
Druckerei zu Altenburg

Herstellungsleitung Production Supervision
Marina Arnoldt

Gedruckt auf chlorfrei gebleichtem Papier
Printed on acid-free paper

Printed in Germany

ISBN 978-3-7913-3811-8

Umschlagabbildung Cover
Bergbauarchiv Clausthal-Zellerfeld
Mining Archive Building, Clausthal-Zellerfeld
Foto Photo
Jürgen Schmidt

von Gerkan, Marg und Partner

Bauten Buildings

Herausgegeben von Edited by
Meinhard von Gerkan und Volkwin Marg

PRESTEL
München · Berlin · London · New York

Inhalt
Content

10 40 Jahre gmp – Veränderung. Reflektion. Neue Wege.
Gert Kähler
40 years of gmp – Change. Reflection. New Paths.
Gert Kähler

1967–1969

32 Stormarnhalle, Bad Oldesloe
Bad Oldesloe Stormarn Hall
Max-Planck-Institut für Aeronomie, Lindau/Harz
Max Planck Institute for Aeronomics, Lindau/Harz
→ 34
Wohnhaus Köhnemann, Hamburg
Köhnemann Residence, Hamburg

1970–1972

36 Sportzentrum Diekirch, Luxemburg
Diekirch Sports Centre, Luxembourg
Wohn- und Bürogebäude Fontenay, Hamburg
Residential and Office Block on the Alster (Fontenay), Hamburg
Apartmenthaus Alstertal, Hamburg
Alstertal Apartment Block, Hamburg

1974–1975

38 Hauptverwaltung Deutsche Shell AG, Hamburg
Deutsche Shell AG Headquarters, Hamburg
→ 42
Flughafen Berlin-Tegel
Berlin-Tegel Airport
→ 44
Tower, Flughafen Berlin-Tegel
Tower, Berlin-Tegel Airport
Brücken, Flughafen Berlin-Tegel
Bridges, Berlin-Tegel Airport
→ 52

Energiezentrale und betriebstechnische Anlagen, Flughafen Berlin-Tegel
Central Energy Station and Operational Facilities, Berlin-Tegel Airport
→ 54
Frachtanlage, Flughafen Berlin-Tegel
Freight Centre, Berlin-Tegel Airport

40 Hauptverwaltung Aral AG, Bochum
Aral AG Headquarters, Bochum
Schulzentrum Friedrichstadt
School Centre, Friedrichstadt
Lärmschutzkabine, Flughafen Berlin-Tegel
Noise Protection Cabin, Berlin-Tegel Airport
→ 58
Flugzeugwartungshalle, Flughafen Berlin-Tegel
Maintenance Hangar, Berlin-Tegel Airport
Streugutlager, Flughafen Berlin-Tegel
Grit Depot, Berlin-Tegel Airport

1976–1977

60 Finanzamt Oldenburg
Oldenburg Revenue Office
Sportforum der Universität Kiel
Kiel University Sports Forum
→ 62
Kreisberufsschule Bad Oldesloe
Bad Oldesloe Vocational School
Psychiatrische Anstalten, Rickling
Psychiatric Hospital, Rickling

1978

64 Stadthäuser, Hamburg BAU 78
City Houses, 'Hamburg BAU 78'
→ 66

Einfamilienhaus-Siedlung, Hamburg BAU 78
Single-Family House Estate, 'Hamburg BAU 78'
Taxistandüberdachung, Flughafen Berlin-Tegel
Taxi Stand Roofing, Berlin-Tegel Airport
Gewerbeschule für Chemie, Pharmazie und
Gartenbau – G 13, Hamburg-Bergedorf
Vocational School for Chemistry, Pharmacy and
Gardening – G 13, Hamburg-Bergedorf

1979

68   Wiederaufbau der „Fabrik", Hamburg-Altona
Reconstruction of 'Fabrik', Hamburg-Altona
Wohnquartier Kohlhöfen, Hamburg
Kohlhöfen Residential District, Hamburg

1980

70   Hanse-Viertel, Hamburg
Hanse Viertel, Hamburg
→ 72
Europäisches Patentamt, München
European Patent Office, Munich
→ 76
Taima und Sulayyil, Saudi-Arabien
Taima and Sulayyil, Saudi Arabia
→ 74
MAK, Kiel
MAK, Kiel
Biochemisches Institut der Universität Braunschweig
Braunschweig University, Biochemical Institute

1981–1982

78   Renaissance-Hotel Ramada, Hamburg
Ramada Renaissance Hotel, Hamburg
Haus „G", Hamburg-Blankenese
House 'G', Hamburg-Blankenese
Psychiatrische Anstalten, Rickling
Psychiatric Hospital, Rickling
Erweiterungsbau der Hauptverwaltung OTTO-Versand, Hamburg
Extension of the OTTO Versand Headquarters Hamburg
Gemeindehaus Ritterstraße, Stade
Ritterstrasse Parish Hall, Stade
Schaulandt „Black Box", Hamburg
Schaulandt 'Black Box', Hamburg

1983

80   Innenministerium Kiel
Ministry of the Interior, Kiel
Wohnanlage für Behinderte, Hamburg-Südring
Residential Estate for the Handicapped, Hamburg-Südring
Kontorhaus Hohe Bleichen, Hamburg
Hohe Bleichen Office Block, Hamburg
Parkhaus Poststraße, Hamburg
Poststrasse Parking Garage, Hamburg
→ 82
DAL-Bürozentrum, Mainz
DAL Office Centre, Mainz
→ 84

1984

86   Verwaltungsgebäude der Deutschen Lufthansa, Hamburg
Deutsche Lufthansa Administration Building, Hamburg
Hillmann-Garage, Bremen
Hillmann Parking Garage, Bremen
→ 90

Marktarkaden, Bad Schwartau
Market Arcades, Bad Schwartau
Energiesparhaus, Internationale Bauausstellung, Berlin
Low-Energy House, International Building Exhibition, Berlin
→ 92

1984–1985

88   Stadthäuser, Berlin-Tiergarten, Internationale Bauausstellung
City Houses, Berlin-Tiergarten, International Building Exhibition
Plaza-Hotel, Bremen
Plaza Hotel, Bremen
Cocoloco – Bar und Boutique im Hanse-Viertel
Cocoloco – Bar and Boutique in the Hanse Viertel, Hamburg
Psychiatrische Krankenhäuser Rickling-Thetmarshof und
Rickling-Falkenhorst
Psychiatric Hospitals, Rickling-Thetmarshof and Rickling-
Falkenhorst

1986–1987

94   Parkhaus der Oberpostdirektion, Braunschweig
Multi-Storey Car Park of the Braunschweig Post Office
→ 96
Wiederaufbau Landhaus Michaelsen als Puppenmuseum
Reconstruction of the 'Michaelsen Country House' as Doll's
Museum, Hamburg
Gewerbeschulzentrum, Flensburg
Vocational School Centre, Flensburg
Grindelallee 100, Hamburg
Grindelallee 100, Hamburg
→ 98

1988–1989

100 Komplex Rose, Rheumaklinik, Bad Meinberg
Rose Complex, Rheumatology Clinic, Bad Meinberg
→ 102
Neugestaltung des Einkaufszentrums Hamburger Straße,
Hamburg
Renovation of the Hamburger Strasse Shopping Centre,
Hamburg
Wohnhaus Saalgasse, Frankfurt/Main
Residential Building, Saalgasse, Frankfurt/Main
Justizbehörden in Flensburg, Um- und Erweiterungsbau
Legal Authority in Flensburg, Conversion and Extension
Wohnbebauung am Fischmarkt, Hamburg
Residential Development at 'Fischmarkt', Hamburg
Innenhofüberdachung des Museums für Hamburgische
Geschichte
Courtyard Roofing of the Museum für Hamburgische
Geschichte

1990

104 gmp Hauptsitz, Elbchaussee 139, Hamburg
gmp Head Office, Elbchaussee 139, Hamburg
→ 108
Restaurant „Le Canard", Elbchaussee 139, Hamburg
Restaurant 'Le Canard', Elbchaussee 139, Hamburg
→ 114
Oberpostdirektion Braunschweig
Post Office Divisional Administration, Braunschweig
Ausbildungszentrum der Hamburgischen Electricitätswerke,
Hamburg
Training Centre of the Hamburgische Electricitätswerke, Hamburg
→ 118
106 Moorbek-Rondeel, Norderstedt
Moorbek Rondeel, Norderstedt
→ 120

106	Parkhaus, Flughafen Hamburg
Multi-Storey Car Park, Hamburg Airport
→ 122
Lazarus Krankenheim, Berlin
Lazarus Hospital, Berlin
Stadthalle Bielefeld
Civic Centre, Bielefeld
→ 126	172	Bayerische Hypotheken- und Wechselbank, Hamburg
Bayerische Hypotheken- und Wechselbank, Hamburg
Flughafen Hamburg, Terminal 2
Hamburg Airport, Terminal 2
→ 176
Wohnstift Augustinum, Hamburg
Augustinum Home for the Aged, Hamburg
→ 182
Flughafen Stuttgart, A-Mitte – Terminal 2
Stuttgart Airport, A-Centre – Terminal 2

1991

134 Justizbehörden in Flensburg, Um- und Erweiterungsbau
Legal Authority in Flensburg, Conversion and Extension
Carl Bertelsmann Stiftung, Gütersloh
Carl Bertelsmann Foundation, Gütersloh
→ 138
Flughafen Stuttgart, Terminal 1
Stuttgart Airport, Terminal 1
→ 146
Groß-Sporthalle, Flensburg
Large Gymnasium, Flensburg
Café Andersen, Hamburg
Andersen Café, Hamburg
Stadtbahnhaltestelle, Hauptbahnhof Bielefeld
Urban Railway Station "Bielefeld Central Station"

136 Kavaklidere Komplex, Ankara, Türkei
Kavaklidere Complex, Ankara, Turkey
→ 142
Saar-Galerie, Saarbrücken
Saar Galerie, Saarbrücken
Stadtzentrum Schenefeld, Hamburg
Schenefeld Town Centre, Hamburg
Wohn- und Geschäftshaus, Buchholz
Residential and Commercial Block, Buchholz
Hillmannhaus, Bremen
Hillmann House, Bremen
Miro Datensysteme, Braunschweig
Miro Data Systems, Braunschweig
→ 152

1992

156 Wohnhaus von Gerkan, Elbchaussee 139, Hamburg
von Gerkan Residence, Elbchaussee 139, Hamburg
→ 158
Jumbohalle der Deutschen Lufthansa, Hamburg
Deutsche Lufthansa Jumbo-Jet Hall, Hamburg
→ 162
Salamander-Haus, Berlin
Salamander House, Berlin
→ 166
S-Bahnhof, Flughafen Stuttgart
Suburban Railway Station, Stuttgart Airport
→ 168

1993

170 Zürich-Haus, Hamburg
Zürich House, Hamburg
→ 174
Steigenberger-Hotel, Fleetinsel, Hamburg
Steigenberger Hotel, Fleetinsel, Hamburg
Arbeitsamt Oldenburg
Oldenburg Labour Exchange
OPD Hannover – Fernmeldeamt 2
Hanover Post Office Divisional Administration –
Telecommunications Office 2
Energie Aktiengesellschaft Mitteldeutschland (EAM), Kassel
Energie Aktiengesellschaft Mitteldeutschland (EAM), Kassel

1994

184 Hillmann-Eck, Bremen
Hillmann-Eck, Bremen
Musik- und Kongresshalle Lübeck
Music and Congress Hall, Lübeck
→ 192
Galeria Duisburg
Duisburg Galeria
→ 198

186 Amtsgericht Braunschweig
Law Court, Braunschweig
→ 200
Wohn- und Geschäftshaus Schaarmarkt, Hamburg
Schaarmarkt Residential and Commercial Building, Hamburg
Deutsche Revision AG, Frankfurt/Main
Deutsche Revision AG, Frankfurt/Main
→ 190
Bank- und Geschäftshaus Brodschrangen, Hamburg
Bank and Commercial Building Brodschrangen, Hamburg
→ 204
Rehaklinik Trassenheide, Usedom
Rehabilitation Clinic, Trassenheide, Usedom
→ 188

1995

206 Deutsch-Japanisches Zentrum, Hamburg
German-Japanese Centre, Hamburg
→ 208
Messe Hannover, Halle 4
Hanover Trade Fair, Hall 4
→ 212
Stadtvilla Dr. Braasch, Eberswalde
Dr. Braasch Town Villa, Eberswalde

1996

216 Solarpavillon, Kiel
Solar Pavilion, Kiel
Neue Messe Leipzig
New Leipzig Trade Fair
→ 218
Allee-Center, Leipzig-Grünau
'Allee-Center', Leipzig-Grünau
Hapag-Lloyd, Hamburg
Hapag-Lloyd Office Building, Hamburg

1997

224 Block 203, Friedrichstraße, Berlin
Block 203, Friedrichstrasse, Berlin
→ 230
Dresdner Bank am Pariser Platz, Berlin
Dresdner Bank at Pariser Platz, Berlin
→ 232

Praxis Dr. Manke, Uelzen
Dr. Manke Practice, Uelzen
→ 252
Sternhäuser, Norderstedt
Star Houses, Norderstedt

226 Restaurant VAU, Berlin
VAU Restaurant, Berlin
→ 236
Typendach für die Deutsche Bahn AG
Serial Platform Roofing for Deutsche Bahn AG
→ 238
Wohnbebauung, Berlin-Friedrichshain
Residential Development, Berlin-Friedrichshain
Geschäftshaus Neuer Wall 43, Hamburg
Commercial Block Neuer Wall 43, Hamburg
Nordseepassage, Wilhelmshaven
Nordseepassage, Wilhelmshaven
→ 242
Forum Köpenick, Berlin
Köpenick Forum, Berlin

228 Ortszentrum Schöneiche bei Berlin
Schöneiche Town Centre, near Berlin
Gerling Haus, Stuttgart
Gerling House, Stuttgart
→ 246
Telekomzentrale, Suhl
Telekom Headquarters, Suhl
Klappbrücke, Kiel-Hörn
Bascule Bridge, Kiel-Hörn
→ 250
Restaurierung des Thalia Theaters, Hamburg
Thalia Theatre Restoration, Hamburg
Umbau und Restaurierung der Hapag-Lloyd AG am Ballindamm, Hamburg
Conversion and Renovation of Hapag-Lloyd AG on Ballindamm, Hamburg

1998

254 Hörsaalzentrum der Universität Oldenburg
Lecture Theatre Centre, Oldenburg University
→ 258
Hörsaal- und Seminargebäude der TU Chemnitz
Auditoria and Seminar Building, Chemnitz Institute of Technology
→ 262
Telekom-Zentrale, Berlin-Tegel
Telekom Headquarters, Berlin-Tegel
S-Bahn-Stationen zur Expo 2000 in Hannover
Suburban Railway Station to the Expo 2000 in Hanover
→ 272

256 Büropark Bredeney, Essen
Bredeney Office Park, Essen
→ 268
Residenz in Jurmala, Lettland
Residence in Jurmala, Latvia
→ 274
Norddeutsche Metall-Berufsgenossenschaft, Hannover
Professional Association of the Metal Industry, Hanover
→ 280
Bahnhof Berlin-Spandau
Berlin-Spandau Railway Station
→ 284
Havelbrücke, Berlin-Spandau
Havel Bridge, Berlin-Spandau
→ 290
Verbindungsbauten zwischen den Hallen 3, 4 und 5 der Messe Hannover
Connecting Buildings between Halls 3, 4 and 5 of the Hanover Exhibition Centre

1999

292 Calenberger Esplanande, Hannover
Calenberg Esplanande, Hanover
→ 298
HTC Kehrwiederspitze, Hamburg
HTC Kehrwiederspitze, Hamburg
→ 300
Metropolitan Express Train, Interieur Design
Metropolitan Express Train, Interior Design
→ 306

294 Messehalle 8/9, Hannover
Trade Fair Hall 8/9, Hanover
→ 310
Philips Messestand
Philips Exhibition Stand
→ 316
Congress Centrum Neue Weimarhalle
'New Weimar Hall' Congress Centre
→ 320

296 Entertainment Center, Hamburg
Entertainment Centre, Hamburg
→ 328
Hotel an der Landsberger Allee – Forum Friedrichshain, Berlin
Hotel at Landsberger Allee – Forum Friedrichshain, Berlin
Fachmarktzentrum, Göttingen
Shopping Centre, Göttingen
Wohn- und Geschäftshaus Friedrichstraße 108–109, Berlin
Residential and Commercial Block Friedrichstrasse 108–109, Berlin
Elbkaihaus, Hamburg
Loft Elbkaihaus, Hamburg
→ 332
Fassade des Wohnhauses von Gerkan, Elbchaussee, Hamburg
Façade of the von Gerkan Residence, Elbchaussee, Hamburg
→ 336

2000

340 Wohnhaus Alvano, Hamburg-Othmarschen
Alvano House, Hamburg-Othmarschen
→ 346
Christus-Pavillon auf der Expo 2000, Hannover
Christ Pavilion at the Expo 2000, Hanover
→ 350
Deutsche Schule Peking, China
German School, Beijing, China
→ 362
Fußgängerbrücken EXPO 2000, Hannover
Expo 2000 Pedestrian Bridges, Hanover
→ 370

342 Messehalle 6, Düsseldorf
Düsseldorf Exhibition Centre, Hall 6
→ 376
Ausstellungspavillon der TU Braunschweig
Exhibition Pavilion for the Braunschweig Institute of Technology
→ 378
Bergbauarchiv, Clausthal-Zellerfeld
Mining Archive, Clausthal-Zellerfeld
→ 382
Lenné-Passagen, Frankfurt/Oder
Lenné Passage, Frankfurt/Oder
Media City, Leipzig
Media Centre, Leipzig

344 Kontorhaus am Altmarkt, Dresden
Office Building, Altmarkt, Dresden
Marshall-Brücke, Berlin
Marshall Bridge, Berlin
Art Kite Museum, Detmold
Art Kite Museum, Detmold

344 Fachhochschule des Bundes, Schwerin
Federal College, Schwerin
→ 386
Umbau des Kesselhauses in der Speicherstadt, Hamburg
Conversion of the Boiler House in the Speicherstadt, Hamburg
→ 392

2001

394 Villa in Reinbek
Villa in Reinbek
→ 400
Chistus-Pavillon, Volkenroda
Christ Pavilion, Volkenroda
Bahnhofsplatz Koblenz
Station Square, Koblenz
Ausstellungshalle für das Xinzhao Residential Area, Peking, China
Exhibition Hall for Xinzhao Residential Area, Beijing, China
Wohnhaus Dr. Manke, Melbeck
Villa Dr. Manke, Melbeck
Villen Kanzleistraße, Hamburg
Villas in Kanzleistrasse, Hamburg
396 Jakob-Kaiser-Haus, Abgeordnetenbüros des
Deutschen Bundestages, Berlin
'Jakob-Kaiser-Haus', Parliamentarians' Offices, Berlin
→ 404
Spielbank Bad Steben
Casino, Bad Steben
→ 410
Ku'damm-Eck, Berlin
Ku'damm-Eck, Berlin
Tennishalle der Jurmala Residenz, Lettland
Tennis Hall of the Jurmala Residence, Latvia
→ 420
Apartmenthaus in Riga, Lettland
Apartment House in Riga, Latvia
→ 422
Neue Messe Rimini, Italien
New Trade Fair, Rimini, Italy
→ 428
398 Swissôtel im Ku'damm-Eck, Berlin
Swissôtel in Ku'damm-Eck, Berlin
→ 414
Neues Tempodrom, Berlin
New Tempodrom, Berlin
→ 436
Landesvertretungen Brandenburg und Mecklenburg-Vorpommern in Berlin
State Authority Offices for Brandenburg and Mecklenburg-Vorpommern in Berlin
→ 440
Flughafen Paderborn/Lippstadt
Paderborn-Lippstadt Airport Extension
Depesche Hochregallager, Geesthacht
Depesche High Bay Warehouse, Geesthacht
Alltours Bürogebäude, Duisburg
Alltours Office Building, Duisburg

2002

446 Bodensee-Messe, Friedrichshafen
Bodensee Trade Fair, Friedrichshafen
Hanse-Messe, Rostock
Hanse Trade Fair, Rostock
Kibbelstegbrücken, Hamburg-Speicherstadt
Kibbelsteg Bridges, Hamburg-Speicherstadt
Restaurant „Bastion" am Binnenhafen, Hamburg-Speicherstadt
Restaurant 'Bastion' at the Inner Harbour, Hamburg-Speicherstadt

448 Hauptverwaltung der HHLA, Hamburg-Speicherstadt
HHLA Headquarters, Hamburg-Speicherstadt
Finca „Es Rafalet", Mallorca, Spanien
Finca 'Es Rafalet', Majorca, Spain
→ 452
Speicherblock X, Hamburg-Speicherstadt
Warehouse Block X, Hamburg-Speicherstadt
Kundenzentrum des Porsche-Werks Leipzig
Customer Centre of the Leipzig Porsche Plant
→ 458
Harburg Arcaden, Hamburg
Harburg Arcades, Hamburg
450 Europäisches Patentamt, Umbau Saal 102, München
European Patent Office, Conversion Hall 102, Munich
Wohnbebauung Xinzhao, 1. Bauabschnitt, Peking, China
Xinzhao Residential Area, 1st Building Phase, Beijing, China
Liquidrom im Tempodrom, Berlin
Liquidrom in the Tempodrom, Berlin
→ 462

2003

466 Warnow-Turm der Hanse-Messe Rostock im IGA Park
Warnow Tower at the Hanse Trade Fair Rostock in the IGA Park
Airbus A 380-Sektionsbauhalle, Hamburg
Airbus A 380 Major Component Assembly Hall, Hamburg
Villa Alexandra, Jurmala, Lettland
Villa Alexandra, Jurmala, Latvia
→ 470
468 Elbkaihaus, Kopfbau West, Hamburg
Elbkai House, Head Building West, Hamburg
Internationales Messe- und Kongresszentrum, Nanning, China
Nanning International Convention & Exhibition Centre, China
→ 474
Königliche Porzellan-Manufaktur, Berlin
KPM Porcelain Manufacturer, Berlin
→ 482
Stadion der Freundschaft, Cottbus
Stadium of Friendship, Cottbus
→ 486

2004

490 Hauptbahnhof Kiel – Renovierung und Neugestaltung
Kiel Central Station – Reconstruction and Redesign
Messebahnhof Rimini, Italien
Railway Station of the New Rimini Trade Fair, Italy
Frischemarkt Frankfurt
Frankfurt Fruit and Vegetable Market
Flughafen Stuttgart, Terminal 3
Stuttgart Airport, Terminal 3
→ 506
Flughafen „Raffaello Sanzio", Ancona-Falconara, Italien
'Raffaello Sanzio' Airport, Ancona-Falconara, Italy
RheinEnergieStadion, Köln
RheinEnergie Football Stadium, Cologne
→ 494
492 Olympiastadion, Berlin– Umbau und Überdachung
Olympic Stadium, Berlin – Conversion and Roofing
→ 498
Xinzhao Wohnbebauung, 2. Bauabschnitt, Peking, China
Xinzhao Residential Area, 2nd Building Phase, Beijing, China
Große Parkrotunde am Flughafen Hamburg
Large Car Park Rotunda at Hamburg Airport
Wohnhaus Luserke, Hamburg
Luserke House, Hamburg
→ 510
Institut für Physikalische Chemie, Aachen
Institute for Physical Chemistry, Aachen

Messe- und Kongresszentrum Shenzhen, China
Shenzhen Convention and Exhibition Centre, China
→ 512

2005

520 Development Central Building, Guangzhou, China
Development Central Building, Guangzhou, China
→ 524
Fußgängerbrücke über den Ryck, Greifswald
Pedestrian Bridge across the Ryck, Greifswald
Vogelbeobachtungsstation auf dem Graswarder in Heiligenhafen
Bird-Watching Tower, Graswarder in Heiligenhafen
Airbus A380 Ausstattungsmontagehalle, Hamburg
Airbus A380 Interior Equipment Assembly Hall, Hamburg
Flughafen Hamburg, Terminal 1
Hamburg Airport, Terminal 1
Commerzbankarena, Frankfurt am Main
Commerzbankarena, Frankfurt am Main
→ 528
522 Fachmarktzentrum II, Göttingen
Trade Market Centre II, Göttingen
Allianz Bürogebäude, Taunusanlage, Frankfurt am Main
Allianz Office Building, Taunusanlage, Frankfurt/Main
Lingang Service Center, bei Shanghai, China
Lingang Service Centre, near Shanghai, China
Erweiterung des Sheraton Hotels, Ankara, Türkei
Extension of the Sheraton Hotel, Ankara, Turkey
Museum Shanghai-Pudong, China
Shanghai-Pudong Museum, China
→ 532
Laboratorium für Werkzeugmaschinen und Betriebslehre der RWTH Aachen
Laboratory of Machine Tools and Production Engineering at RWTH Aachen

2006

536 Abbe-Zentrum, Jena-Beutenberg
Abbe Centre, Jena-Beutenberg
CYTS Plaza, Peking, China
CYTS Plaza, Beijing, China
Zhongguancun Kulturzentrum, Peking, China
Zhongguancun Cultural Centre, Beijing, China
Dixingju Bürogebäude, Peking, China
Dixingju Office Building, Beijing, China
538 Nationales Konferenzzentrum, Hanoi, Vietnam
National Conference Centre, Hanoi, Vietnam
„Beijing Château", Peking, China
'Beijing Château', Beijing, China
Gong Yuan Building, Hanzhou, China
Gong Yuan Building, Hanzhou, China
→ 540
Ausstellung Langemarckhalle, Olympiastadion Berlin
Langemarckhalle Exhibition, Berlin Olympic Stadium
Kapelle im Olympiastadion Berlin
Chapel in the Berlin Olympic Stadium
Berlin Hauptbahnhof
Berlin Central Station
→ 544

Ausblick
Outlook

556 Marriott Hotel, Binjiang Plaza, Ningbo, China
Marriott Hotel, Binjiang Plaza, Ningbo, China
Century Lotus Sportpark, Foshan, China
Century Lotus Sports Park, Foshan, China
Tourismus Center, Hangzhou, China
Tourism Centre, Hangzhou, China
558 Wohnen am Philosophenweg, Innenhafen Duisburg
Residential Buildings, Philosophenweg, Duisburg Inner Harbour
Polizeipräsidium Bonn
Police Headquarters, Bonn
Christliche Kirche Peking, Haidin District
Beijing Christian Church, Haidin District
Herzzentrum der Uniklinik Köln
Centre for Cardiac Medicine, University Hospital, Cologne
China Telecom, Häuser 12 und 13, Shanghai
China Telecom, Buildings 12 and 13, Shanghai
560 Forschungsgebäude auf dem UKE-Campus, Hamburg
Research Building, Hamburg University Hospital
Twin Towers, Dalian, China
Twin Towers, Dalian, China
Internationales Bildungszentrum Hui Jia, Peking, China
Hui Jia International Education Centre, Beijing, China
Internationales Messe- und Kongresszentrum Xi' an, China
Xi' an International Conference and Exhibition Centre, China
Wanda Plaza, Peking, China
Wanda Plaza, Beijing, China

Anhang
Appendix

564 Curricula Vitae
Curricula Vitae
570 Büroprofil
The Practice
572 gmp Philosophie
gmp Philosophy
574 Publikationen
Publications
575 Bildnachweis

Anmerkung zum Gebrauch dieses Buches

In dem Zeitraum 1965-2006 sind über 200 Bauten von den Architekten gmp gebaut worden, die alle in diesem Buch unter der Jahreszahl ihrer Fertigstellung abgebildet sind. Aus jedem Jahr wurden Projekte herausgehoben, die als besonders geeignet erschienen, Ausdrucksstärke im Ganzen und im Detail zu zeigen.
Architektur und Fotografie im Duplexverfahren verschmelzen zu einer eigenen ästhetischen Anmutung, die strukturelle Elemente – vereint mit Licht und Schatten – erlebbar macht, jenseits von farbigen Hochglanz-Sehgewohnheiten. Monochrome Farbeinstreuungen bewirken eine wechselseitige Steigerung der Wahrnehmung. Pläne finden nur Niederschlag aus gestalterischer Sicht und Textinformationen werden auf ein Minimum reduziert.
Ein einleitender Text, begleitet von einer Zeitleiste, ordnet die gmp-Bauten in den politischen und baugeschichtlichen Kontext der letzten vier Jahrzehnte ein.

Annotation on how to use this book

Between 1965 and 2006, more than two-hundred buildings and constructions have been realized by the architects of gmp, which are all presented in this book under the year of their completion. Certain projects from every year have been singled out, which seem to be suitable to show their expressiveness regarding the overall concept as well as the single detail.
Architecture and photography in duplex technique are merged into an individual aesthetic impression that makes structural elements – unified with light and shadow – readily experienced, beyond coloured high gloss standards of vision. Monochrome colour interspersions effect a mutual intensification of the perception. Plans are only presented from a design perspective, and written information has been reduced to a minimum.
An introductory text, which is accompanied by a timeline, relates the gmp buildings to the political and building-historical context of the last four decades.

1964

A » Architektur
    Architecture
P » Politik
    Politics

A Sep Ruf: Kanzlerbungalow, Bonn
   Sep Ruf: chancellor bungalow, Bonn, Germany
   Alvar Aalto: Hochschule Otaniemi, Finnland
   Alvar Aalto: Otaniemi Technical University, Otaniemi, Finland
   James Stirling: Ingenieurfakultät der Universität Leicester, Großbritannien
   James Stirling: Leicester Engineering Building, Leicester, Great Britain
   Kenzo Tange: Bauten für die Olympischen Spiele Tokio, Japan
   Kenzo Tange: Buildings for the Olympic Games, Tokyo, Japan

40 Jahre gmp
Veränderung. Reflektion. Neue Wege.

40 Jahre eines Architekturbüros, mit großen, gelösten Aufgaben hinter sich, mit weiteren, teilweise noch größeren Aufgaben vor sich – das ist Anlass für ein Innehalten. Anlass für einen Augenblick der Reflektion dessen, was man tut, vor dem Hintergrund dessen, was man in der Vergangenheit getan hat – in der Vermutung, man könne daraus Schlüsse für die Zukunft herleiten.

Architekturbüros sind in der Regel merkwürdige Gebilde, weil sie aus einzelnen Personen bei ihrer Gründung im Erfolgsfalle zu Firmen werden, spätestens dann, wenn die Frage der Nachfolge der Personen ansteht. Die vierzig Jahre der Existenz eines Büros wie das von gmp decken sich mit der Lebensarbeitszeit eines Menschen, die ihn zum Bezug einer Rente berechtigt. Der Staat geht, zumindest zurzeit noch, davon aus, dass 40 Jahre Arbeitsleben genug sind.

Das Modell taugt und taugte allerdings in erster Linie für Werktätige, von denen angenommen wurde, sie müssten körperlich leistungsfähig sein und hätten keinen Spaß am Beruf. In allen kreativen Berufen hingegen war es noch nie besonders sinnvoll; dort zählt Erfahrung mehr als Muskelmasse; Komponisten, Dirigenten, Maler oder Schauspieler – oft führt das Alter im Gegenteil zu den höchsten Leistungen. Auch einem Dichter oder Schriftsteller, selbst einem Architekturkritiker wird man das Schreiben im Alter über 65 nicht verwehren können – Goethe sei Dank! Insofern ist konsequent, was die beiden älteren Herren Meinhard von Gerkan und Volkwin Marg tun, die mit ihrer Person und ihrem Namen für das Büro gmp stehen: Sie arbeiten einfach weiter. Sie haben das Rentenalter erreicht, wollen aber dessen zweifelhafte Vorzüge nicht genießen – das Alter gilt ihnen als Sprungbrett, nicht als Ruhekissen.

40 Jahre also, als Zwischenstation betrachtet: Deswegen steht im Mittelpunkt dieses Buches nicht der Blick auf einzelne Bauten, sondern deren Abfolge – fast wie in einem Film. Und wie im Film entstehen Sequenzen; die Bauten-Bilder fügen sich aneinander wie beim Daumenkino. Damit aber entsteht etwas Neues, eine eigene Qualität, die die Entwicklung, die Veränderung der Architektur sichtbar macht, nicht den einzelnen Bau in den Mittelpunkt rückt.

Die Darstellung von Entwicklung aber bietet die Chance zur Reflektion vor einem Hintergrund, den wir alle kennen, auch wenn wir ihn nicht mehr im einzelnen erinnern, nämlich vor dem Hintergrund der allgemeinen politischen und gesellschaftlichen Zeitläufe, denen der Architekturentwicklung im Besonderen. Was geschah zur selben Zeit, als das Haus x entstand? Wo befanden sich Politik, Gesellschaft, die internationale Architektur? Sehen wir unter diesem Blickwinkel das Büro gmp als stilistischen oder architekturtheoretischen Vorreiter oder als dedicated follower of fashion? Sehen wir Titanen, die unbeirrt ihren Weg gehen, oder verändert sich neben der Welt draußen auch die Architektur drinnen? Wird immer nur derselbe Bau variiert, wie man es Mies van der Rohe nachgesagt hat, oder werden neue Lösungen für jedes neue Problem angeboten, wie es Eero Saarinen tat?

Vielleicht sollten Sie, der Leser, tatsächlich einmal das Experiment machen: Nehmen Sie die Blätter dieses Buches, nehmen Sie 40 Jahre Geschichte eines Architekturbüros, auf 560 Seiten reduziert, und lassen Sie sie mit dem Daumen im Schnelldurchlauf an sich vorbei streichen – haben Sie gesehen, wie sich die Architektur verändert? Haben Sie erkannt, wie sich die Architekturauffassung verändert hat? Oder welche Konstanten gibt es?

1965

P Die Bundesrepublik nimmt diplomatische Beziehungen zu Israel auf
The Federal Republic of Germany establishes diplomatic relations with Israel

A † Le Corbusier
† Le Corbusier
Buch: Christian Norberg-Schulz: Logik der Baukunst (1963 in norwegisch)
Book: Christian Norberg-Schulz: Intentions in Architecture (Norwegian edition 1963)
Buch: Alexander Mitscherlich: Die Unwirtlichkeit unserer Städte
Book: Alexander Mitscherlich: Die Unwirtlichkeit unserer Städte
Arne Jacobsen: Nyager Grundschule, Kopenhagen, Dänemark
Arne Jacobsen: Nyager Elementary School, Copenhagen, Denmark

1966

P Der Rücktritt Ludwig Erhardts als Bundeskanzler führt zur ersten großen Koalition unter Kurt Georg Kiesinger
The resignation of Ludwig Erhardt as German chancellor leads to the first grand coalition led by Kurt Georg Kiesinger
Bis 1969 Kulturrevolution in China
Cultural revolution in China; ends 1969

A Buch: Aldo Rossi: L'architettura della città (dt. 1973)
Book: Aldo Rossi: L'architettura della città (German edition 1973)
Buch: Robert Venturi: Complexity and Contradiction in Architecture (dt. 1978)
Book: Robert Venturi: Complexity and Contradiction in Architecture (German edition 1978)
R. + R. Pietilä: Kaleva Kirche, Tampere, Finnland
R. + R. Pietilä: Kaleva Church, Tampere, Finland

40 years of gmp
Change. Reflection. New Paths.

The forty-year history of an architectural firm that looks back on large building problems solved and forward to further tasks, some of them even larger, is a reason to stop and take stock, reason to reflect for a moment on what one does against the background of what one has done in the past – assuming that it is possible to draw conclusions from it for the future.

Generally speaking, architectural offices are curious phenomena as they are founded by individuals and, in case of success, become firms – at the latest when the question of succession of the principals arises. The forty-year existence of an office such as gmp corresponds to the working life of the average person, which entitles him/her to draw a pension. At present, the state still holds that a forty-year working life is enough.

This model applies and applied primarily to industrial workers who, it was assumed, had to be physically fit and did not enjoy their work. In the creative professions, however, experience matters more than muscle. Composers, musical directors, painters or actors have shown that often the best performances came with old age. Poets or writers, even architectural critics cannot be forbidden to write beyond the age of sixty-five – thank Goethe! From that point of view the two senior gentlemen, Meinhard von Gerkan and Volkwin Marg, are consistent in continuing to represent the office of gmp in name and in person. They just carry on working. Despite having reached retirement age, they do not wish to enjoy its dubious advantages. Age, to them, is a springboard, not a comfortable pillow.

Forty years, then, regarded as a stopover, which is why this book focuses not on individual buildings, but on their progression – almost like the sequences in a film. The images of their buildings follow on from each other, like a flip-book. This creates something new, an original quality which reveals the development, the changes in their architectural designs, instead of putting the individual building centre stage.

Tracing a development, however, provides an opportunity for reflection against a background known to all of us, even though we may not remember every detail, that is to say, against the background of the general course of political and social events, in particular with regard to architectural developments. What exactly was happening in the world when house X was built? Where did politics, society and international architecture stand? Do we, from this angle, see gmp as a precursor in terms of style or architectural theory, or (only) as a dedicated follower of fashion? Do we see Titans unswervingly going their own way, or has the architecture inside the office changed, too, and not only the outside world? Do they only ever vary the one building (as critics said of Mies van der Rohe), or do they, like Eero Saarinen, offer a new solution to every new problem?

Perhaps you should really try this: take the pages of this book, the forty-year history of an architectural office reduced to 560 pages, and then thumb through it quickly. See how the concept of architecture has changed? See any constants?

1966–1969

In 1966, the 'office of gmp' won the competition for the new airport at Berlin-Tegel. Sounds pretty straightforward, but the story behind it is much more thrilling as there was virtually no established architectural firm behind it. That was founded only after the competition win and subsequent receipt of the commission. Yet it was quite a remarkable public entry. Even the magazine Der Spiegel, known as a 'grouch' where architecture was concerned, acknowledged gmp's competition

1967

P Studentenunruhen in Berlin und anderen deutschen Städten nach der Erschießung eines Studenten bei einer Demonstration
Student unrest in Berlin and other German cities after the shooting of a student during a demonstration
Putsch der Obristen in Griechenland (bis 1974)
Military coup in Greece (governed until 1974)
6-Tage-Krieg Israel gegen Ägypten endet mit Niederlage Ägyptens
Six-Day War in Israel ends with the defeat of Egypt

A Helmut Striffler: evangelische Versöhnungskapelle, Dachau
Helmut Striffler: Protestant Chapel of Reconciliation, Dachau, Germany
Helmut Spieker und Team: Universitätsbauten Marburg
Helmut Spieker and Team: university buildings in Marburg, Germany
Frei Otto und Rolf Gutbrod: Deutscher Pavillon, EXPO Montreal, Kanada
Frei Otto and Rolf Gutbrod: German pavilion, EXPO, Montreal, Canada
Buckminster Fuller: Geodätische Kuppel, EXPO Montreal, Kanada
Buckminster Fuller: geodesic dome, EXPO, Montreal, Canada

Moshe Safdie: Habitat, EXPO Montreal, Kanada
Moshe Safdie: Habitat, EXPO, Montreal, Canada
James Stirling: Bibliothek Historische Fakultät Cambridge, Großbritannien
James Stirling: history faculty library building, Cambridge, Great Britain
Kongress „Architekturtheorie und Architekturkritik" in Berlin
Conference 'Architectural Theory and Architectural Criticism' in Berlin, Germany

1968

P Andauernde Studentenunruhen in Deutschland und in vielen anderen Ländern; Attentat auf Rudi Dutschke Notstandsgesetze treten in Kraft
Continuing student unrest in Germany and several other countries; assassination attempt of Rudi Dutschke
Emergency legislation goes into effect
„Prager Frühling" in der CSSR und dessen Niederschlagung durch fünf sozialistische „Bruder"länder, darunter die DDR
Prague Spring in Czechoslovakia and its defeat by five socialist 'brother' countries, including the GDR
„Maiunruhen" in Frankreich
'May Events' in France
Ermordung Martin Luther Kings
Assassination of Martin Luther King
Ermordung Robert F. Kennedys
Assassination of Robert F. Kennedy

1966–1969

Im Jahr 1965 gewann das Büro gmp den Wettbewerb für den Neubau eines Flughafens in Berlin-Tegel – das klingt nüchtern genug. Viel spannender ist die Geschichte dahinter, denn „das Büro" gab es praktisch noch nicht; es konstituierte sich erst mit dem Wettbewerb und dem folgenden Auftrag. Aber es war ein bemerkenswerter öffentlicher Auftritt: Selbst das Nachrichtenmagazin Der Spiegel, sonst eher als Architekturmuffel bekannt, würdigte die Wettbewerbserfolge des Jahres – der Flughafen war nicht der einzige – mit einer Geschichte: Das Büro gmp war nicht nur in der Architektenszene, sondern auch in der allgemeinen Öffentlichkeit angekommen und würde in Zukunft nicht daraus verschwinden – übrigens in einer schwer nachvollziehbaren Melange aus Anerkennung (durch die Öffentlichkeit) und eher verhaltener Begeisterung mit Neideinsprengseln (durch die Architekten- und Kritikerszene). Zumindest die ersten dreißig Jahre der Büroexistenz wurden von der unterschwelligen Auffassung der Kritiker begleitet, wer so viel Erfolg habe, könne einfach nicht gut sein. Dabei stellt der Flughafen, der erste große Erfolg, gerade ein Beispiel dafür dar, dass dem nicht so ist: Es war eine völlig neue, bis heute gut funktionierende Flughafenorganisation, die zu einer überzeugenden Form des sechseckigen Terminals entwickelt worden war.

Wovon in diesem Zeitabschnitt in Deutschland noch kein Kritiker, aber auch kein Architekturtheoretiker oder -praktiker Notiz nahm, war etwas, das sich erst Jahre später mit einem journalistisch einprägsamen, aber historisch falschen Datum bemerkbar machte, nämlich die so genannte „postmoderne Architektur". Ihre theoretische Grundlage erhielt sie durch zwei Buchveröffentlichungen im Jahr 1966: Robert Venturis „Complexity and Contradiction in Architecture" und Aldo Rossis „L'Architettura della Città". In das allgemeine Bewusstsein geriet die Postmoderne aber erst 1977/78 durch Charles Jencks' Buch über die „Sprache der postmodernen Architektur", in dem der Beginn der Postmoderne auf 1972 datiert wurde: als die Sprengung eines nur zwanzig Jahre alten Blocks des sozialen Wohnungsbaus eines renommierten Architekten in St. Louis, USA, stattfand.

Die Rückschau ermöglicht jedoch eine andere Perspektive als sie Jencks nahe legt: Zur gleichen Zeit – sogar ein Jahr vor den Büchern von Venturi und Rossi – erschien in Deutschland ein Buch des Architekten und Historikers Christian Norberg-Schulz, der versuchte, in eine brüchig gewordene Moderne eine theoretische Systematik einzubeziehen. Und es erschien ein höchst erfolgreiches, wütendes Pamphlet mit Alexander Mitscherlichs „Unwirtlichkeit unserer Städte". Beide Bücher waren Zeichen für die einsetzende Kritik an einer Moderne, die in Deutschland noch nicht einmal auf ihrem Höhepunkt angekommen war, im Gegenteil noch als ein Stück gesellschaftlichen Fortschritts begriffen wurde: die Lösung gesellschaftlicher Probleme durch (moderne) Architektur. International hatte diese Kritik aus sich selbst heraus – die Kritik der Moderne durch die modernen Architekten – spätestens mit der Tagung der CIAM in Otterlo 1959 begonnen.

Wenige Jahre später, auf dem Höhepunkt der Studentenbewegung in Berlin, wurde die Auseinandersetzung zwischen den Architekten des Märkischen Viertels, einem Neubauquartier für 40 000 Bewohner, und den studentischen Verteidigern der „Kreuzberger Mischung" geführt, die ihren „Kiez" verteidigen wollten. Man begann zu ahnen, dass das WC innerhalb der Wohnung, die Einbauküche und das normgerechte Kinderzimmer nicht alles sind: Architektur ist (auch) Emotion. Das hätten gmp nie geleugnet.

Auf der politischen Ebene waren die Jahre zwischen 1966 und 1969 die der ersten großen Koalition zwischen CDU und SPD in Deutschland. Ebenso wie sich in der Architektur der Umbruch aus einer Zeit scheinbarer Gewissheiten andeutete, so tat er das in Politik und Gesellschaft. Die Zeit Konrad Adenauers, des ersten Kanzlers der Republik, als eine, in der sich eine Gesellschaft finden und definieren musste, indem sie an der Gewissheit einer Vaterfigur festhielt, diese Zeit war endgültig vorbei.

Das war in der gebauten Architektur weder bei gmp noch bei anderen zu spüren – gebaute Architektur eignet sich nicht dazu, Zweifel anzumelden. Der Architekt muss Gewissheiten sehen und vermitteln – ein eindeutig definiertes Raumprogramm, ein eindeutiges konstruktives Gerüst, eine ablesbare ästhetische

1969

A Ludwig Mies van der Rohe: Nationalgalerie Berlin
Ludwig Mies van der Rohe: Nationalgalerie, Berlin, Germany
Gottfried Böhm: Wallfahrtskirche Neviges
Gottfried Böhm: Pilgrimage Church, Neviges, Germany
Dieter Oesterlen: Museum am Hohen Ufer, Hannover
Dieter Oesterlen: Museum am Hohen Ufer, Hanover, Germany
Roche + Dinkeloo: Ford Foundation New York, USA
Roche + Dinkeloo: Ford Foundation New York, United States
Bauausstellung 507 in Berlin
Building Exhibition 507 in Berlin, Germany

P Gustav Heinemann wird erster sozialdemokratischer Bundespräsident
Gustav Heinemann becomes the first social democratic German president
Nach der Bundestagswahl sozialliberale Koalition unter Willy Brandt
Following parliamentary elections, social liberal coalition governs under Willy Brandt
Richard Nixon wird Präsident der USA, tritt nach der „Watergate-Affäre" 1974 zurück
Richard Nixon becomes president of the United States of America, resigns following the Watergate Affair in 1974
Zwei Amerikaner betreten zum ersten Mal den Mond
Two Americans walk on the moon for the first time

A Kallmann, McKinnell + Knowles: Rathaus Boston, USA
Kallmann, McKinnell + Knowles: City Hall, Boston, United States
† Walter Gropius
† Walter Gropius
† Ludwig Mies van der Rohe
† Ludwig Mies van der Rohe

1970

P „Kniefall von Warschau" von Willy Brandt
Willy Brandt kneels in front of the Ghetto Memorial in Warsaw
Brandt und Stoph treffen sich in Erfurt
Brandt and Stoph meet in Erfurt
Gewaltverzichtsvertrag UdSSR-BRD
Non-aggression treaty between the Soviet Union and Federal Republic of Germany
Atomwaffensperrvertrag wird unterzeichnet
Nonproliferation treaty is signed

A Bruce Goff: Harder House, Minnesota, USA
Bruce Goff: Harder House, Minnesota, United States

wins of that year (Tegel was not the only one) with an article. The office of gmp had arrived on the architectural stage, and also in public awareness, not to disappear again – accompanied, incidentally, by a mixture, hard to understand, of appreciation (from the public) and rather restrained enthusiasm mingled with touches of envy (from architects and architectural critics). For at least the first thirty years of its existence, gmp lived with the subliminal attitude of the critics that anyone who is that successful simply cannot be any good. For all that, the office's first major success – the airport – goes to show that this does not apply to gmp. It represented a completely new and, to this day, efficient airport organization, which, at the time, had been developed into a convincing version of the hexagonal terminal.

In all these years, neither critics in Germany nor any fellow architect and theoretician took note of a phenomenon which would surface only years later (though erroneously dated) under the journalistic catchword of 'postmodern architecture'. Its theoretical foundations were laid by two books published the year of the Tegel competition win (1966), namely, Robert Venturi's 'Complexity and Contradiction in Architecture', and Aldo Rossi's 'L'architettura della città' (Architecture of the city). However, the general public was made aware of Postmodernism eleven years later (1977/78) through Charles Jencks's book 'The Language of Post-Modern Architecture', in which he fixed 1972 as the beginning of Postmodernism with the blasting, in St. Louis, USA, of a social housing block built only twenty years previously by a well-known architect.

That was a brilliant and most successful journalistic scoop. Yet looking back opens yet another perspective. At roughly the same time, one year before Venturi's and Rossi's books, architect and architectural historian Christian Norberg-Schulz published a book in Germany, in which he tried to undergird Modernism, which by then had become rather brittle, with a systematical theory. And Alexander Mitscherlich's published his very successful, angry polemic pamphlet 'Our Uninhabitable Cities'. Both publications were signs of mounting criticism of a modern movement that, in Germany, had not even reached its climax, but was, on the contrary, seen as a piece of social progress – solving social problems through (modern) architecture. Internationally, the criticism of modern architecture from among its own ranks started, at the latest, with the Otterlo CIAM Congress in 1959.

A few years later, at the height of the student revolution in Berlin, the debate raged between the architects of the Märkisches Viertel (social housing quarter) and the students who defended the 'Kreuzberg mixture' (old buildings of mixed uses, flats and small industry: translator's note). People began to suspect that indoor toilets, fitted kitchens and standard children's rooms were not everything; that architecture was (also) emotion – something that gmp would never have denied.

At the political level, the years from 1966 to 1969 were those of the first Great Coalition that governed Germany. The end of a time of seeming certainties dawned not only in architecture, but also in politics and society. The times of Konrad Adenauer, when German society had to define itself by holding on to the certainty of a father figure, were definitely over.

The built projects by gmp and other architects conveyed nothing of this. Completed buildings are unsuited to raise doubts. The architect must see and produce the required certainties of a clearly defined spatial programme, a clearly constructed frame, a clearly readable aesthetic expression. This does not say anything about the figures of dialogue from which these certainties emerged, but the work itself is positivist.

1970–1975

Years of change: with the student revolt on the one hand, and Willy Brandt's politics as German chancellor on the other, the post-war period ended in Germany once and for all. Now, following the signing of the so-called 'East treaties' and the Conference for Security and Cooperation in Europe (CSCE) in Helsinki, it was possible to start establishing a new order based on careful consensus and dialogue. The first East and West German meeting at government level took place in Erfurt in 1970. The world approved: in 1971, Willy Brandt was awarded the Nobel Peace Prize, while in 1972, Heinrich Böll received the Nobel Prize for Literature.

Another turning-point: The Club of Rome's report of 1972 warned of a climatic disaster

1971

P Erich Honecker löst Walther Ulbricht als Generalsekretär der SED ab
Erich Honecker replaces Walther Ulbricht as secretary general of the United Socialist Party of East Germany
VR China wird Mitglied der UNO
People's Republic of China becomes a member of the United Nations

A Alvar Aalto: Finlandia Halle, Helsinki, Finnland
Alvar Aalto: Finland Hall, Helsinki, Finland

1972

P Grundlagenvertrag mit der DDR
Basic Treaty with the German Democratic Republic
Der SALT I-Vertrag zwischen den USA und der UdSSR beginnt eine Phase der Abrüstung
The SALT I treaty between the USA and the Soviet Union instigates an initial period of disarmament

A Lucien Kroll: Studentenheim der Medizinischen Fakultät Woluwe St.-Lambert, Belgien
Lucien Kroll: dormitory for medical faculty, Woluwe St.-Lambert, Belgium
Herman Hertzberger: Verwaltung Centraal Beheer Apeldoorn, Niederlande
Herman Hertzberger: Verwaltung Centraal Beheer Apeldoorn, Netherlands

Günter Behnisch: Olympia-Bauten München
Günter Behnisch: structures for Olympic Games, Munich, Germany
Otto Steidle: Wohnbebauung Genter Straße, München
Otto Steidle: apartment house in the Genter Strasse, Munich, Germany
Louis I. Kahn: Kimball Art Institute Fort Worth, USA
Louis I. Kahn: Kimball Art Institute, Fort Worth, United States

Aussage verlangen das. Das sagt nichts darüber aus, in welchen dialogischen Figuren diese entstanden sind – aber das Werk selbst ist positivistisch.

1970–1975

Jahre des Umbruchs: Mit der Studentenrevolte einerseits, der Regierungsübernahme von Willy Brandt andererseits war die Nachkriegszeit in der Bundesrepublik endgültig beendet; jetzt konnte man mit den Ostverträgen und der Konferenz für Sicherheit und Zusammenarbeit in Europa (KSZE) in Helsinki daran gehen, eine neue Ordnung zu etablieren, die auf vorsichtigen Konsens, auf Miteinander-Reden gegründet war: Das erste deutsch-deutsche Treffen zwischen den Regierungsebenen der Bundesrepublik und der DDR fand 1970 in Erfurt statt. Die Welt fand das gut: 1971 erhielt Brandt den Friedensnobelpreis, ein Jahr später Heinrich Böll den für Literatur.

Ein anderer Einschnitt: Der Bericht des „Club of Rome" 1972 beschrieb die künftige Klimakatastrophe, die inzwischen Gewissheit geworden ist. Der „Ölpreisschock" brachte den „autofreien Sonntag" und führte zu einem neuen ökologischen Bewusstsein auch im Bauen.

„Mehr Demokratie wagen", das Motto Willy Brandts aus seiner Regierungserklärung 1969, und das studentische Aufbegehren gegen verkrustete gesellschaftliche Strukturen fanden ihre Parallelen auch in der Architektur. 1972 wurde das Gebäude der Medizinischen Fakultät der Universität Löwen in Woluwe-St.-Lambert (Belgien) fertig gestellt – Ergebnis eines Architekten, der sich als Steuerer demokratischer Prozesse sah, und eines Landschaftsarchitekten, der immer eine Handvoll Wildsamen in der Hosentasche trug, um das (pflanzliche) Chaos in die Welt zu bringen. In Deutschland entstand das Pendant in München mit den aus Industrie-Fertigteilen zusammengebastelten Wohnbauten Otto Steidles – Architektur als gebaute Ideologie. Auch diese Architekturen waren, wiewohl sie andere Gewissheiten ausstrahlten, im Ergebnis eindeutig – an der Eigentümlichkeit des Mediums „Architektur" konnten sie nichts verändern.

In mancher Hinsicht die eigentlichen architektonischen Gewinner dieser Jahre waren die Erbauer der Olympia-Bauten in München: das Büro von Günter Behnisch; nach einer Umfrage aus dem Jahr 2003 sind das die Bauten, die für die Deutschen am ehesten moderne Architektur verkörpern – keine schlechte Wahl. Eine Dachlandschaft wie die dort realisierte spielte auch in den Vorüberlegungen von gmp zu dem Wettbewerb für die Olympia-Bauten eine Rolle – das wäre dann der dritte Entwurf geworden, den sie hätten abgeben können. Stattdessen wurde die eine ihrer beiden Lösungen mit dem 2. Preis, die andere mit einem Ankauf ausgezeichnet.

Die Postmoderne etabliert sich. Dabei meint der Begriff nicht, wie oft missverstanden, nur die dekorative, mehr oder minder ironische Verwendung von historischen Formen, sondern eine Ablösung des modernen Denkens, die bis heute anhält: eines Denkens, das endzeitlich auf eine „Welt freier und gleicher Individuen" zielt und alle anderen gesellschaftlichen (und architektonischen) Entwürfe für im moralischen Sinne falsch hält. Postmoderne – das akzeptiert die Verschiedenheit als geistiges Prinzip, und so stehen architektonische Stilformen wie Rationalismus, High-Tech-Architektur, Regionalismus, Late Modernism und postmoderner Eklektizismus gleichberechtigt nebeneinander. Jedes Gebäude muss seine formale Begründung aus sich selbst heraus entwickeln und seine Qualität beweisen; nur „modern" zu sein, reicht da nicht – aber natürlich waren sie dennoch modern.

Die Ikone des Rationalismus war der – schnell verblasste – Wohnblock in Mailand-Gallaratese von Aldo Rossi: hochgejubelt von der Kritik und den Theoretikern, nicht akzeptiert von den Bewohnern – allein unter diesem Aspekt ein Lehrstück moderner Architektur. Das Gegenstück dazu waren die Hotelbauten von John Portman in den USA – inszenierte Kunstwelten, von der Kritik nicht für voll genommen, aber erfolgreich. Der Gegensatz scheint typisch für die Architektur des 20. Jahrhunderts: Was die Kritiker lobten, fand nur in seltenen Fällen die Anerkennung des Publikums – und umgekehrt.

Das eigentliche architektonische Highlight jener Jahre jenseits aller Stile, auch heute noch ein Ort zum Träumen und Staunen, war das Grabmal der Brion Vega in San Vito di Altivole in Italien von Carlo Scarpa – eintausend Jahre venezianischer Geschichte vereinigen sich in

1973

P Beginn der Konferenz für Sicherheit und Zusammenarbeit in Europa (KSZE)
Organization for Security and Cooperation in Europe (OSCE) conference begins
Waffenstillstand zwischen Nordvietnam und den USA; Beendigung des amerikanischen Engagements
Armistice between North Vietnam and the United States of America; end of American involvement in North Vietnam
Jom-Kippur-Krieg Israel-Ägypten endet mit der Niederlage Ägyptens
Jom Kippur war between Israel and Egypt ends with the defeat of Egypt

A Aldo Rossi: Friedhof San Cataldo, Modena, Italien
Aldo Rossi: San Cataldo Cemetery, Modena, Italy
Aldo Rossi: Wohnblock Gallaratese, Mailand, Italien
Aldo Rossi: Gallaratese apartment building, Milan, Italy
Mario Botta: Wohnhaus, Riva San Vitale, Schweiz
Mario Botta: House, Riva San Vitale, Switzerland
John Portman: Hyatt Regency Hotel San Francisco, USA
John Portman: Hyatt Regency Hotel, San Francisco, United States
Richard Meier, Douglas Haus, Harbor Springs, USA
Richard Meier: Douglas House, Harbor Springs, United States
Candilis, Josic, Woods: FU Berlin
Candilis, Josic, Woods: Freie Universität, Berlin, Germany

1974

P Rücktritt Willy Brandts; Helmut Schmidt wird Bundeskanzler
Resignation of Willy Brandt; Helmut Schmidt becomes German chancellor
Militärputsch in Portugal führt zur Beendigung der Kolonialkriege und zur Demokratisierung des Landes
Military coup in Portugal leads to an end of the wars in the colonies and the democratization of the country
Erste indische Atombombe
India creates its first atomic bomb

A Hans Hollein: Juweliergeschäft Schullin 1, Wien, Österreich
Hans Hollein: jewelry store, Schullin 1, Vienna, Austria
Charles Moore: Cresge College, Santa Cruz, USA
Charles Moore: Cresge College, Santa Cruz, United States
Jorn Utzon: Oper Sydney (seit 1957!), Australien
Jorn Utzon: Sydney Opera House, (begun 1957!), Sydney, Australia

which has since become a certainty. The oil crisis brought with it the 'car-free Sunday' and led to increased ecological awareness also in the building industry.

"Take the plunge for more democracy" demanded Willy Brandt in his 1969 governmental declaration. This slogan also found its way into architecture, as did the student protests against inflexible social structures. In 1972, the new medical faculty building of Louvain University at Woluwé-Saint-Lambert in Belgium was completed, the work of an architect who saw himself as the promoter of democratic processes, and of a landscape architect who always carried a handful of wild flower seeds in his trouser pockets in order to bring (phytogenic) chaos into the world. In Germany, in Munich, Otto Steidle assembled the counterparts, namely, residential buildings constructed out of prefabricated elements: architecture as built ideology. Even these architectures were unambiguously clear (though conveying other certainties), but could not change the singular nature of the medium of architecture.

In some ways the architects of the 1972 Olympic buildings for Munich – Behnisch & Partners – were the real winners of that year. According to an opinion poll of 2003, a majority identifies these structures most easily as truly modern architecture – not a bad choice at all. A roofscape like the one in Munich also played a role in one of gmp's competition designs for the Olympic buildings. This would have been the third design they could have submitted. Of the two they did enter, one was awarded second prize and the other was purchased.

Postmodernism gradually 'set in'. The term has often been misunderstood to mean only the decorative, more or less ironic use of historic forms, but it really means a rejection of modernist thought, of a philosophy which eschatologically aims for a "world of free and equal individuals" and considers all other social (and architectural) designs as ethically wrong. Postmodernism accepts difference as an intellectual principle so that architectural design sensibilities such as Rationalism, High-tech, Regionalism, Late Modernism or postmodern Eclecticism can coexist as equals. Every building had to and must be developed from its own formal logic and prove its quality. Being 'modern' alone was not enough, but, of course, all of them were modern.

Aldo Rossi's apartment block in Milan-Gallaratese was the soon-to-pale icon of rationalism, praised to the skies by critics and architectural theoreticians, but not accepted by the residents. From this perspective alone it is a good piece of modern architectural education. Its counterparts were the hotel buildings in the US by John Portman – dramatically staged art(ificial) worlds and successful, though not taken seriously by the critics. Opposites seem to be typical of 20th-century architecture. What the critics praised seldom met with public recognition – and vice versa.

The real architectonic highlight of those years – beyond all styles and even today a place of wonder and dreaming – was the tomb of Brion Vega which Carlo Scarpa created in San Vito di Altivole so that one thousand years of Venetian history united with architectural Modernism in an upper-Italian village, in a design beyond all 'isms'. It showed that architecture is never a question of style, but exclusively of quality.

"We therefore see all past professions of fundamental principles (that are again blossoming today) critically and with some reservation", wrote Meinhard von Gerkan in 1978. Justifying every formal design through and from its own specific conditions has been the sustained creed of the office right from the beginning. It did not lead to randomness, but to consistent rationality. And buildings such as the Max Planck Institute in Lindau, the residential and office block in Hamburg, or the Esso headquarters in Hamburg testify to this – thoroughly time-related – rationality.

1976–1982

Why take 1976 to 1982 as a period? One, political, reason is: it was Helmut Schmidt's term of office as Federal Chancellor. He was pragmatic, unideological, but forced to take decisions to defend fundamental political positions. Then came the 'German Autumn' of 1977 with many fatal attacks by the RAF terrorists; NATO's rearmament for the purpose of disarmament ('twin-track decision') forced difficult government decisions. The end of the liberal socialist coalition and the beginning of Helmut Kohl's sixteen-year term as

1975

P Tod Francos; Juan Carlos I. wird König in Spanien. Demokratisierung des Landes
Franco dies; Juan Carlos I becomes king of Spain. Democratization of country
Ende des Vietnamkrieges nach der Eroberung des Südens durch den Norden
Vietnam War ends with the conquest of the south by the north

A **Carlo Scarpa: Grabmal Brion Vega San Vito, Italien**
Carlo Scarpa: Brion-Vega Cemetery, San Vito, Italy
Peter Eisenman: Haus VI, USA
Peter Eisenman: House VI, New York, United States
Europäisches Jahr für Denkmalschutz
European Year of Historic Preservation

1976

P Tod Mao tse Dongs
Mao tse Dong dies

A Carlfried Mutschler, Frei Otto: Multihalle, Mannheim
Carlfried Mutschler, Frei Otto: grid shells, Mannheim, Germany
Richard J. Dietrich: Metastadt, Wulfen (1987 abgerissen)
Richard J. Dietrich: Metastadt, Wulfen, Germany (1987 demolished)
Heinz Graffunder u.a.: Palast der Republik, Berlin
Heinz Graffunder and others: Palast der Republik, Berlin, Germany
Jorn Utzon: Bagsvaerd Kirche, Kopenhagen, Dänemark
Jorn Utzon: Bagsvaerd Church, Copenhagen, Denmark
Buch: Rem Koolhaas, Madeleine Vriesendorp: Delirious New York
Book: Rem Koolhaas, Madeleine Vriesendorp: Delirious New York

1977

P „Deutscher Herbst" mit zahlreichen Anschlägen der RAF
'German Autumn'; numerous attacks by the Red Fraction Army

A Renzo Piano und Richard Rogers: Centre Pompidou, Paris, Frankreich
Renzo Piano and Richard Rogers: Centre Pompidou, Paris, France
Josef Paul Kleihues: Wohnbebauung Vinetaplatz, Berlin
Josef Paul Kleihues: apartment complex, Vinetaplatz, Berlin, Germany
Charles Jencks: The Language of Postmodern Architecture (dt. 1978)
Charles Jencks: The Language of Postmodern Architecture (German edition, 1978)

---

einem oberitalienischen Dorf mit der architektonischen Moderne –, eine Anlage, die jenseits aller Ismen angesiedelt war. Sie zeigte, dass Architektur keine Frage von Stilen, sondern ausschließlich eine von Qualitäten ist.

„Entsprechend kritisch und distanziert sehen wir deshalb auch alle vergangenen und heute wieder neu sprießenden architektonischen Grundsatzbekenntnisse", schrieb Meinhard von Gerkan im Jahre 1978 in einem Grundsatzbekenntnis: Die Begründung jedes Entwurfs aus seinen spezifischen Bedingungen heraus war das frühe und andauernde Credo des Büros – eines, das nicht in Beliebigkeit endete, sondern in konsequenter Rationalität. Dazu brauchte es kein gesellschaftliches Gesamtprojekt, wie es die Moderne darstellte. Dazu brauchte es nur gute Architekten; und Bauten wie das Max-Planck-Institut in Lindau, das Wohn- und Bürohaus in Hamburg oder die Hauptverwaltung der Esso AG in Hamburg bezeugen die – durchaus zeitgebundene – Rationalität.

1976–1982

Warum ein Zeitabschnitt von 1976 bis 1982? Eine politische Begründung lautet: Es war die Zeit Helmut Schmidts als Bundeskanzler in Deutschland – pragmatisch, unideologisch, aber in den Entscheidungen doch zu Grundsatzpositionen gezwungen: Der „Deutsche Herbst" 1977 mit zahlreichen Attentaten durch inzwischen bewaffnete Reste der Studentenrevolte, die Aufrüstung der NATO zum Zwecke der Abrüstung („Doppelbeschluss")

erzwangen schwere Entscheidungen des Staates. Das Ende der sozialliberalen Koalition und der Beginn von 16 Jahren Kanzlerschaft von Helmut Kohl geben ihre eigene Antwort darauf.

Aber man kann den Zeitraum auch anders begründen: 1975 war nämlich unter architekturtheoretischen Aspekten vor allem das: das „Europäische Jahr des Denkmalschutzes". Wie schon um 1900, als der Denkmalschutz in seinem heutigen Verständnis entwickelt wurde, ging dem „Schutz" die Zerstörung voraus – durch den Krieg, aber auch durch die Euphorie des Wiederaufbaus und den Bauboom der Nachkriegszeit; es wird gern behauptet, die Zerstörungen durch Abrisse in den ersten Jahren der Bundesrepublik seien größer als die durch die Bomben des Krieges verursachten. Das Bewusstsein, das Neue sei das Bessere, änderte sich in der Bundesrepublik im Laufe der sechziger Jahre – der Protest und Hausbesetzungen gegen den Abriss nicht immer bauhistorisch wertvoller, sondern häufig spekulativer, ausbeuterischer Wohnquartiere des 19. Jahrhunderts, wie es sie in Berlin-Kreuzberg, aber in jeder anderen Stadt ebenfalls gab, hatte als Kern: Das Quartier wurde als „Kiez" empfunden, als funktionierender Stadtteil, der für viele zur Heimat geworden war. „Eine Zukunft für unsere Vergangenheit", hieß das Motto des Denkmalschutzjahres. Es brachte einen mächtigen Schub für die Denkmalpflege der Bundesrepublik; Denkmalschutz wurde von einer – zwar notwendigen – Randdisziplin zu etwas, das selbst von Politikern anerkannt wurde. Es

deutete sich an, was heute Gewissheit geworden ist: Der Rückgriff auf historisierende Formen ist wieder salonfähig geworden – obwohl der das direkte Gegenteil von Denkmalschutz ist.

Es ist keineswegs ein Zufall, dass diese Jahre auch den Höhepunkt der postmodernen Architektur bildeten, denn beiden – Denkmalschutz und Postmoderne – lag eine Ablehnung, zumindest aber eine Problematisierung der Moderne zugrunde. 1982 – im gleichen Jahr wurden Ralph Erskines wie selbst gebastelt wirkende Wohnbebauung in Newcastle/Tyne (Großbritannien) mit der Byker Wall und Ricardo Bofills monumentaler Betonfertigteil-Klassizismus „Palacio d'Abraxas" bei Paris fertig gestellt, und im fernen Hongkong gewann eine bis dahin völlig unbekannte irakische Architektin namens Zaha Hadid einen weltweit ausgeschriebenen Wettbewerb für ein Restaurant: „The Peak". Zusammen mit einer schräg zusammengenagelten Erweiterung eines eher bescheidenen Wohnhauses bei Los Angeles durch den Kanadier Frank O. Gehry und einigen Zeichnungen von mikado-ähnlichen Verwerfungen durch COOP Himmelb(l)au oder Daniel Libeskind war der „Dekonstruktivismus" geboren, der freilich seinen Namen erst mit einer Ausstellung in New York 1988 bekam.

Dekonstruktivismus – das war das vorläufig letzte Mosaiksteinchen einer Postmoderne, die in der Auseinandersetzung mit der Moderne aus eben dieser neue Funken schlug. Es zeigte sich in den folgenden Jahren, dass gerade die Teile, die sich am weitesten von der heroischen

1978

P   Beitritt Großbritanniens, Irlands und Dänemarks zur EG
    Admittance of Great Britain, Ireland and Denmark into
    the European Union
    Karol Wojtyla wird Papst Johannes Paul II.
    Karol Wojtyla become Pope John Paul II
A   Charles Moore: Piazza d'Italia, New Orleans, USA
    Charles Moore: Piazza d'Italia, New Orleans,
    United States
    Frank O. Gehry: Haus Gehry, Santa Monica, USA
    Frank O. Gehry: Gehry House, Santa Monica,
    United States
    Norman Foster: Sainsbury Centre for the Visual Arts,
    Norwich, Großbritannien
    Norman Foster: Sainsbury Centre for the Visual Arts,
    Norwich, Great Britain
    Hans Hollein: Fremdenverkehrsverein Opernring, Wien,
    Österreich
    Hans Hollein: tourist association building, Opernring,
    Vienna, Austria
    Buch: Robert Venturi u.a.: Learning from
    Las Vegas (dt. 1979)
    Book: Robert Venturi: Learning from Las Vegas
    (among others) (German edition, 1979)

1979

P   In Großbritannien wird Margaret Thatcher
    Premierminister (bis 1990)
    Margaret Thatcher becomes prime minister
    of Great Britain (governs until 1990)
    Friedensvertrag zwischen Israel und Ägypten
    Peace treaty between Israel and Egypt
A   **Joachim Schürmann: Wohnbebauung
    Groß-St.-Martin, Köln
    Joachim Schürmann: Groß-St.-Martin apartment
    buildings, Cologne, Germany**
    Beginn der IBA, Berlin
    Start of the International Building Exhibition (IBA),
    Berlin, Germany

Chancellor were to give their own responses to these issues.

Yet one could state other reasons for defining this specific period. From the point of view of architectural theory, for example, 1975 was the 'European Year of Monument Conservation'. As around 1900, when the idea and practice of protecting and preserving monuments was devised as we know it today, protection was preceded by destruction – caused during World War I – but also through the euphoria of reconstruction and the post-war construction boom. There are those who like to maintain that demolitions during the first years of the Federal Republic caused more damage than the bombs of World War II. The notion that the new is always better than the old did not change until the 1960s. Civic protesters and squatters wanted to stop the demolition of old tenement quarters which were not always of valuable architectural quality, but often, as in Kreuzberg (Berlin's East End), the products of 19th-century speculative, exploitative interests. At the core of these protests was that these well-functioning urban neighbourhoods had become 'home' to many of their inhabitants. The year of monument conservation had as its motto, "A Future for our Past", and gave a mighty boost to monument conservation in the Federal Republic, moving from a marginal (though necessary) discipline to a profession recognized even by politicians. This started a trend which, today, has become an established fact: using historicist forms has again become socially acceptable, although it is the exact opposite of monument conservation.

It is by no means a coincidence that these years represent the heyday of postmodern architecture. After all, at the root of both monument conservation and Postmodernism was the rejection of Modernism, or at least an expounding of its problematic aspects. 1982: that year saw the completion of Ralph Erskine's Byker Wall housing complex, which appears somewhat 'DIY'; of Ricardo Bofill's monumental prefab classicist Palacio d'Abraxas near Paris; while in faraway Hong Kong the then unknown Iraqi architect Zaha Hadid won the international competition for a restaurant called 'The Peak'. This, and Canadian Frank O. Gehry's extension, 'nailed' together at a slant, of a rather modest house near Los Angeles and drawings of mikado-type geological faults by COOP Himmelb(l)au or Daniel Libeskind marked the birth of 'Deconstructivism', although it only received this name in 1988 with a first exhibition in New York.

Deconstruction was the latest tessera of Postmodernism which, although it went against Modernism, also drew new sparks of inspiration from it. The following years revealed that precisely that position which diverged furthest from the heroic Modernism of the 1920s, that is, the more or less ironically lightened postmodern Eclecticism, was the most untenable. Just take a look at many buildings of the euphorically celebrated International Building Exhibition Berlin of 1987, regarded as the playground of international architectural trendsetters: how quickly it became outdated!

Who still remembers the 'Strada novissima' at the 1980 Venice Biennale, where fretsaw-worked Eclecticism was happily celebrated as 'new architecture'?

It is sometimes better not to have been present at every event ...

Putting the projects gmp designed and built in these years into the different 'compartments' (which at the time were juggled with in virtuoso fashion) has its attractions. This done, the reconstruction of the Hamburg 'Fabrik' would be labelled as monument conservation (which even the architects did not pretend it to be); the 'Passages' (Walter Benjamin) of the Hanse Viertel in Hamburg would pass as postmodern Eclecticism; the developments at Taima and Sulayyil in Saudi Arabia would be ranged as (critical?) regionalism, and the 'black box' of a store selling audio and video systems would be subsumed under Deconstructivism. For what else can it be when a building appears to sink into the ground at an angle? All this only goes to show that these compartments are inappropriate for classifying architecture.

Something else that had existed before, but not as conspicuously, made itself felt in these years: the trend towards exposed lightweight, filigree structures. Buildings such as the Sports Forum in Kiel (a reference to the Braunschweig school in the person of Dieter Oesterlen), a taxi-rank canopy at Berlin-Tegel Airport and the timber structure of the residential building G. show how they are made, but do not make a

1980

P Einmarsch der UdSSR in Afghanistan
Invasion of Afghanistan by the Soviet Union
Erste unabhängige Gewerkschaft in Polen
(„Solidarnoscz")
First independent union created in Poland
('Solidarnoscz')
Tod Titos
Tito dies

A Karljosef Schattner: Fachbereichsbibliothek
„Ulmer Hof", Eichstätt
Karljosef Schattner: faculty library 'Ulmer Hof',
Eichstätt, Germany
„Strada Novissima" auf der Biennale Venedig, Italien
'Strada Novissima' at the Biennale in Venice, Italy

1981

A Gustav Peichl: 4 ORF-Studios, Österreich
Gustav Peichl: four ORF studios, Austria
Buch: K.C. Bloomer / Charles Moore:
Architektur für den einprägsamen Ort
Book: K.C. Bloomer / Charles Moore: Body, Memory
and Architecture (Original English edition 1978)
Buch: Gert Kähler: Architektur als Symbolverfall.
Das Dampfermotiv in der Baukunst
Book: Gert Kähler: Architektur als Symbolverfall.
Das Dampfermotiv in der Baukunst

1982

P Ende der sozialliberalen Koalition; Helmut Kohl wird
Bundeskanzler
End of the social liberal coalition; Helmut Kohl becomes
German chancellor
Andropow löst Breschnew (†) als Generalsekretär der
KPU ab
Andropow replaces Brezhnev (†) as secretary general
of the CPSU

Moderne der 1920er Jahre entfernten, nämlich der mehr oder weniger ironisch gebrochene postmoderne Eklektizismus, deren am wenigsten haltbarer Teil war. Man sehe sich viele Bauten der euphorisch gefeierten Internationalen Bauausstellung in Berlin an, die als Tummelplatz internationaler architektonischer Trendsetter galt – wie schnell ist das veraltet! Wer erinnert sich heute noch an die „Strada Novissima" auf der Biennale in Venedig 1980, in der der laubsägegeschnitzte Eklektizismus fröhlich als neue Architektur gefeiert wurde?

Bisweilen ist es eben doch von Vorteil, nicht überall dabei gewesen zu sein ...

Es ist nicht ohne Reiz, die Arbeiten des Büros gmp aus dieser Zeit auf die verschiedenen „Schubladen" zu verteilen, wie sie in jenen Jahren virtuos jongliert wurden – dann steht der Wiederaufbau der „Fabrik" in Hamburg-Altona nach einem Brand, der das Haus vollständig zerstört hatte, unter dem Label des Denkmalschutzes (was er nicht ist, was die Architekten auch nicht vorgeben), das „Passagenwerk" des „Hanse-Viertels" in Hamburg geht als „postmoderner Eklektizismus" durch, weil deutlich ins Moderne gewendete historische Bezüge hergestellt werden, die Bebauung in Taima und Sulayyil in Saudi-Arabien würde unter dem Vorzeichen eines (kritischen?) „Regionalismus", und die „Black Box" eines Verkaufslagers für Unterhaltungselektronik in Hamburg unter „Dekonstruktivismus" subsumiert. Denn was kann es anderes sein, wenn ein Gebäude schräg im Boden zu versinken scheint?

Was auch nur zeigt, dass diese Schubladen nicht taugen, um Architektur zu erfassen.

Etwas anderes lässt sich dennoch in diesen Jahren in der Arbeit des Büros beobachten, das vorher vorhanden, aber nicht so offensichtlich war: nämlich eine Tendenz hin zu leichten, filigranen Konstruktionen, die als solche gezeigt werden. Das Sportforum in Kiel – Reverenz an die Braunschweiger Schule in Gestalt von Dieter Oesterlen –, eine Taxistand-Überdachung am Flughafen Tegel oder die Holzkonstruktion des Wohnhauses G. – in Bauten wie diesen, die zeigen, wie sie gemacht sind, aber daraus nicht eine Sensation um ihrer selbst Willen machen, erweist sich die Disziplin des Büros, die modische Lösungen (fast) immer ablehnt.

1983–1989

Im vorigen Abschnitt wurde überlegt, ob und wie ein so vielschichtiges und vielseitiges Œuvre wie das von gmp in „Schubladen" aufgeteilt werden kann, die etwas über ihre Architektur aussagen? Ihre herausragenden Bauten dieses Abschnitts, der in der Bundesrepublik politisch vom Regierungsbeginn Helmut Kohls bis zur Öffnung der Mauer in Berlin verläuft, sind (in einer subjektive Auswahl) das Parkhaus Poststraße, die Innenhof-Überdachung des Museums für Hamburgische Geschichte und die Eckbebauung an der Grindelallee.

Alle drei Objekte liegen in Hamburg. Alle drei sind sehr unterschiedlich – roter Backstein in einer Umgebung, in der es wenig davon gibt; eine filigrane technische Lösung, die auch vom Denkmalschutz begeistert begrüßt wurde; eine absolut zeitgemäße Architektur aus Stahl und Putz als Antwort auf ein eher unbedeutendes gründerzeitliches Wohnhaus. Alle drei sprechen, oberflächlich gesehen, eine unterschiedliche Sprache – Regionalismus, High Tech, Late Modernism. Alle drei gehen intensiv auf den vorhandenen Ort ein. Was besagen dann die „Schubladen"?

Die „Schubladen" werden auch international gern verwendet; ihr Gebrauchswert bleibt eng begrenzt, genauer: Ihr Wert ist auf die Medien beschränkt. Wenn man diesen folgt, dann gibt es eine leicht verständliche Stilfolge. Aber was noch eine gewisse Berechtigung besaß, als Stile mehrere hundert Jahre bis zur endgültigen Spätphase brauchten – Romanik, Gotik, Renaissance –, das taugt in unserer Zeit nicht mehr, wird aber dennoch gern genommen: Konnte die Nachkriegsmoderne noch von 1950 bis etwa 1975 datiert werden – mit einigen Einsprengseln wie Brutalismus oder Metabolismus –, so datierte der postmoderne Eklektizismus offenbar nur bis etwa 1986, als er von der High Tech Architektur abgelöst wurde. 1988 wurde – mit der Ausstellung in New York – der Dekonstruktivismus erfunden, anschließend eine „Neue Einfachheit" proklamiert, und heute befinden wir uns offenbar in der Stilphase – „Epoche" möchte man die kurzen Abschnitte kaum nennen – computergenerierter, amöben-

1983

A Ralph Erskine: Wohnquartier Byker, Newcastle/
   Tyne, Großbritannien
   Ralph Erskine: Byker residential quarter, Newcastle/
   Tyne, Great Britain
   Zaha Hadid: Wettbewerb „The Peak", Hongkong
   Zaha Hadid: competition 'The Peak', Hong Kong
   Ricardo Bofill: Palacio d'Abraxas, Marne-La-Vallée,
   Frankreich
   Ricardo Bofill: Palacio d'Abraxas, Marne-La-Vallée,
   France

A Lech Walesa erhält den Friedensnobelpreis
   Lech Walesa receives the Nobel Peace Prize
P Buch: Oswald Mathias Ungers: Die Thematisierung
   der Architektur
   Book: Oswald Mathias Ungers: Die Thematisierung
   der Architektur

1984

A Berichtstermin IBA Berlin
   First review of IBA Berlin
   Ausstellung im DAM: Die Revision der Moderne
   Exhibition in the German Architecture Museum:
   Die Revision der Moderne
   James Stirling: Staatsgalerie Stuttgart
   James Stirling: Staatsgalerie Stuttgart
   Oswald Mathias Ungers: Deutsches
   Architekturmuseum, Frankfurt/Main
   Oswald Mathias Ungers: German Architecture
   Museum, Frankfurt/Main, Germany

sensation out of it for sensation's sake. They reveal the discipline of the office team who (almost always) reject 'fashionable' solutions.

1983–1989

Having reflected on whether, and how, such a multi-layered and multiform oeuvre as that by gmp can be compartmentalized, we must ask whether these compartments say anything about gmp's architecture. According to the subjective choice of the author, the firm's outstanding buildings of this period – which in terms of politics lasted through Helmut Kohl's term of office up to the opening of the Berlin Wall – are the Poststrasse multistorey car park, the glass-and-steel canopy covering the patio of the Museum für Hamburgische Geschichte (Hamburg History Museum), and a house at the corner of Grindelallee.

All three buildings are in Hamburg, but are very different from each other: red bricks in an otherwise rather brickless context; a filigree engineering solution which even monument conservation hailed with enthusiasm; an absolutely contemporary architecture of steel and rendered façades on top of a rather insignificant, late 19th-century house. Seen superficially, all three speak a different language: regionalist, high-tech, late-modern. And all three are highly 'contextual'. What, then, do the 'compartments' mean?

'Compartments' are popular internationally, too, their utility value is strictly limited – to the media, to be precise. If one goes along with the media, there is an easily understandable style chronology. This was somewhat justified when styles – Romanesque, Gothic, Renaissance – took several centuries to reach their final stages. 'Compartments' cannot be applied to our time, but are still used readily. While it was possible to define the post-war stylistic period as 1950 to c. 1975 (with a few interspersions such as Brutalism or Metabolism), the end of postmodern Eclecticism has obviously been fixed at 1986, when it was replaced by high-tech architecture. The New York exhibition of 1988 marked the invention of Deconstructivism, to be followed by the proclamation of 'new simplicity' while today we seem to be in the middle of the style phase (one hesitates to call these short periods 'epochs') of computer-generated, amorphous blobs of 'architectures of foam', philosophically undergirded by Peter Sloterdijk. None of this says anything about the architectures, their theoretical foundations or logics, but only something about the mechanisms which bring them to the surface.

In fact, most currents, as always, run parallel to each other. Architectural critics and theoreticians might learn from politics that the only thing we can really be certain of is constant, unexpected change. The times of constancy and certainty seem to belong to that past we call the 'good old times'. Constancy (in the person of a chancellor known for 'sitting out' problems) became a type, yet who could have imagined the changes that happened? Who would have thought in January 1989 that the Wall would have fallen by December of that same year? 'Mauerspecht' (wall pecker) became the buzzword of that year (and has long since been on the 'red list' of extinct species).

One certainty that existed for decades after World War II was the East-West 'contrast', less euphemistically called the 'Cold War'. Within a few months it was history! One of the ten leading industrialized states of the world, the GDR, had proved to be a deceptive economic packaging, and the operation to rescue it could not be paid just with a bit of West German petty cash. We have called the years from 1966 to 1969 a time of change. What exactly happened in those years?

Surprisingly, the architecture of the time does not tell of radical change – neither gmp's nor international architecture, distilled by architectural theory. The emerging 'new simplicity' prettified itself by propagating permanence in times when the non-permanent prevailed, in other words, dramatic political changes, and turned our world upside down. Architecture to reassure the world? The term 'with one's back to the wall' used as an architectural metaphor of social conditions which demand that this wall must be of stone and durable, and show that it is so?

In fact, at times, the architecture of 'new simplicity' verges almost desperately on the classical modern architecture of the 1920s which had been abandoned only a short while ago for postmodern variety.

The 'new simplicity' proposed by gmp these last few years is also a form of reasserting something, namely red bricks. From Kiel to

1985

P Verlängerung des „Warschauer Paktes" um 20 Jahre
   Twenty year extension of the 'Warsaw Pack' signed
   Gorbatschow löst Andropow (†) als Generalsekretär
   der KPU ab
   Gorbachev replaces Andropow (†) as secretary general
   of the CPSU

A Bernard Tschumi: Parc de la Valette, Paris, Frankreich
   Bernard Tschumi: Parc de la Valette, Paris, France
   Buch: Heinrich Klotz: Moderne und Postmoderne.
   Architektur der Gegenwart 1960-1980
   Book: Heinrich Klotz: Moderne und Postmoderne.
   Architektur der Gegenwart 1960-1980

1986

P Spanien und Portugal treten der EG bei
   Admittance of Spain and Portugal into the
   European Union
   Ermordung Olof Palmes in Stockholm
   Assassination of Olof Palme in Stockholm
   Reaktorunglück in Tschernobyl
   Chernobyl disaster at the Chernobyl Nuclear
   Power Plant

A Richard Rogers: Lloyd's Versicherung, London,
   Großbritannien
   Richard Rogers: Lloyd's Insurance office building,
   London, Great Britain
   Norman Foster: Hongkong and Shanghai Bank,
   Hongkong
   Norman Foster: Hong Kong and Shanghai Bank,
   Hong Kong
   Rafael Moneo: Museo Nacional de Arte Romano,
   Merida, Spain
   Rafael Moneo: Museo Nacional de Arte Romano,
   Merida, Spain

hafter Blobs oder von „Architekturen des Schaums" – mit philosophischer Unterstützung von Peter Sloterdijk. Alles zusammen sagt nichts über die Architekturen, ihre Theorien oder deren Schlüssigkeit aus, sondern nur etwas über die Mechanismen, die sie emporspülen.

Tatsächlich liefen und laufen die meisten Strömungen parallel.
Dabei könnten die Architekturtheoretiker und -kritiker etwas von der Politik lernen: Das einzige, was wirklich gesichert scheint, ist die ständige und überraschende Veränderung. Die Zeiten von Konstanz und Gewissheit gehören offenbar jener Vergangenheit an, die man die „gute, alte Zeit" nennt. Konstanz – sie wurde in der Person eines aussitzenden Kanzlers zum Typ. Aber welche tatsächlichen Veränderungen gab es! Wer hätte auch nur am Beginn des Jahres 1989 gedacht, die Mauer in Berlin würde an dessen Ende gefallen sein, der „Mauerspecht" würde zum Wort des Jahres (inzwischen ist er längst auf der „roten Liste" ausgestorbener Tierarten angekommen)!

Die Gewissheit der gesamten Nachkriegszeit war der eher euphemistisch so genannte Ost-West-Gegensatz – weniger freundlich hieß er „Kalter Krieg" –, und binnen eines Jahres gehörte dieser der Geschichte an! Eine der zehn führenden Industrienationen der Welt, die DDR, erwies sich als wirtschaftliche Mogelpackung, deren Sanierung man eben nicht so mal eben aus der westdeutschen Portokasse bezahlen konnte! Eine Zeit des Umbruchs hatten wir die Jahre von 1966 bis 1969 genannt.

Ja, was waren dann dieses für Jahre?
Erstaunlich ist, dass man das der Architektur nicht ansieht – weder der von gmp noch der von Architekturtheoretikern destillierten internationalen Entwicklung. Die entstehende „Neue Einfachheit" machte sich begrifflich hübsch, weil sie das Dauerhafte propagierte in Zeiten, da das Nicht-Dauerhafte, der dramatische politische Wandel dominierte und unsere Welt auf den Kopf stellte. Architektur als Vergewisserung der Welt? Der Begriff „mit dem Rücken zur Wand stehen" als architektonische Kategorie gesellschaftlicher Zustände, weshalb diese Wand aus Stein und dauerhaft sein und das nach außen hin zeigen müsse?

Tatsächlich nähert sich die Architektur einer „Neuen Einfachheit" bisweilen fast verzweifelt wieder der Architektur der klassischen Moderne der 1920er Jahre an, die man doch soeben verlassen hatte zugunsten postmoderner Vielfalt.

Die „neue Einfachheit" des Büros gmp, auch das eine Vergewisserung, ist in diesen Jahren der rote Backstein. Von Kiel bis Bremen, mit einem starken Schwerpunkt in Hamburg, wird das traditionelle, beinahe altmodische Material aufgegriffen, um den Bezug zum Ort herzustellen. Im Ergebnis wirken die Bauten vertraut, obwohl sie – zum Glück! – in den Formen keineswegs traditionell sind. Was der Hamburger Oberbaudirektor Fritz Schumacher in den 1920er Jahren geschafft hatte, nämlich die stilistischen Unterschiede zahlreicher Architekten im einheitlichen Material verschwinden zu lassen, das bewährt sich auch hier; die Neuheit der Formen – man nehme das Parkhaus in Hamburgs Poststraße mit einem Fassadenaufbau, der weder mit dem Inneren noch mit der Umgebung zu tun hat! – bekommt einen Einschlag von Vertrautem, er, der Backstein „dämpft alle neuartigen Wirkungen durch einen leisen Einschlag von Überlieferung", wie es Fritz Schumacher gesagt hatte.

Gerade die Tatsache, dass das Büro an anderer Stelle andere Materialien verwendete, beweist die Richtigkeit der Theorie einer Annäherung an einen Ort; im – formal gesehen – polaren Gegensatz zum Parkhaus steht der Bau des eigenen Büros an der Elbchaussee: der weiße Putzbau dort, wo dieser auch in Hamburg zuhause ist. Dass der „Dampfer" quer zur Elbe liegt und damit auf schwerem Havariekurs, mag man dagegen verzeihen. Symbolisch wird es nicht gemeint sein; dagegen sind die Erfolge des Büros gerade in den folgenden Jahren zu eindrucksvoll.

1990–2000

Die politischen Widersprüche setzten sich fort und sind im Rückblick besonders deutlich, auch in ihrer Absurdität: Da „wächst", mit den Worten des ehemaligen Bundeskanzlers Willy Brandt, „zusammen, was zusammen gehört", da bricht mit der UdSSR eine die gesamte Nachkriegszeit in Europa dominierende Großmacht binnen Jahresfrist zusammen, da erweist sich ein ideologisches Konzept wie das des Kommunismus, das viele Jahre lang die halbe Welt geprägt hatte, als Seifenblase, weil es an den simplen Bedürfnissen der Menschen vorbei ging

1987

P   „Barschel-Affäre" in Schleswig-Holstein
    'Barschel Affair' in Schleswig-Holstein, Germany
A   Jean Nouvel: Institut du Monde Arabe, Paris, Frankreich
    Jean Nouvel: Institut du Monde Arabe, Paris, France
    OMA/Rem Koolhaas: Nederlands Danstheater, Den Haag, Niederlande
    OMA/Rem Koolhaas: Nederlands Danstheater, The Hague, Netherlands
    Günter Behnisch: Hysolarinstitut Stuttgart
    Günter Behnisch: Hysolarinstitut, Stuttgart, Germany
    2. Berichtstermin IBA Berlin
    Second review of IBA Berlin

1988

A   Erith + Terry: Richmond Riverside, London, Großbritannien
    Erith + Terry: Richmond Riverside, London, Great Britain
    Kollhoff: Wohnblock Luisenplatz, Berlin
    Kollhoff: apartment buildings on Luisenplatz, Berlin, Germany
    Herzog & de Meuron: Wohnhaus entlang Scheidemauer, Basel, Schweiz
    Herzog & de Meuron: apartment house on a division wall, Basel, Switzerland

Bremen, and especially in Hamburg, gmp again uses this traditional, almost old-fashioned material to relate the buildings to their contexts. This makes them seem familiar although, happily, the forms are anything but traditional. In the 1920s, Hamburg's chief architect, Fritz Schumacher, succeeded in making differences of style between the many architects who built in the city less obvious by ruling that they had to use the same material, that is to say, bricks. This method has proved successful in our time, too. Newness of form (for example, of the car park on Poststrasse with a façade unrelated to either interior or surroundings!) has a touch of the familiar. Bricks, Schumacher said, "soften all novel effects by a subtle admixture of tradition".

The fact that gmp has used other materials in other places confirms the truth of the philosophy of contextual approach. gmp's own offices on Elbchaussee formally represent the opposite pole to the multi-storey car park; it is a white-rendered building in an area of Hamburg where rendered façades are widespread. Observers may forgive the architects for having placed the 'steamer' at an angle to the Elbe – on a serious collision course, so to speak. This is probably not to be taken symbolically; the success the office has had in recent years is too impressive for that.

1990–2000

Political contradictions continued, clearly discernible with hindsight, also in their absurdities. In the words of Willy Brandt, something that "belongs together is growing together again". With the collapse of the USSR, the superpower that had dominated post-war Europe disappeared within a year, and the ideology of Communism, which had shaped half the world for decades, burst like a soap bubble because it neglected the simple needs of the people. (In a wonderful caricature, Marx, in the eternity of heaven, tells Engels that Communism was "just a passing idea".)

Over the course of these years, walls came down – in people's minds – and national borders opened – in reality – after the Schengen Agreement of 1990 had instituted freedom of movement within the European Union. Yet that same year, Europe also experienced the first wars since 1945 (in the Balkans), and beyond Europe the United States rose to become the only global superpower, attempting to set the world to rights by ending Iraqi occupation of Kuwait with the first Gulf War. War again became a reality (which Europeans at least had thought a thing of the past) and a political tool.

But realities change, not only in politics, but in society, art, and in architecture with its changing function. During these years, architectural theory and critique seemed to realize that the different names of the various, ever shorter style periods were no longer helpful in explaining the (architectural) world. This also meant the final acceptance of postmodern thought, which defines the juxtaposition of different architectures as the basic prerequisite for further development.

In consequence, the debate turned from architectural problems to questions of urban design. A random selection of book titles shows the uncertainties involved: 'Die zweckentfremdete Stadt' (1994; Misappropriated city); 'Risiko Stadt?' (1997; The city, a hazard?); 'Macht Stadt krank?' (1996; Does the city make us ill?); 'Streiten für die menschliche Stadt' (1997; Fighting for a humane city); 'Kursbuch Stadt' (1995; Urban timetable); and 'Lebensmodell STADT' (2002), subtitled 'about the lost connections between urban life, society and design'. The list could be extended at will by international publications by Richard Sennett, Saskia Sassen and others.

What was remarkable was that the metropolis, the large city as a social and architectural entity, was an achievement of the 20th century. It had grown in the 19th century, but became a 'quality' only after it had 'physically' existed for some time, when the convergence of great numbers of people led to new forms of humans living together. Sociologist Georg Simmel had observed this as early as the beginning of the 20th century. After World War II, however, when everybody had to make a fresh start, in the Federal Republic and in Central Europe, there emerged the ideal of a 'city for all', represented by mass 'social housing' and the (alleged) solution to every conceivable national problem by means of new institutions – from civic centre to homes for the elderly. Even though today we no longer appreciate the buildings of that time very much, for the first time in living memory the new purpose of

1989

P Bau der Wiederaufbereitungsanlage in Wackersdorf wird eingestellt.
Construction of the reprocessing plant in Wackersdorf is halted
„Montagsdemonstrationen" in Leipzig und anderen Städten führen zum Fall der Mauer
'Monday demonstrations' in Leipzig and other cities lead to the Fall of the Wall
Vaclav Havel wird Staatspräsident in der Tschechoslowakei
Vaclav Havel becomes president of Czechoslovakia
UdSSR beendet den Krieg in Afghanistan
Soviet Union ends its war in Afghanistan
Sturz Ceausescus in Rumänien
Fall of Ceausescu in Romania

Massendemonstrationen auf dem „Platz des Himmlischen Friedens" in Peking werden blutig niedergeschlagen
Mass demonstrations on the Square of Heavenly Peace in Peking end in a massacre

A COOP Himmelb(l)au: Dachausbau Falkestraße, Wien, Österreich
COOP Himmelb(l)au: roof finishing and completion, Falkestrasse, Vienna, Austria
Ieoh Ming Pei: Louvreeingang, Paris, Fankreich
Ieoh Ming Pei: entrance to the Louvre museum, Paris, France
Eisenman: Wexner Centre For the Visual Arts, Columbus, Ohio, USA
Eisenman: Wexner Center for the Visual Arts, Columbus, Ohio, United States

(in einer wunderbaren Karikatur meinte im Himmel der Unsterblichkeit Marx zu Engels, der Kommunismus sei „ja nur mal so eine Idee" gewesen).

Da öffnen sich also Grenzen in den Köpfen, aber auch in der Realität der Landesgrenzen, nachdem mit dem „Schengener Abkommen" 1990 die Freizügigkeit innerhalb der Europäischen Union weitgehend durchgesetzt war. Und dann werden im gleichen Jahr auf dem Balkan die ersten Kriege innerhalb Europas seit 1945 geführt, und außerhalb Europas etabliert sich die USA als einzige ernst zu nehmende globale Ordnungsmacht, indem sie mit dem ersten Golfkrieg die Besetzung Kuwaits durch den Irak beendet – der Krieg wird erneut zur (zumindest in Europa überwunden geglaubten) Realität und zum Mittel der Politik!

Aber Realitäten ändern sich. Das bezieht sich nicht nur auf die Politik, sondern auf die Gesellschaft, die Kunst, auf die Architektur, deren Funktion innerhalb der Gesellschaft sich zunehmend wandelte. In der Architekturtheorie und -kritik schien man während dieser Jahre zu der richtigen Erkenntnis zu kommen, die immer schneller aufeinander folgenden Begriffe für unterschiedliche Strömungen seien als Erklärung der (architektonischen) Welt nicht mehr wirklich hilfreich. Das bedeutete gleichzeitig die endgültige Anerkennung postmodernen Denkens, das das Nebeneinander unterschiedlicher Architekturen als Grundbedingung einer Weiterentwicklung begreift.

Die Fragestellungen verlagerten sich konsequenterweise von den architektonischen auf die städtischen Fragen. Ein beliebiger Griff in den Bücherschrank verrät die Unsicherheit, die sich dort zeigte: „Die zweckentfremdete Stadt" (1994), „Risiko Stadt?" (1995), „Macht Stadt krank?" (1996), „Streiten für die menschliche Stadt" (1997), „Kursbuch Stadt" (1999), „Lebensmodell STADT" mit dem Untertitel: „Über den verlorenen Zusammenhang von Stadtleben, Stadtgesellschaft und Städtebau" (2000), „Was ist los mit den öffentlichen Räumen?" (2002) – man kann die Liste mit den internationalen Titeln von Richard Sennett oder Saskia Sassen beliebig fortsetzen.

Das war schon sehr bemerkenswert: Die Metropole, die Großstadt als soziales und architektonisches Gebilde war eine Errungenschaft des 20. Jahrhunderts. Sie war im 19. Jahrhundert gewachsen, aber zur Qualität erst geworden, als sie schon physisch existierte, als also die Zusammenballung vieler Menschen zu neuen Formen des Zusammenlebens führte. Das hatte der Soziologe Georg Simmel schon am Anfang des 20. Jahrhunderts festgestellt; nach dem Zweiten Weltkrieg aber, unter der Voraussetzung eines Neuanfangs für alle, hatte sich in der Bundesrepublik und in Mitteleuropa das Ideal einer „Stadt für alle" herauskristallisiert; der massenhafte „soziale Wohnungsbau" und die (scheinbare) Lösung jedweden gesellschaftlichen Problems durch neue Institutionen vom Bürgerhaus bis zum Altersheim standen dafür. Das war eine neue Qualität, selbst wenn wir die gebauten Ergebnisse heute nicht mehr besonders hoch schätzen: zum ersten Mal in der Geschichte der Menschheit die menschenwürdige Wohnung, die Stadt für alle realisieren zu wollen und dieses Ziel in weiten Teilen auch zu erreichen!

Dieses Ideal war am Ende des Jahrhunderts so brüchig geworden wie die Sichtbetonbauten der Trabantenstädte – städtische Seniorentreffs wurden von privaten Seniorenresidenzen abgelöst, städtische Stadtteil-Schwimmhallen von privaten „Bäder-Landschaften", das Einkaufen spaltete sich in die Aldi/Penny/Lidl-Baracken einerseits, die „Gallerias" und „Malls" andererseits, und beim Wohnen wurden die Bauten des sozialen Wohnungsbaus in den Trabantenstädten zunehmend zu „sozialen Brennpunkten", während auf der anderen Seite die „Residenzen" mit einem neuen Stilkonservativismus auftrumpften.

Die Gemeinde als Idee eines gesellschaftlichen Zusammenhalts ist unter den Einwirkungen von Migration, Globalisierung, Sesshaftigkeit verhindernder Flexibilisierung des Arbeitsmarktes, aber auch durch anderes Sozialverhalten wie die Verlockungen des Fernsehens, schließlich auch durch den Luxus des Wohnens auf 40 qm pro Person in ihrer traditionellen Form offenbar nicht mehr tragfähig. Die Stadt kann ihre traditionellen Aufgaben der sozialen Vorsorge immer weniger erfüllen, von der intakten Abwasserleitung bis zum Krankenhaus, zumal die Reihenfolge bei der Lösung ihrer Aufgaben heute verzerrt ist: immer weniger Geld für die Kommunen bei gleichen oder – zum Beispiel in der Sozialhilfe oder der Integration verschiedener Gruppen – gar wachsenden Aufgaben. Notwendig wäre dagegen

1990

P Währungsunion zwischen der Bundesrepublik und der DDR
Monetary union between the Federal Republic of Germany and the German Democratic Republic
3. Oktober Beitritt der DDR zur Bundesrepublik
On October 3, the GDR joins the Federal Republic of Germany
Schengener Abkommen öffnet die Grenzen in Europa
Schengen Treaty neutralizes internal borders within the European Community
Gorbatschow erhält den Friedensnobelpreis
Gorbachev receives the Nobel Peace Prize
A Volkskongress in Leipzig
People's Congress in Leipzig

1991

P Nach der Besetzung Kuwaits durch den Irak erster Golfkrieg; endet mit der Niederlage des Irak
The first Golf War begins after the invasion of Kuwait by Iraq; this ends with the defeat of Iraq
Auflösung des „Warschauer Paktes"
Dissolution of the Warsaw Pact
Gründung der GUS aus Russland und acht weiteren Staaten
Establishment of the CIS made up of Russia and eight other countries
Estland, Lettland und Litauen werden unabhängig
Estonia, Latvia and Lithuania become independent
Boris Jelzin wird Staatspräsident Russlands, Gorbatschow tritt zurück
Boris Yeltzsin becomes president of Russia; Gorbachev resigns
Beginn der Balkankriege (bis 1995), nachdem sich Kroatien, Slowenien, Mazedonien und Bosnien-Herzogowina für unabhängig erklären
The war in the Balkans begins (rages until 1995), after which Croatia, Slovenia, Macedonia and Bosnia-Herzegovina declare their independence
A Norman Foster: Stansted Airport, Großbritannien
Norman Foster: Stansted Airport, Stansted, Great Britain

---

architecture and urban planning aimed at urban quality, wanting to build the city for all, and then also achieved it in large parts.

At the end of the 20th century, this ideal had become as brittle as the exposed-concrete housing blocks in the satellite towns. Old people's homes were replaced by senior citizens' residences; neighbourhood public baths by 'fun poolscapes'; shoppers split into those who went to discount stores (Aldi, Lidl, etc.) and those who shopped in 'gallerias' and malls. Public housing estates in the suburbs increasingly turned into 'social hot spots', while on the other side 'residences' were the trump cards of a new conservative style.

The community idea of social togetherness and solidarity can no longer be practised in its traditional form. This is the result of migration, globalization and a flexible labour market which prevents people from settling, but is also due to changing social behaviour following the attractions of television, and finally also due to the fact that on average people have a living space of a luxurious 40 m² per person. The city is no longer able to provide the traditional public services, from keeping sewers in good repair to running hospitals, in particular since the order of means and priorities has changed. While municipalities have dwindling revenues, the services they have to provide (and finance) remain the same or are growing (social benefits, integration of minorities, etc.). One should first define what services citizens expect from the authorities, and then assign the necessary funds to them.

The marketplace, too, is often no longer a public institution – 'city air liberates!'. Instead, it has mutated into a shopping centre with limited liability and private 'sheriffs'. The CentrO in Oberhausen, built on ground once occupied by the industry that shaped the city, is an example of this change. Internationally, the Guggenheim in Bilbao and the namesake 'effect' have shown how architecture can respond to such situations: with spectacular buildings that have nothing in common with their surroundings, but make media events of their locations.

Bilbao became the model for many cities, though the economic benefits of the Guggenheim were short-lived. Still, the 'star architect' came to the fore. What was good for Bilbao must also be good for Bad Oeynhausen or Herford, and if one sensation isn't enough, then one must simply produce several. "Would you like a little more?" as the guiding principle of city fathers who are desperately trying to prevent their cities sinking into insignificance in order to aid business and industry and thus to create jobs. If one 'Gehry' doesn't do it, then let's put a 'Foster' next to him and a 'Herzoganddemeuron' behind – and if all else fails, will a 'Libeskind' perhaps do the trick?

How nice that gmp have – as yet – not submitted a design for the largest, tallest, longest, fastest completed building in the world!

Even without that, measured by the number of completed buildings, the decade from 1990 to 2000 were the office's most successful years. While the office portfolio lists only seven completed buildings per annum for the previous ten years, it lists double that annual number for most years in the current decade.

Figures alone don't say much. After all, buildings are different. On closer inspection, however, the figures reflect the two developments which also affect gmp, namely, globalization and the issue of the significance of the city in our time. From the beginning, international orientation has always been a factor in their work, because architects generally want to measure themselves against fellow architects abroad. Parallel to the general slump in Germany's building industry, however, gmp's international orientation has become its – highly successful – mainstay. Is there another architectural office that has worked as early and successfully as gmp in China, in a country where about a dozen other German architects are now also active? gmp's pioneering role on the international market cannot be overlooked, and its success still exceeds that of every other German office. It started with the winning competition design for the National Library in Teheran (1978), went on to 'Bucharest 2000' (1996), the National Assembly Building in Hanoi (2003) and the National Museum in Beijing (2004).

But what about the city and its changing role in architecture? In this sense, gmp has achieved something unusual. While in the previous paragraphs we have cited buildings which visibly and successfully relate to their contexts, we can now introduce buildings which have created new places.

1992

P Spanien auf der europäischen Bühne zurück: EXPO in Sevilla, Olympische Spiele in Barcelona, Kulturhauptstadt Madrid
Spain reenters the European stage with the EXPO in Seville, the Olympic games in Barcelona and Madrid as Europe's cultural capital
Die Slowakei trennt sich von Tschechien
Slovakia becomes independent of the Czech Republic

A **Santiago Calatrava: TGV-Bahnhof, Lyon, Frankreich**
Santiago Calatrava: TGV train station, Lyon, France
Günter Behnisch: Plenarsaal des Deutschen Bundestages, Bonn
Günter Behnisch: assembly room of the German parliament, Bonn, Germany

1993

P Vertrag von Maastricht tritt in Kraft, Beginn des Europäischen Binnenmarktes
Maastricht Treaty goes into effect; internal European market opens
Bill Clinton wird US-amerikanischer Präsident
Bill Clinton becomes president of the United States
Sprengstoffanschlag auf das World Trade Center in New York
Bomb attack on the World Trade Center in New York City
Erste freie Wahlen in Russland
First free elections in Russia

A Buch: Wolfgang Welsch: Wege aus der Moderne. Schlüsseltexte der Postmoderne-Diskussion
Book: Wolfgang Welsch: Wege aus der Moderne. Schlüsseltexte der Postmoderne-Diskussion

---

eine Definition dessen, was die Gesellschaft von der Kommune verlangt und geleistet sehen will, und dann deren Ausstattung mit den erforderlichen finanziellen Mitteln.

Auch der Markt bildet heute vielfach nicht mehr eine öffentliche Einrichtung – „Stadtluft macht frei!", wie der mittelalterliche Rechtsbegriff hieß –, sondern mutiert zum Einkaufszentrum mit beschränkter Haftung und privaten Sheriffs. Das Einkaufszentrum „CentrO" in Oberhausen, gebaut auf dem Grund, auf dem vorher die die Stadt und Umgebung wirtschaftlich prägende Industrie lag, macht den Wandel deutlich; es firmiert als „neue Mitte" der Stadt. International wurde mit dem Guggenheim-Museum in Bilbao und dem gleichnamigen „Effekt" gezeigt, wie die Architektur darauf reagieren kann: durch spektakuläre Bauten, die mit dem jeweiligen Ort nichts mehr zu tun haben, diesen aber zum Medienereignis machen.

Bilbao wurde zum Vorbild für viele Kommunen, obwohl der wirtschaftliche Effekt nur kurzfristig wirksam war; der „Star"-Architekt war geboren: Was für Bilbao gut war, das muss es doch für Bad Oeynhausen oder Herford auch sein? Und wenn es nicht die eine Sensation tut, dann produziert man eben mehrere – „Darf's ein bisschen mehr sein?" als Prinzip von Stadtvätern, die verzweifelt gegen die Bedeutungslosigkeit ihrer Städte ankämpfen, um der Wirtschaft und damit den Arbeitsplätzen zu helfen; wenn es der eine „Gehry" nicht tut, dann stellen wir noch einen „Foster" daneben, dahinter einen „Herzogunddemeuron", und wenn alles das noch keinen wirtschaftlichen Erfolg bringt, wird es ein „Libeskind" schaffen? Wie schön, dass gmp noch keinen Entwurf für das größte/höchste/längste/schnellste Gebäude der Welt vorgelegt hat!

Dabei war das Jahrzehnt zwischen 1990 und 2000 für das Büro die – gemessen an der Zahl fertig gestellter Bauten – erfolgreichste Zeit. Lag deren Zahl im Jahrzehnt zuvor nach Ausweis ihres Projektverzeichnisses bei höchstens sieben, so kamen sie im Folgenden meist auf die doppelte Anzahl.

Nun besagt eine solche Zahl wenig; Bau ist nicht gleich Bau. Eine nähere Betrachtung zeigt aber, dass sich darin auch für das Büro gmp die beiden genannten Entwicklungen spiegeln: die der Globalisierung und die der Frage nach der Bedeutung von Stadt in der gegenwärtigen Zeit. Denn die internationale Ausrichtung der Arbeit, wiewohl vom Beginn an vorhanden, weil sich die Architekten immer messen wollten an der internationalen Konkurrenz, wurde (parallel zu einer in Deutschland allgemein sinkenden Bauproduktion) zum dominierenden – und extrem erfolgreichen! – Faktor. Welches Architekturbüro hat schon so früh und so erfolgreich in China gearbeitet – dort, wo sich heute ein rundes Dutzend deutscher Büros tummeln? Die Vorreiterrolle von gmp auf dem internationalen Markt ist unübersehbar – und der Erfolg immer noch dem eines jeden anderen deutschen Büros überlegen: angefangen beim Wettbewerbserfolg für die Nationalbibliothek in Teheran 1978 über „Bukarest 2000" im Jahr 1996, den Bau für die Nationalversammlung in Hanoi 2003 und das Nationalmuseum in Peking 2004!

Die Sache mit der Stadt aber und der sich wandelnden Rolle der Architektur? In dieser, der letztgenannten Hinsicht schafft gmp etwas Ungewöhnliches: Nachdem wir im vorigen Abschnitt Bauten hervorgehoben haben, die sich erkennbar und erfolgreich mit dem jeweiligen Ort auseinander setzen, so können wir hier Bauten nennen, die einen neuen Ort erschaffen!

Das Extrem bildet zweifellos der Plan für eine vollständig neue Stadt in China, Lingang bei Shanghai, für zunächst 300 000 Einwohner (heute 800 000) und, mit der Hamburger Alster als Referenz, um einen künstlichen See herum geplant, der hoffentlich wie in Hamburg zum Ort der Identifikation wird. Aber „den Ort schaffen" kann man auch mit kleineren Aufgaben, von denen nur zwei herausgehoben werden sollen, die das unter schwierigen Bedingungen erreichen: Die Neue Messe in Leipzig und der Pavillon der christlichen Kirchen auf der EXPO in Hannover.

Beide Projekte schaffen neue Bilder an Plätzen, die bis dahin keine eigene Identität besaßen. Eine internationale Weltausstellung auf der grünen Wiese, darin die Herstellung eines Ortes der Konzentration, der Besinnung – und, zu allem Überfluss, auch noch demontabel und ohne jede Aussicht auf wirtschaftlichen Profit, bestenfalls auf seelischen? Oder eine Messe irgendwo im Niemandsland am Stadtrand, kein Baum, kein Strauch, kein Geländeprofil? Keine Frage, dass gerade die Schwierigkeit der Aufgabe den Reiz für Architekten (und im Falle der Leipziger Messe auch für die Landschaftsarchitekten!) ausmacht; nichts

1994

P Mit dem Maastrichter Vertrag wird die EG zur EU mit einem Binnenmarkt
With the Treaty of Maastricht the European Community becomes the European Union with a single market
Eröffnung des Eurotunnels zwischen Frankreich und Großbritannien
Opening of the Euro tunnel between France and Great Britain
Beginn des Tschetschenien-Krieges in Russland
Chechnya war begins in Russia

1995

P Österreich, Schweden und Finnland treten der EU bei
Austria, Sweden and Finland enter the European Union
A Rolf Disch: Heliotrop, Freiburg
Rolf Disch: heliotrope, Freiburg, Germany
Dominique Perrault: Nationalbibliothek Paris, Frankreich
Dominique Perrault: National Library, Paris, France
Buch: Christopher Alexander: Eine Mustersprache
Book: Christopher Alexander: A Pattern Language, (original English edition 1977)
Buch: Andreas Feldkeller: Die zweckentfremdete Stadt. Wider die Zerstörung des öffentlichen Raumes
Book: Andreas Feldkeller: Die zweckentfremdete Stadt. Wider die Zerstörung des öffentlichen Raumes

The climax is no doubt the master plan for a whole new city in China, Lingang near Shanghai, initially designed for 300,000 inhabitants (present population: 800,000), with reference to Hamburg's Alster basin laid out around an artificial lake which, like the Alster, will – it is hoped – become a place of identification. Yet it is also possible to 'create places' with smaller structures. Of those projects that achieved this in difficult conditions, only two are mentioned here: the new Leipzig Trade Fair complex and the pavilion of Christian churches at the Hanover EXPO.

Both projects created new images in places that until then had lacked identity. First, a space of concentration and contemplation in the midst of a World Exhibition in the open countryside, in a pavilion designed for easy dismantling and without prospects of economic profit (at best of spiritual benefit). Secondly, a trade fair complex far from the city in the 'outback' – no tree, no shrub, no topographical interest providing a landmark. Without a doubt it was precisely the difficulty of the task which made it attractive to architects (and landscape architects in the case of the Leipzig fair grounds). Nothing is worse for them than a complete lack of contextual relationships. But they must first come up with the solution: the new place. In the case of the pavilion of Christian churches, this was achieved by means of the cloisters, which represented a sort of 'constructed silence' in contrast to the din from the EXPO. At the new Leipzig Trade Fair complex in Leipzig, a new, artificial landscape was built, with the valley creating a noticeable order.

Both the Hanover EXPO and the Leipzig Trade Fair pavilions reveal something else which, though always a part of gmp's work, now set new standards through co-operation with engineers and the use of new technology: the challenge of structural design. The large halls at Hanover and Leipzig show how a structure driven to its logical end creates an aesthetic that needs no additions. It also reveals the difference between high-tech architecture aimed at aesthetic results, and architecture which produces high-tech ones.

Two buildings (compared with the trade fair halls rather small ones) are examples of this: first, the platform canopies rail travellers encounter all over Germany. If built at every station, they could form the corporate identity of the Deutsche Bahn – if the company had a feeling for functional beauty. Secondly, the filigree three-span bascule bridge in Kiel – a toy for adults. ("Any engineer who didn't play with toys in his youth is not cut out to design engineering structures," says its engineer Jörg Schlaich.) It is a work of art in the form of a mobile made of cables, winches and counterweights, which, for the two and a half minutes that it takes to open or close the bridge, shows that there is more to it than mere functionality, but that functionality was the initial aim and not a preconceived aesthetic.

It goes without saying that this could not have been possible without close cooperation with highly competent structural engineers.

2000–2006

Turn of the millennium – an almost mythical term for a New Year's Eve party which differed from others only in the number of fireworks and the intensity of the next morning's hangover! A new millennium – a hope, a promise of change, even of improvement? People will not really have expected this, especially as in Germany 'turns' of events have not always been as positive as the peaceful revolution of 1989 ...

At zero hour between 31 December 1999 and 1 January 2000 instant changes both in politics and in society as a whole failed to appear. As Goethe said in a poem, people ("the world's small gods") still were "of the same breed, as odd as on the first day", and things have not changed that quickly since Goethe's time. Yet suddenly, on 11 September 2001, with the terror attacks on the World Trade Center and the Pentagon, things did instantly change our awareness and consciousness. Whether justifiably or not remains to be seen. The question of whether gradual processes like global warming, the increasing percentages of elderly people in Central Europe, or our use of finite resources will not have much more far-reaching consequences is justified, but our response does not really make a difference, as our preventive actions and awareness are inadequate. This is due to the nature of human consciousness: people react and respond much more strongly to sudden sensational events, published by the media, than to gradual developments. One has to ask what would have

1996

A Rhode, Kellermann, Wawrowsky RKW: CentrO
   Oberhausen
   Rhode, Kellermann, Wawrowsky RKW: CentrO
   Oberhausen, Germany
   Leon Krier: Poundbury, Großbritannien
   Leon Krier: Poundbury, Great Britain
   Peter Zumthor: Thermalbad Vals, Schweiz
   Peter Zumthor: thermal spa in Vals, Switzerland

1997

P Tony Blair wird Premierminister in Großbritannien
   Tony Blair becomes prime minister of Great Britain
   Erste Weltklimakonferenz in Kyoto
   First climate change negotiations in Kyoto
A Frank O. Gehry: Guggenheim-Museum, Bilbao, Spanien
   Frank O. Gehry: Guggenheim Museum, Bilbao, Spain
   MVRDV: Seniorenheim, Amsterdam, Niederlande
   MVRDV: senior housing in Amsterdam, Netherlands

1998

P Erste rot-grüne Regierung unter Gerhard Schröder
   First red-green coalition led by Gerhard Schroeder
   Offensive Serbiens gegen Kosovo-Albaner;
   Niederschlagung durch die NATO
   Serbian offensive against ethic Albanians in Kosovo;
   defeated by NATO
   Das Kyoto-Protokoll über Reduktion von Treibhausgasen
   Kyoto Conference held to discuss the reduction of
   greenhouse gases
   Gründung der Europäischen Zentralbank (EZB)
   Establishment of the European Central Bank (ECB)
A Richard Meier: Getty Center, Los Angeles, USA
   Richard Meier: Getty Center, Los Angeles,
   United States
   Daniel Libeskind: Felix-Nussbaum-Haus, Osnabrück
   Daniel Libeskind: Felix Nussbaum House, Osnabrück,
   Germany
   Eric Owen Moss: Bürohaus, Culver City, USA
   Eric Owen Moss: office building, Culver City,
   United States
   Herzog & de Meuron: Umbau Bankside Power Station
   zur Tate Gallery, London, Großbritannien
   Herzog & de Meuron: conversion of the Bankside Power
   Station into the Tate Gallery, London, Great Britain
   Rafael Moneo: Rathaus Murcia, Spanien
   Rafael Moneo: Murcia City Hall, Murcia, Spain

---

schlimmer für sie, als wenn es keinerlei Bindungen gibt. Aber die Lösung müssen sie erst schaffen: den neuen Ort. Im Falle des Pavillons der christlichen Kirchen wurde das durch den Kreuzgang geschafft, der so etwas wie „gebaute Stille" gegenüber dem Lärm der EXPO darstellte. In Leipzig, bei der Neuen Messe, wird eine neue, künstliche Landschaft hergestellt mit dem Tal, das eine ablesbare Ordnung schafft.

Beide Herausforderungen, die der EXPO auf dem Messegelände Hannover und die der Neuen Messe in Leipzig, zeigen noch etwas anderes, was in den Arbeiten von gmp immer angelegt war, das aber erst jetzt, in der Zusammenarbeit mit Ingenieuren und neuen Techniken wirklich einen neuen Standard setzte: Die Herausforderung der Konstruktion. Die großen Messehallen in Hannover und Leipzig zeigen, wie aus der bis ans Ende getriebenen Konstruktion eine Ästhetik entsteht, die keiner anderen Zutaten bedarf. Sie zeigen auch den Unterschied zwischen einer als ästhetische Absicht verfolgten High Tech Architektur und einer, die höchste Technik als Ergebnis bringt: Erstere löst auf technisch brillante Weise Probleme, die es ohne die ästhetische Vorgabe „High Tech" gar nicht gäbe; sie demonstriert höchste Technik. Die andere, der Weg von gmp, löst anstehende Probleme auf technische Weise und denkt sie zu Ende, so dass High Tech am Ende als Ergebnis entsteht.

Auch hierzu zwei Beispiele, die im Vergleich zu Messen und großen Hallen eher klein sind: die Bahnsteigdächer, die man bei der Fahrt mit dem Zug immer wieder in Deutschland trifft, und die bei konsequenter Realisierung so etwas wie eine corporate identity für die Deutsche Bahn bilden könnten – wenn die Sinn für funktionale Schönheit hätte; und als zweites die Dreifeld-Klappbrücke in Kiel – was für ein Wort für ein so filigranes Gerät! Ein Kinderspielzeug für Erwachsene – („Ein Ingenieur, der in seiner Jugend nicht gespielt hat, taugt nicht zum Entwurf von Ingenieurbauten", meint der Konstrukteur der Brücke, Jörg Schlaich) –, ein Mobile als Kunstwerk aus Seilen, Winden und Gegengewichten, das zweieinhalb Minuten lang bei jeder Öffnung oder Schließung zeigt, dass es mehr gibt als nur den nackten Zweck. Wobei der „nackte Zweck" aber der Ausgangspunkt bleibt, nicht ein vorgefasstes ästhetisches Resultat.

Dass das nur in enger Zusammenarbeit mit herausragenden Ingenieuren gelingen kann, ist dabei selbstverständlich.

2000–2006

Jahrtausendwende: Ein mystischer Begriff für eine Silvesterfeier, die höchstens durch die Zahl der Feuerwerksraketen und die Größe des Katers am nächsten Morgen anders als andere war! Jahrtausendwende: Eine Hoffnung, ein Versprechen, jetzt werde alles anders, oder sogar besser? Beides wird man ernsthaft nicht vermutet haben, zumal in Deutschland die „Wenden" nicht immer so positiv verlaufen sind wie die der friedlichen Revolution 1989...

Sowohl in der Politik wie in der Gesellschaft blieben die schlagartigen Veränderungen zwischen dem 31.12.1999 und dem 1.1.2000 aus – die Menschen, der „kleine Gott der Welt", ist „immer noch vom gleichen Schlag / und ist so wunderlich als wie am ersten Tag"; so schnell änderte sich seit Goethes Zeiten nichts. Erst der 11.9.2001 mit den Anschlägen auf World Trade Center und Pentagon veränderte tatsächlich schlagartig unser Bewusstsein. Ob das sachlich gerechtfertigt war, mag dahingestellt sein; die Frage, ob nicht ein schleichender Prozess wie die Klimaveränderung oder die Vergreisung Mitteleuropas oder allgemein unser Umgang mit endlichen Ressourcen viel weiter reichende Folgen hat, ist zwar richtig gestellt, ihre Beantwortung aber spielt keine Rolle, da die Folgen im Handeln und im allgemeinen Bewusstsein nicht adäquat sind. Das hängt mit dem Bewusstsein der Menschen zusammen, das viel stärker auf plötzliche, über die Medien verbreitete und verstärkte Sensationen reagiert als auf langsame Entwicklungen; man muss sich nur einmal die Frage stellen, was gewesen wäre, wenn es keine hunderte Male wiederholte Fernsehbilder eines in ein Hochhaus fliegenden Flugzeugs gegeben hätte? Die Bilder – und das ist nicht erst seit dem so genannten Fernsehzeitalter so – sind allemal wirkungskräftiger als die Tatsachen.

In seinen skeptischen Überlegungen zum Einfluss von Computer und anderer digitalisierter Technik in der heutigen Architektur reflektiert Meinhard von Gerkan gerade diese Macht der Bilder, in diesem Fall die der am Computer

1999

P Wladimir Putin wird Staatspräsident in Russland
Vladimir Putin becomes president of Russia
A **Daniel Libeskind: Jüdisches Museum, Berlin**
Daniel Libeskind: Jewish Museum, Berlin, Germany
Norman Foster: Deutscher Bundestag im Reichstag, Berlin
Norman Foster: German Reichstag building, Berlin, Germany
1989-1999: IBA Emscher Park
1989-1999: IBA in Emscher Park, Germany
Françoise Jourda, Gilles Perraudin: Fortbildungsakademie Herne
Françoise Jourda, Gilles Perraudin: Academy for Advanced Studies, Herne, Germany

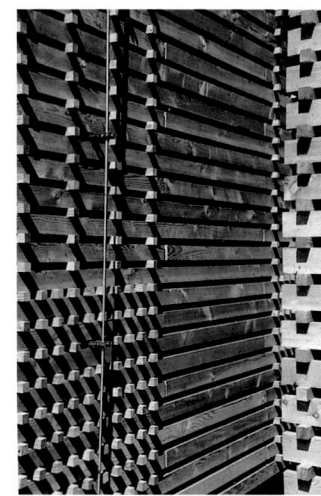

2000

A Herzog & de Meuron: Tate Modern, London, Großbritannien
Herzog & de Meuron: Tate Modern, London, Great Britain
MVRDV: Niederländischer Pavillon, EXPO Hannover
MVRDV: Dutch pavilion, EXPO, Hanover, Germany
Peter Zumthor: Schweizer Pavillon, EXPO Hannover
Peter Zumthor: Swiss pavilion, EXPO, Hanover, Germany
Thomas Herzog: EXPO-Dach, Hannover
Thomas Herzog: roof construction, EXPO, Hanover, Germany
Werner Sobek: Haus R 128, Stuttgart
Werner Sobek: House R 128, Stuttgart, Germany

happened if the moving pictures of aeroplanes crashing into two high-rises had not been televized hundreds of times. Images have always had more impact than the facts themselves – not just since the invention of television.

"The appearance of perfection and materialization promised by the digital media produces a pseudo-objectivity rarely withstood by the contents of the design at hand", wrote Meinhard von Gerkan in his sceptical analysis of the influence of the computer and computerized technology in contemporary architecture. What sounds like a comment on the remarks above was the preface for a gmp exhibition on virtual worlds in current architectural production. The role of computers with their great representational potential for the success of gmp architecture since the 1990s (and of architecture as a whole, which Michael Mönninger then called a "cultural guiding motif") cannot be underestimated. Even the suspended canopies over the Olympic stadium in Munich of 1972 by Günter Behnisch and Frei Otto would not have been possible without early digital technology. There is scarcely an architect today capable of drawing a good perspective. The question of whether such a world is a better place for it remains open.

The start of the millennium did, therefore, mark a change, even though it did not come with one stroke of the clock: from then on, architects the world over (not gmp, though!) increasingly used computers to simulate forms, not just to calculate their dimensions. Daniel Libeskind's 'lightning' Jewish Museum (completed in 1999) was certainly also developed with the aid of computers, but was not its aesthetic result. On 3 October 1990 he straightened the outer walls – still inclined in the competition design – because, said Libeskind, German unification provided justification for this. (Or did the structural designer tell him that perpendicular walls were cheaper?) Buildings like the department store in Birmingham (GB) by Future Systems (2003), Peter Cook's Kunsthaus Graz of the same year, or the strange 'Blobs' of subsequent years would not have been possible without computers either. What is more: they introduced new computer-generated architectural forms and new ways of designing. However, the basic question – why "flowing, flexible and highly complex forms stemming from non-Euclidean geometry" (Wikipedia) should be a desirable aim of architecture – has, unfortunately, remained unanswered.

Many structurally determined buildings by gmp, designed together with engineers of Schlaich, Bergermann and Partners, would not have been possible without computers. Yet there is a big difference between the latest digitally shaped 'blobs' and amorphous 'architectures of foam' (Peter Sloterdijk) on the one hand, and gmp buildings on the other. The office demonstrates forces with gusto – and for all to see! It constructs and does what architecture has always done. For gmp, the Vitruvian triangle of firmitas, commoditas and venustas still forms the basis of an architecture which people can understand, be they observers or users. Critics and colleagues have criticized gmp for an architecture that is just modern enough and populistically close to the current zeitgeist for their clients to understand and recognize as modern and future-oriented. Which explains why it is successful.

In short: gmp architecture is 'lucid'. What an absurd criticism this is! Of course, the office of gmp may be criticized; its portfolio of about 2,000 projects may well include a few architectural flops. Thumbing through the pages covering the last forty years does, indeed, reveal repetitions and some 'weak' designs. But to criticize gmp buildings for being lucid and understandable to the people who have to live and work in them is just the result of a kind of tabloid thinking greedy for new sensations every day. According to the teachings of architecture over five millennia, however, aesthetic and structural changes always happen gradually. The new without precedent, the thing never before seen, is an invention of today's advertising strategists and is out of place in buildings that have to serve for thirty, fifty or one hundred years. Forms that were developed just because they never existed before may be exciting and media-effective, but not necessarily functional, let alone humane. On the contrary, one of the doctrines of 1920s classical Modernism was that formal newness without precedent was to be rejected.

It is not because he is regarded as 'classical' that Vitruvius is so often quoted. He was probably only an average architect whose long-winded books 'De architectura' just had the good

2001

P 11.9.: gekidnappte Flugzeuge werden gezielt ins New Yorker World Trade Center und ins Pentagon gesteuert
September 11th: hijacked airplanes are flown into the World Trade Center in New York and the Pentagon
USA beginnen Krieg gegen Afghanistan
USA begins a war with Afghanistan

A Axel Schultes: Kanzleramt, Berlin
Axel Schultes: Chancellery, Berlin, Germany

2002

P Mehrere EU-Länder schließen sich zur Währungsunion zusammen (Einführung des Euro)
Several EU countries unite to form the monetary union (introduction of the euro)
USA richten ein Gefangenenlager in Guantanamo/Cuba ein
The United States establishes a detainment camp on Guantánamo Bay, Cuba
Die Schweiz wird Mitglied bei den Vereinten Nationen
Switzerland becomes a member of the United Nations
Nach Bundestagswahl Fortsetzung der Koalition SPD und Grüne
The coalition of the Social Democratic and Green parties continue to govern following parliamentary elections
Eröffnung der „Bibliotheca Alexandrina" in Kairo, Ägypten
Opening of the 'Bibliotheca Alexandrina' in Cairo, Egypt
Jahrhundertflut an der Elbe
Flood of the Century on the Elbe

A Stephan Braunfels: Pinakothek der Moderne, München
Stephan Braunfels: Pinakothek der Moderne, Munich, Germany
Richard Rogers: Konzerthaus, Rom, Italien
Richard Rogers: Concert House, Rome, Italy
Steven Holl: Bellevue Art Museum, Seattle, USA
Steven Holl: Bellevue Art Museum, Seattle, United States
Frank O. Gehry: DG Bank, Berlin
Frank O. Gehry: DG Bank, Berlin, Germany
Allmann, Sattler, Wappner: Herz Jesu Kirche, München
Allmann, Sattler, Wappner: Herz Jesu Church, Munich, Germany

---

erzeugten, scheinbar realen, die man inzwischen kaum noch von den Fotos der Wirklichkeit unterscheiden kann: „Der Schein von Perfektion und Konkretion, den die digitalen Medien verheißen, erzeugt eine Pseudoobjektivität, der der Gehalt des jeweiligen Entwurfs selten standhält", schreibt er. Was der Kommentar zu den vorigen Bemerkungen sein könnte, war das Vorwort zu einer Ausstellung des Büros gmp über die virtuellen Welten in der heutigen Architekturproduktion. Wobei der Erfolg von gmp wie der der Architektur überhaupt seit den neunziger Jahren, da sie als „kulturelles Leitmedium" (Michael Mönninger) wahrgenommen wurde, ohne diese Rechner mit ihren Möglichkeiten der Darstellung kaum überschätzt werden kann (schon das Olympiadach 1972 in München von Günter Behnisch und Frei Otto wäre ohne das beginnende Computerzeitalter nicht möglich gewesen). Ob die Welt besser geworden ist dadurch, dass es heute kaum noch jemanden gibt, der als Architekt in der Lage ist, eine anschauliche Perspektive mit der Hand zu zeichnen, sei allerdings dahingestellt...

Insofern markiert die Jahrtausendwende doch einen Umbruch, selbst wenn er nicht schlagartig kam; den Umbruch nämlich, dass in der internationalen Architektur – nicht im Büro gmp! – der Computer verstärkt zur Generierung von Formen herangezogen wird, anstatt diese nur zu berechnen: Des Blitze schleudernden Daniel Libeskinds Jüdisches Museum in Berlin (fertiggestellt 1999) wurde zwar sicherlich auch mit Hilfe der Rechner gebaut, war aber nicht deren ästhetisches Ergebnis; seine im Wettbewerb noch schräg stehenden Wände wurden am 3. Oktober 1990 gerade gerückt, weil die Vereinigung beider deutscher Staaten das, nach Aussage des Architekten, rechtfertigte (oder hat doch nur der Statiker dem Architekten gesagt, senkrechte Wände seien preisgünstiger?). Bauten aber wie das Kaufhaus in Birmingham/GB von Future Systems (2003) oder das Kunsthaus in Graz (Österreich) von Peter Cook im gleichen Jahr oder die merkwürdigen Formen von Blobs in den folgenden Jahren wären nicht nur ohne Rechner nicht möglich gewesen; sie führen neue Formen in die Architektur ein, die im Rechner erzeugt wurden – das ist eine neue Art zu entwerfen. Wobei die eigentliche Kernfrage, warum denn eigentlich „flüssige, wandlungsfähige und hochkomplexe Formen, die der nicht-euklidischen Geometrie entstammen" (Wikipedia über Blobs), ein erstrebenswertes Ziel in der Architektur sein sollen, leider unbeantwortet bleibt.

Ohne Computer wären auch die vielen konstruktiv geprägten Bauten des Büros gmp nicht möglich gewesen, die vor allem in der Zusammenarbeit mit dem Ingenieurbüro Schlaich, Bergermann und Partner entwickelt wurden. Trotzdem besteht ein großer Unterschied zwischen den neuen, computergenerierten Blobs, die amorph daherkommen, und den Bauten von gmp: Letztere führen geradezu lustvoll – und sichtbar! – Kräfte spazieren; sie konstruieren und machen damit das, was die Architektur immer gemacht hat: Die vitruvsche Dreiheit aus firmitas, commoditas und venustas bildet für gmp immer noch die Grundlage einer Architektur, die den Menschen – den Betrachtern wie den Benutzern – verständlich ist. Die Kritiker und Kollegen haben ja dem Büro gern vorgeworfen, ihre Architektur sei gerade so modern und damit dem jeweiligen Zeitgeist so populistisch nahe, dass die Bauherren sie einerseits verstehen, sie andererseits als modern und zukunftsgerichtet erkennen könnten. Daher rühre der Erfolg des Büros.

Mit einem Wort, so der Vorwurf der Kritiker: Ihre Architektur sei verständlich. Aber was ist das für ein absurder Vorwurf! Man kann auch dem Büro gmp einiges vorwerfen; wessen Projektliste etwa bei Nummer 2000 angekommen ist, hat wohl auch architektonische Flops zu verantworten; das „Daumenkino" in diesem Rückblick über 40 Jahre entlarvt Wiederholungen und schwache Entwürfe. Aber der Vorwurf, ein architektonischer Entwurf sei verständlich für die Menschen, die in ihm leben und arbeiten müssen – dieser Vorwurf ist einfach nur das Ergebnis eines Denkens in Bildern der yellow press: Jeden Tag eine neue Sensation. Die Lehre von 5 000 Jahren Architektur ist vielmehr die, dass sich ästhetische und konstruktive Veränderungen immer langsam vollzogen haben. Das voraussetzungslos Neue, das nie Gesehene ist eine Erfindung heutiger Werbestrategen. In der Architektur, die immer noch über dreißig, fünfzig oder einhundert Jahre tauglich sein muss, hat es nichts zu suchen. Formen, die nur deshalb entwickelt werden, weil es sie noch nie gegeben hat, mögen aufregend sein, auch

2003

P 2. Golfkrieg der "Koalition der Willigen" gegen den Irak, weil dieser verdächtigt wird, Massenvernichtungswaffen herzustellen
Second Golf War begins between the "Coalition of the Willing" and Iraq because Iraq is suspected of making arms of mass destruction

A Future Systems: Kaufhaus Birmingham, Großbritannien
Future Systems: department store in Birmingham, Great Britain
P. Cook: Kunsthaus Graz, Österreich
P. Cook: Art House, Graz, Austria

2004

P Erweiterung der EU um acht osteuropäische Staaten sowie Malta und Zypern
Expansion of the European Union to include eight eastern European counties, as well as Malta and Cyprus
Demonstrationen gegen den Reformkurs der Bundesregierung
Demonstrations staged protesting the reformist course of Germany's federal government
Horst Köhler wird Bundespräsident
Horst Köhler becomes the German president
George W. Bush wird erneut für vier Jahre zum Präsidenten gewählt
George W. Bush is re-elected to serve another four years as president of the United States
Erster Versuch in Deutschland mit gentechnisch verändertem Weizen
First tests conducted in Germany with genetically modified wheat

A Henning Larsens Tegnestue: Oper, Kopenhagen, Dänemark
Henning Larsens Tegnestue: Opera, Copenhagen, Denmark
EMBT: Parlament Edinburgh, Schottland
EMBT/RMJM: Scottish Parliament building, Edinburgh, Scotland
Herzog & de Meuron: Uni-Bibliothek Cottbus
Herzog & de Meuron: University Library, Cottbus, Germany
Richard Rogers: Zentrum Paul Klee, Bern, Schweiz
Richard Rogers: Paul Klee Center, Bern, Switzerland

---

fortune to be among the very few surviving texts on architecture from Antiquity. Yet his theoretical triangle, often translated into modern terms, is still appropriate because it is well balanced: convenience (functionality), beauty and stability are not separate, independent qualities of a building; they mutually support and explain each other.

This balance of tradition and modernity lends gmp buildings a quality which others lack, whose often rather short-lived – yet always contemporary – theoretical foundations we have traced here for over forty years. Its best examples are timeless, or at least of sustained aesthetic quality.

The comparison with a particular building may help us to recognize this quality as a high value, a building that has become the sign of a certain trend in architecture and in society's attitude to architecture, for example, the Dresden Frauenkirche (Church of our Lady). Leaving aside the evidently fervent wish for reconstruction by the people of Dresden (who did much fund-raising) and leaving aside the fact that by now several generations of locals know the original Dresden skyline on the Elbe only from paintings or historic photos, the fact remains that a building of the greatest urban significance in our time was erected in the style of 1738 because contemporary architecture was not trusted to create a structure of comparable beauty. The point here is not whether this is really so. The point is that the citizens declared almost unanimously that "the old (building) was more beautiful!" And not only the citizens of Dresden, but also those of Berlin with regard to the Stadtschloss (city palace); of Potsdam with regard to the Garnisonkirche or the Palace; of Braunschweig with regard to their Palace; of Munich with regard to paring down the Alte Pinakothek to its original shape; and of Frankfurt/Main with regard to the Paulskirche.

The Frauenkirche represents the prototype of this trend, which is supported by the public debate about the reconstruction of the Berlin Stadtschloss (which requires the demolition of the 'Palace of the Republic', doubtless also an architectural monument) and about the Berlin 'Inner City' plans with its return to 19th-century patterns. We now have an architectural movement which, partly on a high quality level, adheres to the conviction that old is better than new. The admittedly irritating thing about this is that its proponents also make good use of the computer. They maintain that the old is modern and that, after all, even the Renaissance had revived past architectural models and adapted them to the needs of the 16th century, so that for them the Greek temple-style architecture of Schinkel's Berlin or a baroque-style church appear timeless.

Today, we therefore seem to stand between the extremes of a traditional architecture that serves people's longings for familiar things, and an architecture which strengthens the unfamiliarity of the new without precedent and whose main aim is medial sensation.

Building for the future with architectural history in mind, and thus constantly rebalancing Vitruvius's triangle, represents the position between the two extremes. This is also gmp's approach, and it is not only meaningful in terms of architectural theory, but also successful on account of constantly renewed quality.

'Change. Reflection. New Paths?'
Let us have a look at the work of the two senior gentlemen and their many helpers in recent years. They have added quite a number of stadiums to their portfolio, among them the difficult 'balancing act' of renovating and refurbishing the Berlin Olympic Stadium, and have also started building hospitals. They are testing new constructions and returning to old ones, such as with the wooden roofs of their trade fair halls in Rimini or Friedrichshafen.
The office team has worked and is currently working on projects one could call 'once-in-a-century' projects: Berlin Central Station, Berlin Schönefeld Airport, a new city in China.

That entails a lot of work – work that is done not to secure a pension or the jobs of one's employees, but because one enjoys trying something new, putting something old to the test and bringing order into the world. It certainly needs it.

2005

P Nach einem Seebeben tötet ein Tsunami rund
230 000 Menschen in Südostasien
Nearly 230,000 people are killed in south east Asia by
a tsunami following a seaquake
„Wir sind Papst"
"We are Pope"
Zweite große Koalition, diesmal unter Kanzlerin
Angela Merkel
Second grand coalition forms, led by
Chancelor Angela Merkel

A Zaha Hadid: Phaeno, Wolfsburg
Zaha Hadid: Phaeno, Wolfsburg, Germany
Wiedererrichtung der Frauenkirche, Dresden
Reconstruction of the Frauenkirche, Dresden,
Germany

2006

P Weltbevölkerung: 6,5 Milliarden Menschen
Word population reaches 6.5 billion
Kurt Beck wird Vorsitzender der SPD
Kurt Beck becomes the chairman of the Social
Democratic Party of Germany (SPD)
In Italien gewinnt das Bündnis unter Prodi die Wahlen
gegen Berlusconi
Prodi and his coalition government win elections
against Berlusconi in Italy
Konflikt zwischen Israel und der Hisbollah im Libanon
Conflict between Israel and Hezbollah in Lebanon
Inbetriebnahme des Drei-Schluchten-Damms in China
Opening of the Three Gorges Dam in Sandouping, China
Mozartjahr
Mozart Anniversary Year

A OMA Rem Koolhaas, Sanaa u.a.: Umbau Zeche
Zollverein, Essen
OMA Rem Koolhaas, Sanaa and others: conversion of
Zollverein Mining Complex, Essen, Germany
UN Studio: Mercedes Museum, Stuttgart
UN Studio: Mercedes Museum, Stuttgart, Germany
David Chipperfield: Literaturmuseum, Marbach
David Chipperfield: Literaturmuseum, Marbach, Germany
Le Corbusier: St. Pierre Kirche, Firminy, Frankreich
Le Corbusier: Church of St. Pierre, Firminy, France

medienwirksam, aber sie sind nicht zwangsläufig auch vernünftig oder gar menschlich. Im Gegenteil: Eine der Lehren der klassischen Moderne der 1920er Jahre ist gerade, dass die voraussetzungslose Neuheit von Formen abgelehnt wird.

Vitruv wird ja nicht deshalb so oft zitiert, weil er als „klassisch" gilt; er war vermutlich nur ein durchschnittlicher Architekt, dessen umständlich geschriebenes theoretisches Werk das Glück hatte, als einziges aus der Antike überliefert zu sein. Sein theoretisches Dreieck, oft mit modernisierten Begriffen versehen, taugt aber deshalb heute noch, weil es sich im Gleich-Gewicht befindet: Gebrauchstüchtigkeit, Schönheit und Standfestigkeit sind keine losgelösten, für sich stehende Eigenschaften eines Gebäudes, sondern sie stützen und erläutern sich gegenseitig.

Dieses Gleichgewicht aus Tradition und Modernität verleiht der Architektur von gmp eine Eigenschaft, die andere Architekturen nicht besitzen, deren theoretische Spuren wir hier über vierzig Jahre verfolgt haben, und deren Lebensdauer häufig recht kurz war: Sie ist immer heutig. Und damit ist sie in den besten Beispielen zeitlos oder, etwas niedriger gehängt, von dauerhafter ästhetischer Qualität.

Um das als hohen Wert zu erkennen, mag als Vergleich ein als Signal für eine bestimmte Tendenz in der Architektur und das dem zugrunde liegenden Denken der Gesellschaft wirkender Bau dienen: Die Frauenkirche in Dresden. Lassen wir den offenbar brennenden Wunsch der Dresdner beiseite, den den Bau mit viel privatem Engagement finanziert haben; lassen wir beiseite, dass mehrere Generationen von Bewohnern der Stadt inzwischen das Original der Dresdner Elbsilhouette nur aus einem Gemälde oder aus historischen Fotos kennen. Es bleibt, dass einer der städtebaulich wichtigsten Bauten der Gegenwart in einer Architektur des Jahres 1738 errichtet wurde, weil man der zeitgenössischen Architektur nicht zutraut, etwas vergleichbar Schönes zu schaffen. Dabei geht es nicht um die Frage, ob das tatsächlich so ist – es geht um die Einschätzung der Bürger, die von Dresden bis zu den diskutierten Rekonstruktionen des Stadtschlosses in Berlin, der Garnisonkirche oder dem Schloss in Potsdam, dem Braunschweiger Schloss bis hin zu Überlegungen zum Rückbau der Alten Pinakothek in München oder dem der Paulskirche in Frankfurt/Main sich ziemlich einheitlich artikuliert: Das Alte war schöner!

Der Wiederaufbau der Frauenkirche in Dresden steht prototypisch für diese Tendenz. Es gibt inzwischen eine Architekturströmung, die der Überzeugung folgt, das Alte sei das Bessere – teilweise übrigens auf hohem Niveau. Was irritiert, ist, dass auch deren Architekten sich des Computers bedienen; sie behaupten, das Alte sei vielmehr das Moderne, und schließlich hätte auch zum Beispiel die Renaissance eine vergangene Architektur wiederbelebt, indem sie sie für die Zwecke des 16. Jahrhunderts tauglich gemacht hätte – die Architektur des griechischen Tempels oder eines preußischen Stiles im Berlin um 1800 sei eben zeitlos.

Wir stehen also heute zwischen den Extremen dieser traditionellen Architektur, die den Wunsch der Menschen nach dem Vertrauten bedient, und einer, die die Fremdheit des voraussetzungslos Neuen noch verstärkt, deren wichtigstes Ziel die mediale Sensation ist.

Es ist schön, dass die Position dazwischen: mit der Architekturgeschichte im Hinterkopf für die Zukunft zu bauen, das vitruvsche Dreieck immer aufs Neue auszubalancieren, dass also die Position von gmp nicht nur in architekturtheoretischer Hinsicht sinnvoll, sondern aufgrund der von ihnen immer wieder erneuerten Qualität auch erfolgreich ist.

„Veränderung. Reflektion. Neue Wege"? Sehen wir uns doch die Arbeiten der beiden älteren Herren und ihrer vielen Helfer aus den letzten Jahren an: Eine ganze Anzahl von Stadionbauten ist hinzu gekommen, darunter der schwierige Balanceakt des Umbaus des Berliner Olympiastadions mit seiner belasteten Geschichte; es wurde zu den Olympischen Spielen 1936 errichtet. Neuerdings werden Krankenhäuser gebaut. Neue Konstruktionen werden erprobt und auf alte zurückgegriffen, wie bei den Holzdächern der Messebauten in Rimini oder Friedrichshafen. Projekte waren und sind in Arbeit, die man als „Jahrhundertprojekte" bezeichnen möchte: Der Berliner Hauptbahnhof, der Flughafen Berlin-Schönefeld, die neue Stadt in China.

Das ist ein Haufen Arbeit. Die macht man nicht wegen seiner Rente oder um die Arbeitsplätze im Büro zu sichern. Die macht man, weil man Spaß daran hat, etwas Neues zu wagen. Etwas Altes erneut auf den Prüfstand zu stellen. Und man macht es, um Ordnung in diese Welt zu bringen. Nötig hat sie es.

Gert Kähler
2006

1967
1969

Stormarnhalle, Bad Oldesloe

Die Sporthalle, die auch als kommunale Versammlungsstätte genutzt wird, wurde mit bescheidenen gestalterischen Mitteln und einfachen Materialien realisiert. Eine breite Freitreppe führt auf die obere Erschließungsebene, an der die Zuschauertribünen, eine Garderobe und eine Cafeteria situiert sind.

Bad Oldesloe Stormarn Hall

The sports hall, also being used as a municipal meeting venue, was realized with unassuming means of design and simple materials. A wide flight of stairs leads to the upper circulation level, where the stands, a cloakroom and a cafeteria are situated.

Max-Planck-Institut für Aeronomie, Lindau/Harz

Entsprechend der abgeschiedenen Lage des Forschungsinstituts in der hügeligen Landschaft des Harzvorlandes wurde das Raumprogramm in mehreren pavillonartigen Baukörpern untergebracht, die sich entsprechend dem Geländegefälle in die Landschaft einfügen.

Max Planck Institute for Aeronomics, Lindau/Harz

Corresponding to the secluded location of the research institute in the hilly landscape of the foreland of the Harz Mountains, the room programme was distributed into several pavilion-like buildings, which integrate into the natural fall.

Wohnhaus Köhnemann, Hamburg

Das Gebäude wurde auf dem höchsten Punkt des Grundstücks winkelförmig angelegt, ein kleiner Innenhof öffnet sich nach Süden. Charakteristische Merkmale von Grund- und Aufriss sind gegeneinander versetzte und sich durchdringende kubische Elemente, ergänzt durch mit Betonmauern eingefasste Terrassen.

Köhnemann Residence, Hamburg

The building was designed with an angled plan on the highest point of the site. A small inner courtyard opens up towards the south. Characteristic features of plan and elevation, which alternate towards each other, are cubic elements penetrating each other. Concrete walls enclose the terrace that follows the topography.

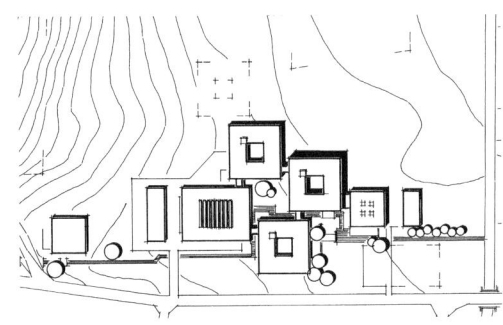

Max-Planck-Institut für Aeronomie, Lindau/Harz
Max Planck Institute of Aeronomics, Lindau/Harz

Wettbewerb Competition
1966 – 1. Peis

Entwurf Design
Meinhard von Gerkan und Volkwin Marg

Partner Partner
Rolf Störmer

Bauherr Client
Max-Planck-Gesellschaft, München

Bauzeit Construction period
1967-1970

BFG Gross floor area
12.000 m²

Die Charakteristik der Landschaft setzt sich in den Innenhöfen der pavillonartigen Baukörper fort. Der vorhandene Bach wurde als künstlicher Wasserlauf durch die Anlage geführt und stellt als lebendiges Element eine spielerische Komponente in der funktionsbetonten Forschungsstätte dar. Die einzelnen Häuser sind über Brücken miteinander verbunden. Die Gliederung in getrennte Einheiten entspricht der Nutzung durch verschiedene Bereiche: Verwaltung, Sondenbereiche, Labors, Werkstattbereich, Sozialbereich, Fahrdienst. Außenstehende Stützen und Betonfertigteile sind die bestimmenden Elemente der Gestaltung, die im Innenbereich durch eine gezielte Farbgebung in den Komplementärfarben grün und rot akzentuiert werden. Das Erschließungsgerüst der windmühlenartig angeordneten Flure, die zu einem addierbaren Netz auch für spätere Erweiterungen verwachsen, kehrt in vielen anderen Entwürfen von gmp wieder.

The characteristics of the surrounding countryside extend into the ensemble of pavilion-type building volumes. The existing natural stream was diverted into an artificial water course running through the building. It adds a 'living' and playful element to this research centre focusing on functionality. The individual pavilions are interconnected by bridges. The interior organization with separate units corresponds to the departmental division into administration, probe department, laboratories, workshops, staff areas, vehicle pool. Exterior supports and prefabricated concrete parts are the determining factors of the design, accentuated inside by the complementary-colour scheme with green and red. The pinwheel structure of the corridors, which forms a circulation network able to "grow" with subsequent extensions, is a recurring theme in gmp's designs.

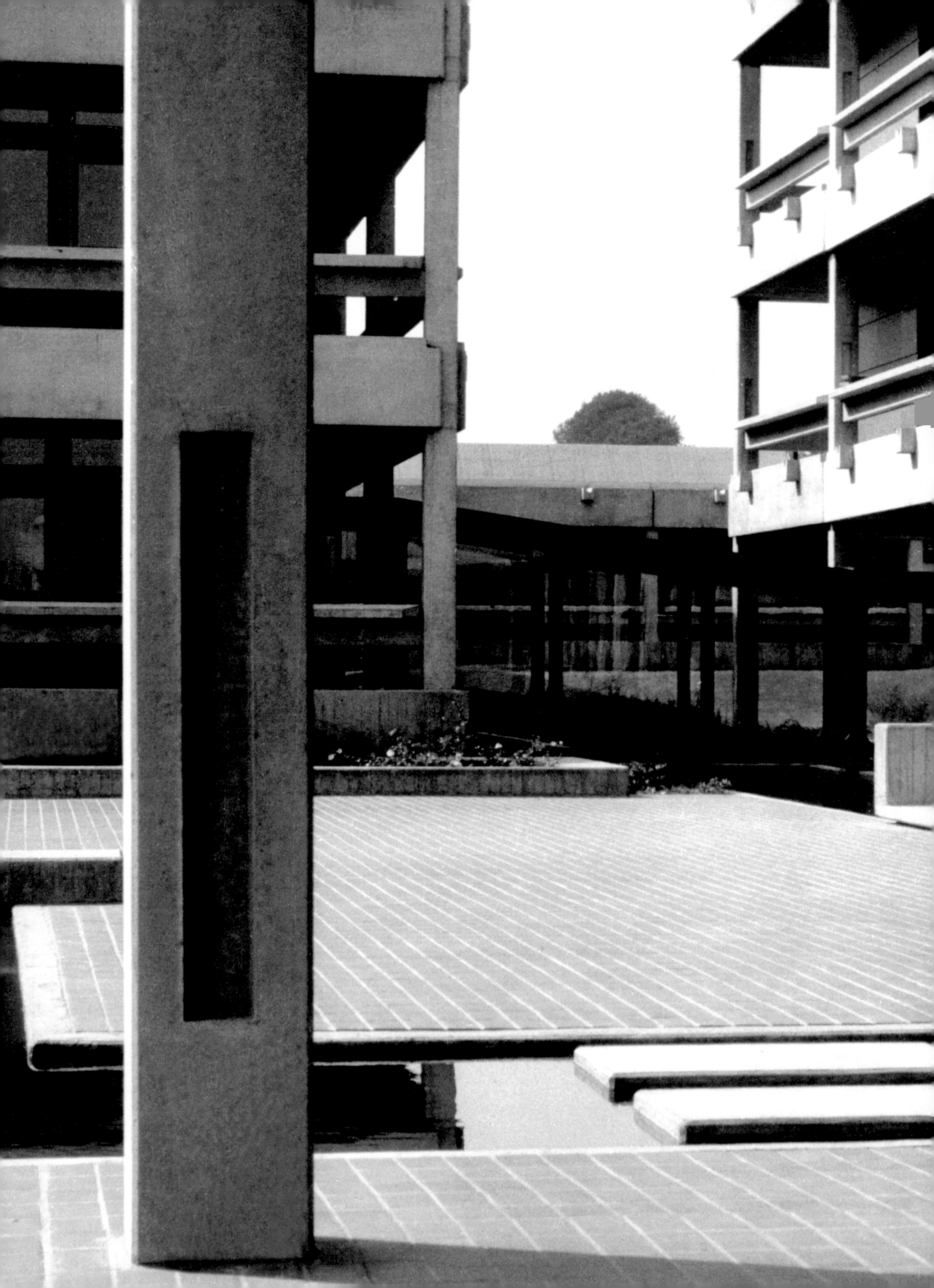

1970
1971
1972

Sportzentrum Diekirch, Luxemburg

Das Sportzentrum besteht aus Hallenfreibad, Sporthalle und Stadion sowie Zuschauertribünen für alle Bereiche. Von einer hochgelegenen Erschließungsebene, auf die eine breite flachgeneigte Rampe führt, erhält der Besucher einen Gesamtüberblick in beide Hallen und durch die Hallen hindurch ins Freie.

Diekirch Sports Centre, Luxembourg

The sports centre is comprised of a combined indoor and outdoor bath, a gymnasium and a stadium as well as stands for all areas. From an elevated circulation level, which is accessible via a wide, slightly inclined ramp, the spectators can look into both halls and simultaneously through the halls' glass façades into the open.

Wohn- und Bürogebäude Fontenay, Hamburg

Der hohe Bodenwert des Grundstücks erforderte eine entsprechende Ausnutzung, die von Villen geprägte Umgebung jedoch eine maßstäbliche Einfügung. Abstaffelung, Höhenversätze, Vor- und Rücksprünge, offene und geschlossene Flächen erzeugen spannungsvolle und lebendige, bis zu 24 m tiefe Baukörper.

Residential and Office Block on the Alster (Fontenay), Hamburg

The high property value of the site requires an appropriate utilization, whilst the neighbouring large-scale villas demand a scaled integration. Staggering, variations in height, projections and recesses, open and solid surfaces generate an interesting and vivid appearance along the up to 24-m-deep building.

Apartmenthaus Alstertal, Hamburg

In den unteren drei Geschossen des Apartmenthauses befinden sich Läden, Praxen und Büros, in den oberen Geschossen Wohnungen. Die plastischen Ausformungen des Staffelgeschosses, des Giebels mit Schornstein und der Zugangsrampe überlagern die additive Regelmäßigkeit der Hauptgeschosse.

Alstertal Apartment Block, Hamburg

Shops, practices and offices are located on the first three floors of the apartment block, whilst apartments are accommodated on the upper floors. The sculptural form of the split-level, the gable with a chimney and the access ramp overlap with the additive regularity of the main storeys.

1974 1975

Hauptverwaltung Deutsche Shell AG, Hamburg

Entgegen dem Wettbewerbsprogramm sollten bei der Ausführungsplanung die meisten Arbeitsplätze in konventionellen Zellenbüros untergebracht werden. Aus mehreren alternativen Projektstudien wurde eine Lösung gewählt, bei der im Grundriss zwei winkelförmigen Bürotrakte versetzt zu einem Kreuz angeordnet sind.

Deutsche Shell AG Headquarters, Hamburg

Contrary to the competition programme, the constructional planning had to accommodate the majority of the workplaces in conventional cell offices. One solution was selected from several alternative project studies, which in plan positions two angle-shaped office wings in a cruciform formation.

Flughafen Berlin-Tegel

Die Ringform des Terminals schafft auf der Luftseite mehr Platz zur Aufstellung der Flugzeuge – an 14 erkerartigen Vorbauten – und reduziert auf der Landseite die Weglängen für umsteigende Fluggäste, zum Zentralbereich mit den übergeordneten Funktionen sowie zum Parkhaus in der offenen Mitte des Sechsecks.

Berlin-Tegel Airport

The ring shape of the terminal generates more spaces for the positioning of aeroplanes on the apron side (at 14 protruding bays). On the street side this ring form simultaneously reduces the distances for transferring passengers, to the central area with super-ordinate functions as well as to the parking garage in the open centre of the hexagon.

Tower, Flughafen Berlin-Tegel

Der Kontrollturm fügt sich in Gestaltung und Funktion in das Gesamtkonzept: Wie beim Terminal sind Dreiecksgeometrie und geneigte Flächen die Komponenten, mit denen sein plastischer Ausdruck geformt wurde. Im obersten Geschoss ist das Kontrollzentrum untergebracht, in den Ebenen darunter befinden sich Büros.

Tower, Berlin-Tegel Airport

In design and function the tower is fully integrated into the overall concept: As with the passenger terminal, triangular geometry and sloped surfaces are a feature of the sculptured design. The top floor houses the control centre whilst the lower floors provide office facilities.

Brücken, Flughafen Berlin-Tegel

Alle Straßen, Brücken und Außenanlagen des Flughafens wurden ebenfalls von gmp mit dem Ziel geplant und gestaltet, diese organisch in die Umgebung einzubinden, wie beispielsweise die Zufahrt zum Terminalgebäude, die unter dem ringförmig geschlossenen Rollweg der Flugzeuge hindurchführt.

Bridges, Berlin-Tegel Airport

All streets, bridges and outdoor facilities of the airport were also planned and designed by gmp with the objective to organically integrate them into the surroundings. One example is the access road towards the terminal building, which runs underneath the ring-shaped closed aircraft taxiway.

Energiezentrale und betriebstechnische Anlagen, Flughafen Berlin-Tegel

Alle Bauten ordnen sich dem Gesamtkonzept, bestehend aus Maßsystem der Baukörper, Fassadengliederung und Farbe, unter. Trotz unterschiedlicher Nutzungen und Größen entsteht eine städtebauliche Einheit. Die Gebäudecontainer haben jochartige Einschnürungen, ein Fugenraster gliedert die Fassaden.

Central Energy Station and Operational Facilities, Berlin-Tegel Airport

All buildings submit to the overall concept that defines the dimensional framework of the buildings as well as the organization and colouring of the façades. An urban unit is realized despite varying uses and dimensions. The container-like buildings have a trestle-like contraction; a joint grid introduces a structure to the façades.

Frachtanlage, Flughafen Berlin-Tegel

Die Frachtanlage ist als Teil der Randbebauung des Flughafens – dem einheitlichen Gestaltungskonzept folgend – in Gebäudecontainer gegliedert. An der landseitigen Rampe schließt ein Riegel mit Büros im Obergeschoss an, zur Luftseite folgt eine Lager- und Umschlagshalle, die über Sheddächer Tageslicht erhält.

Freight Centre, Berlin-Tegel Airport

As part of the airport's edge development, and in accordance with the uniform design concept, the freight centre is divided into building containers. A bar building with offices on the upper level adjoins the landside ramp, whilst a storage and transshipment hall that is daylit by shed roofs follows on the apron side.

1975

Hauptverwaltung Aral AG, Bochum

Hauptziel des Entwurfs war die ausgewogene städtebauliche Einordnung des Gebäudes. Diese wird erreicht durch ein zurückgesetztes Dachgeschoss, eine zweimalige Rückstaffelung entlang der Straßenfront sowie die Gestaltung der Fassade mit spiegelnder Verglasung, die die gegenüberliegenden Bauten reflektiert.

Aral AG Headquarters, Bochum

The primary objective of the design was the building's balanced integration into the urban context. This is achieved with a recessed attic, a double-recess along the street front as well as a façade design with reflective glazing.

Schulzentrum Friedrichstadt

Als erster und zweiter Bauabschnitt wurden Realschule und Sporthalle fertiggestellt. Das als einfacher Dreibund angelegte Schulgebäude kann darüber hinaus linear erweitert werden. Die Sonderräume „wachsen" im Erdgeschoss unter dem Obergeschoss mit den Regelklassenräumen heraus.

School Centre, Friedrichstadt

The middle school and gymnasium were completed in the first and second construction phases. The school building is laid out in a twin-corridor formation and can be extended in a linear direction. On the ground floor the special function rooms 'grow' from underneath the upper floor with the standard classrooms.

Lärmschutzkabine, Flughafen Berlin-Tegel

Die auf der Basis eines akustischen Konzepts entworfene Lärmschutzanlage auf dem Gelände des Flughafens Berlin-Tegel schützt die Anwohner vor den lauten Geräuschen bei Düsentriebwerksprobeläufen. Sie ist für Flugzeuge bis zur Größe einer Boeing 707 konzipiert.

Noise Protection Cabin, Berlin-Tegel Airport

The noise protection facility on the premises of Berlin-Tegel Airport is based on an acoustic concept and protects residents from the noise levels produced during the tests of jet engines. It is laid out for aeroplanes up to the dimensions of a Boeing 707.

Flugzeugwartungshalle, Flughafen Berlin-Tegel

Aufgrund ihrer Höhe von über 40 m wurde ein abgelegener Standort für die Halle gewählt, die dennoch in die übergeordnete städtebauliche Konzeption des Flughafens einbezogen ist. Das gesamte Dach einschließlich der 19,50 m hohen Schiebetore ist an Pylonen aufgehängt, die Wände sind nicht tragend.

Maintenance Hangar, Berlin-Tegel Airport

On account of its height of more than 40 m a remote location was chosen for the hall, which is nevertheless integrated into the priority urban planning concept of the airport. The entire roof, including the 19.5-m-high sliding gates, is suspended from pylons. The walls have no load-bearing function.

Streugutlager, Flughafen Berlin-Tegel

Das Streugutlager wurde mit den gleichen gestalterischen Mitteln den übrigen Bauten angepasst. Das Streugut wird über Schneckenförderanlagen auf die obere Ebene transportiert und dort gelagert. Die Streufahrzeuge fahren unter die aufgeständerten Container und können von oben direkt beschickt werden.

Grit Depot, Berlin-Tegel Airport

The grit depot was adapted to the other buildings by employing the same means of design. Via screw conveyors the grit is transported to the upper level, where it is stored. The gritting vehicles drive underneath the supported containers and can be directly loaded from above.

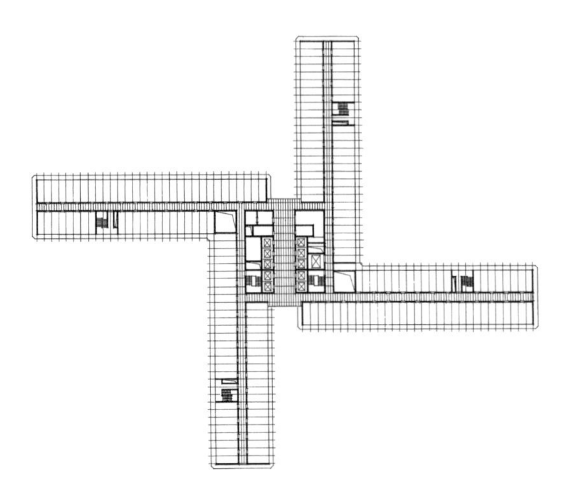

Hauptverwaltung Deutsche Shell AG, Hamburg
Deutsche Shell AG Headquarters, Hamburg

Entwurf Design
Volkwin Marg

Partner Partner
Eike Wiehe

Bauherr Client
Deutsche Shell AG

Bauzeit Construction period
1972–1974

BGF Gross floor area
49.125 m²

Die Gestalt des Bürogebäudes ist durch zwei deutlich voneinander gelöste Bauteile geprägt: zum einen das kreuzförmige Hochhaus mit konventionellen Zellenbüros und zum anderen der zweigeschossige Sockelbereich für Sonderfunktionen und Großraumbüros. Der horizontal gegliederte Sockelbereich mit seinen Stahlbetonbrüstungen bindet an die Plattformstruktur der benachbarten Gebäude an. Demgegenüber hebt sich das Hochhaus mit einer spiegelnden Fassade aus dunkelbraunem Absorptionsglas und umlaufenden Galerien deutlich von der hellen Schichtung des Sockels ab. Die transparente Einschnürung im Kernbereich sowie die Spiegelung des jeweils anderen Baukörperflügels und der Galeriepfosten in der Fassade verleihen dem Hochhaus Leichtigkeit und Eleganz. Die in Elementkonstruktion errichtete Fassade besteht aus Zweischeiben-Isolierglas, die Metallteile aus gezogenen, dunkelbronze eloxierten Aluminiumprofilen.

The mass of this office building has two distinctly different sections: a multi-storey structure on a cruciform plan with conventional cellular offices, and the two-storey plinth containing special functional spaces and large open-plan offices. The horizontally emphasized plinth with its RC parapets makes the link to the platform structures of neighbouring buildings. The high-rise section has a reflecting façade of dark brown actinic glass surrounded by balconies and offsets the pale-coloured plinth layers. Its transparent recessed middle, together with reflections of the other wing and of the balcony pilasters in the façade, make the high-rise appear light and elegant. The façade modules consist of two-piece laminated insulating glass framed by dark-bronze, extruded, anodized aluminium sections.

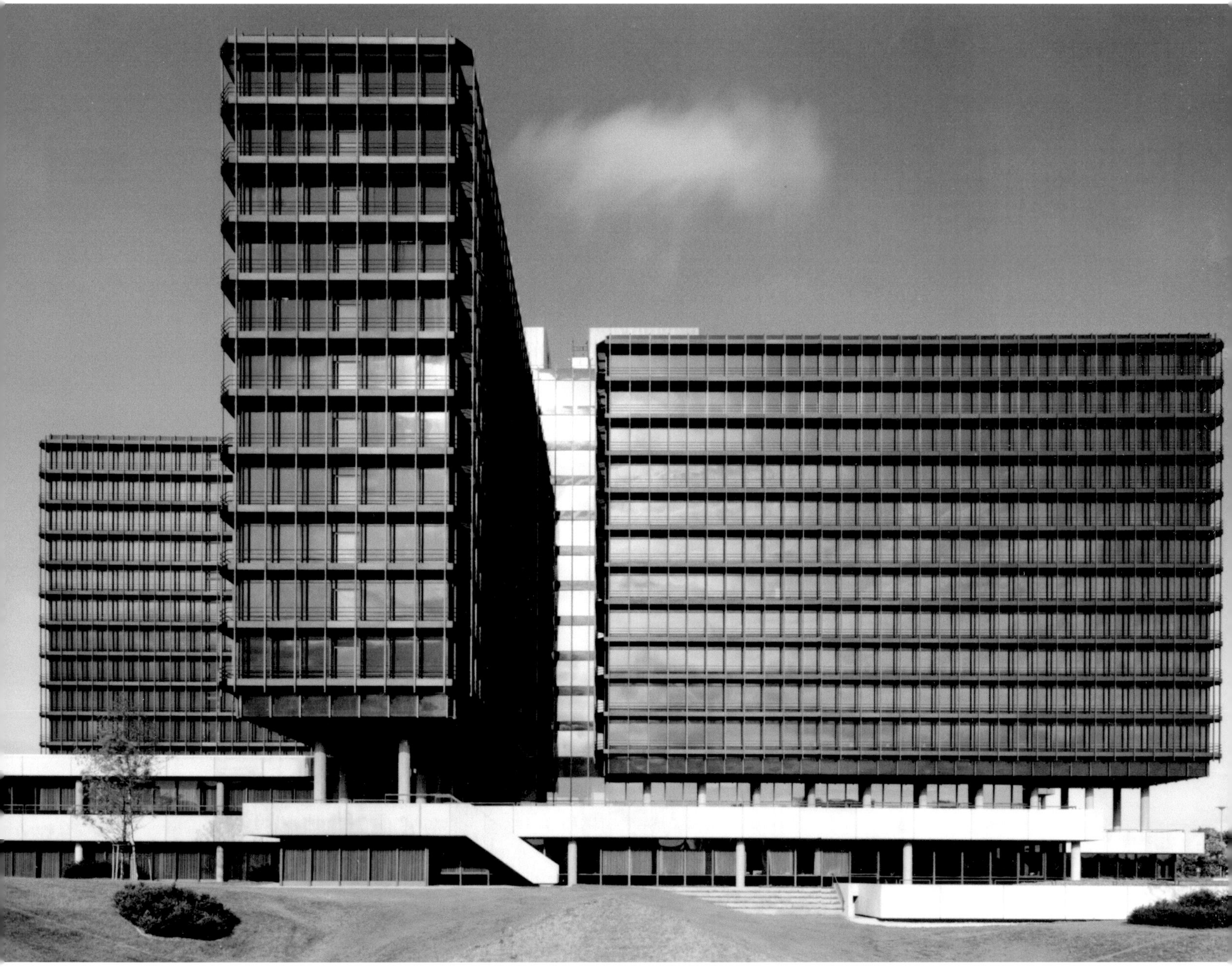

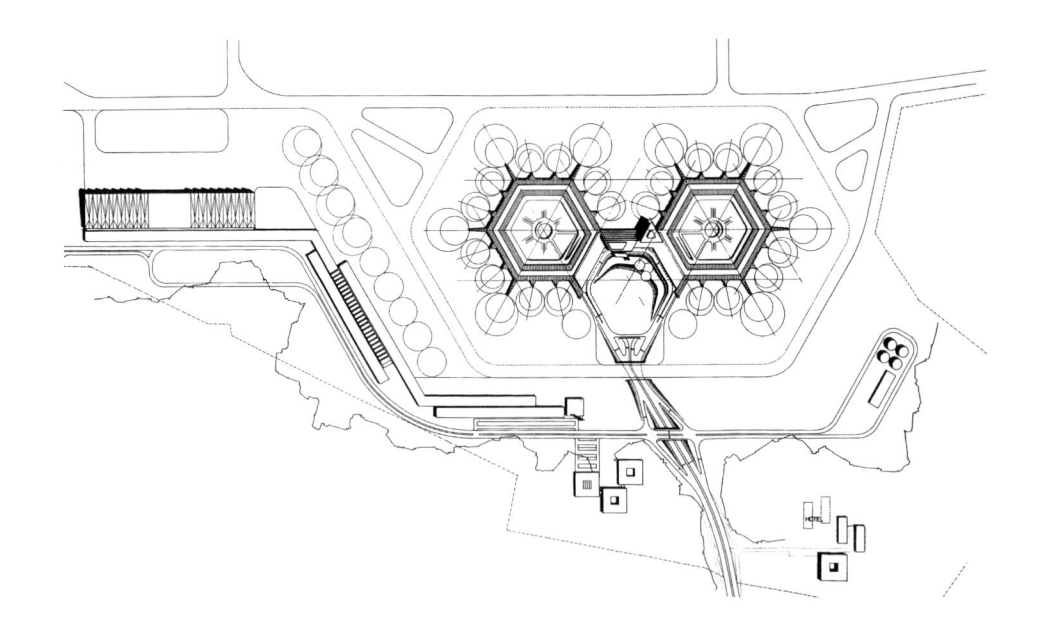

Flughafen Berlin-Tegel
Berlin-Tegel Airport

Wettbewerb Competition
1965 – 1. Preis

Entwurf Design
Meinhard von Gerkan,
Volkwin Marg, Klaus Nickels

Partner Partners
Rolf Niedballa, Klaus Staratzke, Karsten Brauer

Bauherr Client
Berliner Flughafen-Gesellschaft mbH

Bauzeit Construction period
1970–1975

Überbaute Fläche Covered area
28.000 m²

Die Gesamtform wurde soweit vorstrukturiert, dass alle zukünftigen Entwicklungen Teile eines Ganzen bleiben, ebenso wie auch alle Konstruktionen, Decken, Fußböden, Treppen und Einrichtungsgegenstände aus der gleichen geometrischen Logik entwickelt wurden. Das geometrische Ordnungsprinzip des Dreiecksrasters im Grundriss findet seine Entsprechung im Aufriss. Die Rohbaustruktur des Betons ist außen und innen sichtbar belassen. Während im zentralen Bereich alle übergeordneten Funktionen zusammengefasst sind, dient der Flugsteigring vorwiegend der dezentralisierten, direkten Abfertigung von Fluggästen und Flugzeugen. Abflug und Ankunft befinden sich auf einer Ebene. Neben der Planung des Flughafens wurden gmp auch alle Einzelplanungen für die Betriebsgebäude, die Planung für Straßen, Brücken und Rollfelder, die Landschaftsgestaltung, das Informationssystem und die Entwürfe fast aller Inneneinrichtungen übertragen.

The overall shape and layout of this drive-in airport was planned in such a way as to accommodate all future extensions as parts of the whole. Likewise, every structure, ceiling, flooring, stairway and piece of furniture was developed following the same geometric logic. The triangular geometric grid of layout and floor plans was also applied to the elevation. The concrete carcass structure was left exposed both inside and outside. While all the general airport services are concentrated in the middle, the concourse ring serves mainly the decentralized, direct 'handling' of passengers and planes. Arrivals and Departures are on the same level. gmp was commissioned not only to plan the airport, but also to design the technical buildings, roads, bridges, runways, landscaping, information system and almost all interior furnishings.

Abflug-Ankunft
Departures-Arrivals
Flug-
Information
BERLIN-TEGEL
KLÖCKNER-STAHL
AEG-TELEFUNKEN
Abflug Ankunft
Departures-Arrivals
Mietwagen
Car rental
TAXI

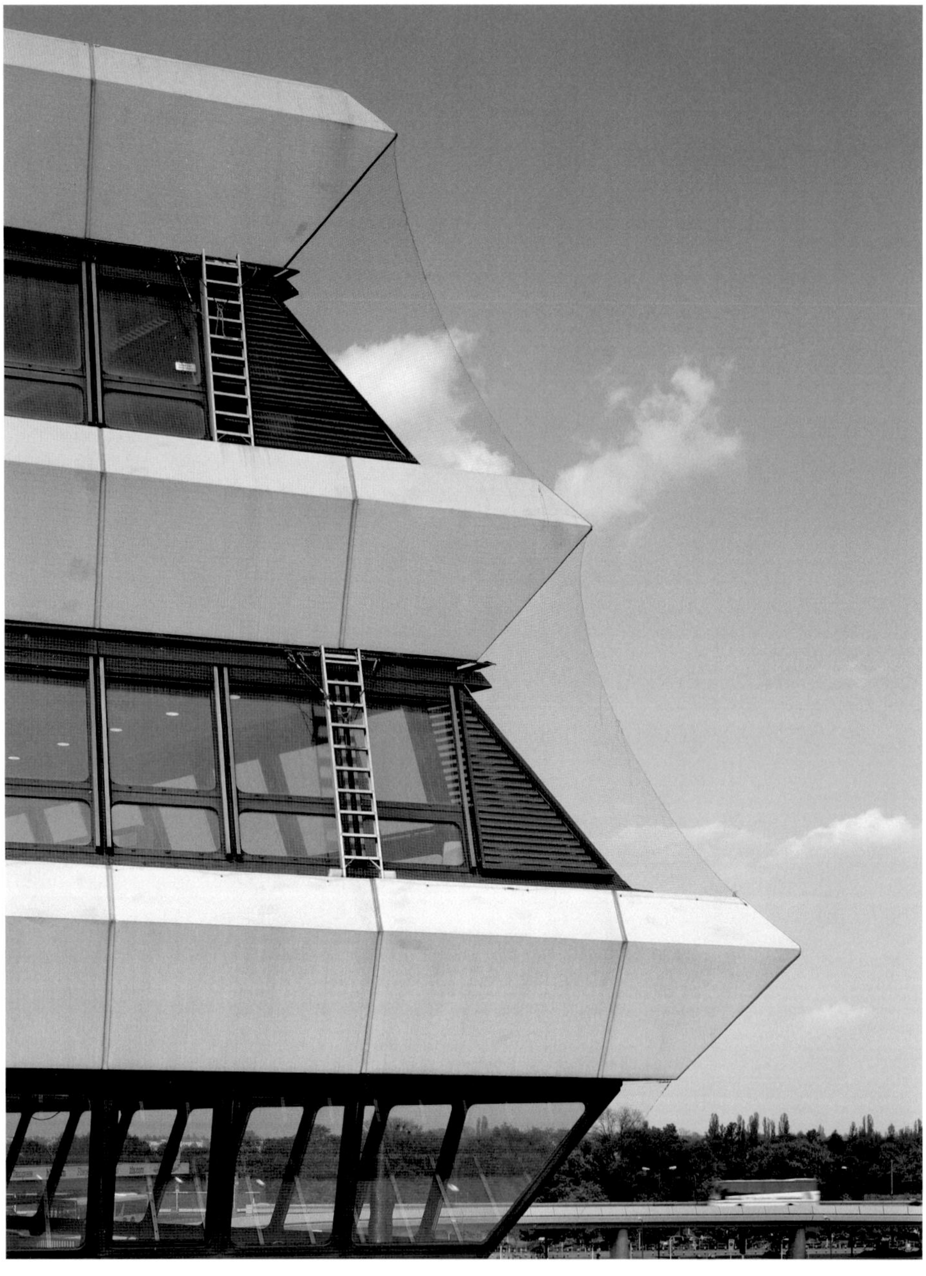

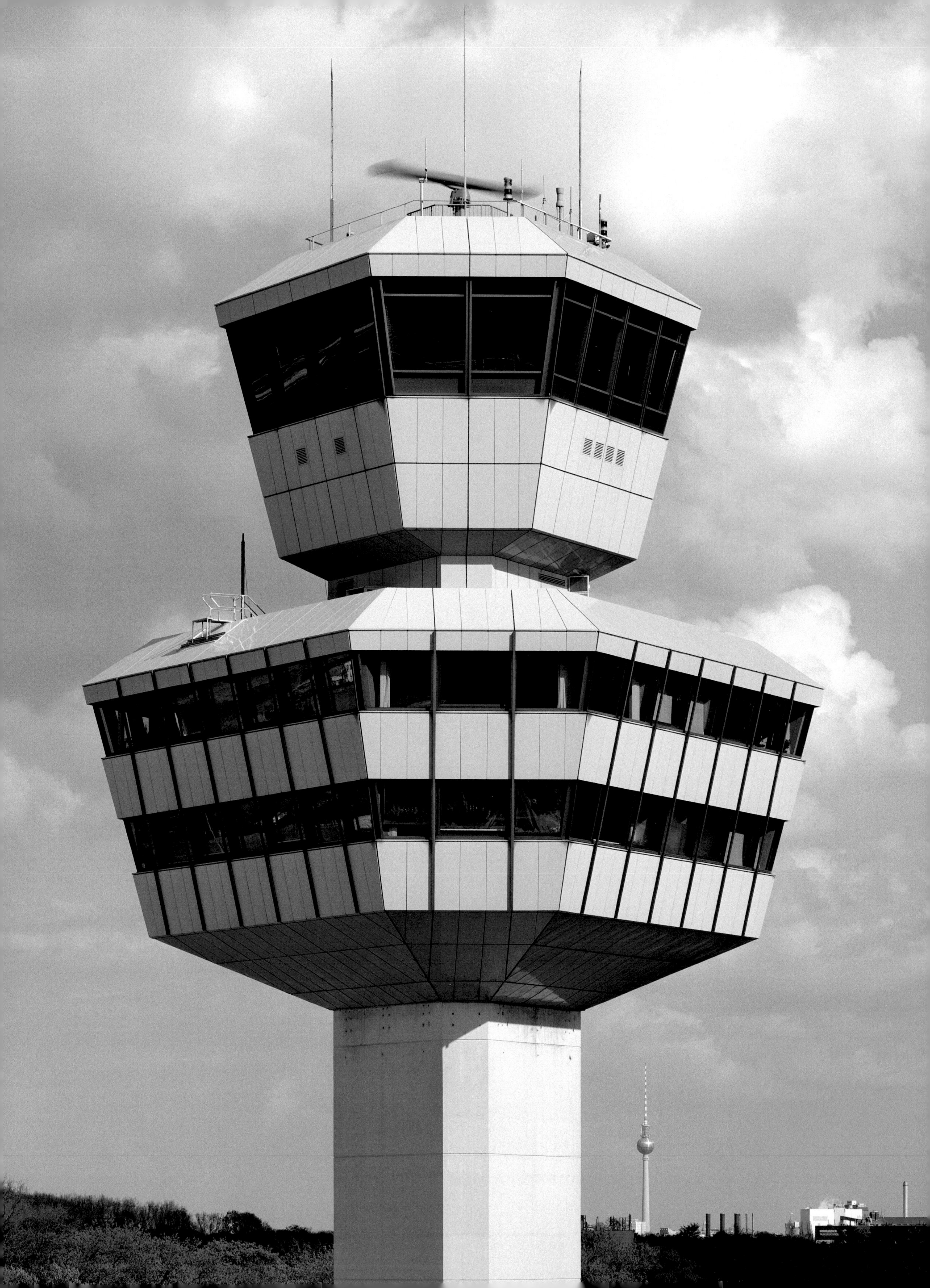

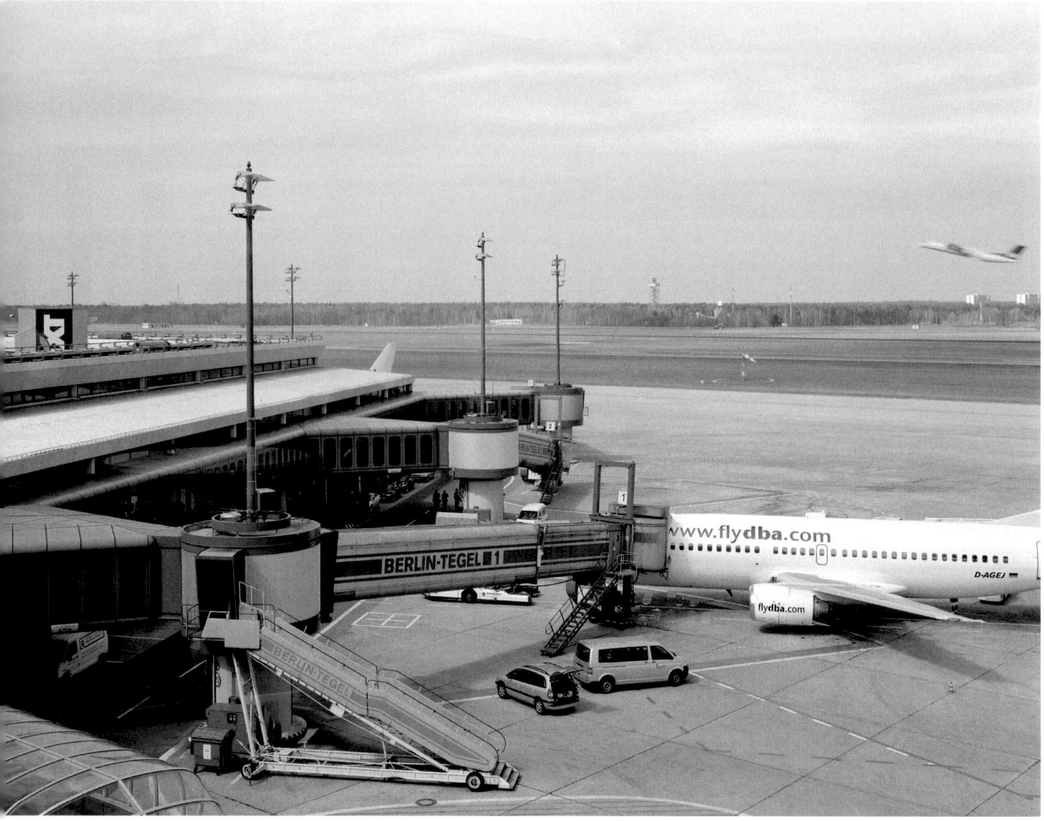

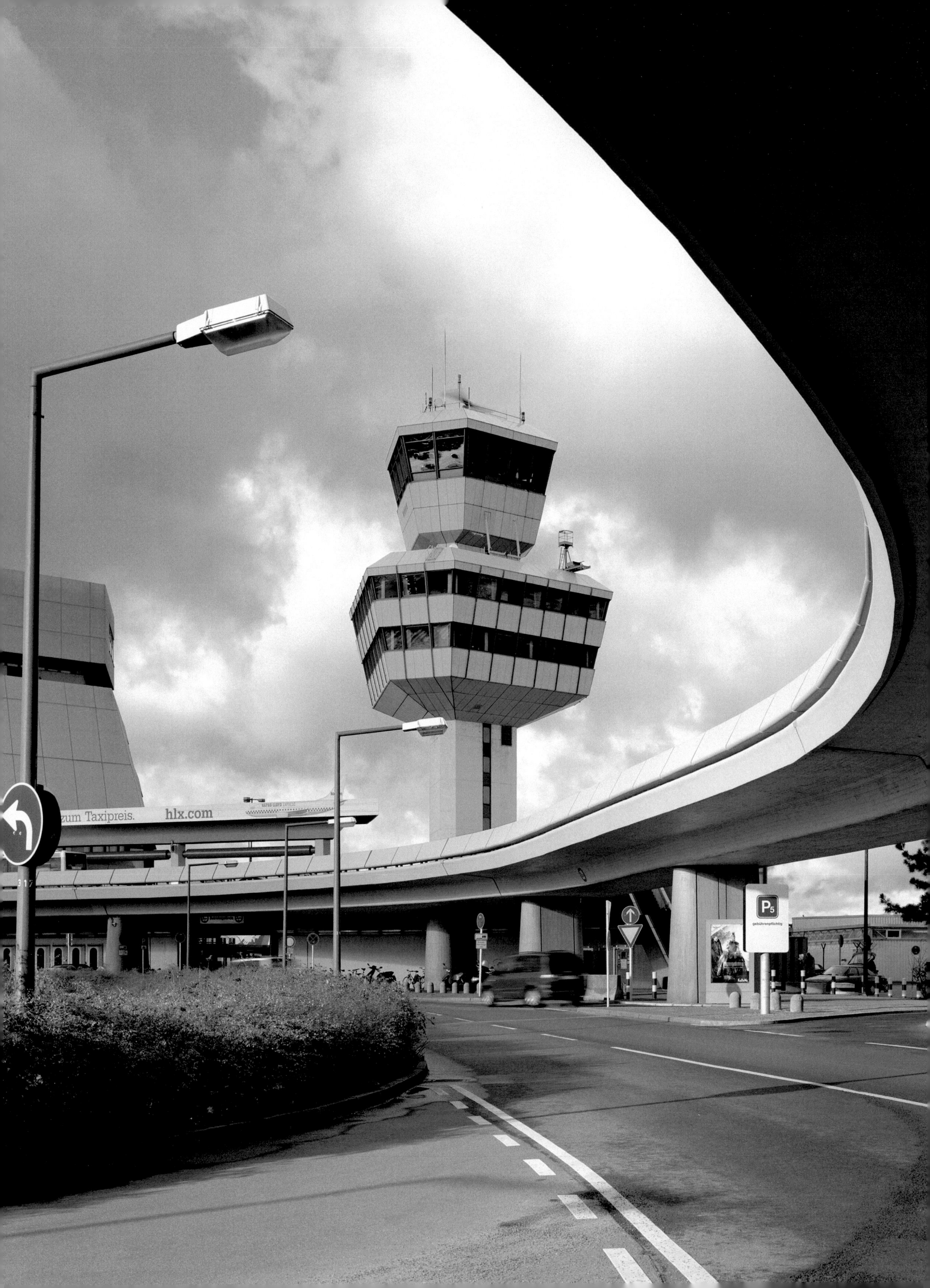
zum Taxipreis.
hlx.com
P5

TAX FREE
P1
WC
7-15
P5
0-6
20-44
TEGEL
BOULEVARD
ZEITSCHRIFTEN
INTERNATIONALE PRESSE
DIE ZEIT

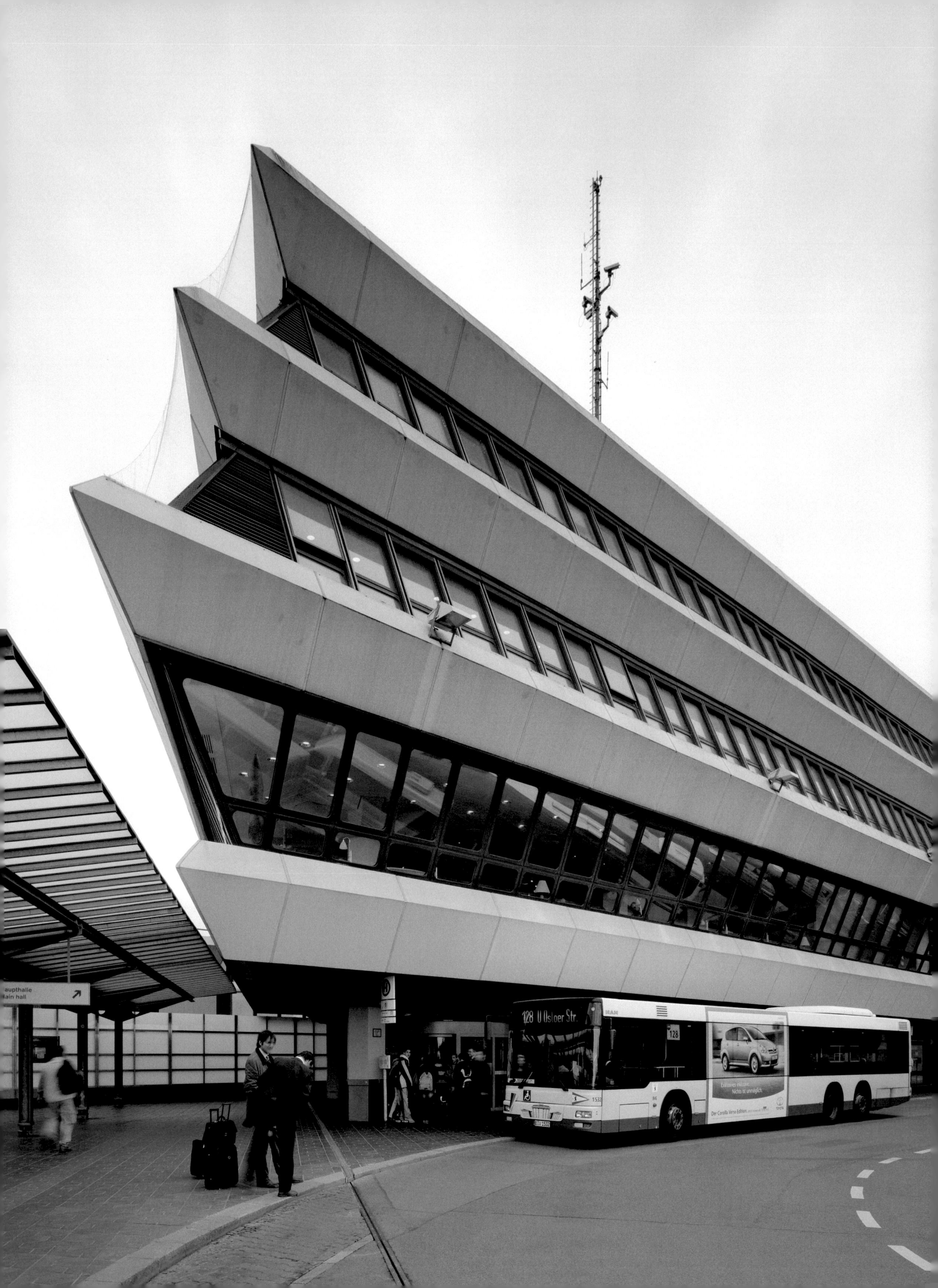
aupthalle
lain hall
128 U Osloer Str.
128

Brücken, Flughafen Berlin-Tegel
Bridges, Berlin-Tegel Airport

Die Taxiwaybrücke besteht aus drei nebeneinander liegenden Brücken, auf denen zwei Verbindungsstraßen und ein Flugzeugrollweg über die Zufahrt zum neuen Empfangsgebäude geführt werden. Zwischen den Bauwerken sind parallel verlaufende Lamellenfelder angeordnet. Die Gesamtbreite von Brücken- und Lamellenfeldern beträgt rund 120 m, wobei die Konstruktion die zweimal dreispurige Zufahrt zweifeldrig mit je rund 16 m Weite überspannt. Die Widerlager aller Brücken und der dazwischen liegenden Lamellenfelder sind durchgehende Fußgängertunnel. Die organische Einbindung in die Umgebung wird erreicht durch leicht schräg gestellte Fronten, die plastisch herausgezogenen Stützmauern, die Ausrundung der Ecken im Auflagerbereich und am Sockel sowie die Abbildung der lasttragenden Funktion bei den Widerlagern. Alle Sichtbetonflächen wurden in Schiffsbodenschalung mit versetzten Stößen ausgeführt.

The taxiway bridge consists of three bridges running next to each other, across which two connecting roads and one aircraft taxiway traverse the access road towards the new terminal building. Parallel louvred areas are positioned between the structures. The total width of bridges and louvred sections is approximately 120 m, with the structure traversing the two three-lane access roads with two spans approximately 16 m wide each. The abutments of all bridges and louvred sections located in between are continuous pedestrian tunnels. The organic integration into the surrounding is achieved with slightly inclined fronts, the sculpturally formed retaining walls, the filleting of corners in the load-bearing areas and at the socle as well as the projection of the load-bearing function at the abutments. All fair-faced concrete surfaces were executed in formwork with alternated butt joints.

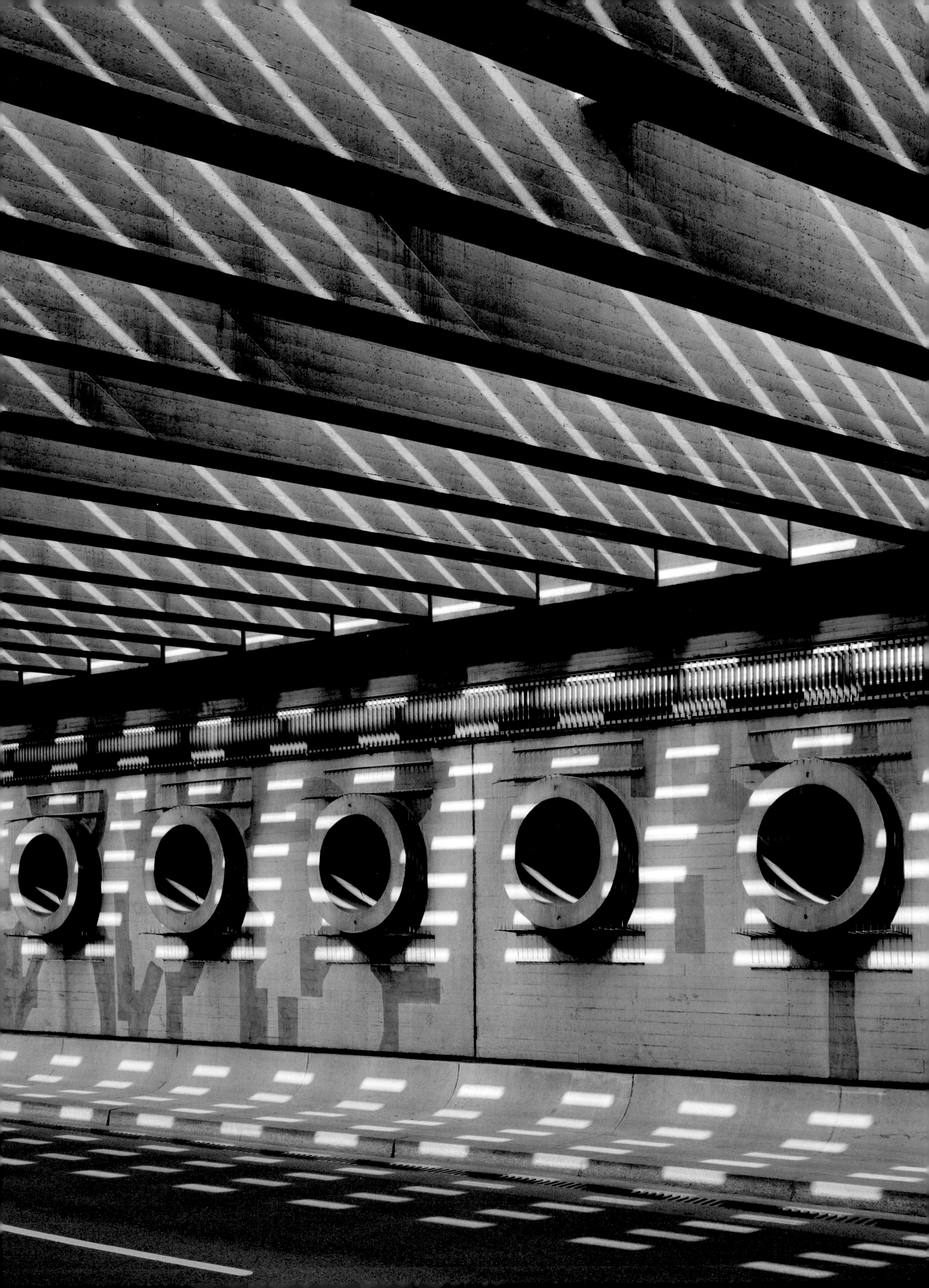

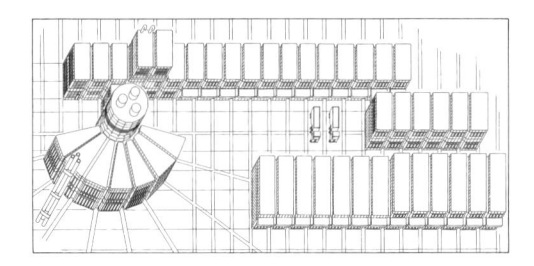

Energiezentrale und betriebstechnische Anlagen, Flughafen Berlin-Tegel
Central Energy Station and Operational Facilities, Berlin-Tegel Airport

Im Rahmen des Gesamtauftrags waren neben dem Fluggastterminal auch die Betriebsbauten für den Flughafen zu planen. Hierbei wurde die Vielfalt der unterschiedlichen Nutzungen und Gebäudegrößen einem einheitlichen Gestaltungskonzept untergeordnet, das gleichzeitig dem permanenten Wachstumsprozess Rechnung trägt; d.h., für spätere Erweiterungen einzelner Bereiche werden nicht nur Flächen vorgesehen, sondern auch ein Gestaltungsrahmen festgelegt, der trotz aller Vielfalt im Einzelnen die Ordnung und Einheit im Ganzen wahrt. Sowohl die einzelnen Bauteile als auch die Gesamtheit der Anlage entstanden aus der Addition gleicher Grundelemente. Aus dieser Maßordnung entwickelte sich ein Bausystem, bei dem die einzelnen Gebäudemodule konstruktiv selbständige Einheiten darstellen, die wie Container nebeneinander stehen. Die Tragstruktur ist variabel und besteht aus Stahl, Stahlbeton oder aus in Ortbeton ausgeführter Mischbauweise. Alle Baukörper sind mit vorgehängten Fassaden aus farbig lackiertem Aluminiumblech verkleidet.

The complete brief was comprised of the planning of the passenger terminal as well as the operational facilities of the airport. The variety of different uses and building scales was subordinated to a uniform design concept that simultaneously considered the permanent growth process; that means that the future extension of single areas was being considered regarding the necessary site area, but also regarding the definition of a design framework, which, despite the variety of single components, maintains the order and clarity of the overall complex. Single building units as well as the unity of the ensemble resulted from the addition of identical basic elements. A structural system was derived from this dimensional framework, where the single building modules appear as constructively independent units, standing next to each other like containers. The load-bearing structure is variable and made of steel, reinforced concrete or in-situ concrete. All buildings are clad with suspended façades from coloured sheet aluminium.

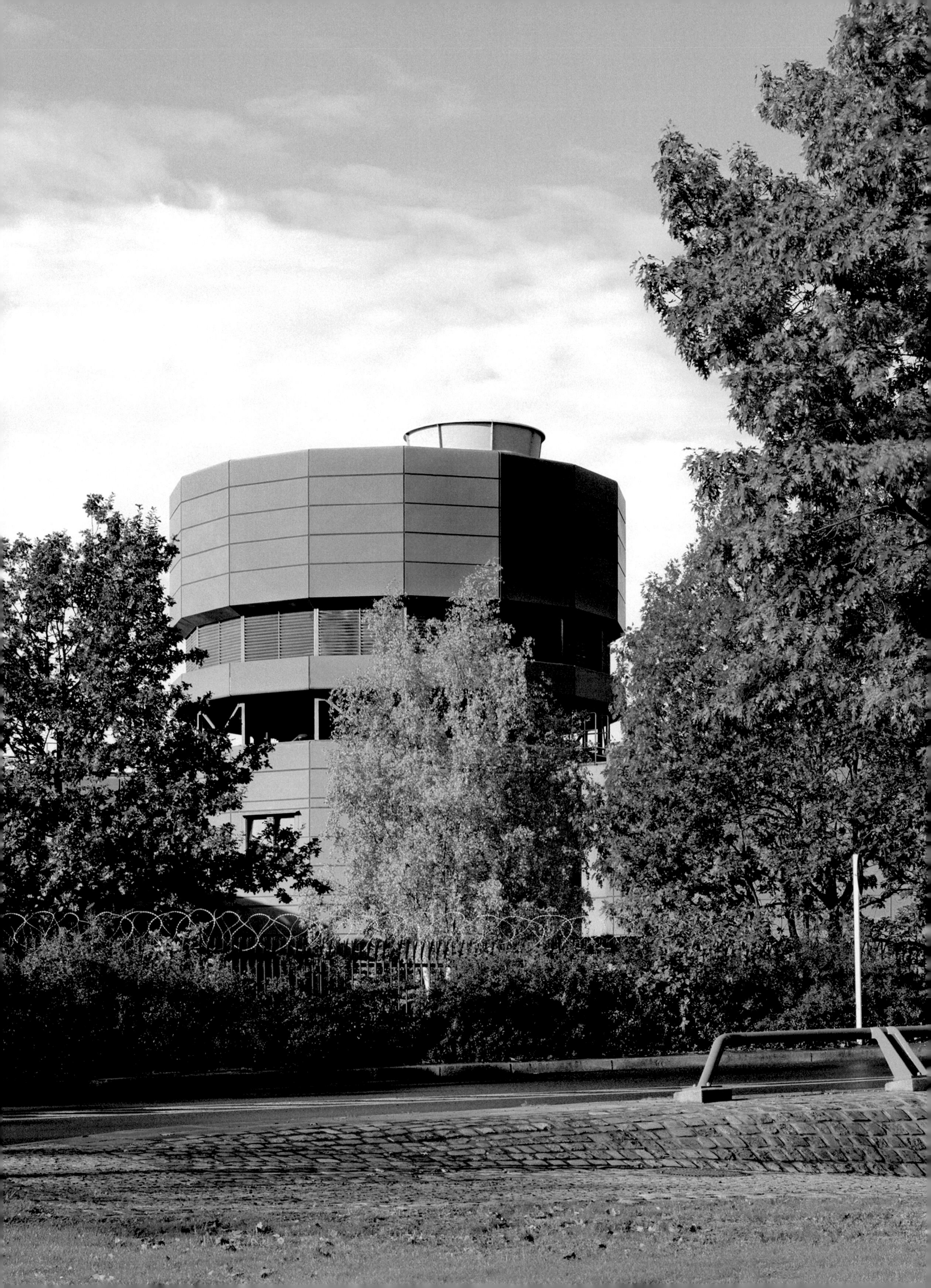

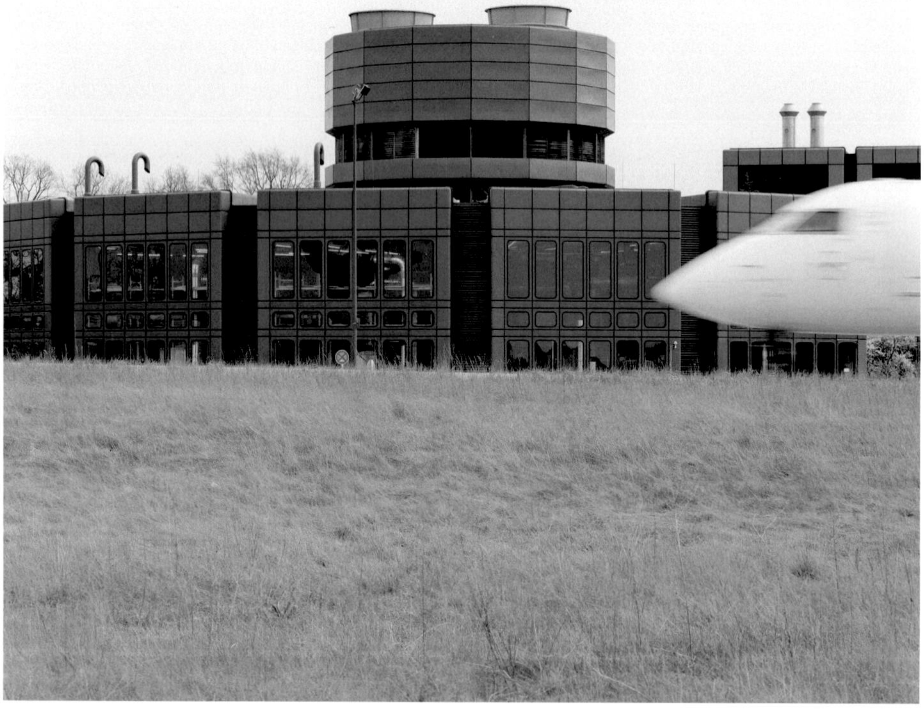

AUTOWÄSCHE
Waschstrasse
Durchfahrtshöhe
max. 2,05 m
STOP
Bitte den Anweisungen
des Personals folgen!

Lärmschutzkabine, Flughafen Berlin-Tegel
Noise Protection Cabin, Berlin-Tegel Airport

Die Lärmschutzhalle des Flughafens Berlin-Tegel gewährleistet insbesondere im Bereich des Schallpegelmaximums, das in einem Winkel von 20 bis 60° seitlich zur Strahlrichtung liegt, eine wirksame Schallreduktion um mehr als 20 dB. Dies wird zum einen dadurch erreicht, dass der Schall durch die umschließende schwere Dach- und Wandkonstruktion gedämmt wird, und zum anderen durch die entsprechende Beugung der frei austretenden Schallwellen über die geneigten Flächen. Der wesentliche Vorteil dieser Lärmschutzhalle besteht gegenüber herkömmlichen Konstruktionen darin, dass die hohen Kosten und technischen Schwierigkeiten einer geschlossenen Halle vermieden werden, gleichzeitig jedoch der günstige flache Beugungswinkel des Schalls gegenüber bisherigen Zäunen oder Kabinen wesentlich durch die nicht nur seitlich sondern auch oberhalb abgeschirmte Schallquelle vergrößert wird.

The noise protection cabin at Berlin-Tegel Airport achieves an effective noise reduction of more than 20 decibels, especially in the area of the maximum noise level at an angle of 20 to 60° lateral to the sound direction. The reduction is achieved by the massive sound-insulated roof and walls, and by their slanted surfaces refracting the sound waves emanating from the aeroplanes. The main advantages of this acoustic hangar construction over conventional hangars are that it does not cost as much and does not pose the same technical problems as a closed hall. Furthermore the flat acoustic refraction angle is made more effective in absorbing sound than the usual barriers or cabins are, essentially by means of the noise being reduced not only by lateral walls, but also by the roof.

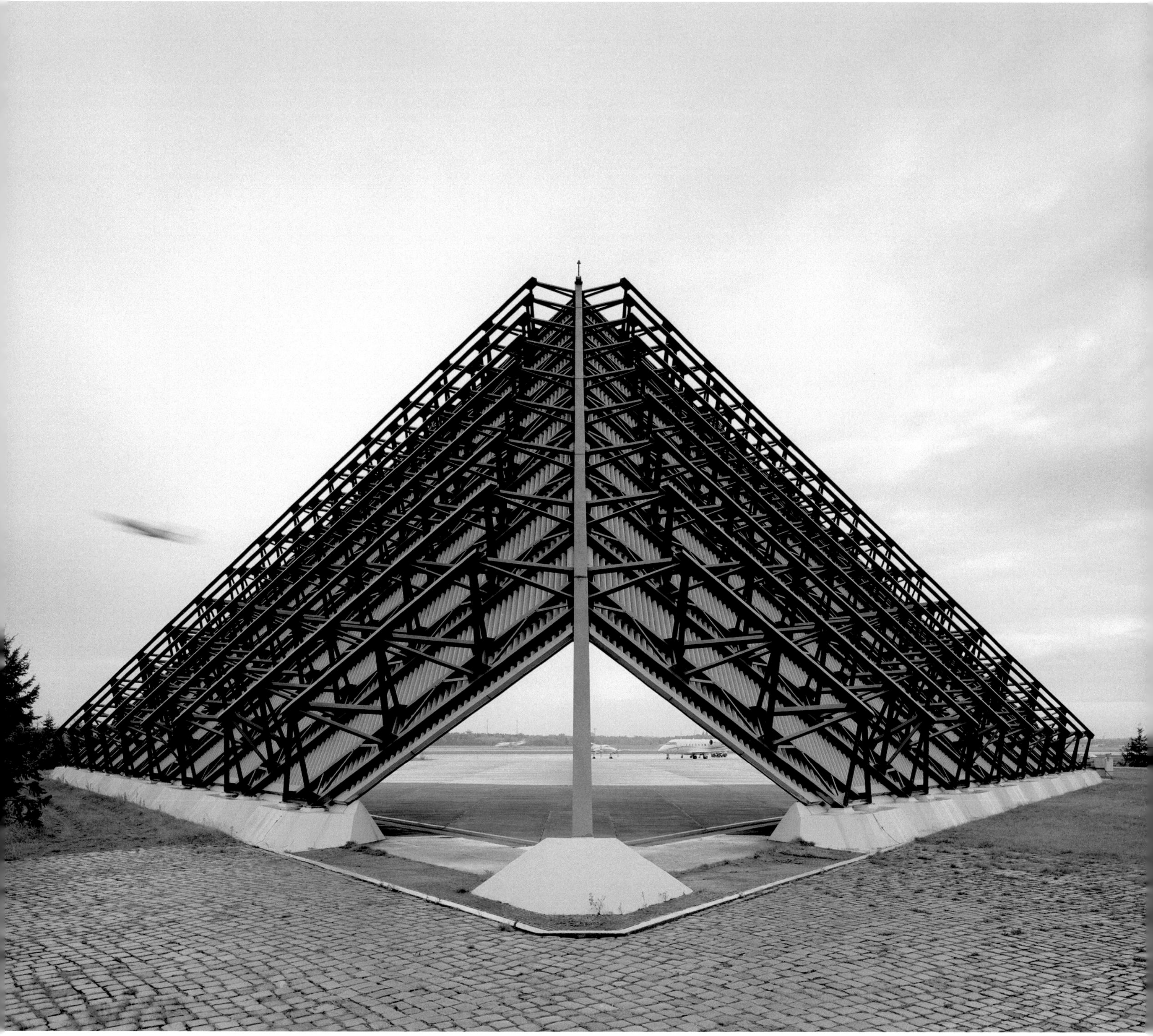

1976
1977

Finanzamt Oldenburg

Der Komplex gliedert sich in drei versetzt positionierte Baukörper unterschiedlicher Höhe. Um einen jeweils mittigen Kern sind die Flure wie Flügel einer Windmühle angeordnet.
An ihren Enden zeichnen sie sich als senkrechte Schlitze in der Fassade ab oder münden in einen Verbindungsgang zum benachbarten Baukörper.

Oldenburg Revenue Office

The complex is divided into three staggered buildings of different height. The corridors are positioned around the respective central core like the sails of a windmill. At their ends they appear as vertical slits in the façade or end in a connecting corridor leading towards the neighbouring building.

Sportforum der Universität Kiel

Die sechs Schwimm- und Sporthallen sind als optisches und räumliches Kontinuum angelegt, das von der Fachwerkkonstruktion des Daches überspannt wird. Die gläsernen Fassaden erlauben allseitigen Einblick in die Hallen, deren transparenter und offener Charakter passive und aktive Teilnahme herausfordert.

Kiel University Sports Forum

Six indoor pools and gymnasiums are laid out as a visual and spatial continuum that is spanned by the framework construction of the roof. The glazed façades allow views into the halls from all sides, their transparent and open character inviting to passive and active participation.

Kreisberufsschule Bad Oldesloe

Dem sehr beengten Hanggrundstück folgend sind die Baukörper L-förmig angeordnet. Im Knickpunkt des Winkels befindet sich eine zentrale Halle mit durchgehendem Luftraum und einem räumlich integrierbaren pädagogischen Zentrum. Die Erschließung erfolgt von der mittleren Ebene.

Bad Oldesloe Vocational School

Following the confined site on a slope the buildings are positioned in an L-shaped formation. A central hall with a continuous void and an educational centre, which can be spatially integrated, is located in the bend of the angle. The circulation starts on the central level.

Psychiatrische Anstalten, Rickling

Die Stahlbetonskelettbauweise bedingt ein straffes äußeres Erscheinungsbild, das durch vielfältige Baukörperkombination und topographisch bewegte Außenanlagen aufgelockert wird. Holz für Fassaden und Decken, Klinker für Wände und Fußböden sowie kräftige Farben innen und Markisen außen vermeiden eine sterile Krankenhausatmosphäre.

Psychiatric Hospital, Rickling

The reinforced concrete skeleton construction demands a concise external appearance, which is loosened up with various building combinations and topographically moved outdoor ceilings, brick used for walls and floors as well as rich colours in the interior and exterior sunblinds avoid a sterile hospital atmosphere.

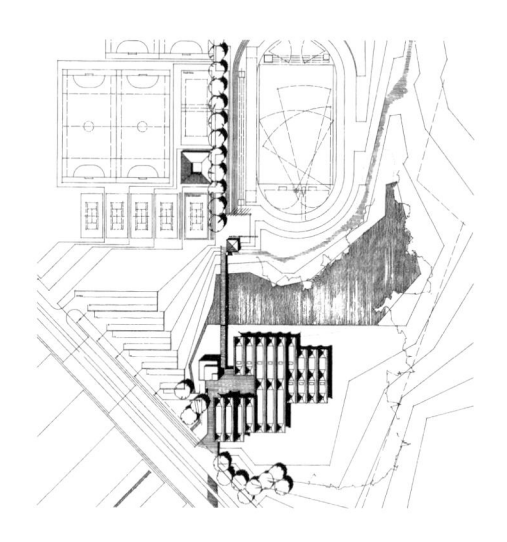

Sportforum der Universität Kiel
Kiel University Sports Forum

Wettbewerb Competition
1966 – 1. Preis

Entwurf Design
Meinhard von Gerkan und Volkwin Marg

Partner Partner
Klaus Nickels

Bauherr Client
Landesverwaltung Schleswig-Holstein

Bauzeit Construction period
1972–1974, 1976

BFG Gross floor area
6.900 m²

Vom Vorplatz aus sind die Übungshallen über eine große Eingangshalle als auch das Institutsgebäude getrennt zugänglich. Über eine Treppe erreicht man die untere Ebene, auf der die Umkleide- und Übungsräume liegen. Bei Publikumsveranstaltungen stehen den Sportlern die Nebeneingänge zur Verfügung, die Besucher verbleiben auf der oberen Ebene, die in allen Hallen als Tribüne abschließt. Die Übungshallen teilen sich in Trockensporthallen für unterschiedliche Disziplinen und die Schwimmhallen mit jeweils direkt zugeordneten Umkleide-, Geräte- und Nebenräumen. Die konzentrierte Grundrissanordnung erlaubt kürzeste Wege zwischen Übungshallen und Institutsgebäude. Im Vordergrund des Entwurfs stand der Anspruch, eine Anlage zu schaffen, die dem spielerischen und pädagogischen Charakter des Geschehens gleichermaßen gerecht wird und dabei eine enge Verzahnung von Innen- und Außenraum herstellt.

Approached from the forecourt, the training halls are separately accessible via a large entrance hall as well as the institute building. A staircase leads to the lower level, accommodating the changing and training rooms. During public events the athletes use the side entrances, whilst the spectators remain on the upper level, which terminates as stands in all halls. The training halls are divided into dry sports halls for various disciplines and the indoor swimming pools with the respective assigned changing, tool and secondary rooms. The dense plan arrangement ensures short distances between the training halls and the institute building. The main focus of the design was placed on the achievement of a complex that equally reflects the playful as well as educational character of the procedures, whilst simultaneously generating a close link between interior and exterior spaces.

63

1978

Stadthäuser, Hamburg BAU 78

Trotz des steigenden Angebots von Eigentumswohnungen hatten auch Ende der 1970er Jahre die Vorzüge des Wohnens im eigenen Haus nicht an Popularität verloren. Aus Anlass der Ausstellung Hamburg BAU 78 entstand daher ein Ensemble von vier Stadthäusern mit unterschiedlichen Grundrissen.

City Houses, 'Hamburg BAU 78'

Despite the increasing availability of owner-occupied flats at the end of the 1970s, the advantages of living in one's own house had not lost their appeal. An ensemble of four city houses with different plans was therefore realized on the occasion of the Hamburg BAU 78 exhibition.

Einfamilienhaus-Siedlung, Hamburg BAU 78

Die acht Häuser in geschlossener Bauweise sind so angeordnet, dass auf beiden Seiten individuell nutzbare Freiflächen entstehen. Die Vielfalt im Einzelnen wird durch die einheitlichen Fassaden aus rotem Klinker und die geneigten Dachflächen zusammengefasst. Dacherker und Gauben beleben die Firstlinie.

Single-Family House Estate, 'Hamburg BAU 78'

The eight houses designed according to a dense construction method are positioned so as to generate individually usable open spaces on both sides. The variety of single details is combined through uniform façades made from red brick and inclined roof surfaces. Gabled windows add diversity to the ridgeline.

Taxistandüberdachung, Flughafen Berlin-Tegel

Eine leichte Stahlprofil-Konstruktion überdacht die Fußgängerinsel unmittelbar vor der Vorfahrt des Abfertigungsgebäudes. Das Dach aus transparenten Plexiglasschalen überdeckt eine Fläche von 8,66 x 65 m und steht auf vier runden Stahlrohrstützen.

Taxi Stand Roofing, Berlin-Tegel Airport

A lightweight steel sectional structure covers the pedestrian island located directly in front of the access road to the departure terminal. The roof, made of transparent acrylic glass shells, covers an area of 8.66 by 65 m and is supported by four round steel tube columns.

Gewerbeschule für Chemie, Pharmazie und Gartenbau – G 13, Hamburg-Bergedorf

Der aus Rücksicht auf drei erhaltenswerte Bäume abgewinkelte Grundriss umfasst eine forumartige Platzanlage und nimmt durch vorgelagerte ein- und zweigeschossige Bauteile und das angegliederte Gewächshaus maßstäblich Bezug zum vorhandenen Fachwerkhaus, das als Gemeinschaftszentrum genutzt wird.

Vocational School for Chemistry, Pharmacy and Gardening – G 13, Hamburg-Bergedorf

The plan, elbowed out of consideration for three trees worth preserving, comprises a forum-like square. With one- and two-storey building units and the adjoining glasshouse the ensemble makes a scaled reference to the existing timber-frame farmhouse, which is used as a common centre.

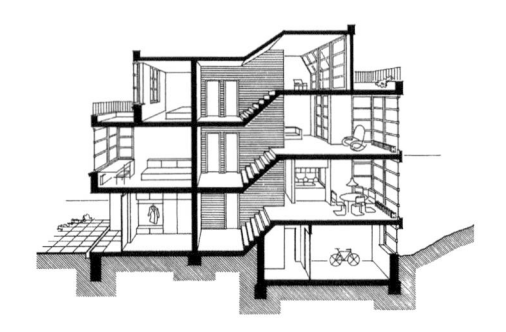

Stadthäuser, Hamburg BAU 78
City Houses, 'Hamburg BAU 78'

Wettbewerb Competition
1977 – 2. Preis

Entwurf Design
Meinhard von Gerkan

Partner Partners
Hans-Eggert Bock, Rolf Niedballa

Bauherr Client
Stadthaus GmbH

Bauzeit Construction period
1977–1978

BGF Gross floor area
ca. 150 m²

Das Einfamilienhaus in der Großstadt lässt sich meist nur dann realisieren, wenn die knappen und teuren städtischen Baugrundstücke intensiv genutzt werden. Die bei der Hamburger Bauausstellung 1978 zur Verfügung stehenden Grundstücke weisen demnach eine Breite von jeweils weniger als 6 m auf. Obwohl die vier Häuser äußerlich ein Ensemble bilden, hat jedes Haus einen anderen Grundriss. Allen gemeinsam ist jedoch die halbgeschossige Versetzung der Ebenen. Die Treppe dient gleichzeitig als Erschließungsflur, so dass die Wohnflächen optimal genutzt werden können und die einzelnen Wohnbereiche miteinander verzahnt sind. Eine vor Einblicken geschützte Dachterrasse ergänzt den knapp bemessenen Garten. Vor- und Rücksprünge, Erker und Rückstaffelungen bewirken eine plastische Differenzierung der Fassaden aus hell gestrichenen Kalksandsteinflächen und farbig lackierten Fensterelementen.

A single-family house in large cities can be realized only when scarce and expensive urban building sites are intensively used. The sites available during the Hamburg Building Exhibition in 1978 had a width of less than 6 m each. Although externally the houses form a unity, each house has a different plan. A common feature, however, is the mezzanine division of the floors. The stairs serve as a circulation corridor, allowing for an optimal use of the floor area and linkage of the single living zones. A roof terrace, shielded from view, adds to the limited garden. Bays, projections and recesses generate a three-dimensional façade structure from brightly painted sand lime brick and coloured window elements.

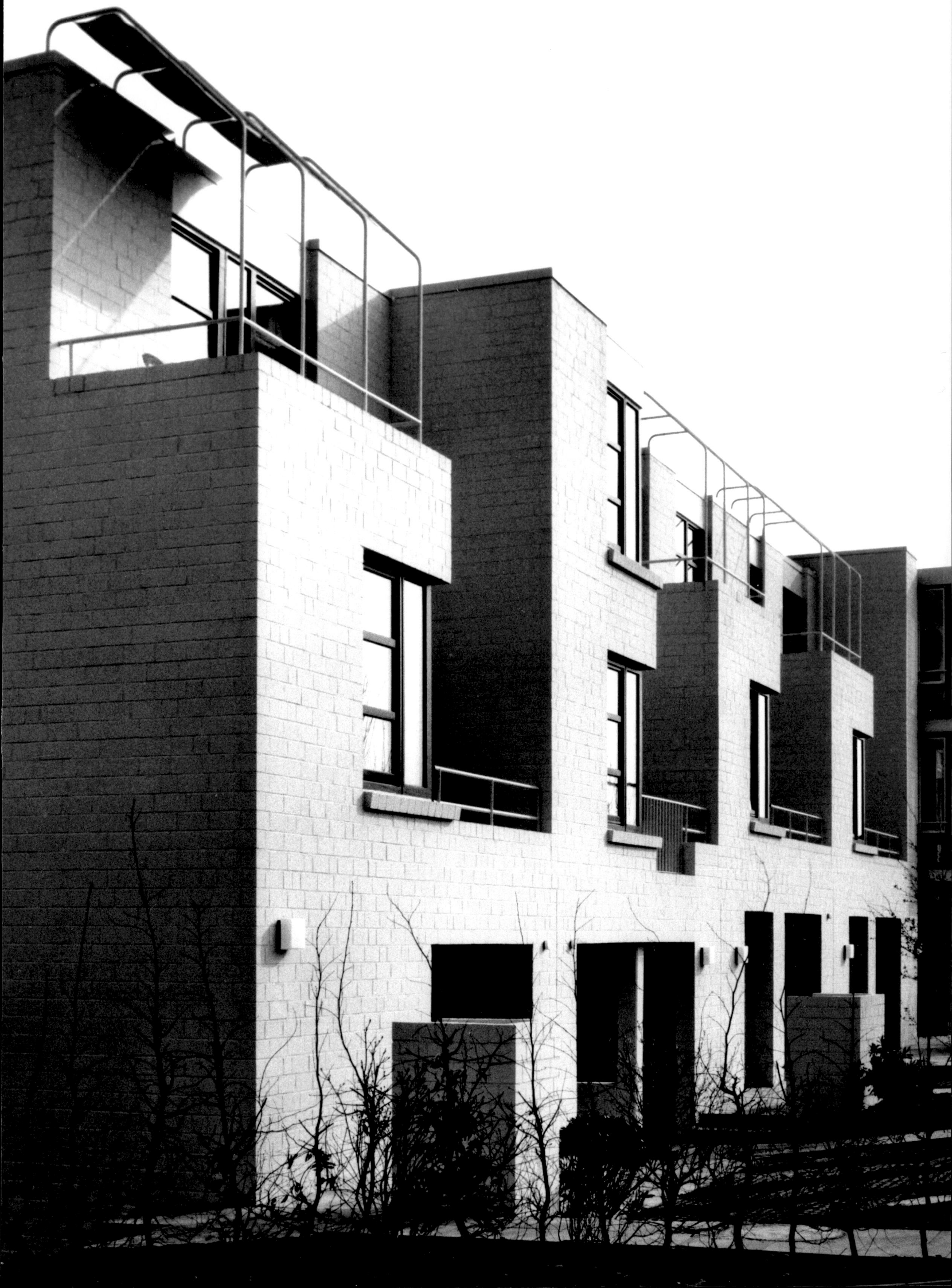

1979

Wiederaufbau der „Fabrik", Hamburg-Altona

Beim Wiederaufbau des abgebrannten Kulturzentrums galt es, die ursprüngliche Atmosphäre wiederzubeleben und, trotz strenger Sicherheitsbestimmungen, die Konstruktion der dreigeschossigen, dreischiffigen Halle in Holz auszuführen. Aufgrund der geringen finanziellen Mittel wurden Abbruchmaterialien und ausrangierte Industriebauteile verwendet.

Reconstruction of 'Fabrik', Hamburg-Altona

The reconstruction of the burnt-down cultural centre aimed to revive its original atmosphere and a realization of the three-storey, three-nave hall as a timber structure despite strict safety regulations. Restricted financial means necessitated the use of demolition material and discarded industrial components.

Wohnquartier Kohlhöfen, Hamburg

Die Dachschrägen und der rote Vormauerstein dienen der Einbindung der in Grund- und Aufriss mehrfach gestaffelten Baukörper in den Charakter der Umgebung. Ein Teil der hauptsächlich als Maisonettes gestalteten Wohnungen steht Alten, Behinderten oder kinderreichen Familien zur Verfügung.

Kohlhöfen Residential District, Hamburg

The roof pitches and the red facing brick adjust the buildings, which in plan and elevation are repeatedly staggered, to the character of the neighbourhood. A number of the flats, primarily laid out as maisonettes, is available to the old, the handicapped or to large families.

1980

Hanse-Viertel, Hamburg

Die vorhandene Straßenrandbebauung wurde saniert und ergänzt und das Blockinnere in niedriger Bauweise genutzt. Das Ziel der Architekten war es, eine Passage im Wortsinne zu schaffen – zum Abkürzen der Wege, aber zugleich attraktiv zum Flanieren, ohne Musikberieselung und aufdringliche Reklame.

Europäisches Patentamt, München

Die Konzeption des Entwurfs ist im wesentlichen funktional bestimmt. Der überwiegende Teil der 1.500 Arbeitsplätze ist in einem kreuzförmigen Bürotrakt mit flexibler Raumaufteilung untergebracht. Im Funktionsschwerpunkt befindet sich die Zentralregistratur, erkennbar an der Fassadeneinschnürung.

Hanse Viertel, Hamburg

The existing roadside development was reconstructed and added to, whilst the block interior was utilized with a low-rise development. The aim of the architects was to create a 'passage': to be used as a short cut, but simultaneously as an attractive walkway without background music and obtrusive advertisements.

European Patent Office, Munich

The design concept is primarily functional. The majority of the 1,500 workplaces is accommodated in a cross-shaped office building with a flexible room layout. The central filing department forms the primary emphasis of the building and is emphasized through the façade contraction.

Taima und Sulayyil, Saudi-Arabien

In der Nachbarschaft zweier Oasenstädte – Taima im Nordwesten und Sulayyil im Süden Saudi-Arabiens – plante das Königreich die Neugründung von Wohnsiedlungen. Beide Projekte umfassen jeweils 25 Doppelhäuser, zwei Grundschulen, ein Theater und eine Moschee sowie weitere Einrichtungen.

Taima and Sulayyil, Saudi Arabia

The kingdom planned the new development of residential settlements in the neighbourhood of two towns located in an oasis: Taima in the northwest and Sulayyil in the south of Saudi Arabia. Both projects are comprised of 25 semi-detached houses, two primary schools, a theatre, a mosque as well as other facilities.

MAK, Kiel

Das große Volumen des Raumprogramms wurde mit Bedacht in einzelne Baukörper aufgelöst, um eine lockere Einbettung in den Park und zugleich eine architektonisch gefasste Eingangssituation zu schaffen. Auf diese Weise wird der spezifischen Situation des Ortes Rechnung getragen.

MAK, Kiel

The large volume of the room programme was considerately divided into single buildings, in order to generate a loose integration into the park and simultaneously an architecturally framed entrance situation. This solution carefully considers the site-specific characteristics.

Biochemisches Institut der Universität Braunschweig

Die Gebäudegruppe nimmt den Maßstab und die Höhenentwicklung der vorhandenen Bebauung auf und gliedert sich um einen introvertierten Freibereich, der über einen Fußweg an das Hochschulforum angeschlossen ist. Die Ausrichtung der Gebäude folgt den Richtungen der begrenzenden Straßenräume.

Braunschweig University, Biochemical Institute

The ensemble relates to the scale and height development of the existing buildings and is laid out around an introverted open space, which is linked to the university forum via a path. The orientation of the buildings follows the directions of the adjoining street courses.

Hanse-Viertel, Hamburg
Hanse Viertel, Hamburg

1974

Entwurf Design
Volkwin Marg

Partner Partners
Klaus Staratzke, Rolf Niedballa

Bauherr Client
Allianz Lebensversicherungs AG

Bauzeit Construction period
1978–1980

BGF Gross floor area
27.300 m²

Die Passage soll als öffentlicher Kommunikationsraum attraktiv sein und als eindeutiges Architekturerlebnis gleichwertig neben dem Kommerz stehen. Der gesamte Entwurf war von der Zielsetzung geprägt, den Inhalt der Bauaufgabe mit den spezifischen Bedingungen des Ortes durch eine architektonische Entsprechung zu einem Ganzen zu verschmelzen. Analog zu den Außenfassaden und den benachbarten Altbauten sind im Innern die Böden und Wände in ortstypischem Backstein errichtet. Die innenräumliche Wirkung wird von Kuppeln und Bogengängen auf Ziegelpfeilern beherrscht. Da die Passage als öffentlich genutzter Straßenraum verstanden wird, weist sie eine Geradlinigkeit mit Blick auf die Ein- und Ausgänge auf und ist nach oben transparent gehalten. Sie soll gleichermaßen abends und am Wochenende belebt bleiben, daher befinden sich unterhalb der beiden Kuppeln Restaurants.

The shopping arcade has to be an attractive public place of communication, whilst simultaneously presenting a clear architectural experience equivalent to commerce. The whole concept is characterized by the aim to unify the building task and the site-specific conditions through an architectural analogy. In tune to the exterior façades and the existing neighbouring buildings, the floors and walls in the interior are constructed from locally used brick. Domes and brick columns dominate the interior effect. The understanding of the shopping arcade as a public streetscape leads to its regularity towards the entrances and exits and transparency towards the ceiling. The arcade has to be busy at night and at the weekends, and so restaurants are located underneath the domes.

GEOGRAPHISCHE LÄNGE · 9 GRAD 59 MINUTEN
SEKUNDEN OST
MINUTEN 18 SEKUNDEN NORD

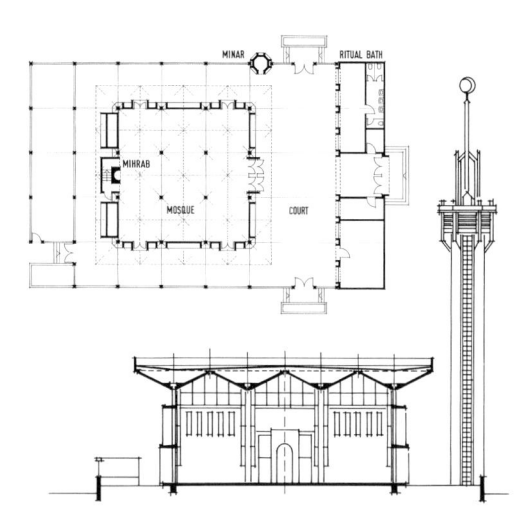

Taima und Sulayyil, Saudi-Arabien
Taima and Sulayyil, Saudi Arabia

1977

Entwurf Design
Meinhard von Gerkan und Karsten Brauer

Partner Partner
Klaus Staratzke

Bauherr Client
Königreich Saudi-Arabien

Bauzeit Construction period
1977-1980

Die beiden Gesamtanlagen sind jeweils durch ein rechtwinkliges Ordnungssystem um einen zentralen quadratischen Grünraum, der von öffentlichen Gebäuden gesäumt ist, gegliedert. Die Wohnhäuser wurden als Gartenhofhäuser konzipiert. Die Hofmauern, die auch die Schulen umschließen, sind zugleich wichtiges Entwurfsmotiv: Sie vergrößern einerseits optisch das Volumen der Häuser und bilden eindeutige Straßenräume, andererseits wird durch das treppenartige Aneinanderstoßen der waagerechten Mauerkronen die leichte Neigung des Geländes ablesbar. Es ergeben sich vielfältige Höhenstaffelungen, die trotz des einheitlichen Materials – Betonholsteine als Sichtmauerwerk – und der monochromen Farbgebung eine kleinteilige und belebte Silhouette erzeugen. Während alle Gebäude der gleichen Formensprache mit nur leichten Variationen entsprechen, bilden die Moschee und das Theater zwei völlig anders gestaltete Solitärbauten.

The complexes are both organized as a rectangular system around a central square green area surrounded by public buildings. The residential blocks are designed as garden courthouses. The courtyard walls, which also enclose the schools, are simultaneously an important design motif: they visually increase the volumes of the houses and form clear streetscapes, whilst the stair-like colliding horizontal wall crowns make the slight natural fall perceptible. The results are manifold variations of levels, which produce a small-scale and vivid silhouette despite the uniform materials (A-blocks as fair-faced masonry) and the monochrome colouring. Whilst all buildings adhere to the same formal expression with only slight variations, the mosque and the theatre are solitaires with a completely different design.

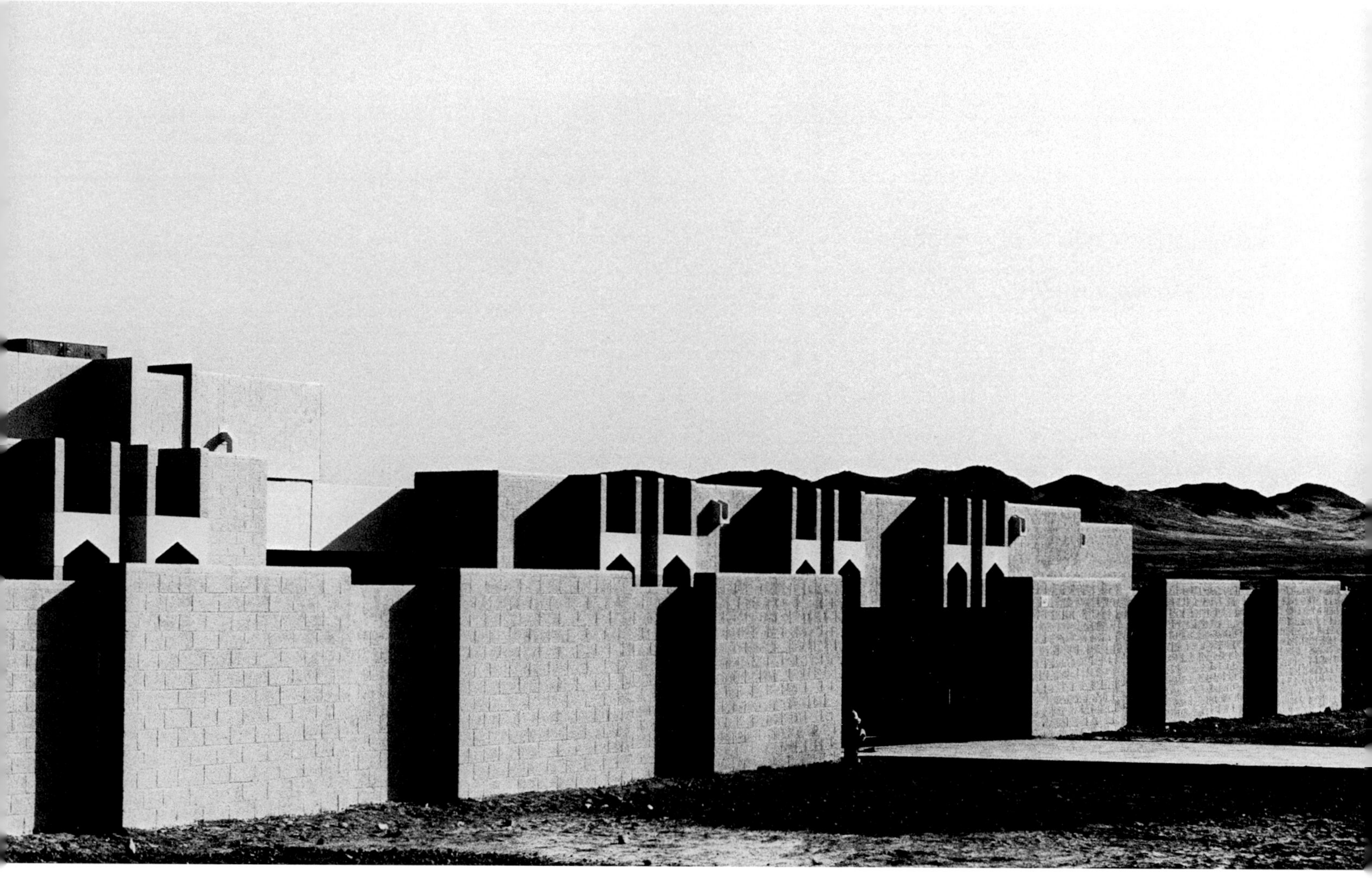

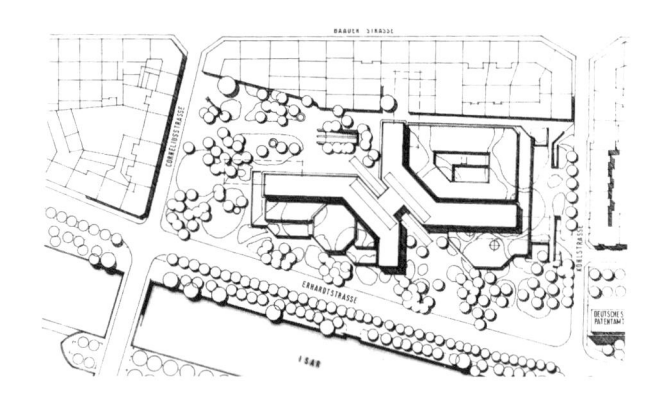

Europäisches Patentamt, München
European Patent Office, Munich

Wettbewerb Competition
1971 – 1. Preis

Entwurf Design
Volkwin Marg und Andreas Sack

Partner Partner
Rolf Niedballa

Bauherr Client
Bundesrepublik Deutschland

Bauzeit Construction period
1975–1979

BGF Gross floor area
81.000 m²

Der Gebäudekern löst, unterstrichen durch einen Wechsel in der Verglasung, die beiden geknickten Büroflügel voneinander. Im Innern dieser gläsernen Verbindungsbrücke mit Ausblick auf die Isar und die Stadt München befinden sich die Rolltreppen, während durch das Erdgeschoss ein öffentlicher Fußweg führt. Alle publikumsintensiven Bereiche sind in den beiden Sockelgeschossen untergebracht. Die Gebäudeform schafft durch ihre Differenzierung in kleinteilige Flachbauten und die beiden Hochbauten eine spannungsreiche Massengliederung. Die Besonderheit wird durch die Lage des Gebäudes an der Isar und die Ausweitung des Grünraums unterstrichen. Seine gestalterische Zurückhaltung in der Farb- und Materialwahl steht in beabsichtigtem Kontrast zu der Vielgestaltigkeit des Hauses, der lebendigen Freiraumgestaltung und Begrünung sowie zu der vielfältigen und aufwendigen Ausstattung mit Kunstobjekten.

Supported by a change in the type of glazing, the central building section separates and connects the two angled office wings. This glazed bridge, which affords a view of the Isar river and the city of Munich, contains the escalators while the ground floor includes a public pedestrian passage. All areas frequented by visitors are on the ground floor of the two wings. As the building is divided into small-scale flat-roofed sections and the two higher wings, the overall impression is that of diversity. The special configuration is enhanced by the location on the Isar and the extended park. Its aesthetic restraint in terms of colours and materials unintentionally contrasts with the building's multiformity, varied landscaping and planting as well as with the many works of art displayed inside.

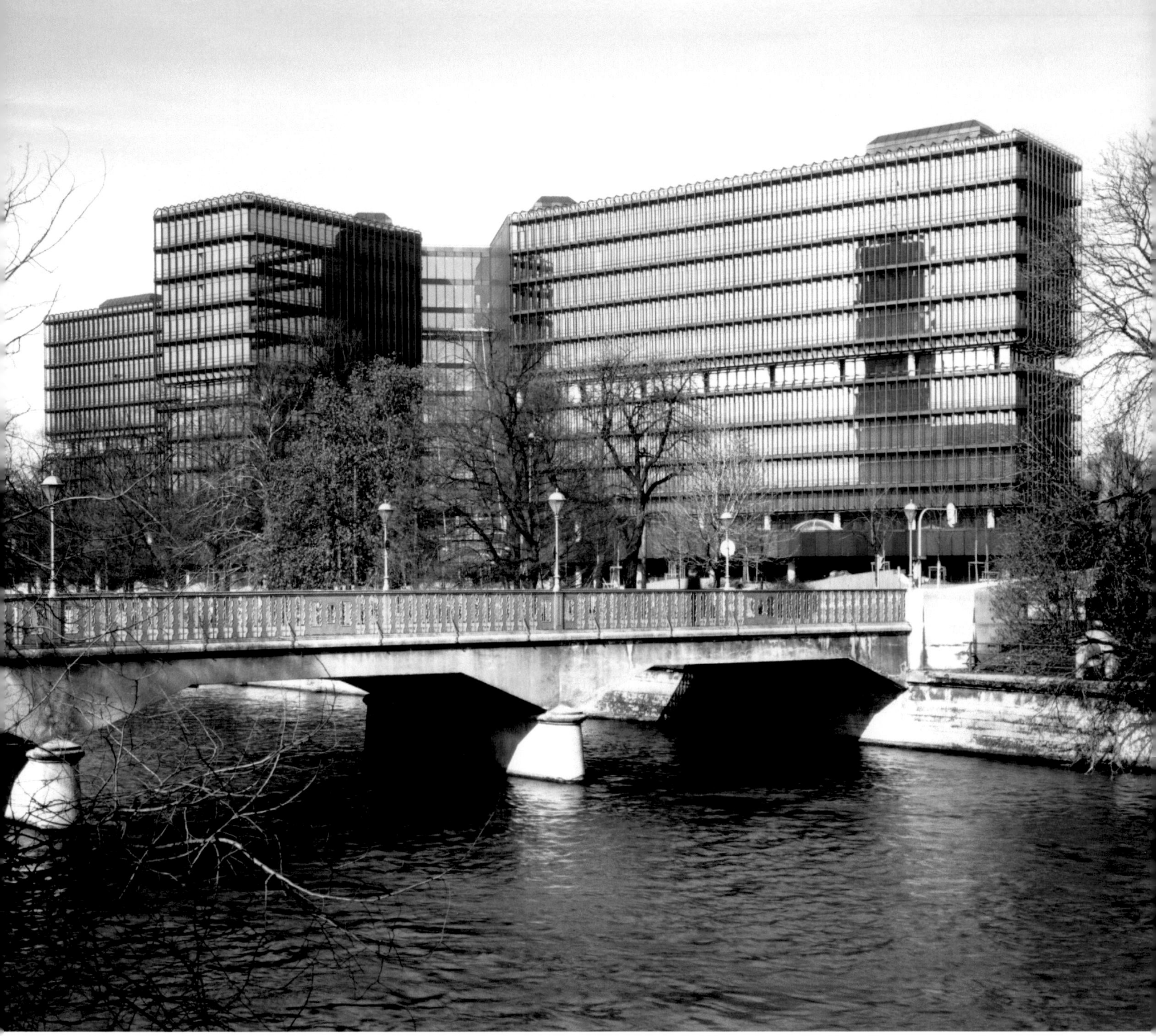

1981
1982

Renaissance-Hotel Ramada, Hamburg

Für die Neuplanung des Hotels wurden zwei vorhandene Hausscheiben von Fritz Höger zusammengefasst. Die sinngemäße Rekonstruktion des Högerschen Baus beschränkt sich auf das Eckgebäude; die daran anschließenden Neubauten sind lediglich in Höhe, Staffelung und Maßstabsbildung der Umgebung angepasst.

Ramada Renaissance Hotel, Hamburg

Two existing building slabs designed by Fritz Höger were combined in the new hotel concept. The analogous reconstruction of the Höger building is restricted to the corner building; the new adjoining units adapt to their surroundings only regarding their height, alternation and scale.

Haus „G", Hamburg-Blankenese

Die gestalterischen und bautechnischen Gesetzmäßigkeiten einer Holzkonstruktion wurden bei diesem Wohnhaus konsequent befolgt: Auch in den Innenräumen dominiert die Konstruktion mit sichtbaren Stützen und Balken. Durch die Gliederung der Baumasse und die versetzten Pultdächer fügt sich das Gebäude in die Umgebung ein.

House 'G', Hamburg-Blankenese

The design and constructional regularities of a timber structure were consequently adhered to for this residential house: the construction method with visible columns and beams also dominates the interior. The division of the building mass and the staggered monopitch roofs harmoniously integrate the building into the neighbourhood.

Psychiatrische Anstalten, Rickling

Die Gesamtanlage gliedert sich in drei Stationen mit jeweils vier Wohngruppen für zehn Patienten. Die Gemeinschaftsräume sind zu einem hofbildenden Flachtrakt zusammengefasst, an den die einzelnen Bettenhäuser angehängt sind. Die Baukörperformen entsprechen der Grundrissgliederung.

Psychiatric Hospital, Rickling

The complete facility is divided into three wards with four housing groups of ten patients each. The common rooms are combined in a low-rise wing forming a courtyard, to which the single dormitories adjoin. The building forms correspond to the plan layout.

Erweiterungsbau der Hauptverwaltung
OTTO-Versand, Hamburg

Der Neubau hat acht Geschosse um einen mittigen Hauptkern. Der zweifach abgewinkelte Baukörper verbindet die Richtung des vorhandenen Verwaltungsgebäudes mit dem Straßenverlauf. Hierdurch und durch die Materialwahl und Gestaltung der Fassaden ließ sich die Massigkeit des großen Volumens differenzieren.

Extension of the OTTO Versand Headquarters, Hamburg

The new building is comprised of eight storeys located around a central core. The double-bent building connects the direction of the existing administration building to the street course. Together with the selected materials and the façade design, this solution makes it possible to differentiate the large volume and mass.

Gemeindehaus Ritterstraße, Stade

Die überwiegend vertikal gegliederte Baukörperstruktur schafft eine maßstabsgerechte Anpassung an die anschließende kleinbürgerliche Bebauung. Im Innenraum setzt sich die zweigeschossige Halle optisch in den begrünten Hof fort. Bei festlichen Anlässen können die Begrenzungswände zum Saal aufgeklappt werden.

Ritterstrasse Parish Hall, Stade

The primarily vertical building structure allows a scaled adaption to the adjoining bourgeois development. In the interior the two-storey hall is continued into the planted courtyard. The partition walls can be opened up for festive occassions.

Schaulandt „Black Box", Hamburg

Die mehrgeschossigen Ausstellungs- und Verkaufsflächen wurden wie ein begehbares „Industrieregal" ohne äußere Berührung mit der schräg gestellten Gebäudehülle offen um einen von oben erleuchteten Zentralraum angeordnet. Mittige Rampen verbinden die versetzten Ebenen.

Schaulandt 'Black Box', Hamburg

The multi-storey exhibition and shop areas were openly positioned like an accessible 'industrial shelf' around a central space lit from above and without any contact to the inclined building envelope. Central ramps connect the mezzanine levels.

1983

Innenministerium Kiel

Dem fünfgeschossigen Neubau ist eine Deichlandschaft vorgelagert, die die Höhe des Gebäudes reduziert und zugleich einen sicheren Hochwasserschutz für tiefer gelegene Räume bildet. Die in allen Ebenen vorgesehenen Anschlüsse an die vorhandenen Altbauten treten als gläserne Erker aus der Ziegelfassade hervor.

Ministry of the Interior, Kiel

Located in front of the new five-storey building is a dyke landscape, which reduces the building's height, whilst simultaneously providing a secure flood protection for rooms located at a lower level. The links to the existing buildings, which are planned on all levels, project from the brick façade as glazed bays.

Wohnanlage für Behinderte, Hamburg-Südring

Die Wohnanlage mit Tagesförderstätte, Jugendclub und Veranstaltungsräumen umschließt einen arkadengesäumten Innenhof. Alle Aufenthaltsräume haben einen Austritt ins Freie. Die kubische Strenge des Backsteinbaus steht im Kontrast zu den bepflanzten Dachflächen und den grün eingewachsenen Fassaden.

Residential Estate for the Handicapped, Hamburg-Südring

The residential estate with a day-care centre, a youth club and function rooms encloses an inner courtyard, which is surrounded by arcades. All common rooms have an exit leading into the open. The cubic strictness of the brick building contrasts the planted roof surfaces and the façades overgrown with plants.

Kontorhaus Hohe Bleichen, Hamburg

Das eingefügte Kontorhaus gleicht nicht nur den 16 m tiefen Versprung der Straßenfront aus, sondern stellt auch einen Übergang vom siebengeschossigen Altbau im Norden zum viergeschossigen neuen Anschlussbau im Süden her. Gebäudeform und Grundrissausbildung wurden aus diesen Bedingungen entwickelt.

Hohe Bleichen Office Block, Hamburg

The embedded office block evens out the 16-m-deep difference in the street level, whilst simultaneously providing a transition from the existing seven-storey building in the north to the new four-storey connecting building in the south. The building volume and plan were derived from these conditions.

Parkhaus Poststraße, Hamburg

Das Parkhaus mit 442 Stellplätzen dient als Ergänzung des Hanse-Viertels in der Hamburger Innenstadt. Gestalterisches Ziel der Baulückenschließung war, die bei Parkhäusern übliche gleichförmige Horizontalgliederung der Fassade zu vermeiden und einen formalen Dialog mit den Bauten der Umgebung einzugehen.

Poststrasse Parking Garage, Hamburg

The multi-storey car park with 442 places functions as an addition to the Hanse Viertel in Hamburg's city centre. The design of this gap site development tries to avoid the uniform horizontal façade fenestration typical of multi-storey car parks and to enter into a formal dialogue with the neighbouring buildings.

DAL-Bürozentrum, Mainz

Das städtebauliche Konzept sah eine flächige Bebauung des Grundstücks mit kreuzförmigen Gebäudesternen vor, die zu einer netzförmigen Gesamtstruktur zusammengefügt sind. Die Höhe der Gebäude ist auf drei bis fünf Geschosse begrenzt. Der Haupteingang orientiert sich zu einem kreisförmigen Platz.

DAL Office Centre, Mainz

The urban planning concept proposed a low-rise development with cross-shaped, star-like buildings that are combined to form a net-shaped overall structure. The building height is restricted to three to five storeys. The main entrance is orientated towards a circular square.

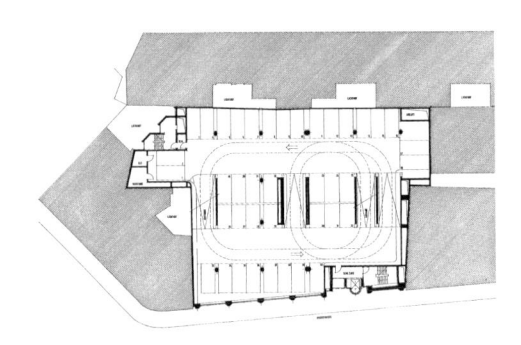

Parkhaus Poststraße, Hamburg
Poststrasse Parking Garage, Hamburg

1978

Entwurf Design
Volkwin Marg

Partner Partner
Klaus Staratzke

Bauherr Client
Allianz Lebensversicherungs AG

Bauzeit Construction period
1981–1983

Stellplätze Parking sites
442

Das Parkhaus nimmt mit seiner Ziegelfassade die überwiegend vorhandenen Materialien und vertikalen Strukturen der umliegenden Gebäude auf, ohne eine andere Nutzung vorzutäuschen. Es schließt an die benachbarten Traufhöhen an, wobei durch eine Rückstaffelung der obersten Geschosse die volle Höhe – insgesamt zwölf Geschosse mit versetzten Ebenen – straßenseitig nicht erkennbar ist. Um den Erlebnisbereich der Passantenzone nicht durch eine geschlossene Gebäudefront zu unterbrechen, befinden sich im Erdgeschoss zwei Läden. Die Fassade besteht aus vorgeblendetem Ziegelmauerwerk. Zwischen den tragenden, sich schichtenförmig nach oben verjüngenden Säulen sind Mauerwerksbögen gespannt, auf denen die gitterförmig gemauerten Ziegelflächen mit ihren breiten, offen gelassenen Stoßfugen lagern. Ein gläserner, außenliegender Fahrstuhl dient ebenfalls der vertikalen Gliederung.

The brick façade of the multi-storey car park repeats the predominantly existing materials and vertical structures of the neighbouring buildings, without pretending to have another use. It connects to the neighbouring eaves heights, whereas an offset of the highest storeys conceals the actual height (a total of twelve storeys with staggered levels) from the street front. Two shops on the ground floor avoid a closed building front and maintain a continuous shopping atmosphere for pedestrians. The façade consists of faced brickwork. Masonry arches span between the load-bearing columns, tapering in layers towards the top, which support the mash-like laid bricks with their wide, open vertical joints. An external glazed lift also emphasizes the vertical structure.

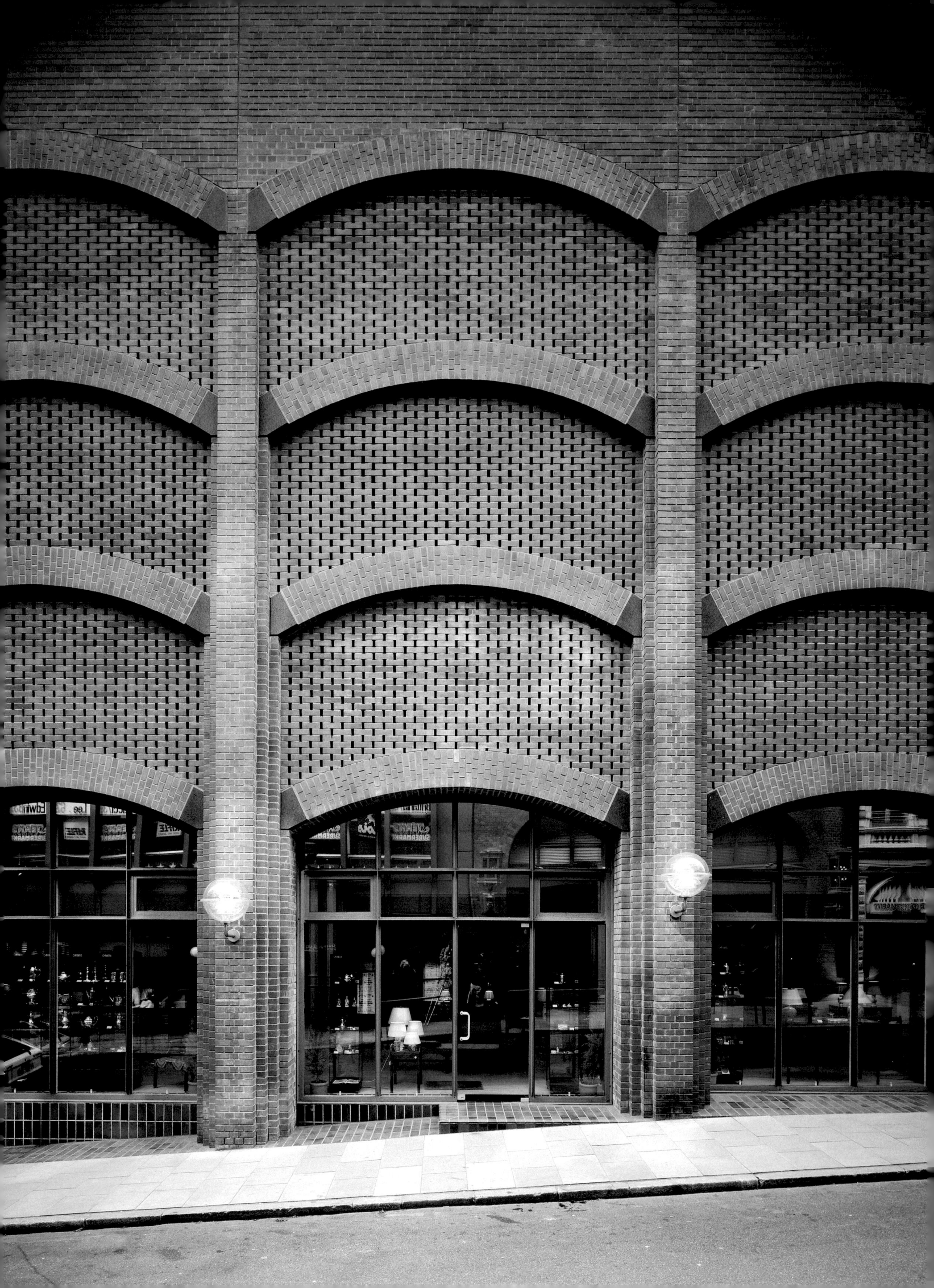

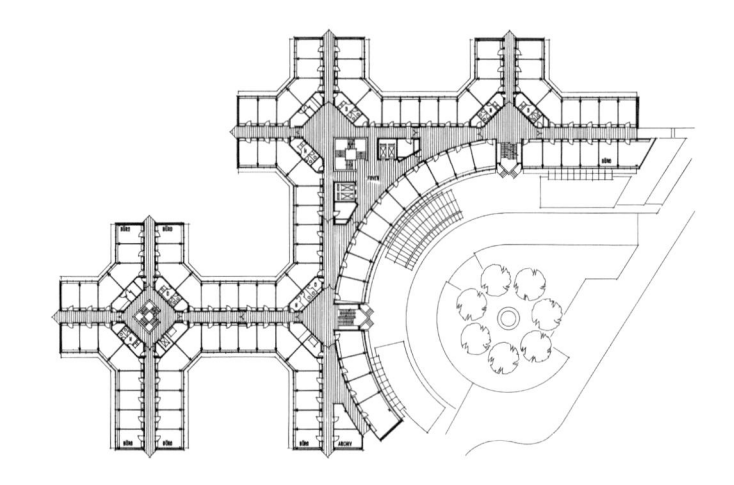

DAL-Bürozentrum, Mainz
DAL Office Centre, Mainz

Wettbewerb Competition
1981 – 1. Rang

Entwurf Design
Meinhard von Gerkan, Jürgen Friedemann, Gerhard Tjarks

Bauherr Client
DAL Deutsche Anlagenleasing

Bauzeit Construction period
1981–1983, 1992

BGF Gross floor area
23.760 m^2

Das Grundelement des Bürozentrums bildet ein kreuzförmiger Gebäudestern, in dessen Mitte ein Kern mit Treppenhaus und Nebenräumen liegt. Oberhalb der Treppe versorgt ein Glasoberlicht die Innenzone mit Tageslicht. Von diesem Zentrum führen in rechtwinkliger Anordnung vier Flure zu den im Zweibund angelegten Zellenbüros. Der gerundete Zentralbaukörper mit Eingangshalle und Sondernutzungen weicht von diesem Schema ab und nimmt die Form des Vorplatzes auf. Die Fassaden sind mit weiß-einbrennlackierten Aluminiumblechen verkleidet, in der vorgelagerten zweiten Ebene sind starre Beschatter aus Lochblech sowie umlaufende Galeriegänge angeordnet. Auch im Innern beschränkt sich die Farbwahl im wesentlichen auf Weiß und Grau: Zu den grauen Sichtbetonflächen gesellen sich Fußböden und Treppen in weißem Marmor. Treppengeländer und abgehängte Decken bestehen aus weiß lackierten Metallelementen.

The basic element of this office complex is a cruciform building with a staircase and ancillary spaces in the middle. A roof skylight provides the staircase with daylight. The corridors with the cellular offices on both sides run perpendicular from and to this core. The rounded central section with entrance hall and special functional spaces depart from the rectangular scheme, taking up the shape of the outdoor entrance area. The façades are clad in white stove-enamelled aluminium sheeting; the second, outer layer includes fixed perforated metal shading slats and maintenance catwalks. The interior colour scheme is basically restricted to white and grey; the grey exposed concrete surfaces are offset by floors and stairs of white marble. Stair railing and suspended ceilings consist of white enamelled metal elements.

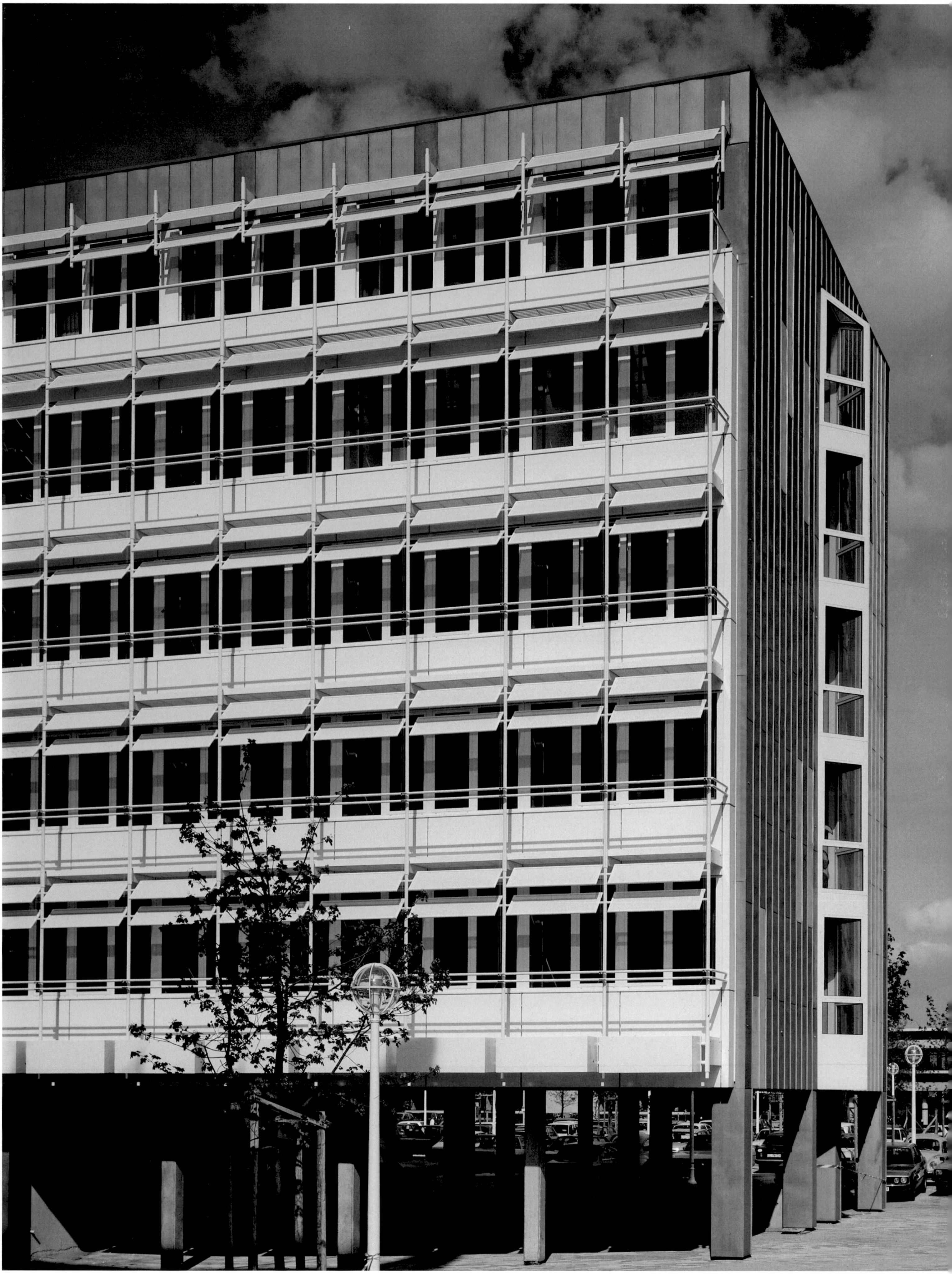

1984

Verwaltungsgebäude der Deutschen Lufthansa, Hamburg

Ein Solitärgebäude mit dreieckigem Grundriss bildet den ersten Bauabschnitt. Die weiteren stereometrisch geformten Bauabschnitte ergänzen sich zu einem Block mit Rücksicht auf den Baumbestand und die vorhandene Bebauung. Wie bei der Umgebungsbebauung dominieren auch bei dem Neubau braun-gelbe Klinker.

Deutsche Lufthansa Administration Building, Hamburg

A solitaire with a triangular plan forms the first construction phase. Further construction phases add up to form a block, whilst considering the existing trees and architectural development. The surrounding buildings as well as the new structure are dominated by brown-yellow brick.

Hillmann-Garage, Bremen

Die 529 Stellplätze sind auf sieben halbgeschossig versetzten Ebenen angeordnet, während in einem Teilbereich des Erdgeschosses eine Fläche für gewerbliche Nutzung vorgesehen ist. Die Einordnung des Parkhauses in den innerstädtischen Raum gelingt durch die charakteristische Fassadengestaltung.

Hillmann Parking Garage, Bremen

Seven alternating mezzanine levels accommodate 529 parking spaces, whilst a partial area for commercial use is proposed on the ground floor. The integration of the multi-storey car park into the inner city fabric is achieved via the characteristic façade design.

Marktarkaden, Bad Schwartau

Im Erdgeschoss befinden sich Läden und ein Supermarkt, im ersten Obergeschoss Büros und Praxen, darüber Maisonettewohnungen. Das Erscheinungsbild wird von dem ortstypischen roten Ziegelmauerwerk geprägt, das durch die Einschnitte der Treppenhäuser, Loggien und Arkaden eine starke Plastizität erhält.

Market Arcades, Bad Schwartau

Shops and a supermarket are located on the ground floor, whilst the first floor accommodates offices and practices, with maisonettes are located above. The external appearance is defined by the red brick masonry common in this area. The recesses of staircases, loggias and arcades add a three-dimensional quality to the façade.

Energiesparhaus, Internationale Bauausstellung, Berlin

Aufgrund der ungünstigen Randbedingungen sind die Wohnungen nur nach Süden und Norden orientiert, die Flanken bleiben mit Ausnahme kleiner Lüftungsfenster geschlossen. Die Nordseite wird, mehr als für die Belichtung erforderlich, geöffnet, um den Ausblick auf den Kanal und das städtische Leben einzufangen.

Low-Energy House, International Building Exhibition, Berlin

The apartments are north-south orientated because of unfavourable edge conditions. The flanks remain massive with the exception of small vent windows. The north side is opened up to a greater extent than necessary for natural lighting, in order to offer a view over Landwehrkanal and the urban activity.

1984
1985

Stadthäuser, Berlin-Tiergarten, Internationale Bauausstellung

Das Projekt umfasst drei Doppelhäuser mit je zwei Wohnungen. Durch die im Grundriss halbgeschossig gegeneinander versetzten Ebenen entstehen in den viergeschossigen Häusern insgesamt jeweils neun Wohnebenen, die die einzelnen Bereiche räumlich miteinander verzahnen.

City Houses, Berlin-Tiergarten, International Building Exhibition

The project is comprised of three semi-detached houses with two flats each. The mezzanine layout of levels produces a total of nine floors in the four-storey houses, which spatially interlink the single areas.

Plaza-Hotel, Bremen

Das Hotel ist entsprechend der historischen Stadtstruktur als geschlossener Baublock konzipiert, durch den diagonal eine Fußgängerpassage führt. Diese weitet sich zu einer glasüberdeckten Rotunde, die sowohl der räumliche Mittelpunkt als auch die Drehscheibe für Erschließung und Orientierung ist.

Plaza Hotel, Bremen

Corresponding to the historic urban fabric, the hotel is designed as a dense development. Traversing the block is a pedestrian passageway, which is widened to form a rotunda with a glass roof and which functions as the spatial centre and pivotal point of circulation and orientation.

Cocoloco – Bar und Boutique im Hanse-Viertel

Eine Modeboutique und eine Cocktailbar liegen diagonal durch eine Glaswand voneinander getrennt im Erdgeschoss, eine Minidisco auf einem rückwärtigen Zwischenniveau. Während der Geschäftszeiten wird die Glaswand zusammengeschoben, so dass ein großer Raum entsteht.

Cocoloco – Bar and Boutique in the Hanse Viertel, Hamburg

A fashion boutique and a cocktail bar located on the ground floor of the shopping arcade are diagonally separated by a glass wall; a small discotheque is situated on the rear mezzanine level. During shopping hours the glass wall is slid away to produce a larger space.

Psychiatrische Krankenhäuser Rickling-Thetmarshof und Rickling-Falkenhorst

Die fünf neuen Gebäude fügen sich mit eineinhalb bzw. zwei Geschossen in Höhe, Form, Gruppierung und Material in die ländliche Umgebung mit ihren bestehenden Bauten ein. Beide Anlagen umschließen jeweils einen Hof oder Anger. Ziegelfassaden und das Holz der Galerien prägen das äußere Erscheinungsbild.

Psychiatric Hospitals, Rickling-Thetmarshof and Rickling-Falkenhorst

With one and two storeys the five new buildings integrate into the rural landscape with the existing buildings regarding their height, form, grouping, and material. Both complexes enclose a courtyard or meadow. Brick façades and the timber used for the galleries characterize the external appearance.

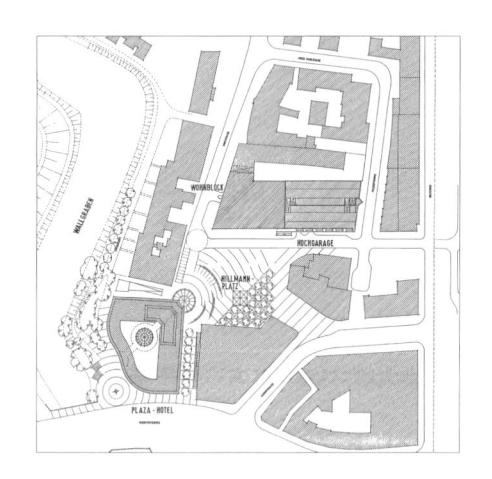

Hillmann-Garage, Bremen
Hillmann Garage, Bremen

1983

Entwurf Design
Meinhard von Gerkan

Partner Partner
Klaus Staratzke

Bauherr Client
Steffens KG

Bauzeit Construction period
1983-1984

Stellplätze Parking sites
529

Der Kontrast geschlossener und durchbrochener Fassadenflächen und die Anordnung einer diagonal über die Hauptfassade verlaufenden Erschließungstreppe vermeidet die Monotonie einer gleichförmigen Gliederung, verleugnet gleichzeitig jedoch nicht die Nutzung als Parkhaus. Die Fassaden bestehen aus drei Ziegelsorten: Für die großen Mauerwerksflächen wurden zwei monochrome Farben „wild" gemischt, so dass durch die nur geringe Farbdifferenz eine Lebendigkeit ohne Sprenkelwirkung entsteht; Stürze, Konsolen und Sockel wurden aus einem dunkelgebrannten Klinker gefertigt. Die Mauerwerksflächen haben offene Querschnitte, die eine natürliche Lüftung gewährleisten, jedoch keinen Einblick von außen ermöglichen. Die Fassade zum Hillmannplatz ist mit etwa 3,60 m² großen Öffnungen versehen, die durch zurückliegende Mauerwerkskassetten mit quadratischen Zuluftöffnungen geschlossen werden.

The contrast between open and closed façade elements, and the access stairway, which forms a diagonal in front of the main façade, avoids the monotony of repetitive structuring while not denying the use of the structure as a car park. The exterior walls consist of three types of bricks. For the large sections, two monochrome bricks were mixed haphazardly. As the colours differ only slightly, these façade surfaces appear vibrant, but not 'spotty'. Lintels, corbels and base course are of dark clinker bricks. The masonry walls have open sections, which provide natural ventilation, but do not allow passers-by to look inside. The façade to Hillmannplatz includes recessed masonry cassettes of approx. 3.6 m² with square openings which let in fresh air.

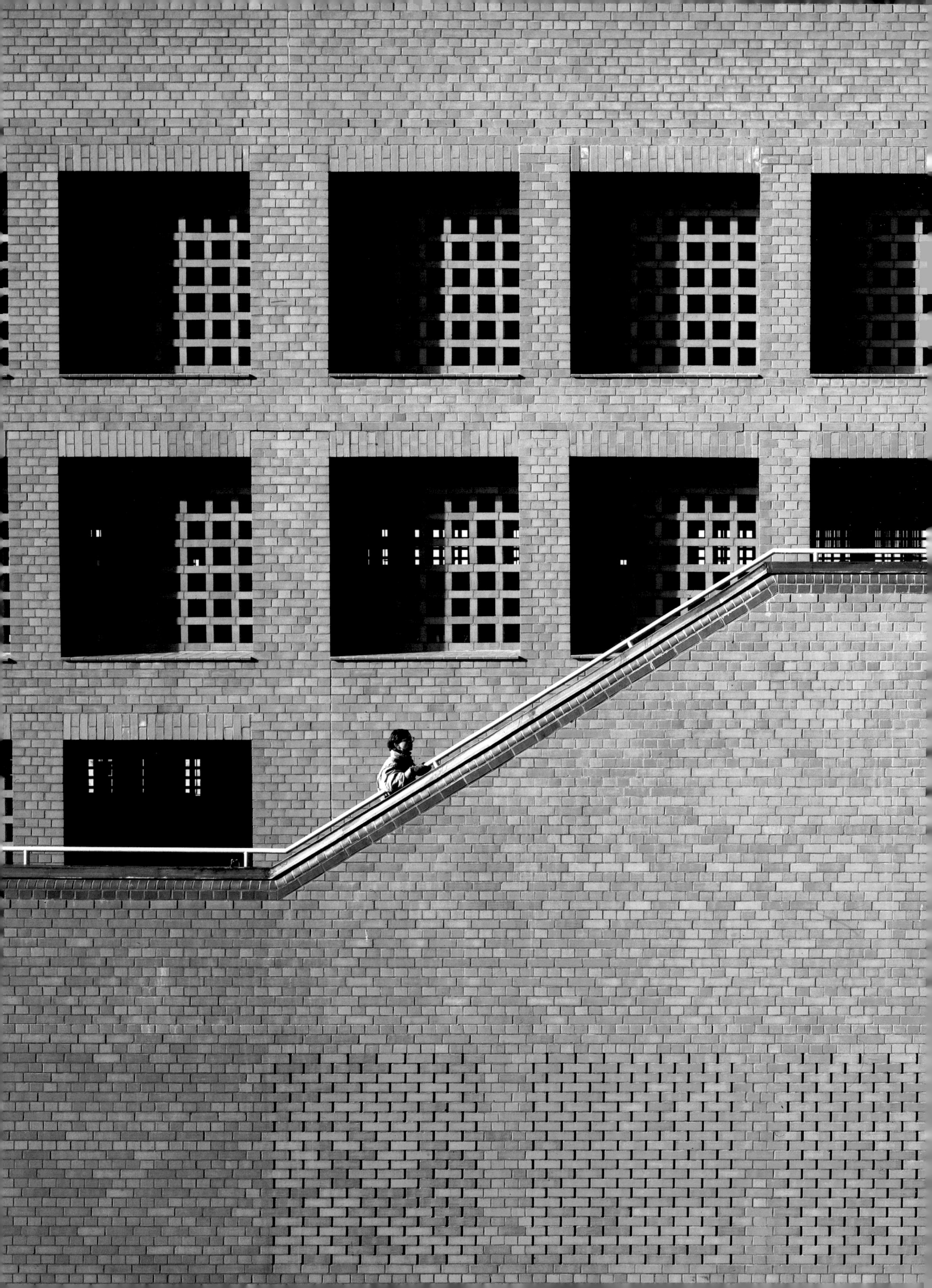

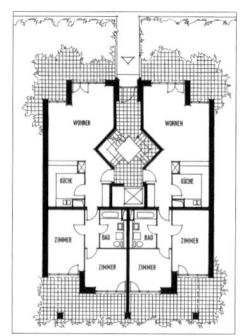

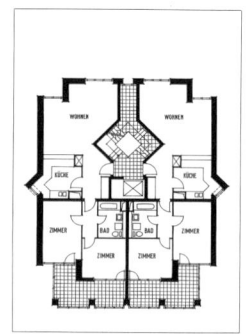

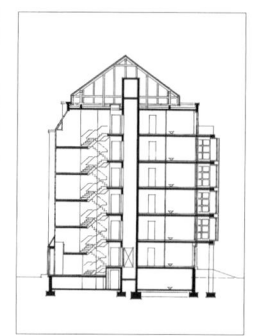

Energiesparhaus, Internationale Bauausstellung, Berlin
Low-Energy House, International Building Exhibition, Berlin

Wettbewerb Competition
1981 – ausgewählt

Entwurf Design
Meinhard von Gerkan

Bauherr Client
Dr. Herbst Ingenieur
Gesellschaft mbH & Co.

Bauzeit Construction period
1983–1984

BGF Gross floor area
1.000 m²

Die Nordfassade ist mit Rücksicht auf den urbanen Maßstab und die Einbindung in die Umgebung ruhig und streng symmetrisch gestaltet, um die Individualität des Hauses und nicht die der einzelnen Wohnungen zu betonen. Die Südseite erhält Balkone, die als Wintergärten verglast sind und eine klimatische und optische Zwischenzone zum Hof bilden. Ein einheitliches filigranes Fenstermodul kennzeichnet die fast vollständig verglaste Fassade und bindet die individuelle Handhabung von Öffnung und Begrünung der Wohnungsloggien in ein übergeordnetes Ganzes ein. Zur Gliederung des Gebäudes und zur Verbesserung der Belichtungsverhältnisse sind die Ecken des Hauses stark zurückgesetzt. Erdgeschoss und oberstes Geschoss unterscheiden sich von den vier Regelgeschossen durch Varianten der Wohnungsgrößen und erlauben die betonte Gestaltung von Sockel und oberem Anschluss des Baukörpers.

With respect to the urban scale and the insertion of the building into its surroundings, the north façade has a quiet, strictly symmetrical structure in order to emphasize not the individual flats but the individuality of the house itself. To the south, the flats have glazed loggias, which form a climatic buffer zone to the courtyard. The almost entirely glazed façade is characterized by the repetition of a filigree window module. Both windows and loggia glazings can be opened individually. In order to 'diversify' the building mass and improve lighting conditions, the corners of the block have been set back considerably. The ground and top floors differ from the four standard floors in that they contain apartments of varying sizes, as well as in their different façade designs.

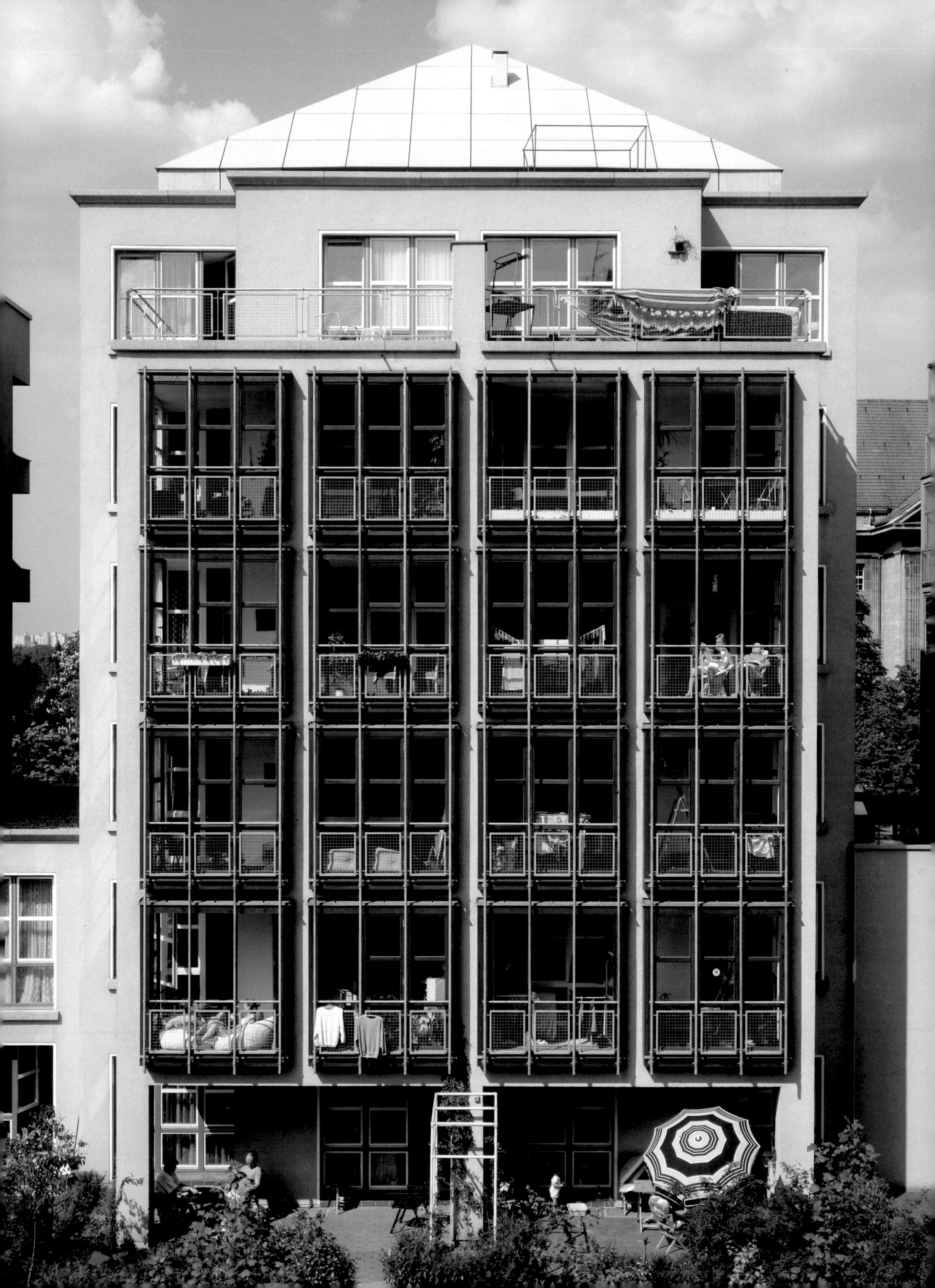

1986
1987

Parkhaus der Oberpostdirektion, Braunschweig

Das Parkhaus mit 240 Stellplätzen ist mit versetzt angeordneten Parkebenen angelegt, sodass eine übersichtliche Erschließung und wirtschaftliche Aufstellung der Autos gewährleistet ist. Um eine freie Durchlüftung sicherzustellen, ist die Fassade, trotz ihrer geschlossenen Wirkung, weitgehend offen.

Multi-Storey Car Park of the Braunschweig Post Office Divisional Administration

The multi-storey car park with 240 spaces is laid out with alternating parking levels, ensuring a clear circulation and economic parking of vehicles. In order to guarantee unrestricted ventilation the façade is primarily open despite its solid appearance.

Wiederaufbau Landhaus Michaelsen als Puppenmuseum

Das im Jahr 1923 von Karl Schneider im Stil der Moderne erbaute Landhaus diente als Treffpunkt für Künstler der Hamburger Sezession. Der Wiederaufbau stellt nun mit knappem Bauaufwand den äußerlichen Bauzustand von 1927 wieder her. Die Puppenpräsentation der Bauherrin findet im Erdgeschoss statt.

Reconstruction of the 'Michaelsen Country House' as Doll's Museum, Hamburg

The country house built in 1923 by Karl Schneider in a modernistic style served as a meeting place for artists of the Hamburg secession. The reconstruction restores the external structural condition of 1927 with minimal construction expenses. The client's doll exhibition is presented on the ground floor.

Gewerbeschulzentrum, Flensburg

Aus den Elementen Klassentrakt, Werkstätten und Sportforum wurde ein spannungsvolles Baukörperensemble entwickelt, dessen Zentrum ein diagonal erschlossener achteckiger Innenhof ist. Zwischen dem eingeschossigen Werkstatttrakt und dem dreigeschossigen Klassentrakt findet eine klare Trennung statt.

Vocational School Centre, Flensburg

The building elements of classroom wing, workshops and sports forum were combined to form an interesting ensemble, its centre being a diagonally accessible octagonal inner courtyard. A clear separation was made between the one-storey workshop section and the three-storey classroom wing.

Grindelallee 100, Hamburg

Das neue Büro-, Geschäfts- und Wohngebäude tritt mit der gegenüberliegenden gründerzeitlichen Bebauung in Dialog, indem es die Eckbetonung durch eine Rotunde mit ausladendem Dachschirm akzentuiert und die plastische Fassadengliederung mit einer vorgesetzten Stahl-Glas-Konstruktion variiert.

Grindelallee 100, Hamburg

The new office, shopping and residential building enters a dialogue with the late-19th-century development on the other side of the street by accentuating the corner with a rotunda and a cantilevered roof as well as by varying the sculptural façade division with a steel-glass structure placed in front.

Parkhaus der Oberpostdirektion Braunschweig
Multi-Storey Car Park of the Braunschweig Post Office Divisional Administration

1984

Entwurf Design
Meinhard von Gerkan

Bauherr Client
OPD Hannover-Braunschweig

Bauzeit Construction period
1985–1986

Stellplätze Parking sites
240

Die freie Durchlüftung der versetzten Parkebenen bei gleichzeitiger optischer Geschlossenheit wird erreicht durch ein modulares Wabensystem als Fassade. Die durch die Waben entstehende starke Plastizität und Kulissenwirkung gibt dem Gebäude zum einen, trotz massiver Ausbildung, filigrane Leichtigkeit und transparente Durchlässigkeit und verhindert zum anderen Einblicke in den Innenraum. Zur Kontrastierung der gerasterten Fassadenfläche verlaufen die äußeren Erschließungstreppen diagonal mit einem direkten Zugang auf jeder Ebene. In der Mitte zwischen den Parkebenen befindet sich ein zentrales Treppenhaus, das auf der obersten Ebene mit einem Glasdach abschließt. Das Traggerüst und die Parkebenen bestehen aus Ortbeton, die Wabenelemente sowie die Fassadenplatten vor den Treppenläufen sind Betonfertigteile. Farbige Stahlkonstruktionen bilden die Treppenstufen und Handläufe.

Despite its solid appearance, the modular honeycomb system of the façade allows for the unrestricted ventilation of the alternated parking levels. Regardless of their massive formation the honeycombs generate a strong three-dimensional effect as well as a filigree and transparent lightness, simultaneously it prevents views into the interior. The diagonal positioning of the external circulation stairs with direct access to each level contrasts with the façade surface. A central staircase is positioned in the middle of the parking levels and terminated with a glass roof. The supporting framework and the parking levels are made from in-situ concrete; the honeycomb elements as well as the façade panels in front of the stairs are pre-cast concrete units. Coloured steel structures form the steps and handrails.

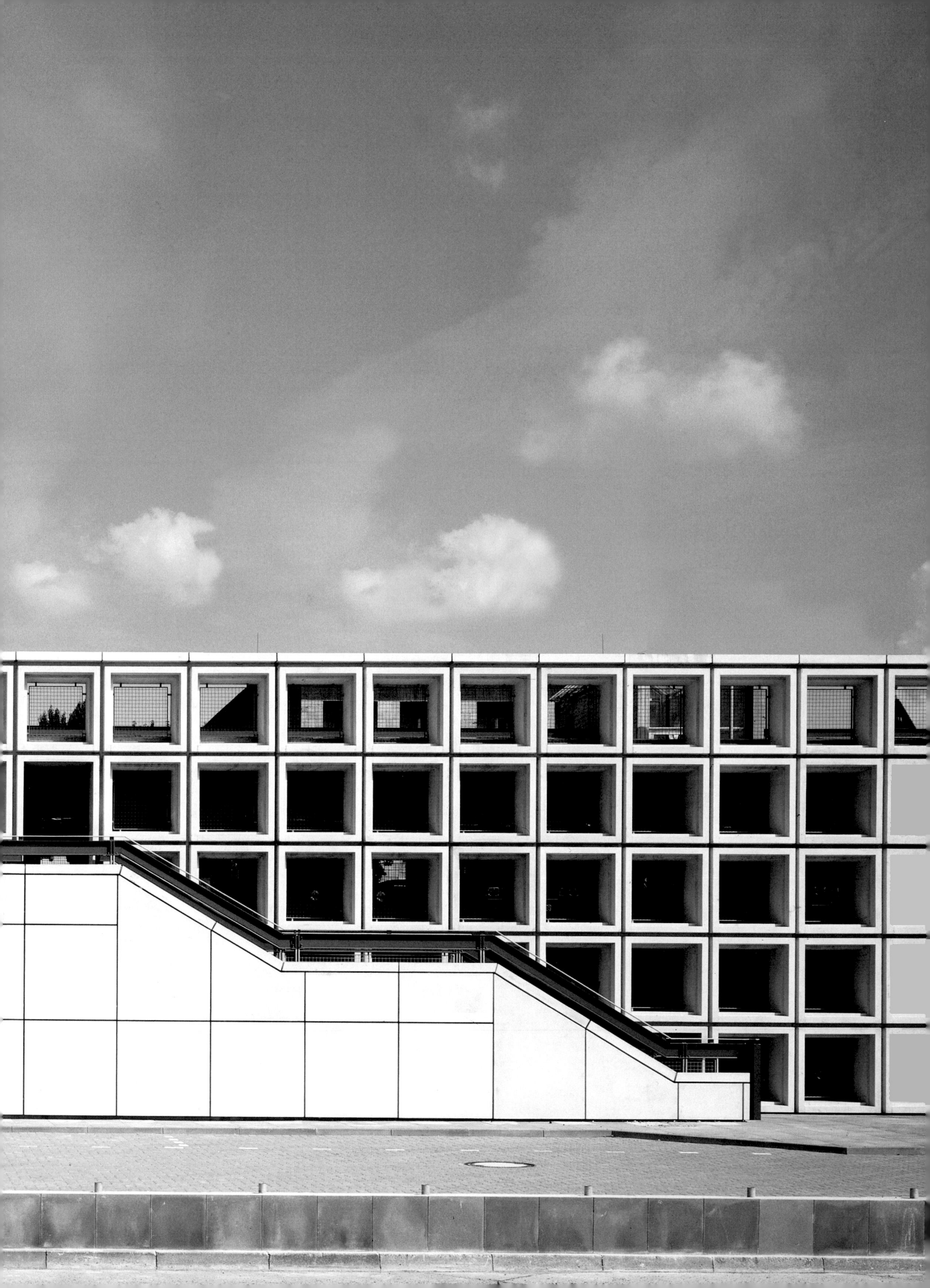

Grindelallee 100, Hamburg
Grindelallee 100, Hamburg

1982

Entwurf Design
Meinhard von Gerkan und Klaus Staratzke

Bauherr Client
Bauen + Wohnen
Baubetreuungsgesellschaft mbH

Bauzeit Construction period
1985–1987

BGF Gross floor area
2.420 m²

Eine Stahl-Glas-Konstruktion legt sich als zweite Fassadenschicht vor die monolithischen Außenwände. Die Wintergärten dienen zugleich als Lärmschutz und erweitern die Wohnräume und Gewerbeflächen. Ihre Fensterkonstruktion wurde in einfacher Verglasung mit thermisch ungetrennten Stahlprofilen ausgeführt, um ein Höchstmaß an Transparenz und Filigranität zu erzielen im Gegensatz zu den blockhaft geschlossenen Wandflächen. Der Grundriss ist in allen Ebenen symmetrisch zur winkelhalbierenden Diagonale des Eckgrundstücks ausgebildet. Die Erschließung führt entlang dieser Diagonale zu dem rückwärtigen, kreisrunden Treppenhaus, das durch eine Glasbausteinwand trotz der Hinterhofsituation licht und hell wirkt. Das Erdgeschoss und Teilflächen des Kellers werden von Läden genutzt, im ersten und zweiten Obergeschoss befinden sich Büroflächen, die drei oberen Geschosse sind dem Wohnen vorbehalten.

A steel-glass structure forms a second façade layer in front of the monolithic exterior walls. The winter gardens serve as noise protection, whilst simultaneously extending the living and commercial areas. Their window design with single glazing and thermally non-separated steel sections aims for a maximum of transparency and filigree appearance, contrasting with the solid block-like wall surfaces. On all levels the plans are designed symmetrically to the diagonal of the corner site. The main circulation route follows this diagonal towards the rear circular staircase, its glass block wall generating a light appearance despite the courtyard situation. The ground floor and partial areas of the basement are occupied by shops. Offices are located on the first and second levels; the upper three levels are reserved for living accommodation.

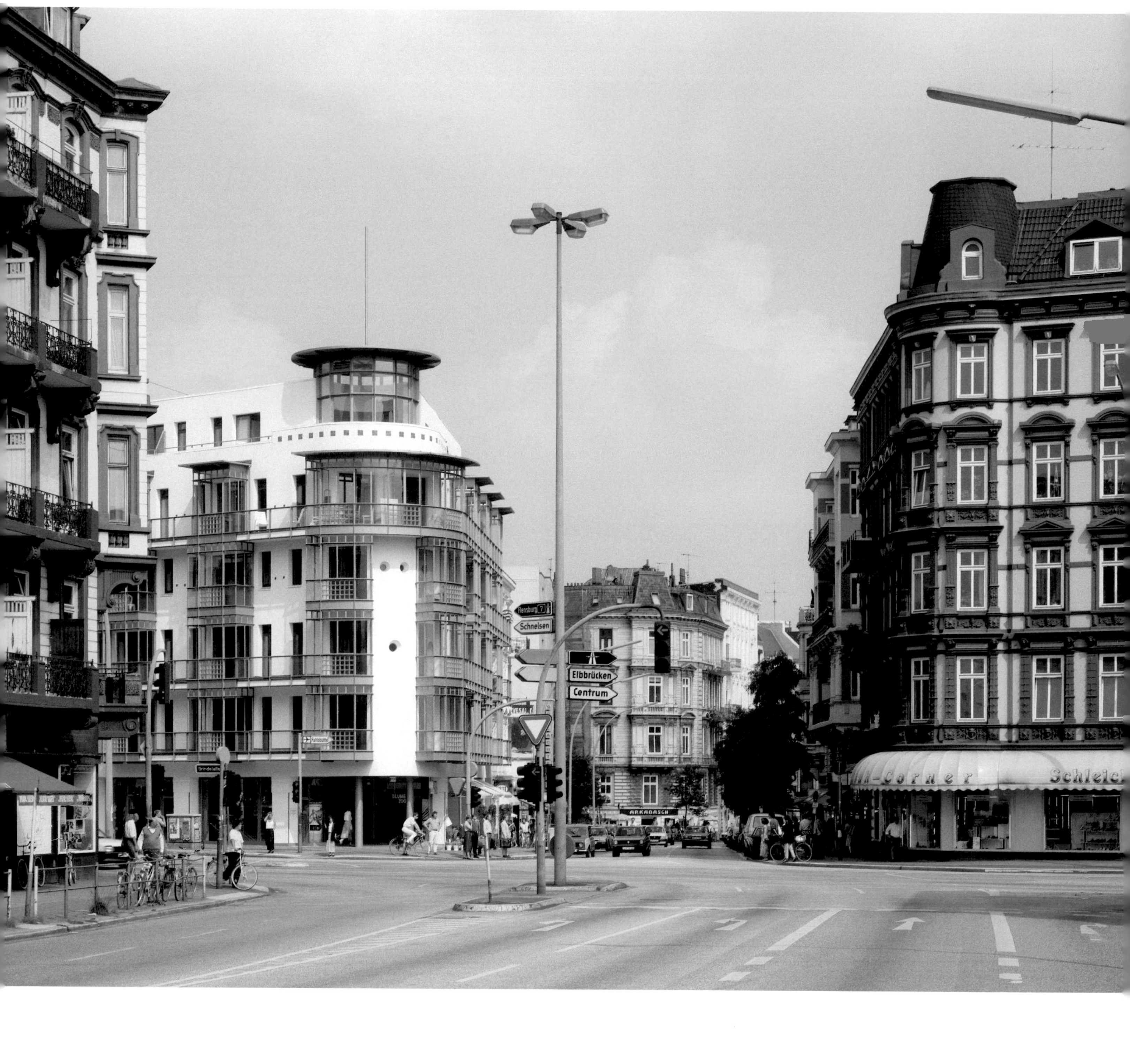
Schnelsen
Elbbrücken
Centrum

1988
1989

Komplex Rose, Rheumaklinik, Bad Meinberg

Der Entwurf entwickelt sich aus der barocken städtebaulichen Achse, die das Kurhaus Stern über den Mittelpunkt des Kurparks auf das denkmalgeschützte Haus Rose bezieht. Die Achse des Kurparks wird im inneren Erschließungssystem des Klinikkomplexes aufgenommen und weitergeführt.

Rose Complex, Rheumatism Clinic, Bad Meinberg

The design concept is derived from the baroque urban axis, relating the Stern Spa House via the centre of the health resort park to Rose House, which is under a preservation order. The axis of the health resort park is continued into the interior circulation system of the clinic complex.

Neugestaltung des Einkaufszentrums Hamburger Straße, Hamburg

Die beiden Passagenteile mit einer Gesamtlänge von 256 Metern werden über eine transparente, gewölbte Glasüberdachung natürlich belichtet. Die hellen Materialien schaffen eine angenehme, lichte Raumatmosphäre. Im Bereich der Halle wurde eine Aktionsfläche für Modenschauen, Ausstellungen, Konzerte etc. angelegt.

Renovation of the Hamburger Strasse Shopping Centre, Hamburg

A transparent, curved glass roof allows natural light into both parts of the arcade with a total length of 256 metres. Bright materials generate a pleasant, light spatial atmosphere. An event zone for fashion shows, exhibitions, concerts, etc. was integrated into the hall area.

Wohnhaus Saalgasse, Frankfurt/Main

Das fünfgeschossige Haus mit ausgebautem Dachgeschoss enthält zwei Zwei- und eine Vierzimmerwohnung über drei Ebenen sowie ein Atelier im Dachgeschoss. Da die Straßenfront auf der Südseite liegt, wurde das Treppenhaus in den hinteren Teil platziert. Der Erker zur Straße nimmt kleine Wintergärten auf.

Residential Building, Saalgasse, Frankfurt/Main

The five-storey house with a converted attic accommodates one four-room and two two-room flats over three levels as well as an atelier in the attic. The street front on the south side led to the location of the staircase in the rear of the building. The bay facing towards the street accommodates small winter gardens.

Justizbehörden in Flensburg, Um- und Erweiterungsbau

Die Neubauten sind dem Geesthang folgend in der Höhe gestaffelt und stellen eine einfache Verlängerung der vorhandenen Gebäude dar. Eine Treppenhalle verbindet Alt- und Neubau und bietet freien Blick auf den Park im Norden. Von der Halle aus gelangt man in die kurzen, kammartig angeordneten Büroflügel.

Legal Authority in Flensburg, Conversion and Extension

Following the fall of the 'Geesthang' the new buildings are staggered in their height and form a simple extension of the existing buildings. A stairwell connects the existing and new building and offers a view of the park to the north. The short, comb-like office wings are accessible from the hall.

Wohnbebauung am Fischmarkt, Hamburg

Die Platzrandbebauung des Fischmarktes entspricht im Maßstab der ursprünglichen Bebauung, die im 2. Weltkrieg bis auf wenige Häuser zerstört wurde. Die Fassadengestaltung der Neubauten nimmt die Vorgaben des Bestandes in Form von Erkern und waagerechten Gliederungen aus Betonfertigteilen auf.

Residential Development at 'Fischmarkt', Hamburg

The scale of the houses at the 'Fischmarkt' square corresponds to the original development that was almost completely destroyed in World War II. The façades of the new buildings take reference from the existing architecture in the form of bays and horizontal divisions from pre-cast concrete components.

Innenhofüberdachung des Museums für Hamburgische Geschichte

Das Museum für Hamburgische Geschichte wurde in den Jahren 1914 bis 1923 von Fritz Schumacher erbaut. Das neue Glasdach über dem Innenhof nimmt Rücksicht auf das zu schonende Baudenkmal, schützt die bislang dem Witterungsverfall ausgesetzten Exponate und schafft attraktive neue Nutzungsmöglichkeiten.

Courtyard Roofing of the Museum für Hamburgische Geschichte

The Museum für Hamburgische Geschichte (Hamburg History Museum) was built from 1914 to 1923 by Fritz Schumacher. The new glass roof covering the inner courtyard takes into account this architectural monument to be preserved, protects exhibits previously exposed to the weather and creates new attractive uses.

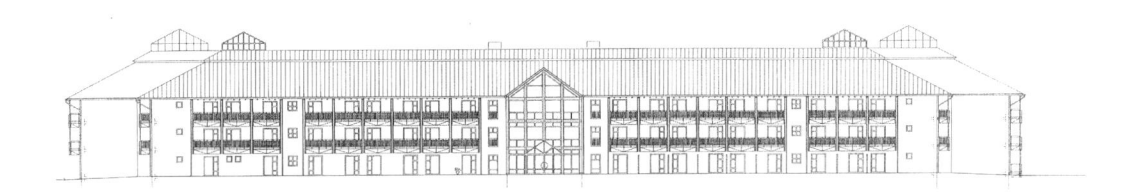

Komplex Rose, Rheumaklinik, Bad Meinberg
Rose Complex, Rheumatology Clinic, Bad Meinberg

Wettbewerb Competition
1981 – 1. Preis

Entwurf Design
Meinhard von Gerkan

Partner Partner
Karsten Brauer

Bauherr Client
Landesverband Lippe
vertreten durch Hurrle GmbH

Bauzeit Construction period
1987–1989

BGF Gross floor area
17.000 m²

Die symmetrische, U-förmige Anordnung des Neubaus wird bestimmt durch die Achse des Kurparks, die als Ordnungs- und Erschließungselement durch das Haus bis in die Außenanlagen weitergeführt wird und sich als öffentlicher Weg in das Kurgelände fortsetzt. Mit Rücksicht auf den funktionalen Zusammenhang zwischen den Altbauten und dem Neubau wurde der Gebäudekomplex nach Norden an die bestehenden Bauten heran geschoben. Dadurch entsteht im Süden eine größtmögliche zusammenhängende Freifläche zur Nutzung als Klinikgarten und für Parkplätze. Der Neubau setzt sich aus einem dreigeschossigen Bettentrakt und einem darunter liegenden Sockelbau mit den Behandlungseinrichtungen zusammen. Der eingeschossige Sockel schließt im Erdgeschoss ebenengleich an die Altbauten an und verschwindet aufgrund des ansteigenden Geländes mit seinem unter dem Bettentrakt liegenden Teil vollständig im Erdreich.

The symmetrical U-shape of the new building is determined by the axis of the health resort gardens. It is the ordering and access element of the building and a public passage that extends to the spa gardens on the other side. Taking into account the functional relationship between the existing buildings and the new one, the latter approaches the entire complex to the neighbouring buildings to the north. This left the largest possible area to the south for use as a garden and parking lots for the clinic itself. The new building consists of a three-storey block of wards rising from a plinth which contains the diagnostic and therapy facilities. At ground-floor level, the one-storey plinth adjoins the old buildings and then, because of the rising ground, completely disappears from view to form the basement of the block of wards.

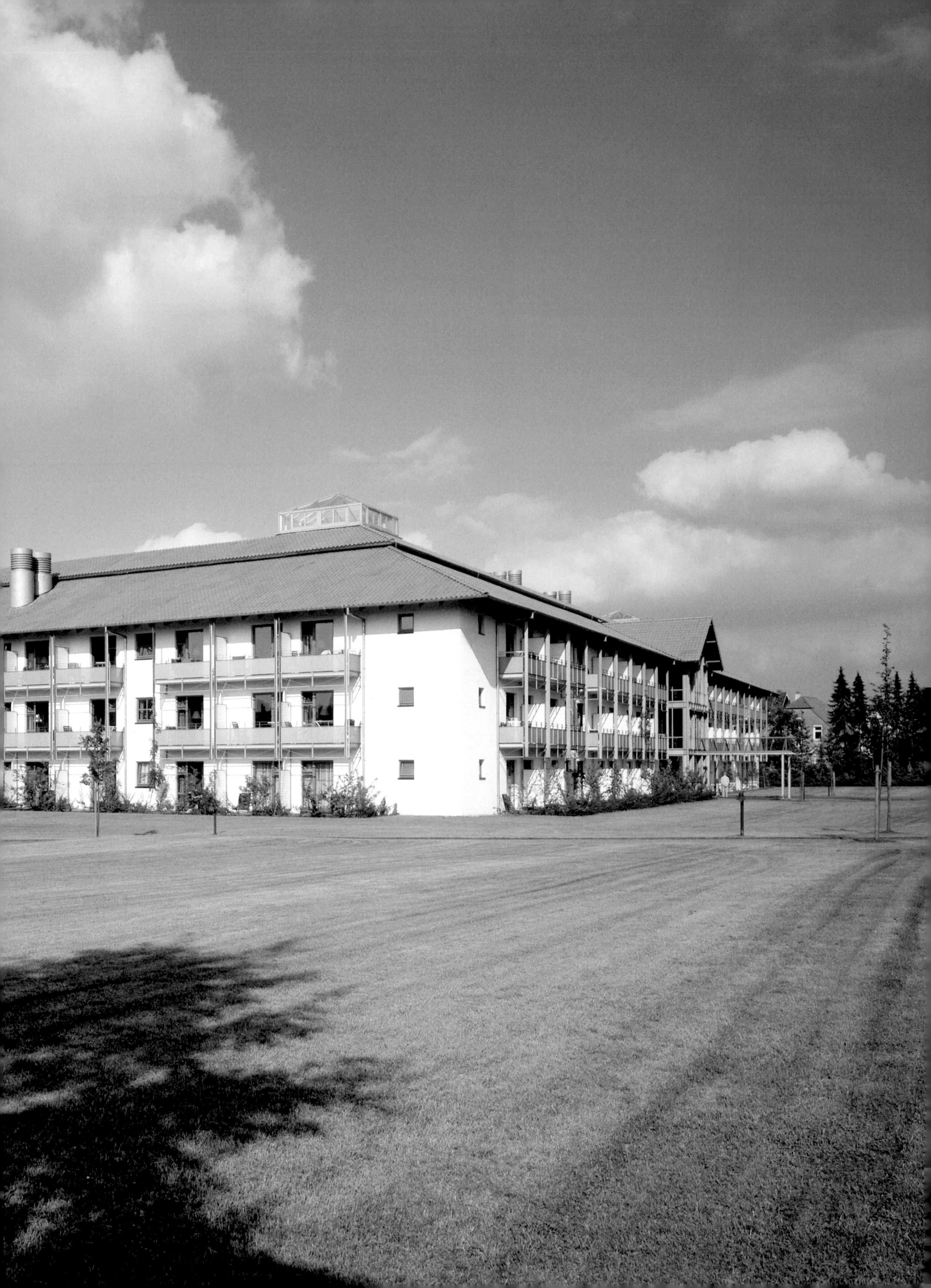

1990

gmp Hauptsitz, Elbchaussee 139,
Hamburg

Der weiße, langgestreckte Baukörper erinnert an einen 50 Meter langen Dampfer, der quer zum Elbstrom, längsseits der Mauer am Oevelgönner Mühlenweg treibt und mit einem klassizistischen Türmchen an der Elbchaussee anlegt. Ein öffentlicher Platz zwischen Büro und Wohnhaus erlaubt den freien Blick auf die Elbe.

gmp Head Office, Elbchaussee 139,
Hamburg

The white, elongated building is reminiscent of a 50-m-long steamer, drifting sideways to the river Elbe alongside the wall on Oevelgönner Mühlenweg and landing on the Elbchaussee with a classical turret. A public square between the practice and the house allows a generous view over the Elbe.

Restaurant „Le Canard", Elbchaussee 139,
Hamburg

Bereits in den 1880er Jahren befand sich hier das Ausflugslokal „Elbschlucht", ein Restaurant mit Biergarten. Hundert Jahre später sah der Bebauungsplan nach wie vor Gaststättennutzung vor, so dass neben Architekturbüro und Wohnhaus auf gleichem Grundstück ein neues Restaurant entstand.

Restaurant 'Le Canard', Elbchaussee 139,
Hamburg

A restaurant with a beer garden was located here as far back as the 1880s. A hundred years later the city development plan still provided for a restaurant use, resulting in the realization of a new restaurant on the same site and located next to the architectural practice and the house.

Oberpostdirektion Braunschweig

Eine Besonderheit des dreieckigen Hochhauses und der anschließenden Flachbauten ist die Fassadenteilung: Die strukturelle Gliederung überspielt die repetierende Gleichförmigkeit kleiner Fensteröffnungen, indem sie jeweils vier Fenster zu einem dominierenden Grundelement zusammenfasst.

Post Office Divisional Administration, Braunschweig

The special feature of the triangular tower block and the adjoining low-level buildings is the façade division: the structural division conceals the repetitive uniformity of small window openings by combining four windows each, thereby generating a domineering basic element.

Ausbildungszentrum der HEW, Hamburg

Das neue Berufsbildungszentrum ergänzt das vorhandene Weiterbildungszentrum und ist mit diesem über einen internen Gang verbunden. Werkstätten, Unterrichts- und Büroräume sowie eine Kantine sind in zwei Geschossen um eine zentrale Ausstellungshalle gruppiert, in der sich auch die Cafeteria befindet.

HEW Training Centre, Hamburg

The new training centre adds to the existing education centre. Both buildings are connected via an internal corridor. Workshops, classrooms and offices as well as the canteen are grouped on two storeys around a central exhibition hall, which also accommodates the cafeteria.

1990

Moorbek-Rondeel, Norderstedt

Das viergeschossige Gebäude präsentiert sich zur städtischen Seite als streng gegliederter Mauerwerksbau mit einer aufgeständerten Erdgeschosszone, während es sich zum Moorbek-Park im Nordwesten mit einer leichten und transparenten Glas-Stahl-Fassade in Form eines Zylindersegments öffnet.

Moorbek-Rondeel, Norderstedt

The four-storey building presents itself towards the city side as an austere masonry construction with an elevated ground-floor zone supported by columns. A light-weight and transparent glass-steel façade shaped like a cylinder segment opens up the building towards the Moorbek Park to the north-west.

Parkhaus, Flughafen Hamburg

Das Parkhaus bildet durch seine Lage und Formensprache den städtebaulichen Dreh- und Gelenkpunkt zwischen den unterschiedlichen Gebäudeausrichtungen und Bereichen des Flughafens. Neun Parkebenen mit insgesamt ca. 800 Stellplätzen sind beidseitig an einer ringförmigen Fahrgasse angeordnet.

Multi-Storey Car Park, Hamburg Airport

With its location and style the multi-storey car park forms the urban planning pivot point between the variously orientated buildings and areas of the airport. Nine parking levels with a total of approximately 800 spaces are located on both sides of the roadway.

Lazarus Krankenheim, Berlin

Der neue fünfgeschossige Hochbau mit Pflegeabteilung und physikalischer Therapie ist vom Bestand abgesetzt und durch eine Glasbrücke mit diesem verbunden. Die über eine Glaslaterne im Dachgeschoss belichtete zentrale Treppenhalle bildet den gemeinsamen „öffentlichen" Ort für die Bewohner.

Lazarus Hospital, Berlin

The new five-storey building with a nursing ward and physical therapy unit is set off against the existing complex and connected to it via a glass bridge. The central stairwell, lit by a glass lantern in the roof, forms the common 'public' space for the patients.

Stadthalle Bielefeld

Der solitäre Baukörper der Stadthalle schwimmt wie ein großer Dampfer im Bahnhofspark mitten in Bielefeld. Der halbkreisförmige Bug des axialsymmetrischen Gebäudes weist, einige Erdwellen vor sich herschiebend, zur Innenstadt. An der Rückseite des Gebäudes ist das Parkhaus angedockt.

Civic Centre, Bielefeld

The secluded civic centre floats like a great steamer in the railway station park right in the centre of Bielefeld. The building lies in axial symmetry with its semicircular bow pointing to the inner city, pushing a few earth waves before it. The multi-storey car park adjoins the rear of the building.

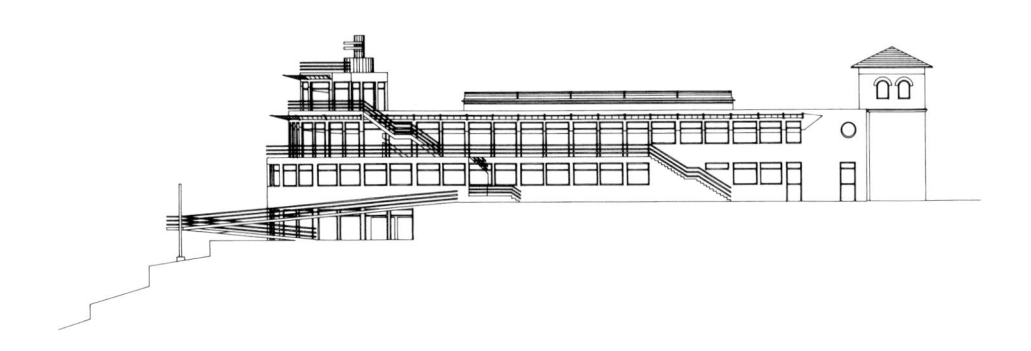

gmp Hauptsitz, Elbchaussee 139, Hamburg
gmp Head Office, Elbchaussee 139, Hamburg

1986

Entwurf Design
Meinhard von Gerkan

Bauherr Client
Meinhard von Gerkan

Bauzeit Construction period
1987–1990

BGF Gross floor area
ca. 2.000 m²

Das dampferähnliche, dominierende Gebäude des Ensembles aus Büro, Wohnhaus, Restaurant und öffentlichem Platz beherbergt den Hauptsitz der Architektensozietät. Das zylindrische Staffelgeschoss als Pendant zum klassizistischen Türmchen des Altbaus überragt den „Dampferbug" wie eine Kommandobrücke. Die mittige Wendeltreppe erschließt den großen, fast rundum verglasten Besprechungsraum. In den beiden Geschossen darunter sind die Büros der Geschäftsleitung und das Foyer untergebracht. Die Arbeitsplätze der Architekten befinden sich im verbindenden Längstrakt. Ein Tonnendach mit sichtbarer Stahlkonstruktion gibt dem großen Zeichensaal im Obergeschoss den Charakter einer Werkstatt. Begehbare, in die Platzebene eingefügte Glasoberlichter lassen Tageslicht in die darunter liegende Garage. Am Abend dringt Kunstlicht nach außen und akzentuiert in Verbindung mit den vier Lichtstelen den öffentlichen Platz.

The dominant, steamer-like building of the complex consisting of an office, a house, a restaurant and a public outdoor area houses the main office of gmp architectural partnership. The cylinder of the top recessed storey – a counterpart of the small classical turret of the old building – towers over the 'steamer's forecastle' like a navigating bridge. The central spiral staircase provides access to the large, almost entirely glazed conference room. The partner offices and the foyer take up the two floors beneath it, while the studios of the employed architects form the connecting tract to the old building. A barrel vault with exposed steel structure lends workshop character to the large drafting studio on the upper floor. Walk-on glass skylights set flush in the floor of the public forecourt let daylight into the garage underneath. At night, the light from inside penetrates the darkness and, together with the four light steles, accentuates the public forecourt.

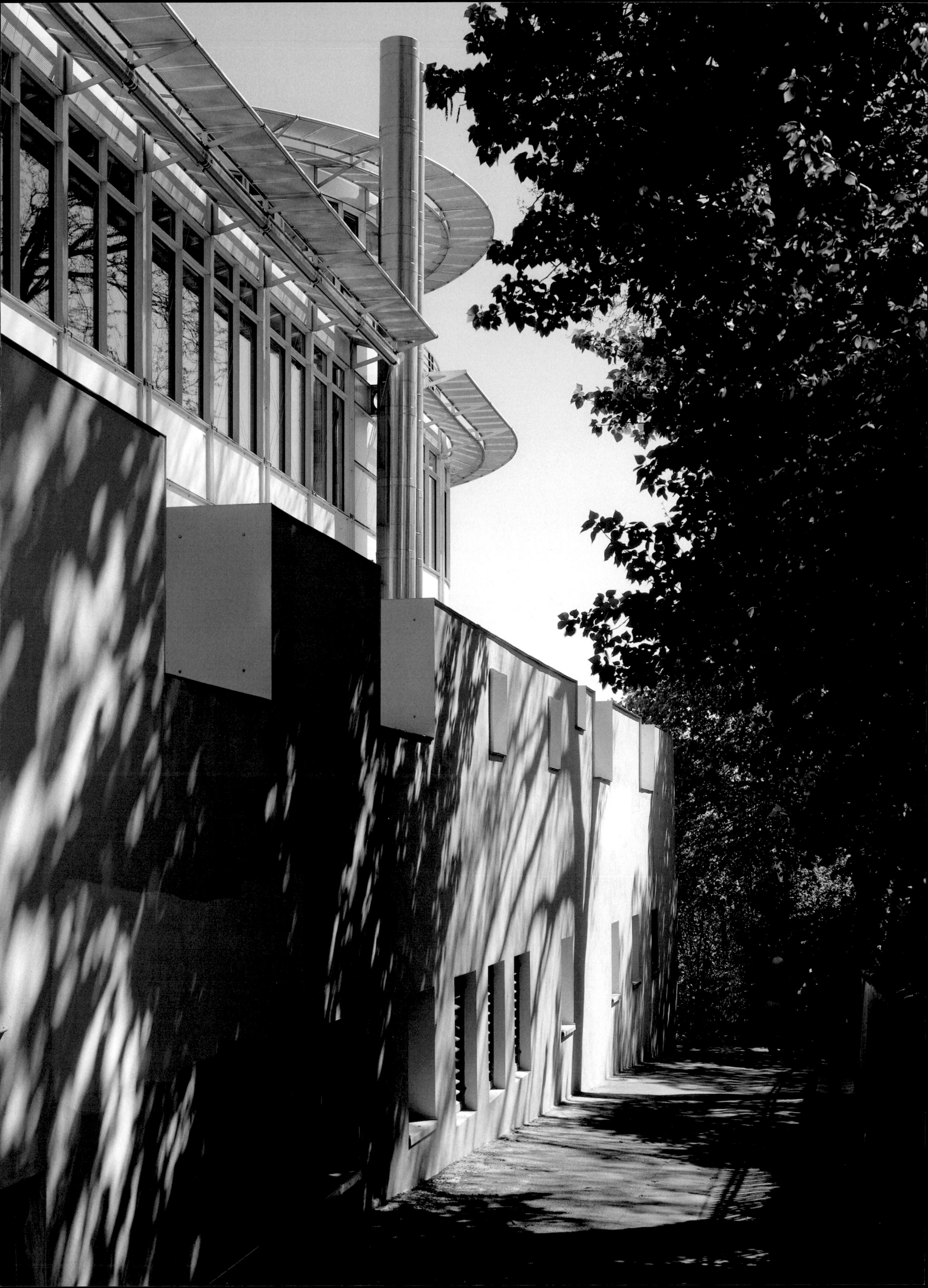

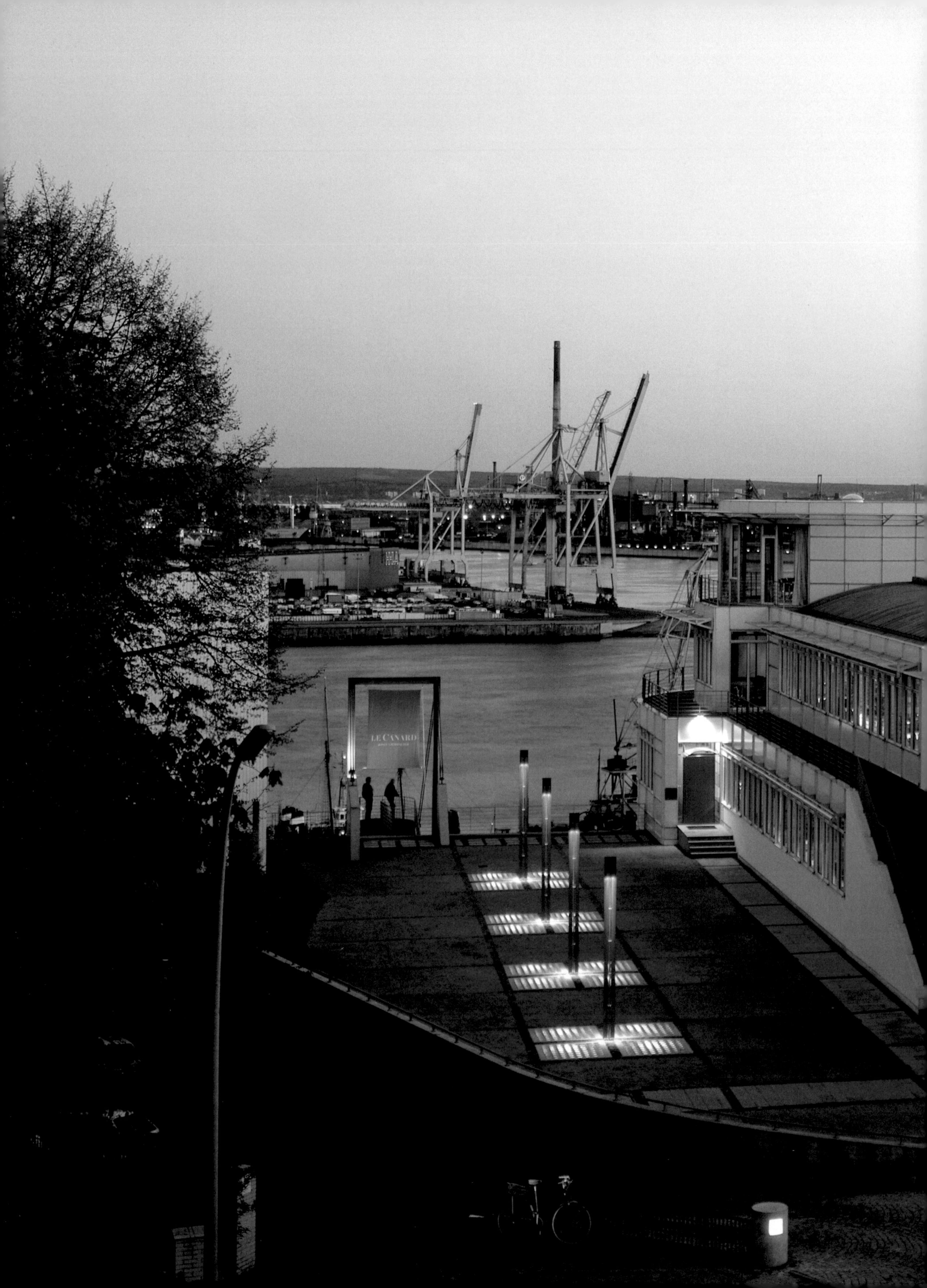
LE CANARD

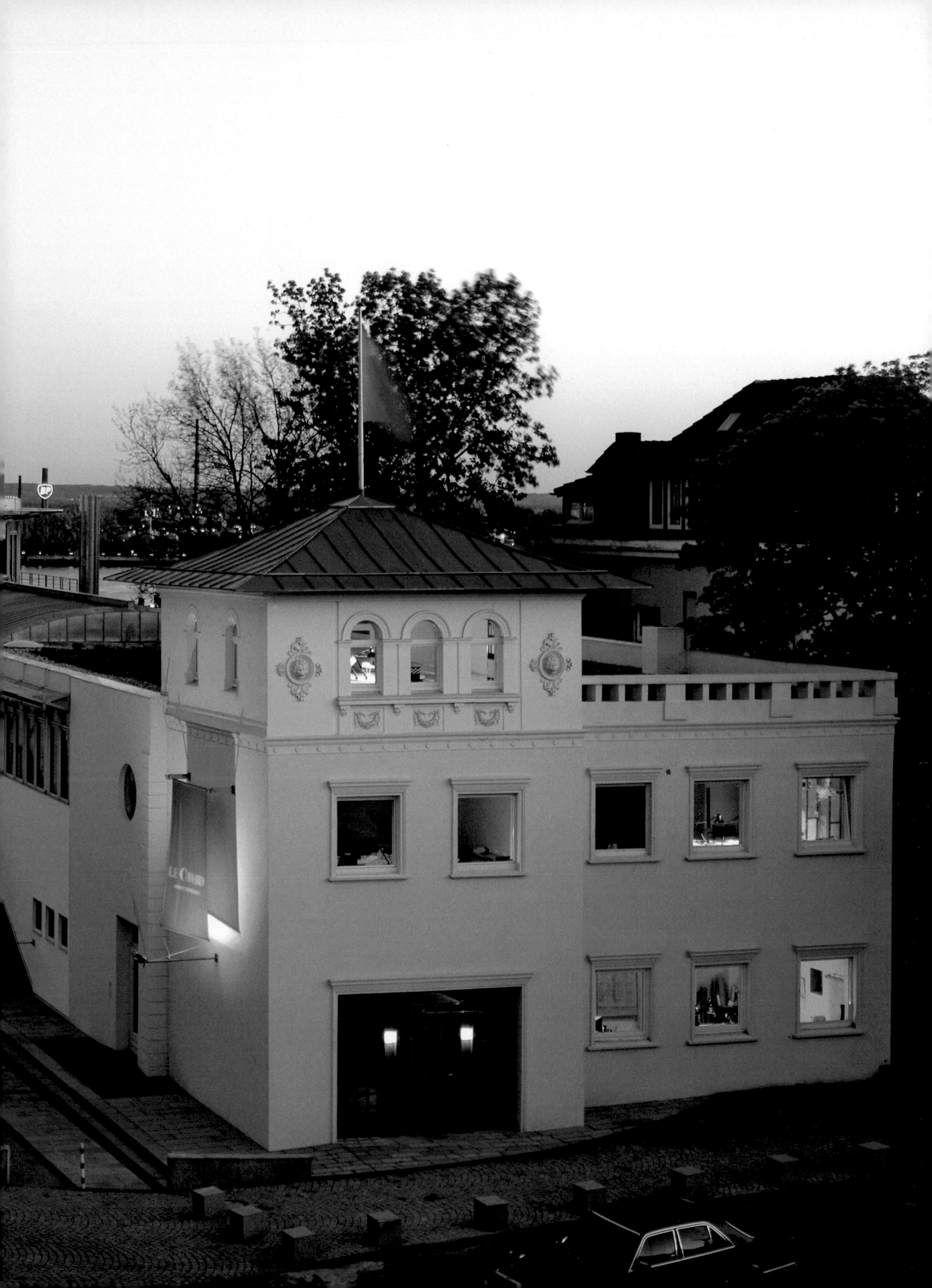

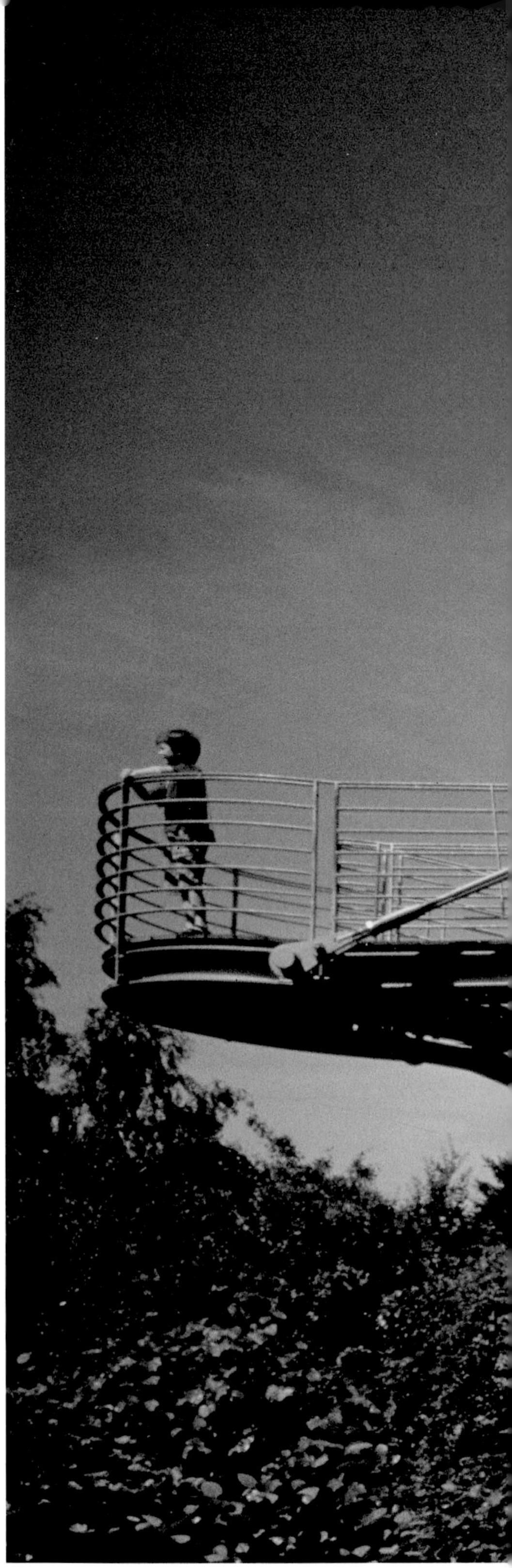

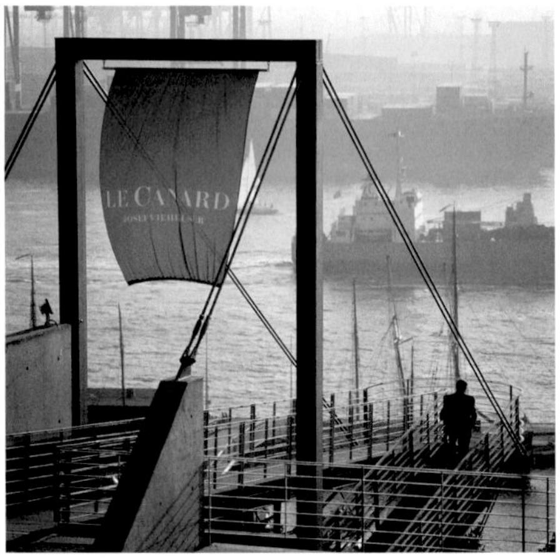

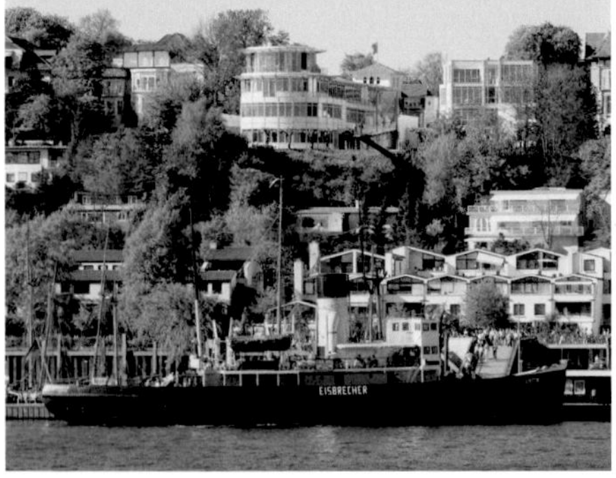

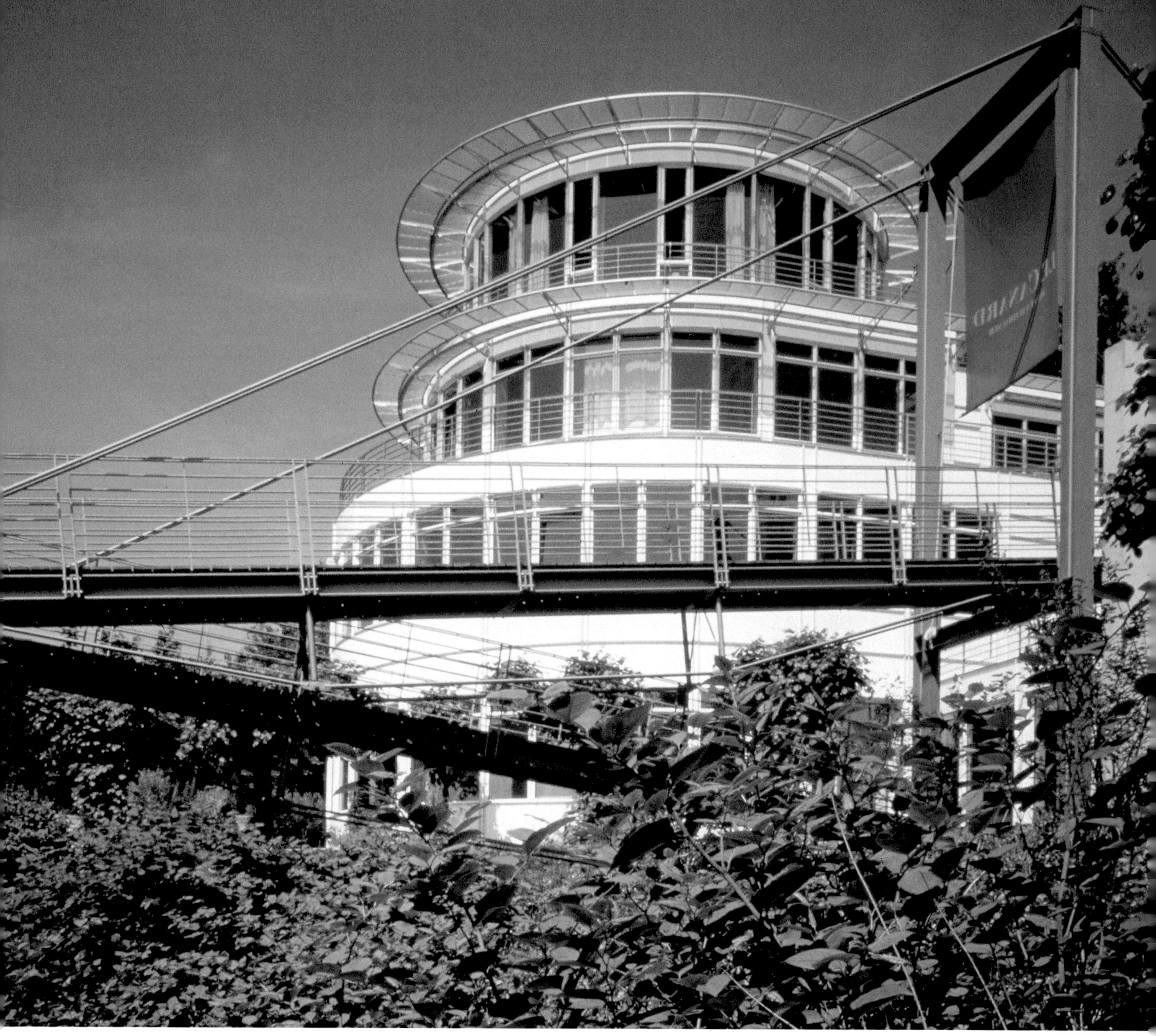

Restaurant „Le Canard", Elbchaussee 139, Hamburg
Restaurant 'Le Canard', Elbchaussee 139, Hamburg

1986

Entwurf Design
Meinhard von Gerkan

Bauherr Client
Meinhard von Gerkan

Bauzeit Construction period
1987–1990

BGF Gross floor area
ca. 2.000 m²

Von der Elbchaussee gelangt man durch ein stählernes Tor zu einer Rampe, die weit über den steilen Hang ausladend zunächst auf die Elbe weist, um sich dann auf der Hälfte der Strecke um 180° zu wenden und zum Eingang des Restaurants zu führen. Dessen Raumkonzeption ist aus der Kreisgeometrie des Gebäudes entwickelt. Wie der Bug eines Dampfers orientieren sich die Gasträume zum Hafenpanorama. Die kaskadenartige Abstaffelung der Decke zum Mittelpunkt macht die Kreisform auch im Innenraum erlebbar. In der Wahl der Materialien, der Beleuchtung und Farben ist hanseatisches Understatement und die Schönheit des Einfachen angestrebt. Das Holz des Fußbodens, der Wandvertäfelungen und der Jalousien geben dem Raum Wärme und Behaglichkeit. Der Clubraum mit seinen Lichtwänden ist eine Hommage an die edle Einfachheit japanischer Raumgestaltung. Die in Vitrinen gezeigten Modelle sind Leihgaben des Architekten.

From the Elbchaussee, guests reach the entrance of the restaurant through a steel gate and down a ramp which cantilevers over the cliff, pointing to the Elbe, and then takes a 180-degree turn half way up. The spatial geometry of the restaurant spaces was developed from the circular shape of the building. Like the prow of a steamer, they are oriented to the harbour panorama. The ceiling which cascades down to the centre makes it possible to experience the circular geometry inside too. The choice of materials, lighting system and colours was geared to Hanseatic understatement and the beauty of simplicity. The wooden floors, panelling and blinds make the restaurant appear warm and welcoming. The club lounge with its back-lit walls is a homage to the elegant simplicity of Japanese interior design. The architectural models displayed in the showcases are on loan from the architect.

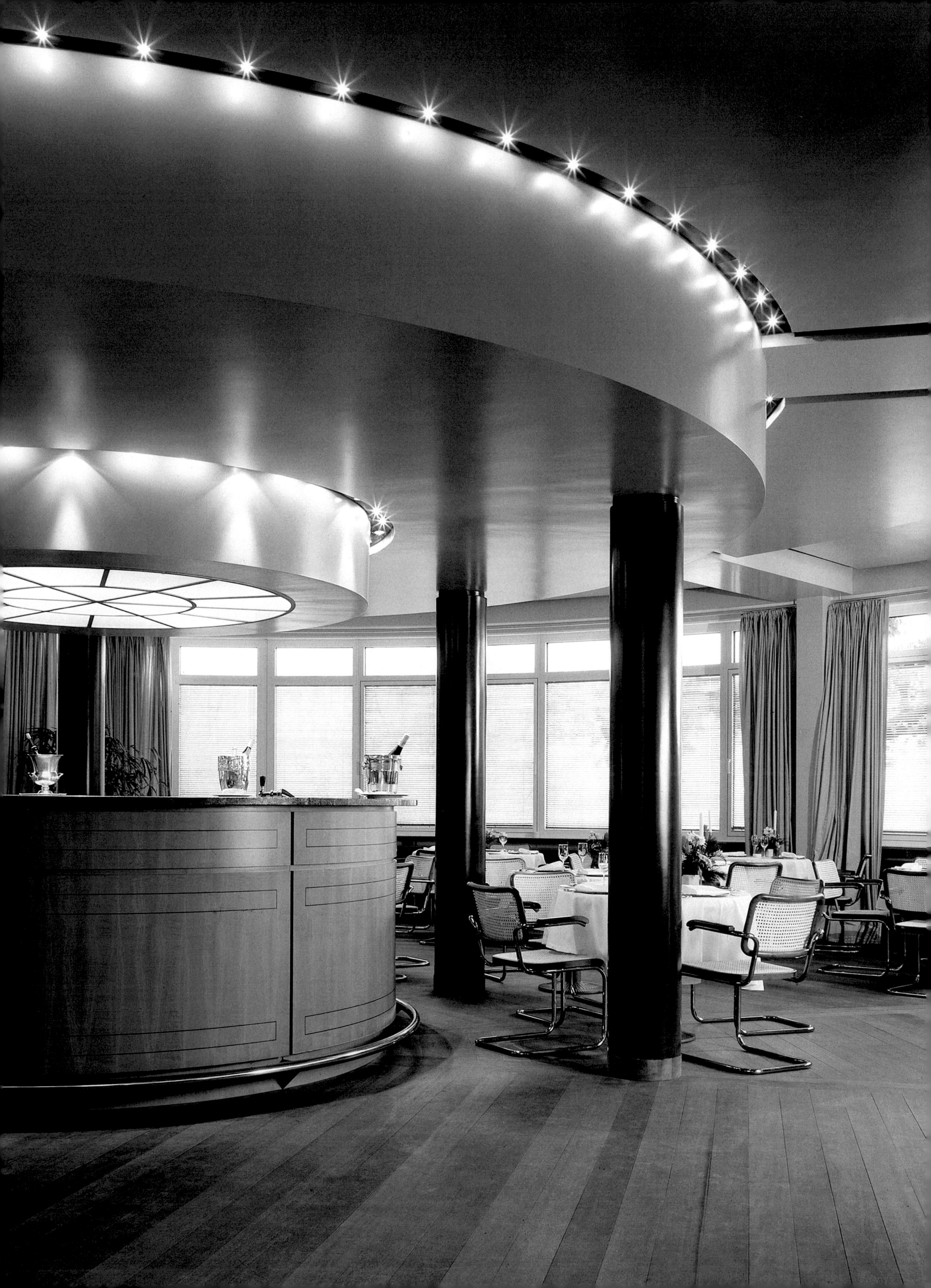

116

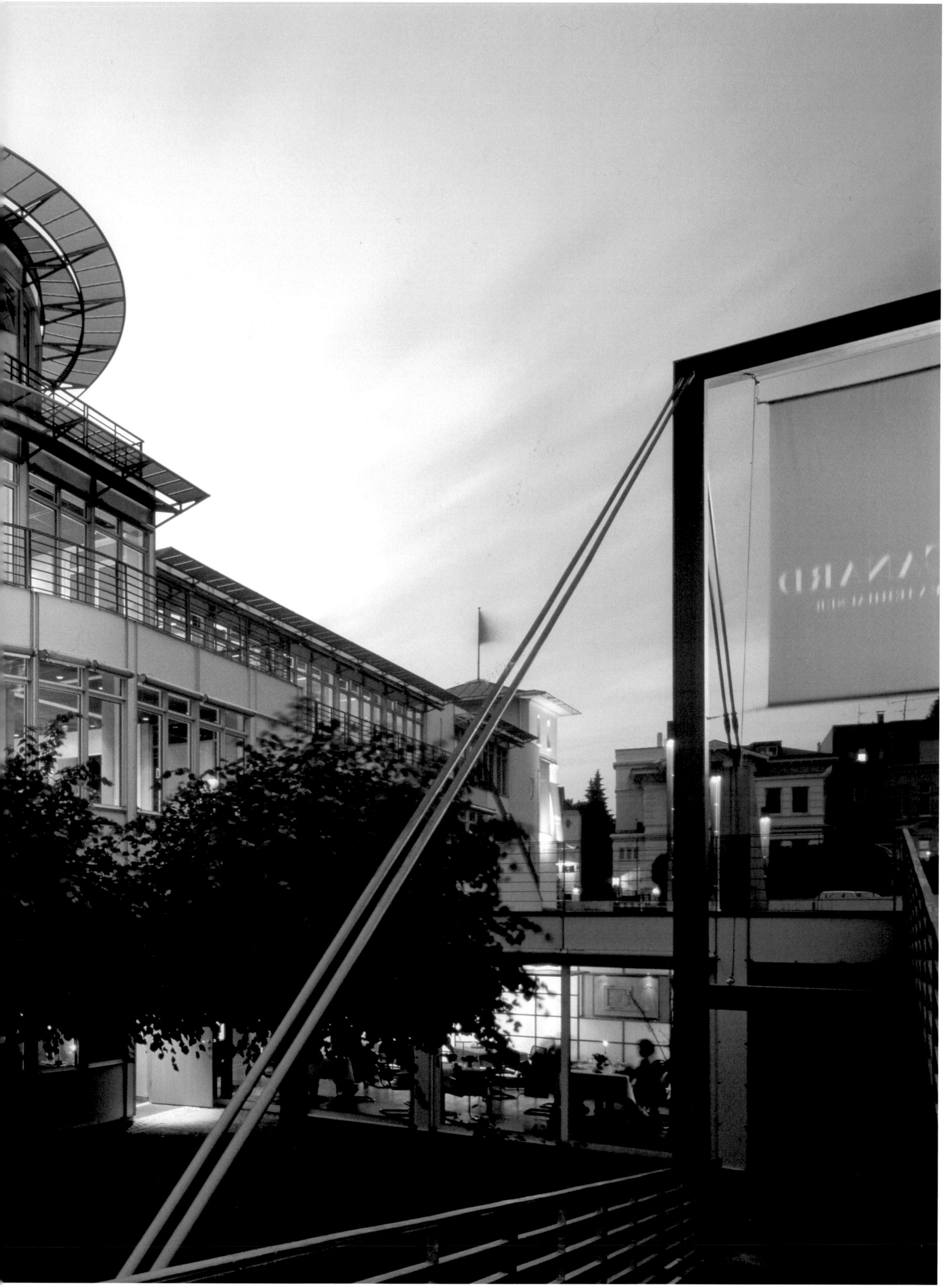

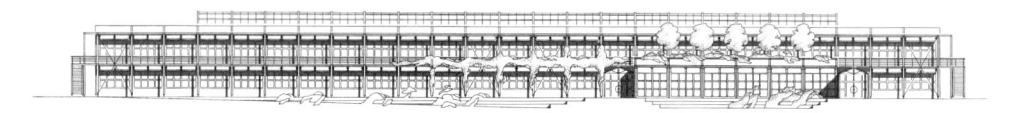

Ausbildungszentrum der Hamburgischen Electricitätswerke, Hamburg
Training Centre of the Hamburgische Electricitätswerke, Hamburg

1987

Entwurf Design
Volkwin Marg

Bauherr Client
Hamburgische Electricitäts-Werke AG

Bauzeit Construction period
1988–1990

BGF Gross floor area
7.000 m²

Die Stahlskelettbauweise des Neubaus schafft zusammen mit dem gelblichen Klinkermauerwerk der Fassade eine Verbindung zu dem Ziegelmaterial des vorhandenen Gebäudes für Weiterbildung. Die verglaste Pausen- und Ausstellungshalle, in der große Demonstrationsmodelle, Darstellungen zur ökologischen Bauweise und Ausstellungsvitrinen stehen, wird zum kommunikativen Mittelpunkt, während der von Pergolen und Umgängen eingefasste Vorplatz vor den beiden Eingängen auch dem Pausenaufenthalt im Freien dient. Die überwiegende Verwendung natürlicher Materialien aus energiearmer, umweltschonender Produktion zur Erzielung eines gesunden Raumklimas stellt neben natürlicher Belichtung und Belüftung, wo immer dies möglich ist, und der Verwendung massiver Bauteile zur Speicherung von Sonnenenergie nur einen Aspekt der ökologisch und biologisch begründeten Zusatzmaßnahmen dar.

The steel skeleton structure and the yellowish clinker brick façade of the new extension both relate to the masonry of the older building of the training centre. The glazed recreation and exhibition hall – containing large-format demonstration models, displays on ecological construction methods and showcases – becomes the communicative focus while the outdoor areas at the two entrances, framed by pergolas and paths, also form recreational spaces. Largely natural materials from low-energy, environmentally friendly production were used to achieve a healthy interior climate. Combined with daylighting and natural aeration wherever possible and with massive elements able to store heat from solar energy, they are responsible for the ecological and organic quality of the extension.

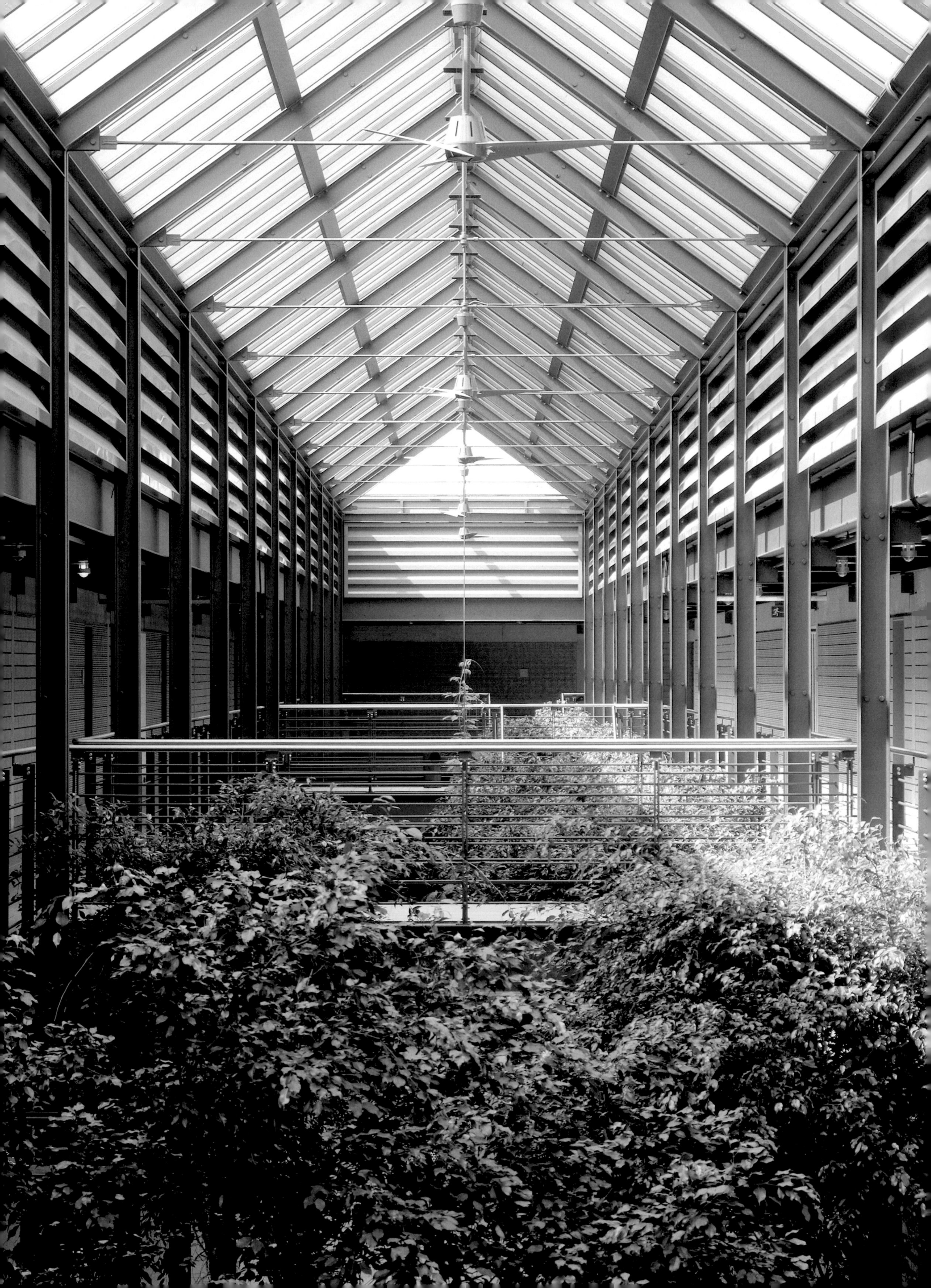

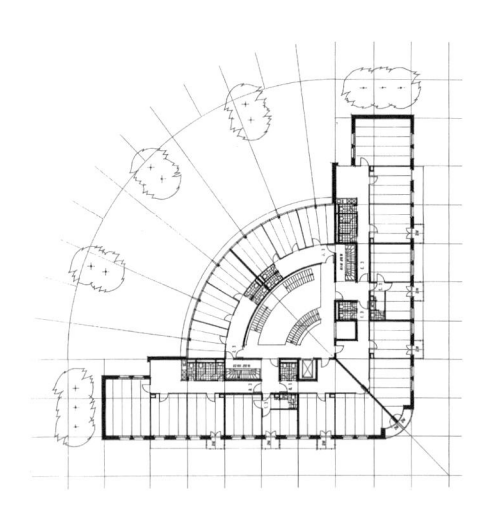

Moorbek-Rondeel, Norderstedt
Moorbek Rondeel, Norderstedt

1987

Entwurf Design
Meinhard von Gerkan
mit Joachim Zais, Uwe Hassels

Bauherr Client
Wohnungsunternehmen Plambeck

Bauzeit Construction period
1987–1990

BGF Gross floor area
7.200 m²

Von der Gebäudeecke an der Bahnhofsplatzseite führt eine kurze Passage ins Innere zu einem Lichthof, der die Gewerbeflächen im zurückliegenden Bereich, und über eine geschwungene Treppe die Obergeschosse, erschließt. Der Entwurf ist so ausgelegt, dass ein hohes Maß an Nutzungsflexibilität mit unterschiedlich großen Einheiten ermöglicht wird. Im Erdgeschoss befinden sich Läden, eine Bankfiliale und ein Restaurant, die Obergeschosse bieten Platz für Büros oder Wohnungen. Der zur Stadt orientierte Teil ist als Mauerwerksbau mit roter Ziegellochfassade und einer Stahlkonstruktion als zweiter Ebene ausgebildet. Die geschwungene Fassade zum Park ist als filigrane Glas-Stahl-Konstruktion mit vorgelagerten Sonnenschutzelementen gestaltet. Feststehende Beschatter mit Füllelementen aus Lochblech bilden den oberen Abschluss des Gebäudes.

A short interior passage leads from the street corner on the side of the station square to the central atrium, which gives access to the business premises at the back and, via a curved stairway, to the upper floors. The design aimed to create a high measure of operational flexibility by providing units of varying sizes. On the ground floor, there are shops, a bank and a restaurant; the upper floors offer office and residential spaces. The building section facing the city has a lower perforated red brick, and an upper steel-framed façade. The curved façade to the park is a filigree glass-and-steel structure with exterior sun-shading elements. Fixed shading elements with perforated sheeting gap fillers mark the top of the building.

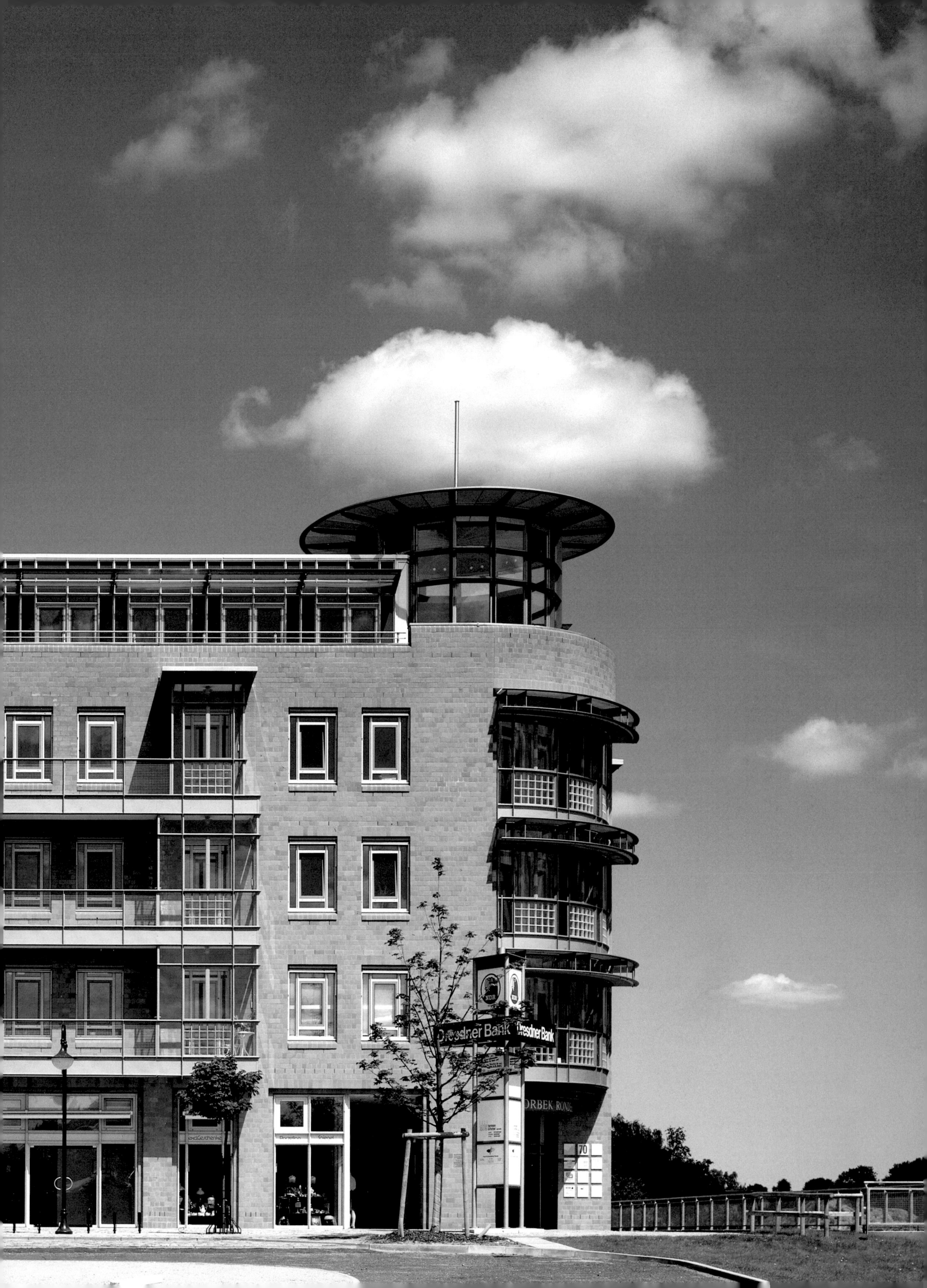
Dresdner Bank
Dresdner Bank
ORBEK RONDE
70

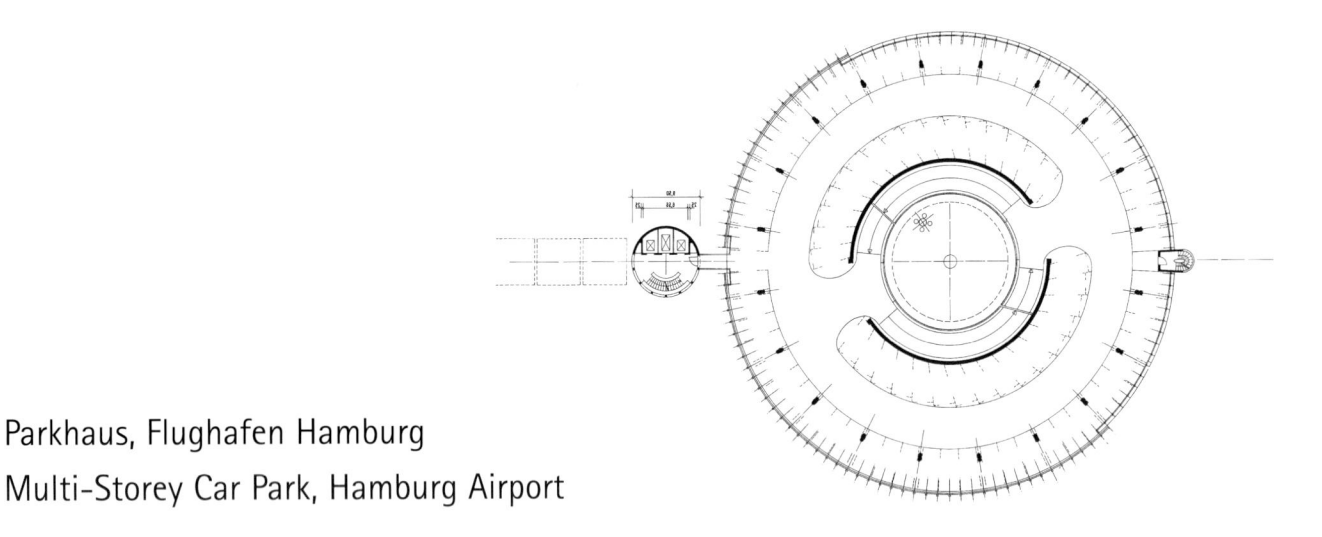

Parkhaus, Flughafen Hamburg
Multi-Storey Car Park, Hamburg Airport

Wettbewerb Competition
1986 – 1. Preis

Entwurf Design
Meinhard von Gerkan

Partner Partner
Karsten Brauer

Bauherr Client
Flughafen Hamburg GmbH

Bauzeit Construction period
1989–1990

Stellplätze Parking sites
800

Die neun Ebenen des Parkhauses werden durch zwei gegeneinander versetzte, spindelförmige Rampen für Auf- und Abwärtsverkehr im Mittelpunkt des Kreises erschlossen. Auf den Rampen und den Parkdecks herrscht Einbahnverkehr, Verkehrsüberschneidungen gibt es nur an Ein- und Ausfahrten. Die Fußgängererschließung erfolgt an der Nordseite über einen separaten Treppenturm, der durch leichte Brücken mit dem Parkhaus verbunden ist. Wesentliches Gestaltungsmerkmal ist neben der dominierenden Kreisgeometrie die Gliederung der Geschosse durch einen teilweise vorgehängten Screen aus Stahlrosten. Hierdurch wird einerseits der Ausblick und die Durchlüftung gewährleistet, andererseits ein akzentuierter Abschluss erzeugt. In den Ein- und Ausfahrtsgeschossen sowie den oberen beiden Parkebenen wurde auf den Screen verzichtet, um die Leichtigkeit des gesamten Gebäudes zu unterstützen und das Konstruktionsprinzip ablesbar zu machen.

Two spiral ramps for upward and downward traffic are alternated towards each other in the circle core and provide access to the nine levels of the multi-storey car park. One-way traffic predominates on the ramps and park decks; traffic intersections occur only at the access and exit routes. Pedestrians access the building on the north side via a separate staircase tower, which is connected to the car park via lightweight bridges. Fundamental design characteristics are the dominant circular geometry as well as the division of the storeys with a suspended screen of steel mesh. This ensures views and ventilation, whilst simultaneously generating a clear division. The screen is not used on the access and exit levels and the two upper parking levels, in order to reinforce the lightweight appearance of the building and make its structural principle detectable.

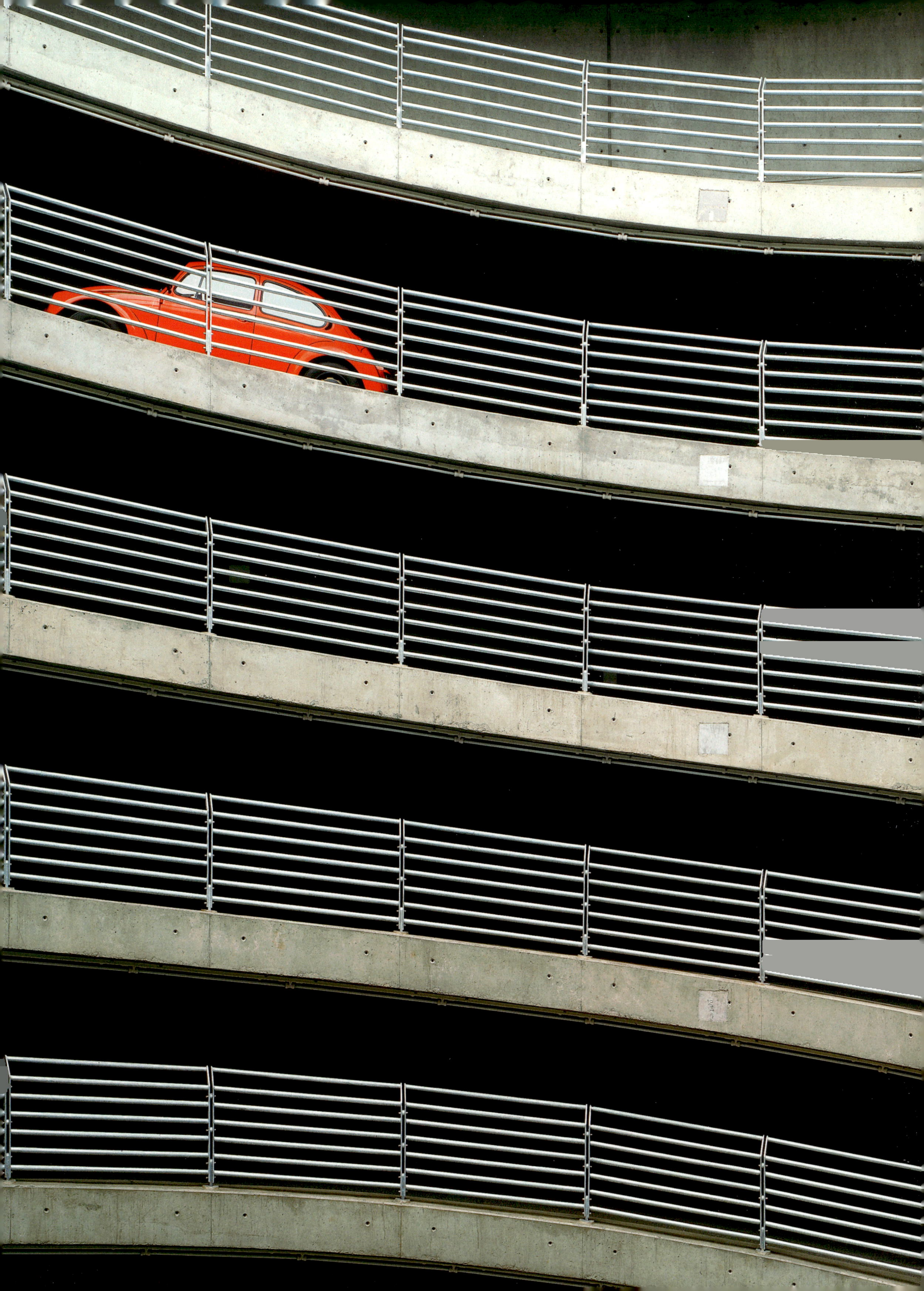

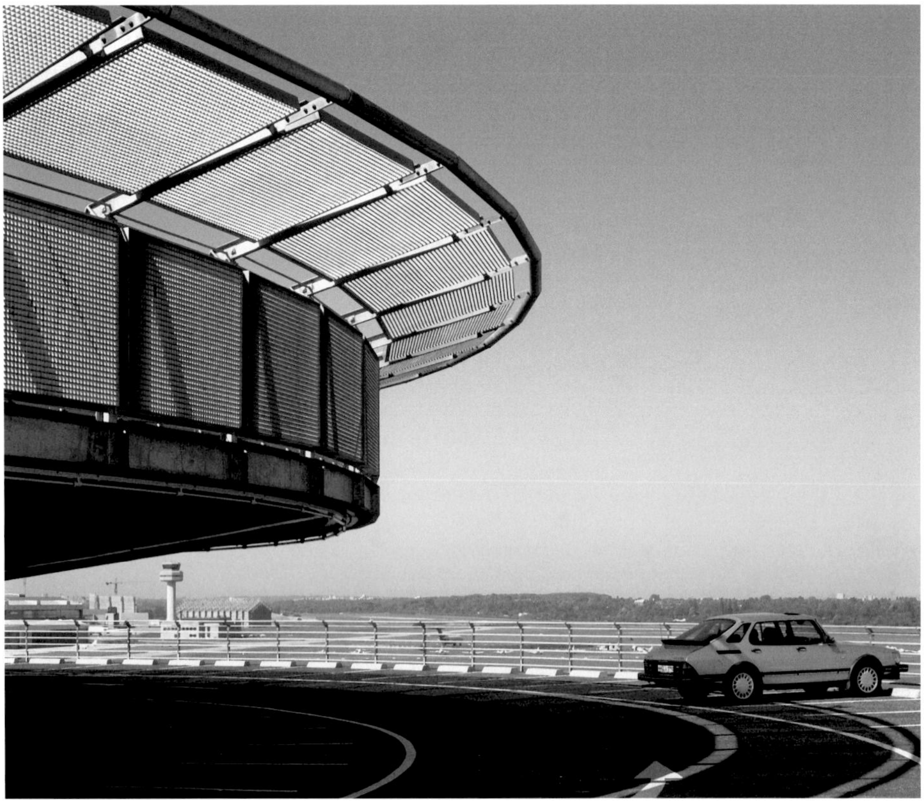

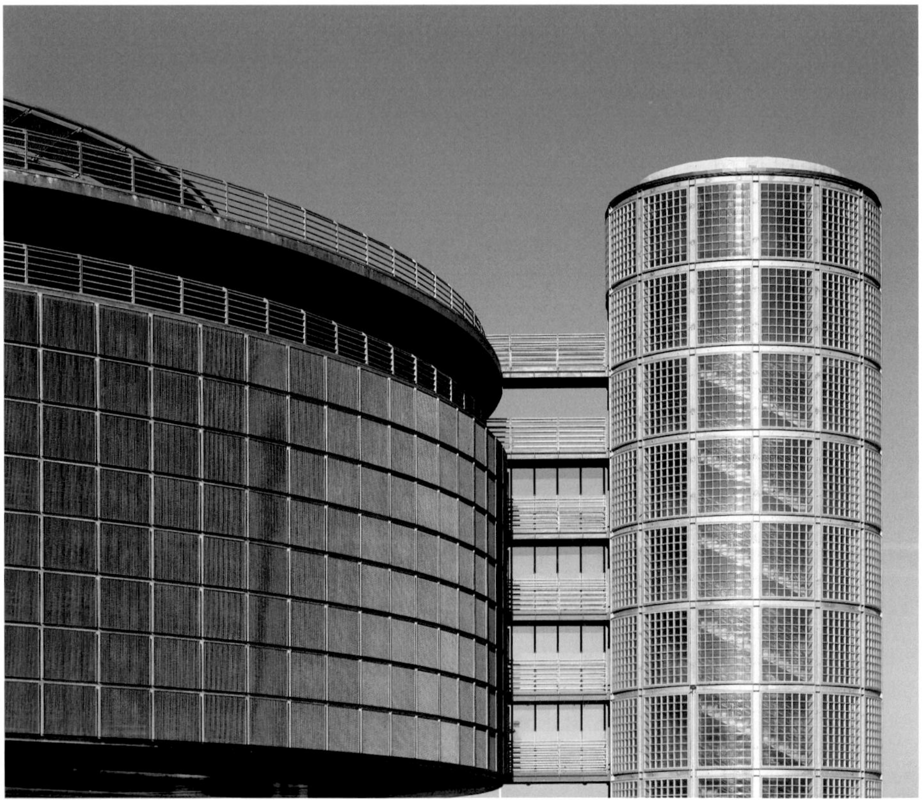

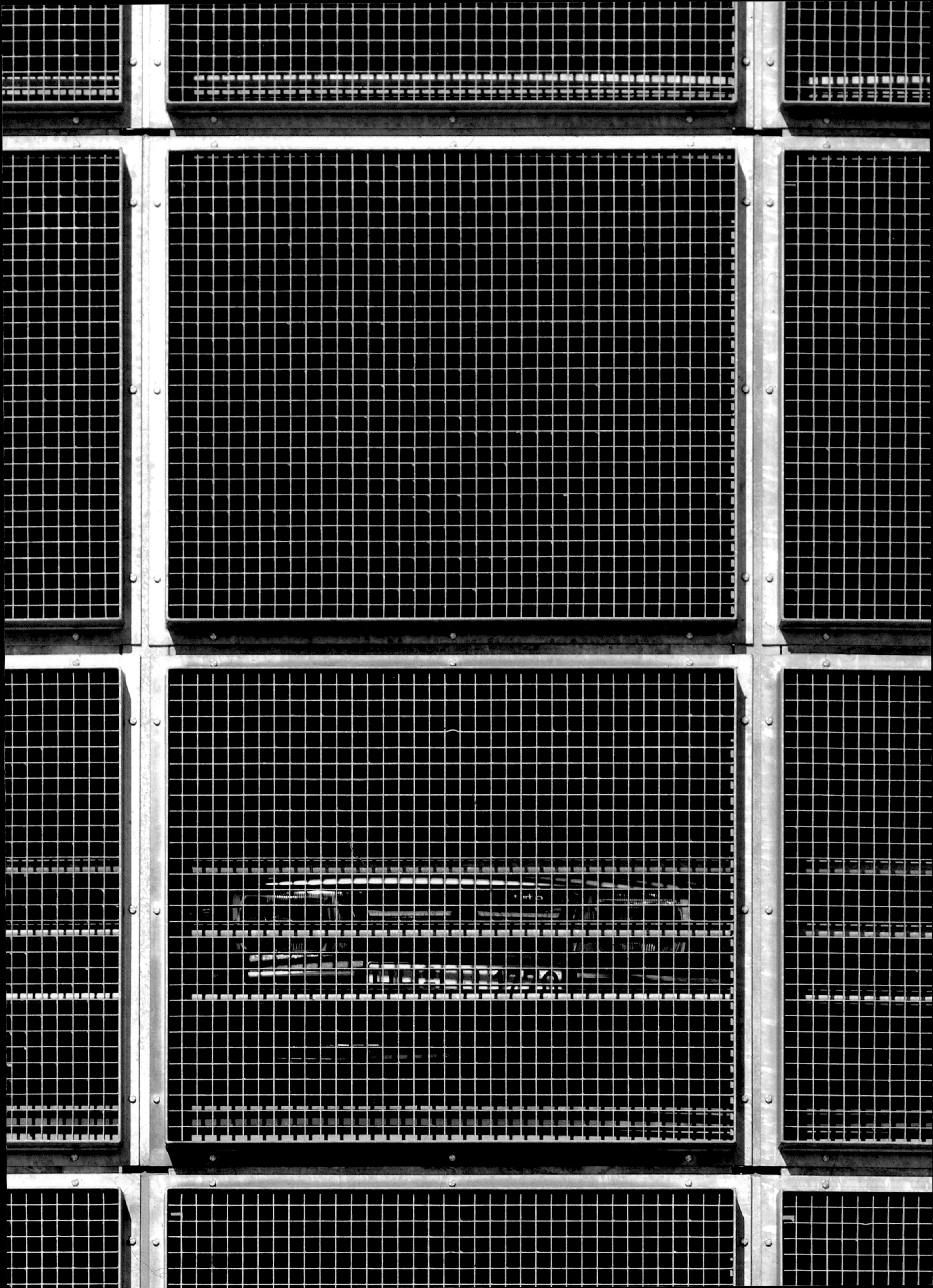

Stadthalle Bielefeld
Civic Centre, Bielefeld

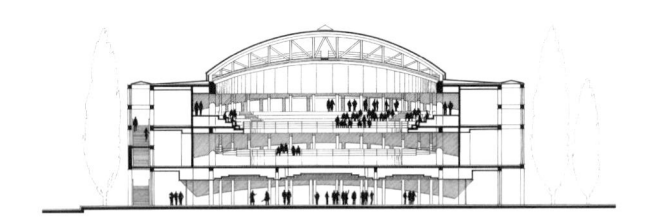

Wettbewerb Competition
1980 – 1. Preis

Entwurf Design
Meinhard von Gerkan

Partner Partner
Michael Zimmermann

Bauherr Client
Stadt Bielefeld

Bauzeit Construction period
1987–1990

BGF Gross floor area
18.400 m²

In der Mitte des einfach konzipierten Gebäudes liegen axialsymmetrisch ausgebildet und umgeben von der Foyerzone der große und der kleine Saal, die auch als Einheit genutzt werden können. Das Prinzip der Einfachheit betrifft ebenso Materialien und Farbkonzept: Weiß und Lichtgrau sorgen dafür, dass die Stadthalle hell und freundlich wirkt und als Hülle neutral genug bleibt, um der Vielfalt des Veranstaltungsgeschehens Freiraum zu geben. Die geometrische Großform gibt zugleich die gliedernde Struktur des Gebäudes in all seinen Teilen vor. Die längsgerichtete Achse des Tonnendachs und die als halbrund ausgebildete Rückfront des großen Saales betonen die Klarheit der strukturellen Ordnung. Die Treppenaufgänge in der zweischichtigen Fassade liegen im Übergang zwischen Innen und Außen, so dass die Bewegung der Besucher für den Innenraum wie für die Passanten ein charakteristisches Element dieses öffentlichen Gebäudes ist.

In the centre of the building, which is based on a simple design concept, are the large and the small hall, arranged in axial symmetry and surrounded by a foyer. Both halls can be used as a unified whole. The principle of simplicity also concerns the material choice and the colour concept. White and light grey ensure that the civic centre receives a bright and inviting atmosphere; the envelope, however, remains neutral enough to accommodate a variety of events. The great geometric form reflects the divisional structure of each part of the building. The long axis of the vaulted roof and the rear of the hall, which is semicircular, sustain the clarity of form. The stairs set in the two-layer façade are in a transition area between the interior and the exterior. Visitor flow is thus a characteristic element of this public building both towards the inside and for passers-by.

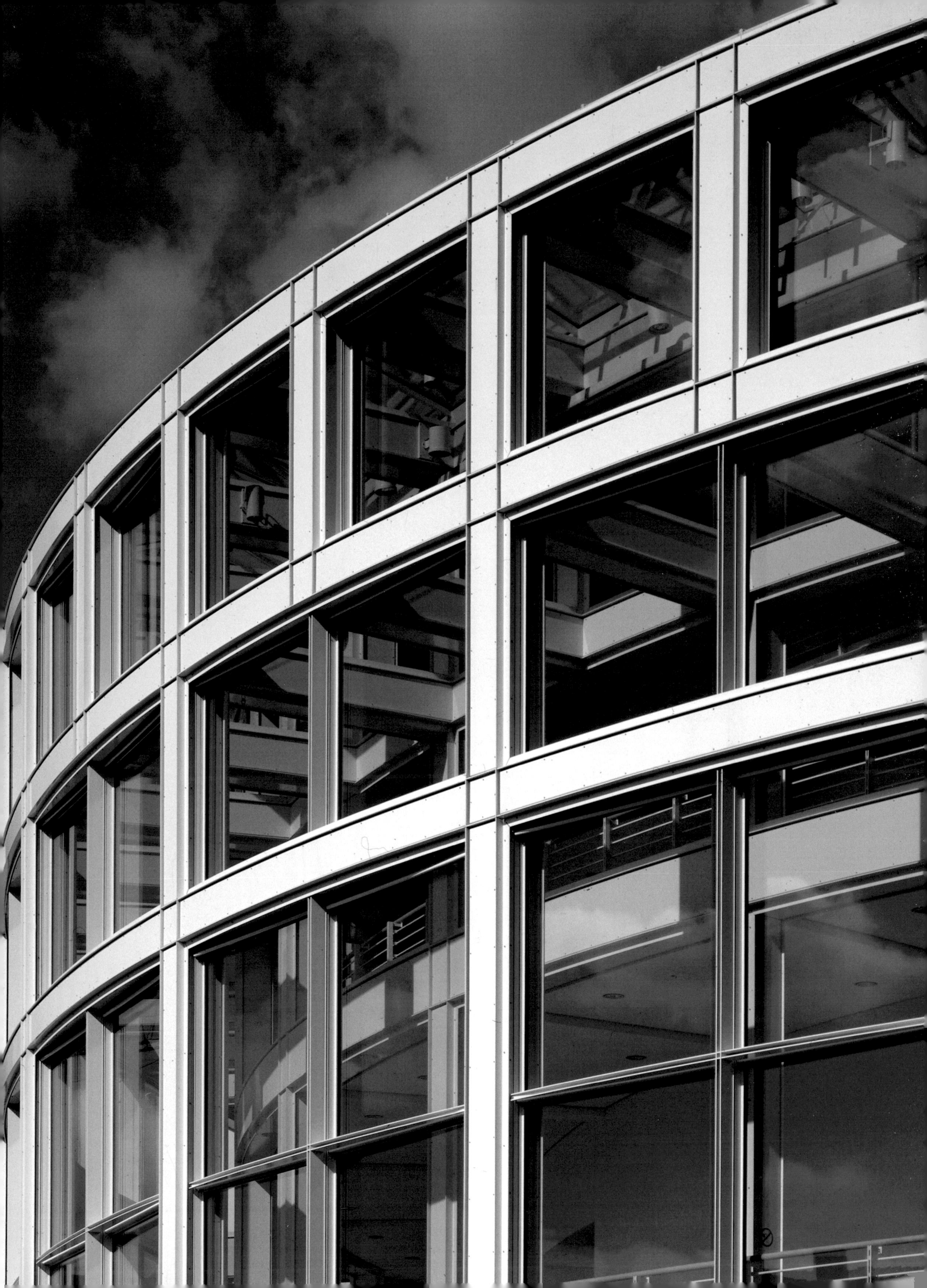

128

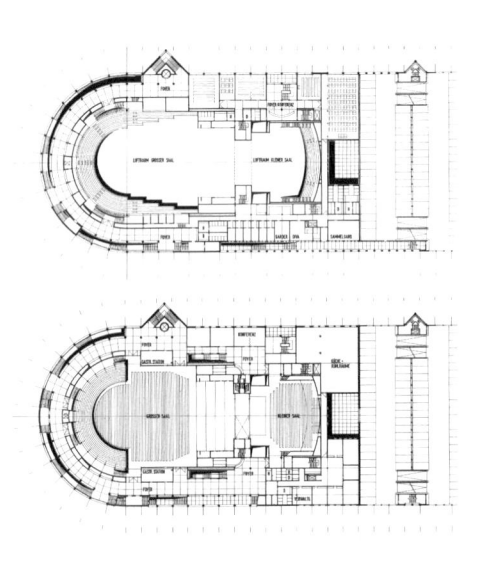

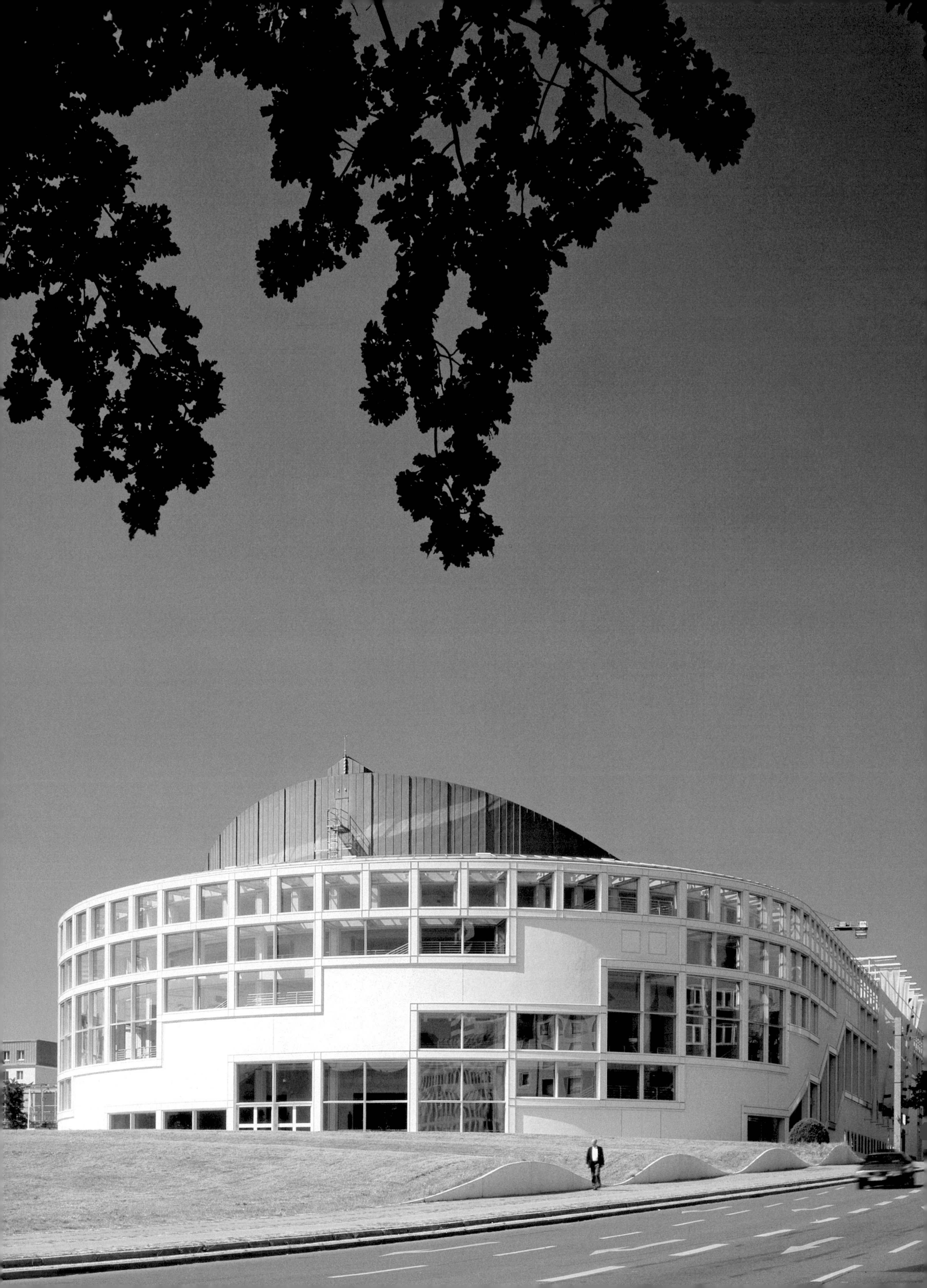

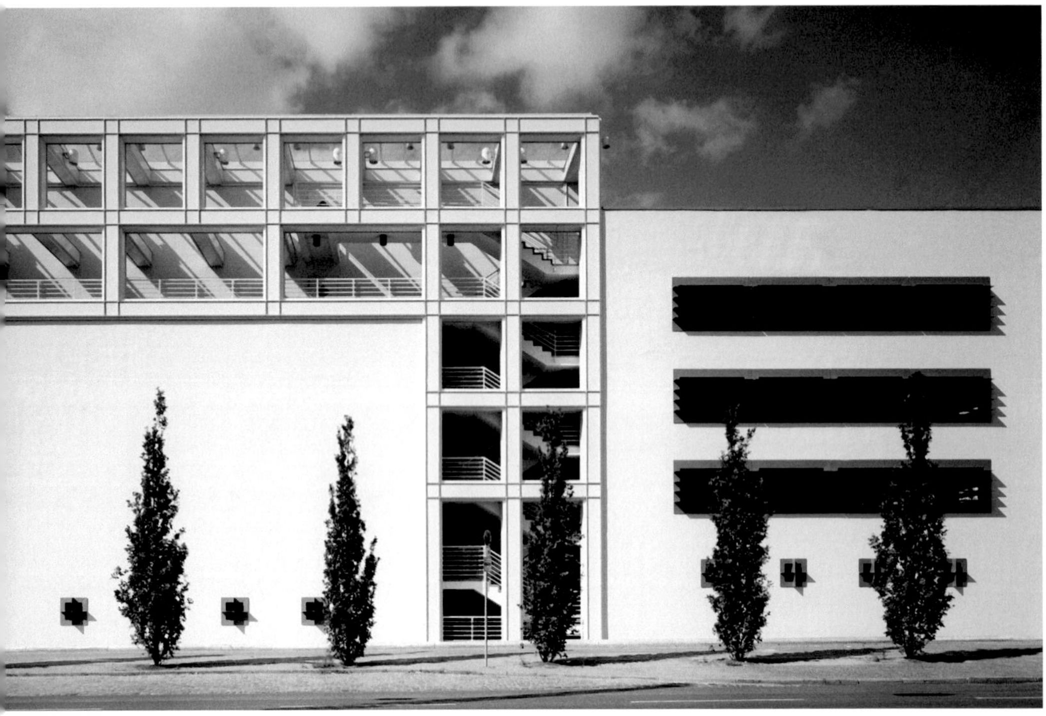

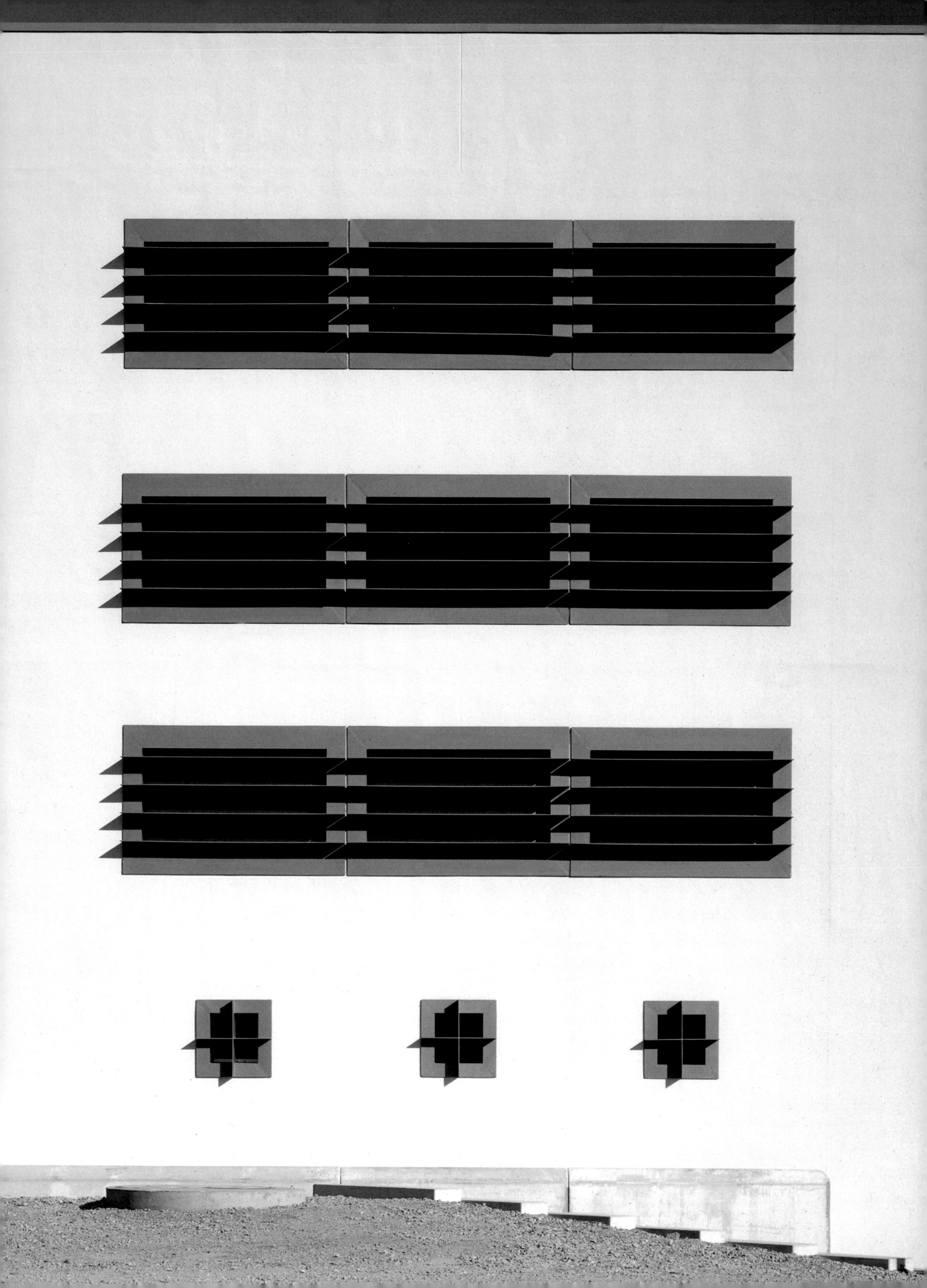

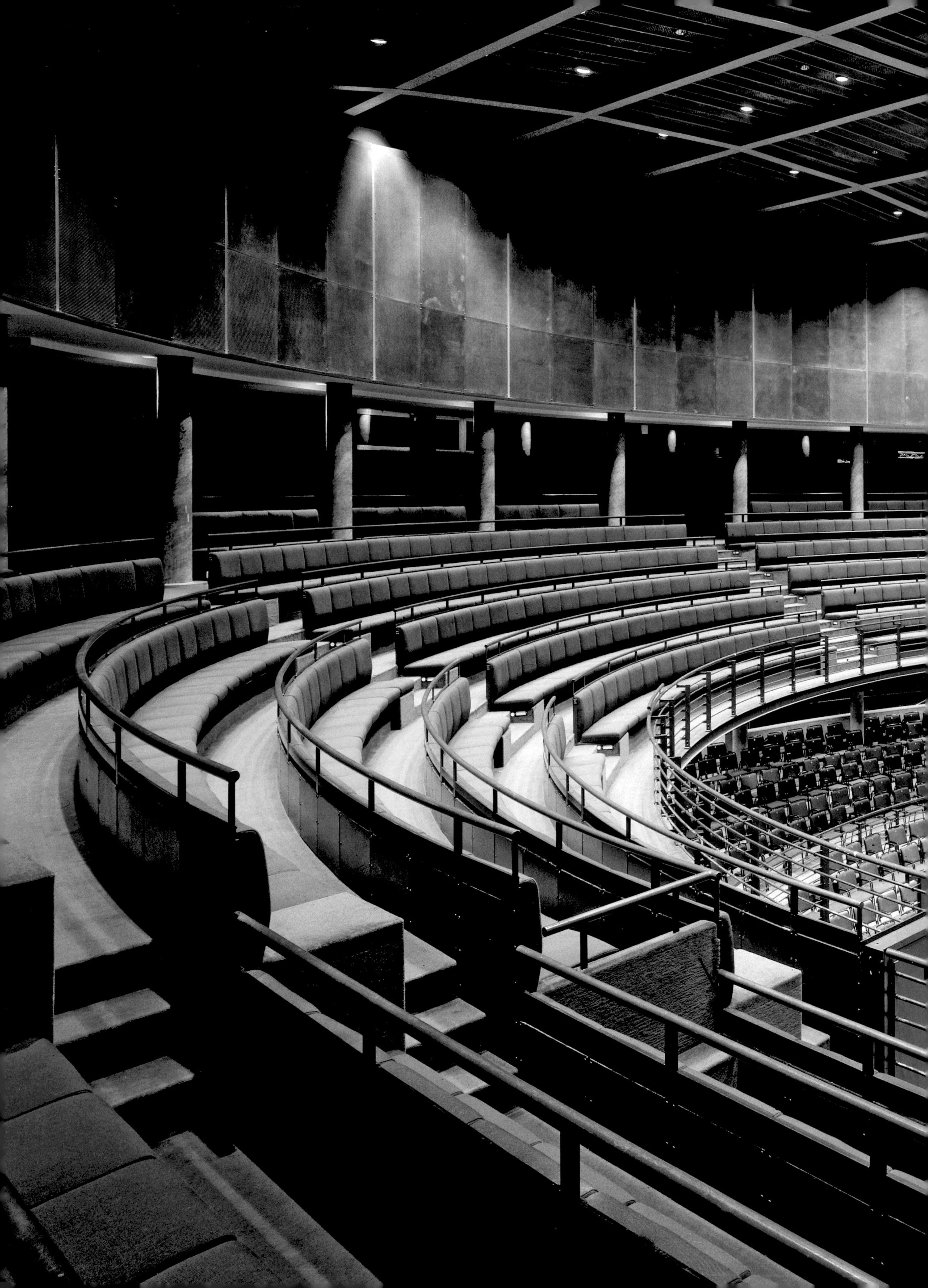

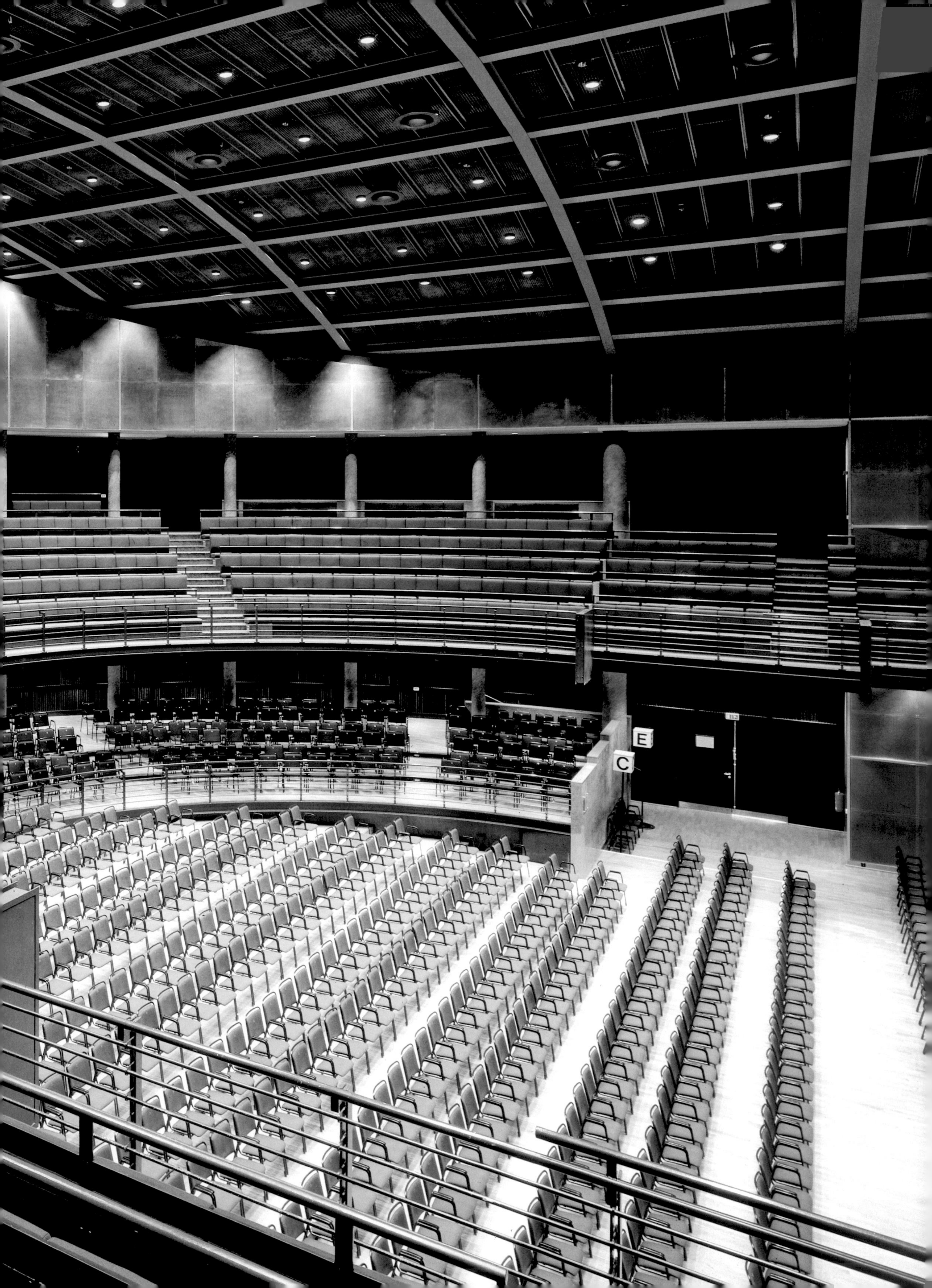
E
C

1991

Justizbehörden in Flensburg, Um- und Erweiterungsbau

Die Neubauten sind dem Geesthang folgend in der Höhe gestaffelt und stellen eine einfache Verlängerung der vorhandenen Gebäude dar. Eine Treppenhalle verbindet Alt- und Neubau und bietet freien Blick auf den Park im Norden. Von der Halle aus gelangt man in die kurzen, kammartig angeordneten Büroflügel.

Legal Authority in Flensburg, Conversion and Extension

Following the fall of the 'Geesthang' the new buildings are staggered in their height and form a simple extension of the existing buildings. A stairwell connects the existing and new buildings and offers a view of the park to the north. The short, comb-like office wings are accessible from the hall.

Carl Bertelsmann Stiftung, Gütersloh

Die transparent und leicht wirkenden Pavillons sind Teil eines neuen Parks um einen künstlich angelegten, kreisrunden See. Sie unterscheiden sich in ihrer Kleinmaßstäblichkeit deutlich von der großen Bertelsmann Hauptverwaltung, setzen die strenge, orthogonale Rationalität jedoch fort.

Carl Bertelsmann Foundation, Gütersloh

The transparent and light pavilions are part of a new park set around an artificial, circular lake. With their small scale they clearly differ from the large Bertelsmann Headquarters, whilst simultaneously taking reference from the strict, orthogonal rationality.

Flughafen Stuttgart, Terminal 1

Das Terminalgebäude ist auf die elementaren Formen des Längstraktes mit Dreiecksquerschnitt und der rechteckigen Halle reduziert. Die konstruktive Baumstruktur des Hallendaches, dessen Traggerüst der Bauart einer Dolde entspricht, ist das charakteristische Merkmal des Flughafens.

Stuttgart Airport, Terminal 1

The terminal building is reduced to the basic forms of the longitudinal wing with triangular cross-section and the rectangular hall. The structural 'trees' supporting the roof are the inimitable characteristic of the airport building. The skeleton corresponds to the structure of a compound umbel.

Groß-Sporthalle, Flensburg

Die neuen Hallen ergänzen die vorhandene Halle zu einem Sportzentrum. Eine filigrane Stahlkonstruktion aus abgespannten Seitenschiff- und aufgelegten Fachwerkbindern überbrückt die große Spannweite. Unterstützt wird der Habitus der Leichtigkeit durch großzügige Verglasungen in den Außenwänden und im Dach.

Large Gymnasium, Flensburg

The new halls extend the existing gymnasium into a sports centre. A lightweight steel truss structure bridges the large span. The lightweight appearance is emphasized by generous glazing of the exterior walls and the roof.

Café Andersen, Hamburg

Licht wird von Industriescheinwerfern gegen die Tonnendecke aus Profilblech geworfen und reflektiert, so dass der Raum hell ausgeleuchtet ist. Ein kreisrunder Tresen dominiert den Verkaufsraum, während die Nebenräume als metallischer Wagon in der Mitte des Raumes angeordnet sind.

Andersen Café, Hamburg

Industrial floodlights cast light against the barrel roof made from steel profiles where it is reflected, thereby brightly filling the space with light. A round bar dominates the sales room, whilst the secondary rooms are centrally positioned and formed like a metal carriage.

Stadtbahnhaltestelle, Hauptbahnhof Bielefeld

Das in Form eines Glasprismas aus dem Boden wachsende, transparente Zugangsgebäude des unterirdischen Bahnhofs zeigt weithin sichtbar seine Funktion. Hauptgestaltungselement sowohl in diesem Eingangsbauwerk als auch im Verteilergeschoss und auf den Bahnsteigen ist der Einsatz von Licht.

Urban Railway Station "Bielefeld Central Station"

The transparent access building to the underground station grows from the ground in the form of a glass prism, with its function being clearly visible from a distance. The primary design element in the entrance building as well as on the circulation floor and the platforms is the use of light.

1991

Kavaklidere Komplex, Ankara, Türkei

Architektonisch wird der 3,4 ha große Gesamtkomplex von dem 24-geschossigen zylindrischen Turm des Sheraton Luxushotels bestimmt. Als optisches Gegengewicht wirken das große, horizontal angelegte Einkaufs- und Geschäftszentrum und die Wohnbebauung mit 92 Apartments.

Saar-Galerie, Saarbrücken

Ein 38 m hohes Oktogon bildet den Abschluss der sechsgeschossigen Passage. Stahldetails prägen den Charakter des Bauwerks und stehen in Kontrast zu den wabenartigen Stahlbetonfertigteilen, die in Form lichtdurchlässiger, gestaffelter Quadratmodule die äußeren Parkhauswände oberhalb der Arkaden bilden.

Stadtzentrum Schenefeld, Hamburg

Das Einkaufszentrum steht in der Tradition der großen Markthallen und Galerien des 19. Jahrhunderts: Ein gläsernes Tonnendach überdeckt die beiden sich im rechten Winkel kreuzenden Passagen. Die terrassierte Anordnung der drei Ebenen sorgt für ausreichend Tageslicht bis hinunter ins Erdgeschoss.

Kavaklidere Complex, Ankara, Turkey

The 24-storey cylindrical tower of the luxury Sheraton Hotel architecturally characterizes the 3.4-hectare-large complex. The large, horizontally laid-out shopping and commercial centre and the residential development with 92 apartments present a visual counterbalance.

Saar Galerie, Saarbrücken

A 38-m-high octagon forms the termination of the six-storey arcade. Steel details characterize the building and create a contrast to the honeycomb, pre-cast, reinforced concrete units, which form the external walls of the multi-storey car park above the arcades as staggered, light-admitting square modules.

Schenefeld Town Centre, Hamburg

The shopping centre follows the tradition of the large market halls and galleries of the 19th century: a glazed barrel roof covers both arcades intersecting each other at a right angle. The terraced positioning of the three levels allows sufficient daylighting all the way down to the ground floor.

Wohn- und Geschäftshaus, Buchholz

Das Gebäudeensemble gliedert sich in einen linearen Hauptbaukörper entlang der Straße und einen gläsernen Pavillon im Blockinnern. Farb- und Materialwahl unterstreichen die unterschiedliche Gestaltung des introvertierten, abschirmenden Hauptbaukörpers gegenüber dem extrovertierten, transparenten Pavillon.

Hillmannhaus, Bremen

Das Bürohaus bildet den Schlussstein zur Arrondierung des Hillmannplatzes. Die Strenge des Baukörpers wird durch eine starke horizontale Gliederung der Fassade in einen zweigeschossigen Sockel und ein Staffelgeschoss mit auskragendem Flugdach strukturiert.

Miro Datensysteme, Braunschweig

Produktion und Dienstleistung befinden sich unter einem Dach: In der Mitte des langgestreckten Gebäudes liegen die zentrale Halle und der Werkstattraum, seitlich flankiert von den einbündig angeordneten Büros. Die Räume der Geschäftsführung schweben als zylindrische Kanzel über dem Haupteingang in der Halle.

Residential and Commercial Block, Buchholz

The ensemble consists of a linear main building stretching along the street and a glazed pavilion in the block centre. The colour and material selection underlines the varying design of the introverted, shielded main building against the extroverted, transparent pavilion.

Hillmann House, Bremen

The office building forms the termination of the enclosure around the 'Hillmannplatz' square. A strong horizontal division of the façade into a two-storey socle and a roof level with a cantilevered shed roof structure the building's severity.

Miro Data Systems, Braunschweig

Production and service are combined under the same roof: the central hall and the workshop are situated in the centre of the long building, flanked on both sides by the offices, which are arranged along galleries. The managers' rooms hover as a cylindrical control box over the main entrance and the hall.

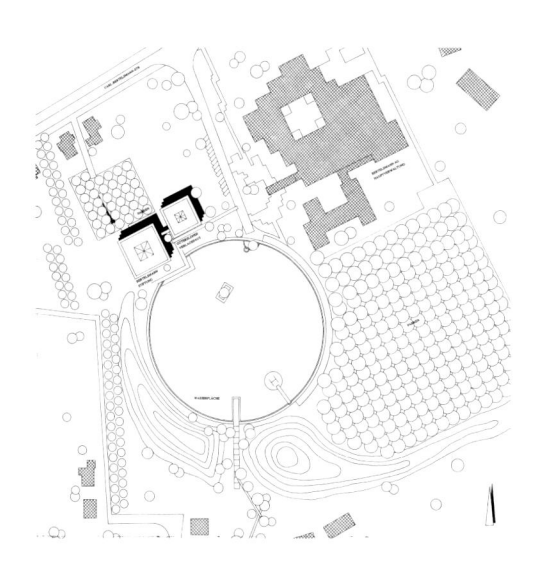

Carl Bertelsmann Stiftung, Gütersloh
Carl Bertelsmann Foundation, Gütersloh

Wettbewerb Competition
1980 – 1. Preis

Entwurf Design
Meinhard von Gerkan und Karsten Brauer

Partner Partner
Klaus Staratzke

Bauherr Client
Flughafen Stuttgart GmbH

Bauzeit Construction period
1986–1991

BGF Gross floor area
36.000 m^2

Die pavillonartigen, transparenten Baukörper öffnen sich zur Parklandschaft, während die verglasten Treppenhallen mit ihren Umgängen zur zwanglosen Kommunikation einladen. Um die Transparenz und Leichtigkeit im Innern noch zu steigern, sind die Bürotrennwände nach oben verglast und im Anschluss an die Außenfassaden gänzlich in Glas aufgelöst. Neben dem Eingangsfoyer mit seiner Terrasse am See befindet sich ein teilbarer Versammlungssaal, der gegenüber dem Niveau des umliegenden Parks leicht abgesenkt ist, so dass man gleichsam in einer Mulde im Grünen sitzt. Der Bau ist technisch und architektonisch äußerst sparsam: Lüftungsanlagen und abgehängte Decken gibt es nicht, Knappheit, Prägnanz und Transparenz waren gleichermaßen inhaltliche wie ästhetische Zielsetzung. Das Stiftungsgebäude samt Park und See wurde in einer Rekordzeit von nur gut einem Jahr gebaut und dem Nutzer übergeben.

The pavilion-like, transparent structures open up towards the park landscape, whilst the glazed stairhalls with their transitions invite one to indulge in casual communication. In order to further reinforce the transparency and lightness in the interior, the office partition walls are glazed at the top and completely dissolved in glass at the connection to the exterior façades. A separable assembly hall, located next to the entrance foyer with its lakeside terrace, is slightly lowered in comparison to the level of the surrounding park, so that people sit in a green trough. The building is technically and architecturally very frugal: ventilation systems and suspended ceilings do not exist. Succinctness, conciseness and transparency have been the content-related and aesthetic objective. The foundation building, including the park and lake, were completed within a record time of approximately one year and handed over to the user.

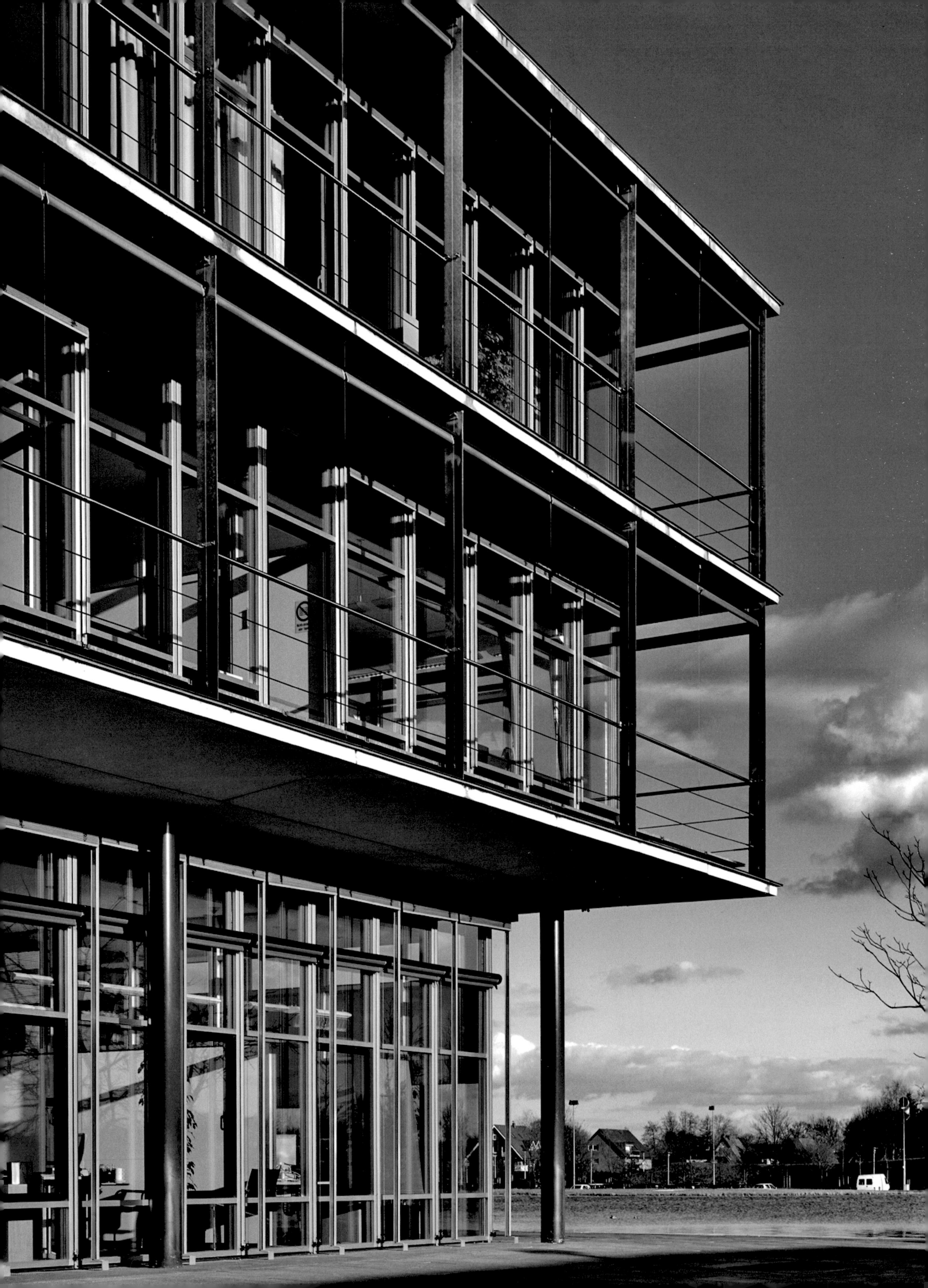

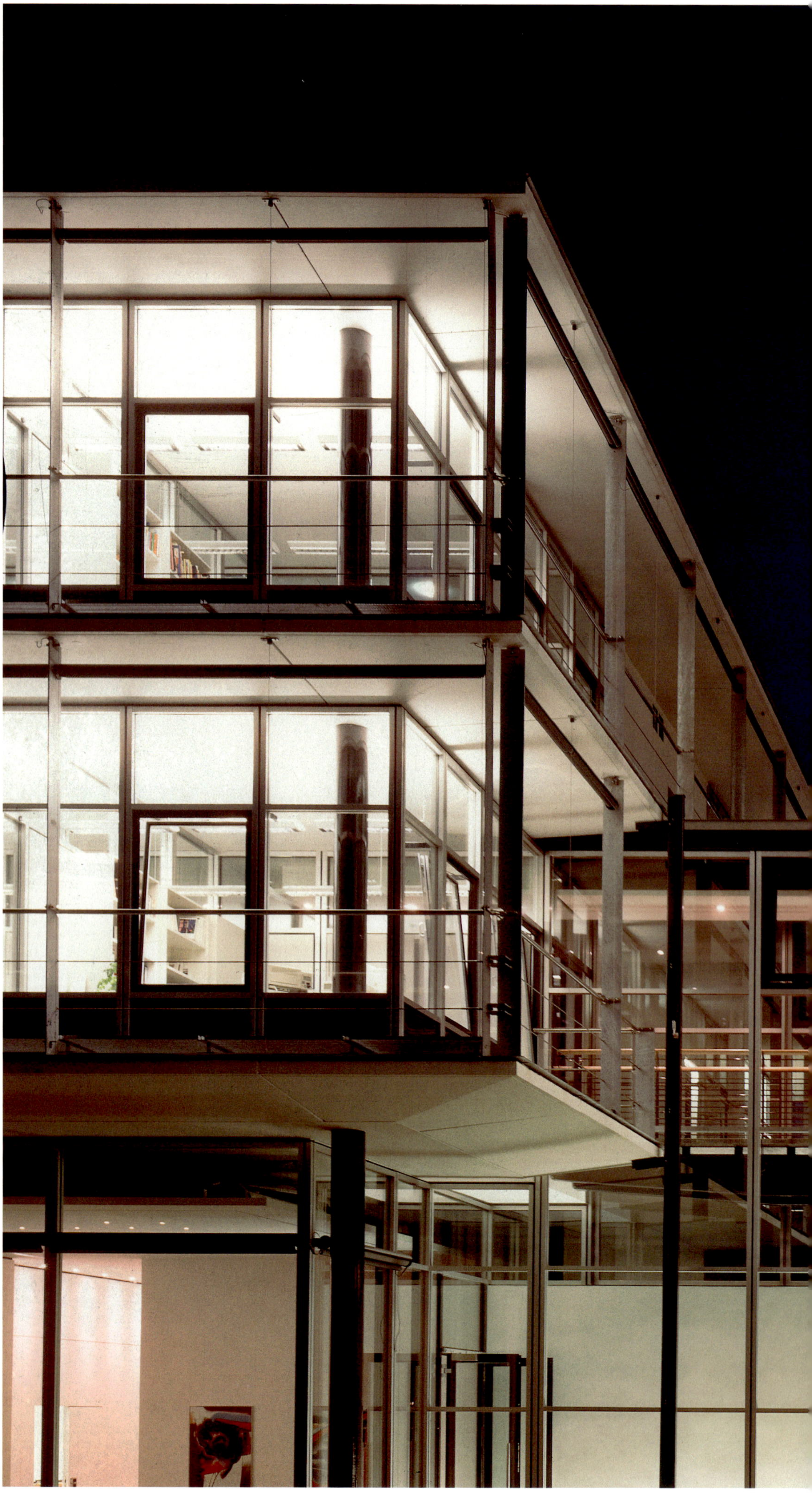

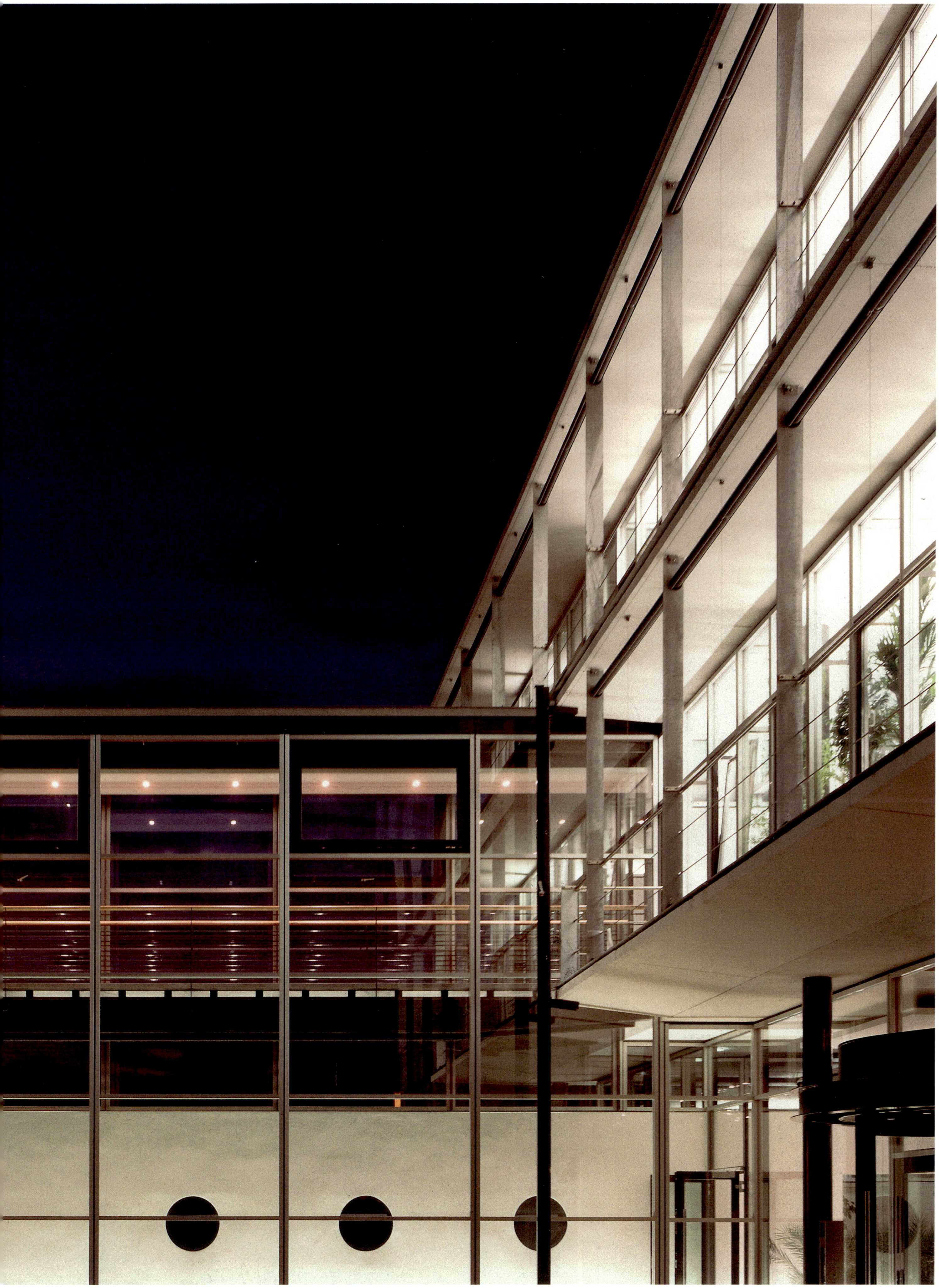

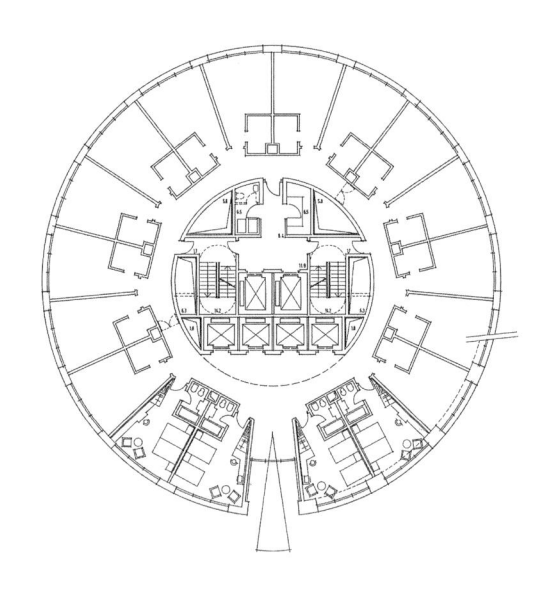

Kavaklidere Komplex, Ankara, Türkei
Kavaklidere Complex, Ankara, Turkey

1984

Entwurf Design
Volkwin Marg und Karsten Brauer

Bauherr Client
Turser A. S.

Bauzeit Construction period
1988-1991

BGF Gross floor area
96.000 m²

Das Sheraton Hotel ist in zwei Bereiche gegliedert: den Bettenturm mit Rezeption, Foyers und Restaurant als extrovertiertes Gebäude und den Flachbau mit Veranstaltungs- und Konferenzräumen, Läden, Casino, Schwimmbad und Fitnessbereich als introvertiertes Gebäude. Die zweigeschossige Eingangshalle bildet ein Bindeglied zwischen beiden Bereichen. Sie befindet sich in der Verlängerung der von der Hauptstraße heraufführenden Treppenkaskade und bildet eine Fortsetzung des öffentlichen Raumes. Zur maßstäblichen Gliederung der Turmfassaden wurden je zwei übereinander liegende Gästezimmer in einem zweigeschossigen Fensterelement zusammengefasst. Das Material der Fassade besteht aus gestrichenen Betonfertigteilen bzw. Ortbeton. Am Fuße des Turmes öffnen sich das ringförmige Foyer und die aufgrund der Hanglage ein Geschoss tiefer liegenden Restaurants in einem herausgeschobenen fächerförmigen Sockel zum Park.

The Sheraton Hotel is divided into two areas: the bedroom tower with the reception, foyers and restaurant designed as an extroverted building, and the low block with event and conference rooms, shops, casino, indoor swimming pool and fitness area conceived as an introverted building. The two-storey entrance hall functions as a link between these areas. It is located in the extension of the stair cascade leading up from the main road and forms a continuation of the public space. The combination of two guest rooms located above each other into one two-storey window element reinforces the scaled layout of the tower façade. The façade material consists of painted pre-cast concrete components or in-situ concrete. At the tower base the ring-shaped foyer and the restaurants, located one level further down on account of the hillside location, open up towards the park in a pushed out, fan-shaped socle.

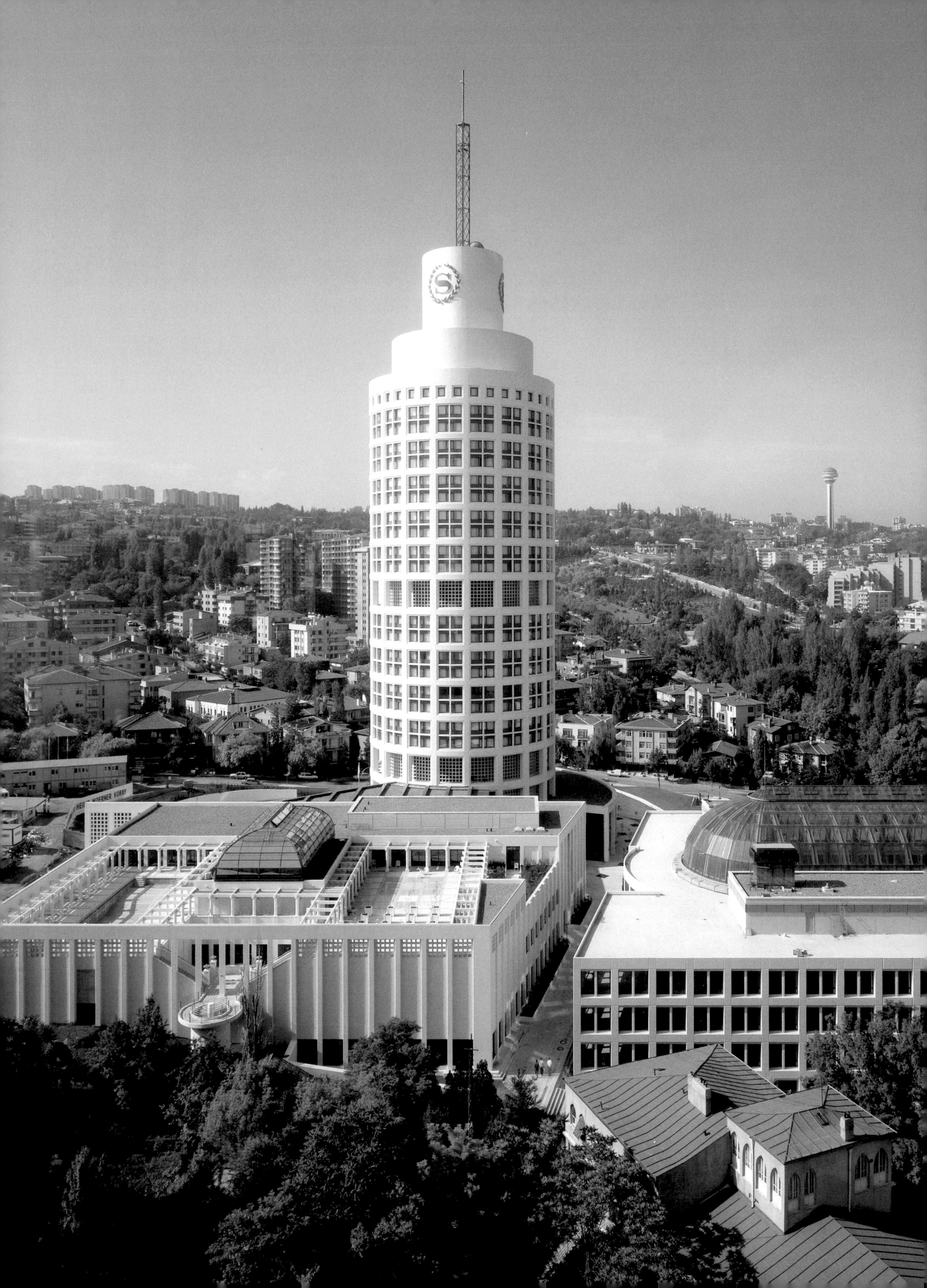

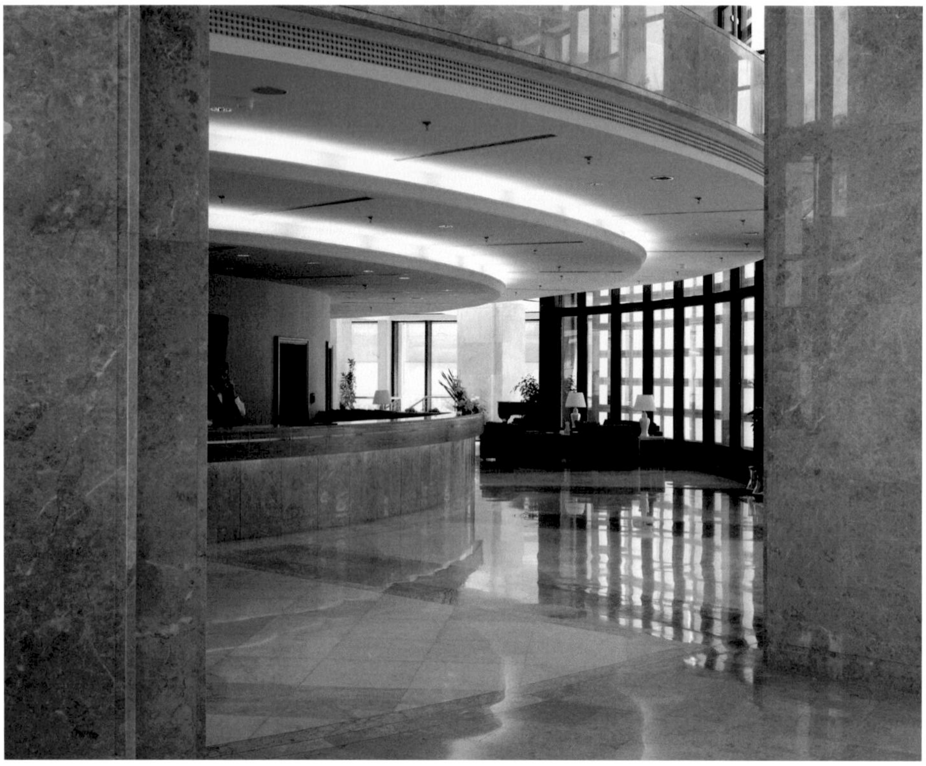

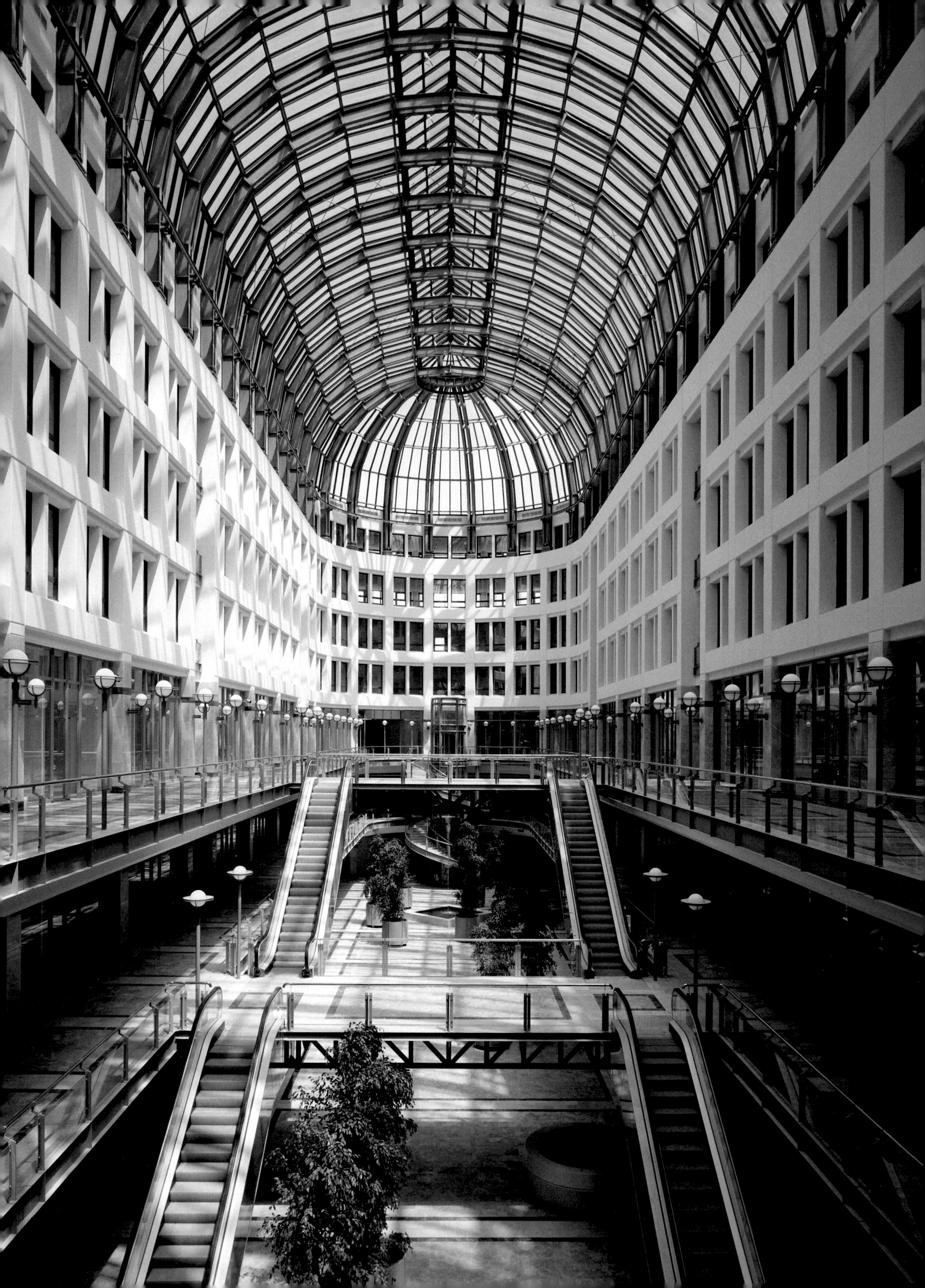

Flughafen Stuttgart, Terminal 1
Stuttgart Airport, Terminal 1

Wettbewerb Competition
1980 – 1. Preis

Entwurf Design
Meinhard von Gerkan und Karsten Brauer

Partner Partner
Klaus Staratzke

Bauherr Client
Flughafen Stuttgart GmbH

Bauzeit Construction period
1986–1991

BGF Gross floor area
36.000 m²

Die Last des Hallendaches wird über ein enges Stützenraster in die Zweige der Baumstruktur geleitet, von denen jeweils vier von einem Ast getragen werden. Zwölf Äste aus Rohrprofilen werden in einem Stamm vereinigt, der in das Fundament eingespannt ist. Die Oberlichter mittig über den Stützen sind mit Heliostaten ausgerüstet: Bewegliche Spiegel lenken dem Sonnenstand folgend das Licht auf die Kronen der Stahlbäume sowie auf die wiederum nach oben reflektierenden Bodenplatten. Die Lüftungsanlagen stehen frei im Raum. Entsprechend der linearen Aufstellung der Flugzeuge sind die Warteräume und Verbindungswege zwischen Land- und Luftseite in einem langgestreckten, als Lärmschutzwall dienenden Gebäude angeordnet. Auf der Vorfeldseite überlagern und durchdringen sich beide Baukörper. Der verglasten Südfront der Halle sind bewegliche Verschatter vorgelagert, die an Tragflächen und Landeklappen von Flugzeugen erinnern.

Force flowing from the hall's roof loads is transmitted into the twigs of the tree structure via a narrow grid of supporting members, each group of four twigs being supported by a thicker branch. Twelve tube-section branches combine to form a tree trunk, which ties into the base. The skylights directly above the supports are equipped with heliostats. Movable mirrors follow the sun and deflect sunrays onto the steel treetops and down onto the floor, from where reflectors throw the light back up. The ventilating system is a free-standing installation. Corresponding to the linear arrangements of the aircraft, the waiting halls and connecting passages are aligned in a long element, which serves as a noise barrier towards landside. On the apron side both buildings overlap and interpenetrate. The glazed south front of the hall is equipped with movable shading devices, which are reminiscent of aircraft wings and landing flaps.

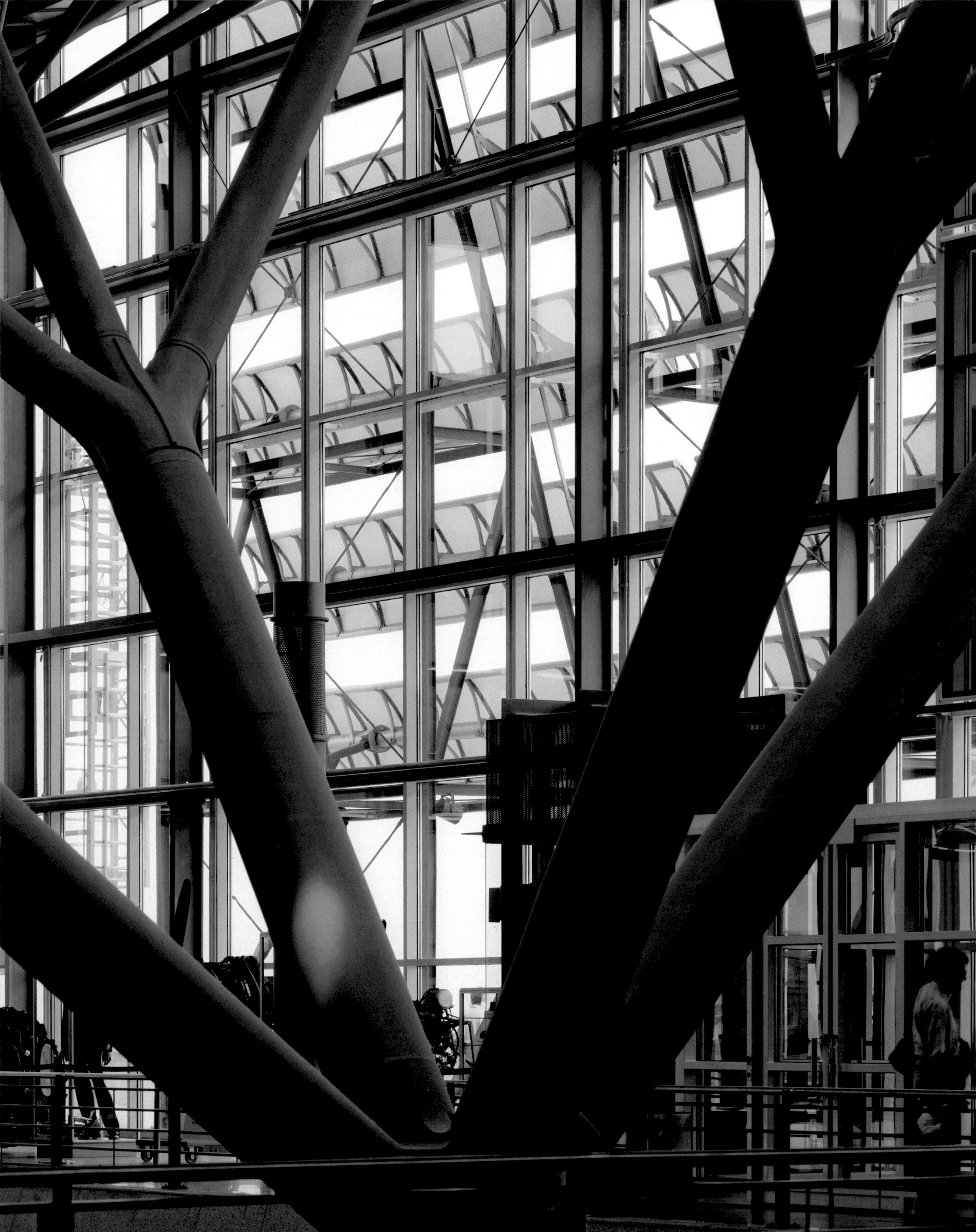

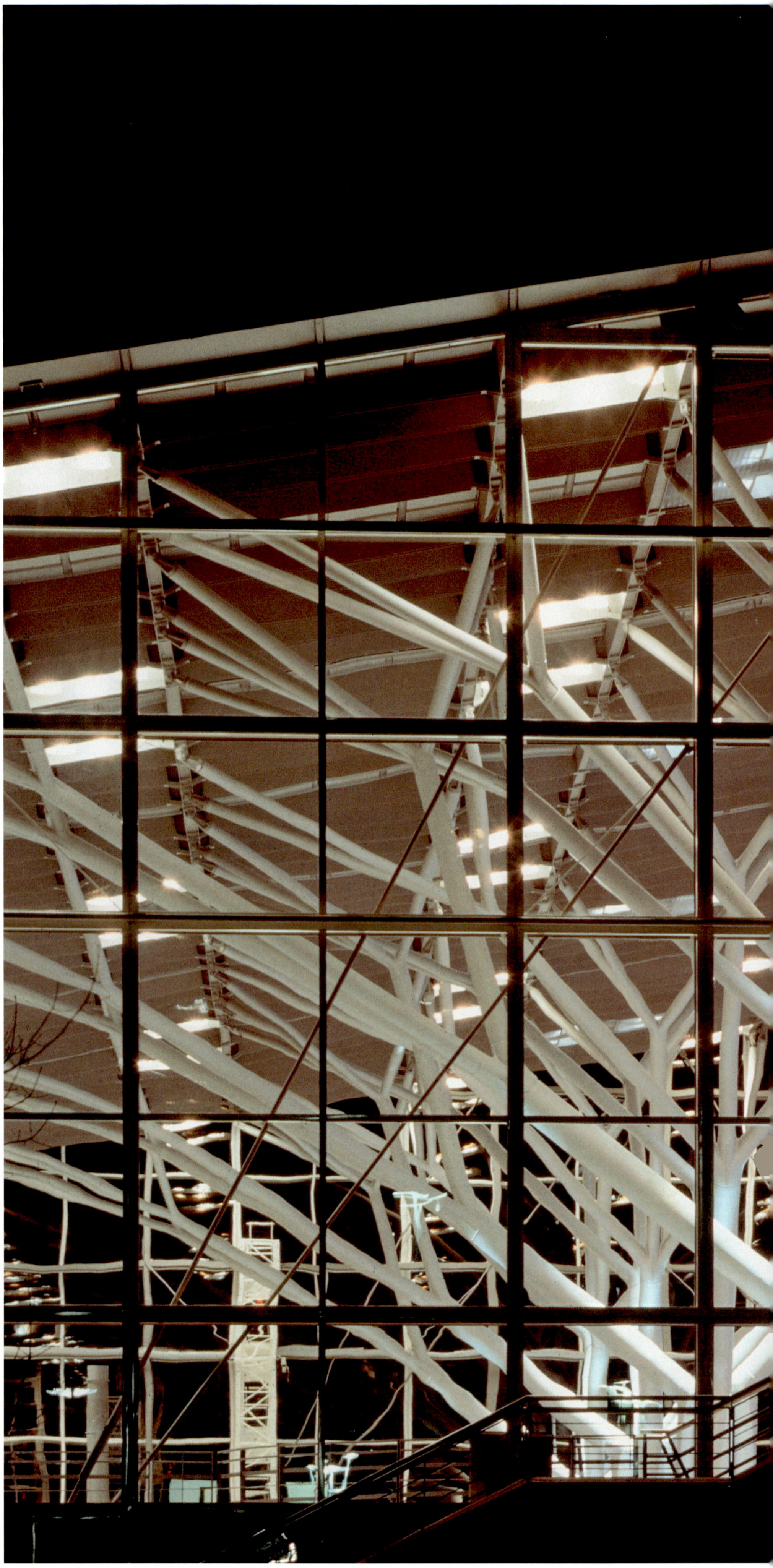

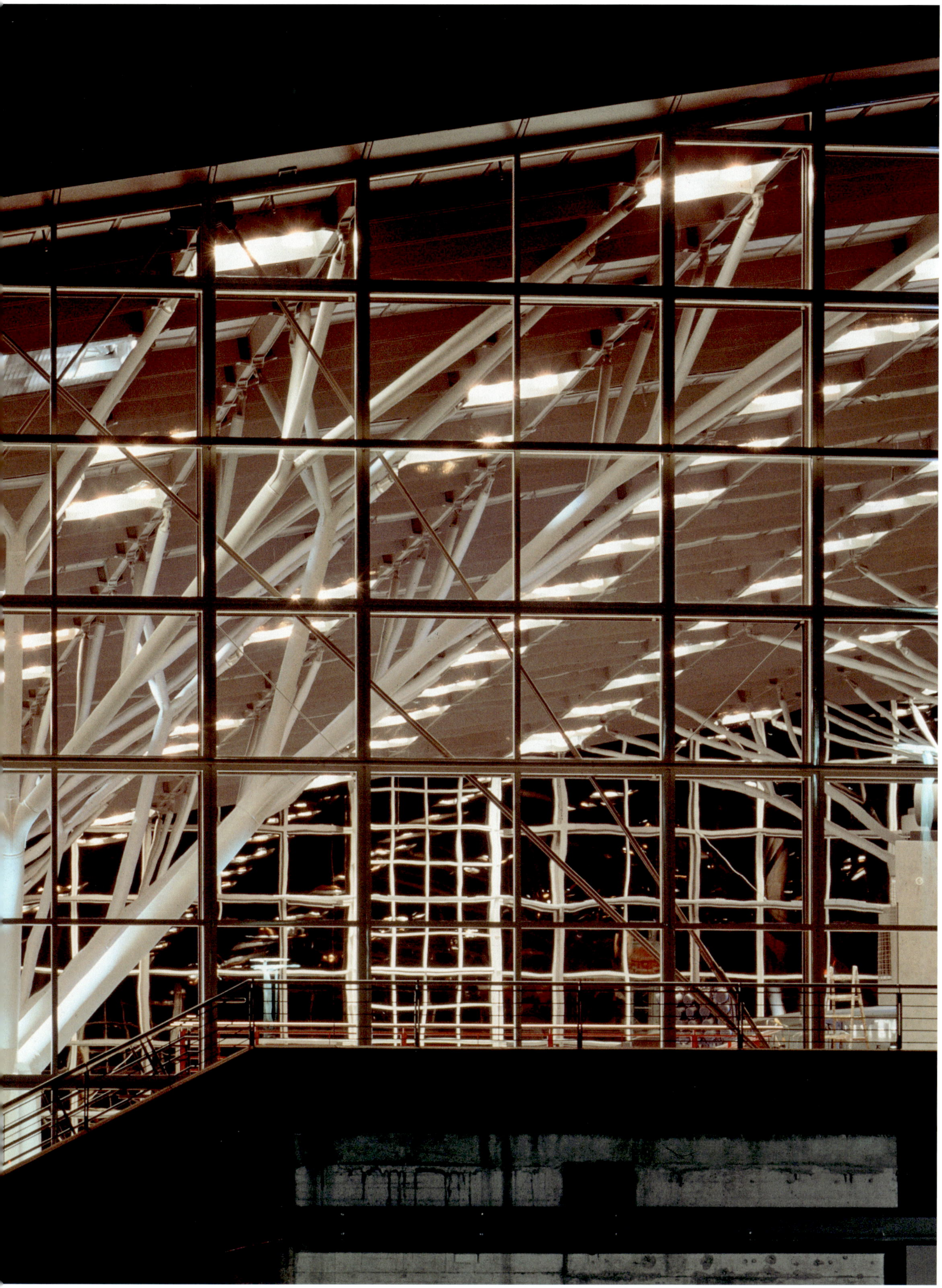

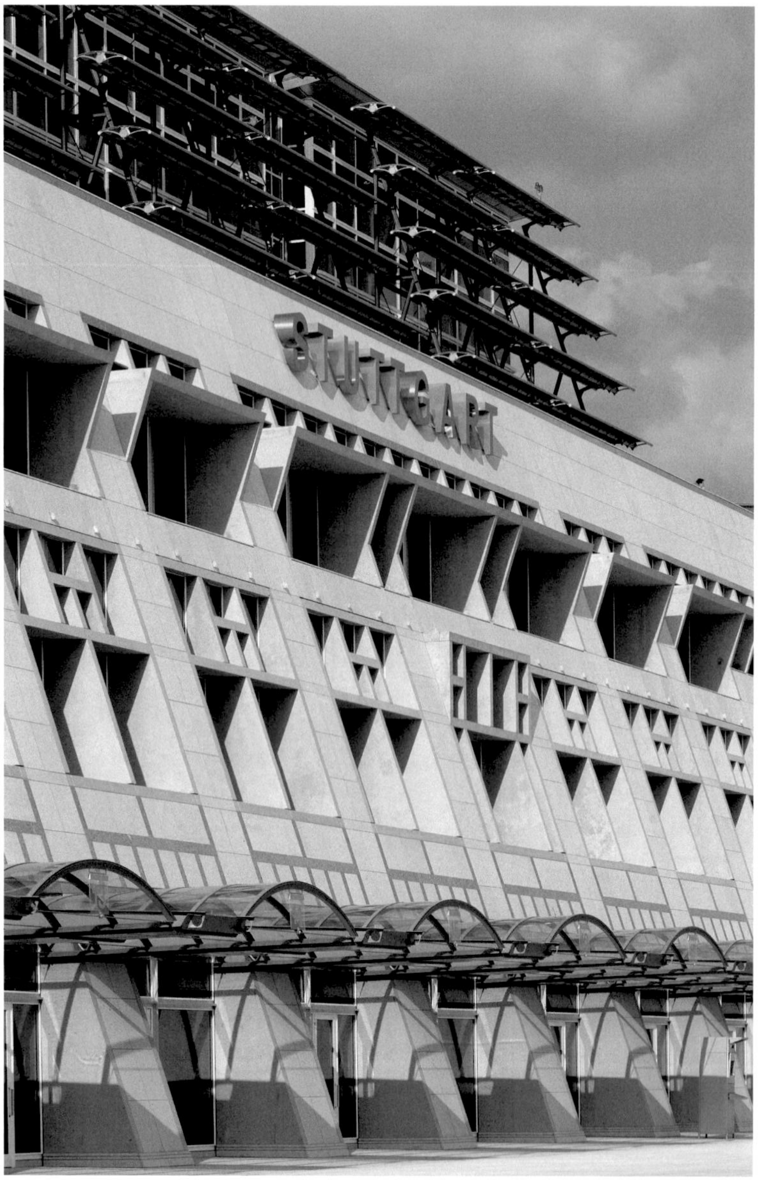
STUTTGART

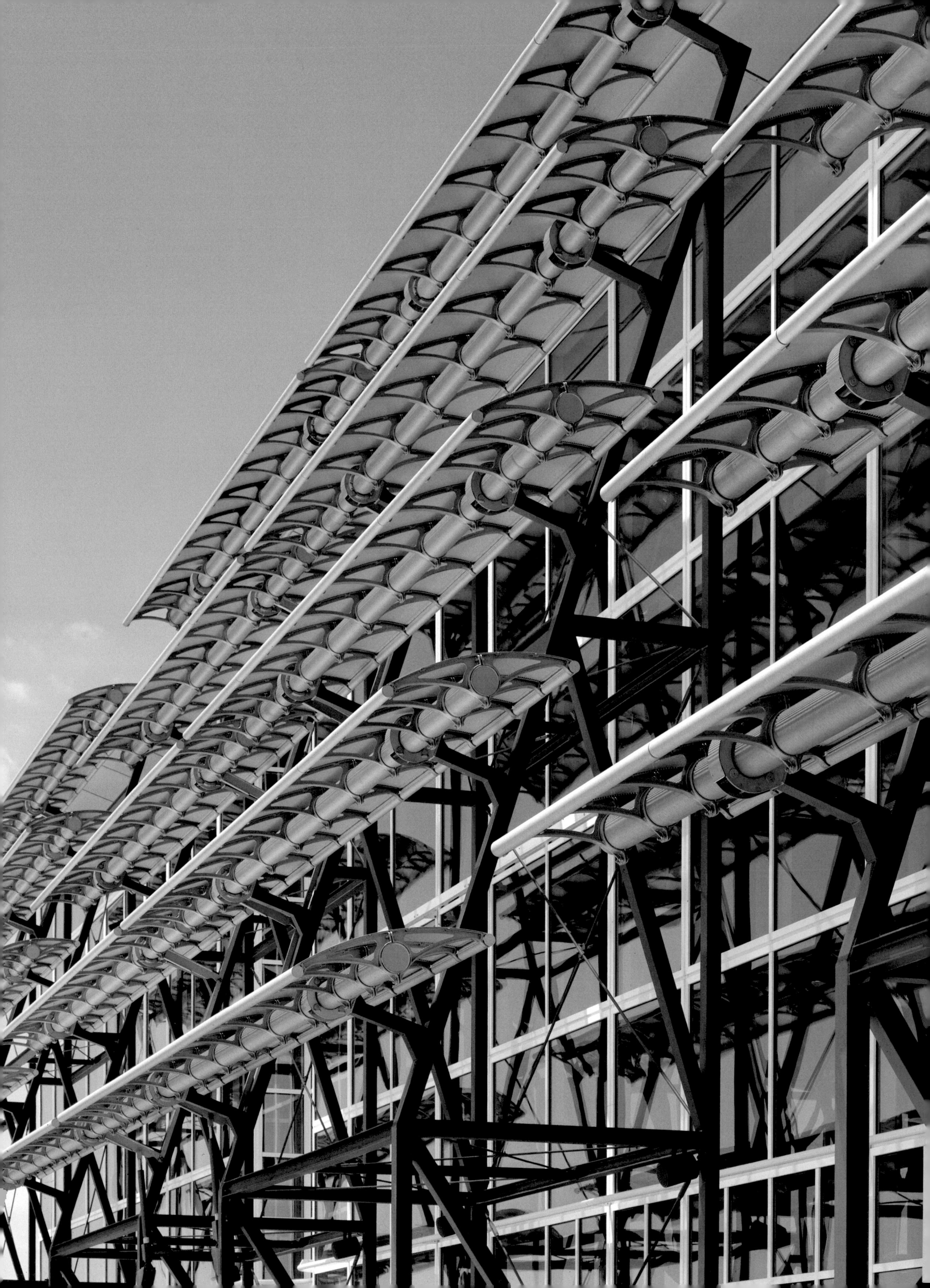

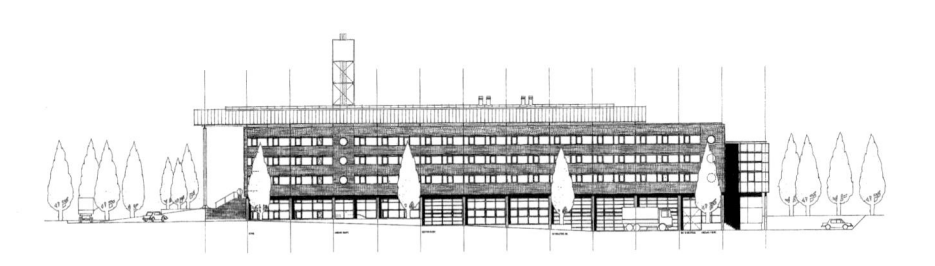

Miro-Datensysteme, Braunschweig
Miro Data Systems, Braunschweig

1990

Entwurf Design
Meinhard von Gerkan

Bauherr Client
Miro Datensysteme GmbH

Bauzeit Construction period
1990–1991

BGF Gross floor area
9.500 m²

Um eine zentrale Halle, die zugleich als Empfangs-, Ausstellungs- und Schulungsraum dient, lagern sich „Denkzellen", in denen neue Computerbausteine entwickelt, Produkte vermarktet und das Geschäft kaufmännisch organisiert wird. Die Räume sind zur gemeinsamen Mitte hin – nur durch Glaswände getrennt – offen. Produktionsstätte und Dienstleistung befinden sich unter einem Dach: Im rückwärtigen Gebäudeteil liegt die zweigeschossige Werkhalle. Im Obergeschoss flankieren die Bürozellen diesen Produktionsraum; die Flure sind als offene Galerien ausgebildet. Typologisch entspricht der Bau einer dreischiffigen Halle, deren Mittelschiff von einer Tonnenschale abgeschlossen wird, die zugleich die Empfangszone überdacht. Die Materialien – Sichtbeton, Wellblech, unverkleidete Stahlkonstruktion – entsprechen bewusst dem technischen Gestus der Nutzung.

Positioned around a central hall, which also serves as reception, exhibition, teaching and celebration area, are 'thinking cells' in which the new computer chips are developed, products marketed and the business organisation managed. The rooms – divided only by glass partitions – are open towards a common middle. Production and service are combined under the same roof: a two-storey workshop is situated in the rear of the building. The office cells on the upper level surround these production areas. The corridors are designed as open galleries. Typologically, the building is a three-aisled hall, with the middle aisle having a barrel roof, which at the same time covers the projecting entrance foyer. The materials – exposed concrete, corrugated metal cladding, raw steel structure – correspond to the technical nature of the building.

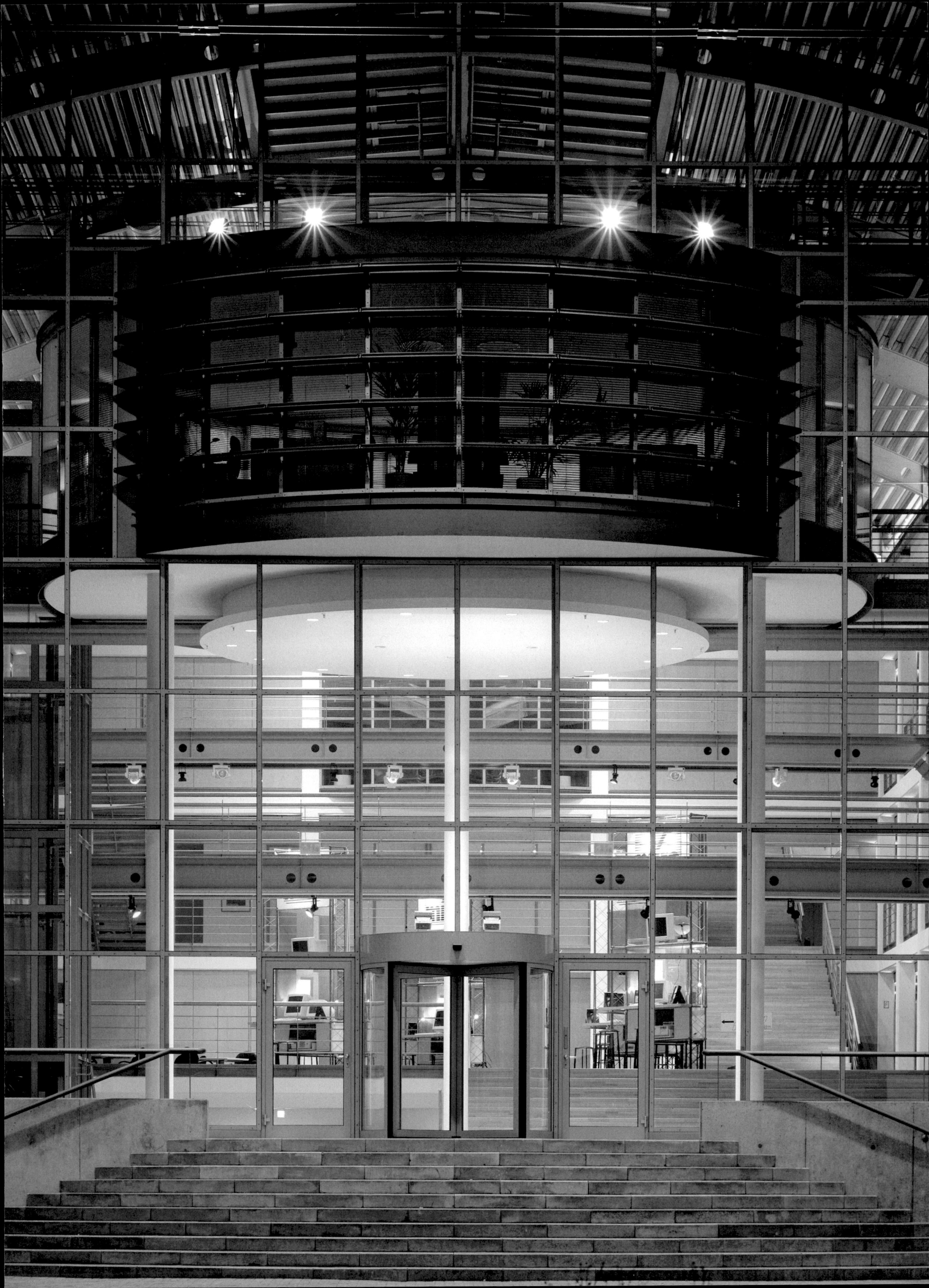

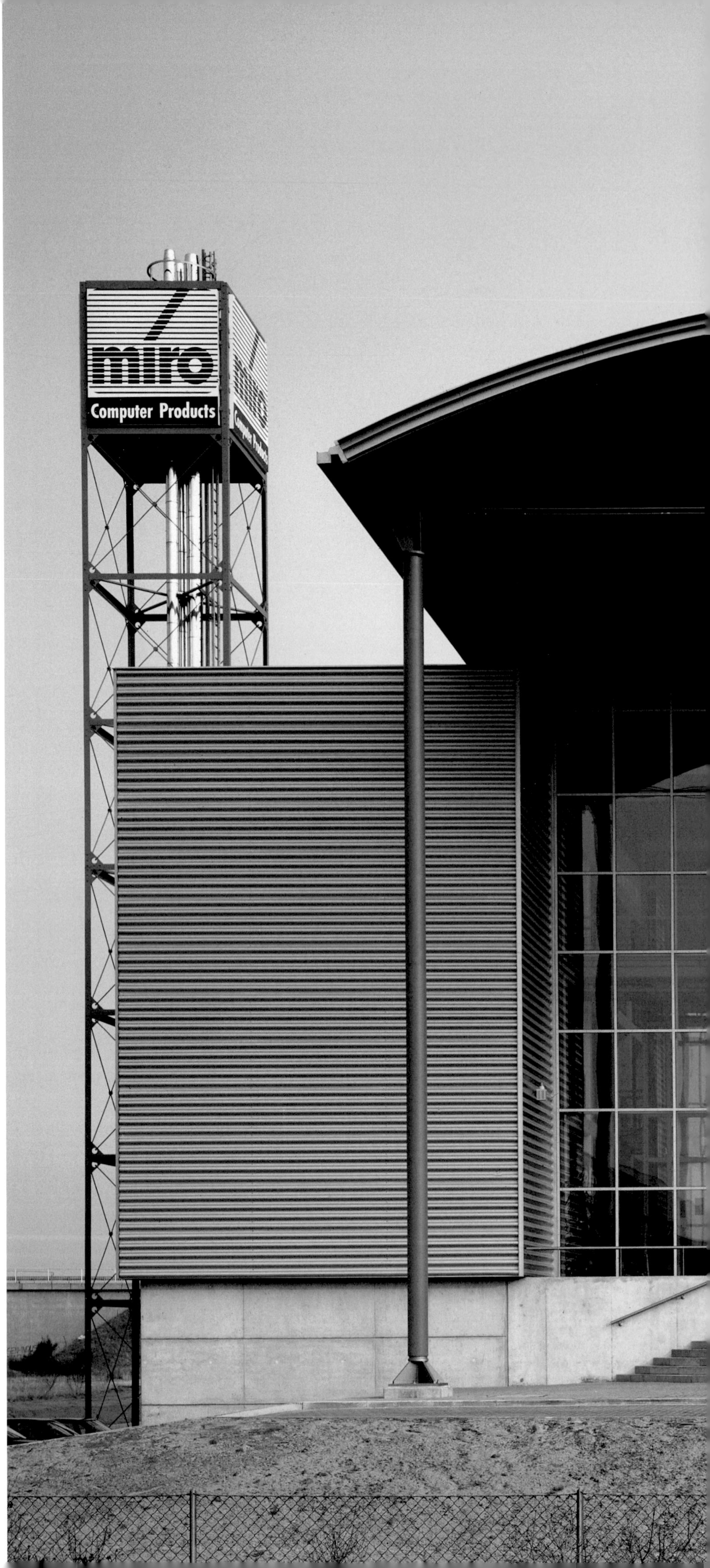
miro
Computer Products

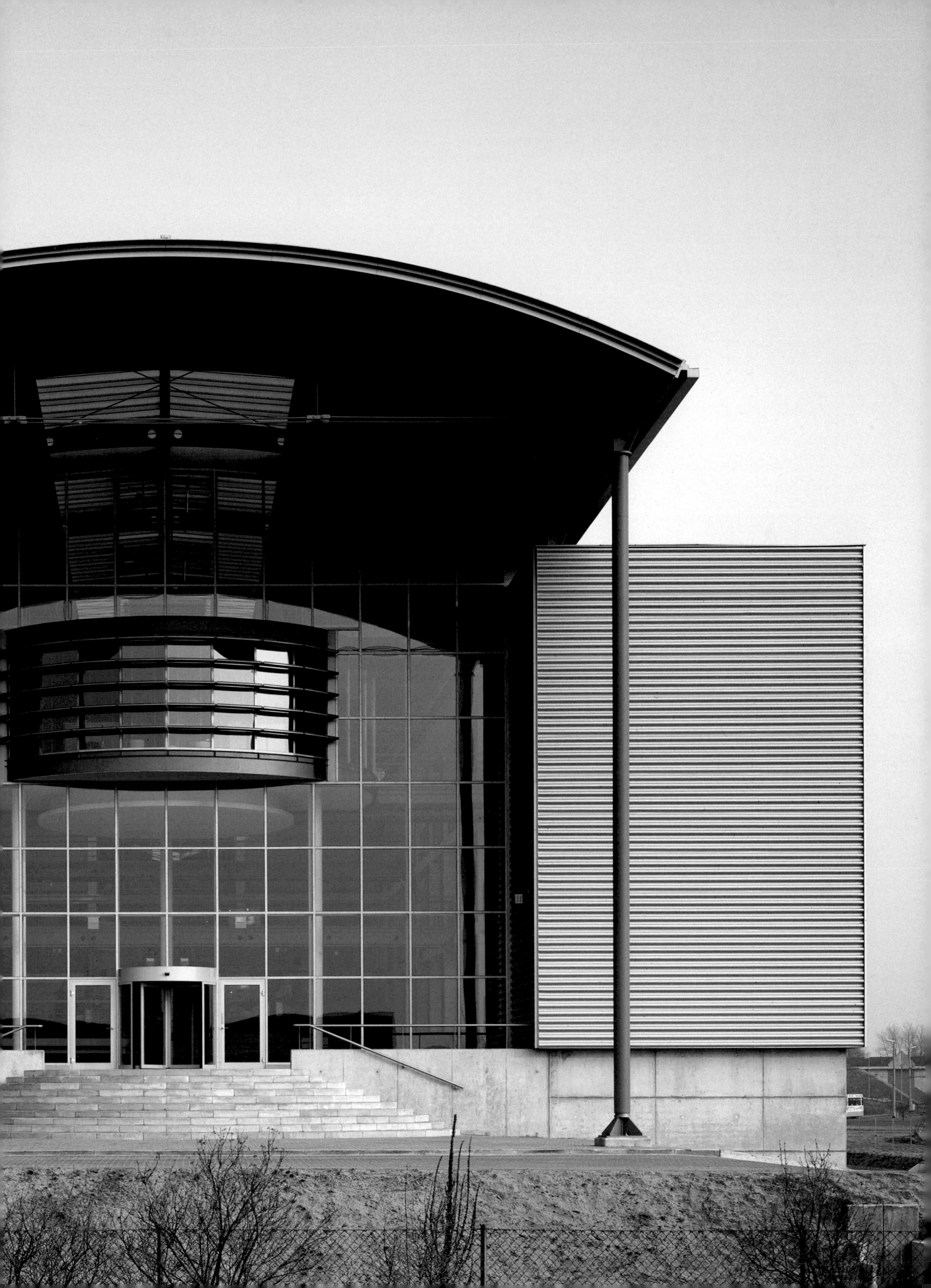

1992

Wohnhaus von Gerkan, Elbchaussee 139, Hamburg

Der würfelförmige Baukörper des Wohnhauses zeigt sich zur Straßen- und Stadtseite als eine überwiegend geschlossene „Kiste", deren Einfachheit durch eine Holzverkleidung aus Sibirischer Lärche betont wird. Nach Süden mit Ausblick auf Elbe und Hafen ist das Haus fast komplett verglast.

von Gerkan Residence, Elbchaussee 139, Hamburg

The cube-shaped residential building presents itself towards the street and city as a primarily solid 'box', its simplicity being emphasized by Siberian larch timber cladding. Towards the south the house is almost entirely glazed, offering a generous view over the Elbe and the harbour.

Jumbohalle der Deutschen Lufthansa, Hamburg

Die Jumbohalle auf dem Hamburger Flughafen dient der Deutschen Lufthansa zur Wartung ihrer Großraumflugzeuge vom Typ Boeing 747 und Airbus. Ein stählerner, 175 Meter langer Tragbogen überspannt wie bei einer Brückenkonstruktion die ca. 12.000 m² große, stützenfreie Halle.

Deutsche Lufthansa Jumbo-Jet Hall, Hamburg

Deutsche Lufthansa uses the jumbo-jet hall at Hamburg Airport for the maintenance of wide-bodied aircrafts of the types Boeing 747 and Airbus. Comparable to a bridge construction, a 175-metre steel subarch spans the approximately 12,000 m² large, column-free hall.

Salamander-Haus, Berlin

Das Büro- und Geschäftshaus des Schuhhauses Salamander befindet sich an einer belebten Tauentzien-Kreuzung im Stadtteil Charlottenburg. Besonderes Merkmal des Gebäudes ist die vertikal strukturierte, zweischalige Glasfassade, die sich in den unteren beiden Geschossen in einen Arkadengang auflöst.

Salamander House, Berlin

The office and commercial building of the Salamander shoe company is located at a busy intersection in Berlin's Charlottenburg district. The special characteristic of the building at the Tauentzien crossing is the vertically structured, double-skin glass façade, which turns into an arcade on the first two floors.

S-Bahnhof, Flughafen Stuttgart

Der unterirdische Bahnhof am Stuttgarter Flughafen ist nach dem Prinzip des Röhrenschildvortriebs gestaltet, d.h. die Bahnsteige präsentieren sich in Form einer Röhre, Wände und Decken sind gebogen und gehen ineinander über. Diese Form wird durch die lineare Ausleuchtung zusätzlich betont.

Suburban Railway Station, Stuttgart Airport

The platforms of the underground station at Stuttgart Airport are laid out like a tube, with curved walls and ceilings merging into each other. This form is additionally emphasized by the linear illumination.

Wohnhaus von Gerkan, Elbchaussee 139, Hamburg
von Gerkan Residence, Elbchaussee 139, Hamburg

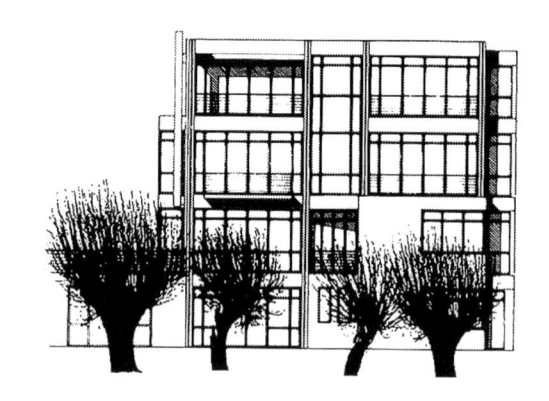

1986

Entwurf Design
Meinhard von Gerkan

Bauherr Client
Meinhard von Gerkan

Bauzeit Construction period
1987–1992

BGF Gross floor area
480 m²

Das Wohnhaus mit 12 m Kantenlänge und 12 m Bauhöhe steht parallel zur östlichen Grundstücksgrenze und ist somit gegenüber der Ausrichtung der anderen Bauten leicht gedreht. Der rechtwinklige Grundriss, in dessen Mitte eine elliptische Treppe alle vier Geschosse miteinander verbindet, basiert auf einem Raster von 1,20 m. Der Haupteingang im 1. Obergeschoss wird über eine lange, einläufige Treppe erreicht, die von der Garage über das Platzniveau zum Wohnhaus führt. Ein zweiter Eingang liegt in den Baukörper eingeschnitten auf dem Vorplatz. Die Einliegerwohnung, das Gästeappartement sowie der Kinderbereich können von hier separat erreicht werden. Im Staffelgeschoss ist aus dem kubischen Baukörper eine große Terrasse herausgeschnitten, die Kanten des Würfels bleiben jedoch durch Konstruktionsprofile betont. Alle Einbauten sowie der größte Teil der Möbel wurden von Meinhard von Gerkan entworfen.

This private residence – 12 m long and 12 m high – is placed parallel to the eastern property border and therefore stands at a slight angle to the other gmp buildings. The orthogonal floor plans, with a central elliptical staircase interconnecting all four levels, are based on a grid of 1.2 m. The main entrance on the first upper floor is accessed via a long single-flight stairway that leads from the garage to the forecourt level and up to the house. A second, recessed entrance gives direct access, from the forecourt, to a small separate flat, the guest apartment and the children's rooms. One storey is stepped back because a large terrace has been cut out of the building volume, while the cube edges are retraced by means of structural profiles. All the fitted interior elements, as well as most of the furniture, were built to designs by Meinhard von Gerkan.

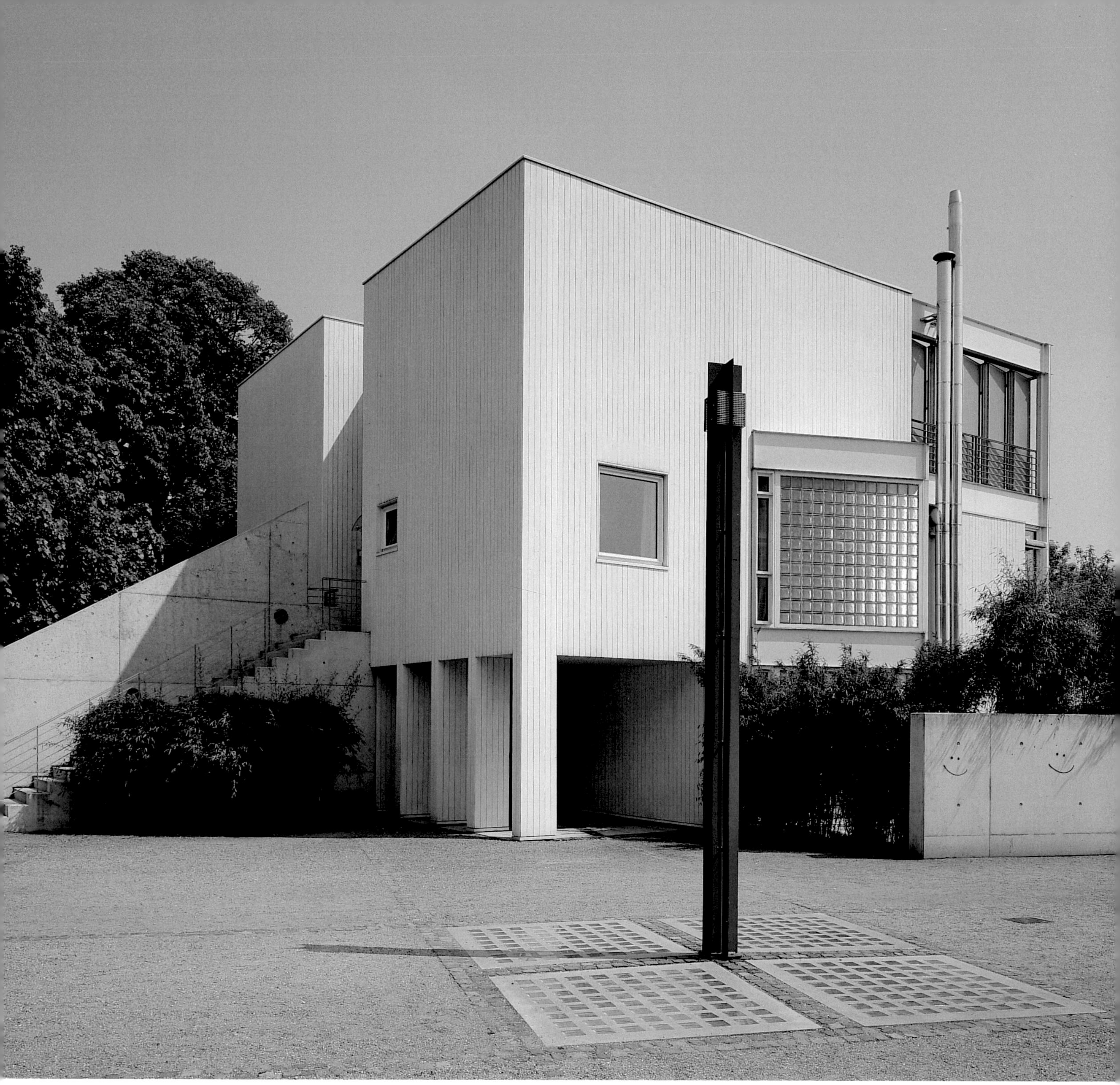

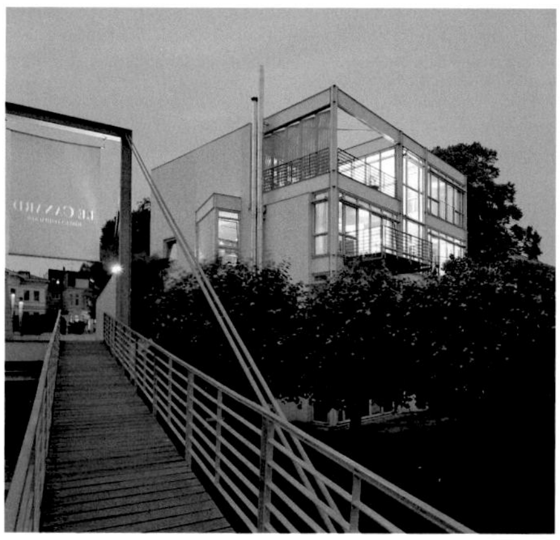

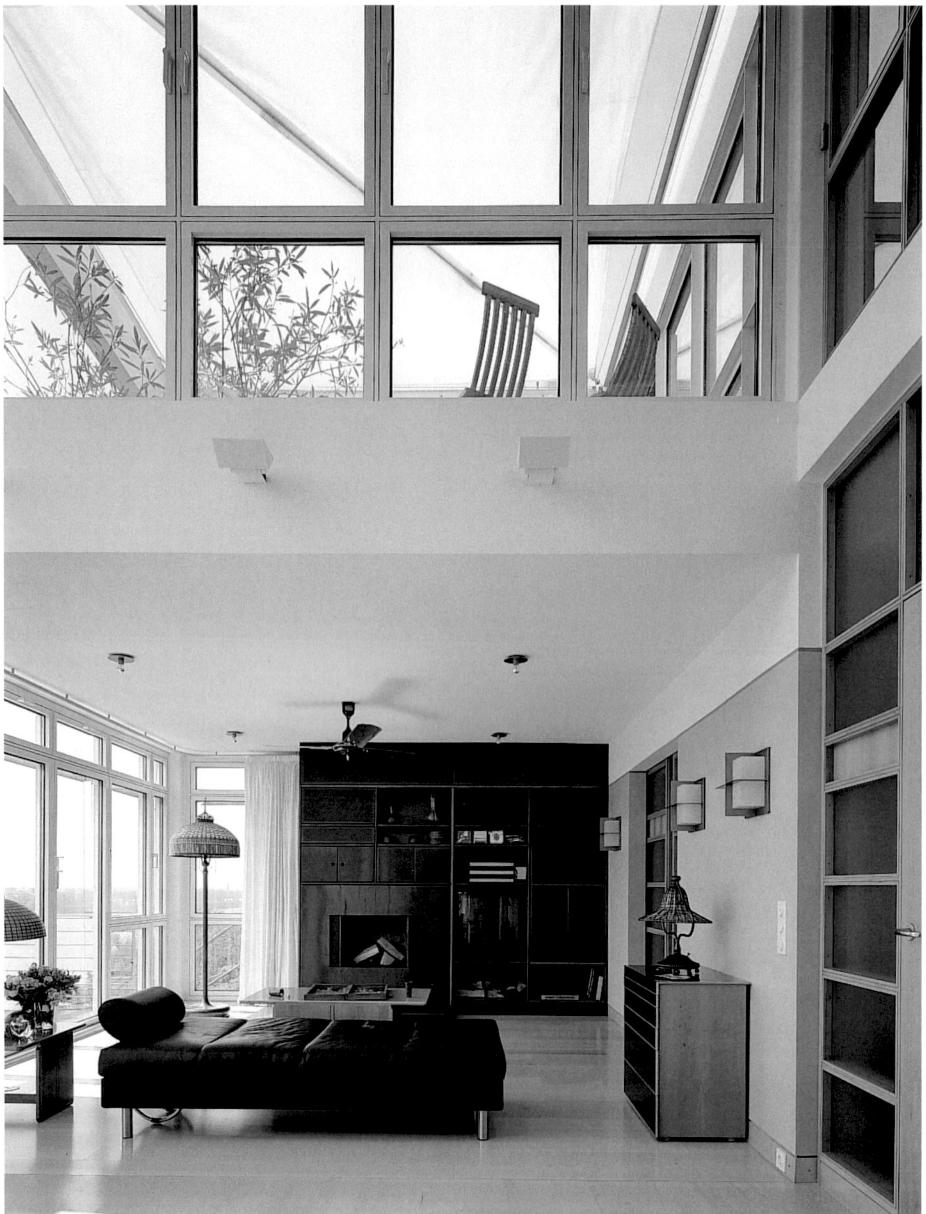

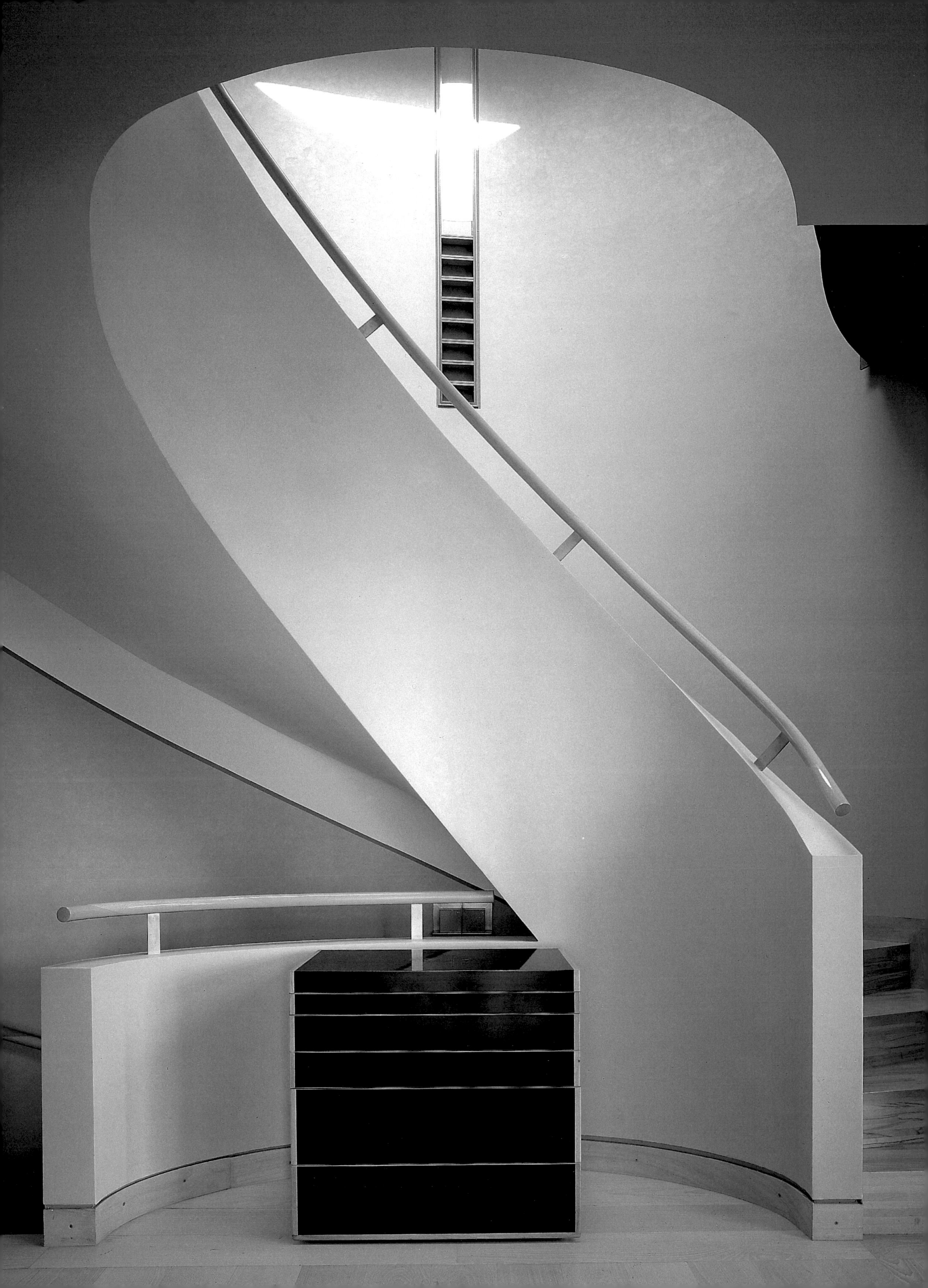

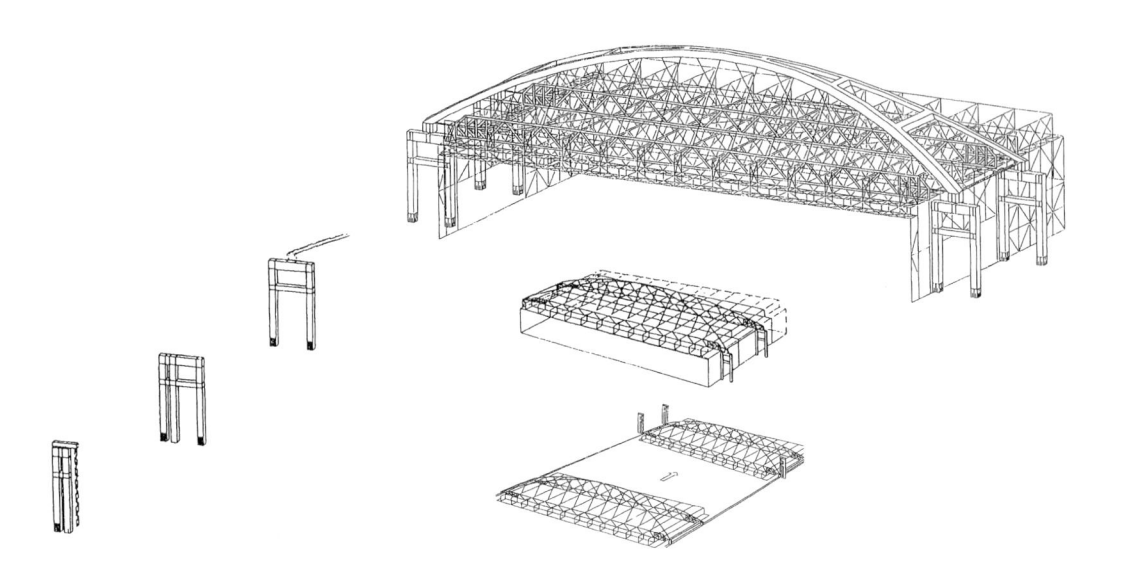

Jumbohalle der Deutschen Lufthansa, Hamburg
Deutsche Lufthansa Jumbo-Jet Hall, Hamburg

Gutachterliche Studie Consultancy
1986

Entwurf Design
Meinhard von Gerkan und Karsten Brauer

Partner Partner
Klaus Staratzke

Bauherr Client
Hamburger Gesellschaft für Fluganlagen mbH

Bauzeit Construction period
1989–1992

BGF Halle Gross floor area hall
18.000 m²

BGF Betriebstrakt Gross floor area workshops
13.000 m²

Unübersehbar ist die am Südrand des Flughafengeländes gelegene Wartungshalle. Der Hallenraum ist 150 m lang, 81 m tief und hat eine lichte Höhe von 26 m. Er ermöglicht das gleichzeitige Arbeiten an zwei Jumbojets und einem Airbus. Um diese gewaltige Halle stützenfrei zu überdachen, bildet ein 175 m weit gespannter, aus zwei gegeneinander geneigten Einzelbögen bestehender Tragbogen das Primärtragwerk. An diesem Bogen, der seine Last auf zwei Betonkonstruktionen seitlich der Halle abträgt, hängt das gesamte Hallendach. Die Bogenform gleicht einer großen Hängebrücke und bestimmt das Erscheinungsbild der Halle, während die Außenwände mit einer silbergrauen Metallfassade verkleidet sind. Die Hallentore sind bei einer Gesamtlänge von 150 m und einer Höhe von 22 m vollständig verglast und erlauben als überdimensioniertes „Schaufenster" den im Flugzeug vorbeirollenden Passagieren einen Einblick in die Großwerkstatt.

The maintenance hangar on the southern side of the airport cannot be missed. With its hangar space 150 m long, 81 m deep and a clear working height of 26 m, two jumbo jets and an Airbus can be dealt with simultaneously. In order to provide a column-free gigantic hall, a primary structural system was created by two bows leaning against one another with a total span of 175 m. The whole roof hangs on these bows, the main load being transferred to two buttress constructions at the side of the hangar. The arch form is similar to a large suspension bridge and determines the appearance of the new hall, while the façades are covered with a silver-grey metal cladding. The hangar doors, with a total length of 150 m and height of 22 m, are fully glazed. This gigantic 'window' allows passengers rolling past in an aircraft to look inside the massive workshop.

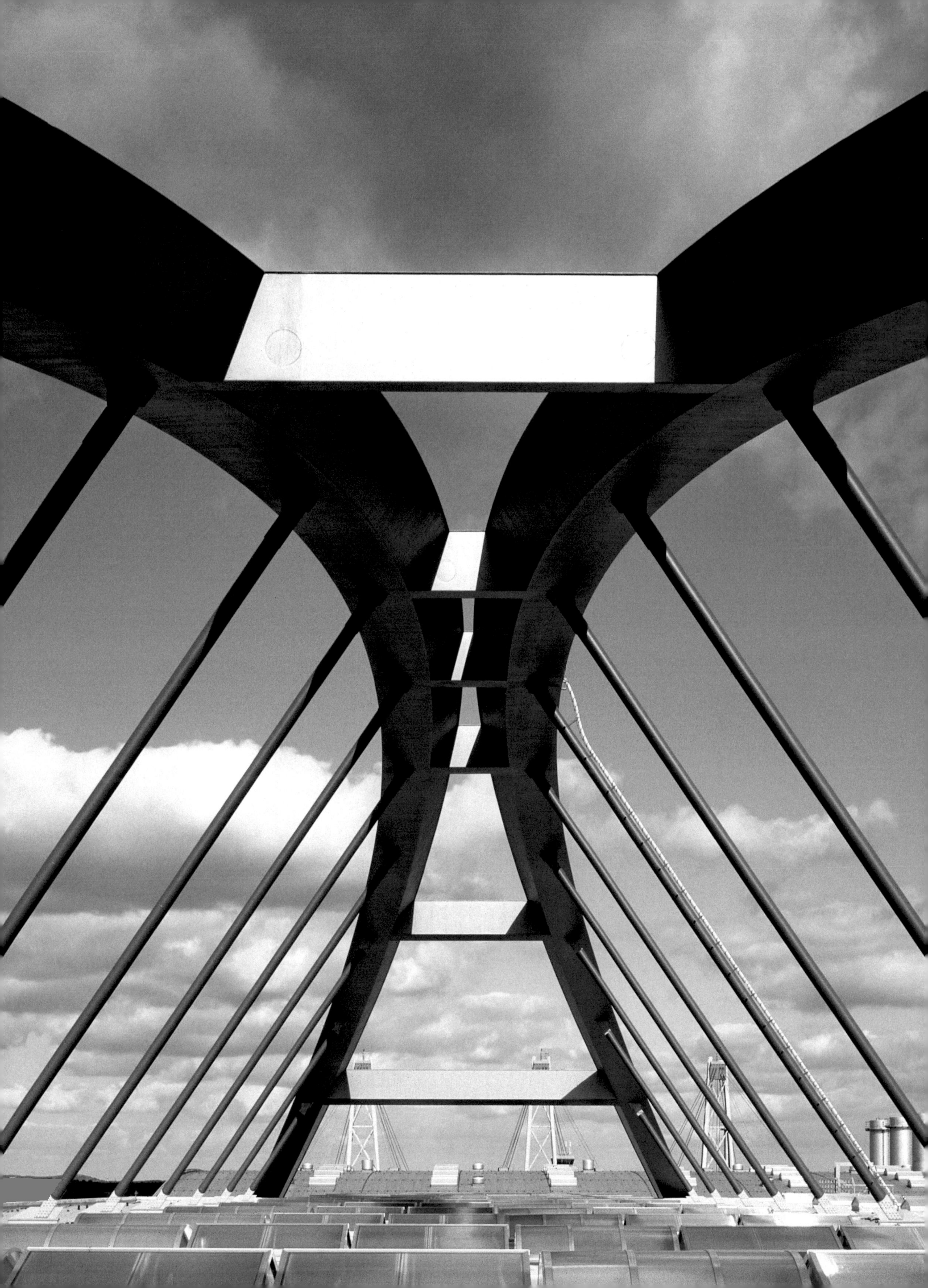

Lufthansa Technik

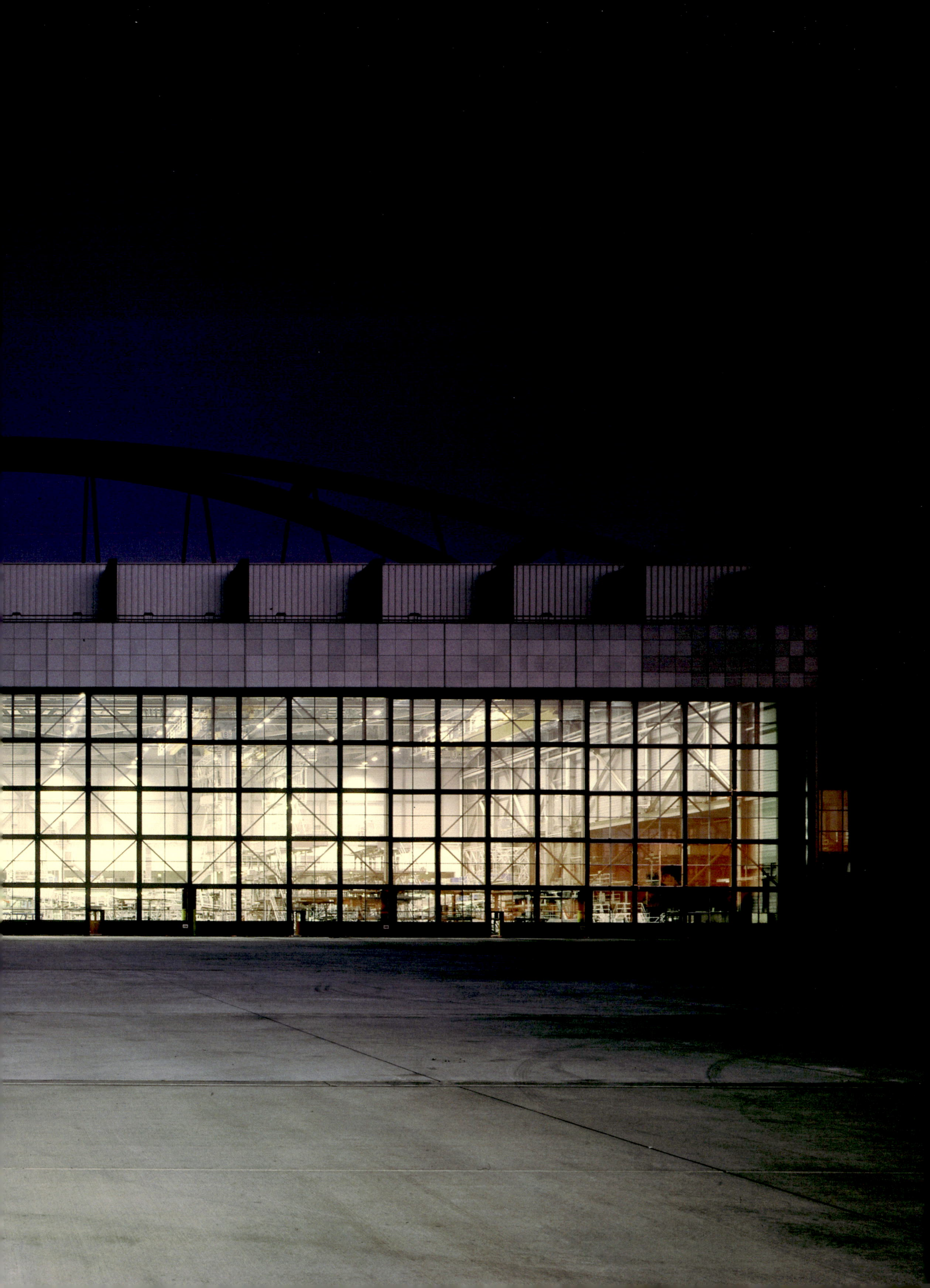

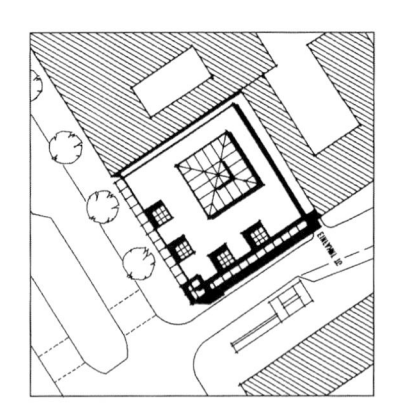

Salamander-Haus, Berlin
Salamander House, Berlin

Gutachten Consultancy
1988 – 1. Rang

Entwurf Design
Volkwin Marg

Bauherr Client
Salamander AG

Bauzeit Construction period
1990–1992

BGF Gross floor area
8.800 m²

Die doppelschalige Fassade umgibt das Gebäude mit ihrer äußeren Glasebene wie eine „zweite Haut". Diese begrünte und bei Nacht hell erleuchtete Wintergartenfassade ist zugleich gestalt- und identitätsprägend. Die Straßenecke wird durch einen „Werbeturm" im Fassadenraster akzentuiert. Die transparenten zweigeschossigen Ladenfronten mit zurückgesetzten Galerien im Obergeschoss sind als Arkaden ausgebildet. Im Innern des Hauses befindet sich ein öffentlich zugänglicher Brunnenhof, der von einem pyramidenförmigen Glasdach überdeckt wird. Alle Büros sind optimal belichtet sowie natürlich be- und entlüftbar. Sie orientieren sich zum begrünten Wintergarten der Außenfassade bzw. zum inneren Brunnenhof. Der Wintergarten bewirkt nicht nur eine freundliche Atmosphäre, sondern dient zugleich als Kälte- und Schallpuffer zur belebten Tauentzienstraße.

The double-skin façade surrounds the building with its outer glass layer like a 'second skin'. This greened and at night brightly lit winter garden façade, is both design and identity. The street corner is landmarked by an 'advertising tower' in the grid of the façade. The transparent double-storey shop fronts with recessed galleries on the upper level are developed as arcades. The interior of the complex has a glazed public court with fountain, covered by a pyramid-shaped glass roof. All offices are well lit, naturally ventilated and orientated to the green winter garden or the interior fountain court. The winter garden not only creates a friendly atmosphere but also serves as a thermal and acoustic buffer to the lively Tauentzienstrasse.

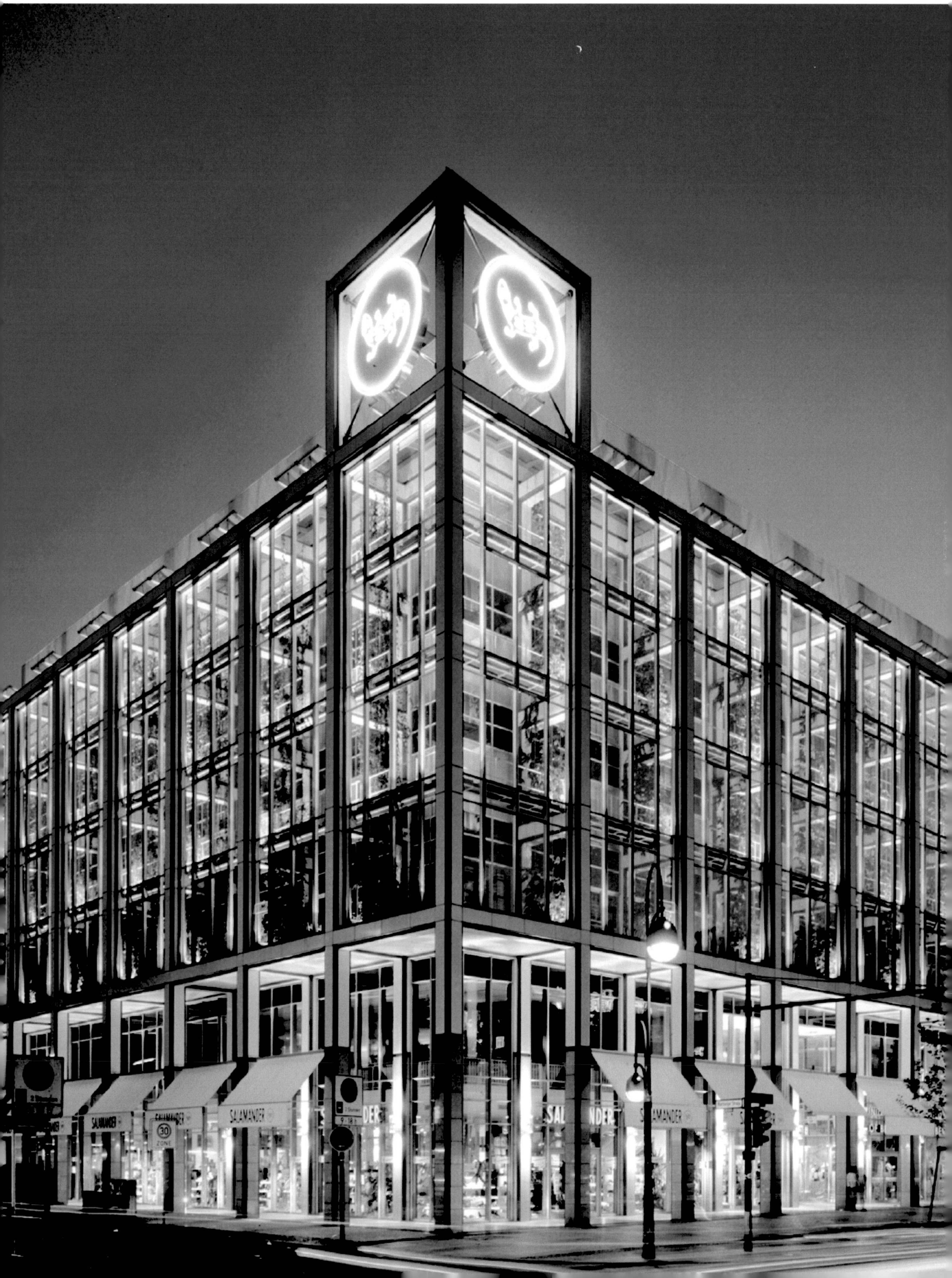
SALAMANDER
30
ZONE

S-Bahnhof, Flughafen Stuttgart
Suburban Railway Station, Stuttgart Airport

1989

Entwurf Design
Meinhard von Gerkan und Klaus Staratzke

Bauherr Client
Deutsche Bahn AG

Bauzeit Construction period
1991-1992

Von der Stuttgarter Innenstadt erreicht man den relativ weit außerhalb gelegenen Flughafen bequem mit der S-Bahn. Der unterirdische Bahnhof präsentiert sich in Form einer Röhre: Die gebogenen Wand- und Deckenflächen gehen ineinander über, während die Gleisanlagen sowie deren Wände und Decken weitgehend im Dunkeln verbleiben. Die Decke über dem Bahnsteig schließt mit einem Leuchtenband ab, das durch seine lineare Anordnung die Röhrenform des Bahnhofs unterstreicht. Wände und Decken sind mit Edelstahl verkleidet und reflektieren das Licht unterschiedlich, je nachdem ob sich gerade ein Zug am Bahnsteig befindet. Die Fußböden bestehen aus Granit. Runde Pfeiler sorgen für eine räumliche Zonierung des Bahnsteigs, während Mittelstützen die Axialität betonen. Der Bereich des kopfseitigen Eingangs wird durch die in Boden und Decken gleichermaßen aufgenommene Kreisgeometrie akzentuiert.

Stuttgart airport, located relatively far from the city centre, can be comfortably reached from downtown Stuttgart by the suburban railway. The underground station is tube-shaped: the curved wall and ceiling surfaces merge into one another, whilst the train tracks and their walls primarily remain in the dark. The ceiling above the platform is terminated with a luminous row, its linear arrangement emphasizing the tubular shape of the station. Walls and ceilings are clad in stainless steel and reflect the light in various ways, depending on whether a train is presently stopping in the station. The floors are made of granite. Round columns form a spatial zoning of the platform, whilst central columns reinforce the axial character. A circular geometry on the floor and ceilings emphasizes the area of the primary entrance.

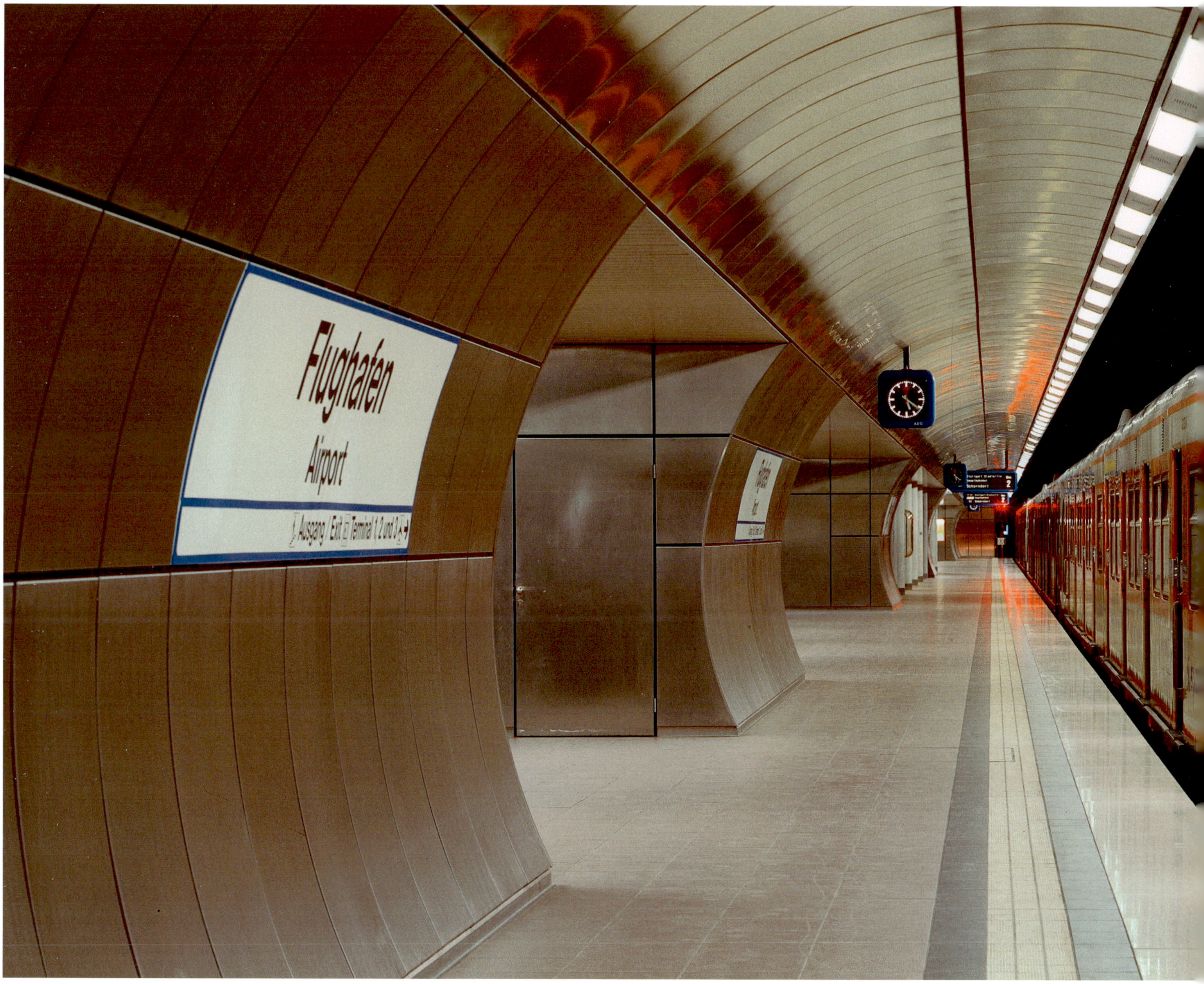
Flughafen
Airport
Ausgang / Exit Terminal 1, 2 und 3

1993

Zürich-Haus, Hamburg

Das Bürogebäude der Zürich Versicherungsgesellschaft führt die architektonische Tradition des frühen hamburgischen Kontorhauses sowohl in der Zonierung als auch in den verwendeten Materialien fort. Introvertierte Lichthöfe werden vermieden und von allen Büros genießt man den Ausblick auf die Stadt.

Zürich House, Hamburg

The office building of the Zürich insurance company continues the architectural tradition of the former Hamburg Kontorhaus both in terms of zoning and materials. Introverted light wells are avoided and a view of the city can be enjoyed from all offices.

Steigenberger-Hotel, Fleetinsel, Hamburg

Zwei- bis dreigeschossige Arkaden bilden die Sockelzonen des Gebäudes, während die über die durchschnittliche Blockhöhe hinausragenden Geschosse, in Anlehnung an die Bautradition der Schumacherzeit, gestaffelt sind. Mauerwerkslisenen gliedern den Baukörper vertikal im Rhythmus der Arkadenstützen.

Steigenberger Hotel, Fleetinsel, Hamburg

Two- to three-storey arcades form the building's socle zones, whilst the staggered storeys protruding above the average block height are a reference to the architectural tradition of the Schumacher period. Masonry lesenes vertically divide the building in the rhythm of the arcade columns.

Arbeitsamt Oldenburg

Ein viertelkreisförmiger Baublock, der sich um einen Innenhof herumlegt, folgt der Wasserlinie und bildet auf der dem Wasser abgewandten Seite einen gebogenen Straßenraum. Die Kombination von Klinkermauerwerk und Stahl bezieht sich auf die Tradition im Gewerbe- und Industriebau.

Oldenburg Labour Exchange

A quadrant-shaped building block that is laid out around an inner courtyard follows the watercourse and forms a curved street space on the side facing away from the water. The combination of brick masonry and steel refers to the tradition of commercial and industrial construction.

OPD Hannover – Fernmeldeamt 2

Ein horizontal gegliederter, langgestreckter Baukörper parallel zum Mittellandkanal ergänzt das vorhandene Hochhaus. Der zweibündige neue Büroriegel wird von einem zylindrischen Baukörper unterbrochen, der den Eingang wie die vertikale Erschließung akzentuiert.

Hanover Post Office Divisional Administration – Telecommunications Office 2

A horizontally divided, elongated building stretching parallel to the Mittellandkanal adds to the existing tower block. A cylindrical building interrupting the new office bar emphasizes the entrance as well as the vertical circulation.

Energie Aktiengesellschaft Mitteldeutschland (EAM), Kassel

Die Kammstruktur der Büroflügel, deren Fassaden Leichtigkeit und Transparenz ausstrahlen, verläuft parallel zu den Höhenlinien und folgt durch ein geschossweises Abtreppen wie selbstverständlich der Topographie. Die massiver wirkende Erschließungs- und Versorgungsachse bildet das Rückgrat der Anlage.

Energie Aktiengesellschaft Mitteldeutschland (EAM), Kassel

The comb structure of the office wings, their façades radiating lightness and transparency, runs parallel to the contour lines and is accompanied by a staggered profile, which naturally follows the topography. The circulation and supply axis with a seemingly massive appearance forms the spine of the complex.

1993

Bayerische Hypotheken- und Wechselbank, Hamburg

Eine öffentliche Passage teilt das Gebäude, das den Fluchten der Kaianlagen, der Fleete und der Straßen folgt, in zwei Hälften. Der Kontrast zwischen den beiden mit Muschelkalk verkleideten massiven Gebäudehälften und der filigranen metallischen Fassadenstruktur der Passage bestimmt die Gestaltung.

Bayerische Hypotheken- und Wechselbank, Hamburg

A public arcade divides the building into two halves. Its plan results from the shape of the quays, the canals and the roads. The contrast between the two massive building halves clad in shell-lime and the delicate metallic façade structure of the arcade defines the design.

Flughafen Hamburg, Terminal 2

Das neue Passagierterminal ist als weite luftige und tageslichtdurchflutete Halle konzipiert. Das große geschwungene Dach fasst die Abflugebene mit den sich nach oben staffelnden Laden- und Konferenz- sowie Restaurant- und Besucherebenen zu einem großen räumlichen Kontinuum zusammen.

Hamburg Airport, Terminal 2

The new passenger terminal was designed as a spacious and naturally-lit hall. The large curving roof combines the departure hall with its stacked shopping, meeting, restaurant and visitor levels into one spatial unit.

Wohnstift Augustinum, Hamburg

Das Wohnstift für Senioren befindet sich an der Stelle eines ehemaligen Kühlhauses direkt am Hamburger Hafen unterhalb der vornehmen Elbchaussee. Nach dem Abriss des Kühlhauses wurde auf dem gleichen Grundriss und mit gleicher Höhe ein ebenfalls mit Backsteinen verkleidetes Seniorenheim errichtet.

Augustinum Home for the Aged, Hamburg

The home for the aged is located on the site of a former cold-storage depot directly at the Hamburg Harbour and below the noble Elbchaussee. Following the demolition of the cold store, the home for the aged was realized with the same plan and height and was also finished in brick.

Flughafen Stuttgart, A-Mitte – Terminal 2

Das langgestreckte, zum Vorfeld hin orientierte Gebäude wird verlängert und bildet das Rückgrat, an dem sich der Neubau des Terminals 2 anlehnt. Im Gegensatz zum verglasten Terminal 1 ist die Fassade geschlossen mit Granit verkleidet. Die zentrale Halle wird über Oberlichter belichtet.

Stuttgart Airport, A-Centre – Terminal 2

The long building orientated towards the apron is extended and forms the spine, against which the new Terminal 2 leans. As opposed to the glazed Terminal 1, the façade is solid and clad in granite. The central hall is lit via skylights.

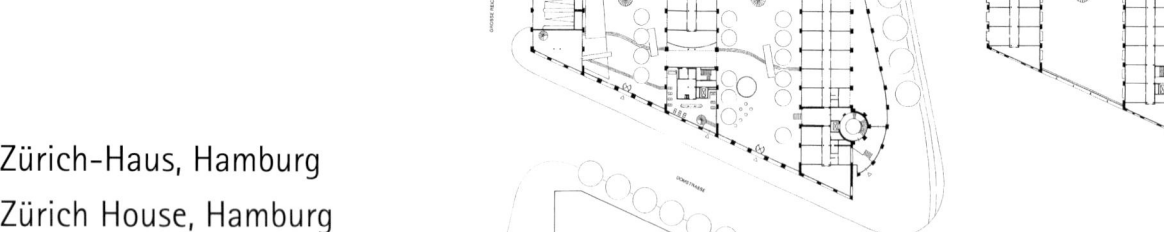

Zürich-Haus, Hamburg
Zürich House, Hamburg

Wettbewerb Competition
1988 – 1. Preis

Entwurf Design
Volkwin Marg und Nikolaus Goetze

Partner Partner
Klaus Staratzke

Bauherr Client
Zürich-Versicherungsgesellschaft

Bauzeit Construction period
1990–1993

BGF Gross floor area
26.400 m²

Die Gestaltung des Zürich-Hauses orientiert sich bewusst an der Hamburger Kontorhausarchitektur. Dies zeigt sich zum einen in der Betonung der Vertikalstruktur durch starke Pfeiler und der Horizontalgliederung in Sockel, Mittelbau und Dachgeschoss sowie zum anderen in der Wahl der Materialien Klinkermauerwerk und Stahl. Verglaste und bepflanzte Wintergärten mit Glasliften, offenen Etagentreppen und Galeriefluren bilden die repräsentativen Eingangssituationen. Sie dienen in erster Linie dazu, die ausschließlich natürlich belüfteten Büroräume gegen den Straßenlärm zu schützen, zudem eignen sie sich vorzüglich für Feste, Konzerte und große Versammlungen. Städtebaulich bildet der runde Treppenturm ein Pendant zum Turm des Messberghofes und markiert die wichtige Straßengabelung der Ost-West-Straße und der Domstraße.

The design of Zürich House is deliberately orientated to the architecture of the Hamburg Kontorhaus. This is evident, on the one hand, in the way the strong pillars emphasize the vertical structure, as well as in the horizontal division using base, middle structure and roof level, and, on the other hand, by the choice of the clinker brickwork and steel as materials. Glazed and planted winter gardens with glass elevators, open staircases and gallery corridors form the formal entrance foyer. Their primary function is to serve as noise barriers protecting the naturally ventilated offices from the street noise. They also serve as excellent areas for parties, concerts and large meetings. In urban planning terms the staircase tower forms a pendant to the tower of the Messberghof and mark the important junction of Ost-West-Strasse and Domstrasse.

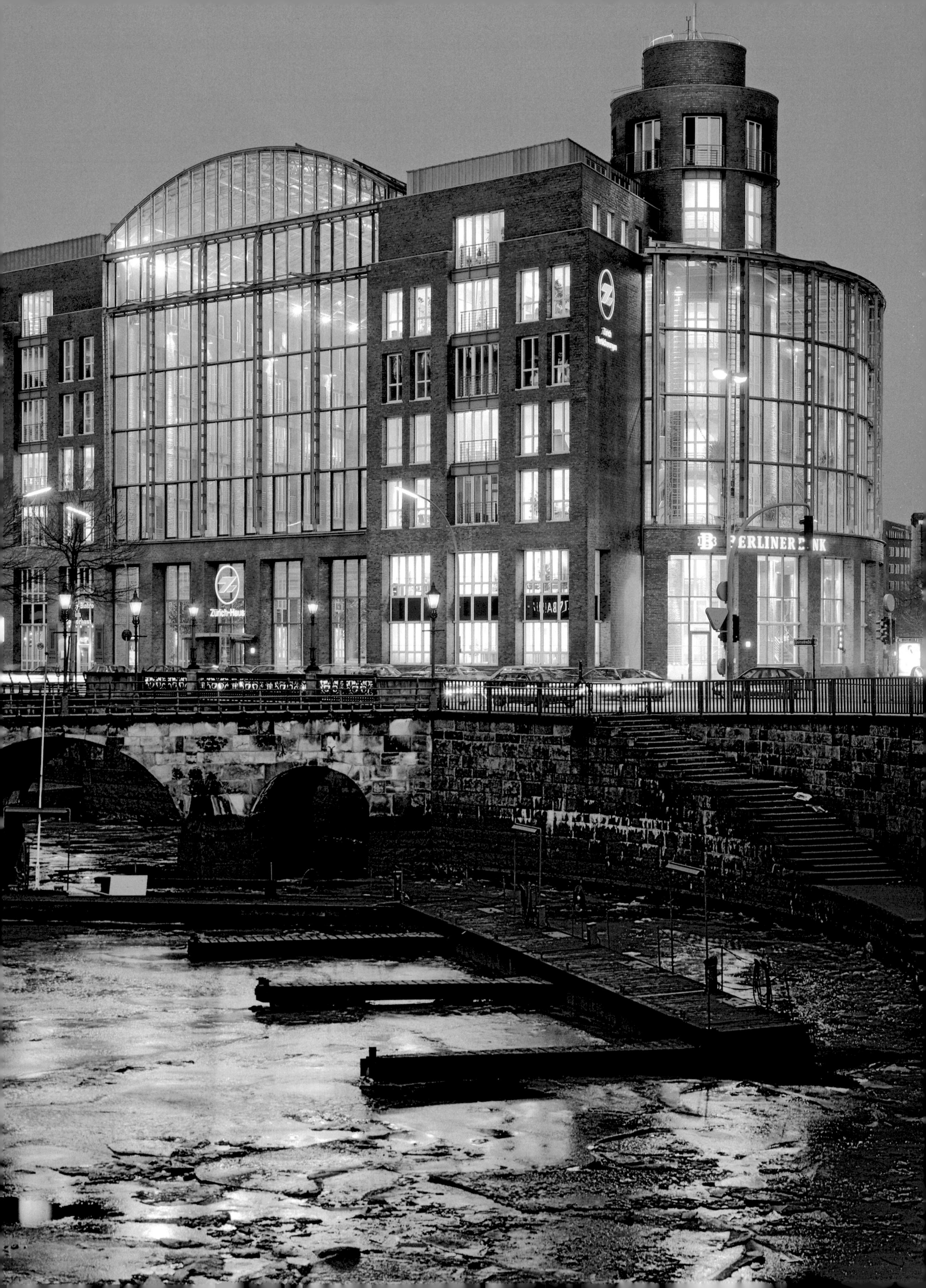
Zürich-Haus

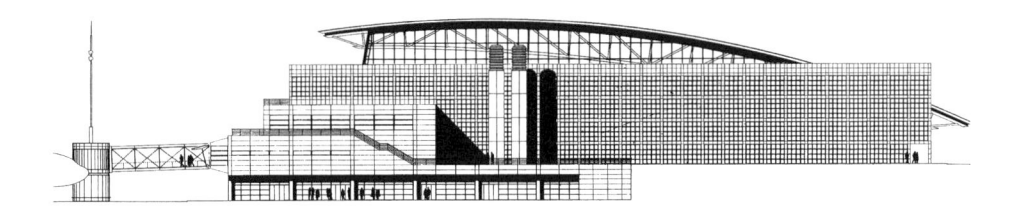

Flughafen Hamburg, Terminal 2
Hamburg Airport, Terminal 2

Wettbewerb Competition
1986 – 1. Preis

Entwurf Design
Meinhard von Gerkan und Karsten Brauer

Bauherr Client
Flughafen Hamburg GmbH

Bauzeit Construction period
1990–1993

BGF Gross floor area
72.000 m²

Die vor den Terminals liegende Flugzeugspange stellt das zusammenbindende „Rückgrat" der gesamten Anlage dar. Quer hierzu angeordnete Gebäudescheiben bilden strukturelle Zäsuren, die der landseitigen Bebauung eine einheitliche Fassung geben – ein städtebauliches Ordnungsprinzip ohne vorzeitige Festlegung weiterer Entwicklungsstufen. Das große geschwungene Dach des Terminals steht als dynamisch geformte Stahlkonstruktion im bewussten Gegensatz zu den seitlichen, monolithisch blockhaften Gebäudescheiben. Form und Konstruktion des Daches stellen eine Analogie zu einer Flugzeugtragfläche her. Trotz der lichten Spannweite von 62 m ist das Dach eine leichte und wirtschaftliche Konstruktion, die ohne Fugen als einheitliche Schale ausgebildet ist. Glasoberlichter sorgen für die gewünschte Tageslichtqualität in der oberen Abflug- wie der unten liegenden Ankunftshalle und lassen von unten die unverkleidete Konstruktion im Gegenlicht ablesbar werden.

The linking 'back-bone' of the complex is the aircraft docking zone in front of the terminals. The building blocks placed across form structural intervals, ensuring that the various architectural elements have a common framework. This gives them an urban planning concept without predetermining their future stages of development. The large, curved roof of the terminal as a dynamically formed steel construction stands in deliberate contrast to the monolithic building blocks on both sides. The form and construction of the roof is based on an aircraft wing. Its construction, which consists of a shell without joints, is light and economic in spite of its span of 62 m. Roof lights provide the required daylighting for the departure hall on the upper level and the arrival hall on the lower level, and allow the uncovered structure to be viewed lit from behind.

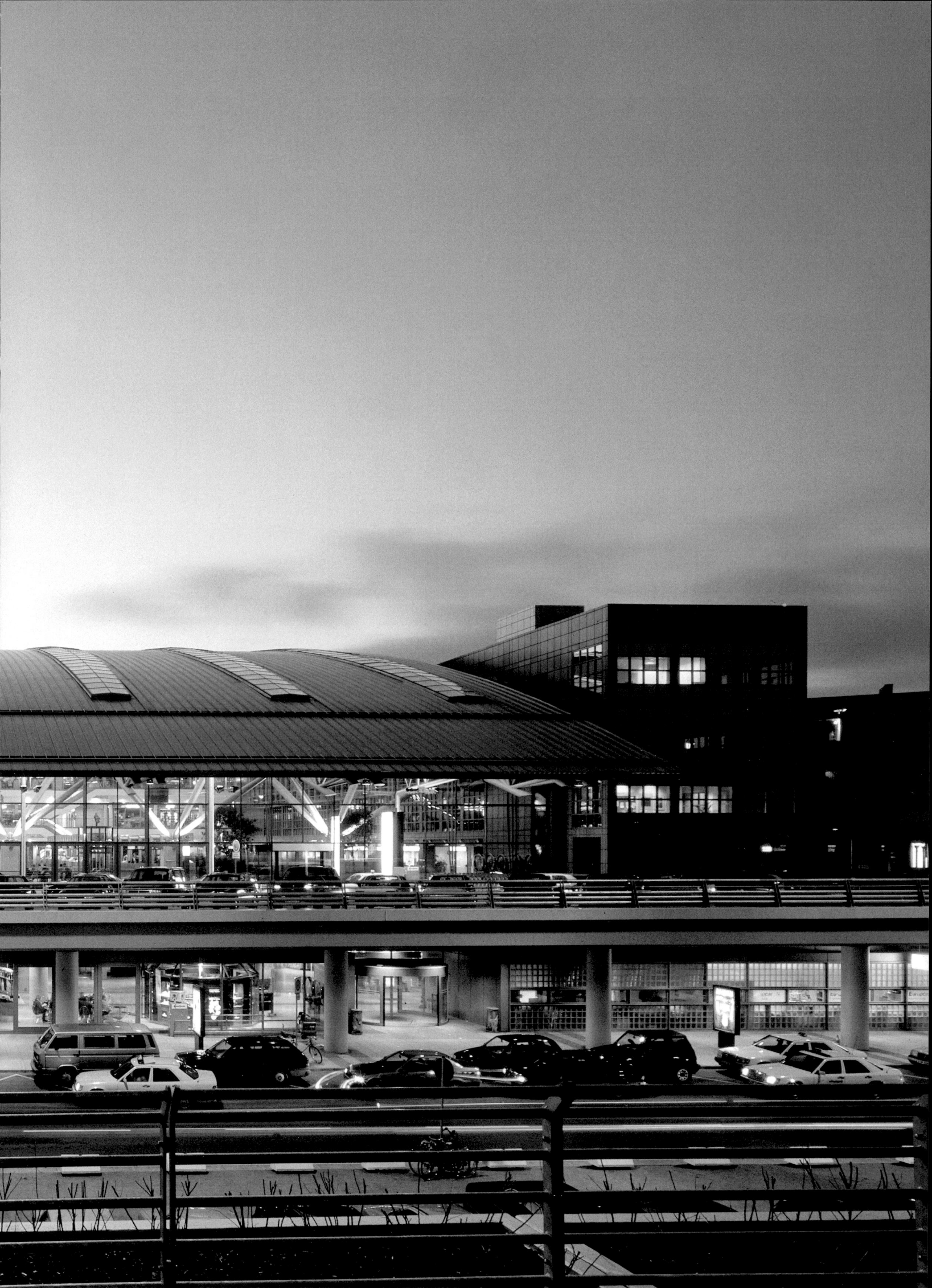

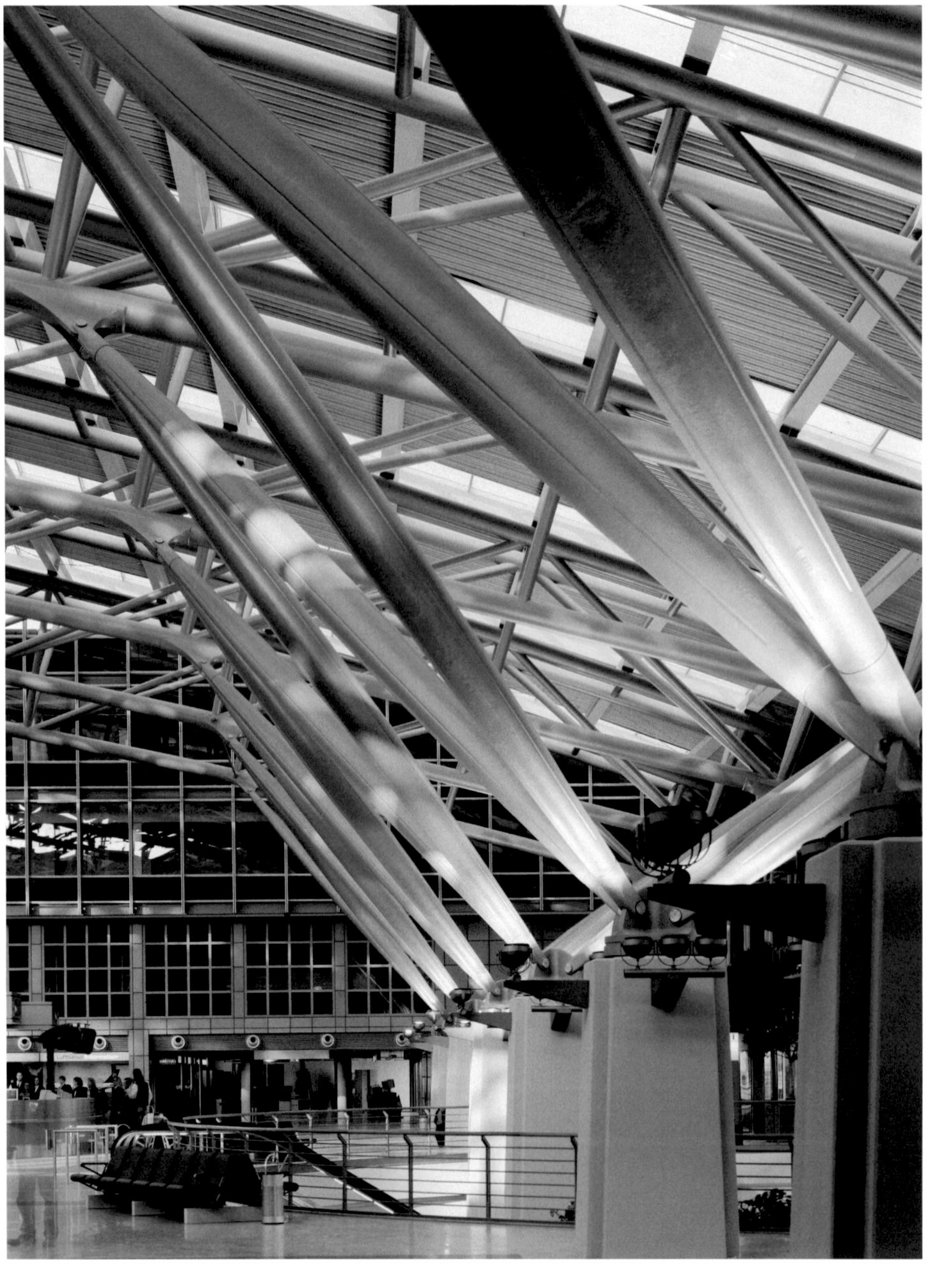

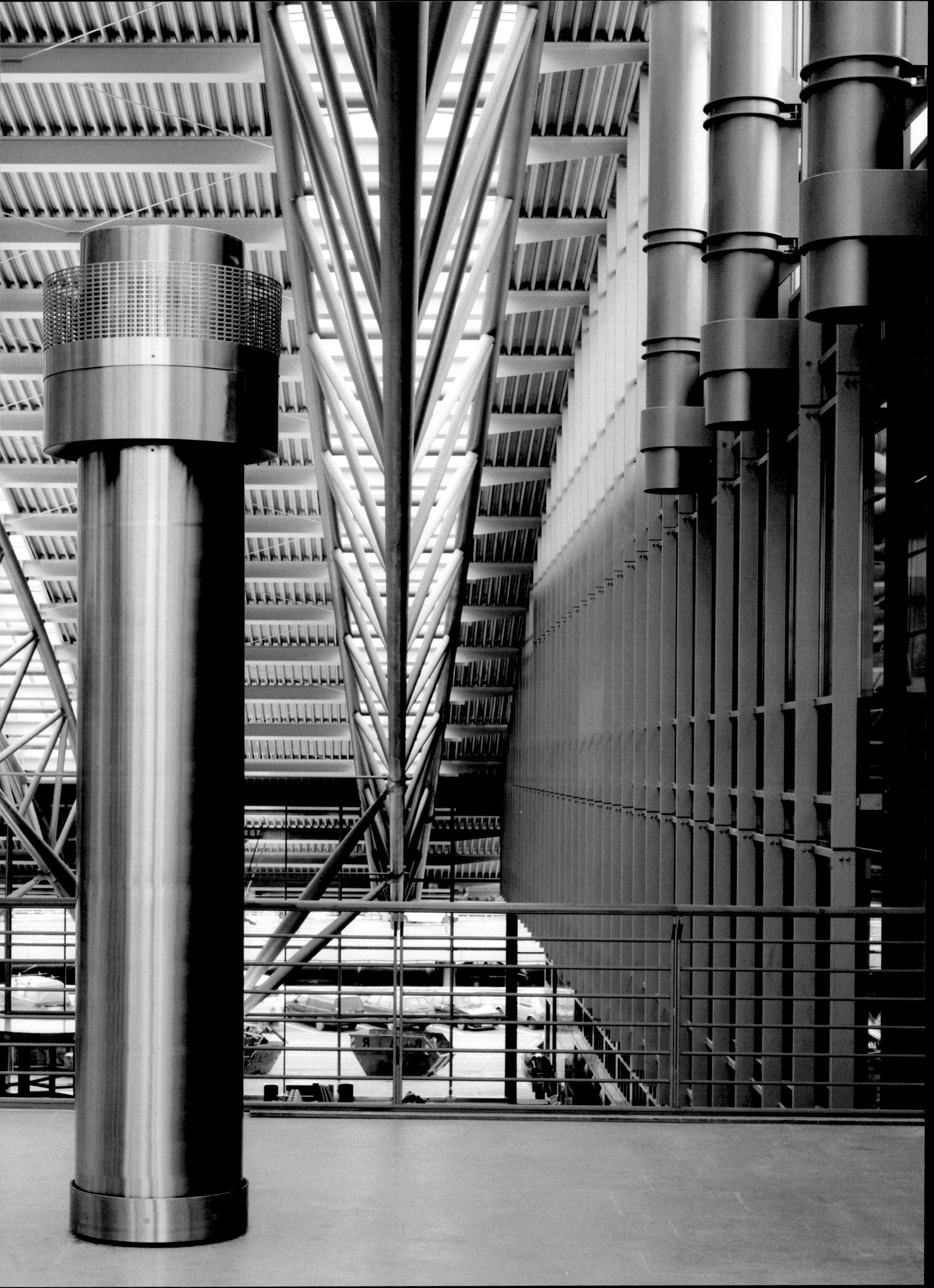

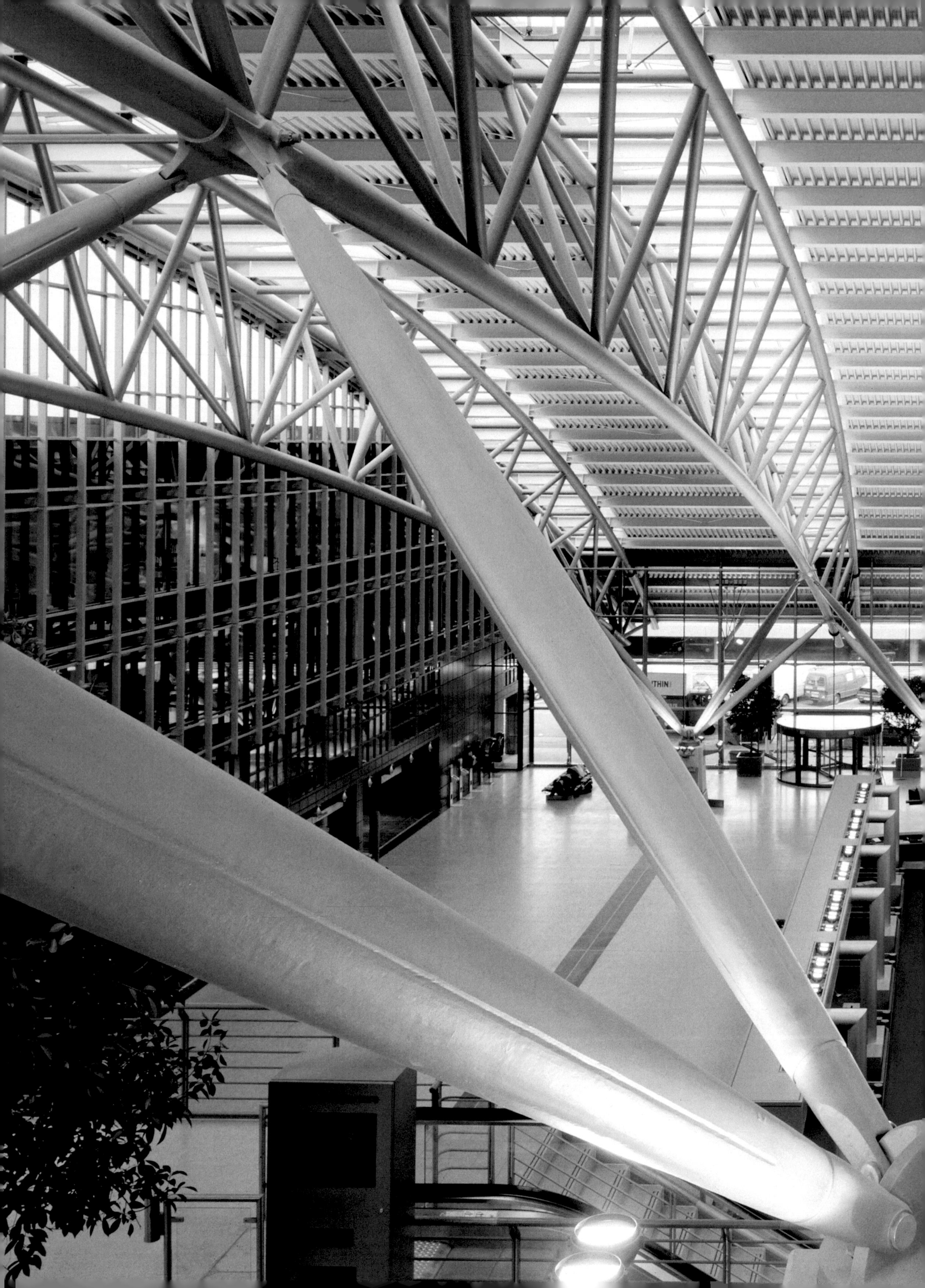

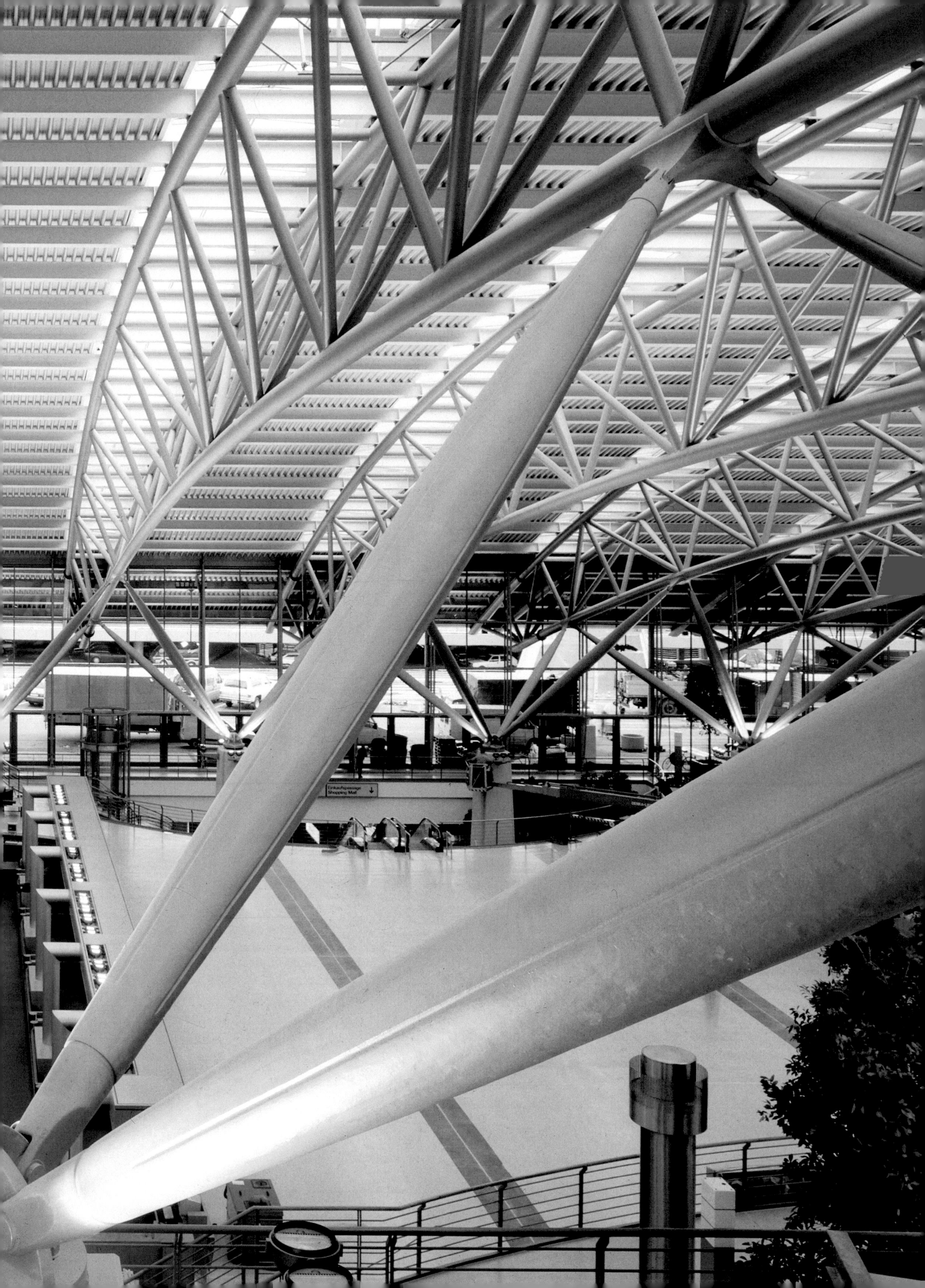

Wohnstift Augustinum, Hamburg
Augustinum Home for the Aged, Hamburg

Gutachten Consultancy
1985/1991

Entwurf Design
Volkwin Marg

Partner Partner
Klaus Staratzke

Bauherr Client
Collegium Augustinum

Bauzeit Construction period
1991–1993

Apartments
145

Das alte Kühlhaus stand unter Denkmalschutz, wurde jedoch seit Jahrzehnten nicht mehr genutzt. Da der Zustand der Bausubstanz keinen Umbau zuließ, wurde das Kühlhaus abgerissen. Dem Totalabriss folgte eine in Volumen und Charakter „zitierte" Neubebauung: ein würfelförmiger Baukörper mit einer Lochfassade aus Klinkermauerwerk. Ähnlich dem alten Kühlhaus wird die Fassade durch horizontale, helle Streifen gegliedert, das oberste Geschoss ist ebenfalls zurückgesetzt. Der besonderen städtebaulichen Bedeutung des Standortes zwischen steinernem Hafenpanorama und dicht bewachsenen Hängen des Urstromtals der Elbe wird durch eine Glaskuppel, unter der sich ein Restaurant befindet, Rechnung getragen. Das Restaurant ist als öffentlich zugänglicher Aussichtspunkt konzipiert. Bei Hochwasser wird das Erdgeschoss durch wasserdichte Schotten abgeschirmt, ein wasserdichter Tunnel kann im Notfall als Fluchtweg dienen.

The old cold-storage depot on the site, though a listed monument, had not been used for decades. As its condition precluded a conversion, it was finally demolished and replaced by a new building that 'quoted' the cold store in terms of mass and character, that is to say, by a cube with a punctuated clinker brick façade. Similarly to the old cold store, the façade is divided by pale horizontal strips, and the top floor steps back. A glass-domed restaurant does justice to the special urban significance of the location between the dockland panorama of stone and the dense vegetation covering the flanks of the Elbe glacial valley. The restaurant was also conceived as a public viewing point. The ground floor is protected from high water by water-tight crosswalls, and a water-tight tunnel serves as an emergency exit.

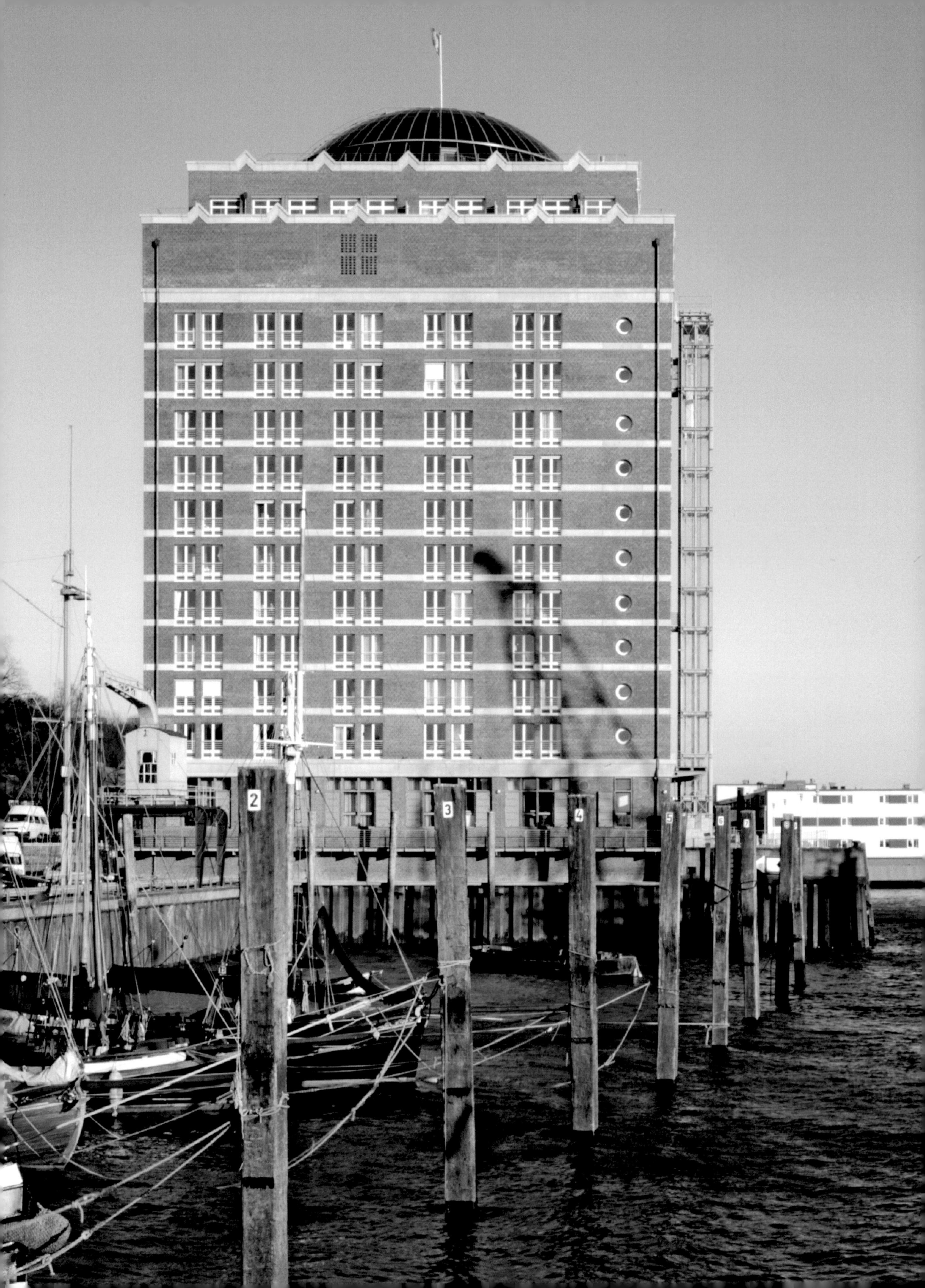
2
3
4
5

1994

Hillmann-Eck, Bremen

Die geschwungene Form des Baukörpers folgt der Grundstücksgrenze. Im Kontrast zu den umgebenden Ziegelfassaden erhielt das Haus eine metallische Fassade, deren Horizontalbetonung mit durchlaufenden Brüstungsbändern und freistehenden Beschattern das kleine Haus größer erscheinen lässt.

Hillmann-Eck, Bremen

The curved building follows the site boundary. Contrasting the surrounding masonry façades the building is finished with a metal façade, its horizontal emphasis with continuous fenestration and detached shading devices seemingly enlarging the small house.

Musik- und·Kongresshalle Lübeck

Der Bau passt sich bewusst nicht in die Kleinmaßstäblichkeit der Altstadt Lübecks ein. Er legt vielmehr semantisch, maßstäblich und ästhetisch ein Bekenntnis zur heutigen Zeit ab. Die Orientierung des Gebäudes und seine öffentlichen Funktionen sind jedoch in das städtische Gefüge einbezogen.

Music and Congress Hall, Lübeck

The building is not conceived to fit into the small-scale atmosphere of the old town of Lübeck. It is much more a commitment to present-day semantics, scale and aesthetics. The orientation of the building with its public facilities is, however, integrated into the urban structure.

Galeria Duisburg

Das Einkaufszentrum erschließt ein bisher ungenutztes „Filetstück" in der Innenstadt. Die leichte Stahl-Glas-Konstruktion schafft im Innern eine angenehme Atmosphäre, während die Verwendung dunklen Backsteins in strenger rhythmischer Architektur ein Stück der alten Hansestadttradition Duisburgs aufnimmt.

Duisburg Galeria

The shopping centre makes use of an undeveloped 'choice' site in the city centre. The lightweight steel-glass structure generates an inviting interior atmosphere, whilst the strictly rhythmical brick architecture responds to part of the historic Hanseatic tradition of Duisburg.

1994

Amtsgericht Braunschweig

Das städtebauliche Ensemble der Gebäude des Amtsgerichts basiert auf der äußerlichen Wiederherstellung des klassizistischen „Landschaftlichen Hauses", das im Jahre 1799 vom Architekten Christian Gottlieb Langwagen erstellt und 1944 durch Kriegseinwirkung zerstört worden ist.

Law Court, Braunschweig

The urban planning ensemble is based on the external reconstruction of the classical 'Landschaftliches Haus', built in 1799 by the architect Christian Gottlieb Langwagen and destroyed in 1944 during World War II.

Wohn- und Geschäftshaus Schaarmarkt, Hamburg

Der in Winkelform konzipierte Neubau nimmt die städtische Struktur der Blockrandbebauungen auf, ein Turm betont die zurückgesetzte Blockecke mit dem Haupteingang. Die Loggien der Obergeschosse bewirken im Zusammenspiel mit den Arkaden der gleichmäßig gerasterten Fassade eine deutliche Tiefenwirkung.

Schaarmarkt Residential and Commercial Building, Hamburg

The new building with an angled plan respects the urban structure of high-density developments; a tower emphasizes the recessed block corner with the main entrance. The loggias of the upper floors interact with the arcades of the uniformly structured façade to generate depth.

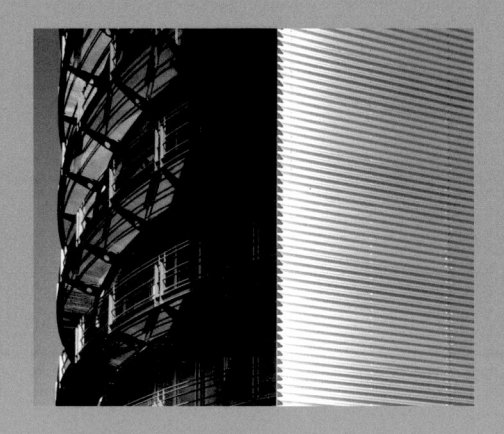

Deutsche Revision AG, Frankfurt/Main

Der Baukörper schmiegt sich der ungewöhnlich polygonal „gebogenen" Grundstückssituation an und gewinnt durch die geschwungene Form eine dynamisch spannungsvolle Geste ohne direkte und tiefe Symbolik oder vordergründig dramatische Baukörpergebärden.

Bank- und Geschäftshaus Brodschrangen, Hamburg

Der siebengeschossige Büro- und Geschäftshausneubau im historischen Börsenviertel Hamburgs schließt die Baulücke in einer Blockrandbebauung. Die Ecktürme bilden den Abschluss der Häuserzeilen entlang des ehemals im Blockinnern verlaufenden Fleets.

Rehaklinik Trassenheide, Usedom

Zwar bedingte das Raumprogramm der Klinik die Realisierung erheblicher Baumassen, doch das ebenso behutsam wie gekonnt horizontal und vertikal gegliederte Gebäude fügt sich sensibel in die Landschaft ein. Architektur und Natur korrespondieren im Sinne einer wechselseitigen Überhöhung.

Deutsche Revision AG, Frankfurt/Main

The building fits smoothly into the unusual polygonal 'curved' site form and gains a dynamic exciting element through the sweeping form without direct and deep symbolism or superficial dramatic building gestures.

Bank and Commercial Building Brodschrangen, Hamburg

The seven-storey office and commercial building in Hamburg's historic stock exchange quarter closes a gap in an existing block development. The corner towers form the end of the row of buildings along the canal, which formerly ran through the interior of the blocks.

Rehabilitation Clinic, Trassenheide, Usedom

Although the clinic's room scheme required considerable structural mass, the building – as cautious as it is masterly in its horizontal and vertical sectionalization – it is carefully integrated into the landscape. Architecture and nature correspond in the sense of a mutual exaggeration of heights.

Rehaklinik Trassenheide, Usedom
Rehabilitation Clinic, Trassenheide, Usedom

Gutachten Consultancy
1992

Entwurf Design
Meinhard von Gerkan

Bauherr Client
Klinik GmbH + Co. Dünenwald KG

Bauzeit Construction period
1992–1995

Betten Beds
256

Am Rande des Ortes inmitten eines dichten Kiefernwaldes befindet sich das Grundstück, auf dem ein beträchtliches Bauvolumen mit allein 256 Zimmern untergebracht werden sollte. Die landschaftliche Situation gebot Respekt und Zurückhaltung, die Nutzungsanforderungen einen klar und einfach gegliederten Baukörper. Die niedrige Bauhöhe „duckt" sich in die Dünen, die geneigten Dächer vermitteln den landschaftlichen Bezug, ohne die Größe zu leugnen. Die Patientenzimmer liegen im 1. und 2. Obergeschoss, die betrieblichen Räume im Erdgeschoss, das im Hauptbau durch eine von oben belichtete „innere Straße" erschlossen wird. Sowohl die Klarheit der Architekturform mit ihrer visuellen Erfassbarkeit und räumlichen Orientierung als auch die Bescheidenheit in der Wahl der Materialien verzichten auf jegliche überzogene Geste.

The site choosen to accommodate the considerable building volume of 256 rooms is located on the outskirts of the town, in the middle of a dense pinewood. The landscape commands respect and restraint, whilst the usage requirements call for a clearly and simply structured building. The low building height 'nestles' into the dunes, with the inclined roofs conveying the relation to the landscape without denying the scale. The rooms for the patients are located on the 1st and 2nd levels; the service rooms are on the ground floor. In the main building the ground floor is arranged along an 'internal street', which is lit from above. The clarity of the architectural form, with its visual qualities and spatial orientation as well as the modest choice of materials, is achieved without the use of excessive gestures.

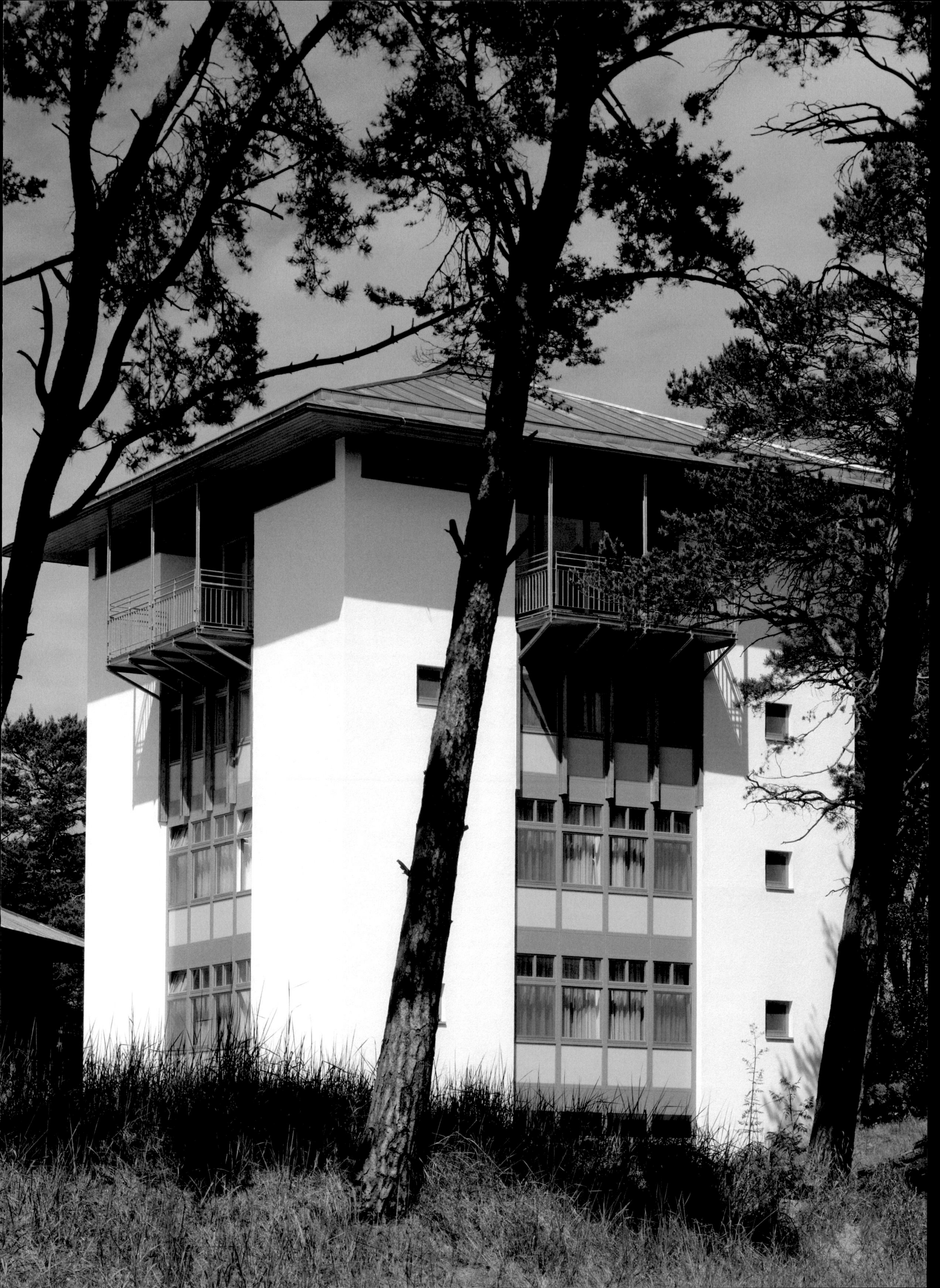

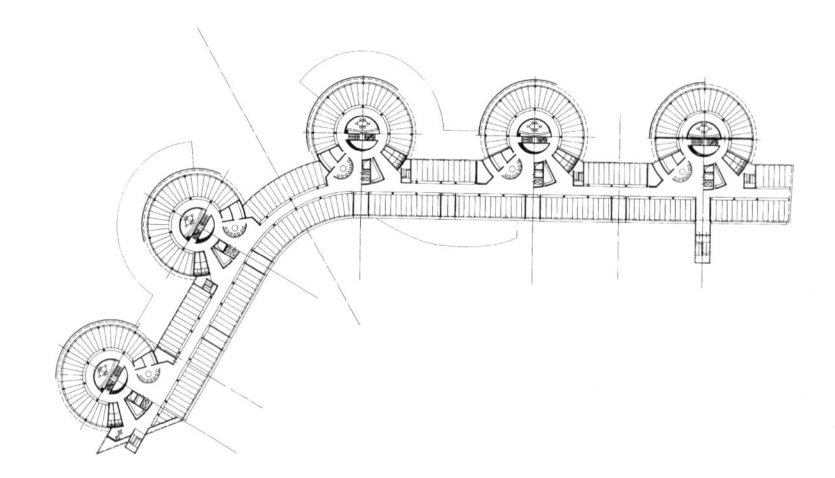

Deutsche Revision, Frankfurt/Main
Deutsche Revision, Frankfurt/Main

Wettbewerb Competition
1990 – 1. Preis

Entwurf Design
Meinhard von Gerkan

Partner Partner
Klaus Staratzke

Bauherr Client
C + L Treuhand Vereinigung AG

Bauzeit Construction period
1992–1994

BGF Gross floor area
44.680 m²

Der geschwungene Hauptbaukörper der Deutschen Revision bildet entlang der Erschließungsstraße gleichsam das Rückgrat, dem fünf zylindrische Haustürme angelagert sind. Das funktionale Konzept, auf dem die Grundrissfigur beruht, gliedert das Bürohaus in Einheiten. Glasoberlichter in den mittigen „Kommunikationstreppenhäusern" gewährleisten Tageslicht. Die Geometrie der Flurzonen aus der Überlagerung des gebogenen Rückgrats mit dem Zylinder bietet erlebnisreiche Räume und geborgene Verweilzonen. Die trapezförmige Ausweitung zur Peripherie begünstigt durch Vergrößerungen natürlich belichteter Flächen die Arbeitsräume in den zylindrischen Bauteilen. Als ergänzende Schallschutzmaßnahme zur modellierten Erdwallanlage besteht die Option zweier „Fassadenmäntel", die zunächst nur als Rahmengerüst ausgebildet sind. Die Fassaden des Rückgrats sind mit Wellblech verkleidet und mit festen Beschattern bestückt.

The curved main building of the Deutsche Revision along the access road forms the spine for five cylindrical towers. The functional concept of the floor plan splits the office building into units. Glass roof lights in the central 'communication staircases' provide natural daylight. The shape of the corridors offers exciting spaces and sheltered rest areas created by the superimposition of the spine with the cylinders. The trapeze-shaped extension to the periphery of the site improves the work areas in the cylindrical buildings by increasing the natural lighting. An additional noise protection alternative to the embankment is the option of using second 'façade coats', which are initially erected only as framework. The façades of the spine are covered in corrugated metal and have fixed shades.

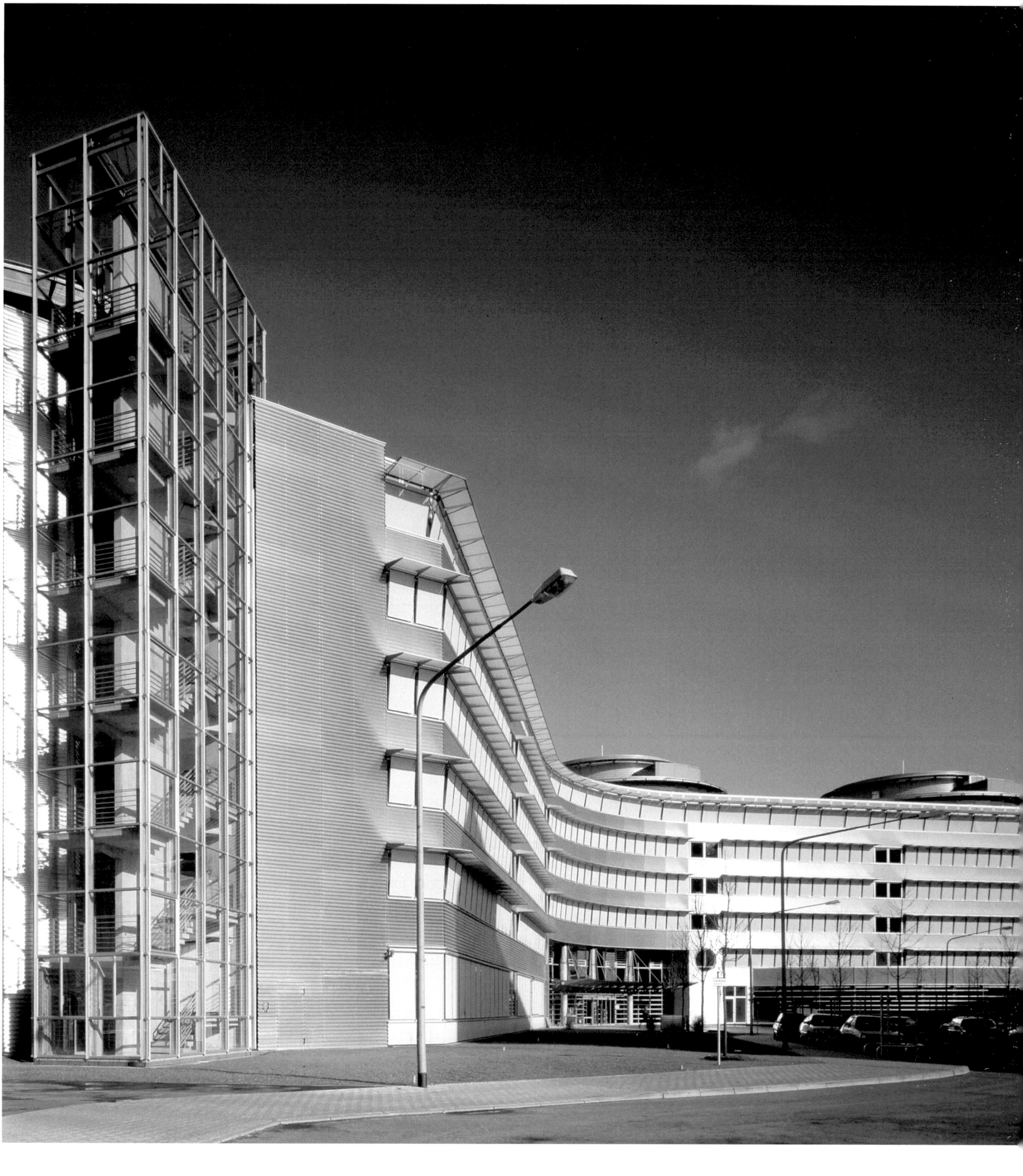

Musik- und Kongresshalle Lübeck
Music and Congress Hall, Lübeck

Wettbewerb Competition
1990 – 1. Preis

Entwurf Design
Meinhard von Gerkan mit Christian Weinmann

Partner Partner
Wolfgang Haux

Bauherr Client
Hansestadt Lübeck, Hochbauamt

Bauzeit Construction period
1992–1994

BGF Gross floor area
18.400 m²

Gegenüber der Lübecker Altstadt zeichnet sich der Baukörper, mit einer Länge von 120 m und einer Breite von 55 m, durch seine relativ geringe Höhe aus. Während sich im Norden die gläserne Foyer-Halle dem Publikum öffnet, wird der eigentliche Kern des Gebäudes, der große Musik- und Kongress-Saal, von der nach Süden ansteigenden Sockelzone umschlossen. Lediglich im Dach wird er in Form einer großen Tonne, die den sonst ruhigen Gebäudekubus durchstößt, ablesbar. Der Saal selbst ist wie ein großes Schmuckkästchen ringsum in edlem Schweizer Birnenholz nach konzertakustischen Gesichtspunkten verkleidet. Das vollständig verglaste, sich nach außen öffnende Veranstaltungsfoyer als städtischer, öffentlicher Platz wurde mit klarem Bezug zum Altstadtkern positioniert. Das ausladende Dach überspannt wie ein Baldachin einen Teil des Stadtraums, hohe Arkaden unterstreichen die öffentliche Geste des Gebäudes.

Opposite Lübeck's historic town quarter the new building, which is 120 m long and 55 m wide, is characterized by its comparatively low height. Whilst the glazed foyer hall in the north opens up for the public, the actual core of the building, the music and congress hall, is enclosed by the socle zone ascending towards the south. Only in the roof is the hall visible as a large barrel, penetrating the otherwise calm building cube. The hall itself is clad in precious Swiss pear wood all around like a large jewellery box. The cladding has been specially applied according to concert-acoustic requirements. The completely glazed event foyer opening up towards the exterior has been positioned with a clear relation to the historic town centre as an urban public space. The projecting roof spans part of the urban space like a baldachin, the high arcades underlining the building's public gesture.

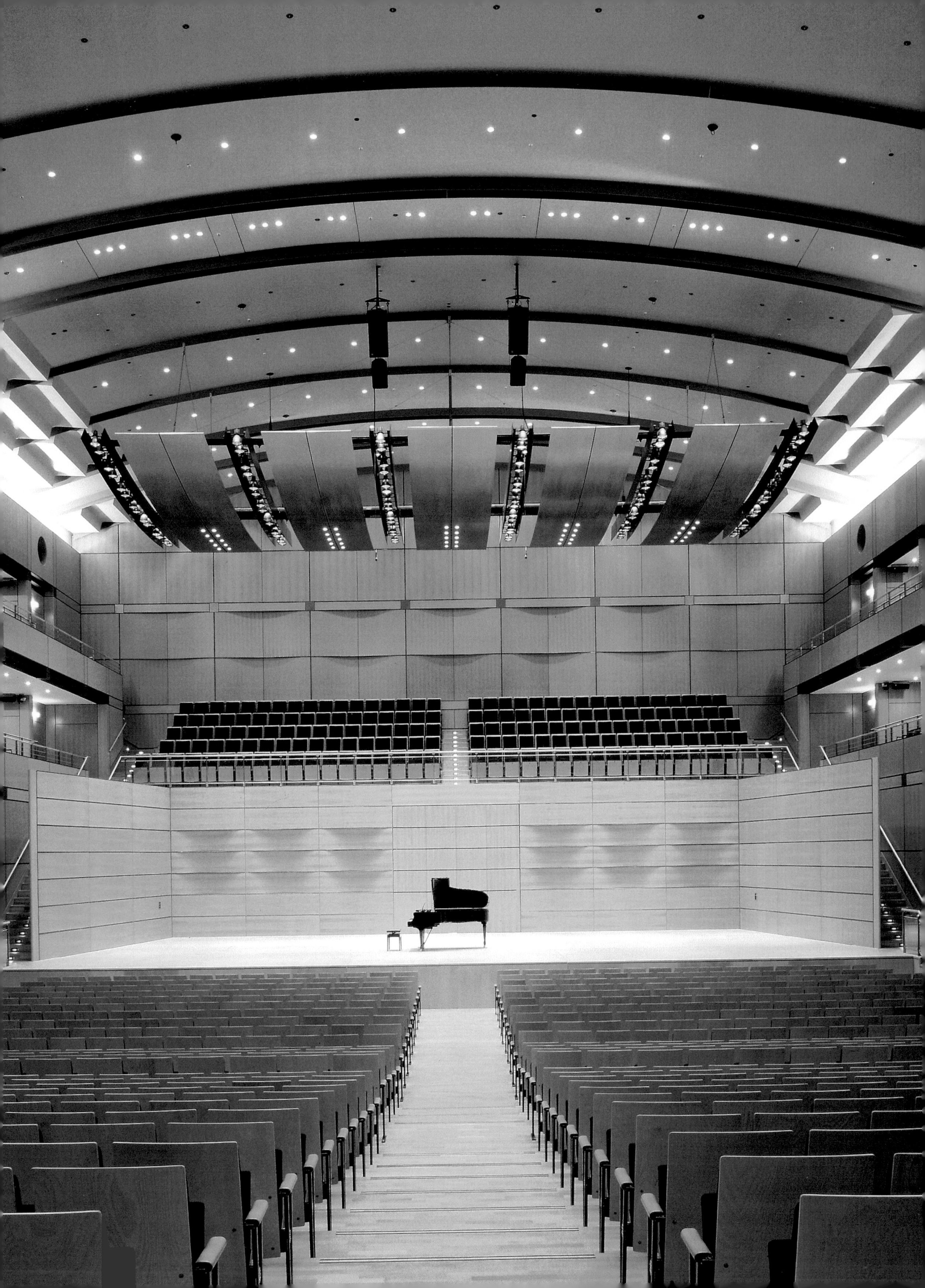

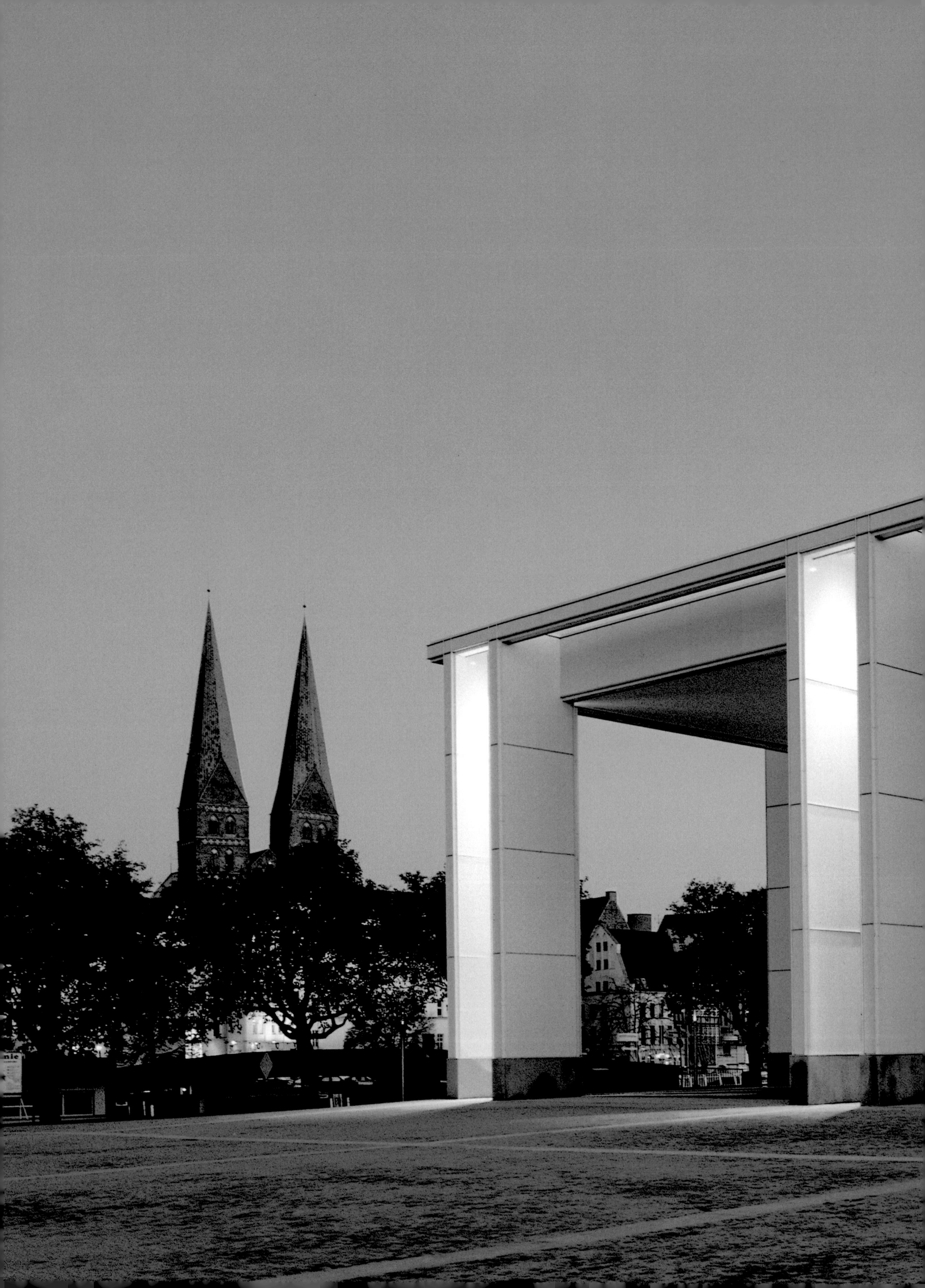

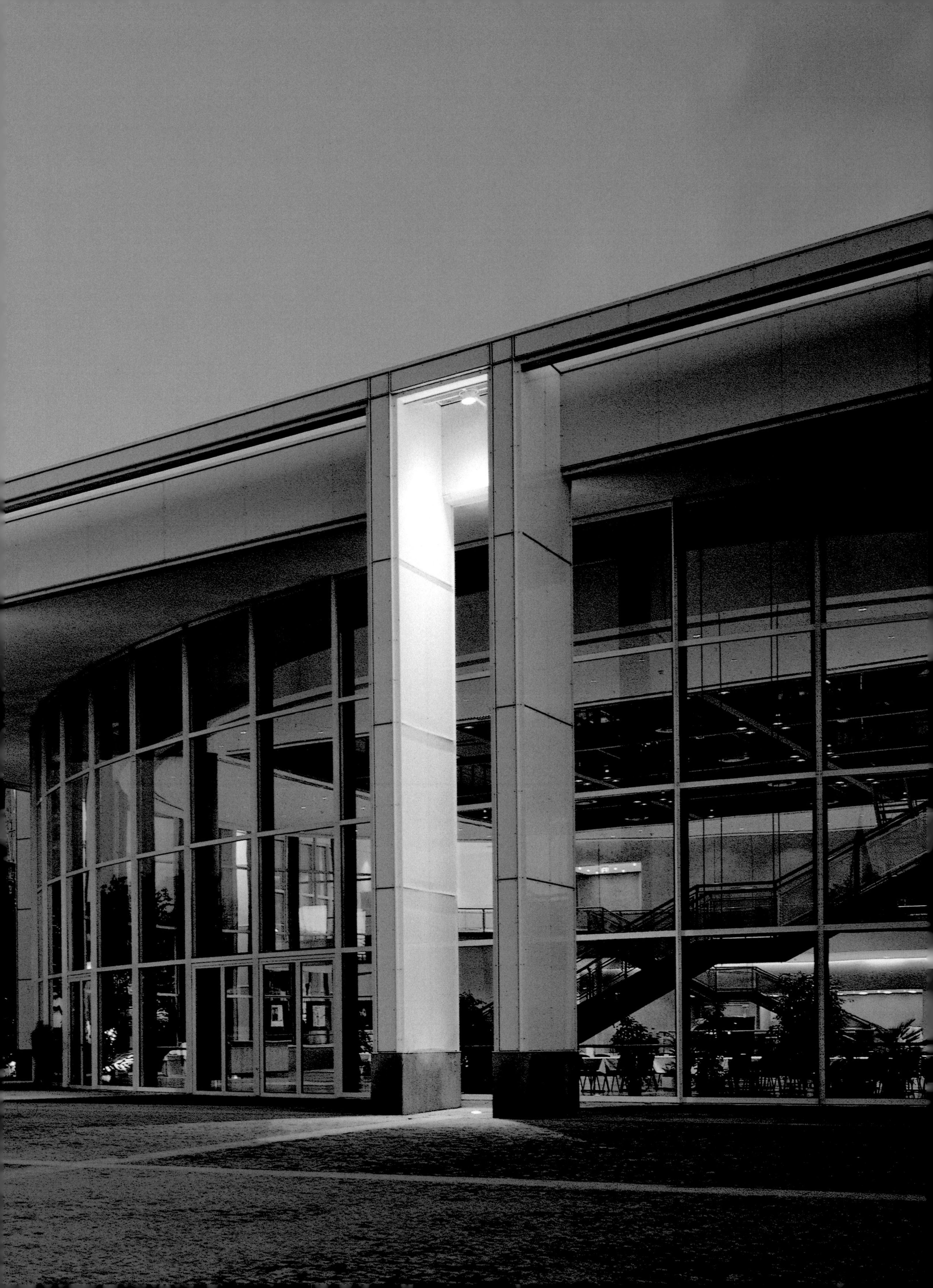

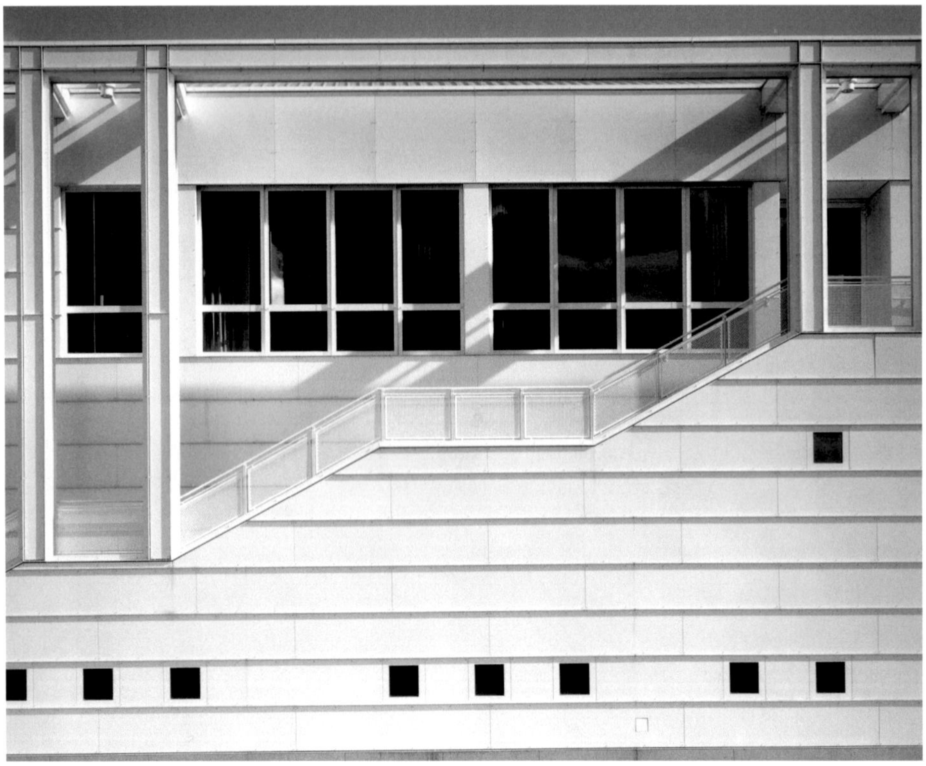

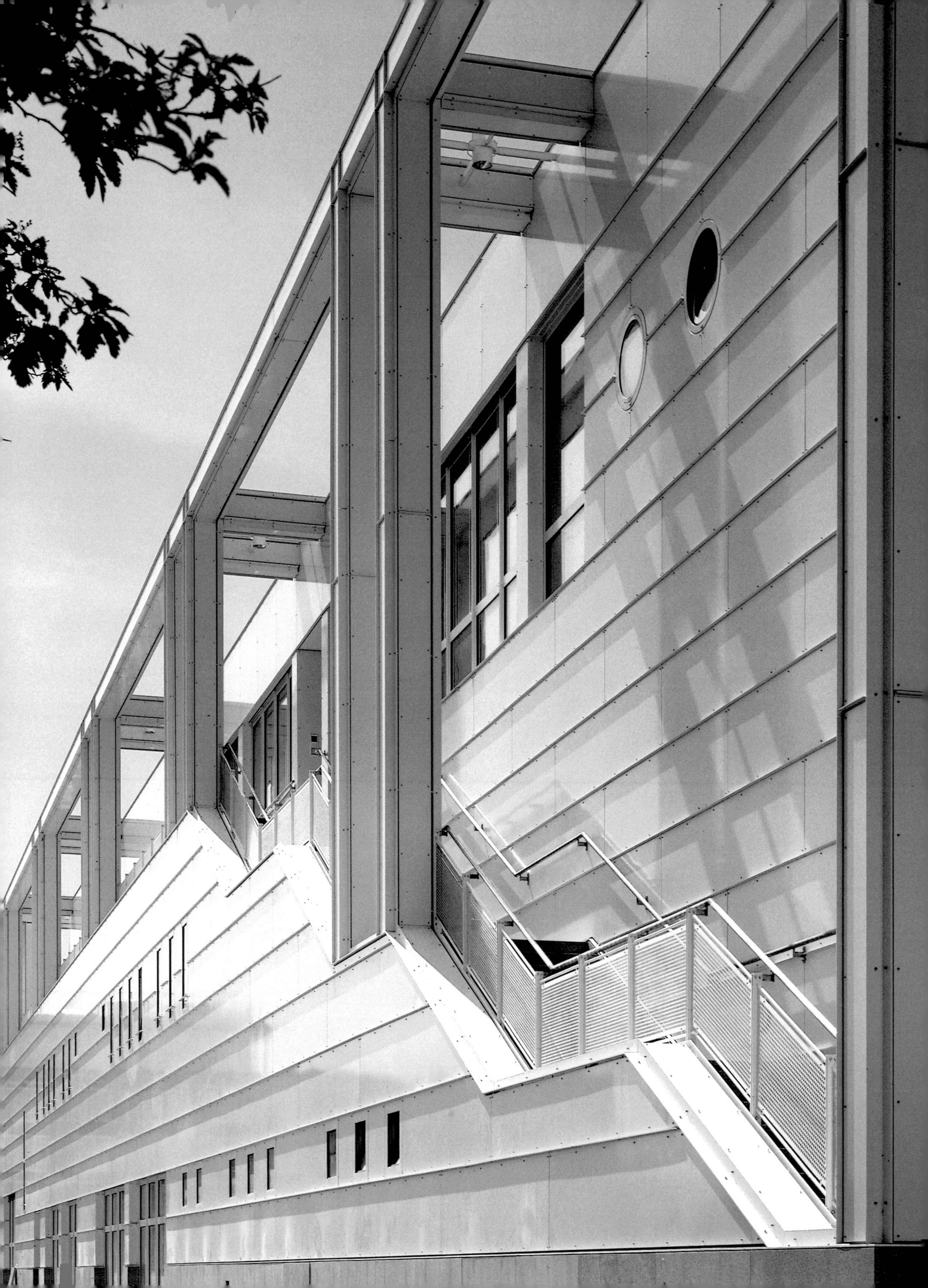

Galeria Duisburg
Duisburg Galeria

1988

Entwurf Design
Meinhard von Gerkan mit Klaus Staratzke und Otto Dorn

Bauherr Client
IVG Immobilien Verwaltungs GmbH

Bauzeit Construction period
1991–1994

BGF Gross floor area
32.000 m²

Die neue städtische Verbindung zu schon vorhandenen Einkaufsschwerpunkten steigert die städtebauliche und architektonische Qualität des unmittelbaren Umfeldes der Galeria Duisburg. Die großzügige Glaspassage wird durch zwei gläserne elliptische Baukörper akzentuiert. Die so vorgewölbten „Türme" sind städtebauliche Orientierungspunkte mit Fernwirkung, die der Betonung der Eingangssituation dienen. Über offene Stahltreppen, verglaste Treppenhäuser und Aufzüge sind die Obergeschosse mit eingehängten Stahlemporen zu erreichen. Blaubunte, dunkel verfugt gemauerte Torfbrandklinker, Stahl und Glas kennzeichnen den Bau außen, Granit, Edelstahl und Holz innen. Axialität und Symmetrie werden im Innern durch die asymmetrische Konstruktion des Glasdachs in ihrer Strenge gebrochen. Im Obergeschoss liegen die Wege als Galerien hinter Arkaden, um die hohe Front der Innenfassaden nicht zu stören.

The new urban link to existing major shopping locations improves the urban planning and architectural quality of the immediate surroundings of the Duisburg Galeria. The spacious glass arcade is accentuated by two glazed elliptical building elements. Vaulted in this way, the 'towers' are urban landmarks visible from a distance, thus accentuating the entrance situation. The upper floors with suspended foyers can be reached by open steel stairs, glazed staircases and lifts. Varied blue bricks with dark pointing, steel and glass characterize the exterior of the building; granite, stainless steel and wood the interior. Axialism and symmetry are interrupted in the interior by the asymmetric structure of the glass roof. On the upper floor the paths are located behind galleries to maintain the height of the inner façade.

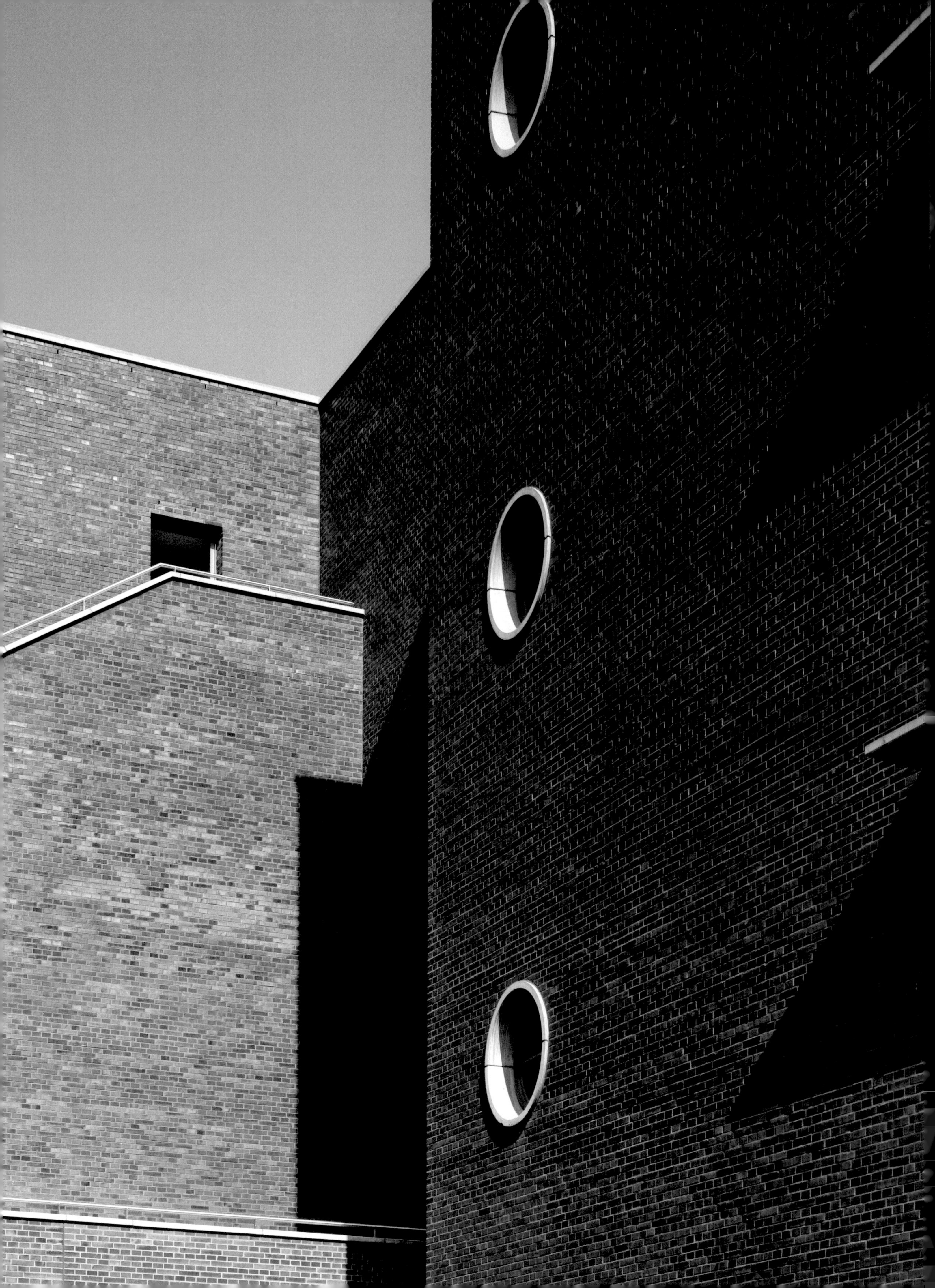

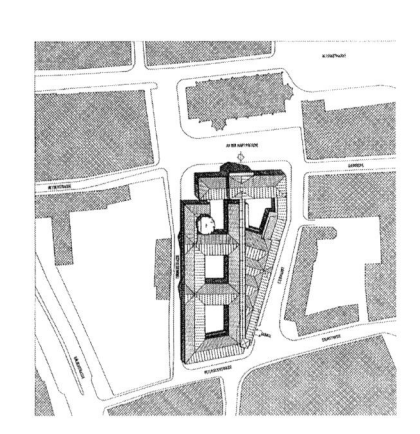

Amtsgericht Braunschweig
Law Court, Braunschweig

Gutachten Consultancy
1981 – 1. Rang

Entwurf Design
Meinhard von Gerkan mit Hans-Eggert Bock
und Manfred Stanek

Bauherr Client
Land Niedersachsen

Bauzeit Construction period
1990–1994

BGF Gross floor area
23.803 m²

Der Wiederaufbau des „Landschaftlichen Hauses" wurde vom Landtag in Hannover gegen das Votum der Architekten beschlossen. Die Neubauten fügen sich mit Respekt gegenüber dem historischen Bestand maßstäblich ein. Der Entwurf erweist der historischen Bausubstanz Referenz ohne zu historisieren. In der Achse des Portikus ist als „rue interieur" eine glasgedeckte dreigeschossige Galeriehalle angelegt. Sie dient der Erschließung und zugleich als Nutzungstrennung. Im Osten sind in zwei Geschossen die Gerichtssäle angeordnet; die Wartezonen öffnen sich zur Halle. Im Westen schließen sich dreigeschossig und durch drei Innenhöfe gegliedert die Arbeitsräume der Verwaltung an. Alle Gebäude orientieren sich in der Höhe an dem historisch geprägten Maßstab. Sie haben Satteldächer, die traufständig zu den Straßen verlaufen und durch Giebel rhythmisiert sind. Fenstergewände, Sockel und Säulen sind in Naturstein, die Fassadenflächen sind in Glattputz ausgeführt.

The reconstruction of the 'Landschaftliches Haus' was politically approved by the state parliament in Hanover against the opinion of the architects. The new buildings blend in according to scale out of deference to the existing historic buildings. The design reflects the past without being historic. A three-storey glazed gallery hall is built along the axis of the portico as a 'rue interieur'. It serves the access and at the same time separates the different uses. The courtrooms are located in two storeys to the east; the waiting foyers open up to the hall. To the west are the three storeys of the administration offices grouped around three inner courtyards. All buildings adhere to the height of the historic scale. They have pitched roofs, with eaves to the streets, and are rhythmically modulated by gables. The wall surfaces of the façades are of smooth plaster; plinths and columns are of natural stone.

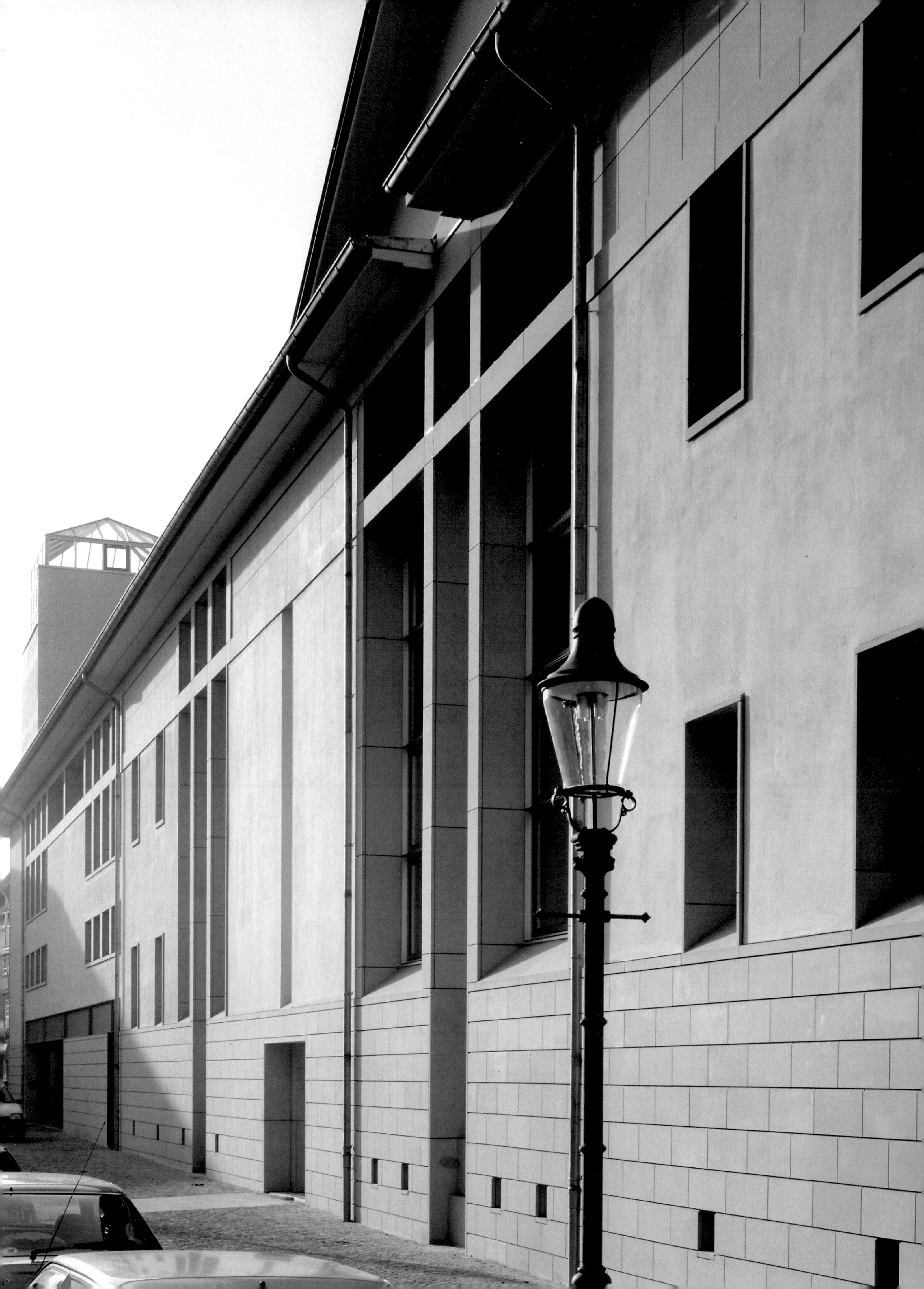

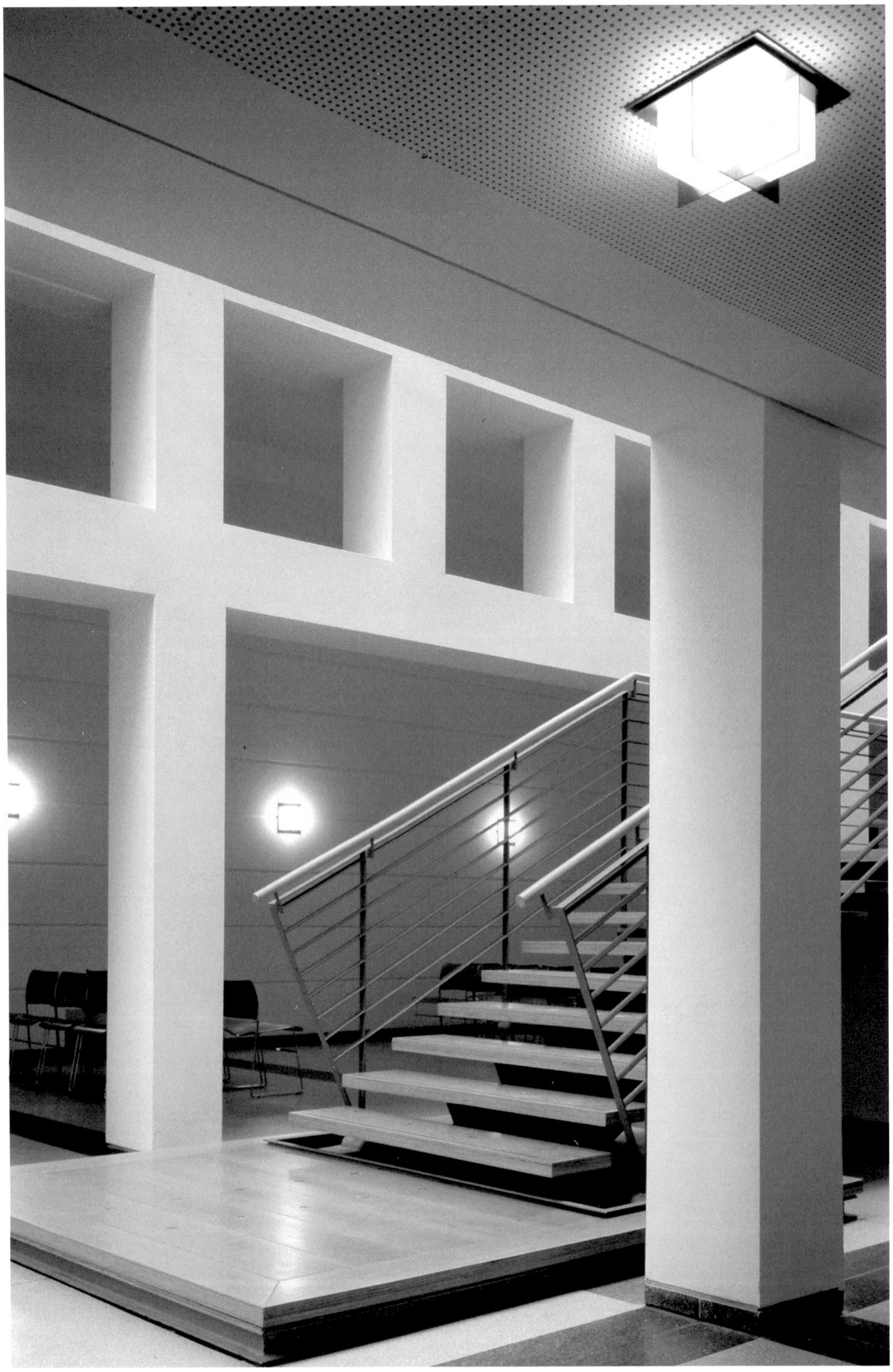

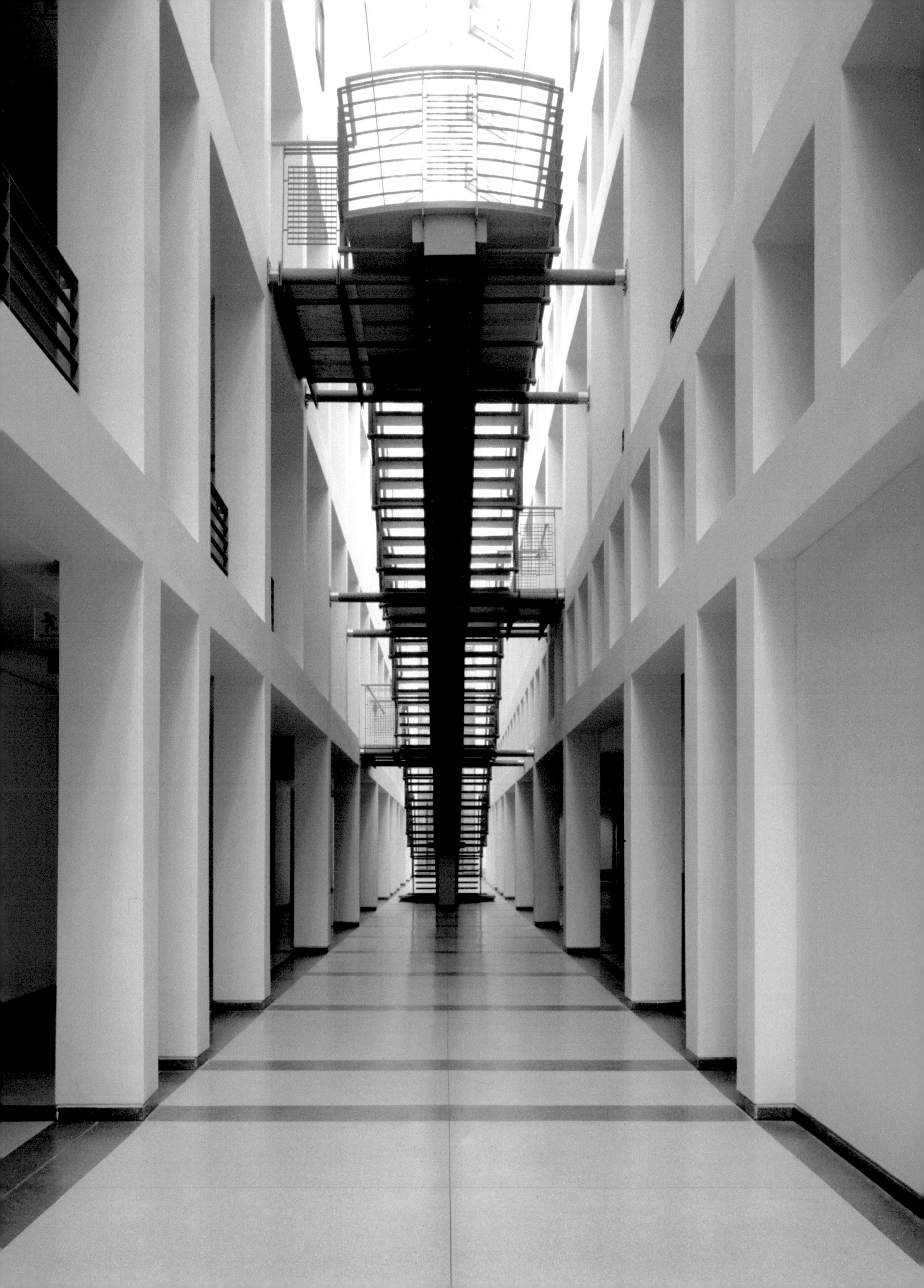

Bank- und Geschäftshaus Brodschrangen, Hamburg
Bank and Commercial Building Brodschrangen, Hamburg

Studie Study
1988

Entwurf Design
Volkwin Marg und Klaus Staratzke

Bauherr Client
A. Büll + Dr. Liedtke

Bauzeit Construction period
1992–1994

BGF Gross floor area
6.600 m²

Die dreigeschossigen, raumhoch verglasten Fassadenerker sowie die achtgeschossigen Ecktürme des Büro- und Geschäftshauses schaffen helle, transparente Arbeitsräume und kompensieren die Enge des Straßenraums. Eine durchgehende Metall-Glas-Fassade in der Gebäudeachse stellt eine Sichtverbindung vom Blockinnen- zum außenraum her. Die Filigranität scharfkantiger Metallprofile und die Transparenz der großen Glasflächen bestimmen die Struktur der Fassade. Die geneigten und mit Atelierfenstern versehenen Dachflächen bestehen aus einem Zink-Stegblech-Dach, die Fassaden- und Attikapfeiler sind mit Naturstein und profiliertem Aluminiumblech verblendet. Die inneren Erschließungsflächen werden durch das Wechselspiel farblicher Akzentuierungen und filigraner Strukturen betont, während die Besprechungsräume in den Ecktürmen durch Glasschiebewände weit geöffnet werden können.

The three-storey, room-high, glazed window oriels as well as the eight-storey glass towers create light, transparent working rooms and compensate for the narrowness of the street space. A continual metal-glass façade on the axis of the building creates a visible link between the interior of the block and the exterior. The delicacy of sharp-angled metal window sections and the large glass areas dictate the structure of the façade. The sloping roof areas, fitted with atelier windows, are made of zinc sheeting; the façade and parapet pillars are covered with natural stone and aluminium panels. The interior entrance zones are defined by an interplay between colour accentuations and delicate structures, while the meeting rooms in the corner tower can be expanded by sliding glass partitions.

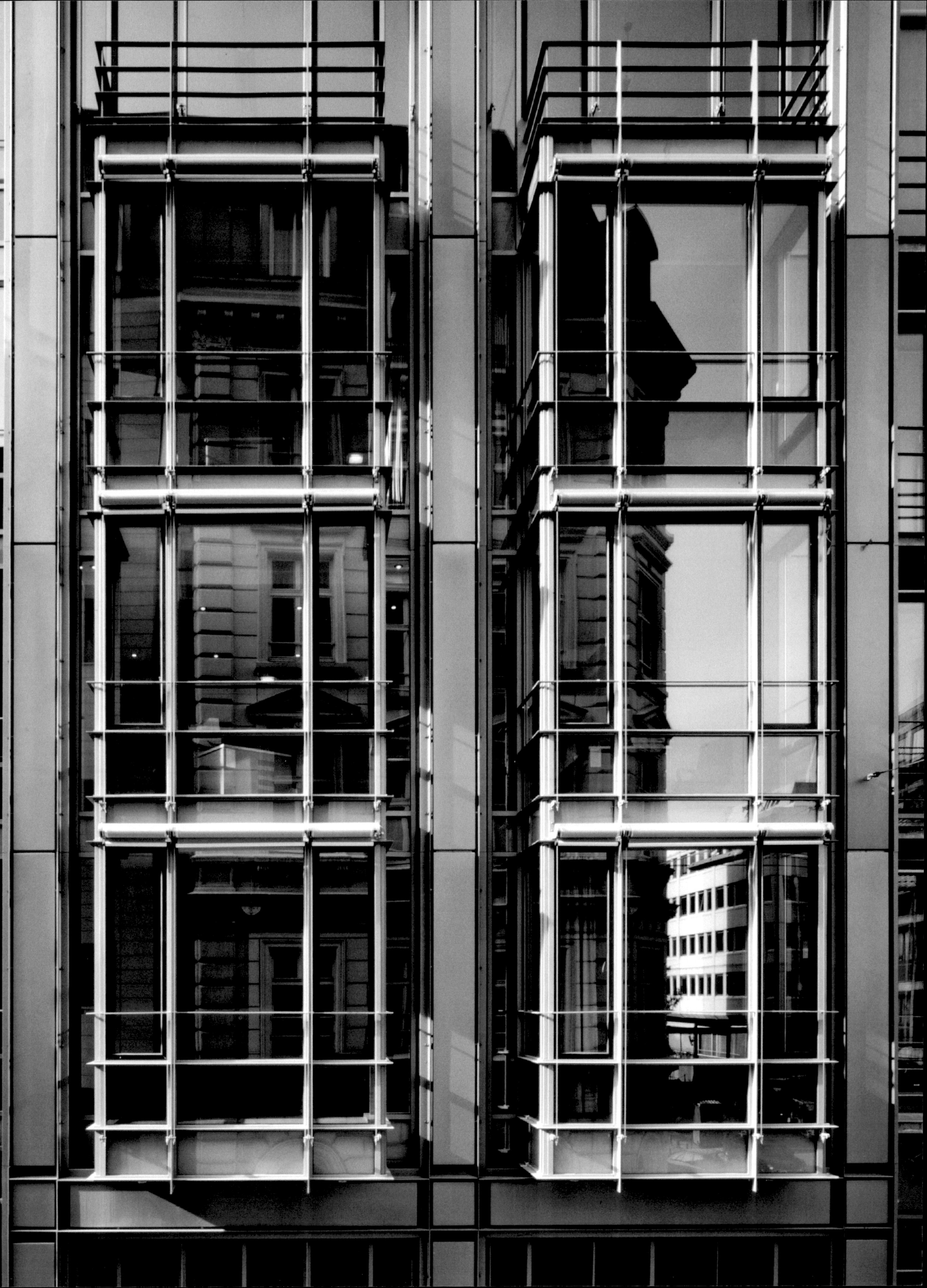

1995

Deutsch-Japanisches Zentrum, Hamburg

Der realisierte Entwurf des Deutsch-Japanischen Zentrums wird durch zwei typologisch sehr unterschiedliche, jedoch in ihrer architektonischen Charakteristik verwandte Baukörper repräsentiert, die jeweils auf die spezifische Grundstückssituation reagieren.

German-Japanese Centre, Hamburg

The implemented design of the German-Japanese Centre presents itself with two typologically very different, albeit architecturally related building volumes, which both react to their specific site conditions.

Messe Hannover, Halle 4

Die Halle 4 ersetzt einen ursprünglich aus dem Jahr 1957 stammenden Vorgängerbau, dessen Konzept als geschlossene Halle ohne Tageslicht nicht mehr der heutigen Auffassung extrovertierter, taghellerAusstellungsbauten entspricht. Große Fischbauchträger bestimmen das Erscheinungsbild der neuen transparenten Halle.

Hanover Trade Fair, Hall 4

Hall 4 replaced a building originally dating from 1957. The original building, conceived as an enclosed shed with no daylight, no longer met the modern trade fair idea of extroverted, day-lit exhibition buildings. Large fish-belly girders determine the appearance of the new transparent hall.

Stadtvilla Dr. Braasch, Eberswalde

Typologisch bezieht sich der Entwurf auf die Villenbebauung der Nachbarschaft, transformiert sie jedoch in eine neue Gestaltsprache. Alle Wohnungen werden separat über eine Außentreppe erschlossen. Den durchgehenden Wohnraum im Staffelgeschoss der obersten Wohnung überspannt ein Tonnendach.

Dr. Braasch Town Villa, Eberswalde

Typologically, the design refers to the neighbouring villa development, simultaneously transforming it into a new architectural expression. All apartments are separately accessible via an exterior staircase. A barrel roof covers the continuous living space on the stepped top floor.

Deutsch-Japanisches Zentrum, Hamburg
German-Japanese Centre, Hamburg

Wettbewerb Competition
1990 – 1. Preis

Entwurf Design
Meinhard von Gerkan

Partner Partner
Klaus Staratzke

Bauherr Client
Deutsche Immobilien Anlagengesellschaft mbH,
HANSEATICA Unternehmens Consulting GmbH,
Kajima Development GmbH

Bauzeit Construction period
1993–1995

BGF Gross floor area
22.000 m²

Das Ensemble des Deutsch-Japanischen Zentrums sollte geschlossen wirken als signifikanter Bau für einen für die Stadt wichtigen Zweck, andererseits mit seinen einzelnen Baukörpern auf die spezifische Grundstückssituation reagieren. Aus diesen Vorgaben wurde eine Baukörpergruppierung mit einer Art „doppelter Symmetrie" zur Stadthausbrücke hin entwickelt: Ein mittlerer, sechsgeschossiger Baukörper wird von zwei schmalen Seitenflügeln flankiert und durch Brücken verbunden. Der linke Teil wird am Fleetrand weitergeführt, der rechte bildet eine neue Platzwand. Leider fiel dieser Bauteil dem Rotstift zum Opfer und blieb nur als Rudiment eines „gläsernen Erkers". Der mittlere Bauteil wiederum wird durch zwei vertikale Schlitze und das im Mittelteil zurückgestaffelte oberste Geschoss sowie eine großformatige Fassade noch einmal kräftig symmetrisch gegliedert.

The German-Japanese Centre consists of two buildings, one of them a slim bar of a house which curves along the Fleet (narrow canal), as if bowing to the urban situation. Slimness and bowing are both metaphors for Japanese culture. The second house, however, appears like a sharp-edged block firmly attached to the ground, representing virtues one might ascribe to the Germans. At the same time, this building, at the rear, opens out into stepped, semi-open courtyards. A pedestrian arcaded passage along the Stadthausbrücke forms a stretch of weather-protected urban street space. The façades also show a marked duality: the street fronts are clad in dark clinker bricks, in deliberate contrast to the filigree transparent glazing to the rear. The functional interior organization was developed as a synthesis of German and Japanese elements, in other words, the typical office cubicle and the open-plan office landscape.

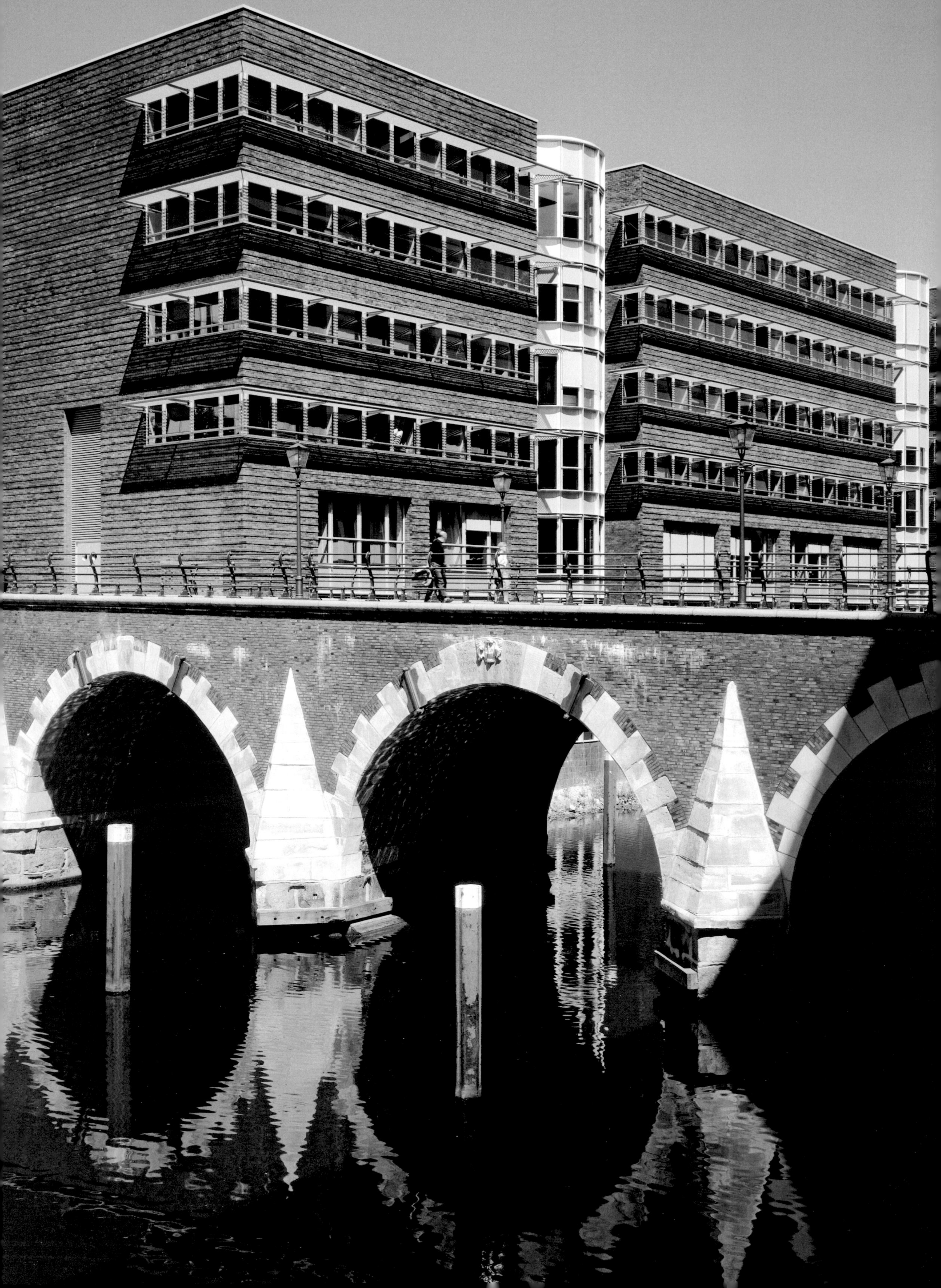

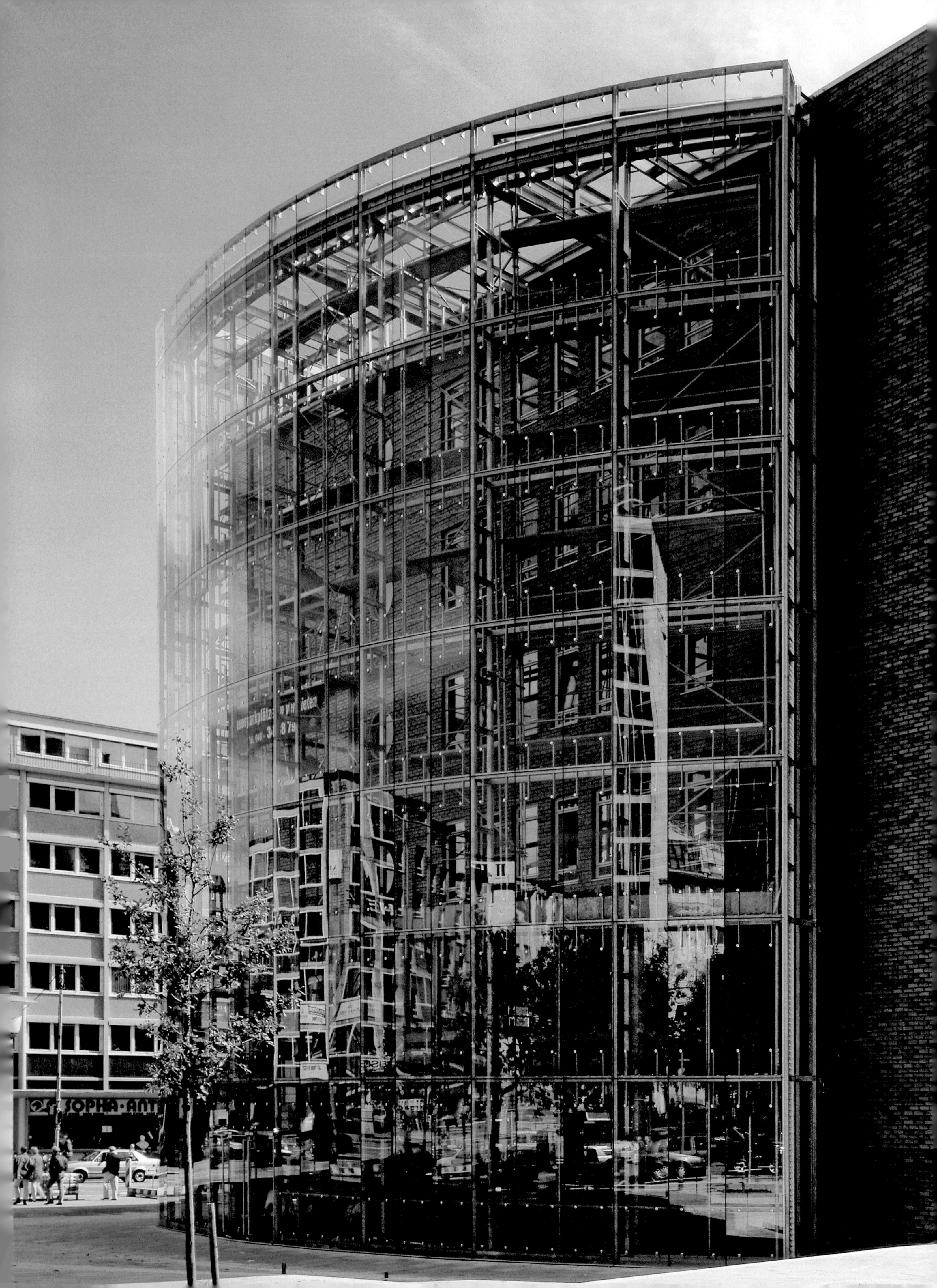
SOPHA-ANT

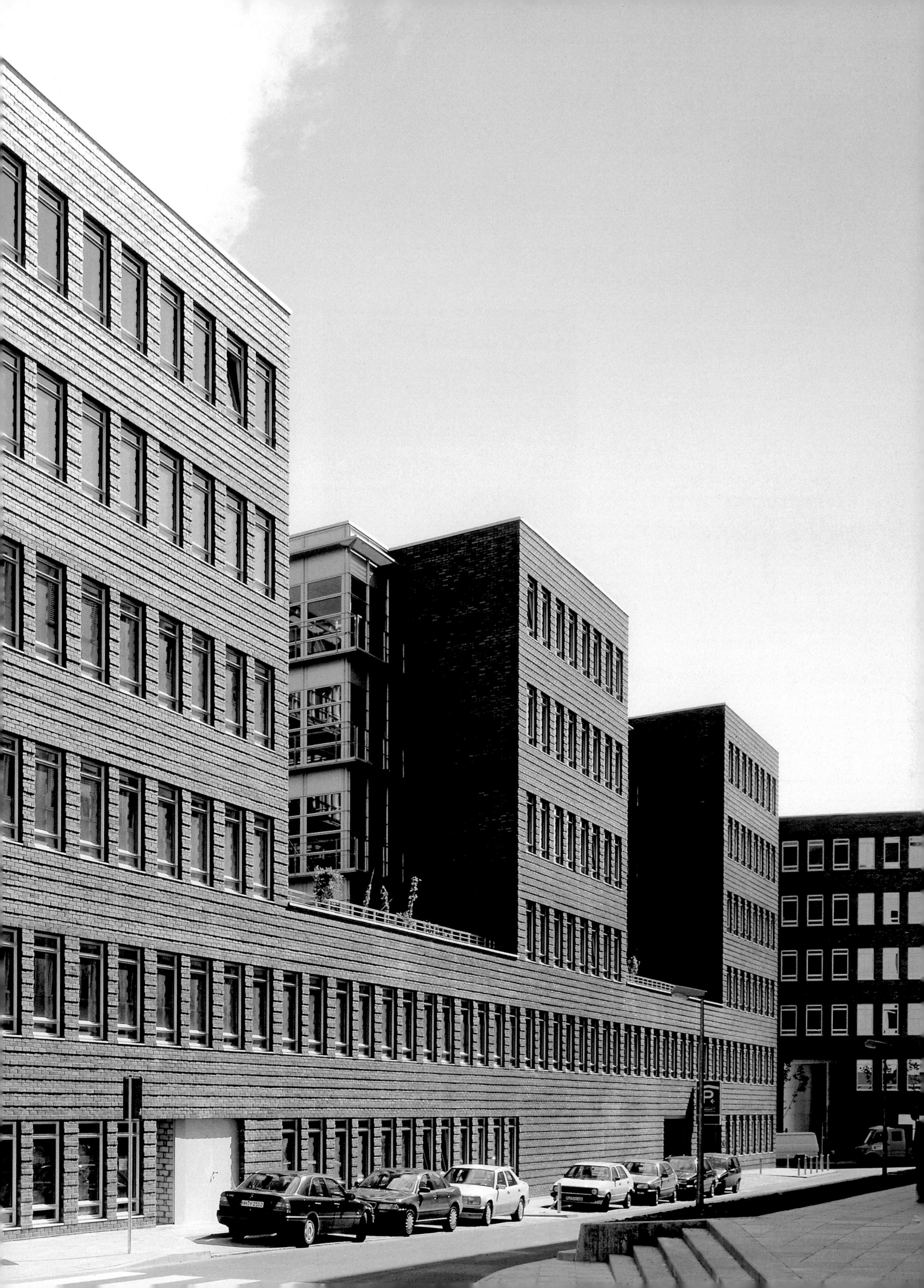

Messe Hannover, Halle 4
Hanover Trade Fair, Hall 4

Wettbewerb Competition
1994 – 1. Preis

Entwurf Design
Volkwin Marg und Jörg Schlaich

Partner Partner
Klaus Staratzke

Bauherr Client
Deutsche Messe AG

Bauzeit Construction period
1995–1996

BGF Gross floor area
35.650 m²

Die Halle 4 wurde als weitgespannte, stützenfrei überdachte Halle mit großzügigen Verglasungen und zweiseitig angeordneten Riegelbauten konzipiert. Die eingeschossige Ausstellungsfläche wird über 122 m stützenfrei überspannt. Linsenförmige Dachhohlkörper bilden die Konstruktion. Sie nehmen in ihrem Inneren raumluft- und elektrotechnische Installationen auf und sind für Wartungszwecke begehbar. Die lichte Höhe unterhalb der Binder, die aus seilunterspannten Druckbogenpaaren bestehen, beträgt 11 bis 15 m. Die Form des Trägers stellt gleichzeitig eine Hommage an Hannovers großen Architekten des Klassizismus dar, an Georg Ludwig Friedrich Laves, der den „Fischbauchträger" für Brückenkonstruktionen erfand. Die verglaste Giebelfassade wirkt bei innerer Beleuchtung wie ein großes Schaufenster und entspricht in besonderem Maße dem Thema des Ausstellungsbaus.

The Hall 4 was created as a wide-span, support-free, roofed-over hall with generous areas of glazing and buildings arranged parallel to each other on two sides. The single-storey exhibition area spans without support over 122 m. It is constructed from hollow, lens-like roof elements, which accommodate the air handling and electrical installation equipment, and which are accessible for maintenance. The clear height created under the bow string trusses and their lower-tensile rod members is 11 to 15 m. The truss form used pays homage to Hanover's great classical architect Georg Ludwig Friedrich Laves, who invented the double-bow truss for use in bridge construction. When illuminated, the glazed gable and elevations create a huge shop window, a quintessential exhibition theme.

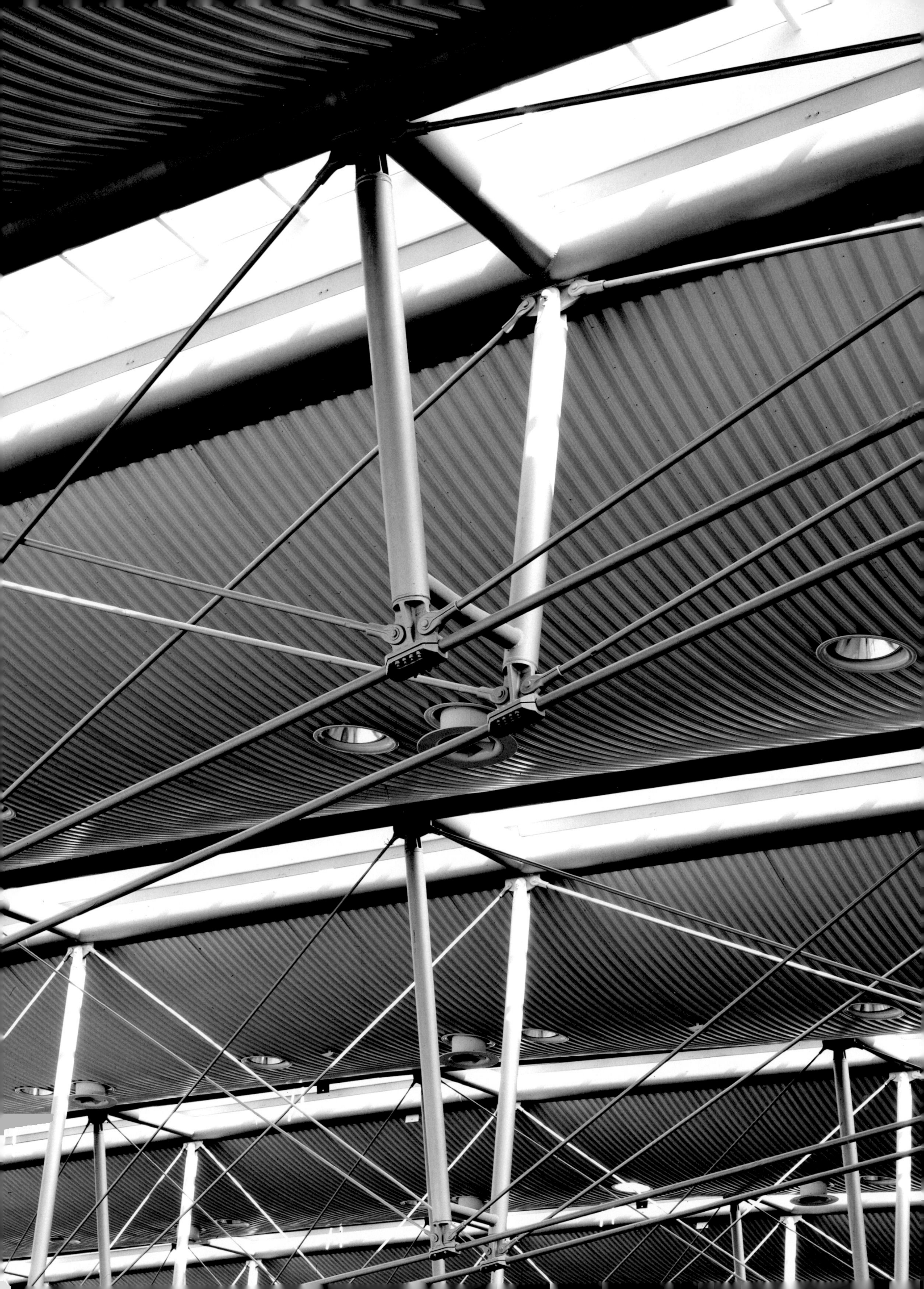

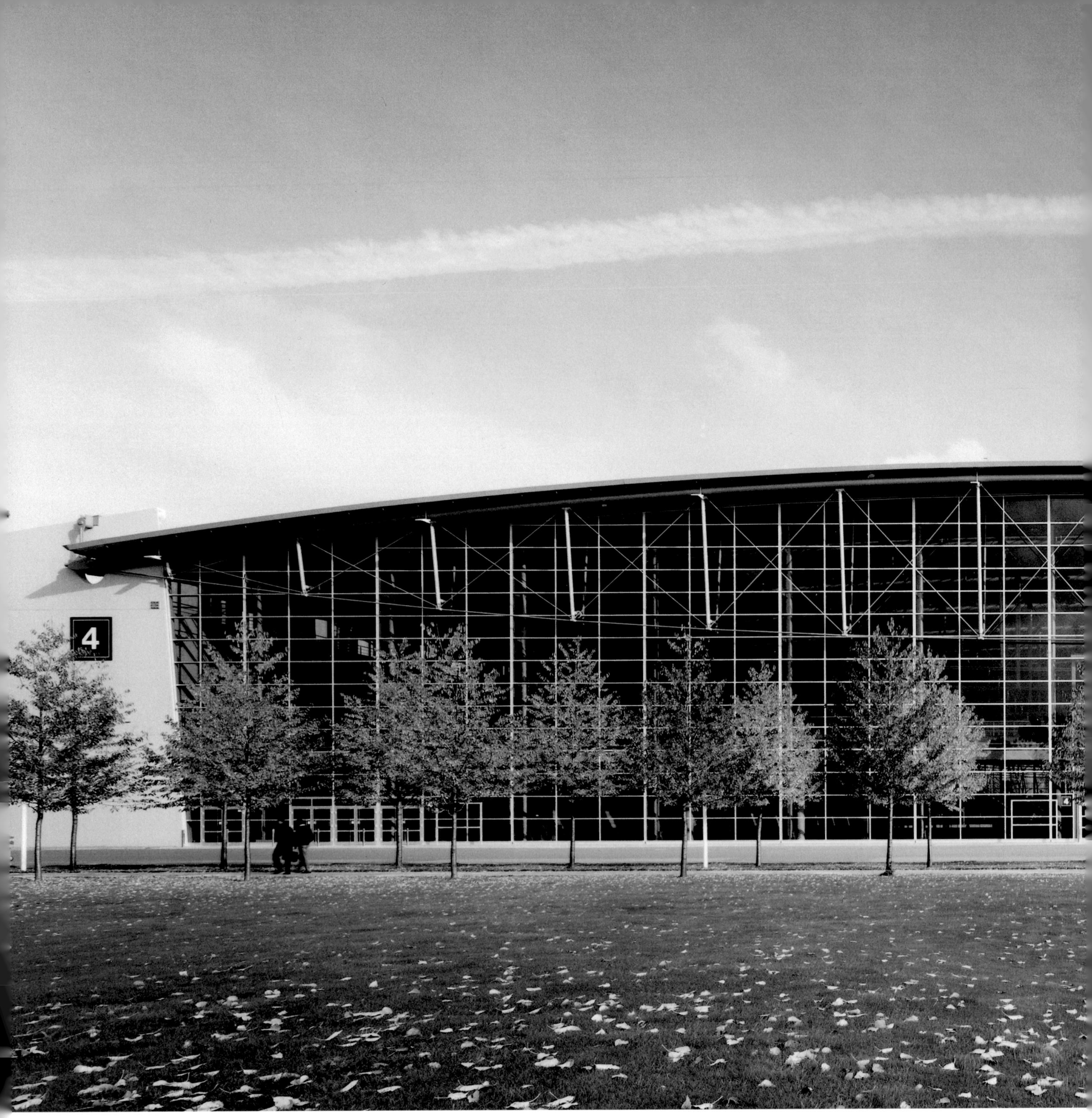
4

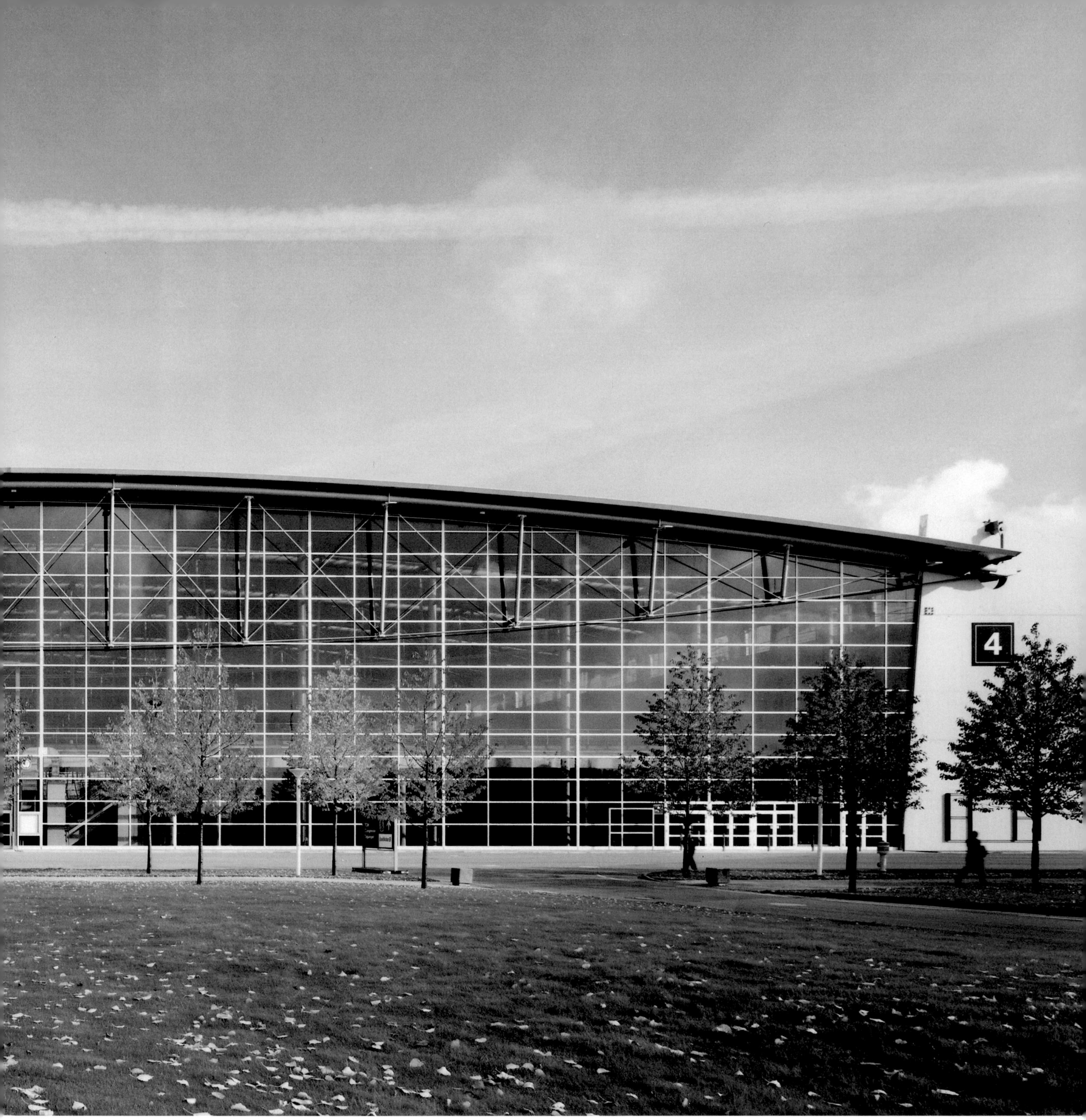
4

1996

Solarpavillon, Kiel

Der Beratungs- und Informationspavillon der Stadtwerke ist als reines Stahlskelett mit vor der Fassade stehenden Stützen konstruiert. Eine innenliegende Ausstellungshalle wird über ein Oberlicht erhellt, dessen transparente Verglasung bereichsweise durch Photovoltaik-Elemente ergänzt wird.

Solar Pavilion, Kiel

The information pavilion of the city's municipal works is designed as a pure steel skeleton with columns placed in front of the façade. An exhibition hall placed inside receives daylight via a roof light, with photovoltaic elements complementing parts of the transparent glazing.

Neue Messe Leipzig

Am neuen Standort der Leipziger Messe in der Nähe von Flughafen und Autobahnanschluss wurde ein neuer, künstlicher Ort geschaffen, ein „Gesamtkunstwerk" aus Stadt- und Landschaftsplanung, Architektur und Ingenieurbaukunst, in einer Umgebung, die durch gestalterischen Wildwuchs gekennzeichnet ist.

New Leipzig Trade Fair

At the new site of the Leipzig Trade Fair, in close proximity to the airport and the motorway a new, artificial place has been developed, a "synthesis of the arts" of urban and landscape planning, architecture and engineering skills in surroundings that are characterized by uncontrolled growth.

Allee-Center, Leipzig-Grünau

Die glasüberdeckte Rotunde mit einem Durchmesser von 40 Metern bildet den Mittelpunkt des Stadtteilzentrums. Sie dient als Aktionsfläche und Schnittpunkt der glasüberdeckten „Straßen" und Galerien der Passage. Die Nutzung entspricht der eines urbanen Kerngebietes mit Geschäften, Büros und Freizeitangeboten.

'Allee-Center', Leipzig-Grünau

The glass-covered rotunda with a 40-metre diameter forms the focal area of the community centre. It serves as activity area and intersection of the glass-covered 'streets' and galleries of the passage. The way it is used corresponds to that of an urban core area with shops, offices and leisure facilities.

Hapag-Lloyd, Hamburg

Die Erweiterung des Verwaltungsgebäudes an der Rosenstraße schreibt den Typus des Hamburger Kontorhauses in die heutige Zeit fort. Der frühere Lichthof im Innern erhält hier als Wintergarten und Treppenhaus eine neue Qualität und wird zur halböffentlichen Eingangs- und Aufenthaltshalle.

Hapag-Lloyd Office Building, Hamburg

The extension of the administration building on Rosenstrasse continues the typology of the traditional office building into modern times. The former inner courtyard acquires a new quality as a winter garden and staircase and becomes a semi-public entrance and waiting area.

Neue Messe Leipzig
New Leipzig Trade Fair

Wettbewerb Competition
1992 – 1. Preis

Entwurf Design
Volkwin Marg und Hubert Nienhoff

Bauherr Client
Leipziger Messegesellschaft mbH

Bauzeit Construction period
1993–1996

BGF Gross floor area
273.000 m²

Das Grundkonzept der Anlage ist einfach: Der Besucher gelangt zunächst in ein zentrales, als zusammenhängender Landschaftspark ausgebildetes Tal, das ein Geschoss tiefer liegt als die Ausstellungshallen. Die größte Halle, die Hochhalle, wird als Mehrzweckhalle genutzt. Ihr Gegenstück ist das Tagungs- und Kongresszentrum. Eine großzügige Treppenanlage verbindet die Foyers vor den Sälen. Die Reihen von Kolonnaden verleihen dem Kongresszentrum seine angemessene Bedeutung. Zusammen mit dem filigranen Turm bildet die Eingangshalle West mit 80 m Spannweite und 240 m Länge das Wahrzeichen der neuen Messe. Sie wird von großen Fachwerkbögen überspannt, von denen eine gläserne Hülle abgehängt ist. Jede der 1,50 x 3,00 m großen Glasscheiben ist an vier Punkten befestigt; sie ergeben zusammen eine riesige, von innen vollständig glatte, profillose Glastonne – ein neuer Kristallpalast am Ende des 20. Jahrhunderts.

The underlying design principle is simple: the visitor arrives in a central valley, which is designed as a continuous landscaped park and runs one level below the exhibition halls. The largest so-called High Hall is used as a multi-purpose hall. Its counterpart is the congress centre. A generous flight of stairs forms a linkage to the foyers in front of the conference halls. A sequence of arcades lend appropriate prominence to the congress centre. In combination with the delicate tower, the Entrance Hall West, with a span of 80 m and a length of 240 m, is the landmark of the new exhibition centre. The roof of this hall is spanned by majestic steel arches with a suspended glass envelope. Every single 1.5 x 3-m glass panel is fixed externally at four points, resulting in a grand, internally smooth glass surface – a new Crystal Palace at the end of the 20th century.

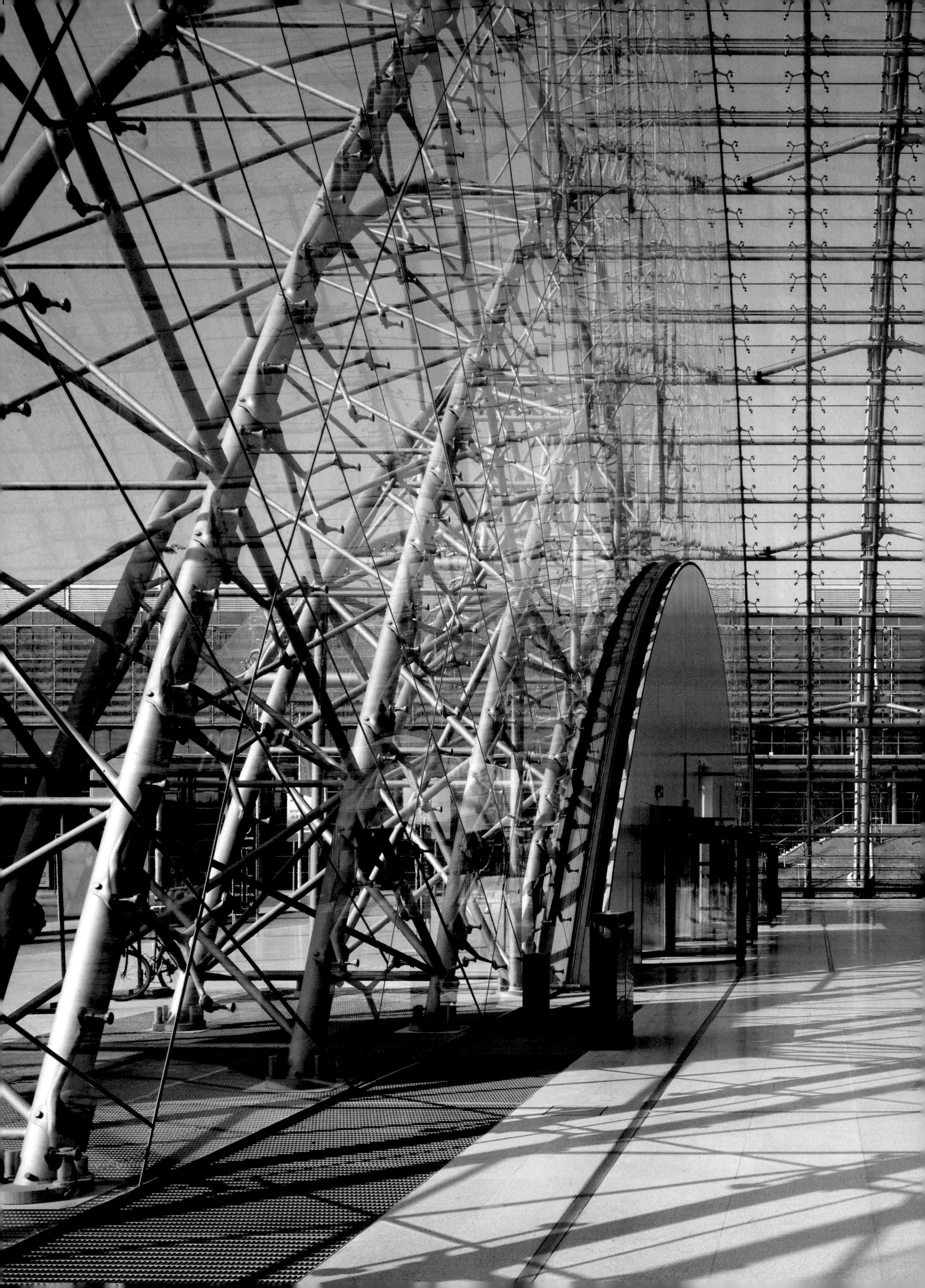

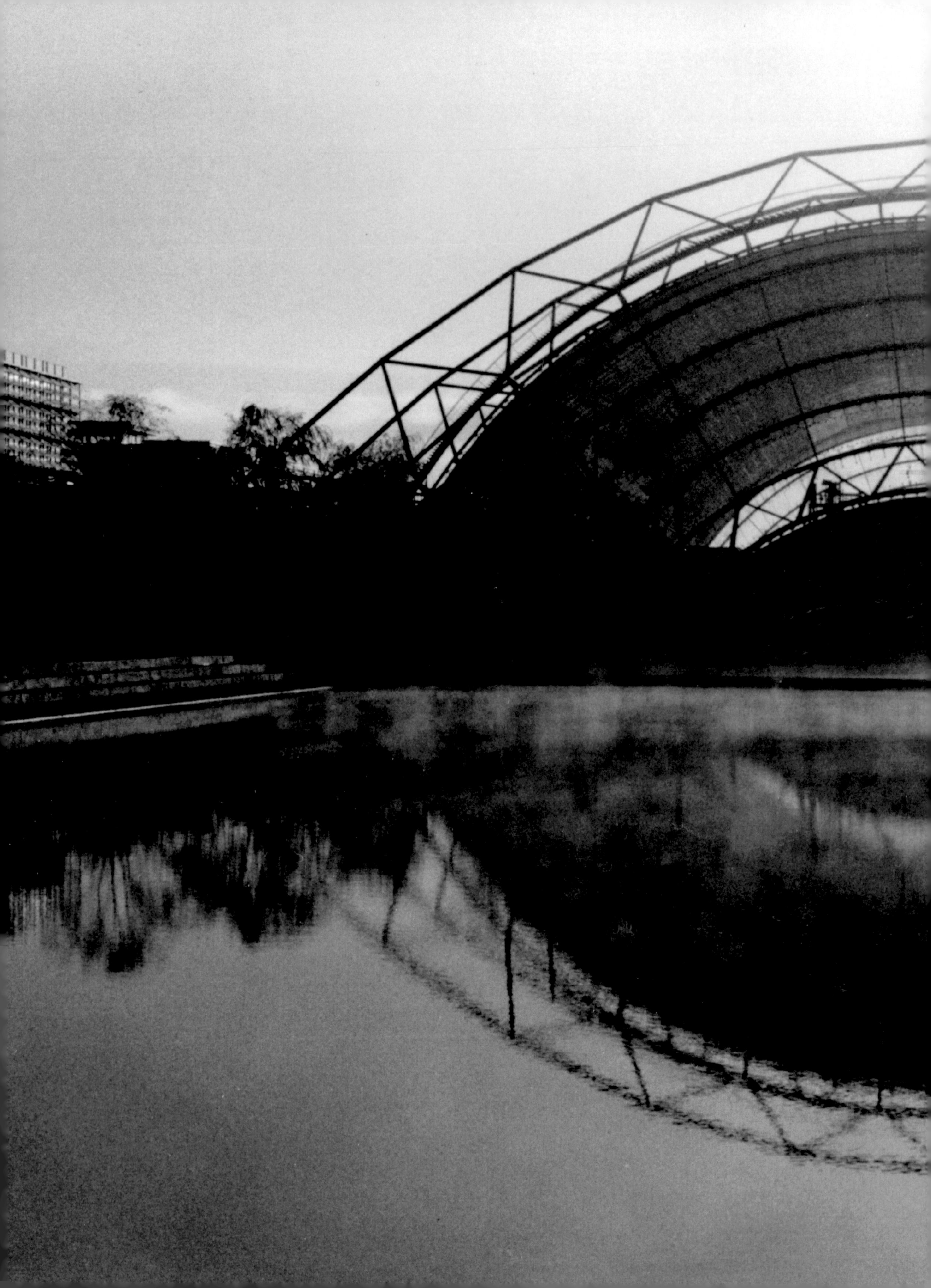

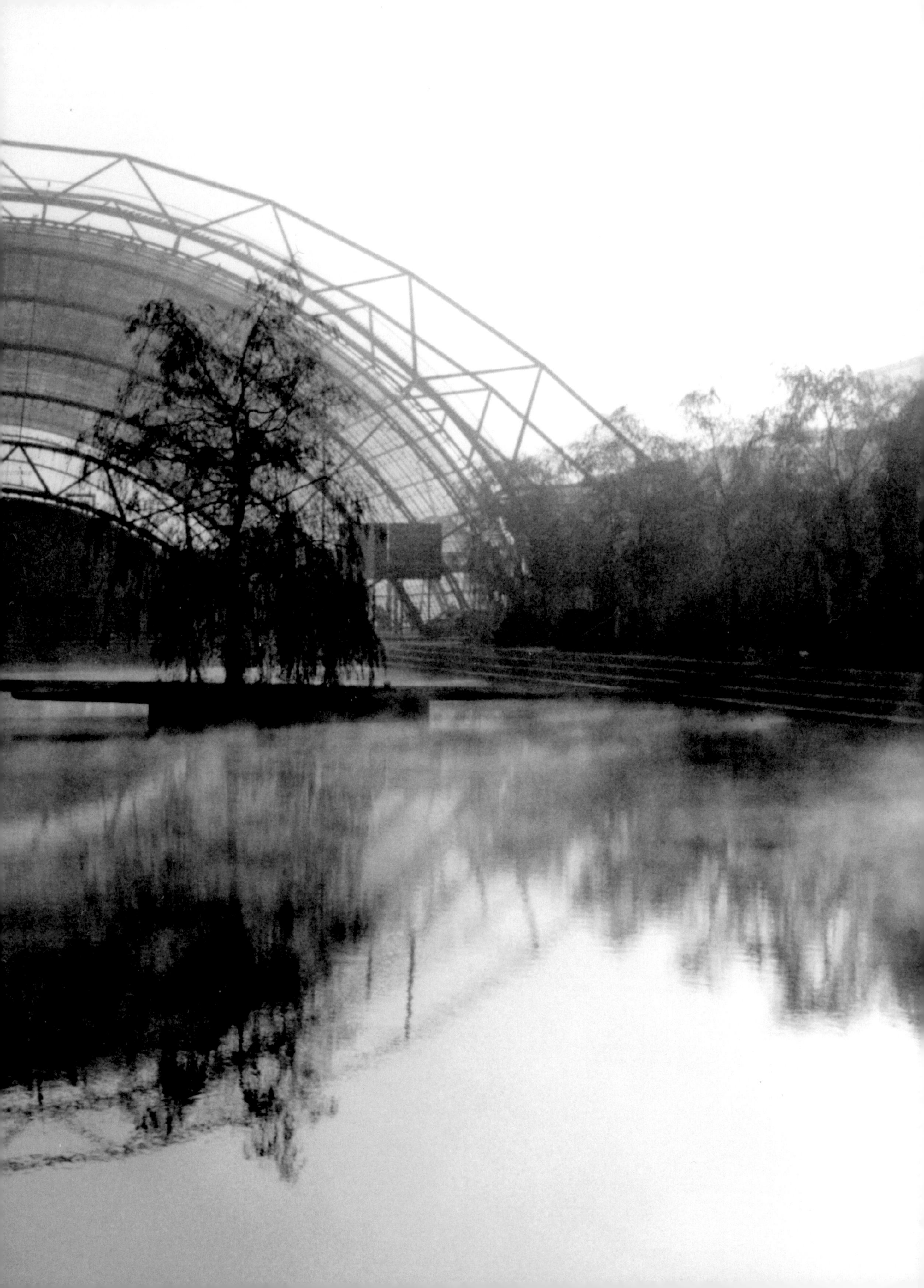

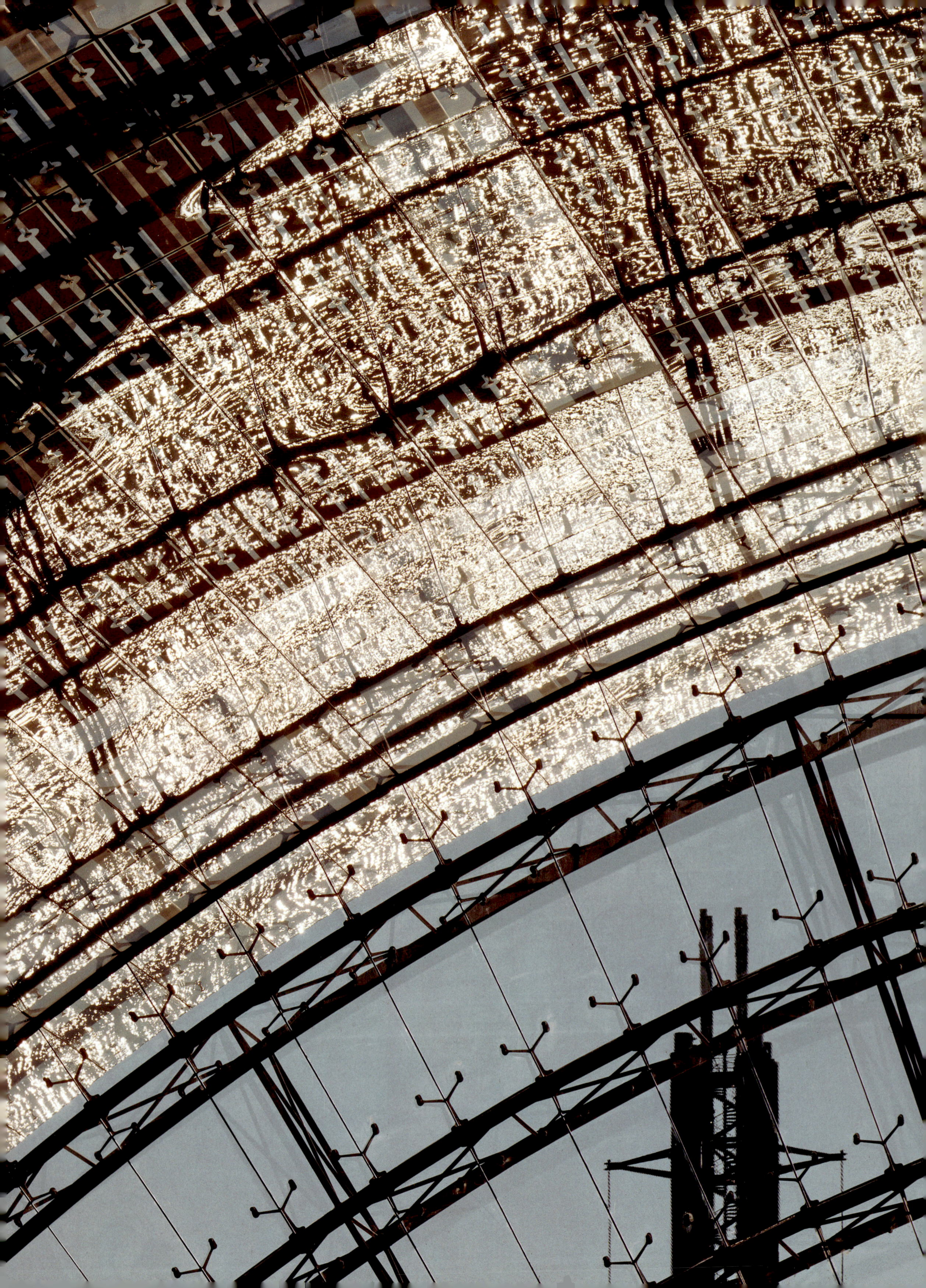

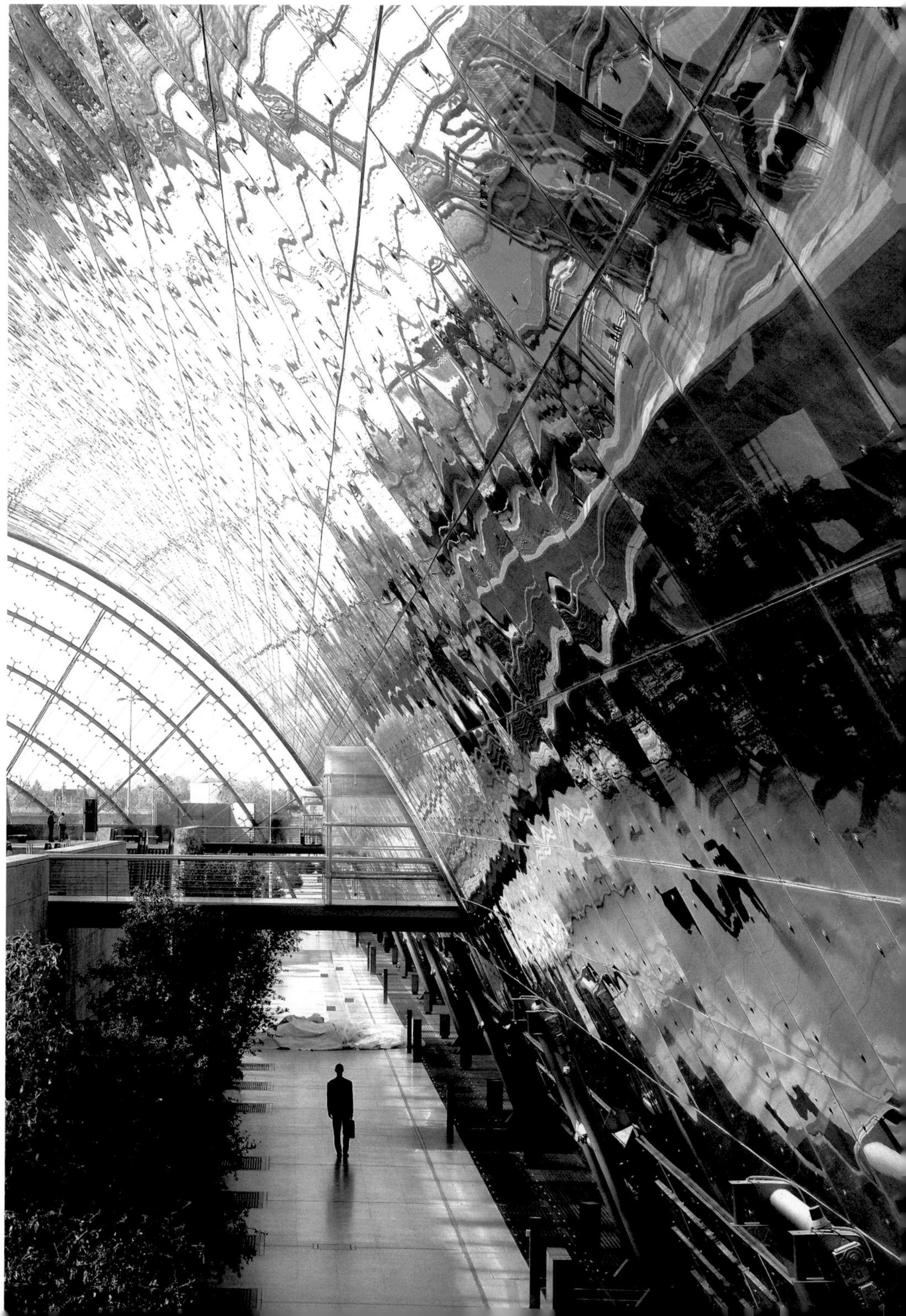

1997

Block 203, Friedrichstraße, Berlin

Für den „Block 203" in der östlichen Innenstadt Berlins wurde ein Büro- und Geschäftshaus mit einem Anteil Wohnungen entwickelt, das die städtebaulichen Rahmenbedingungen der Friedrichstadt berücksichtigt und unter Einbeziehung der Altbauten das Quartier in seinem historischen Stadtprofil neu definiert.

Block 203, Friedrichstrasse, Berlin

Block 203 in the eastern centre of Berlin has been developed as an office and shop centre with a number of apartments. The redevelopment of the historic city profile had to respect the urban context of Friedrichstadt and integrate the existing old buildings.

Dresdner Bank am Pariser Platz, Berlin

Die repräsentative „Gute Stube" Berlins, der traditionsreiche Pariser Platz am Brandenburger Tor, wird im Sinne der „kritischen Rekonstruktion" wiederhergestellt. Einen Teil der Platzwand bildet der Neubau der Dresdner Bank, der sich in Höhe und Grundriss zurückhaltend in das Konzept der Neubebauung einfügt.

Dresdner Bank at Pariser Platz, Berlin

Berlin's representative 'front parlour', the historically rich Pariser Platz at Brandenburger Tor was re-established in the spirit of 'critical reconstruction'. Dresdner Bank's new building forms one segment of the square whilst complying with the restrictive height and plan regulations.

Praxis Dr. Manke, Uelzen

In der heterogenen Umgebung aus Ein- und Zweifamilienhäusern bildet das zweigeschossige Haus mit zurückgestaffeltem Obergeschoss einen Ruhepunkt. Die Außenwände in matt-silbriger Red-Cedar-Holzverkleidung unterstreichen den Charakter des Hauses als ebenso dauerhaft wie einfach.

Dr. Manke Practice, Uelzen

The two-storey house with a recessed upper floor forms a repose in the heterogeneous neighbourhood of single- and twin-family houses. The exterior walls with a matt silver, red-cedar panelling emphasize the permanent as well as the simple character of the building.

Sternhäuser, Norderstedt

Die Grundrissstruktur der drei Solitärbauten besteht aus jeweils zwei um 45° gegeneinander verdrehten Quadraten, die auf diese Weise achteckige „Sterne" bilden. Die Zacken der Sterne sind als verglaste Erker ausgebildet, die die Backsteinfassaden der kubischen Baukörper zu durchbrechen scheinen.

Star Houses, Norderstedt

The plan structure of each of these three solitaires turned towards each other at an angle of 45°, thereby forming octagonal 'stars'. The tips of the stars are designed as glazed bays, which seem to break through the brick façades of the cubic buildings.

1997

Restaurant VAU, Berlin

Das Restaurant befindet sich in einem gründerzeitlichen Haus in direkter Nachbarschaft zum Gendarmenmarkt in der Mitte Berlins. Elemente traditioneller Restaurantarchitektur, die in zeitgemäßer Weise transformiert wurden, prägen die Räume des VAU und erzeugen eine Atmosphäre moderner Behaglichkeit.

VAU Restaurant, Berlin

The restaurant is located in a house originating from the early 20th century in the immediate neighbourhood of Gendarmenmarkt in central Berlin. Elements of traditional restaurant architecture, which were transformed to meet present requirements, characterize the rooms at VAU and generate a cosy modern atmosphere.

Typendach für die Deutsche Bahn AG

Eine sanft geschwungene Stahl-Glas-Konstruktion überdacht die Bahnsteige. Diese Konstruktion ruht auf einer Doppelstützenreihe im Abstand von 9 Metern. Durch die wirbelartige Segmentierung lässt sich die Konstruktion in der Länge variieren. Die Breite kann durch Verlängerung der Querträger angepasst werden.

Serial Platform Roofing for Deutsche Bahn AG

A slightly curved steel-glass structure roofs the platforms. It sits on a row of doubble columns at 9-m intervals. The length of the structure can be varied by the spine-like segmentation. The width can be adjusted by lengthening the transverse girders.

Wohnbebauung, Berlin-Friedrichshain

Der soziale Wohnungsbau an der Friedensstraße bildet den ersten Bauabschnitt des Projektes „Forum Friedrichshain". Der winkelförmige Baukörper ist in acht Einzelhäuser gegliedert, deren zurückgesetztes Dachgeschoss die traditionelle Berliner Traufhöhe respektiert.

Residential Development, Berlin-Friedrichshain

The public housing along Friedensstrasse forms the first construction stage of the 'Friedrichshain Forum' project. The angular volume is subdivided into eight detached houses, their staggered attic storeys respecting Berlin's traditional eaves height.

Geschäftshaus Neuer Wall 43, Hamburg

Die Geschäftshäuser Neuer Wall 41 und 43 wurden von Godber Nissen 1951 bis 1958 als erste Gebäude mit einer Vorhangfassade errichtet. Der Um- und Neubau bietet ein attraktives Laden-Kaufhaus neuen Typs, bei dem um eine Glashalle herum auf drei Galerien von unten einsehbare Läden angeboten werden.

Commercial Block Neuer Wall 43, Hamburg

From 1951 to 1958 Godber Nissen constructed the commercial blocks Neuer Wall 41 and 43 as the first buildings with a suspended façade. The renovation and extension offers an attractive new kind of department store, where shops are located on three galleries around a glass hall and can be looked into from below.

Nordseepassage, Wilhelmshaven

Der Komplex entsteht auf dem Gelände des ehemaligen Wilhelmshavener Bahnhofs, dessen vier Hauptgleise integriert werden und in deren Verlängerung die Hauptpassage verläuft. Die Überdeckung der Einkaufspassagen erfolgt mittels einer aus Dreiecksflächen „gefalteten" Shedstruktur.

Nordseepassage, Wilhelmshaven

The complex was built on the site of the former Wilhelmshaven railway station. The four main tracks of the station are integrated and define the main passage. The shopping arcades are covered by a 'folded' shed structure of triangles.

Forum Köpenick, Berlin

Die glasgedeckte, langgestreckte Halle des Einkaufszentrums bildet als große, einfache Markthalle den Mittelpunkt für Aktionen, Gastronomie und fliegende Märkte. Nach außen bietet sie freie Sicht auf die Bahnhofstraße und das durch Aufstauung des Flusses entstandene Wohnquartier am neuen Wuhle-Becken.

Köpenick Forum, Berlin

The glass-covered, linear shopping hall, designed as a large, simple market hall, forms the focus for various events, restaurants and travelling markets. The hall offers a clear view towards Bahnhofstrasse and the residential district that was built on the new Wuhle Basin by blocking the path of the river.

1997

Ortszentrum Schöneiche bei Berlin

Eine bauliche Mitte als Identifikationspunkt der kleinstädtischen Waldsiedlung fehlte bislang. Die neue zwei- bis dreigeschossige Bebauung gliedert sich in zwei Hälften aus je vier Einzelbaukörpern, die auf Höhe des ersten Obergeschosses Gartenhöfe umschließen. Im Erdgeschoss befinden sich Läden.

Schöneiche Town Centre, near Berlin

What this small-town housing estate set in a forest lacked was an architectural centre to provide a point of identification. The new two- to three-storey development is divided into two halves consisting of four detached buildings each. These houses enclose garden courts at the first upper floor level.

Gerling Haus, Stuttgart

Das Gebäude reagiert in Form und Konzept auf die städtebauliche Situation mit dem sich verjüngenden Grundstück zwischen der Heilbronner und der Presselstraße. Der Baukörper in Form eines rechtwinkligen Dreiecks ragt mit seiner Spitze zur Innenstadt und markiert den Auftakt zu den anschließenden Bürogebäuden.

Gerling House, Stuttgart

The design and form of the building is based on the tapering site between Heilbronner Strasse and Presselstrasse and on the surrounding urban context. The building's shape resembles a rectangular volume, marking the beginning of the adjacent office blocks.

Telekomzentrale, Suhl

Für das gesamte Gebäude wurde eine kammartige, sich nach Süden öffnende, orthogonale Baustruktur entwickelt, die von einem zweiten, ringförmigen Baukörper überlagert wird. Die aus der Überlagerung entstehende Sonderform beinhaltet eine knapp bemessene, zweigeschossige Verteilerhalle.

Telekom Headquarters, Suhl

A comb-like, orthogonal structure opening up towards the south and overlapped by a second, ring-shaped structure, was developed for the entire building. The special form resulting from this overlap accommodates a spatially restricted, two-storey circulation hall.

Klappbrücke, Kiel-Hörn

Die Dreifeld-Klappbrücke stellt im Ruhe- wie im Bewegungszustand eine signifikante Landmarke dar, die im Brückenbau bisher einmalig ist. Sie bietet im Bewegungszustand einen kinetischen Ablauf von großer Attraktion, während sie als Seesteg eine optimale Nähe zum Wasser schafft.

Restaurierung des Thalia Theaters, Hamburg

Das Theater wurde 1912 von Georg Kallmorgen erbaut und nach der teilweisen Zerstörung im Krieg von seinem Sohn Werner 1960 modernisiert. Die unterschiedlichen Handschriften, die die verschiedenen Architekturepochen widerspiegeln, wurden sorgfältig in Abstimmung mit dem Denkmalschutz restauriert.

Umbau und Restaurierung der Hapag-Lloyd AG am Ballindamm, Hamburg

Die repräsentative Eingangszone des 1912/13 von Fritz Höger umgebauten und erweiterten Firmensitzes wurde unter Berücksichtigung denkmalpflegerischer Belange den heutigen funktionalen und repräsentativen Ansprüchen der großen Firma entsprechend saniert und restauriert.

Bascule Bridge, Kiel-Hörn

Whether moving or at rest, the three-span bascule bridge represents a significant landmark, which is unique in bridge construction. During the opening and closing it offers a kinetic procedure providing an attraction, whilst simultaneously generating an optimal proximity to the water as a seaside footbridge.

Thalia Theatre Restoration, Hamburg

The theatre was built in 1912 by Georg Kallmorgen and, after being partially destroyed during World War II, was modernized in 1960 by his son Werner. The different personal styles, reflecting the different architectural periods, were carefully restored in accordance with the requirements for the protection of historic buildings.

Conversion and Renovation of Hapag-Lloyd AG on Ballindamm, Hamburg

The prestigious entrance zone of the company headquarters, which was converted and extended by Fritz Höger 1912/13, was renovated and restored to meet the functional and prestige-related demands of this large firm, whilst taking into consideration the requirements for the preservation of this monument.

Block 203, Friedrichstraße, Berlin
Block 203, Friedrichstrasse, Berlin

Gutachten Consultancy
1992

Entwurf Design
Volkwin Marg

Bauherr Client
Grundstücks-Kommanditgesellschaft
Kullmann & Co., Quartier 203

Bauzeit Construction period
1995–1997

BGF Gross floor area
34.900 m²

Der Block 203 vermeidet jede Historisierung; entsprechend der Normalität der Nutzungen wird eine nicht spektakuläre Architektursprache gewählt. An der Kronenstraße sind Wohnungen angeordnet, um einen Beitrag zum Erhalt der Friedrichstadt als Wohnstandort zu leisten. Der Block selbst mit seinen flexibel aufteilbaren Geschäfts- und Büroflächen wird durch zwei Atrien im Innern aufgewertet. Ein zweigeschossiger Eingang erschließt die etwa 45 m lange Halle mit filigranem Glasdach. Rolltreppen und Pflanzarkaden verbinden die Eingangshalle mit dem als Haupterschließungsebene dienenden Mezzaningeschoss. Die verglasten Innenhöfe mit Wasserbrunnen bilden eine Verweilzone für Besucher abseits der lauten Straße. Die Fassade mit ihren im Stützraster von 7,50 m angeordneten Pfeilern bildet ein massiv horizontal gegliedertes Fassadenraster, das aus der Fußgängerperspektive durch seine Profilierung hervortritt und sehr geschlossen wirkt.

Block 203 avoids any historicism using a rational architetural language to reflect the normality of its functions. Apartments are located along Kronenstrasse to make a contribution to the preservation of Friedrichstadt as a residential quarter. The introduction of two atria enhances the quality of the block with its flexible floor plans for shops and offices. The hall, which is sheltered by a lightweight glass roof, stretches 45 m and is accessible via an entrance two storeys high. Escalators and planted arcades link the entrance hall with the main circulation area on the mezzanine level. The glazed atria with water fountains act as recreational areas for visitors away from the noisy street. The façade is defined by a vertical column grid of 7.50 m and forms a massive horizontal framework, which from the pedestrians' perspective appears solid.

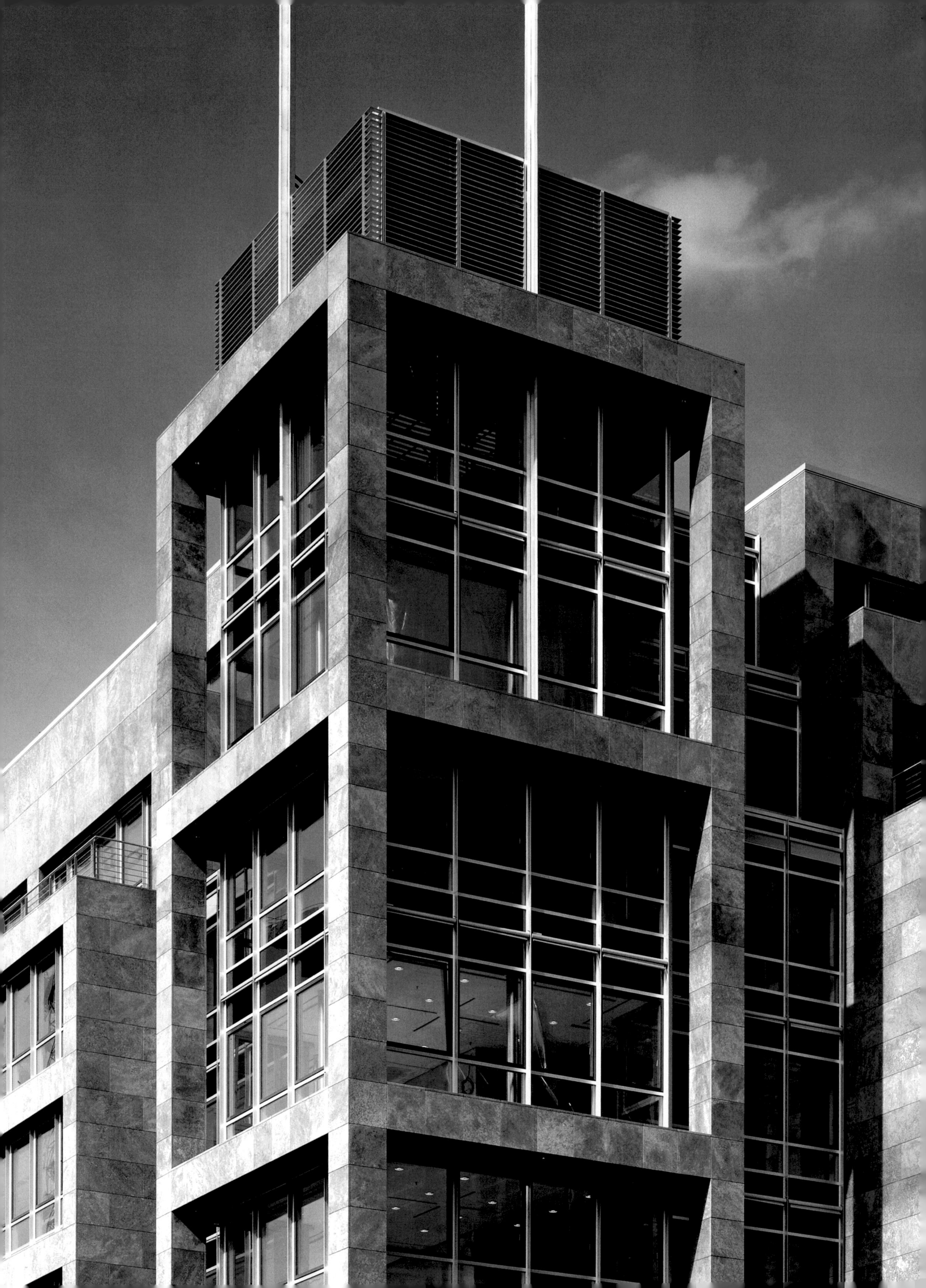

Dresdner Bank am Pariser Platz, Berlin
Dresdner Bank at Pariser Platz, Berlin

Wettbewerb Competition
1995 – 1. Preis

Entwurf Design
Meinhard von Gerkan

Bauherr Client
Schweitzer Grundbesitz-
und Verwaltungs GmbH & Co. KG

Bauzeit Construction period
1996–1997

BGF Gross floor area
11.600 m²

Die schwach ockerfarben getönte Sandsteinfassade des Bankhauses mit den senkrecht betonten Fensteröffnungen vermittelt zusammen mit den Bronzeprofilen der Fenster und den verstellbaren Verschattern sowie den patinierten Kupferplatten des Staffelgeschosses einen Gesamteindruck von vornehmer, verhaltener Repräsentanz. Hinter dem Foyer öffnet sich eine runde Halle mit 31 m Durchmesser und einem linsenförmigen, gläsernen Dach. Eine frei ausladende Spiraltreppe und zwei Aufzüge erschließen die Geschosse, deren Büros zur Halle hin orientiert sind. Ihnen sind gläserne Galerien vorgelagert, die der inneren Hülle eine filigrane Gliederung verleihen. Die Halle selbst ist um einige Stufen gegenüber dem Eingangsniveau abgesenkt; die Stufen laufen arenaartig um und betonen die geometrische Grundform. Inzwischen hat sich die Halle als ein hervorragender und sehr begehrter Ort für Veranstaltungen aller Art erwiesen.

The slightly ochre-toned sandstone façade, with its vertically accentuated window openings and bronze profiles, adjustable shading and patinated copper panels to the staggered floors, communicates a general impression of nobility and restrained presence. The main hall opens up behind the foyer space with a 31-m-diameter lens-like glazed roof. The offices are orientated towards the hall void and are approached through a free-standing spiral stair and two lifts. Glazed galleries are located in front of the offices, which give the interior façade a delicate quality. The hall itself has been lowered by a few steps from entrance level; these steps rotate in layout to form an arena, thereby emphasizing the basic geometric form. The hall has proven to be an excellent and much sought-after place for all sorts of events.

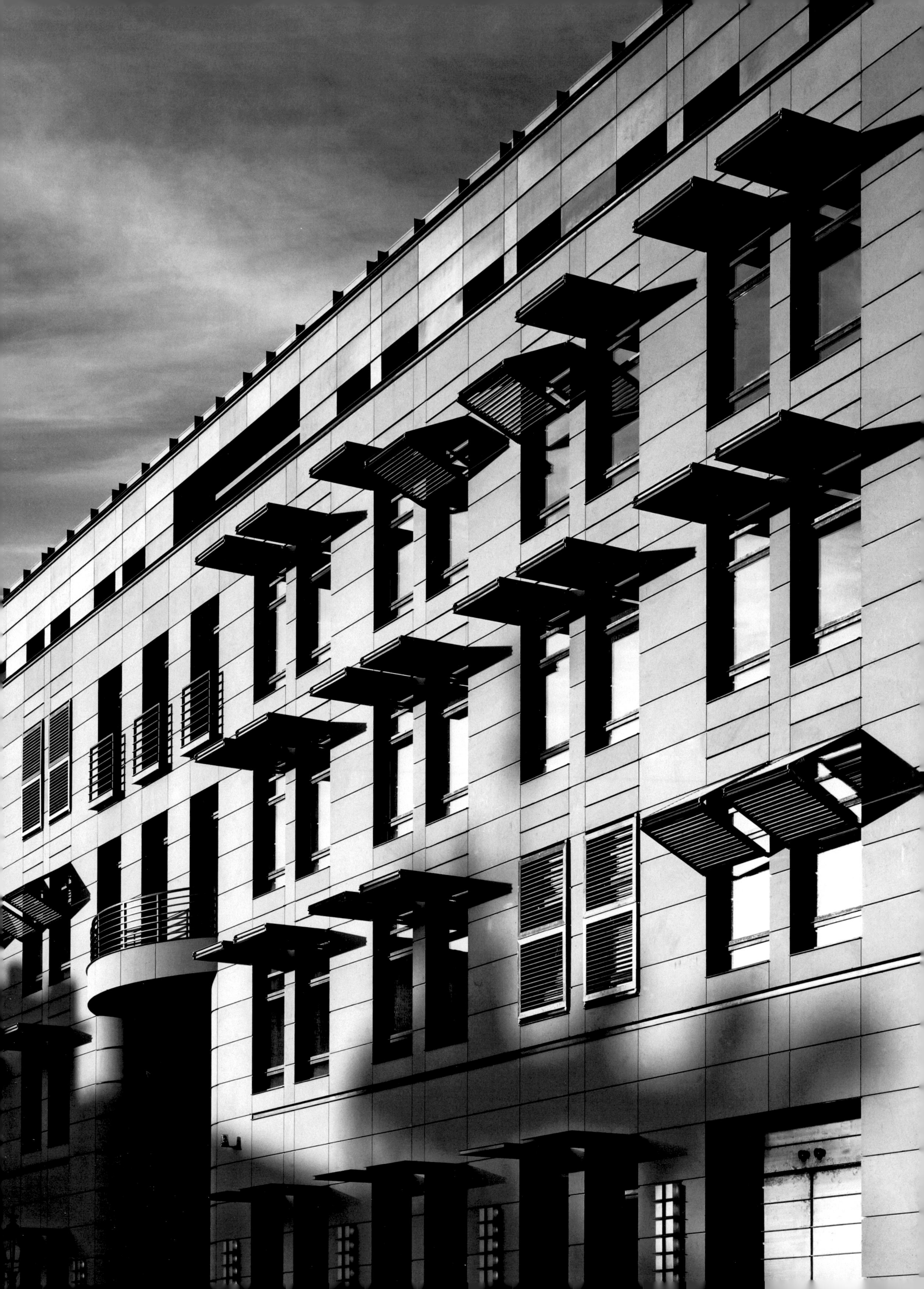

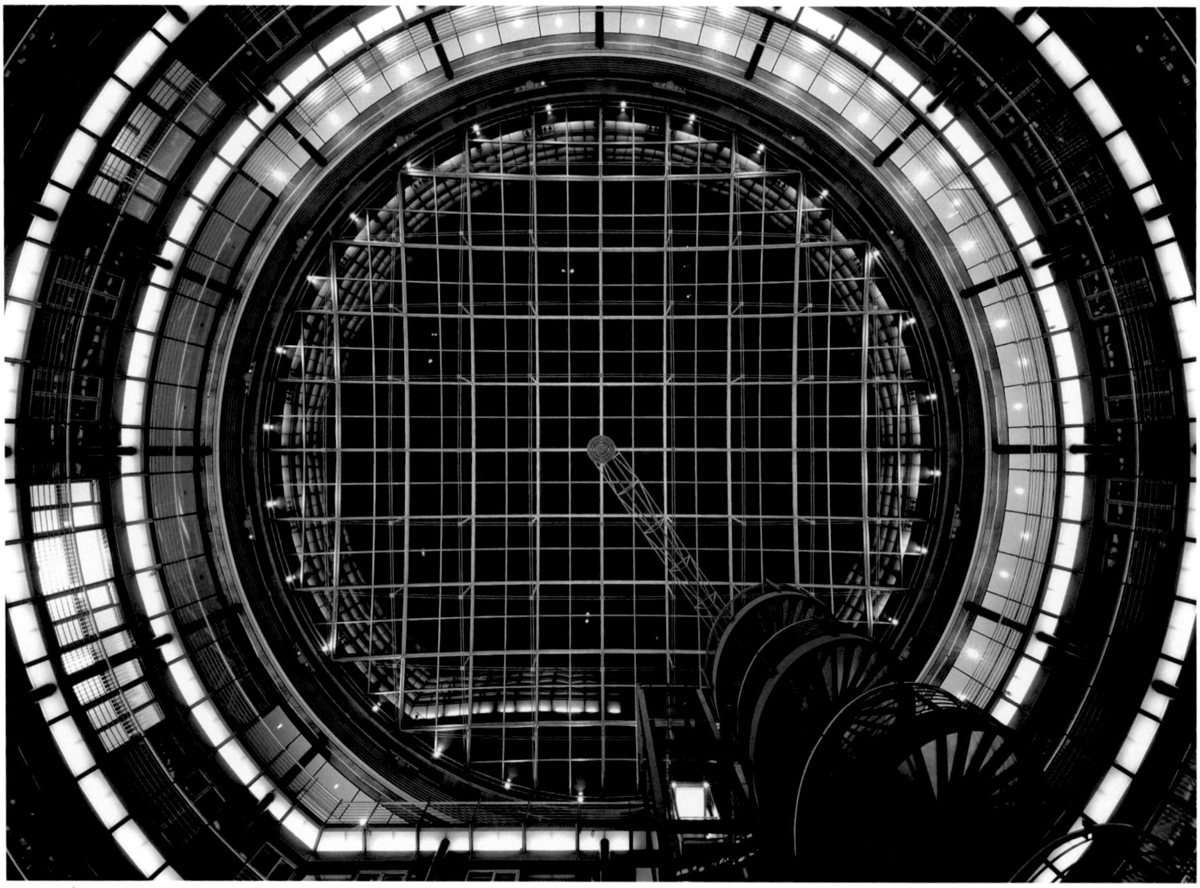

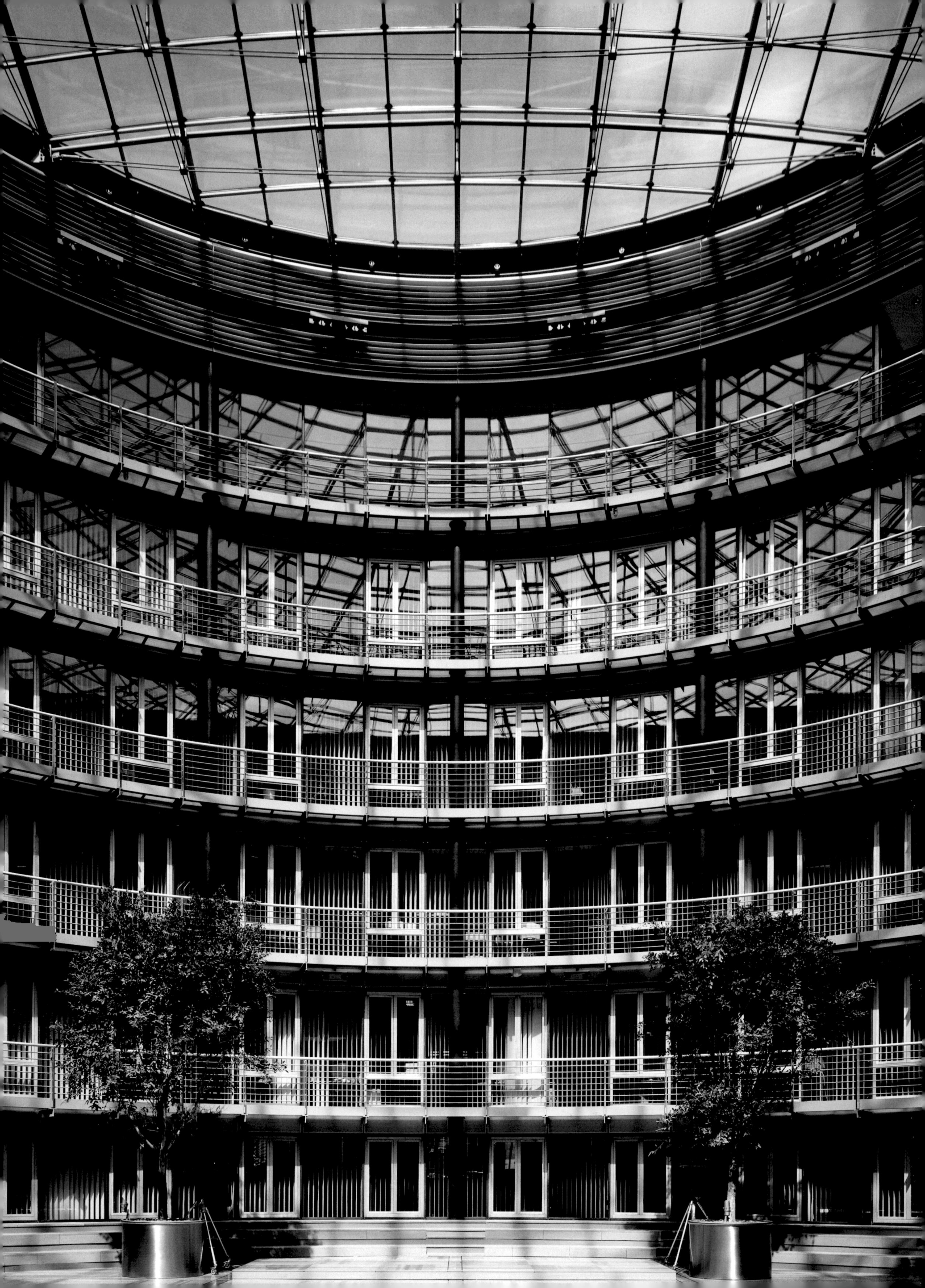

Restaurant Vau, Berlin
Vau Restaurant, Berlin

1996

Entwurf Design
Meinhard von Gerkan mit Doris Schäffler
und Stephan Schütz

Bauherr Client
QUOTAC GmbH Grundstücksentwicklungsgesellschaft

Bauzeit Construction period
1996–1997

BGF Gross floor area
400 m²

Die Gäste betreten das Restaurant von der hellerleuchteten Hofdurchfahrt. Rechts vom Eingang befindet sich ein Salon mit Wänden aus rotem venezianischen stucco lustro. Raumhohe Schiebetüren separieren den Raum für geschlossene Gesellschaften. Eine Treppe aus dunklem Nussbaumholz führt hinab zu einem unter dem Innenhof gelegenen Gastraum. Im Gegensatz zum repräsentativen Restaurant treffen sich hier Nachtschwärmer in intimerer Atmosphäre. Kabinettartige Fächer prägen den Charakter der Bar. Erleuchtete Gefache enthalten insgesamt eineinhalb Tonnen ostdeutscher Braunkohlebriketts als Erinnerung an das ehemals größte private Kohlenlager der Welt in den Kellern Berlins. Walzstahlbezogene Stehtische und eigens für den Raum entworfene Clubsessel aus massivem Birnbaumholz schaffen individuelle Sitzmöglichkeiten; der kühle Fußbodenbelag aus geschliffenem Schiefer betont die unterirdische Lage.

The guests enter the restaurant from the brightly lit courtyard passage. A drawing room with walls of red Venetian stucco lustro adjoins to the right of the entrance. Floor-to-ceiling sliding doors separate the room for private parties. A stair made of dark nutwood leads down to the guest area located underneath the courtyard. In contrast to the prestigious restaurant, this bar attracts night owls with its more intimate atmosphere. Cabinet-like boxes form the character of the bar. Illuminated compartments hold a total of one and a half tons of East German brown coal briquettes as a reminder of what was once the largest private coal storage in the world in the cellars of Berlin. Standing tables covered with rolled steel and club chairs made of massive pear wood, designed especially for this room, allow for individual seating; the cool flooring of polished slate emphasizes the underground location.

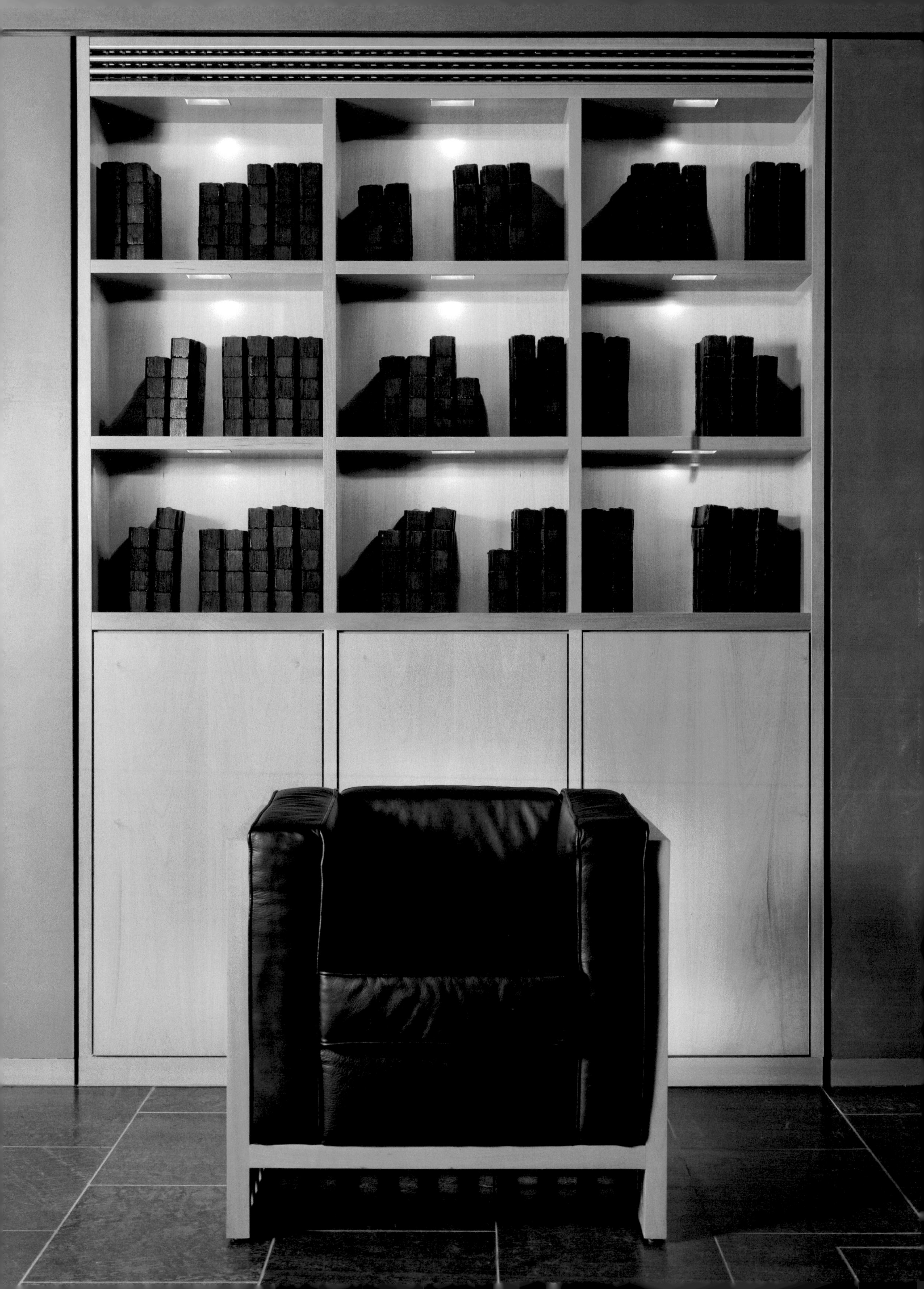

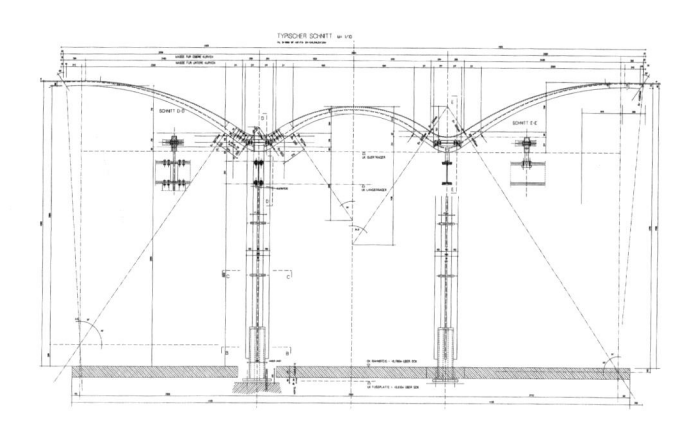

Typendach für die Deutsche Bahn AG
Serial Platform Roofing for Deutsche Bahn AG

Prototypenentwicklung Prototype development
1994

Entwurf Design
Meinhard von Gerkan und Jürgen Hillmer

Bauherr Client
Deutsche Bahn AG

Bauzeit Construction period
1995–2002

Die Rahmenkonstruktion des Typendaches besteht aus modular elementierten Stahlseilen, die Untersicht aus gewelltem Edelstahlblech. Diese Struktur stabilisiert das Tragverhalten und erzeugt lebendige Lichtreflexe. Das Dach teilt den Bahnsteig in drei Zonen: die Mittelzone als Aufenthaltsbereich, die beiden äußeren Zonen als Einstiegs- und Gehbereiche. Die Anpassung an verschiedene Bahnsteigbreiten erfolgt durch proportionales Wachsen der Querträger. Durch Kappen der Querträger passt sich das Dach verjüngenden Bahnsteigen an. Auch Kurven folgt die Konstruktion durch Brechung der Längsachse. Dominierend ist die Eigenfarbe des Materials mit den Reflexen der Wellenstruktur. Tageslicht fällt durch die Glasstreifen entlang der Wellentäler, bei Nacht wird der Bahnsteig von den Dachrändern beleuchtet, während indirektes Licht die Form des Dachs betont.

The framework of the platform roofing consists of modular steel rods, with the underside clad in corrugated, stainless-steel sheeting. This both stabilizes the structure and produces lively light reflections. The roof divides the platform into three zones: the central area for waiting, and two outer zones for boarding and circulation. A proportional lengthening of transverse girders extends the roof cover over widening platforms. The transverse girders are shortened to adapt to narrowing platforms. The structure follows the curve along its longitudinal axis. What dominates is the material's natural colour, enhanced by reflections of light from the corrugated sheeting. Daylight is transmitted through glass strips along the roof 'valley'. At night, the platform lighting comes from the roof edges whilst indirect lighting brings out the shape of the roof.

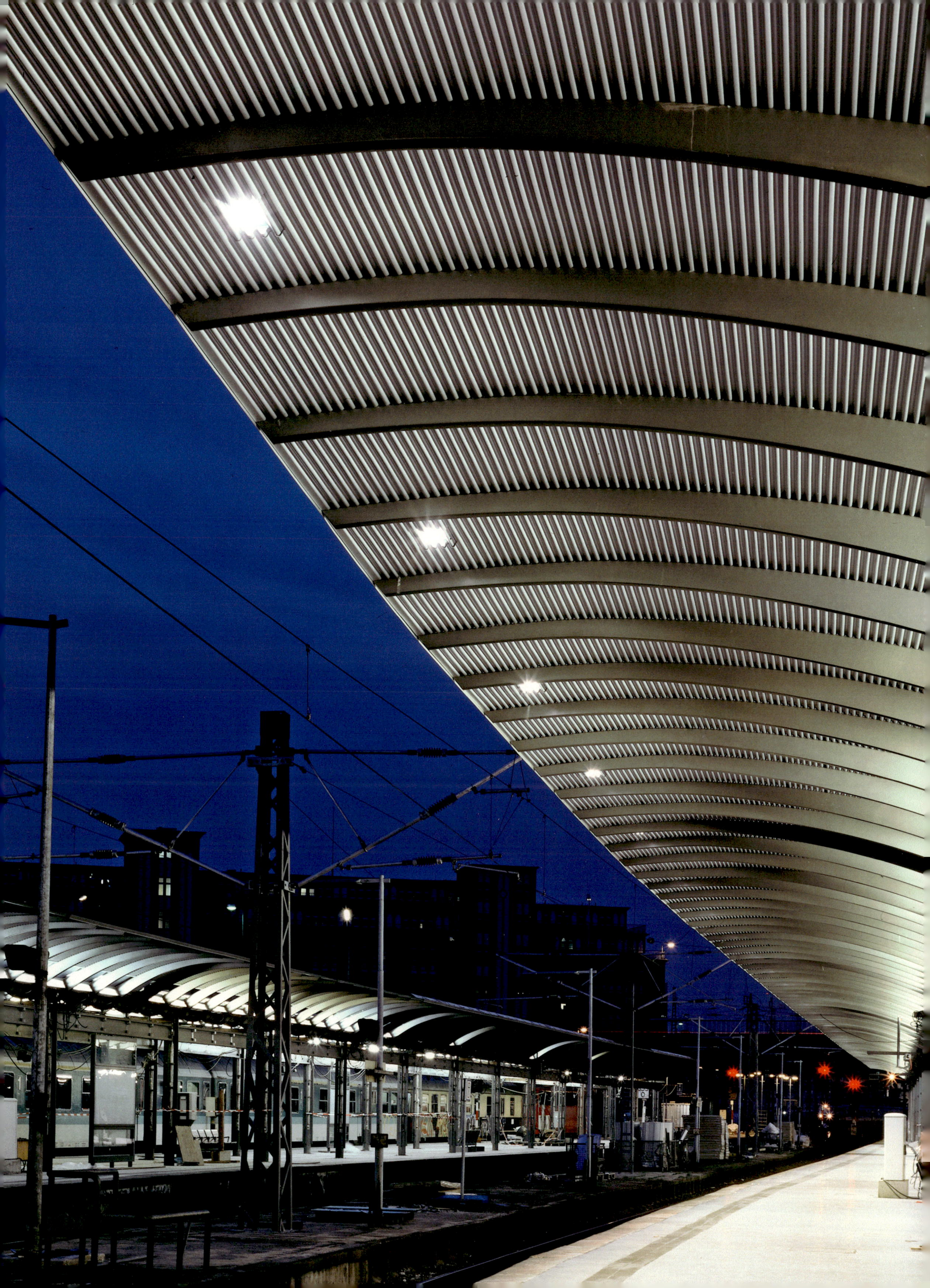

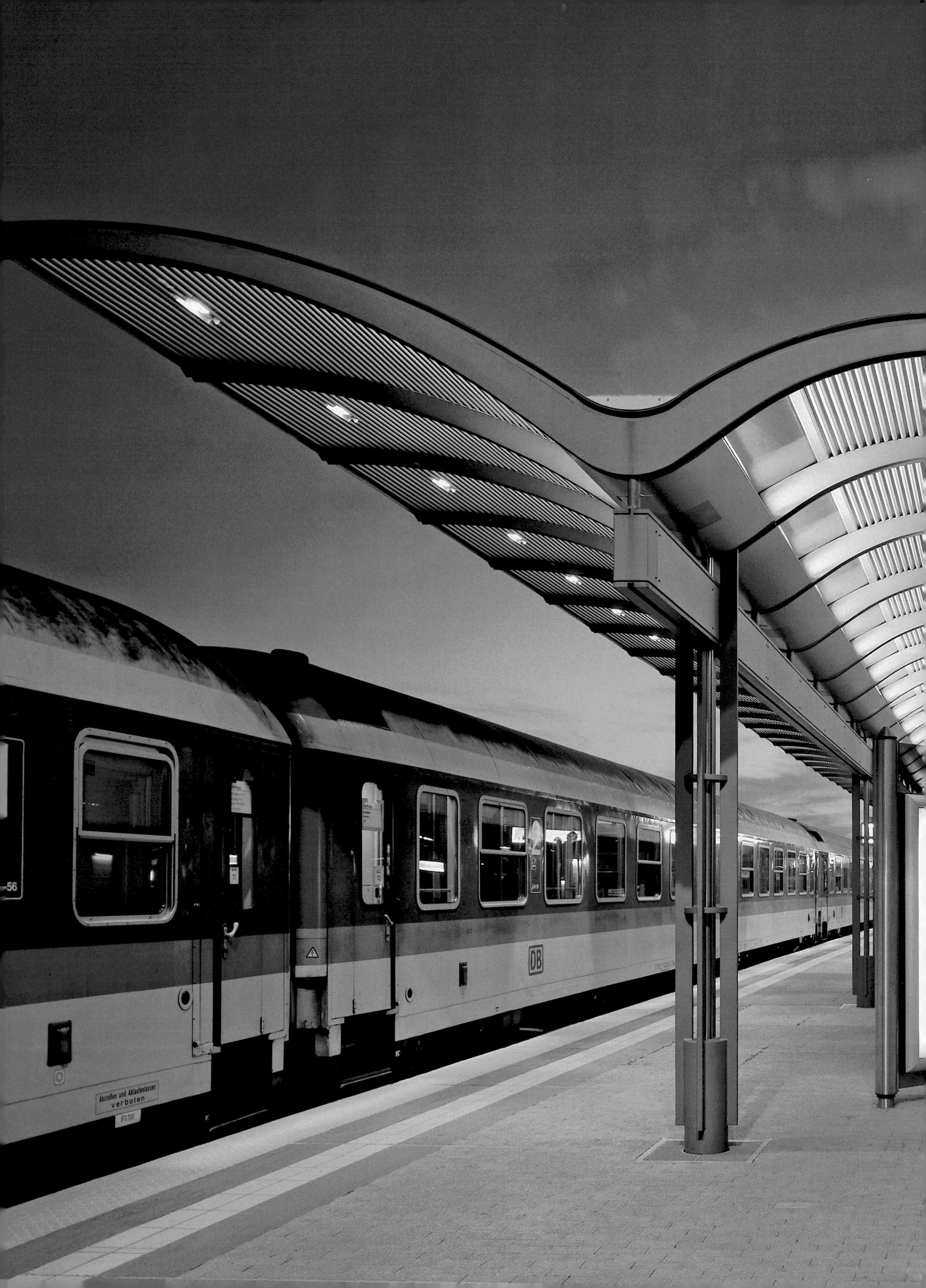
56
DB
Abstoßen und Ablaufenlassen
verboten
F6700

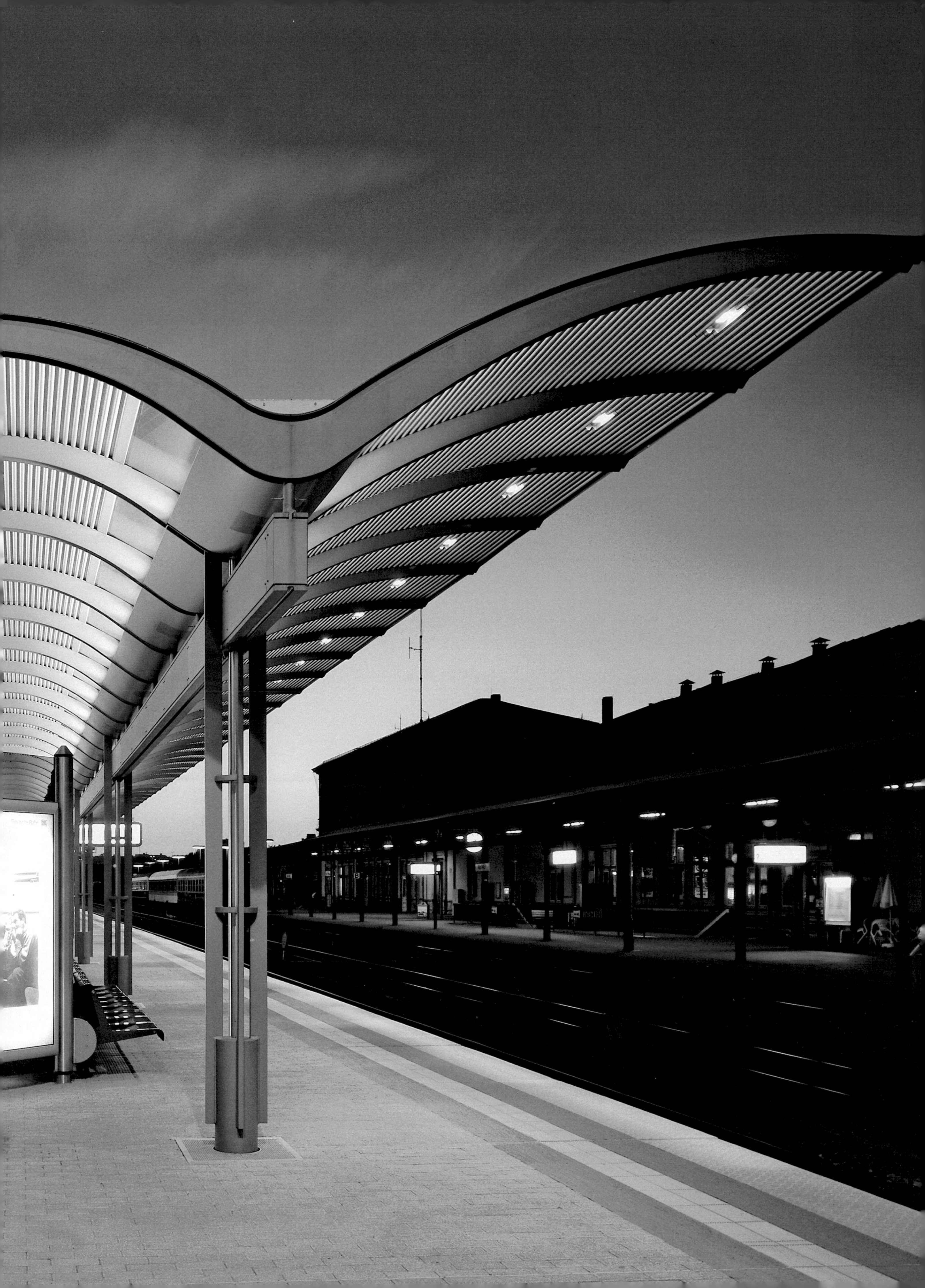

Nordseepassage, Wilhelmshaven
'Nordseepassage', Wilhelmshaven

Gutachten Consultancy
1991

Entwurf Design
Meinhard von Gerkan mit Volkmar Sievers

Partner Partner
Klaus Staratzke

Bauherr Client
Kusto-Immobilienprojektentwicklung GmbH + Co. KG

Bauzeit Construction period
1994–1997

BGF Gross floor area
73.300 m²

Mitten im Zentrum von Wilhelmshaven liegt der Kopfbahnhof, der durch die neue Bebauung eng mit dem Wegesystem der Stadt verknüpft wird. Eine zweigeschossige Hauptpassage bildet die Verlängerung der Schienenstränge in die Stadt hinein; zwei Querpassagen stellen Verbindungen zu den anschließenden Straßen her. Zur Virchowstraße wird ein etwas 25 m tiefer Vorplatz geschaffen, der den neuen Busbahnhof aufnimmt und damit die Funktion des gesamten Komplexes als Verkehrs- und Verkaufsdrehscheibe vervollständigt. Die vier Geschosse des Baukörpers passen sich in der Höhe an die umgebende Bebauung an; die hellroten Ziegel der Fassaden innen wie außen nehmen das ortstypische Material auf. In den Obergeschossen liegen Büros und Wohnungen; zwei Parkhäuser parallel zu den Bahngleisen im Westen ergänzen das Ensemble.

The proposed development connected the centrally located terminus station in Wilhelmshaven to the surrounding road network. The main two-storey passage forms the extension of the tracks into the city. Two secondary passages intersect along this route, linking the adjacent streets. In the direction of Virchowstrasse a 25-m-deep forecourt is introduced and with the inclusion of the new bus terminal the development's function as a focus of traffic and commerce is completed. The four-storey building adapts in terms of height to the surrounding development; the light-red brickwork, characteristic of this area, is used both externally and internally. Offices and apartments are located on the upper floors; two multi-storey car parks, sitting parallel to the train tracks in the west, complete the ensemble.

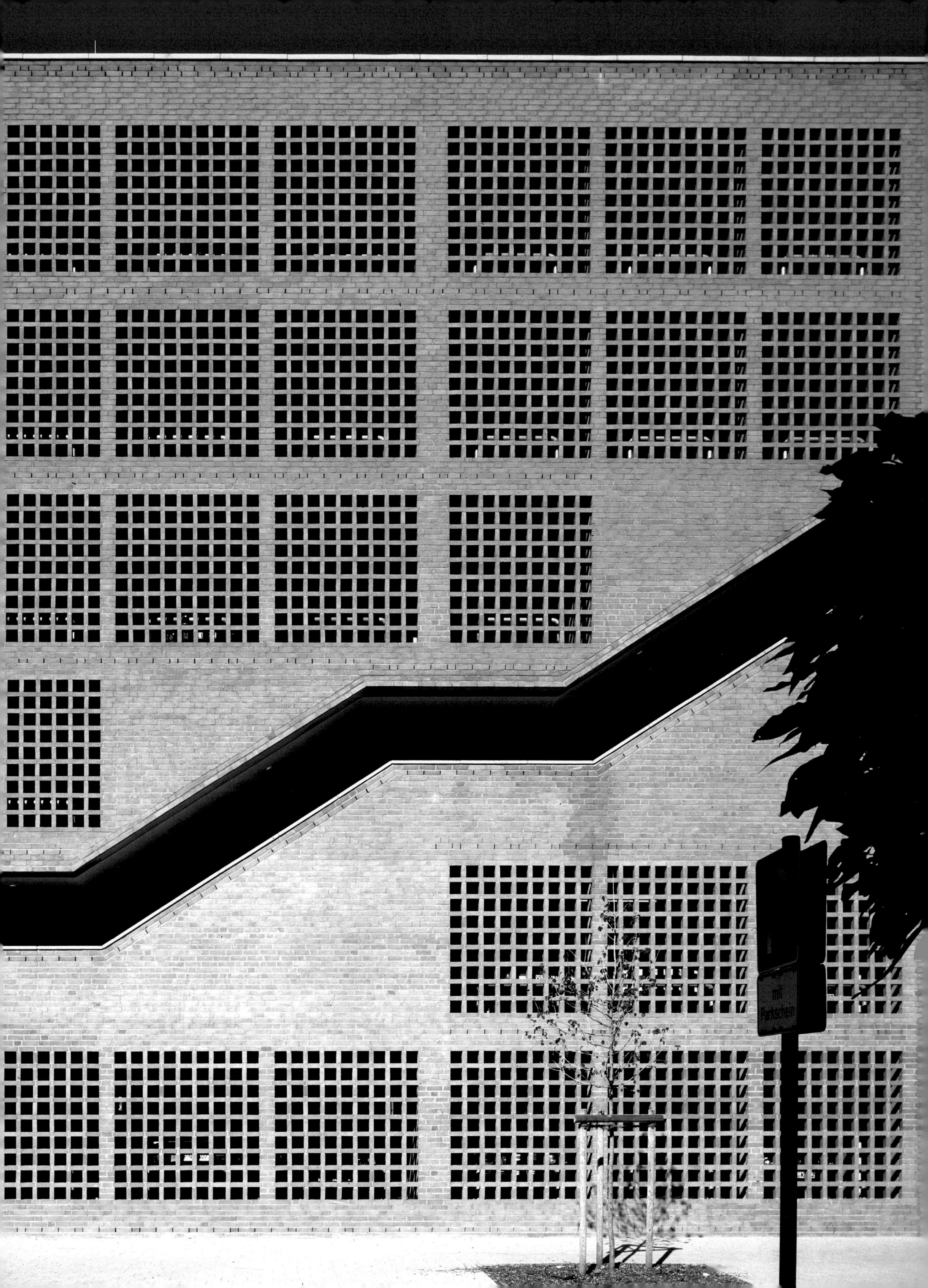
mit
Parkschein

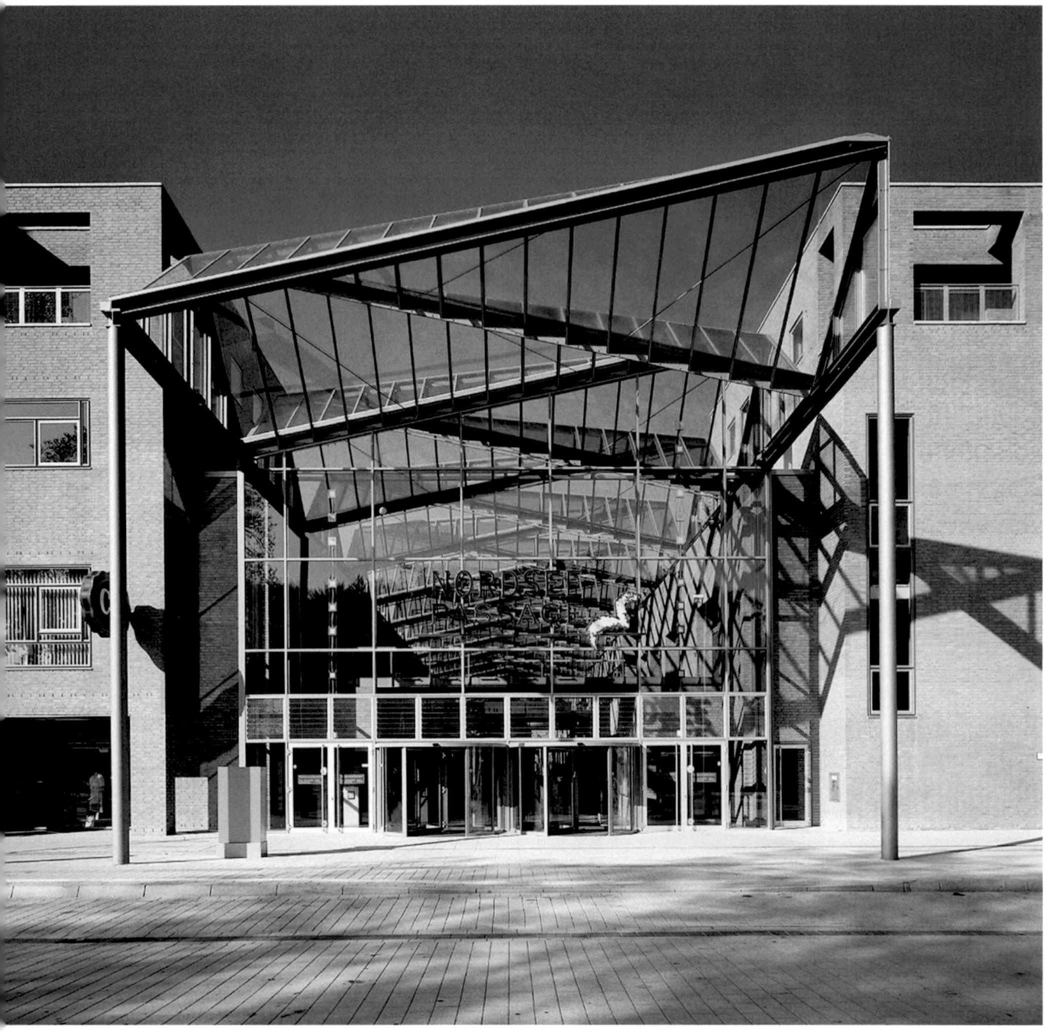

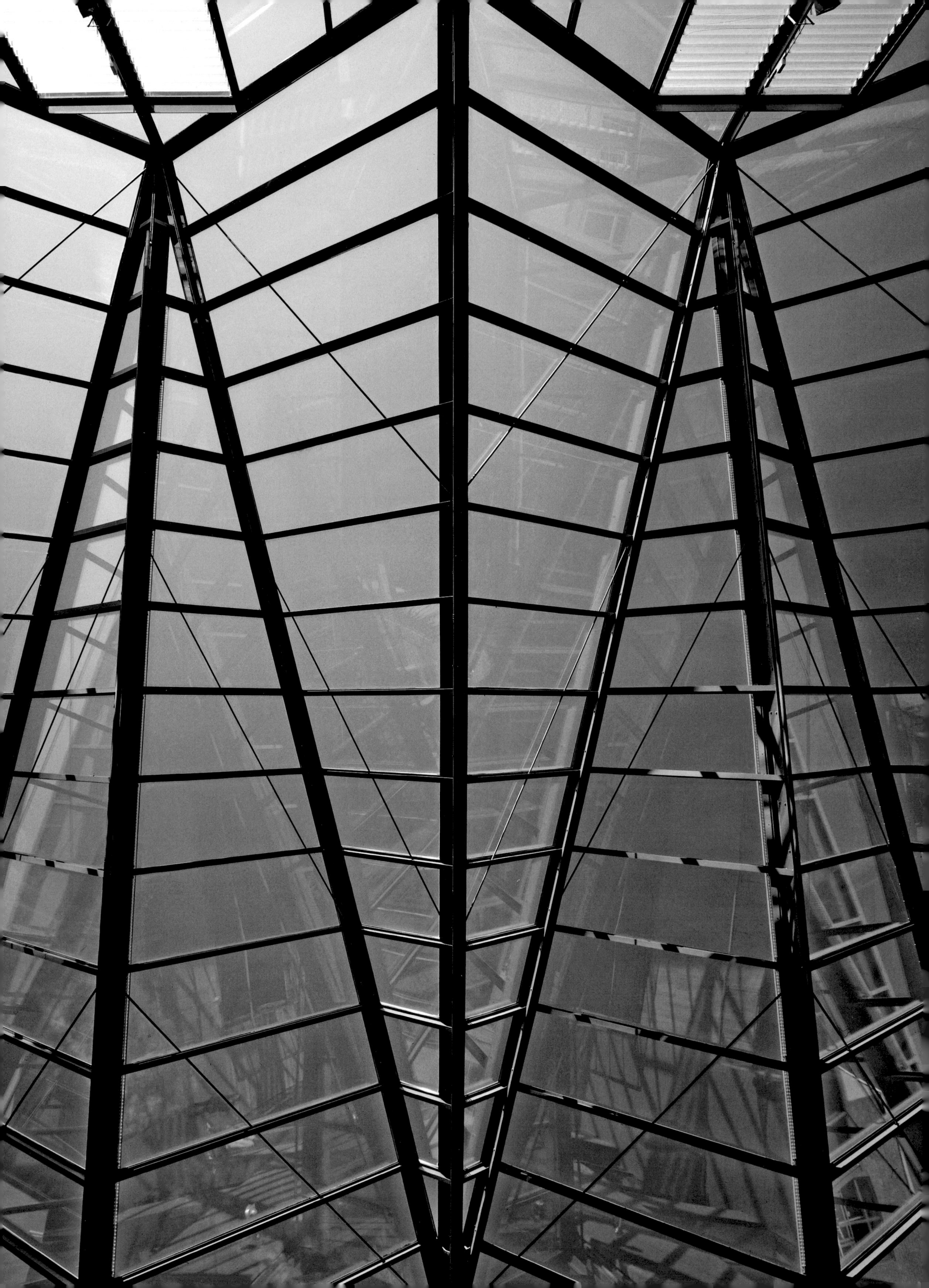

Gerling Haus, Stuttgart
Gerling House, Stuttgart

Gutachten Consultancy
1996

Entwurf Design
Meinhard von Gerkan und Nikolaus Goetze

Bauherr Client
Gerling Konzern, Köln

Bauzeit Construction period
1996–1997

BGF Gross floor area
10.280 m²

Die geschlossenen Fassaden und verglasten Wintergärten des Bürohauses orientieren sich zur stark befahrenen Heilbronner Straße; offene Höfe mit zu ihnen hin orientierten Büros ragen ins Tal. Die der Straßengabelung zugewandte Spitze betont mit ihrer geschlossenen Fassade zur einen Seite und der vollverglasten zur anderen Seite hin die Thematik des Gebäudes. Die Bürotrakte werden zur Heilbronner Straße durch transparente Glashallen verbunden. Sie schützen die Büros vor den Straßenemissionen und bilden zugleich großzügige Treppenhäuser. Der Bau ist so konzipiert, dass er je nach Bedarf auch für Fremdmieter verfügbar gemacht werden kann. Eine besondere Attraktion in einer Umgebung, die durch zahlreiche Bürobauten geprägt ist, stellt das Casino im Erdgeschoss dar, das die intime Atmosphäre des grünen Hofes nutzt. Die Schließung der Attika durch „Luftbalken" fasst die Figur des Dreiecks zusammen.

The solid façades and glazed winter gardens of the office building are positioned along busy Heilbronner Strasse, whilst open courts, together with the offices orientated towards them, look down onto the city centre. The building's sharp profile towards the fork in the street emphasizes the theme of the building – a solid façade on one side and a glazed surface on the other. Glazed halls connect the offices, which are orientated towards Heilbronner Strasse, protect the work spaces from traffic emissions and house generous staircases for circulation. The flexible building design allows usage by third parties. A distinct quality in an area otherwise characterized by numerous office buildings is the staff restaurant, which takes advantage of the landscaped court. The closure of the roof parapet with an 'air beam' frames the triangular form.

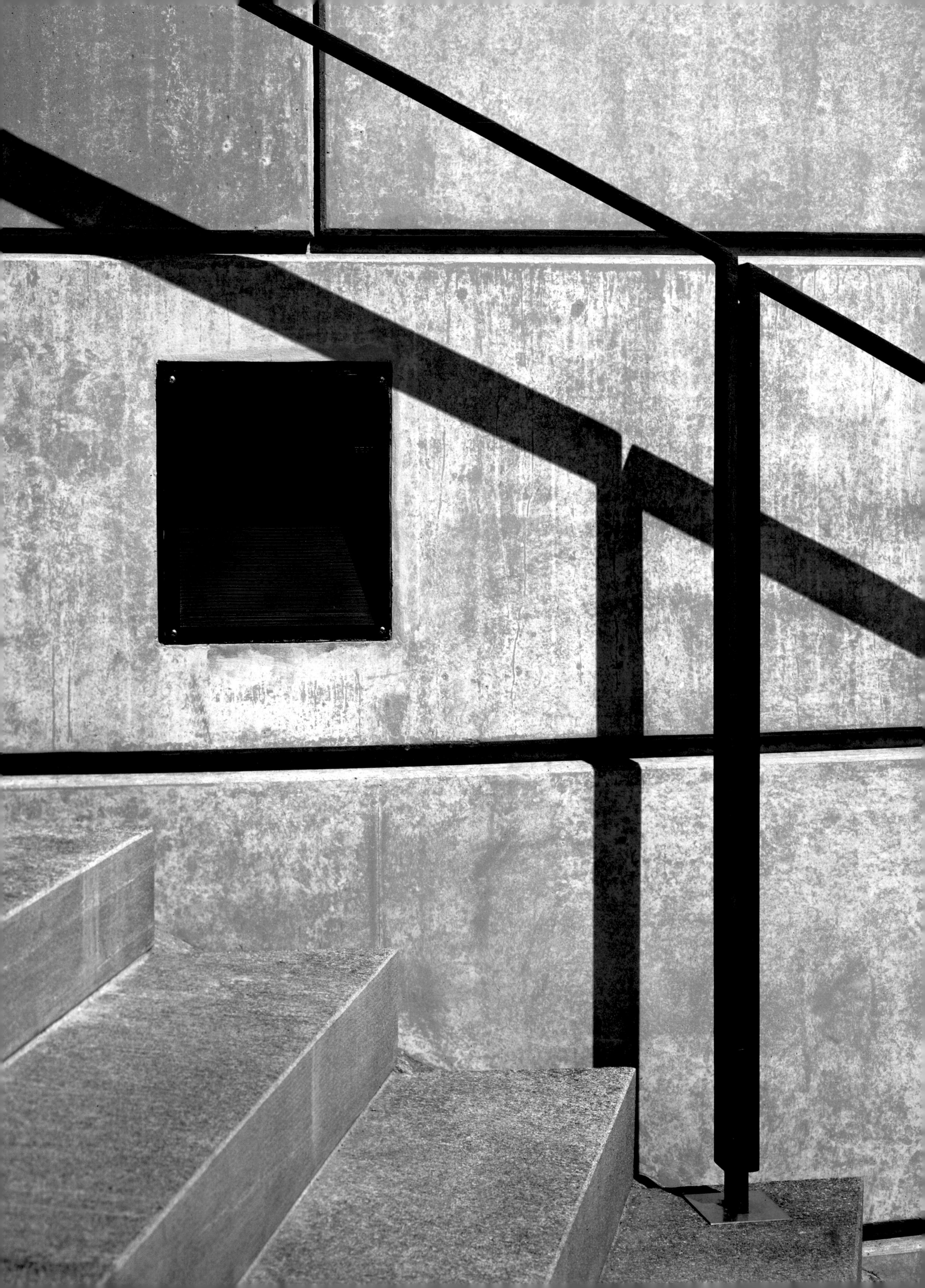

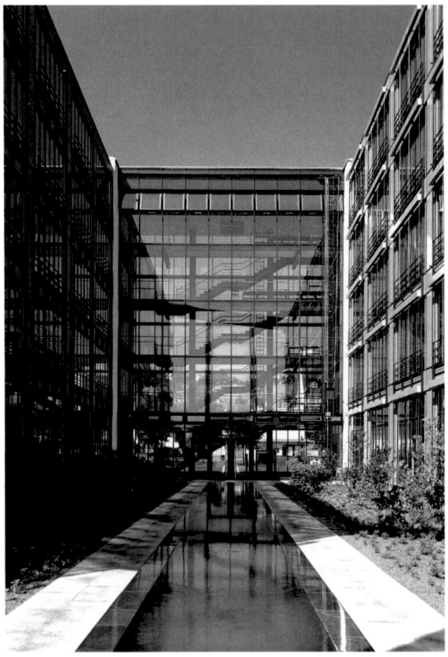

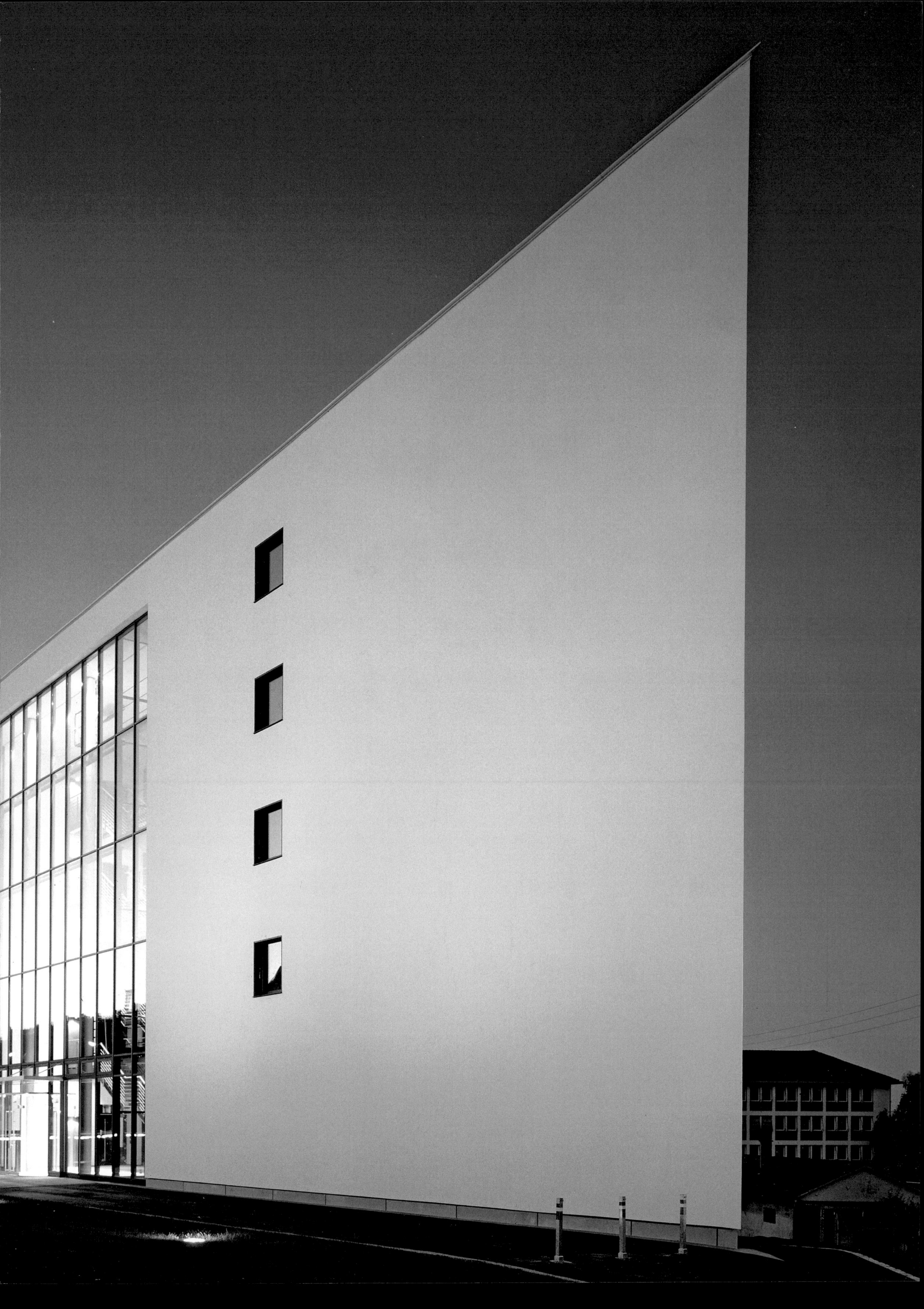

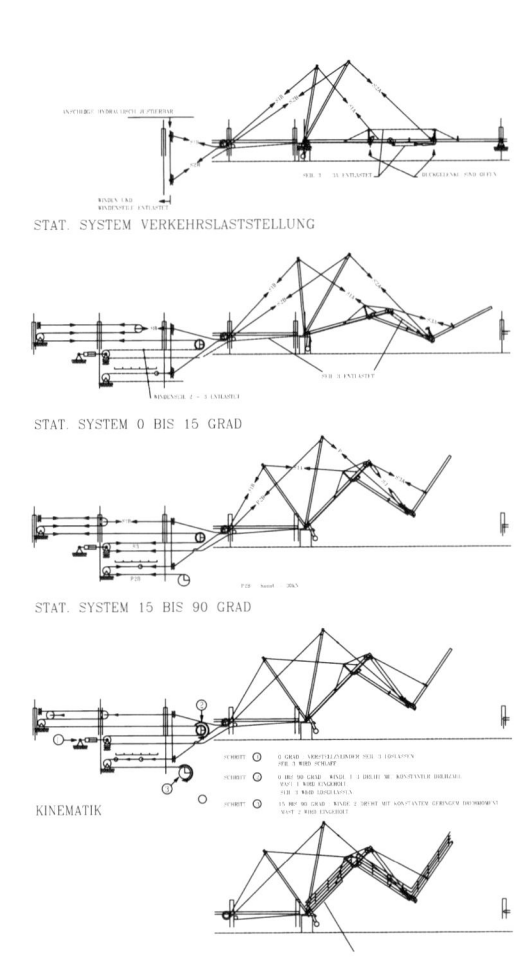

Klappbrücke, Kiel-Hörn
Bascule Bridge, Kiel-Hörn

Gutachten Consultancy
1994

Entwurf Design
Volkwin Marg mit Jörg Schlaich

Bauherr Client
Magistrat der Stadt Kiel

Bauzeit Construction period
1996–1997

Länge Length
116 m, davon ca. 25 m als Faltbrücke

Breite Width
6 m

Der ehemalige Werftstandort am Ostufer der Hörn, unmittelbar gegenüber von Innenstadt und Hauptbahnhof, wird in einem städtebaulichen „Jahrhundertprojekt" saniert und zu einem neuen Quartier aus Wohnen, Büro und Gewerbe umgenutzt. Als Teil davon wird der Stadtteil Gaarden mit einer beweglichen Brücke über die Hörn an die Innenstadt angebunden. Zweifeld-Klappbrücken gehören heute im Schiffsbau zum technischen Standard; als Zeichen von Innovation wirkt deren weltweit neue Weiterentwicklung zu einer „Dreifeld-Klappbrücke" als kunstvolles, maritimes Zeichen für die Bürger. Architektur, Ingenieurbau und kinetische Kunst gehen hier eine neue, sinnfällige und gleichzeitig nutzbare Verbindung ein.

The former dockyard location on the eastern shore of the Hörn is set immediately opposite the city centre and the main railway station. The area will be regenerated as a 'millennium project' of urban planning and transformed into a new area for housing, offices and commerce. As a part of this new area the Gaarden district will be connected to the city centre by a new flexible bridge over the Hörn. The two-span bascule bridge is today a common technical feature of the ship building industry. This new further development of a three-span bridge creates a strong maritime-inspired symbol for the citizens of the city. Architecture, engineering and kinetic art here enter into a new, striking and simultaneously effective fusion.

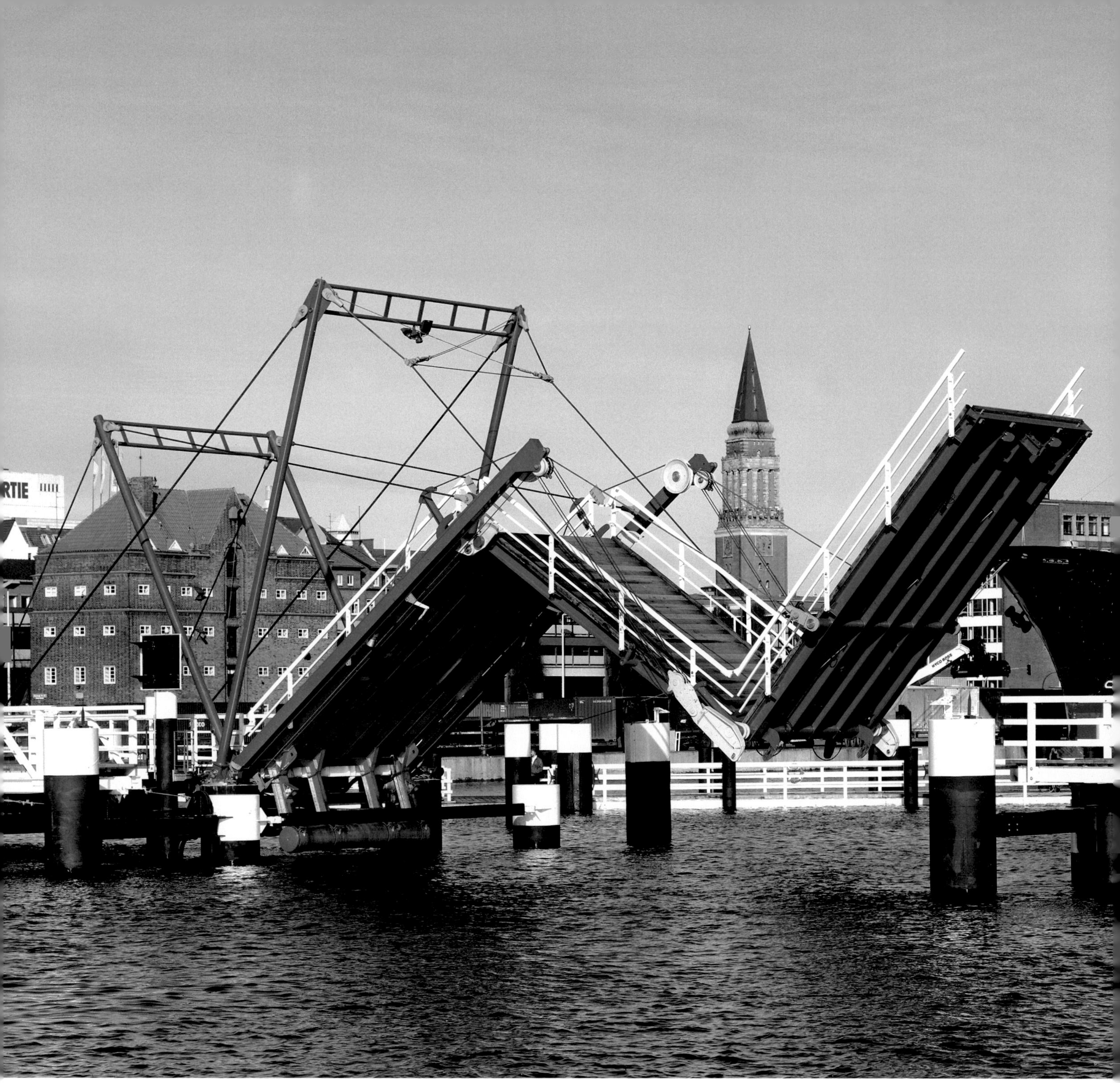

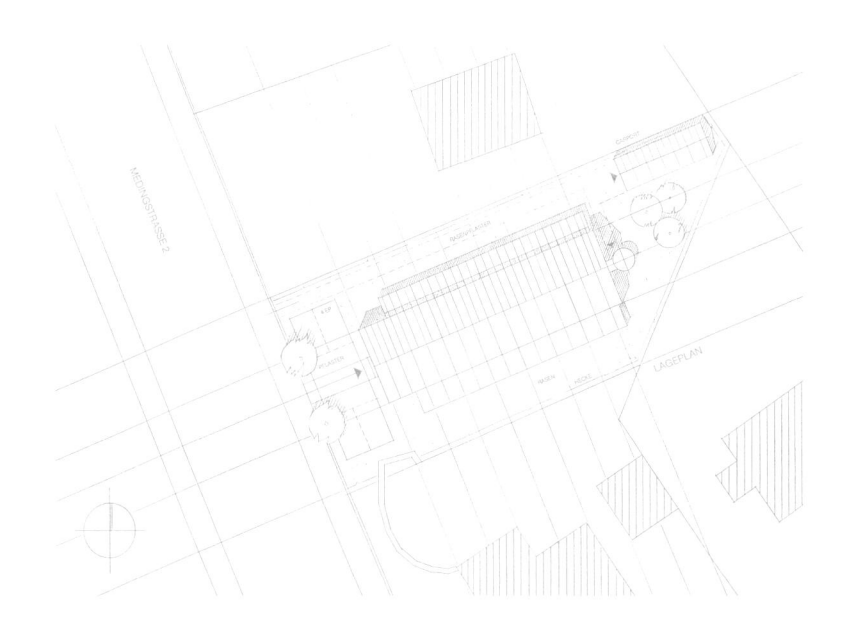

Praxis Dr. Manke, Uelzen
Dr. Manke Practice, Uelzen

1995

Entwurf Design
Volkwin Marg und Joachim Zais

Bauherr Client
Dr. Manke

Bauzeit Construction perod
1996–1997

BGF Gross floor area
470 m²

Eine kieferorthopädische Praxis als klassisch-einfaches, zweigeschossiges Haus, dessen Obergeschoss zurückgestaffelt ist: Das Ergebnis aus einem Raumprogramm, dessen Fläche im Obergeschoss um etwa ein Drittel geringer ist als die des Erdgeschosses, und einer Umgebung, die aus Ein- und Zweifamilienhäusern besteht. In dieser heterogenen Umgebung sollte das neue Haus einen Ruhepunkt bilden, der in seiner größtmöglichen Zurückhaltung liegt. Das Obergeschoss wird an der straßenseitigen Giebelfront vorgezogen, so dass sich ein eindeutiger, die Symmetrie betonender Eingang bildet. Die Außenwände in matt-silbriger Red-Cedar-Holzverkleidung unterstreichen den Charakter des Hauses als ebenso dauerhaft wie einfach.

The orthodontic surgery as a classic two-storey house with a backward-staggered upper floor: the result of the original brief, which required the area on the top floor to be one third less than the ground floor, and a neighbourhood consisting of one- and two-storey family houses. In this disparate environment, the new house will form a necessary 'calm' addition, gaining much from its highly reserved nature. On the street side elevation, the upper floor is drawn out in order to create a clear, symmetrically arranged entrance. Exterior walls are finished in a silvered-matt red cedar panelling underscoring the essence of the house as equally durable and simple.

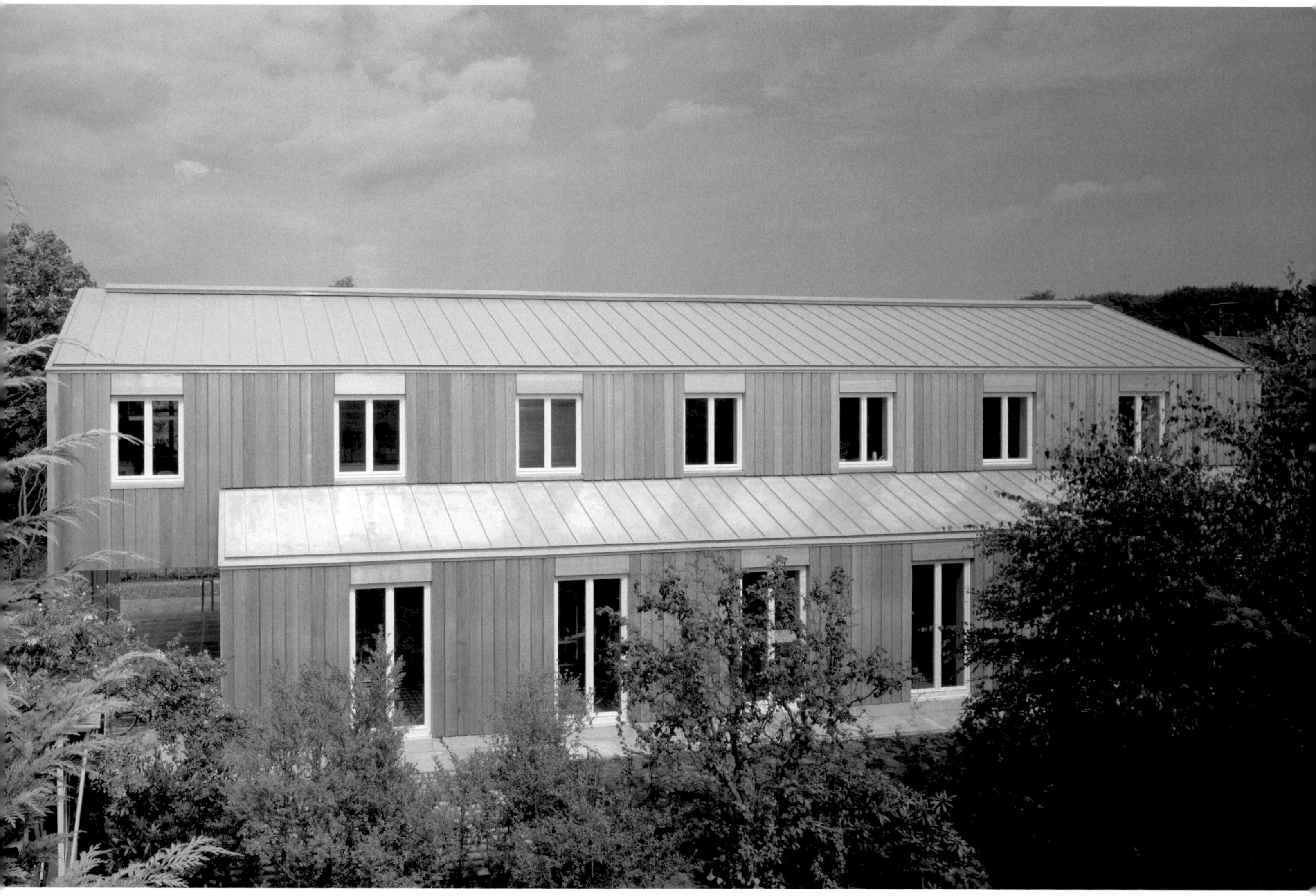

1998

Hörsaalzentrum der Universität Oldenburg

Der Entwurf des Auditorium Maximum reagiert auf die disparate Situation – geschaffen durch kleinteilige Bauten und einige maßstabsprengende Großbauten der 60er Jahre – mit einem kraftvollen, zweigeschossigen, zylindrischen Baukörper, der markant der Bedeutung einer fakultätsübergreifenden Einrichtung gerecht wird.

Lecture Theatre Centre, Oldenburg University

The concept of the main lecture hall reacts against the disparity of a mix of small-scale buildings and town blocks from the 1960s with a strong, cylindrical two-storey form, which fulfils the significance of an institution used by various facilities.

Hörsaal- und Seminargebäude der TU Chemnitz

Ein Winkel aus Seminarräumen fasst ein großes Foyer, dessen Decke durch den schrägen, den ansteigenden Sitzreihen folgenden Boden der großen Hörsäle gebildet wird. Zwischen Winkelbau und Hörsälen lässt eine breite Baukörperzäsur Tageslicht durch Oberlichter über eine Galerie bis ins Foyer fallen.

Auditoria and Seminar Building, Chemnitz Institute of Technology

An angular building with seminar rooms frames a large foyer, its roof formed by the inclined floor following the ascending seating rows of the auditoria. A void between this building and the auditoria allows daylight to enter the complex down to the foyer through top lights above a gallery.

Telekom-Zentrale, Berlin-Tegel

Das Gebäude besteht aus fünf parallel stehenden, sich entsprechend dem Grundstücksschnitt verkürzenden Bürotrakten von je sechs Geschossen. Diese sind über eine sogenannte Magistrale, ein einbündiges Rückgrat, miteinander verbunden. Ein Kopfbau hebt den Eingangsbereich hervor.

Telekom Headquarters, Berlin-Tegel

The complex is composed of five parallel six-storey office bars, their respective length following the site boundary. These bars are interlinked via a so-called 'thoroughfare', laid out as a single corridor building. The head building emphasizes the entrance area.

S-Bahn-Stationen zur Expo 2000 in Hannover

Um einen bestimmten Haltestellentyp in unterschiedlichen Situationen anwenden zu können, wurde für die S-Bahn-Station eine quadratische Grundform gewählt, die ungerichtet ist. Dies ermöglicht den Zugang von allen Seiten entsprechend der Lage der Bahngleise und den Möglichkeiten vor Ort.

Suburban Railway Station to the Expo 2000 in Hanover

The concept of being able to use a certain station type in various situations resulted in the development of a square form with a neutral orientation. This allows the access from all sides corresponding to the location of the railway tracks and the site's possibilities.

1998

Büropark Bredeney, Essen

Der Karstadt-Konzern erhält mit diesem Bau ein Haus mit eigener Identität und einem repräsentativen, eigenen Eingang. Aber auch Fremdmieter kommen zu einer eigenen „Adresse" und haben Anteil am parkartigen Gelände.

Bredeney Office Park, Essen

This complex offers the Karstadt Group a building with an individual identity and a representative, separate entrance. Other tenants also have access via a separate 'address' and share the park-like ground.

Residenz in Jurmala, Lettland

Ausstellungen, Empfänge, Feste und Konzerte sollen in diesem Gästehaus einer Villa nahe des Rigaer Ostseestrandes stattfinden. Dabei ist nicht ein Prunkbau in der Tradition des 19. Jahrhunderts entstanden, sondern ein Gebäude, das die örtliche traditionelle Holzbauweise aufnimmt und zeitgemäß fortschreibt.

Residence in Jurmala, Latvia

This guest house belonging to a villa near Riga's Baltic coast was intended as a venue for exhibitions, receptions, parties and concerts. What emerged was not a grand edifice in the 19th-century tradition but a building that incorporates the local tradition of timber constructions and updated it in keeping with the times.

Norddeutsche Metall-Berufsgenossenschaft, Hannover

Fünf parallel zueinander stehende Gebäudescheiben werden durch eine diagonal angeordnete Magistrale verbunden. An eine gläserne Eingangshalle mit Vorfahrt und zentraler Erschließung lagern sich über dem durchgehenden Erdgeschoss einbündige Bürozonen mit offenen Galerien an.

Professional Association of the Metal Industry, Hanover

A diagonally positioned main axis links five parallel building slabs. Above the continuous ground floor, office zones with open galleries join the glazed entrance hall with an access road and a central circulation area.

Bahnhof Berlin-Spandau

Der durch eine ebenerdige Passage erschlossene Bahnhof Spandau ist Teil der Fernbahnstrecke Hannover–Berlin. Die eigentliche Bahnhofshalle ist 430 Meter lang und vollständig mit parallel laufenden gläsernen Tonnendächern gedeckt.

Berlin-Spandau Railway Station

Spandau railway station is part of the main-line service Hanover–Berlin and runs in an elevated position close to Spandau's town hall. It was developed with a ground-floor arcade. The main hall is 430 m long and completely covered with parallel, glazed, vaulted roofs.

Havelbrücke, Berlin-Spandau

Die Stege der dreifeldrigen stählernen Trogbrücke werden der Beanspruchung folgend geformt und führen zu einer schlanken und gestreckten Konstruktion, die das übliche Durcheinander vieler versetzt angeordneter Brückenträger vermeidet und die Havel in einer schwungvollen Welle überbrückt.

Havel Bridge, Berlin-Spandau

The single bridges of the sectional steel trough bridge are formed according to the loading. This results in a slender and stretched structure, avoiding the usual mess of many alternating bridge girders and bridging the Havel River like a sweeping wave.

Verbindungsbauten zwischen den Hallen 3, 4 und 5 der Messe Hannover

Die Übergänge zwischen den einzelnen Messehallen dienen als Wetterschutz und ermöglichen den Messebesuchern einen angenehmen, witterungsunabhängigen Wechsel von Halle zu Halle. Gleichzeitig steht der Straßenraum in den Auf- und Abbauphasen für den Lieferverkehr uneingeschränkt zur Verfügung.

Connecting Buildings between Halls 3, 4 and 5 of the Hanover Exhibition Centre

The transitions between the single exhibition halls function as protection from the weather, allowing a pleasant change from hall to hall. Simultaneously, the street space can be used continuously for deliveries during the assembly and dismantling periods.

Hörsaalzentrum der Universität Oldenburg
Lecture Theatre Centre, Oldenburg University

Wettbewerb Competition
1992 – 1. Preis

Entwurf Design
Meinhard von Gerkan mit Klaus Lenz

Bauherr Client
Staatshochbauamt Oldenburg

Bauzeit Construction period
1996–1998

BGF Gross floor area
5.163 m²

Die geometrisch reine Form des Auditorium Maximum wird aufgebrochen durch Vor- und Rücksprünge und die unterschiedliche Behandlung der Fassaden zwischen der offenen Foyer- und der Bühnenseite. An die vorhandenen Bauten der Universität wird der Zylinder durch eine Brücke angebunden, die auf der anderen Seite, an der Straßenkreuzung, in einem langgestreckten Baukörper mit den Seminarräumen endet. Der Abstraktheit der geometrischen Form entspricht das Weiß der geputzten Fassade. Nur zwei Flächen der Außenwand werden farblich differenziert und wirken wie eine Kulisse vor dem weißen Hintergrund. Innen ist es der Behindertenaufzug als frei stehender Baukörper mitten im Foyer, der mit einem kräftigen Blau gegen die Farben natürlicher Materialien wie Holz, Gussasphaltboden und Sichtbetonstützen besteht. Der Veranstaltungssaal im Obergeschoss ist mit allen technischen Einrichtungen ausgestattet, um für Theater, Kongresse und Kulturereignisse dienen zu können. Er ist in drei Raumabschnitte unterteilbar, in denen gleichzeitig Veranstaltungen stattfinden können.

The pure geometry of the main lecture hall is fragmented with projecting and recessing elements and through various façade aesthetics between the open foyer and stage side. A bridge links the cylinder to existing university buildings. A longitudinal building consisting of lecture rooms terminates the bridge. The white plastered façade corresponds to the clear building geometry. Two areas on the external façade are emphasized with colour and appear to be scenery in front of the white background. Internally, the lift for the disabled designed as a free-standing element in the foyer, is painted a powerful blue, contrasting with the natural materials like wood, the poured asphalt floor and fair-faced columns. The function hall on the upper floor is equipped with the required technology to serve for theatre, congress and cultural events. It can be subdivided into three sections, to allow events can take place simultaneously.

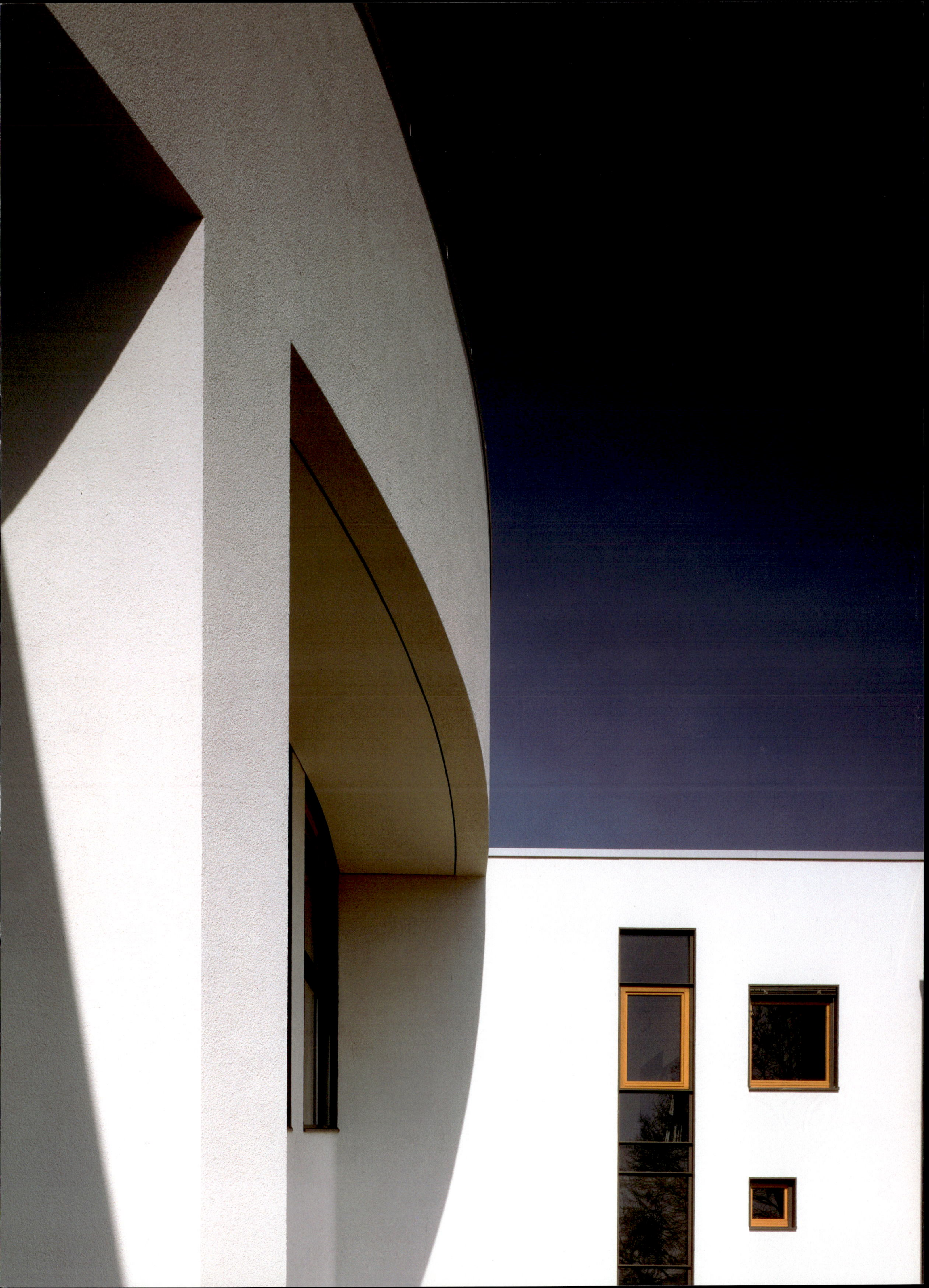

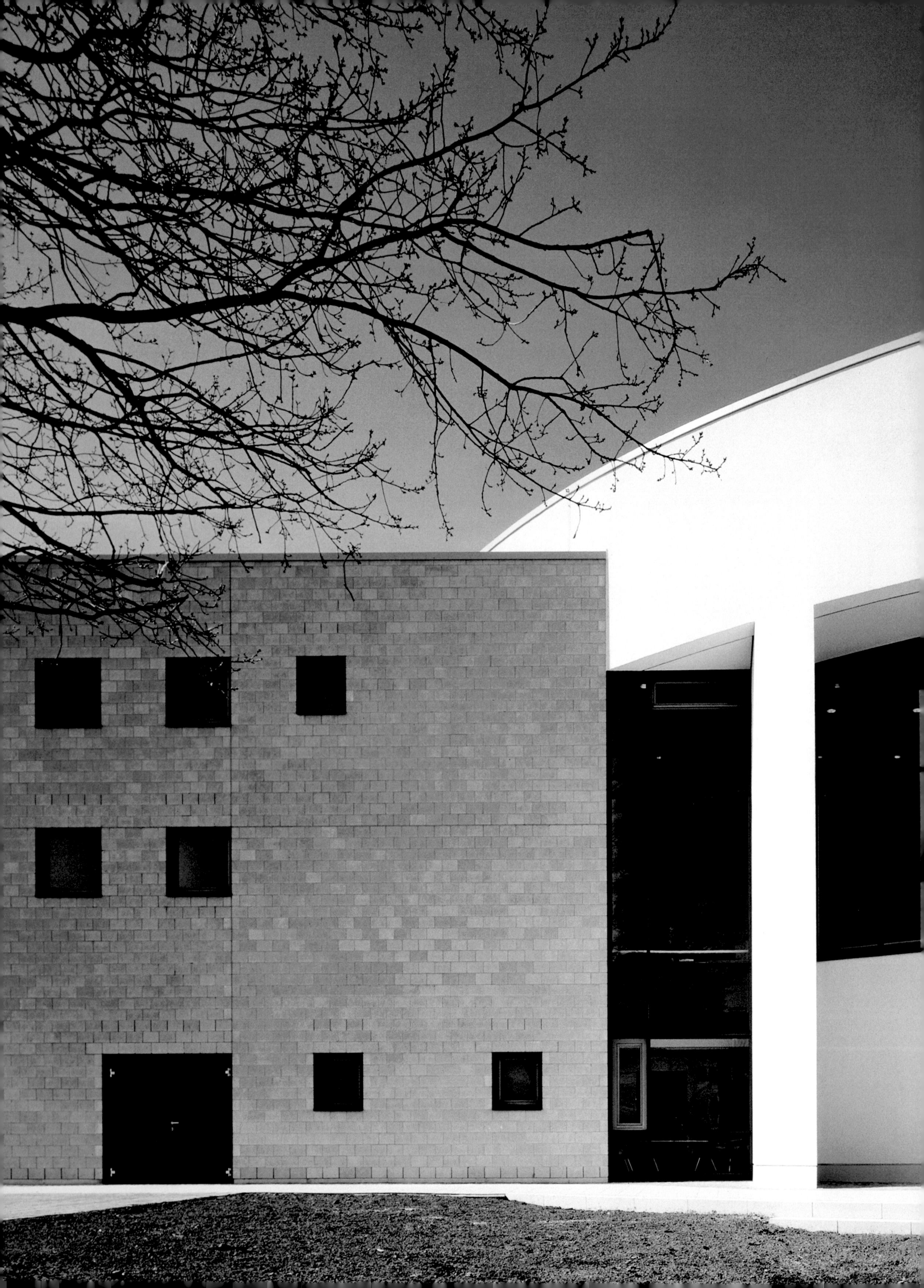

Hörsaal- und Seminargebäude der TU Chemnitz
Auditoria and Seminar Building, Chemnitz Institute of Technology

Wettbewerb Competition
1994 – 1. Preis

Entwurf Design
Meinhard von Gerkan

Bauherr Client
Staatshochbauamt Chemnitz

Bauzeit Construction period
1996–1998

BGF Gross floor area
8.850 m²

Der zentrale Bereich des Hörsaalzentrums ist nach einem durchgehenden Farbkonzept gestaltet – der Hörsaalbaukörper in hellem Gelb „schwebt" in der zweigeschossigen Eingangshalle mit ihrem rötlichen Erdgeschoss und dem kräftig-blauen Obergeschoss. Die einzelnen Bauteile sind in blauen, gelben und braun-rötlichen Farben voneinander abgesetzt und gleichzeitig zueinander in eine farbliche Beziehung gestellt. Die Farbwirkung entsteht dabei aus dem Zusammenstoß verschiedener Wand- oder Deckenteile mit überraschenden Verschneidungen. Die kubische Wirkung der Baukörper wird durch die Farben gesteigert und schafft so einen neuen Ort mit einer eigenen Identität. Das Vorlesungsgebäude ist als erster Teil einer weiteren Bebauung zu sehen, das aber bereits heute einen starken Akzent setzt, um sich gegen die Tristesse der Umgebung zu behaupten.

The core area of the auditoria centre was designed using a continuous colour concept: the main auditorium is coloured in a light yellow and 'hovers' in the two-storey entrance hall with its reddish ground floor and rich-blue upper floor. The single building units stand out from each other clearly in account of their blue, yellow and brown-red shades, whilst this colouring simultaneously generates an inter-relation. The colour effect results from the combination of different wall or ceiling parts with surprising intersections. The colours reinforce the cubic effect of the buildings, thereby generating a new location with an individual identity. The seminar building should be regarded as the first step of a future development – a building that is already setting a new course in order to hold its ground against the dreariness of its surroundings.

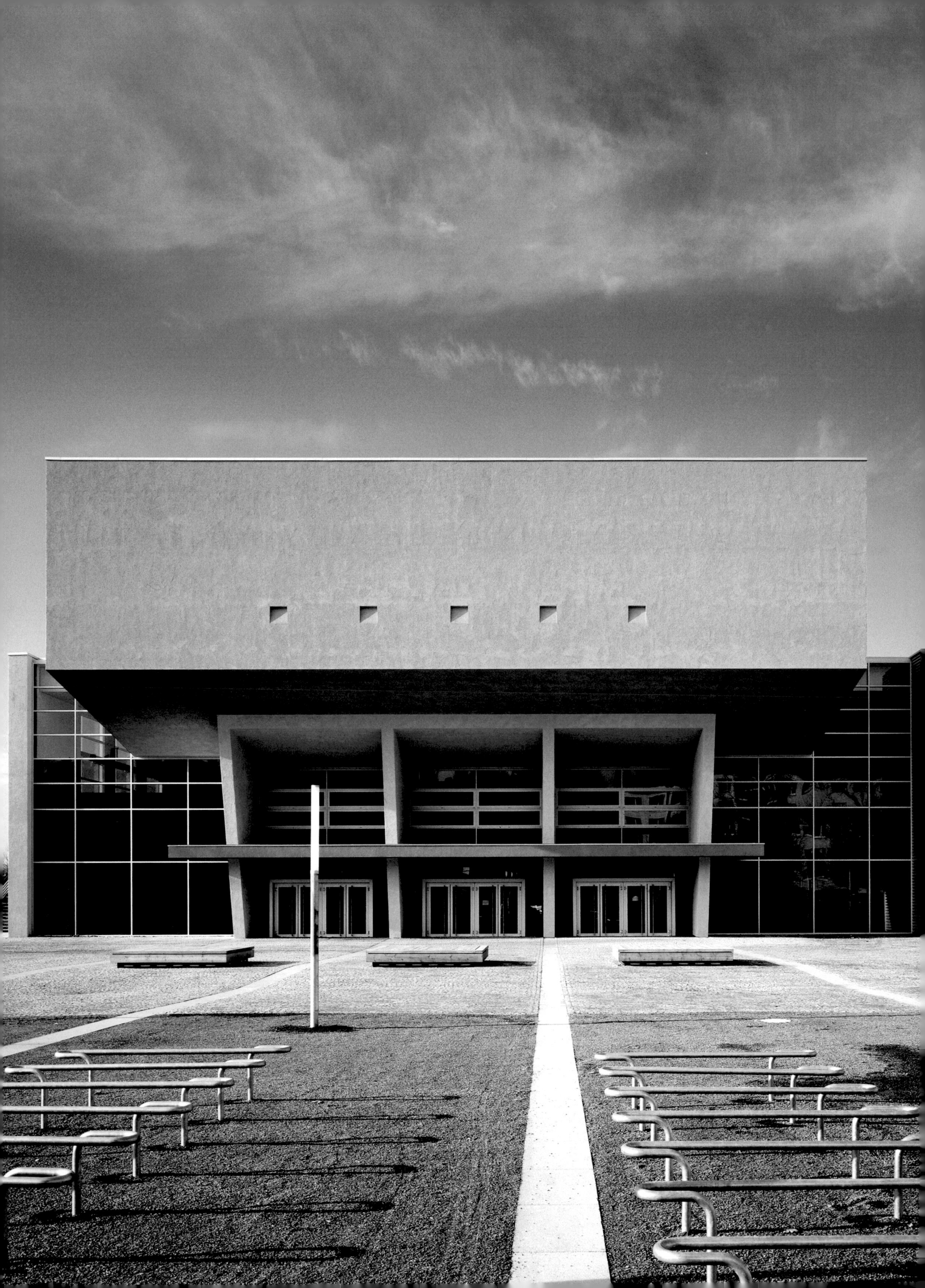

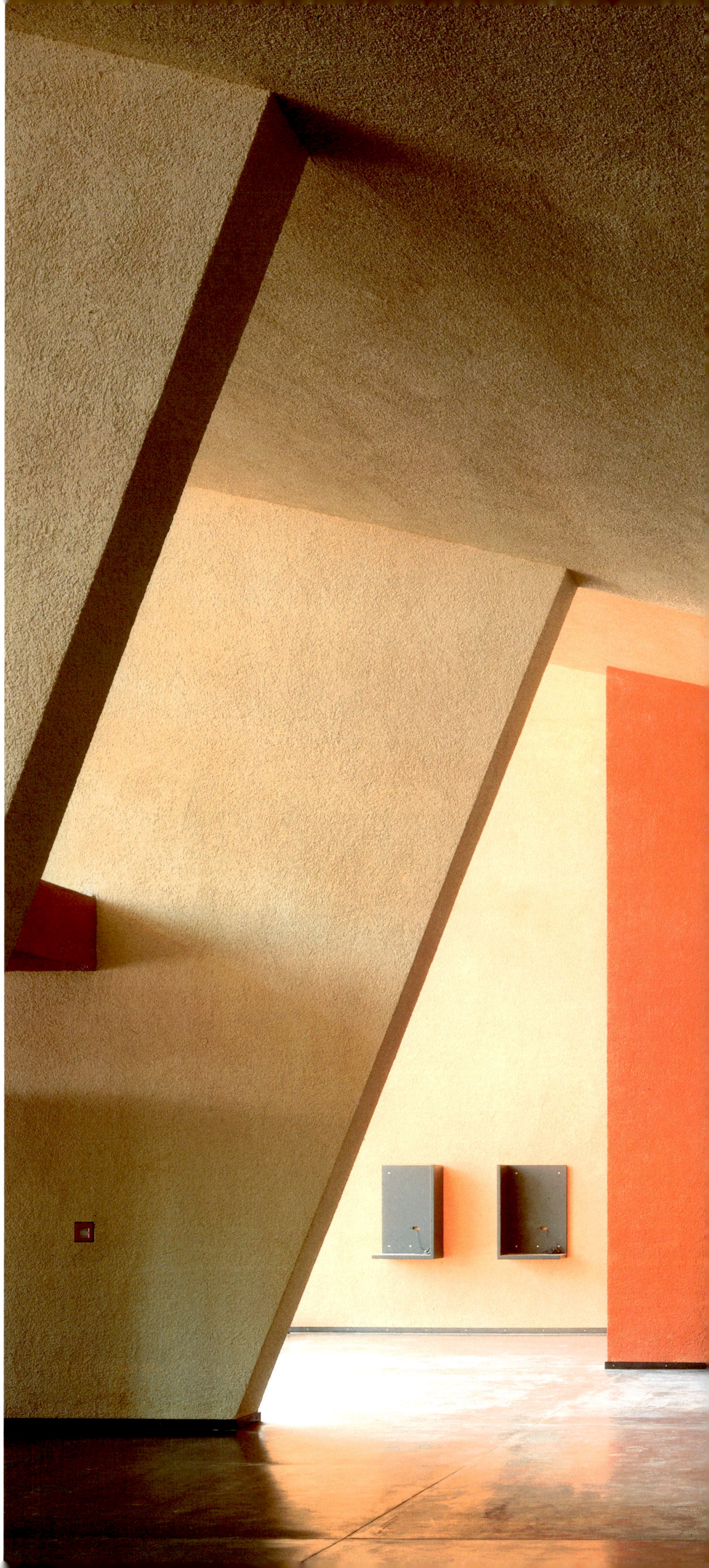

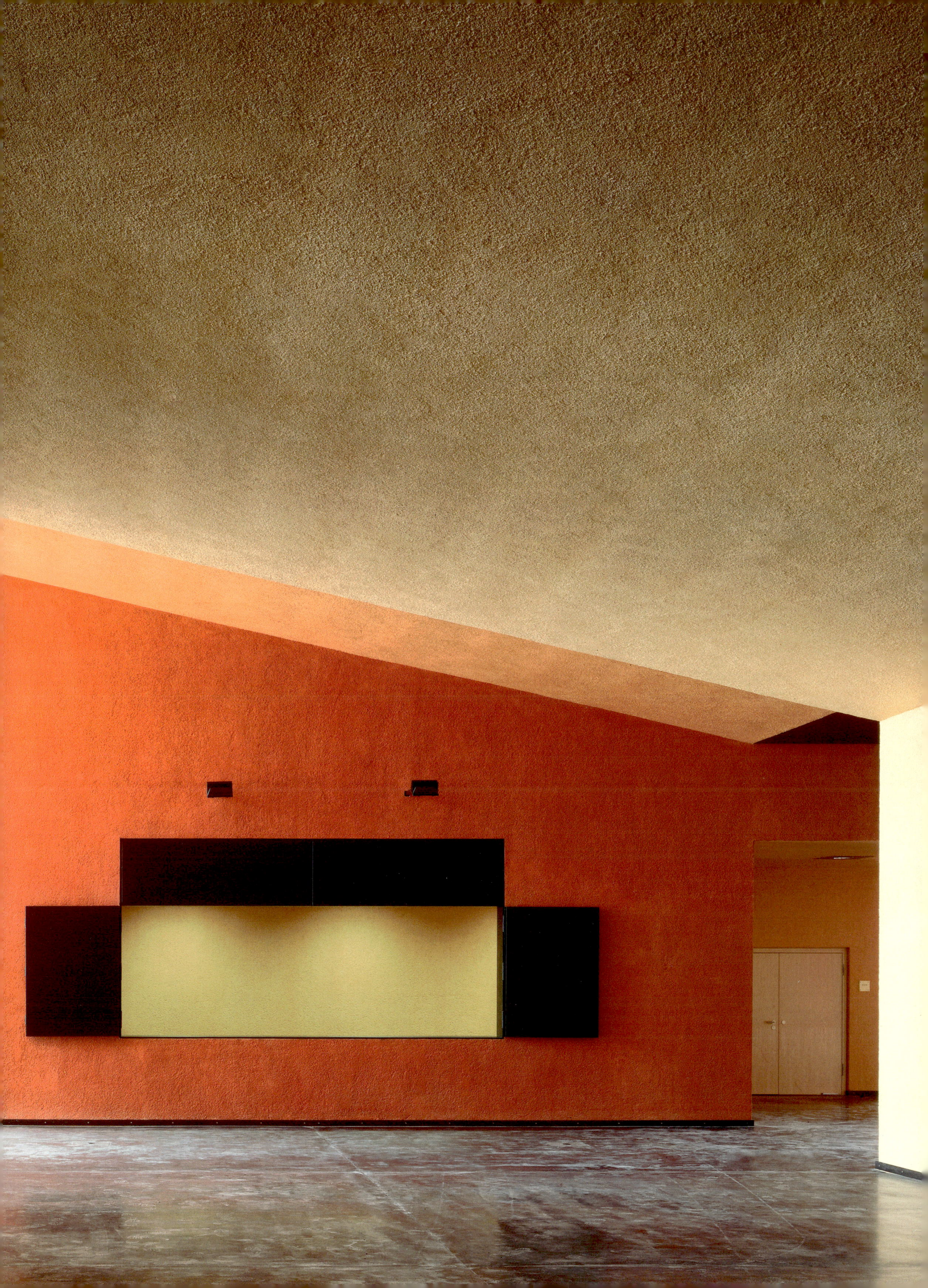

266

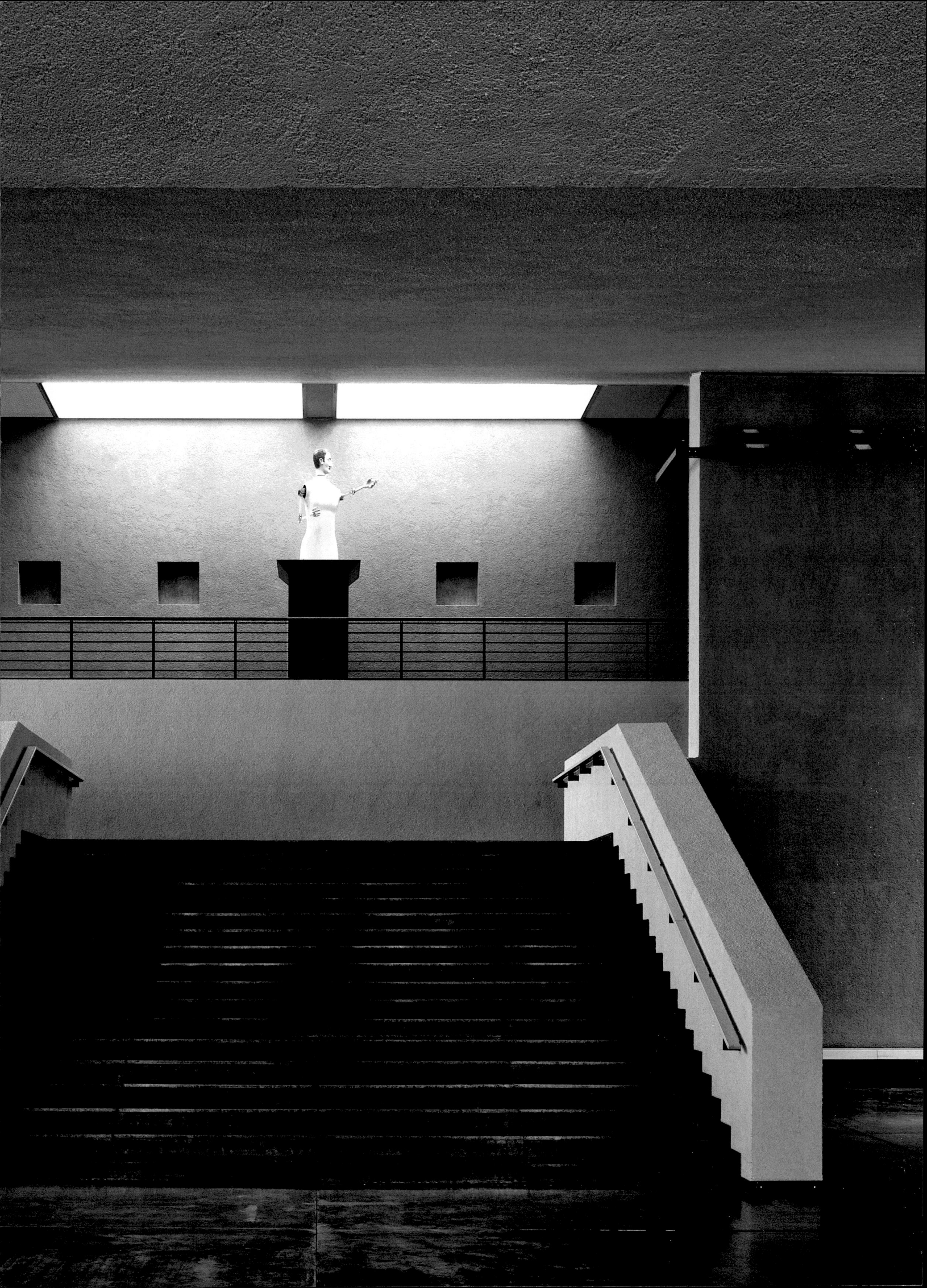

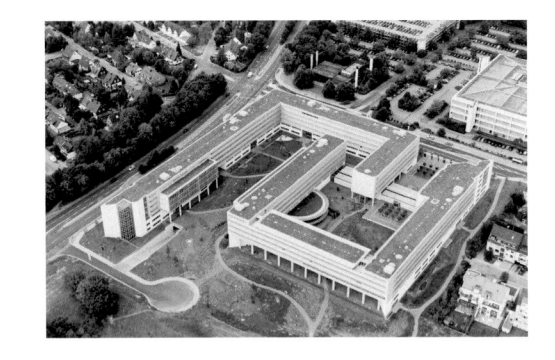

Büropark Bredeney, Essen
Bredeney Office Park, Essen

Wettbewerb Competition
1993 – 1. Preis

Entwurf Design
Meinhard von Gerkan

Partner Partner
Klaus Staratzke

Bauherr Client
MC Immobilien Verwaltungs GmbH + Co. Essen,
Mielesheide Kommanditgesellschaft, Düsseldorf

Bauzeit Construction period
1996–1998

BGF Gross floor area
80.000 m²

Dem parkartigen Charakter des Grundstücks trägt die Konzeption des Gebäudeensembles mehrfach Rechnung: Zum einen sind alle Bauteile auf den Grünzug der Auenlandschaft bezogen, zum anderen setzt sich die Grünanlage bis in die Freiflächen zwischen den Gebäuden fort. Die Baukörperfiguration besteht aus zwei ineinander verschränkten, U-förmigen Bürotrakten. Der um einen quadratischen Gartenhof angelegte Karstadt-Teil öffnet sich in einer Höhe von drei Geschossen auf der ganzen Länge des auf der Südseite gelegenen Flügels. Der Hauptzugang bietet sich mit einladender Geste zur Theodor-Althoff-Straße hin an und stellt so eine optische Verbindung zum Altbau her. Eine zweigeschossige, transparente Halle bindet die drei Erschließungskerne übersichtlich an. Die Grundrissausbildung wechselt von zwei- zu dreibündiger Anordnung, was sich analog in der Fassade abbildet.

The design of the complex took the park-like character of the site into account in several ways. For one thing, every building section is oriented to the green strip of the alluvial landscape, for another, the green strip continues into the open areas between the building sections. The structure consists of two interlocked, U-shaped office wings. The Karstadt wing to the south surrounds a square garden patio; its three storeys open to the surroundings over the entire length of the wing. The main entrance is an inviting element on Theodor-Althoff-Strasse and offers a sight connection to the old building. A two-storey transparent hall provides clear orientation to the three interior circulation and service cores. Floor plans range from rows of offices with one central passage or two corridors in between, and the façade design hints at this interior arrangement.

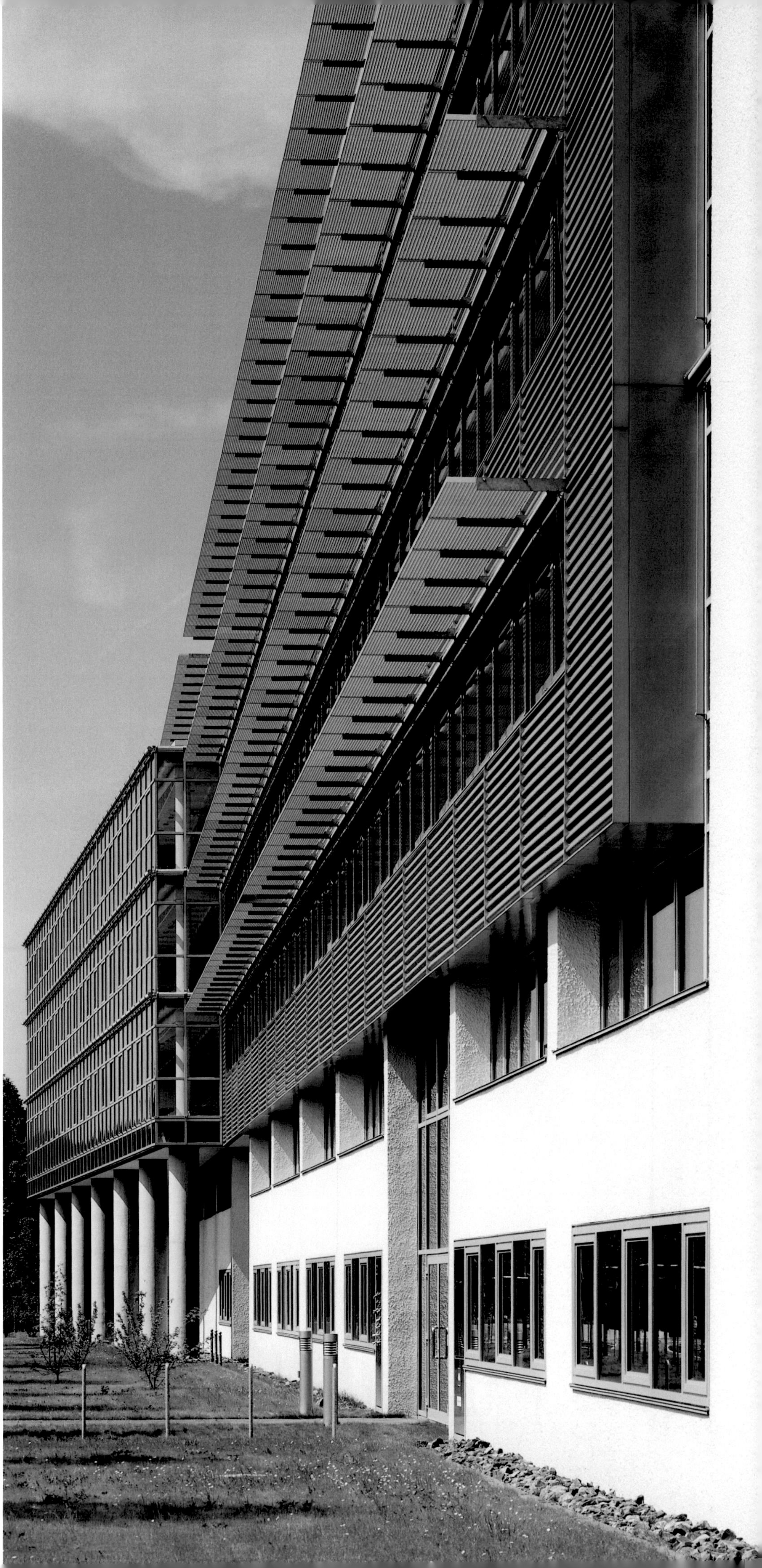

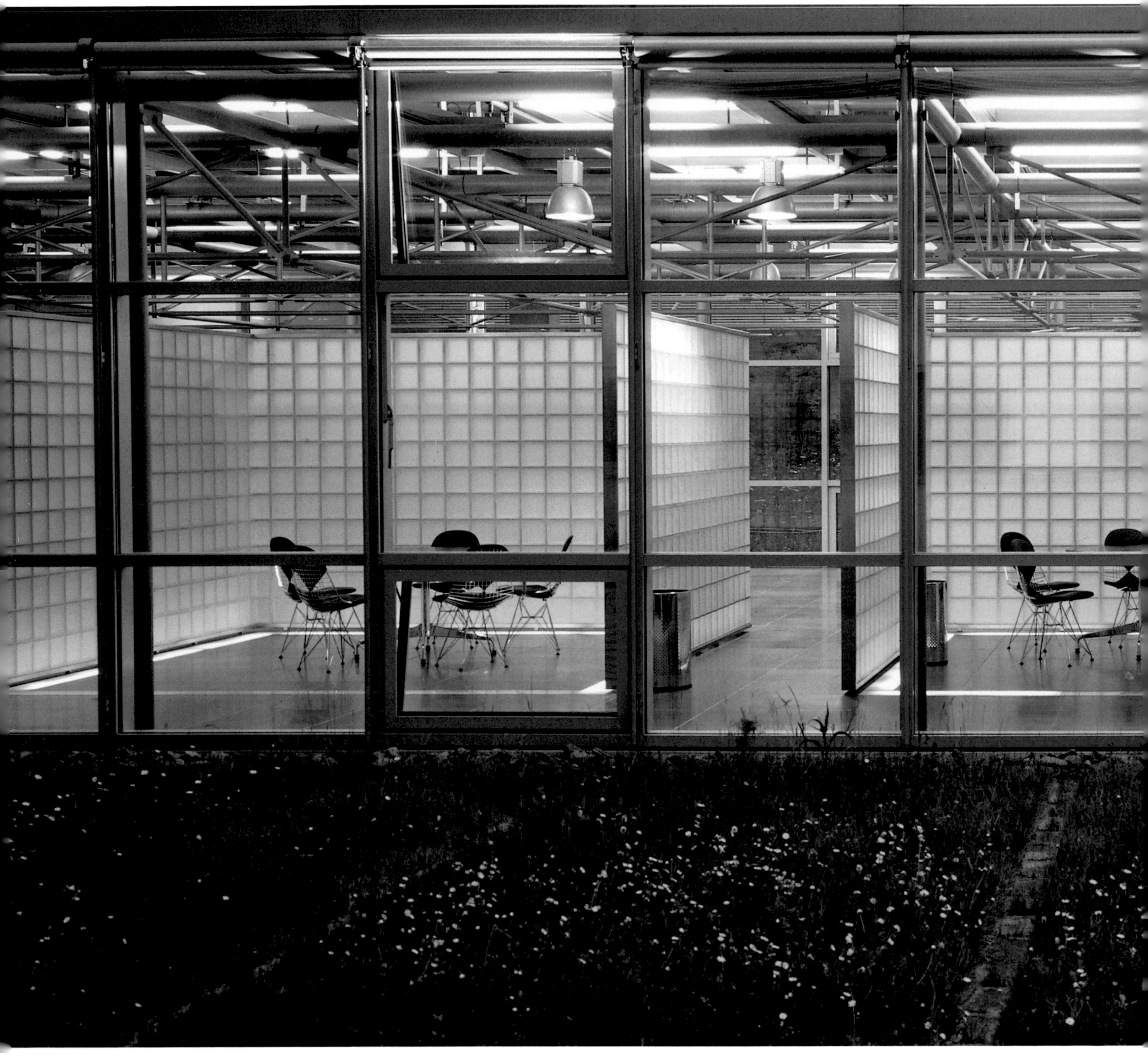

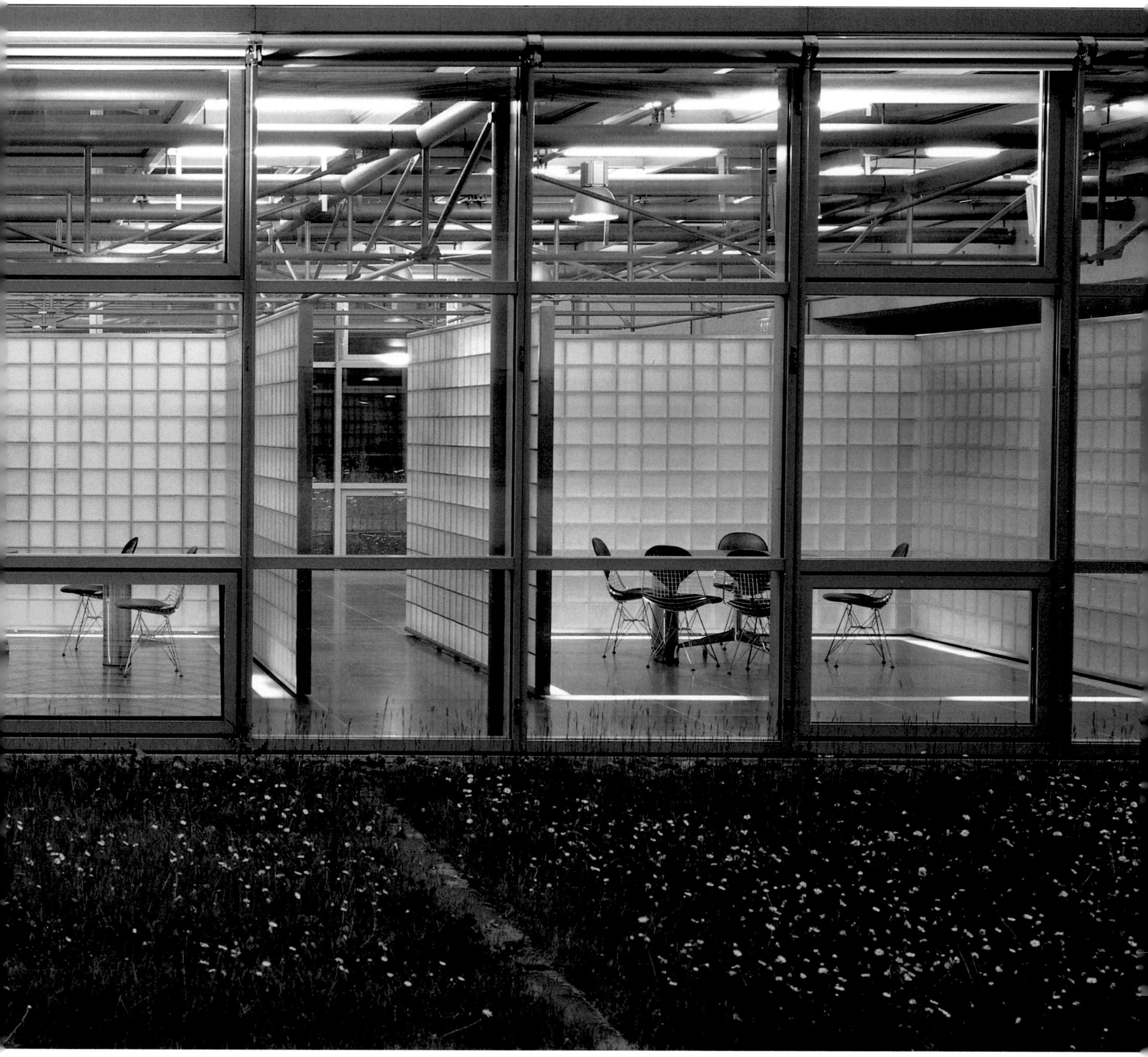

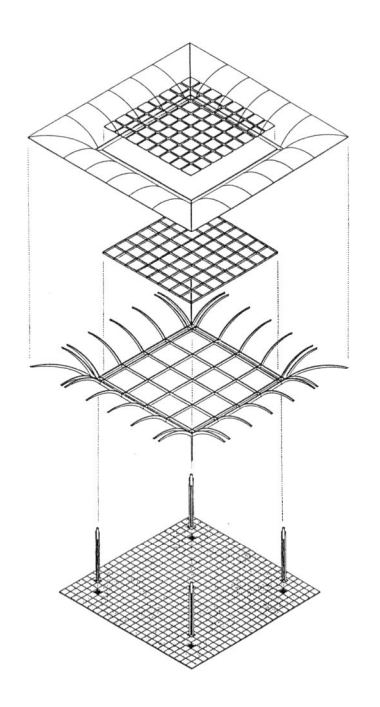

S-Bahn Stationen in Hannover
Suburban Railway Station in Hanover

1996

Entwurf Design
Meinhard von Gerkan

Partner Partner
Jürgen Hillmer

Bauherr Client
Deutsche Bahn AG

Bauzeit Construction period
1997–1998, 7 Dächer

Grundfläche Base area
9 x 9 m

Die ungerichtete, quadratische Haltestelle, die entsprechend der jeweiligen spezifischen Bedingungen vor Ort angeordnet werden kann, ist durch ein 9 x 9 m großes Flachdach definiert, das auf vier aufgelösten Kreuzstützen ruht. Die Stützen haben einen Achsabstand von 5,10 m, zwischen ihnen ist das Dach verglast. Nach außen verlaufen die Stahlprofile des Tragwerks in einem sanften Bogen nach oben. Sie sind mit einem für die Deutsche Bahn AG entwickelten Wellblech gedeckt, so dass ein leicht geschwungener bzw. „beschwingter" Kragen entsteht. Die Beleuchtung fällt aus den in den Stützenachsen angeordneten Downlights auf das darunter befindliche Mobiliar. Durch einen im Bereich der Blechkrempe helleren Bodenbelag wird das Licht vom Boden wiederum an das Wellblech reflektiert, um auch nachts die geschwungene Form erlebbar zu machen.

The square station, which can be positioned according to the specific requirements of the location on account of its neutral orientation, is defined by a 9 by 9 m large flat roof supported by four cruciform columns at 5.10-m centres. The roof in between is glazed. Towards the outside the steel sections of the supporting structure stretch upwards with a slight arch. They are covered with corrugated sheet metal that was developed for Deutsche Bahn AG, forming a slightly curved collar. The illumination from downlights positioned in the column axes falls onto the furnishings placed below. A light flooring in the area of the sheet metal brim reflects the light onto the corrugated sheet metal, illuminating the curved form at night.

Richtung Lehrte 2

Residenz in Jurmala, Lettland
Residence in Jurmala, Latvia

1996

Entwurf Design
Meinhard von Gerkan

Bauherr Client
Familie Krasovicky

Bauzeit Construction period
1997–1998

BGF Gross floor area
1.400 m²

Der Grundriss des großzügigen Gästehauses ist streng axialsymmetrisch aufgebaut. Der Mittelteil in der Achse baut sich aus einer Folge von Empfangshalle, einem Atrium unter einem Glasdach bis zum großen Speiseraum auf und mündete in einen von seitlichen Baukörpern gefassten Gartenhof, in dessen Mitte ein Zierbecken mit einem Wasserfall angelegt ist. Die zwei flankierenden Gebäuderiegel nehmen neben einer Ausstellungsfläche, einem Billardzimmer sowie zwei Gästeapartments im Obergeschoss auch noch die Personal- und Nebenräume auf. Der gesamte Bau ist als Holzkonstruktion mit Holzfassaden aus kanadischer Lärche entwickelt; die Dachfläche aus Pult- und Satteldach ist mit Zinkblech eingedeckt. In weiteren Bauabschnitten sind eine Veranstaltungshalle sowie ausgedehnte Garten- und Freizeitanlagen mit Gästehäusern geplant.

The plan of the spacious guest house is strictly axial symmetric. The central part in the axis is formed by a sequence from the foyer, an atrium underneath a glass roof and, finally, a large dining hall, terminating in a garden courtyard embraced by lateral buildings and a central decorative basin with a waterfall. Two building bars flank the central part, accommodating the exhibition areas, a billiard room as well as two guest apartments and additionally the staff and secondary rooms on the upper level. The whole building is designed as a timber construction made of Canadian larch; the roof surface consisting of monopitch and saddle roof is clad in sheet zinc. An event hall as well as an extensive garden and leisure complex with guest houses are planned in further construction stages.

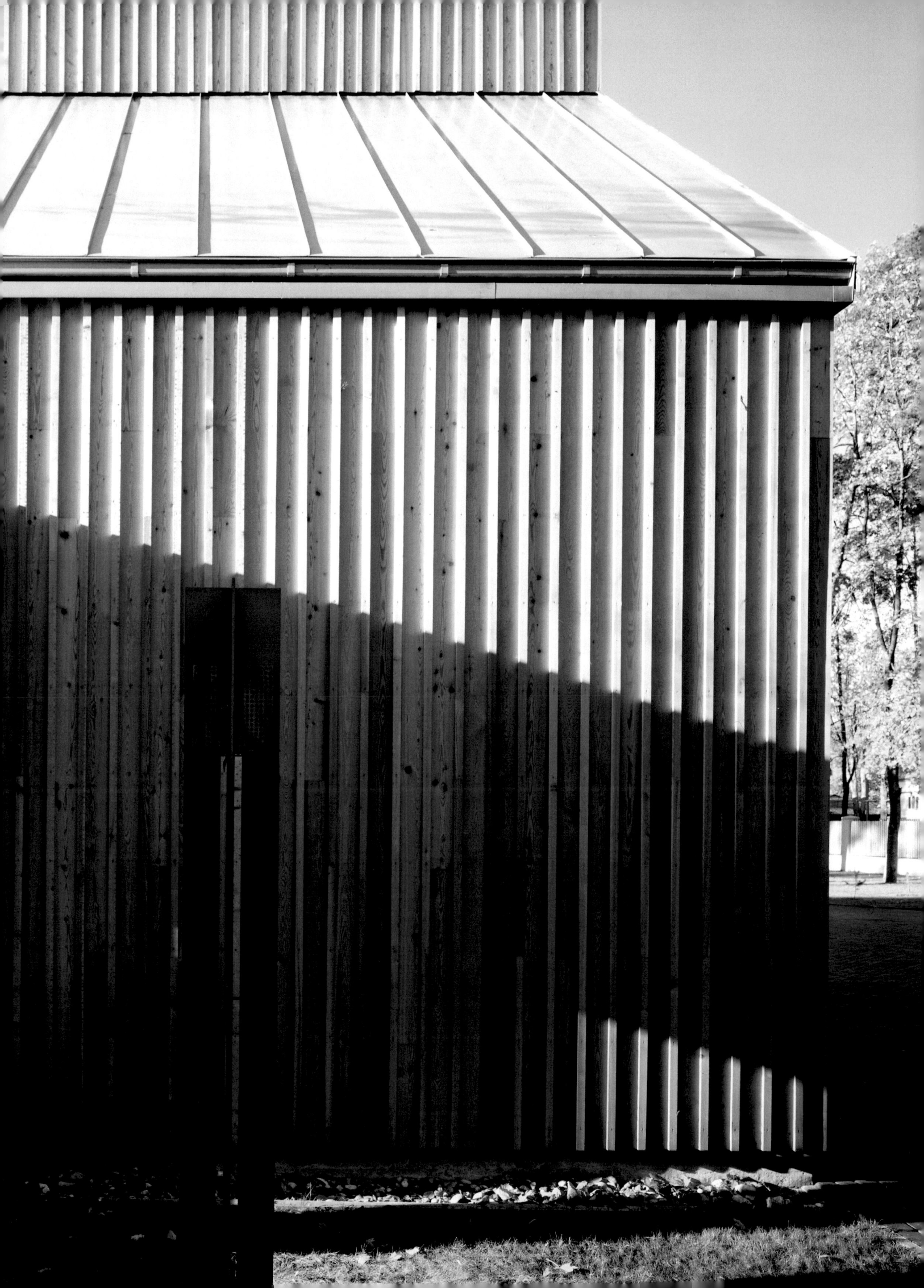

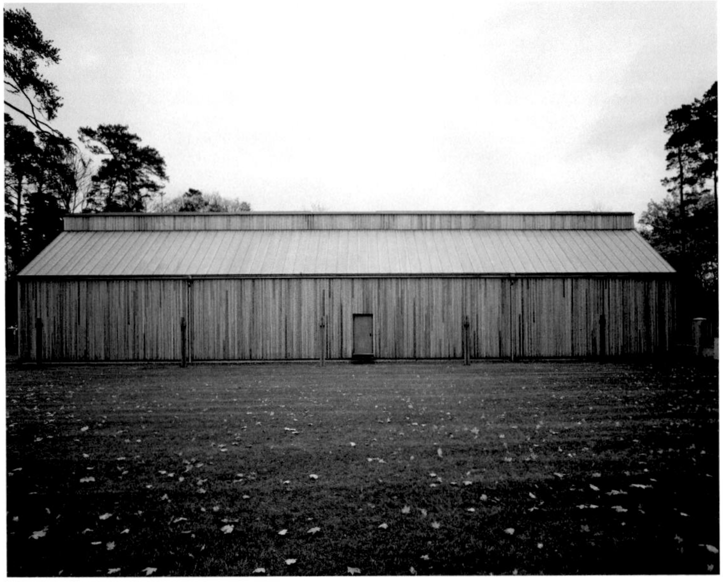

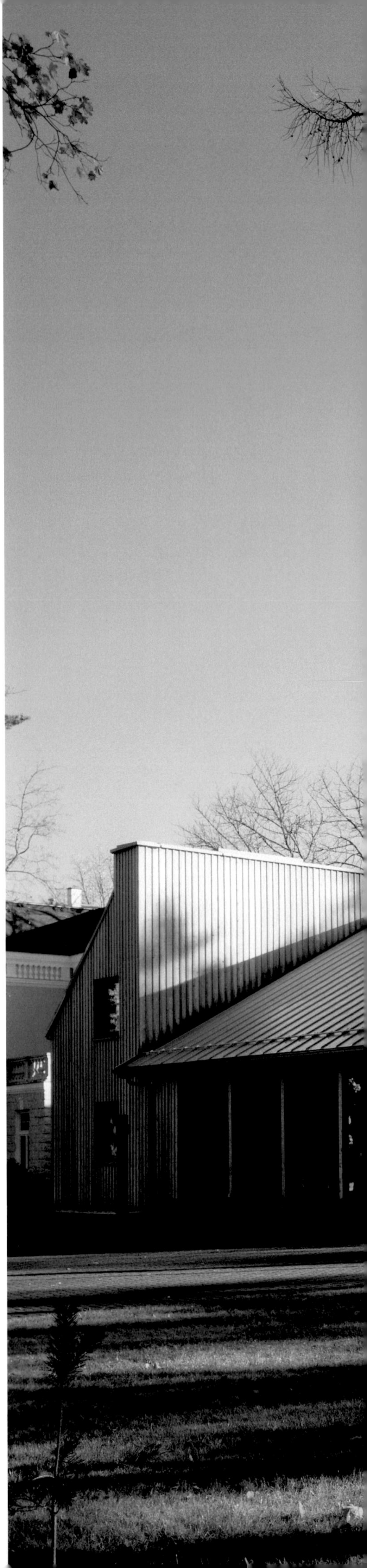

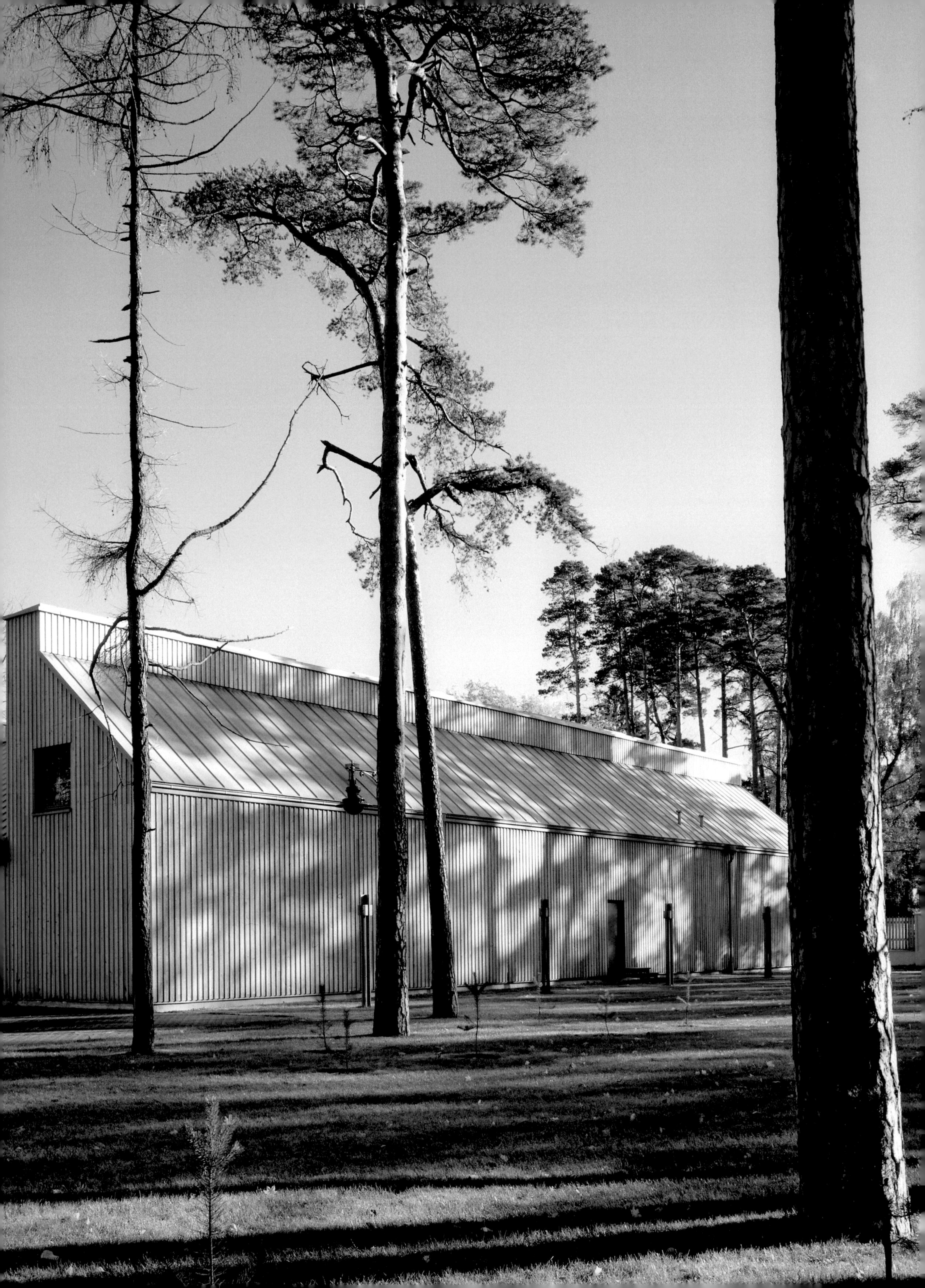

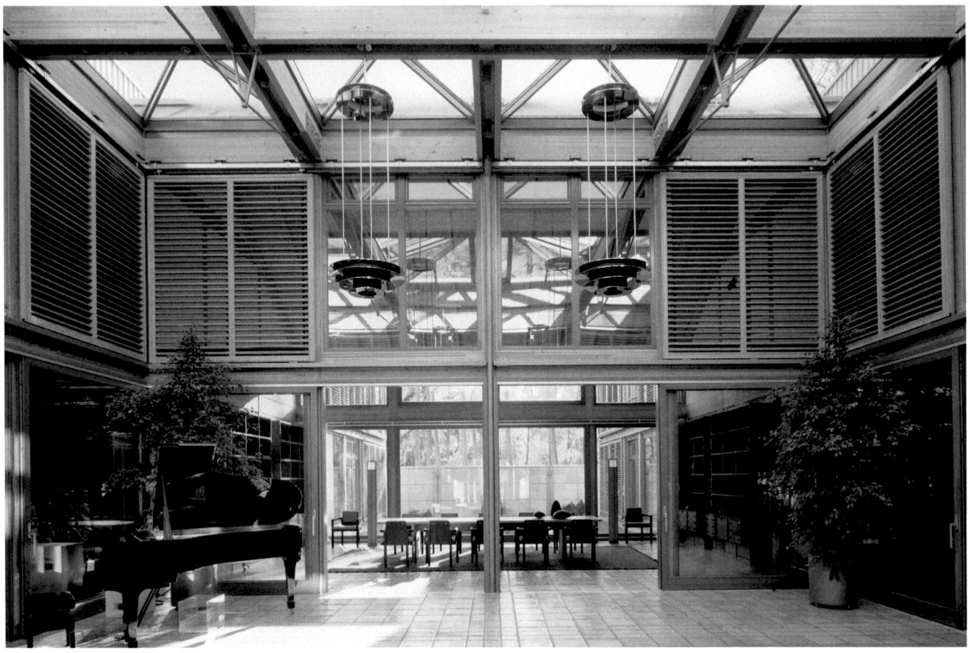

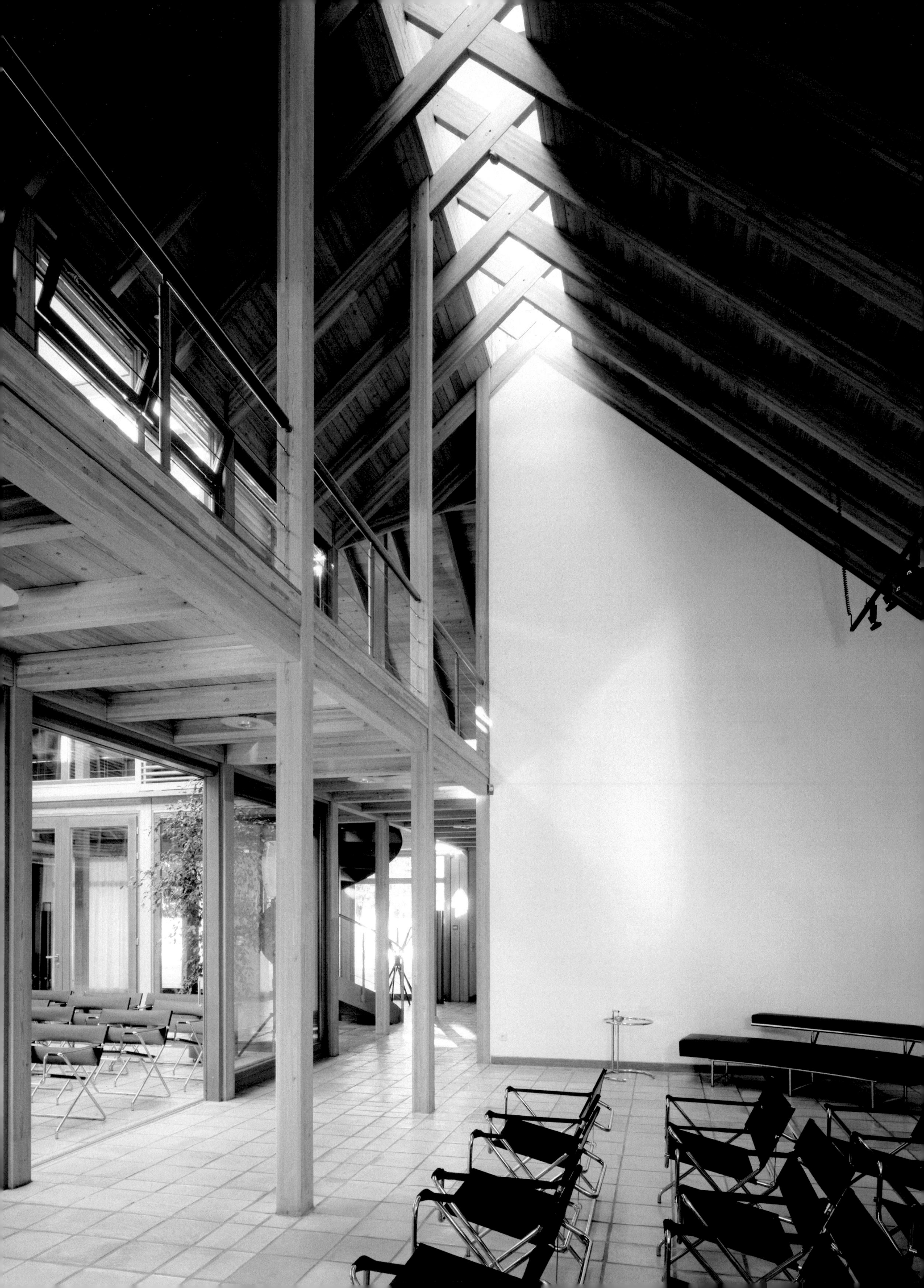

Norddeutsche Metall-Berufsgenossenschaft, Hannover
Professional Association of the Metal Industry, Hanover

Wettbewerb Competition
1994 – 1. Rang

Entwurf Design
Meinhard von Gerkan

Partner Partner
Klaus Staratzke

Bauherr Client
Norddeutsche Metall BGN

Bauzeit Construction period
1995–1998

BGF Gross floor area
23.900 m²

Dass sich die Norddeutsche Metall-Berufsgenossenschaft als Bauherr mit einem metallverkleideten Gebäude gut repräsentiert, ist naheliegend. Gewählt wurde die Pfosten-Riegel-Konstruktion aus Aluminium mit der abschließenden Edelstahlwelle aber auch wegen ihres hüllenartigen Charakters, der dem Gebäudetypus entspricht. Anders als z.B. dem Klinker, sieht man diesem Material die ihm zugedachte Rolle des Verkleidens an. Diese Auffassung der Fassade – als Haut über einem tragenden Skelett – liegt auch der Detailausbildung zugrunde. Die minimierte Aluminium-Pfosten-Riegel-Konstruktion hält die Verglasung und bildet so die Klimahülle, während eine filigrane Stahlkonstruktion die tragende Rolle übernimmt. Die Halle bildet einen Klimapuffer, der die Fläche der Gebäudehülle reduziert und ein großvolumiges, differenziertes Binnenklima in einem Großteil des Gebäudes ermöglicht. Der fünfschiffige Gebäudetypus ist flexibel in der Nutzung; für eine mögliche Fremdvermietung bieten sich separate Zugänge mit eigener Adresse an.

It stands to reason that a metal-clad building as headquarters would be an appropriate calling card for the client, the Professional Association of the Metal Industry. But the post-and-beam aluminium structure with a curving stainless-steel façade was also chosen for its 'sheathing' character which suited the building type. Clinker bricks are not an obvious cladding material, whereas steel sheets are. The conception of the façade as a skin covering the load-bearing skeleton was also the basis of the detailing. The minimized aluminium post-and-beam construction holds up the glazing and thus forms a climatic skin, while the filigree steel structure assumes the load-bearing role. The great hall forms a climatic buffer which reduces the surface area of the building skin and serves to achieve differentiated interior climates in large sections of the building. The five-span building can be used flexibly. Separate entrances make it possible to rent out parts of the building with their own postal addresses.

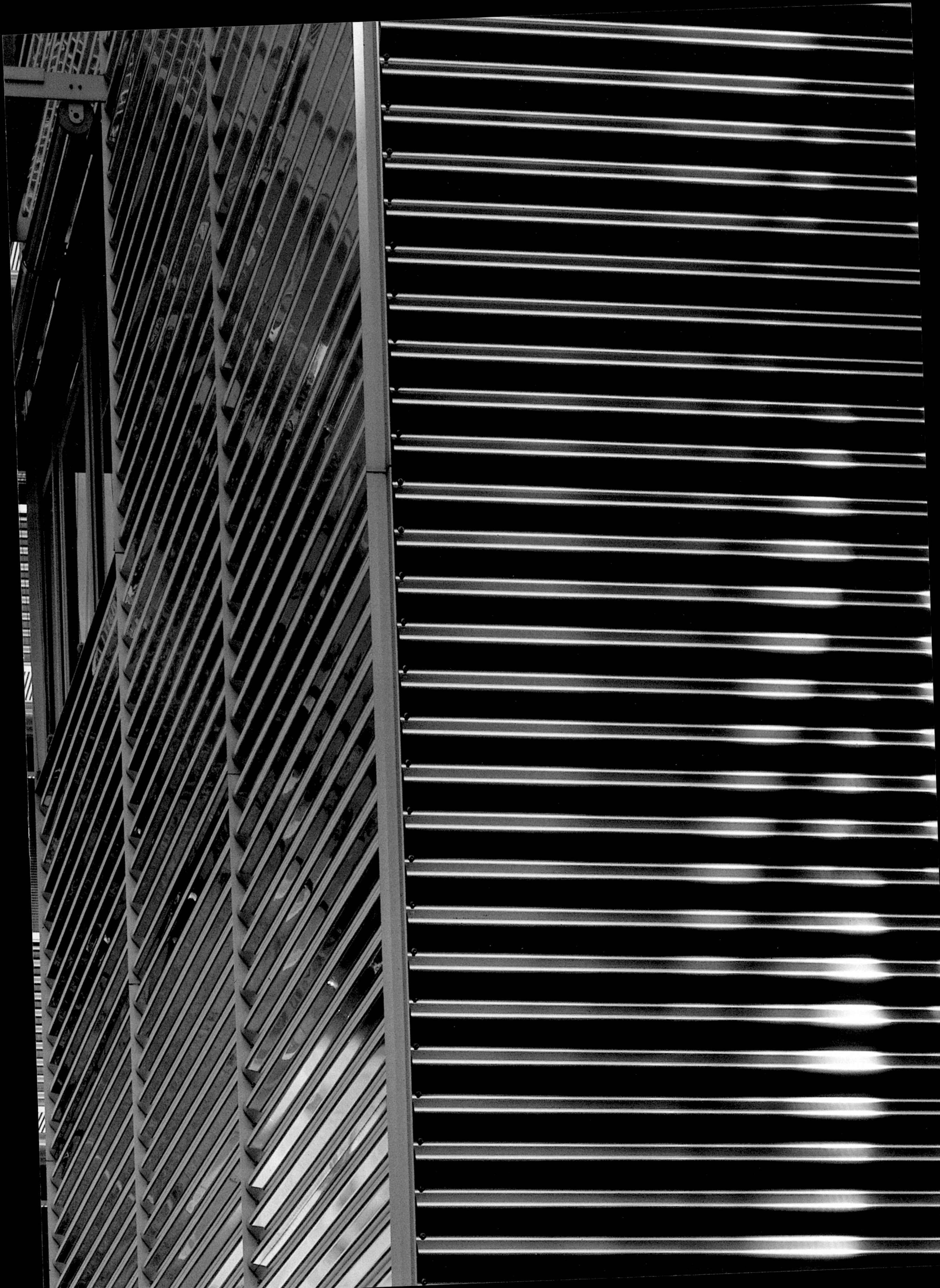

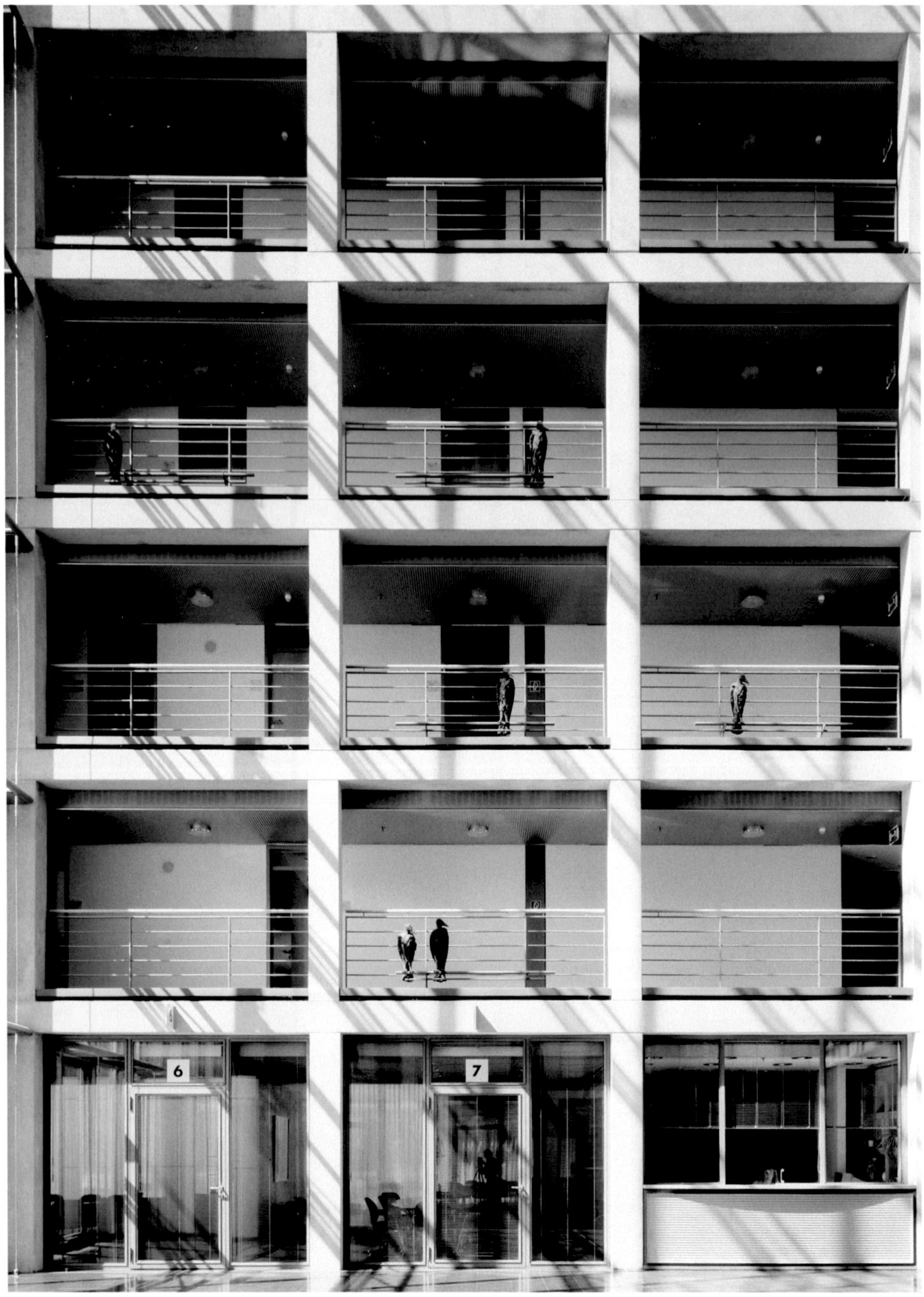
6
7

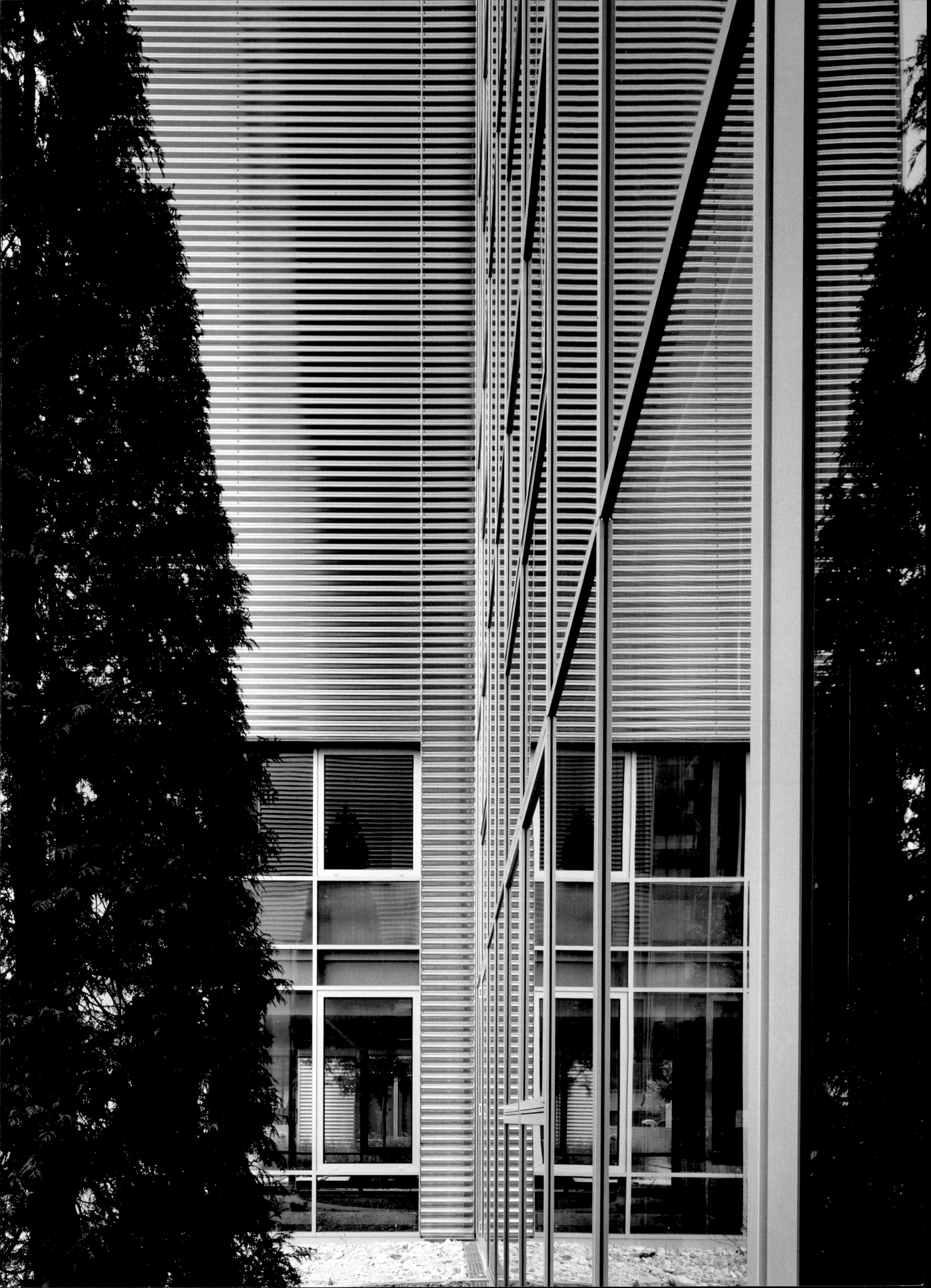

Bahnhof Berlin-Spandau
Berlin-Spandau Railway Station

Wettbewerb Competition
1993 – 3. Preis

Entwurf Design
Meinhard von Gerkan

Partner Partner
Hubert Nienhoff

Bauherr Client
Deutsche Bahn AG

Bauzeit Construction period
1996–1998

BGF überdacht Gross floor area roofed
20.600 m²

Während der Typus der Bahnhofshalle in Spandau an die Tradition historischer Bahnhofshallen anknüpft, ist die Konstruktion der Halle dem 21. Jahrhundert verpflichtet. Die Tonnenkonstruktion ruht auf Längsträgern, die in der Mittelachse der Bahnsteige von Stützen im Abstand von 18 m getragen werden. In der Querachse jeder Stütze liegen der Aussteifung dienende, bogenförmige Rippen. Die Eindeckung der Tonnen erfolgte mit planen Glasscheiben, die infolge der komplizierten Geometrie der Bahnsteige jeweils geringfügig voneinander abweichen. Die gesamte Konstruktion wird durch diagonale, unter der Dachfläche verlaufende Seile stabilisiert. Im Abstand von 3 m angeordnete Lampenausleger geben nachts Licht auf die Bahnsteigebene und erzeugen mit nach oben gerichteten Strahlen Reflexionen in der Glastonne. Dadurch entsteht auch bei Dunkelheit ein eindrucksvolles Raumerlebnis der filigranen Stahl-Glasstruktur.

While the typology of the station hall in Spandau continues the tradition of historical station halls, the construction is committed to the 21st century. The roof construction rests on longitudinal beams, supported by columns positioned at 18-m centres in the central axis of the platforms. The cross axis of each column holds curved stiffening ribs. The glass panel cladding varies slightly owing to the complex geometry of the platforms, but nevertheless appears identical. The overall construction is stabilized by tensile cables, running diagonally below the roof surface. Cantilevered lights at 3-m centres illuminate the platform level at night and create reflections in the glass vault with upward beams, resulting in an impressive spatial experience of the delicate steel-glass structure.

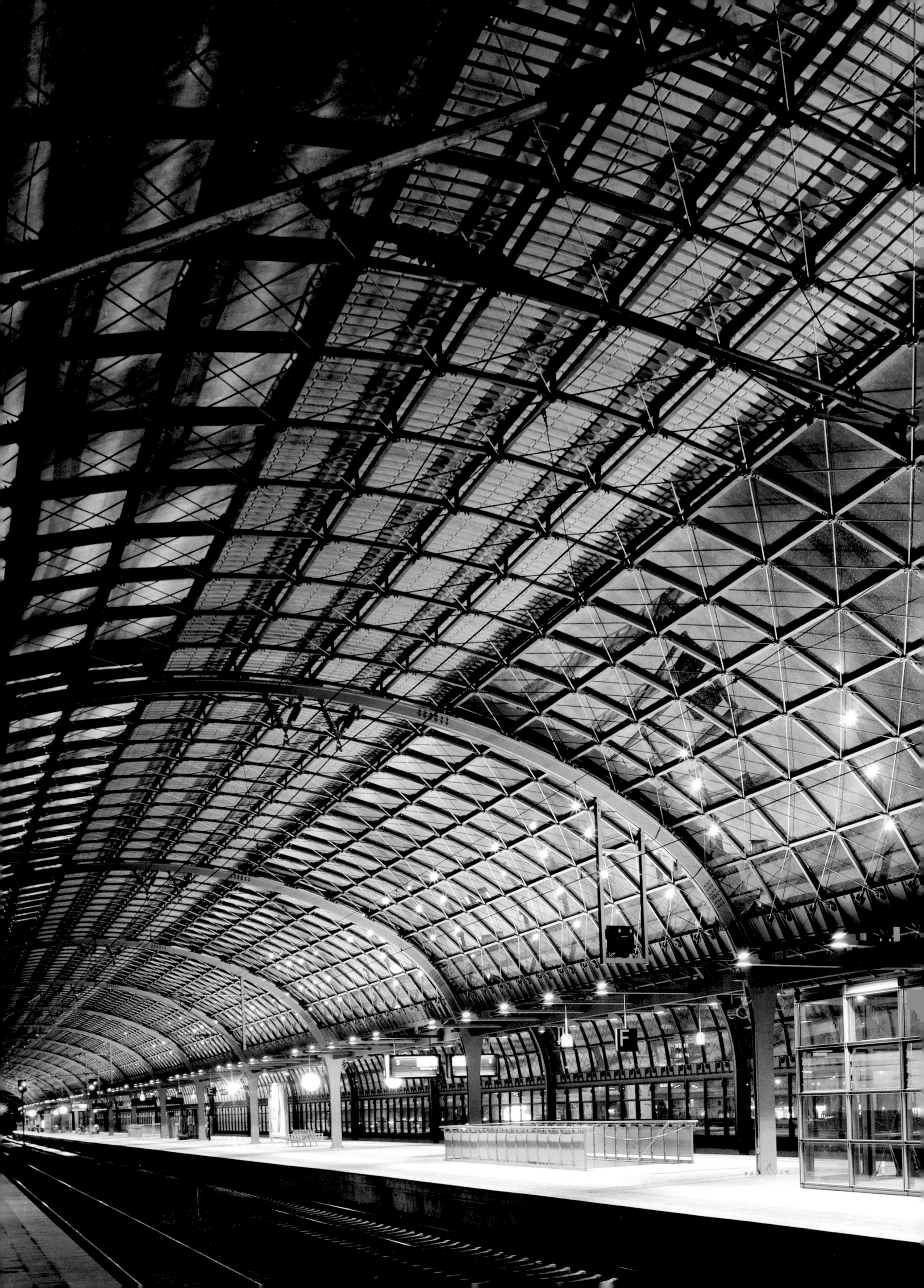
F

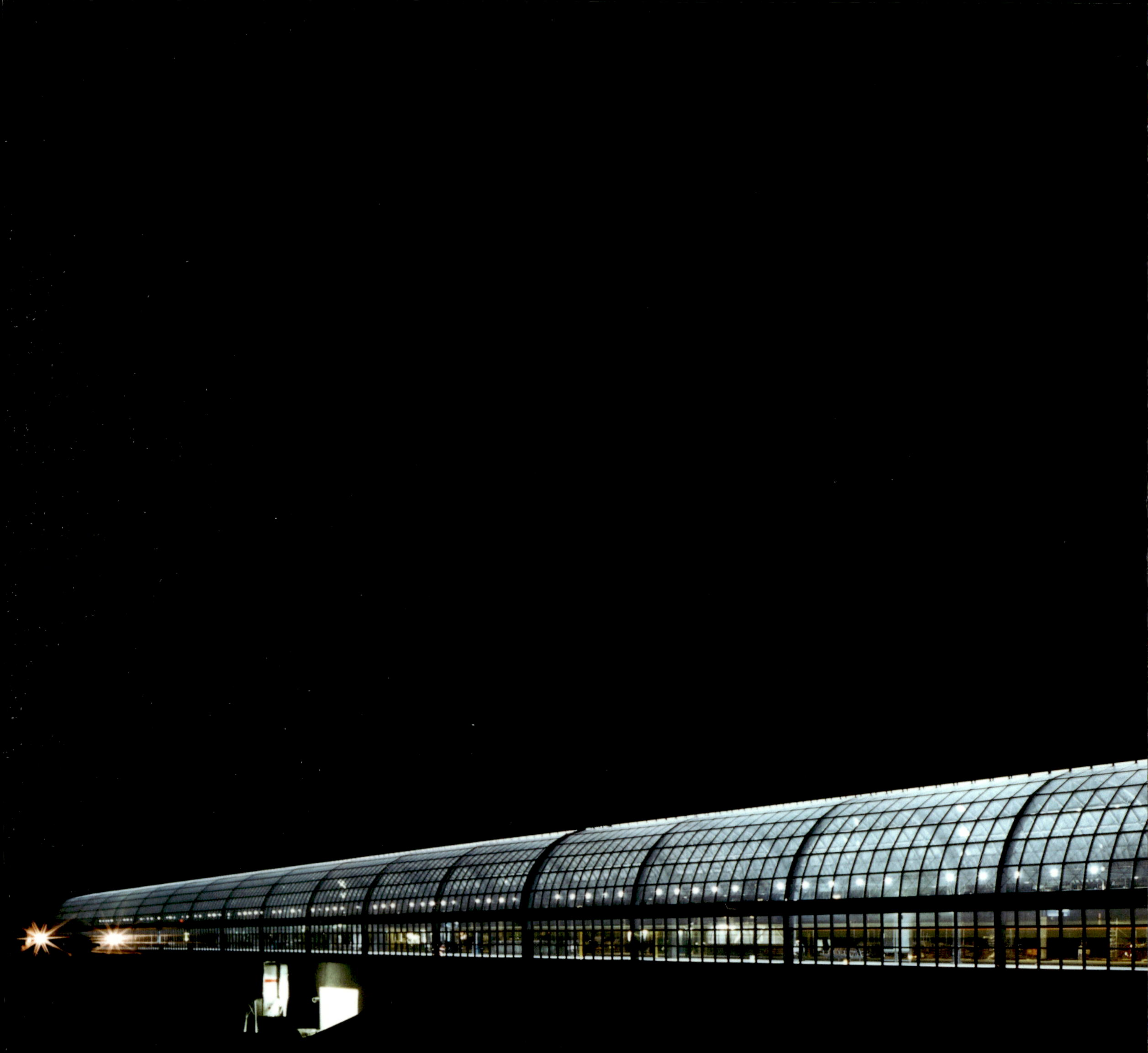

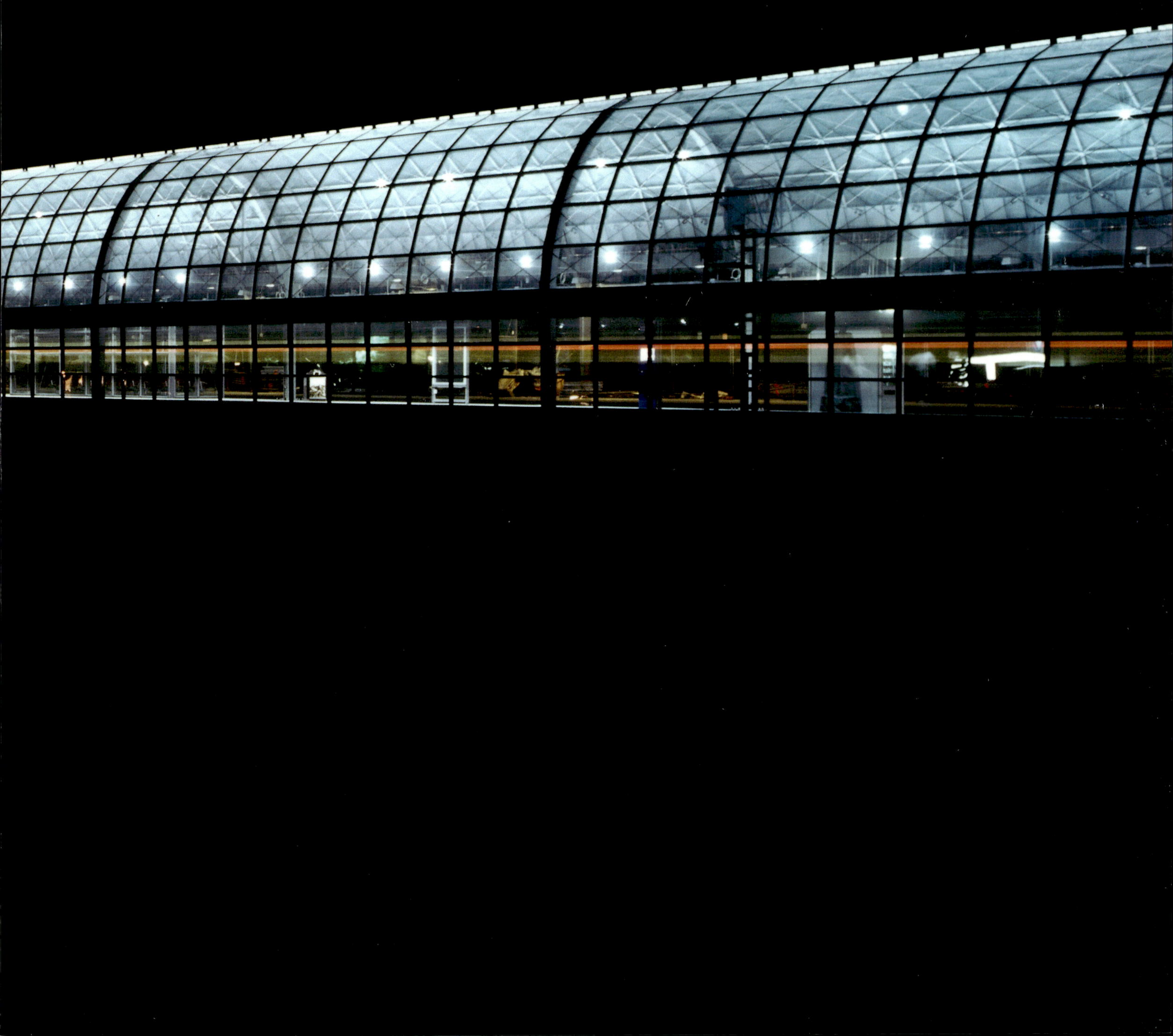

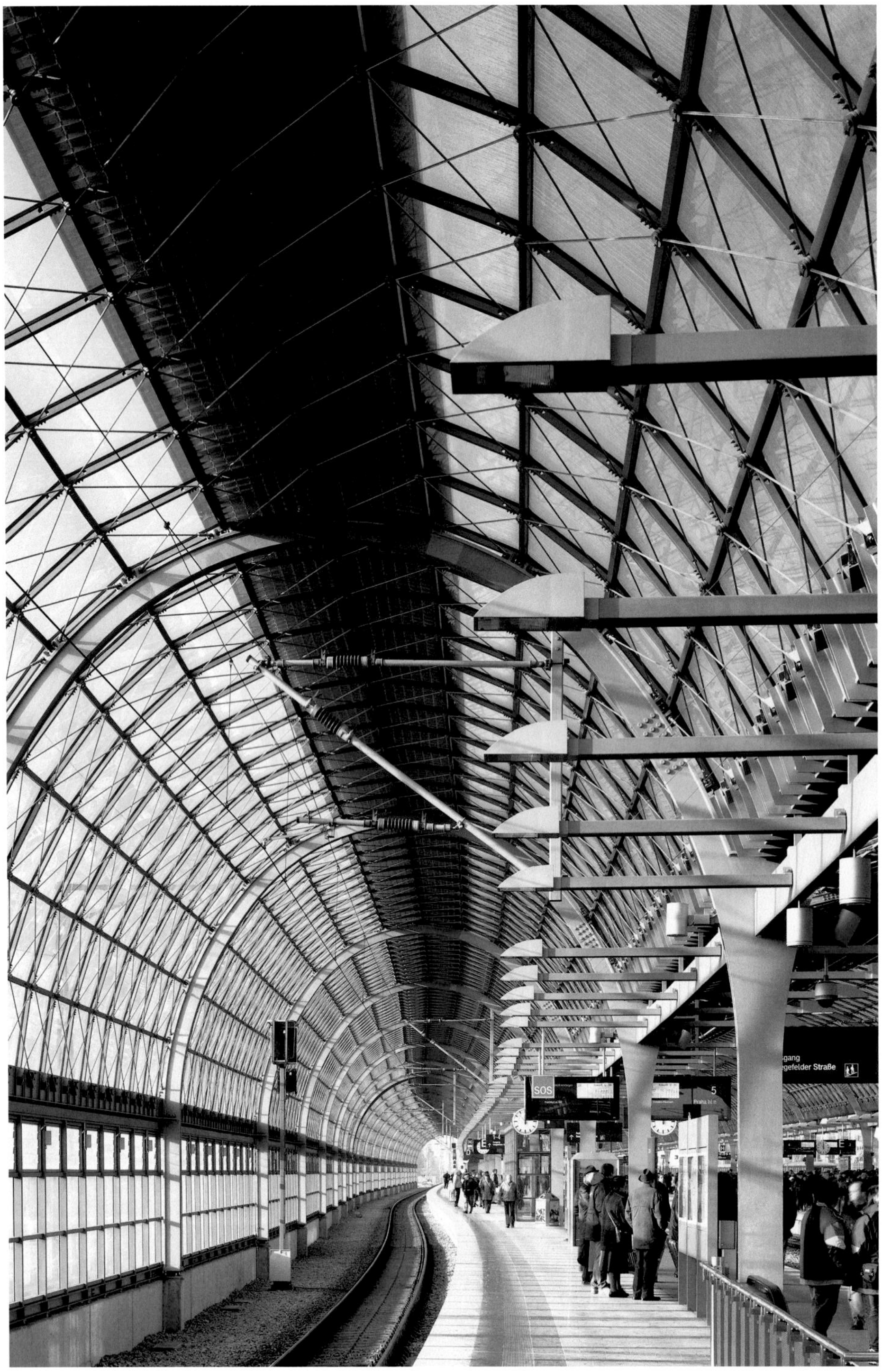
SOS

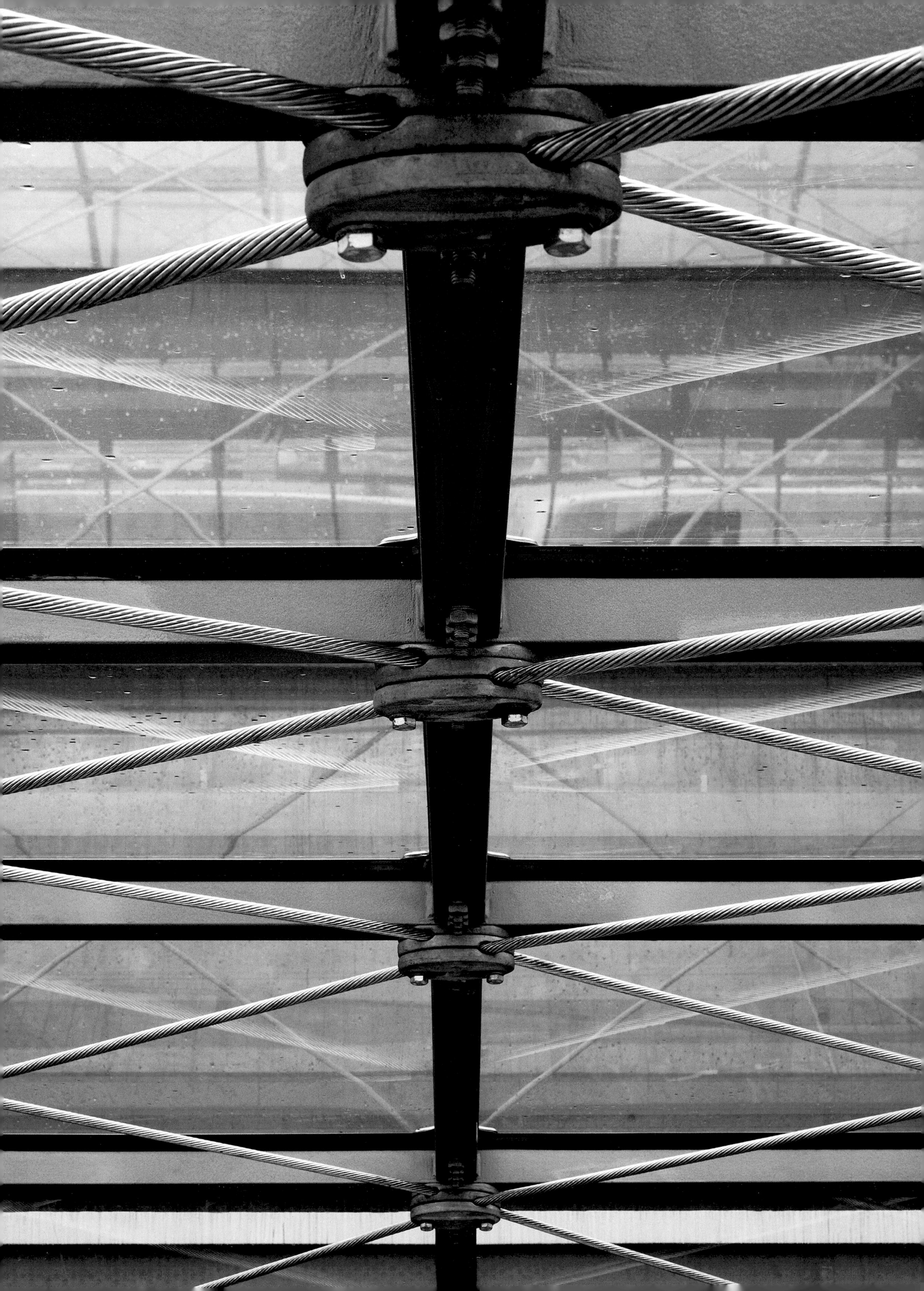

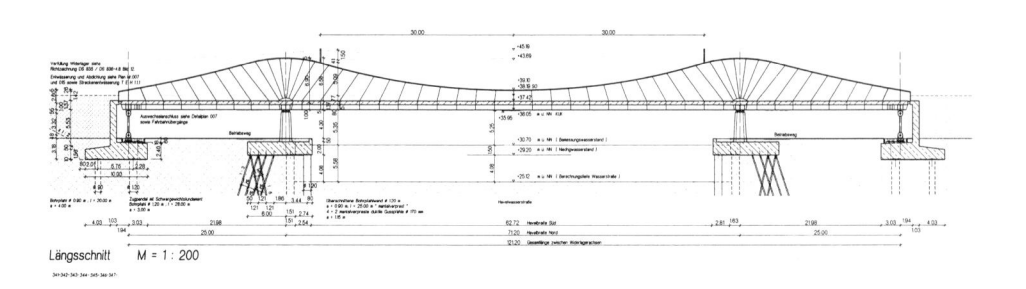

Havelbrücke, Berlin-Spandau
Havel Bridge, Berlin-Spandau

1994

Entwurf Design
Meinhard von Gerkan und Jörg Schlaich

Bauherr Client
Deutsche Bahn AG

Bauzeit Construction period
1996–1998

Länge Length
124,2 m

Breite Width
47,5 m

In Berlin-Spandau wurden im Zuge des Ausbaus der West-Ost-Verbindungen und speziell der Bundesbahnstrecke Hannover–Berlin für den ICE-Verkehr sieben Gleise über die Havel geführt. Die Planungen der Bahn sahen eine weitgehend genormte, unabhängig vom jeweiligen Ort verwendete Bogenbrücke vor, die nicht nur recht unglücklich proportioniert war, sondern auch die Stadtgestalt Spandaus empfindlich gestört hätte. Als Gegenstück wurde in intensiver Zusammenarbeit von Ingenieur und Architekt eine Eisenbahnbrücke entwickelt, die ihre Doppelschwingung durch den Verlauf an den jeweiligen Enden eingespannter Seile herleitet. Die markante Wellenform der drei stählernen Trogbrücken ergibt sich dabei aus einer dem Schnittkraftverlauf folgenden Querschnittshöhe.

Parallel to the development of east-west connections and especially with the extension of the Hanover–Berlin railway link for the ICE (InterCityExpress) service, seven train tracks were built across the river Havel. German Rail's concept was to employ a largely standardized arch bridge construction, which was not only rather badly proportioned and would also have severely disturbed the urban context of Spandau. Contrary to this, intensive working cooperation between engineer and architect produced a classic suspension bridge, its form derived from a tensile cable structure mounted at both ends. The salient wave form of the three-trough bridge results from the section height considering the course of the static forces.

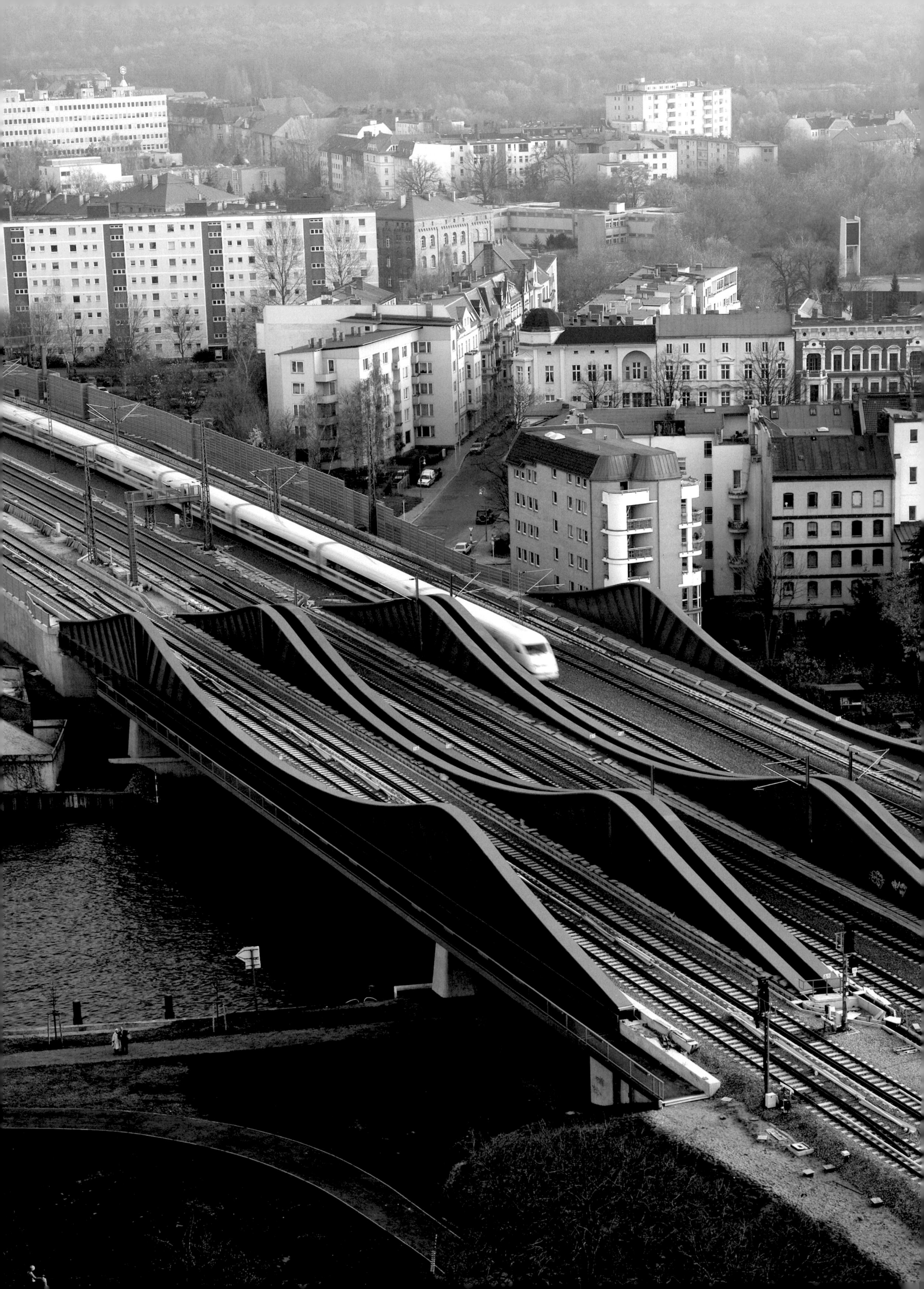

1999

Calenberger Esplanande, Hannover

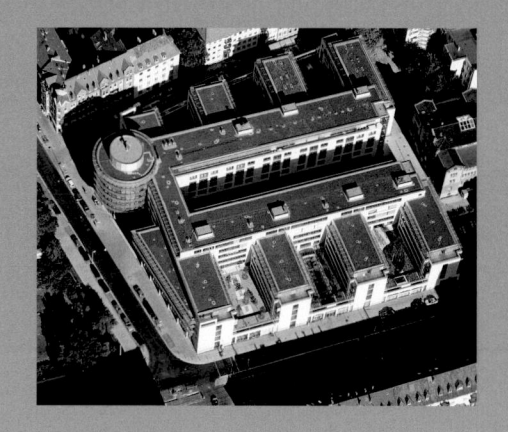

Das neue Ensemble der „Calenberger Esplanade" ergänzt die Calenberger Neustadt in Hannover mit einer städtischen Nutzungsmischung von Wohnen, Büros, Läden und Arztpraxen. Es ist aus einer doppelten Kammstruktur entwickelt, deren Rücken zueinander orientiert sind und dadurch eine ruhige Wohnstraße bilden.

Calenberg Esplanande, Hanover

The new ensemble of the 'Calenberg Esplanade' adds to the 'Calenberg Neustadt' in Hanover with an urban mix of housing, offices, shops and practices. The design is based on a double comb structure whose spines are orientated towards each other, thereby generating a calm residential street.

HTC Kehrwiederspitze, Hamburg

Mit dem Bau des Hanseatic Trade Centers wird das Ensemble der historischen Speicherstadt baukörperlich wiederhergestellt. Diese Bauphase IV ersetzt die ehemalige Kaibebauung; das Bürogebäude mit seiner Länge von 208 m öffnet sich mit vier großen, verglasten Atrien zum Binnenhafen und der Stadt.

HTC Kehrwiederspitze, Hamburg

With the building of the Hanseatic Trade Center the historical Speicherstadt ensemble is structurally restored. This so-called Building Phase IV replaces the original quayside development. The office building, which stretches over 208 m, opens up towards the city centre and the river port with four generous glazed atria.

Metropolitan Express Train, Interieur Design

Der Metropolitan bietet eine komfortable Schnellverbindung zwischen Hamburg und Köln. In formaler Hinsicht bilden der Innenraum, der mit natürlichen Materialien wie Leder und Holz ausgestattet ist, und das Äußere des Zuges eine gestalterische Einheit mit unverwechselbarer Ästhetik.

Metropolitan Express Train, Interior Design

The Metropolitan offers a comfortable shuttle connection between Hamburg and Cologne. In formal respects the interior, which is furnished with natural materials like leather and timber, and the exterior form a stringent unit with distinctive aesthetics.

1999

Messehalle 8/9, Hannover

Der in nur zehn Monaten errichtete Neubau ersetzt die alten, nicht mehr zeitgemäßen Hallen 8 und 9. Er gliedert sich in die niedrige, monolithische Halle 8 sowie die auf großer Länge von flachen Riegelbauten umfasste, voll verglaste Hochhalle 9, die von einer Hängedachkonstruktion stützenfrei überspannt wird.

Philips Messestand

Durch seine Geschlossenheit nach außen und sein Corporate Design macht der zweigeschossige Pavillon der Philips Licht AG das Messepublikum neugierig und bietet dem eintretenden Standbesucher innen offene Ausstellungsbereiche. Die Aufmerksamkeit des Betrachters wird ungestört auf die Exponate gelenkt.

Congress Centrum Neue Weimarhalle

Die Weimarhalle in der Klassikerstadt bildet mit der hellen Westfassade den Abschluss zu der breiten Parkanlage an der Ilm. Die Halle ist transparent und offen konzipiert, um einen Ausblick in die Landschaft zu ermöglichen und gleichzeitig von allen Seiten Einblicke zu gewähren.

Trade Fair Hall 8/9, Hanover

The new building, completed in only ten months, replaces the old exhibition halls 8 and 9, which did not comply with the latest building standards. It is divided into the low-rise, monolithic hall 8 and the completely glazed high-rise hall 9, which is spanned, column-free, by a suspended roof structure and framed alongside by low-level bar buildings.

Philips Exhibition Stand

The external closure of the two-storey 'Philips Licht AG' pavilion arouses the public's curiosity and offers open spaces internally for visitors. The attention of the viewer is drawn exclusively to the exhibits.

'New Weimar Hall' Congress Centre

The bright façade of the Weimar Hall gives a termination to the wide park landscape at the river Ilm running through this classical town. The hall is characterized by a transparent and open design, offering views onto the landscape and simultaneously allowing for views into the interior from all sides.

1999

Entertainment Center, Hamburg

Ein komplett verglastes mehrstöckiges Foyer verbindet neun Kinosäle miteinander und zeigt sich mit all seinen Aktivitäten zur Straßenseite hin transparent. Die Passanten werden so in die im Inneren stattfindenden Aktivitäten miteinbezogen, während der Kinobesucher vom Foyer aus die belebte Straße beobachten kann.

Entertainment Centre, Hamburg

A completely glazed multi-storey foyer connects nine cinemas and presents itself with all its activities completely transparent towards the streetscape. Passersby are thus incorporated into the activities taking place inside, while cinemagoers can look out onto the busy street from the foyer.

Hotel an der Landsberger Allee – Forum Friedrichshain, Berlin

Als zweiter Bauabschnitt setzt das Hotel die Wohnbauten nach Norden fort und schließt die dreieckige Blockbebauung. Eine öffentliche Treppe überwindet den Höhenunterschied von 12 m. Der Biergarten des ehemaligen „Böhmischen Brauhauses" blieb ebenso erhalten wie dessen unterirdische Gewölbe.

Hotel at Landsberger Allee – Forum Friedrichshain, Berlin

As a second construction phase, the hotel continues the residential development towards the north and closes the triangular block development. The public stairs bridge the 12-metre difference in height. The beer garden of the former brewery and its underground vaults have been maintained.

Fachmarktzentrum, Göttingen

Zur Kasseler Landstraße präsentiert sich das Fachmarktzentrum mit einer gegliederten, transparenten Gewächshauszone; eine städtebaulich signifikante Kolonnade orientiert sich zu den Kundenparkplätzen. Die Mall erweitert sich innen im Bereich des mittleren Eingangs zu einer dreischiffigen Halle.

Shopping Centre, Göttingen

The spacialist shopping centre presents itself with a sectionalized, transparent greenhouse zone towards the Kasseler Landstrasse. A colonnade, which has considerable urban planning significance, is orientated towards the customer car park. The mall widens in the central entrance zone to form a three-naved hall.

Wohn- und Geschäftshaus Friedrichstraße 108–109, Berlin

Ein weithin sichtbarer Turm akzentuiert die städtebaulich markante Ecke. Die umlaufende Arkade ermöglicht den fließenden Übergang von öffentlichem Raum mit Verweilqualität zu privaterem Handel. Ein großer verglaster Innenhof bildet das räumliche Zentrum.

Residential and Commercial Block Friedrichstrasse 108–109, Berlin

A tower visible from afar accentuates this urbanistic striking corner. The continuous arcade allows a fluent transition from the public space, which invites one to linger, to more private business. A generous glazed inner courtyard forms the spatial centre.

Elbkaihaus, Hamburg

Das Elbkaihaus mit seiner breiten Glasfront zur Wasserseite der Elbe ist eine in seiner ursprünglichen Bausubstanz entkernte umgebaute Etagenkühlhalle von 1965. Dieser Umbau im Hamburger Fischereihafen Altona mit unverstellbarem Elbblick bietet heute überwiegend jungen Computerfirmen sowie einem Restaurant Platz.

Loft Elbkaihaus, Hamburg

The Elbkaihaus, with its wide glass front towards the River Elbe, is a multi-storey cold store, built in 1965, which has had its original core building structure removed. This conversion in the fishing harbour of Hamburg-Altona now offers young computer firms office space with unobstructed views to the Elbe.

Fassade des Wohnhauses von Gerkan, Elbchaussee, Hamburg

Nach dem Entschluss, dem 1992 fertiggestellten Wohnhaus ein neues Äußeres zu geben, wurden 1999 die Fassaden des Gebäudes umgebaut. Vor der Südfassade, die zur Elbe ausgerichtet komplett verglast ist, wurde ein Stahlgerüst errichtet, das die Terrasse vergrößert und den Sonnenschutz optimiert.

Façade of the von Gerkan Residence, Elbchaussee, Hamburg

After the decision was made to realize a new exterior of the house, which was originally completed in 1992, the façade was altered in 1999. A steel scaffolding was built in front of the completely glazed south façade facing towards the Elbe, enlarging the terrace and optimizing its protection against the sun.

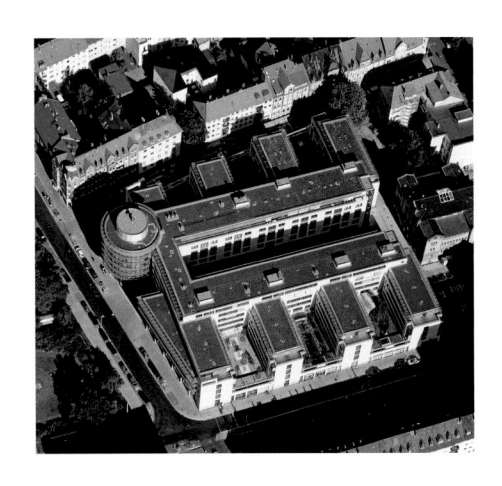

Calenberger Esplanade, Hannover
Calenberg Esplanade, Hanover

Gutachten Consultancy
1991 – 1. Rang

Entwurf Design
Meinhard von Gerkan

Partner Partner
Nikolaus Goetze

Bauherr Client
NILEG mbH, Hannover

Bauzeit Construction period
1996–1999

BGF Gross floor area
44.000 m²

Die Calenberger Esplanade wird als weißstrahlender Putzbau in Kombination mit eingelegten Natursteinelementen errichtet. Ein durchgehender 4,5 m hoher Sockel verbindet alle Elemente des homogenen Gebäudekomplexes miteinander. Im westlichen Teil sind flexible Ladeneinheiten und Restaurants sowie die großzügigen Büroeingänge vorgesehen – der östliche Teil dient einer Reha-Klinik im Zusammenspiel mit Praxen, Läden und Wohnungseingängen. Die hellen, intensiv begrünten Höfe öffnen sich zu den engen Straßen der Blockrandbebauung. Eine Baumallee durch die Wohnstraße hindurch bildet eine Achse zum Baudenkmal an einem Ende des Ensembles. Auf der anderen Seite, zur Calenberger Straße hin, wird der Zugang durch einen 7-geschossigen Turm und einen filigran verglasten Stahl-Glas-Erker definiert. Die Wohnstraße wird beidseitig durch hohe Arkaden begrenzt, an denen die Läden und Restaurants liegen.

The Calenberg Esplanade was erected as a building with façades of white plaster 'inlaid' with natural stone. An uninterrupted 4.5-m-high base structure connects all the parts of the homogeneous complex. Its western section contains flexible retail and restaurant spaces as well as the offices with spacious entrances, while the eastern section houses a rehab clinic, doctors' surgeries, shops and residential units with separate entrance halls. The light-flooded planted patios open to the narrow streets between the peripheral blocks. A tree-lined residential street forms an axis which leads to the listed monument at one end of the complex. At the other end, on Calenberger Strasse, access to the site is marked by a seven-storey tower and a filigree steel-and-glass oriel. The residential street is flanked by a high arcaded passage behind which are the shops and restaurants.

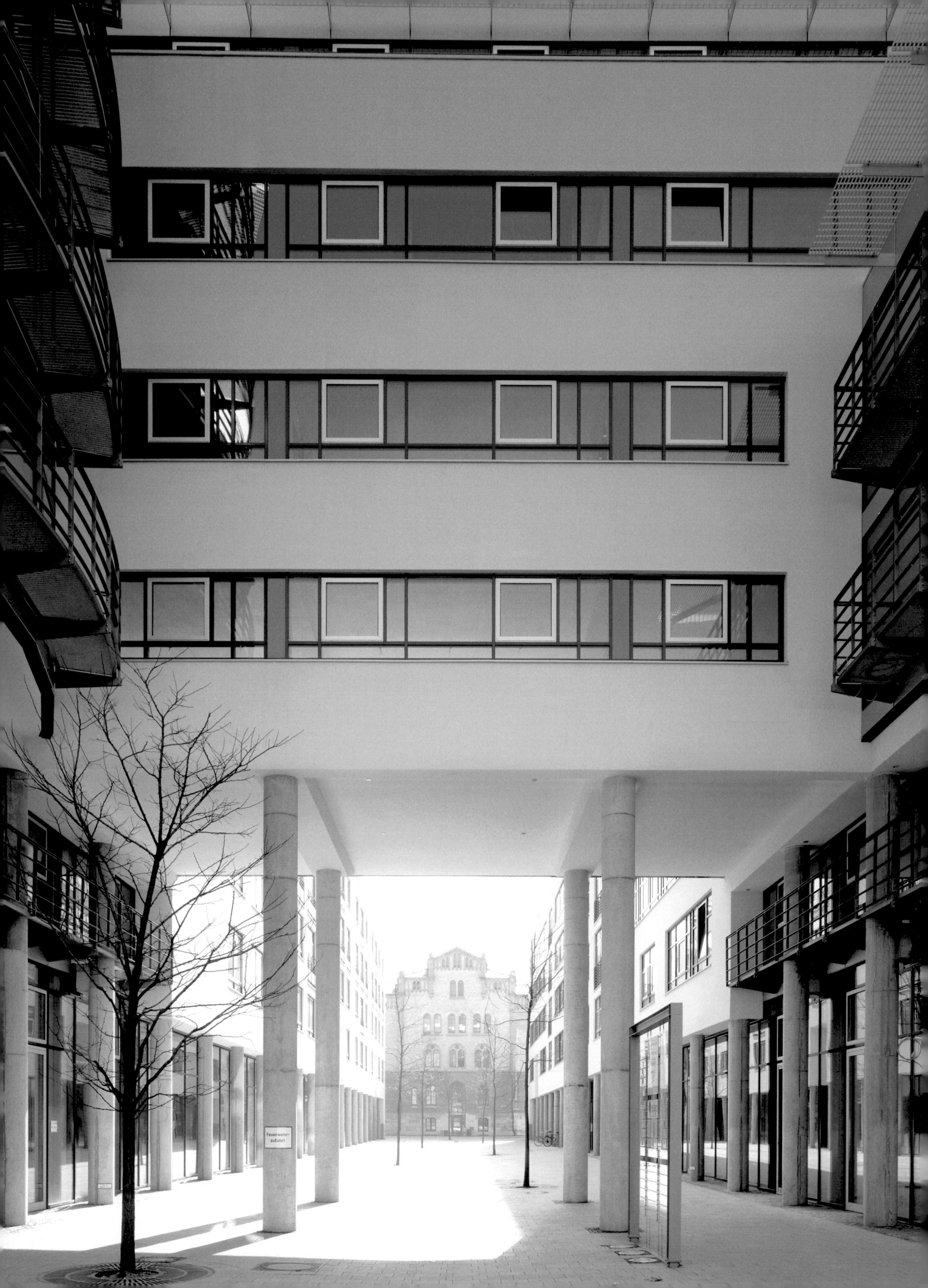
Feuerwehr-
zufahrt

Hanseatic Trade Center, Kehrwiederspitze, Hamburg
Hanseatic Trade Center, Kehrwiederspitze, Hamburg

1992

Entwurf Design

Partner Partners
Volkwin Marg, Klaus Staratzke

Bauherr Client
Hanseatic Trade Center GmbH + Co., Hamburg

Bauzeit Construction period
1997–1999

BGF Gross floor area
45.375 m²

Die verglasten Atrien des Hanseatic Trade Centers bilden mit einer Fläche von je 250 m² die Eingangshallen und Adresse der Büroeinheiten. Zudem tragen sie positiv zur Gesamtenergiebilanz bei, indem die eingefangene Sonnenenergie von den internen steinernen Fassaden gespeichert und phasenverschoben ins Gebäudeinnere weitergeleitet wird. Über zwei freistehende Glasaufzüge werden die Bürogeschosse erschlossen. Diese, teilweise mit Blick in die Stadt, teilweise zum Fleet oder in die großen Glashallen, sind bis zu einer kleinsten Einheit von ca. 100 m² frei aufteilbar. Der Baukörper nimmt die angrenzenden Höhen der alten Speicherstadt sowie der benachbarten Neubauten auf. Die Außenwände sind als klassische Mauerwerksfassaden in der Ziegelfarbe der Speicherstadt ausgebildet und rhythmisiert durch unterschiedliche Fenstergrößen. Die tragende Konstruktion der Hallen sowie der Fensterauskreuzung besteht aus verzinktem Stahl.

With a floor area of 250 m² each, the glazed atria are entrance hall and address of the office units. The atria also contribute to an economic use of energy, with the interior stone façades storing the captured solar energy and conducting it to the inside of the building. The office floors are accessible via two free-standing glazed lifts. The offices are individually dividable up to the smallest unit of approximately 100 m², offering views towards the city or the canal, or into the large glazed halls. The structure corresponds to the adjacent heights of the Speicherstadt and other modern buildings. External walls are finished in masonry with the brick colour of the Speicherstadt, whilst varied window dimensions introduce a rhythm. The load-bearing hall structure and the window frames are made of galvanized steel.

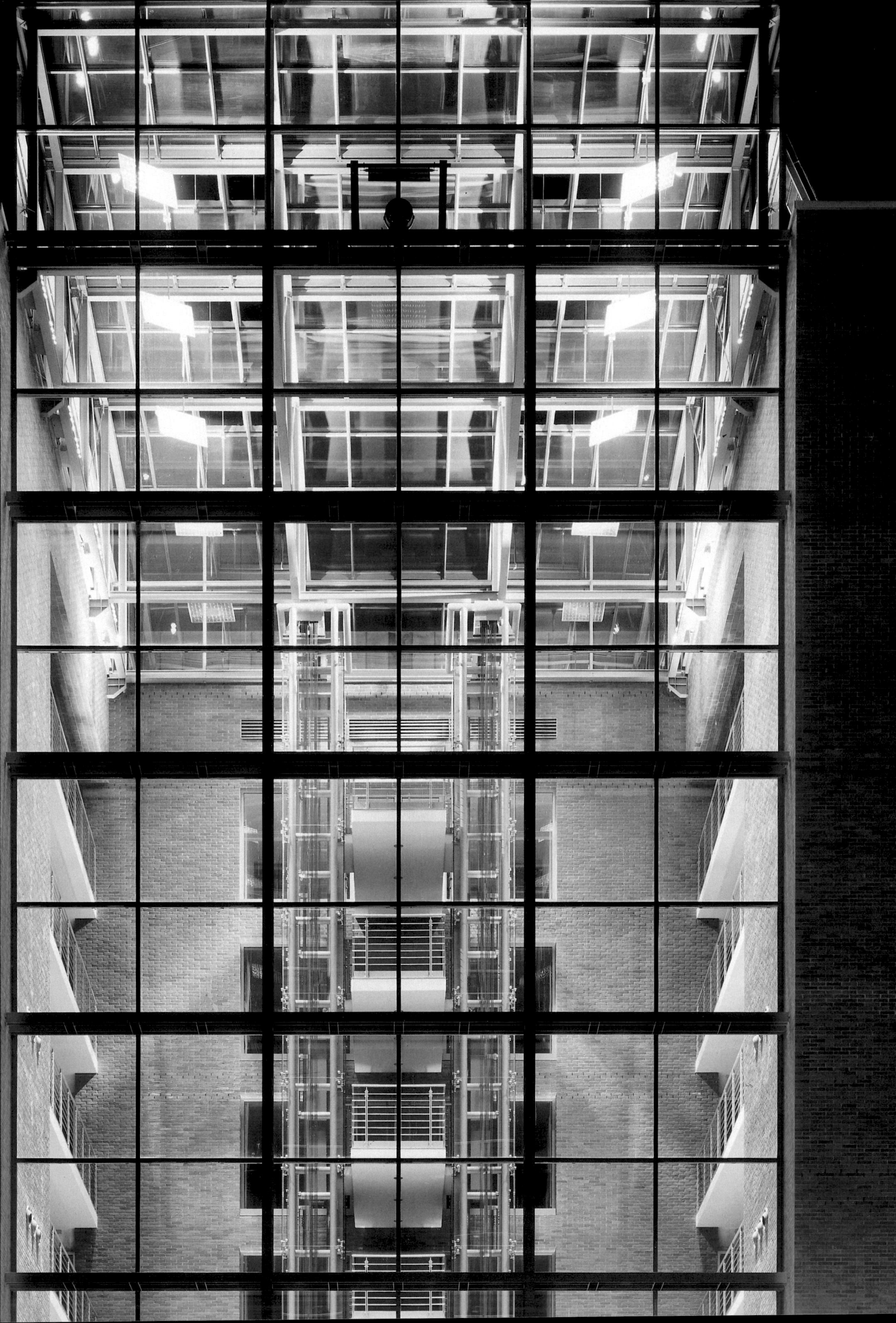

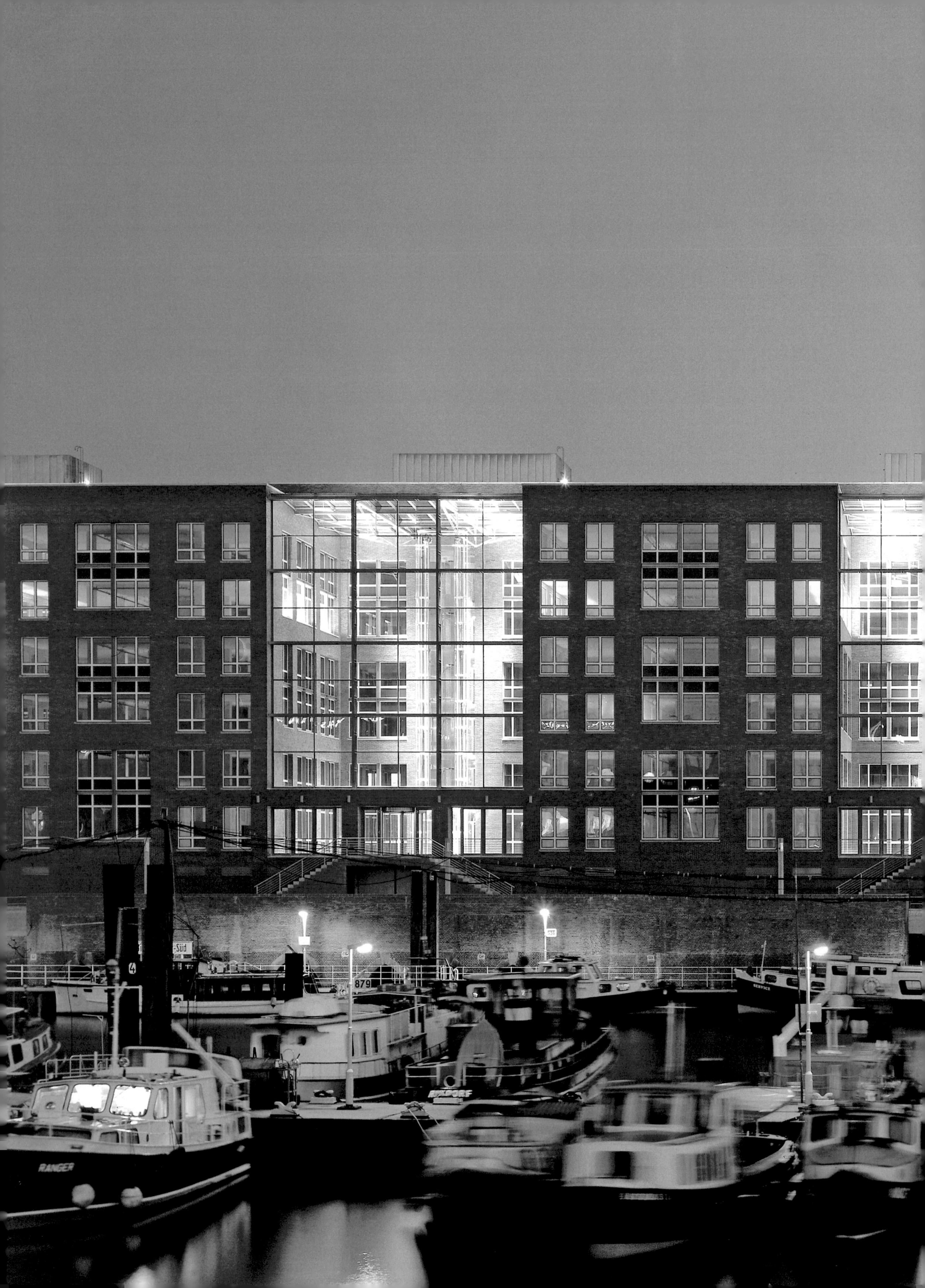
879
RANGER

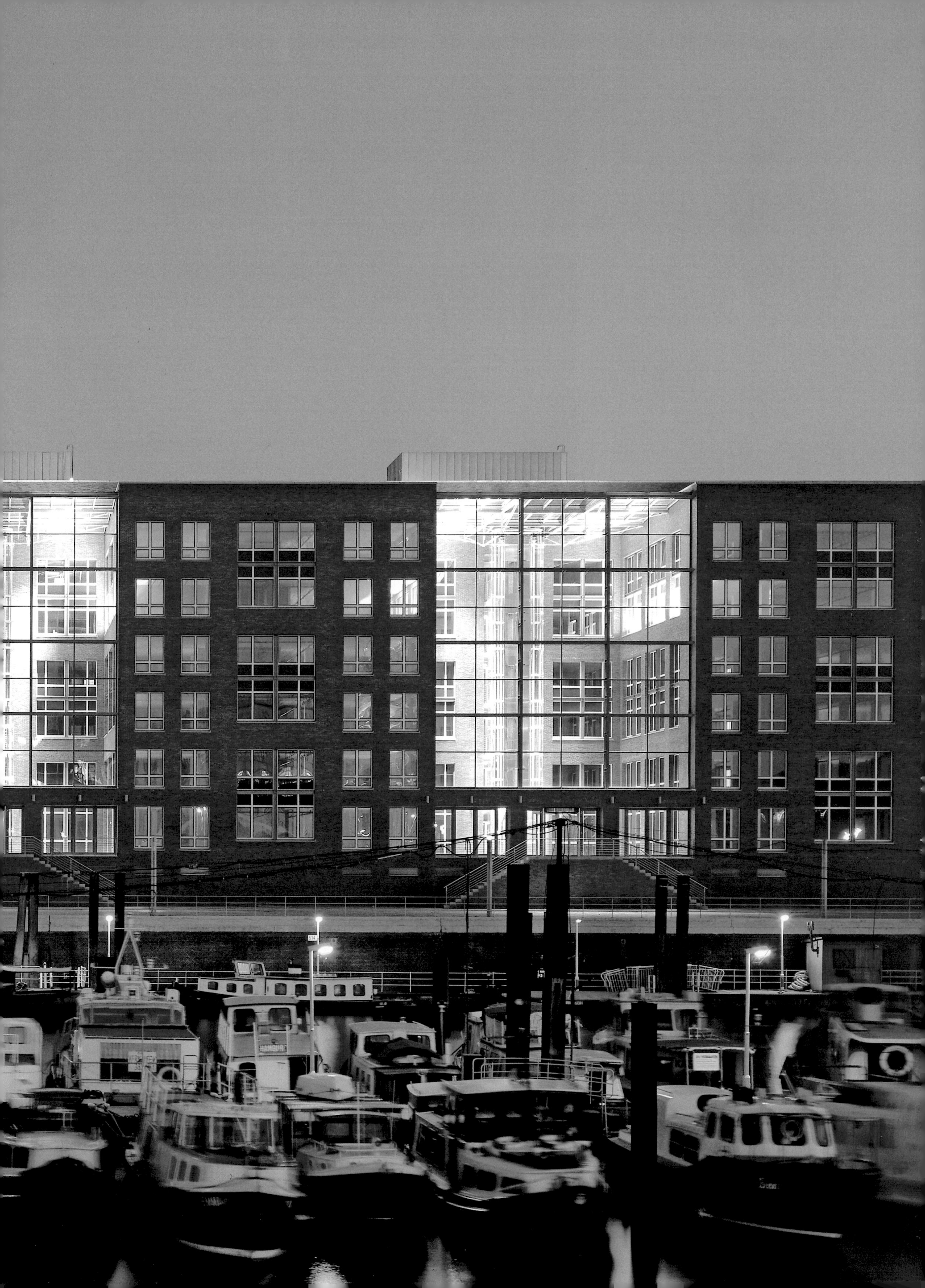

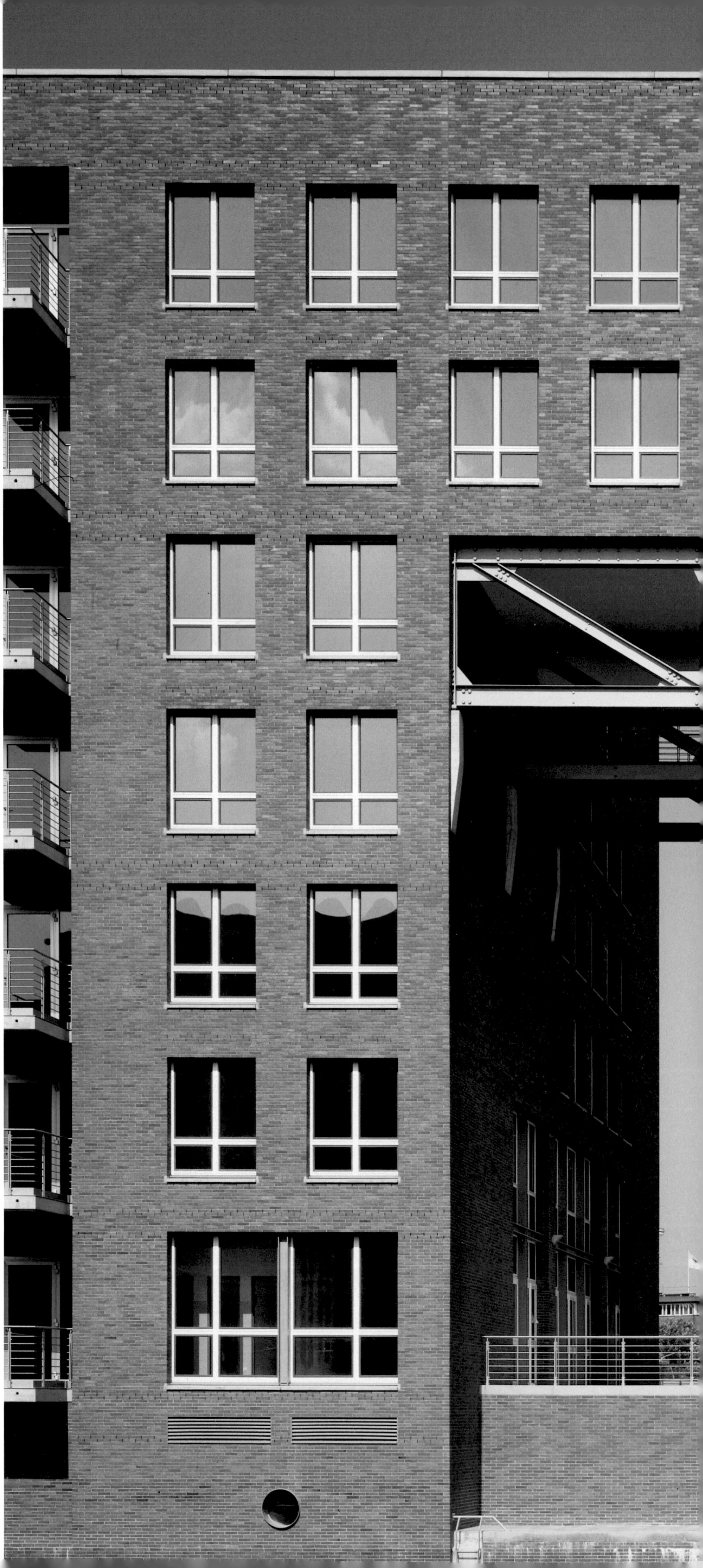

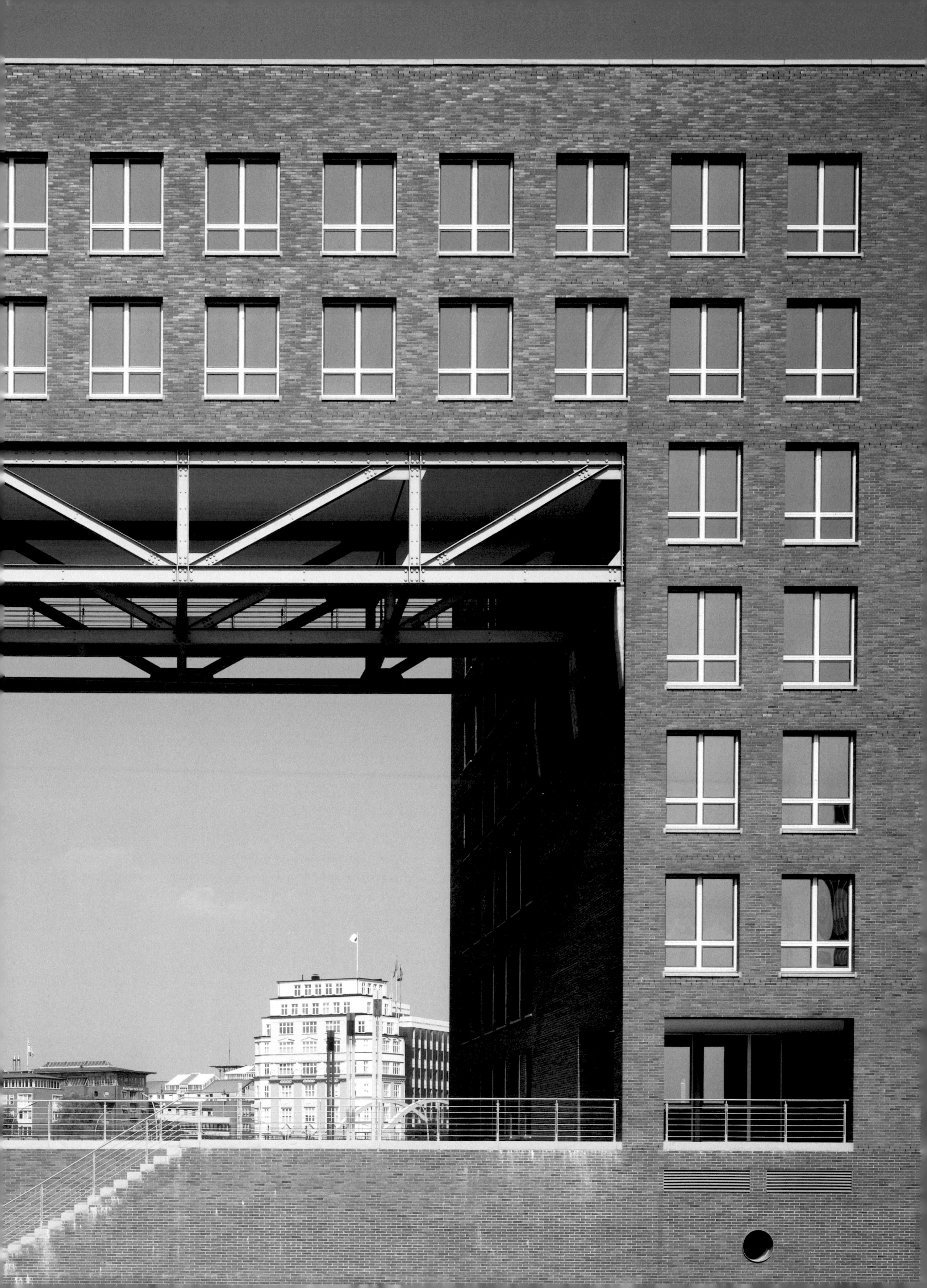

Metropolitan Express Train, Interieur Design
Metropolitan Express Train, Interior Design

Wettbewerb Competition
1996 – 1. Preis

Entwurf Design
Meinhard von Gerkan
und Jürgen Hillmer

Bauherr Client
Deutsche Bahn AG

Bauzeit Construction period
1998–1999

Der metallische Charakter der Außenhülle des Metropolitan steht für Geschwindigkeit und Hochwertigkeit. Ihr dynamischer Eindruck setzt sich in der horizontalen Gliederung und Akzentuierung des durchlaufenden Fensterbandes bis in den Innenraum fort. Durchgängig für alle Wagen gibt es eine 3er Bestuhlung aus zwei Sitzen auf der einen und einem auf der anderes Seite des Ganges. Wichtiger Bestandteil der Ausstattung ist die Verwendung natürlicher Materialien; Schichtholz, Edelstahl und Leder schaffen eine Atmosphäre des Echten und Vertrauten, zudem altern sie „würdevoller"; Kunststoffe wurden vermieden. Entsprechend ist das Farbkonzept auf die natürliche Beschaffenheit der Materialien mit ihrer je eigenen Nuancierung, Zeichnung und Textur reduziert. Das Gepäck wird oberhalb des Fensterbandes auf einer Ablage gestaut. In diese sind zusätzlich zur indirekten Beleuchtung punktgerichtete Leseleuchten integriert.

The metal character of the envelope of the Metropolitan represents speed and quality. Its dynamic impression is continued in the interior with horizontal sections and a continuous row of windows. All carriages are equipped with rows of two seats on one side and one seat on the opposite side of the aisle. An important characteristic of the equipment is the use of natural materials: multiplex boards, stainless steel and leather create a comfortable atmosphere, and these are also materials that age with 'grace'; plastics are avoided. Accordingly, the colour concept is reduced to the natural texture and nuances of these materials. Luggage is stored above the windows on a shelf which integrates indirect lighting and reading lamps simultaneously.

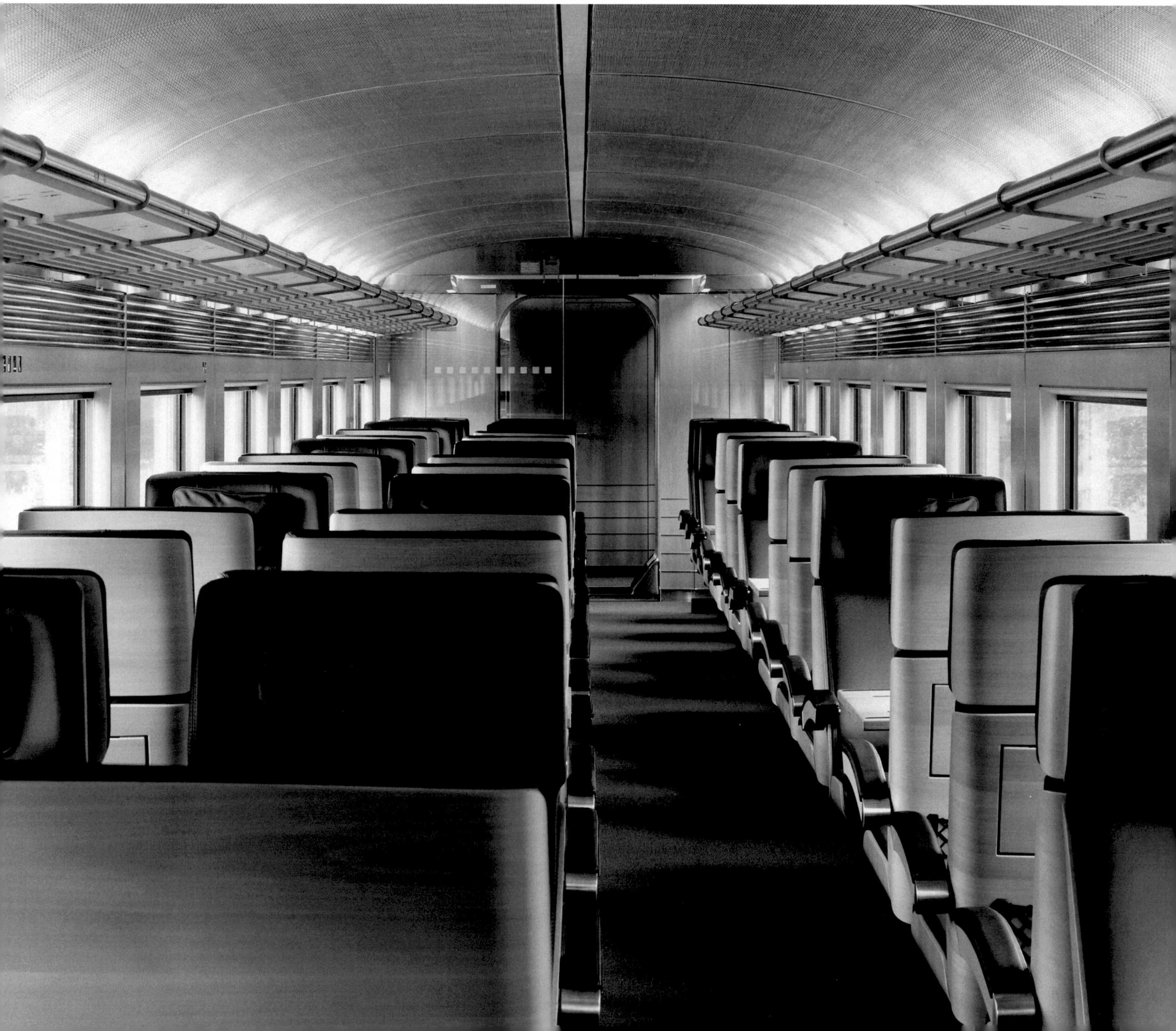

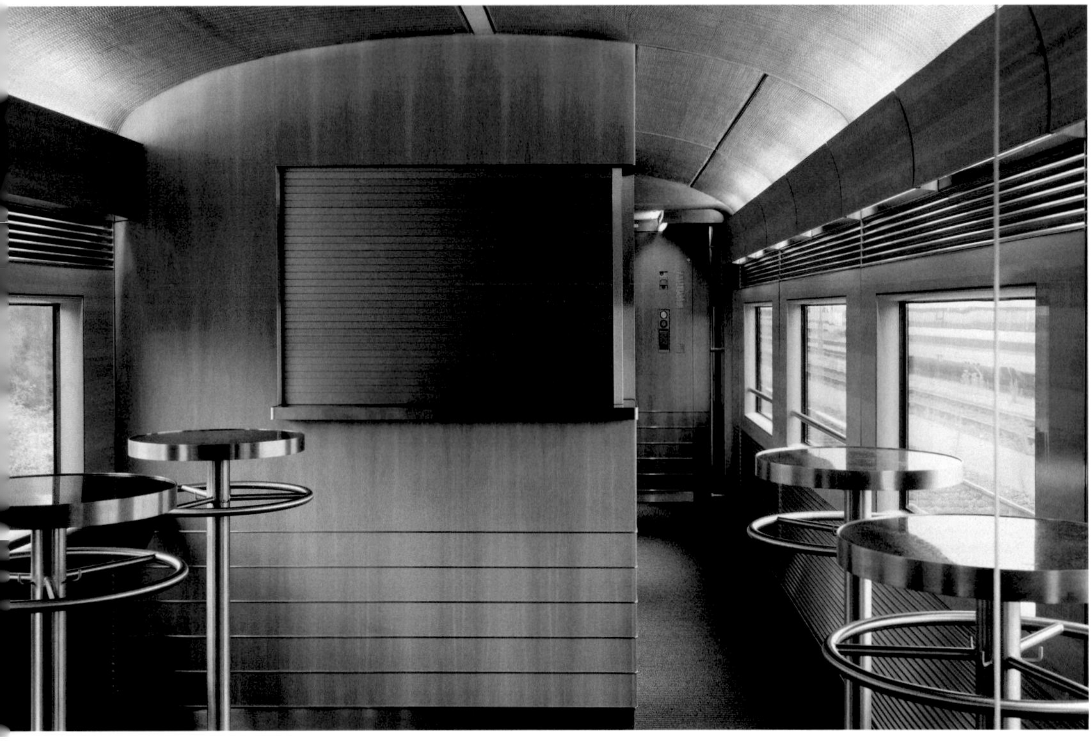

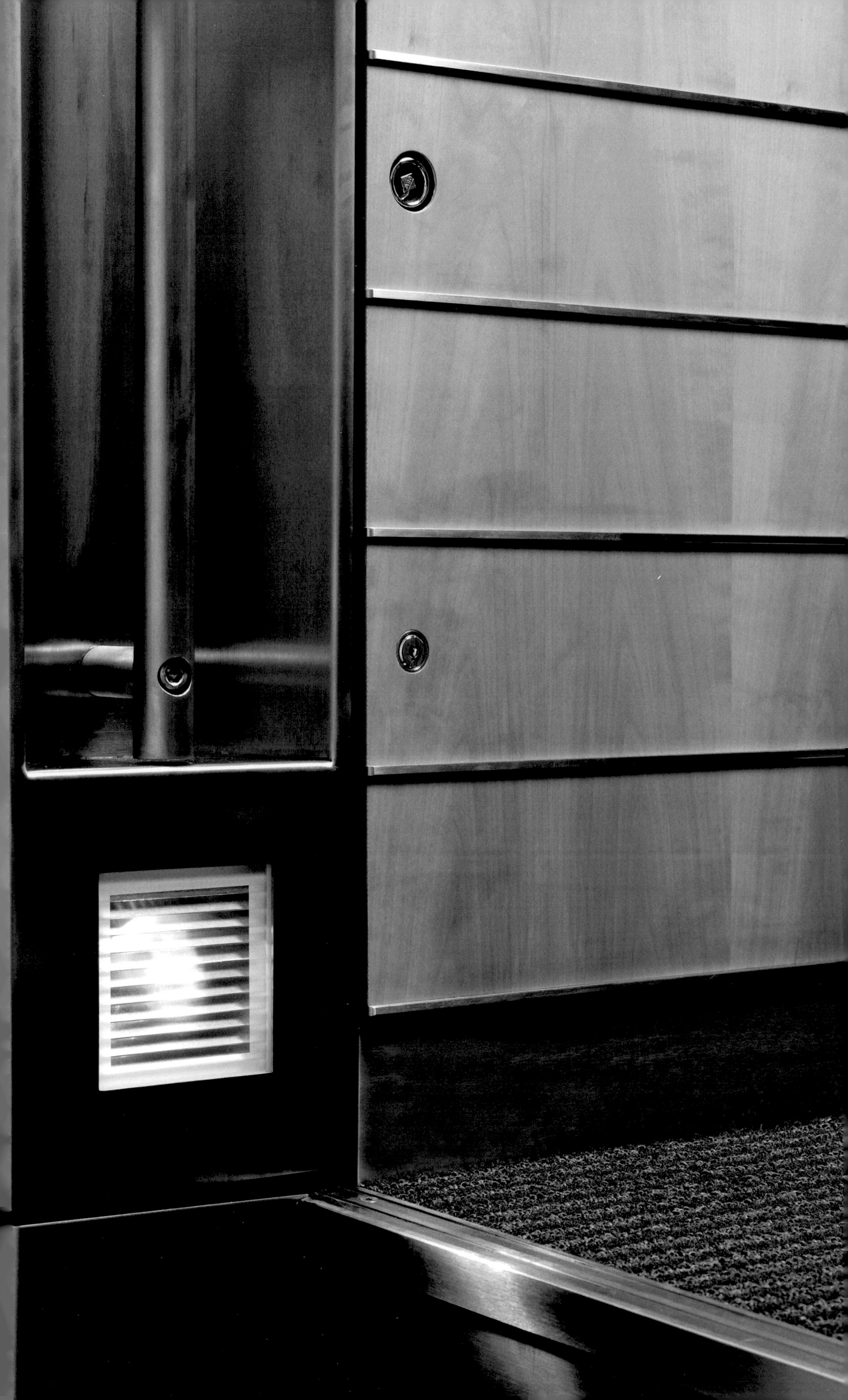

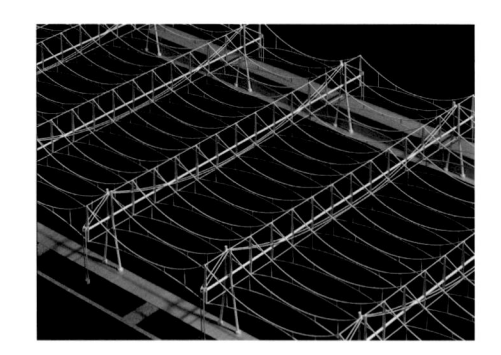

Messe Hannover, Halle 8/9
Trade Fair Hall 8/9, Hanover

Wettbewerb Competition
1997 – 1. Preis

Entwurf Design
Volkwin Marg mit Jörg Schlaich

Bauherr Client
Deutsche Messe AG mit Expo 2000 Hannover GmbH

Bauzeit Construction period
1998–1999

Hallenmaße Hall dimensions
Halle 8: 100 m x 120 m x 8,7 m
Halle 9: 137 m x 240 m x 26 m

Die mit Kunstlicht belichtete Halle 8 mit ihrer begehbaren Dachfläche verbindet gleichzeitig Treppe und Brücke zur Expo-Plaza und vermittelt zur „Allee der Vereinigten Bäume" hin. Die allseitig tageslichtdurchflutete Halle 9 wird von einer fünfschiffigen, scheinbar schwebenden Dachkonstruktion über 105 m stützenfrei überspannt. Die fünf Hauptträger sind wie Hängebrücken konstruiert, mit Tragseilen, Hängeseilen, Böcken als Mast und jeweils einem dicken Rohr als Druckriegel. Als eigentliches Tragsystem für die Dachfläche dienen Hängebänder aus Flachstahl mit gegengekrümmten Stabilisierungsseilen. In der aus Holzkästen bestehenden, leicht konstruierten Dachfläche befinden sich sämtliche Verteilinstallationen der Haustechnik mitsamt der Klimatisierung, deren vertikale Verbindung zur Technikzentrale durch gläserne Steigschächte gebildet wird.

The artificially illuminated Hall 8, with its accessible roof surface, simultaneously connects stairs and bridge towards the Expo Plaza and forms a link towards the 'Avenue of United Trees'. Hall 9, light-flooded from all sides, is spanned column-free across 105 m by a five-nave, seemingly hovering roof construction. The five main girders are constructed like suspended bridges, with supporting cables, vertical suspension hangers, trestles as masts and one thick circular section each as compression bar. The actual load-bearing system for the roof surfaces is provided by suspended struts from flat steel with counter-curved stabilizing cables. The lightweight roof surface, consisting of wooden boxes, houses all technical distribution installations, including ventilation; its vertical connection to the technical centre is formed by glazed shafts.

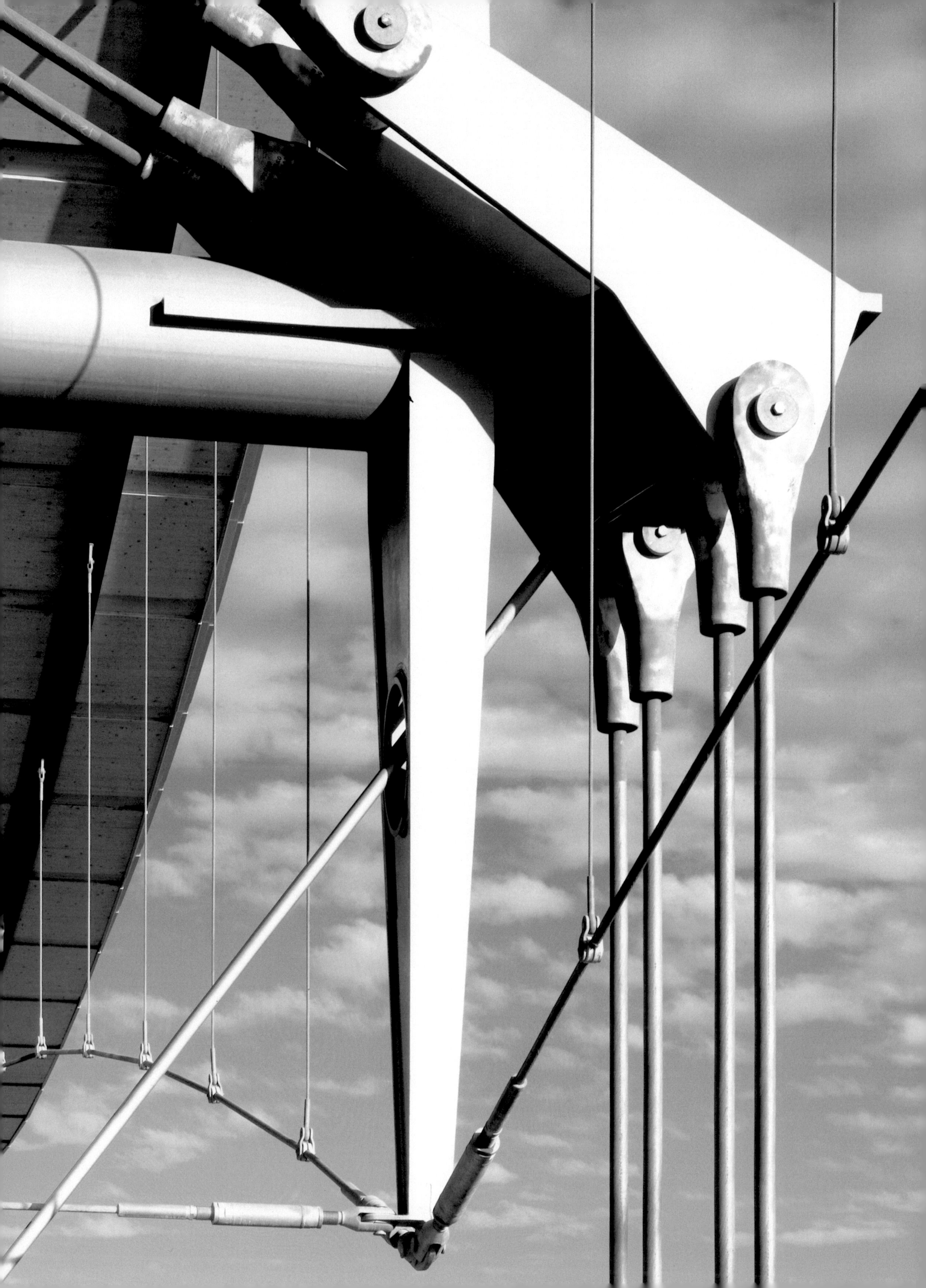

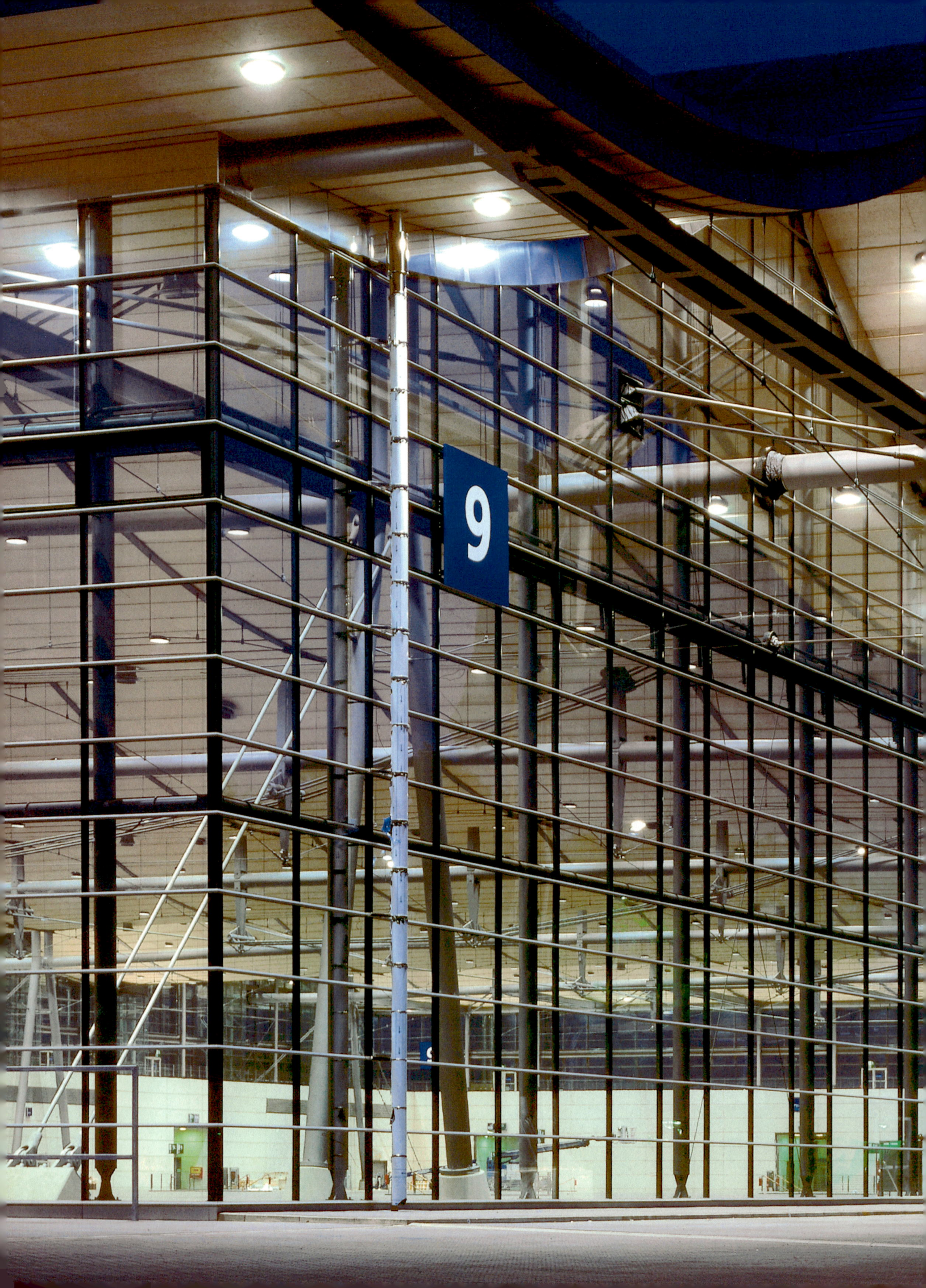
9

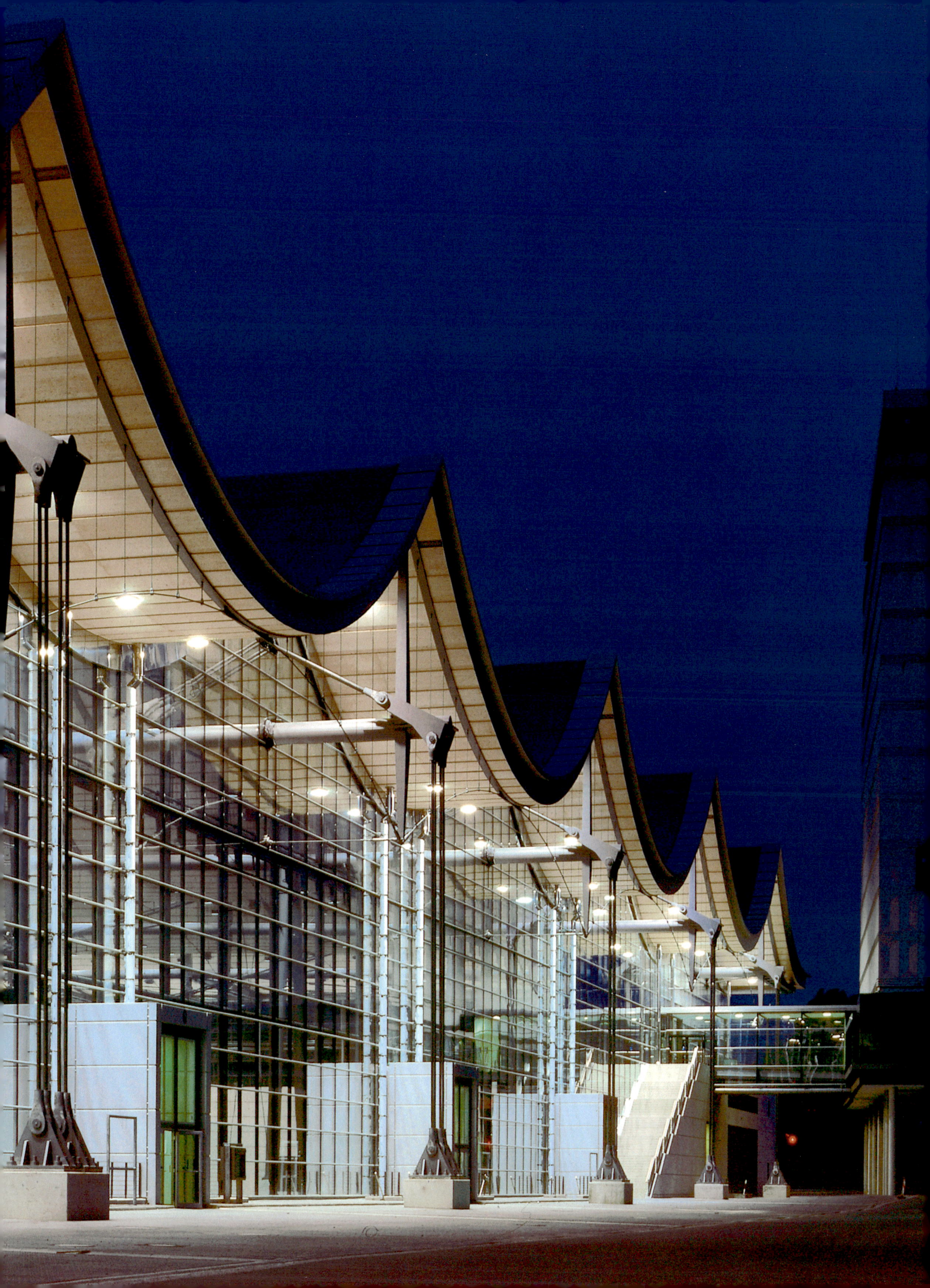

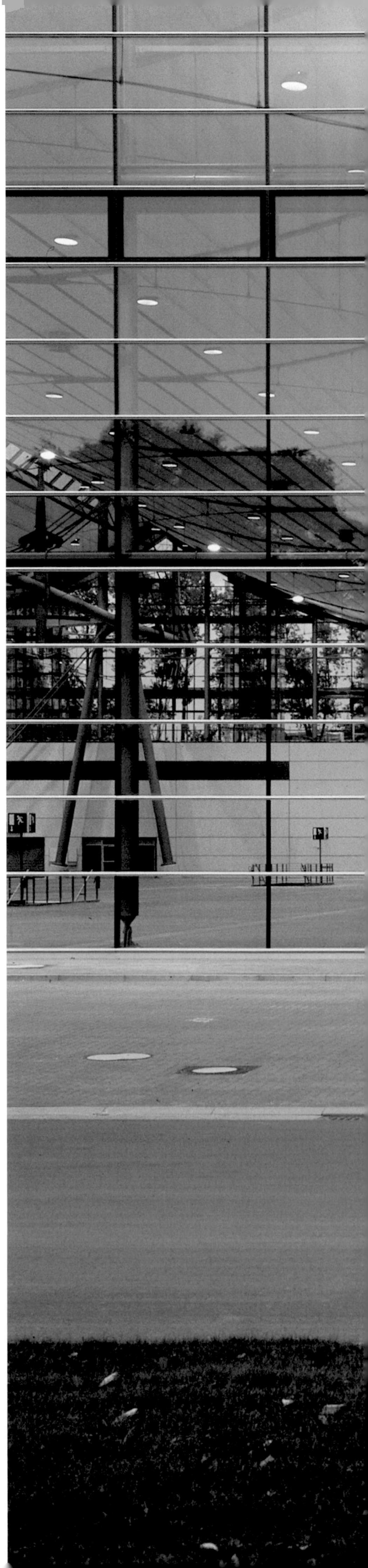

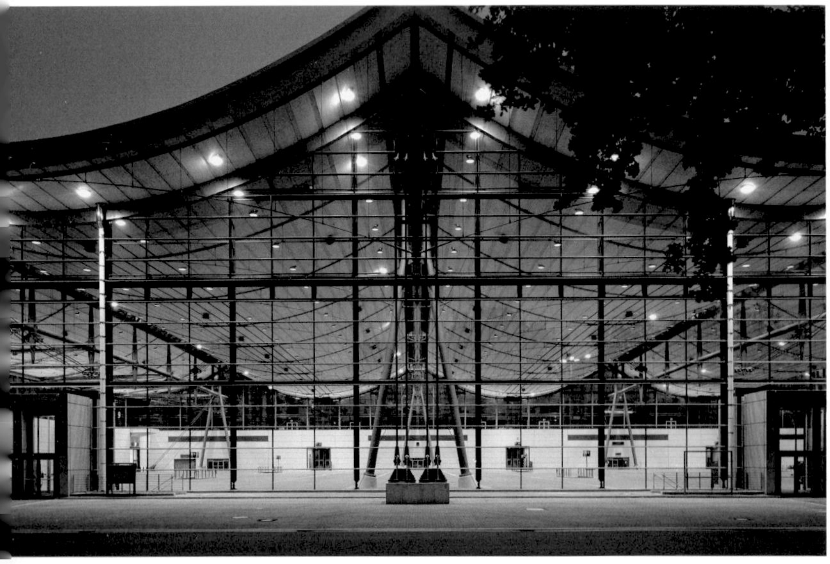

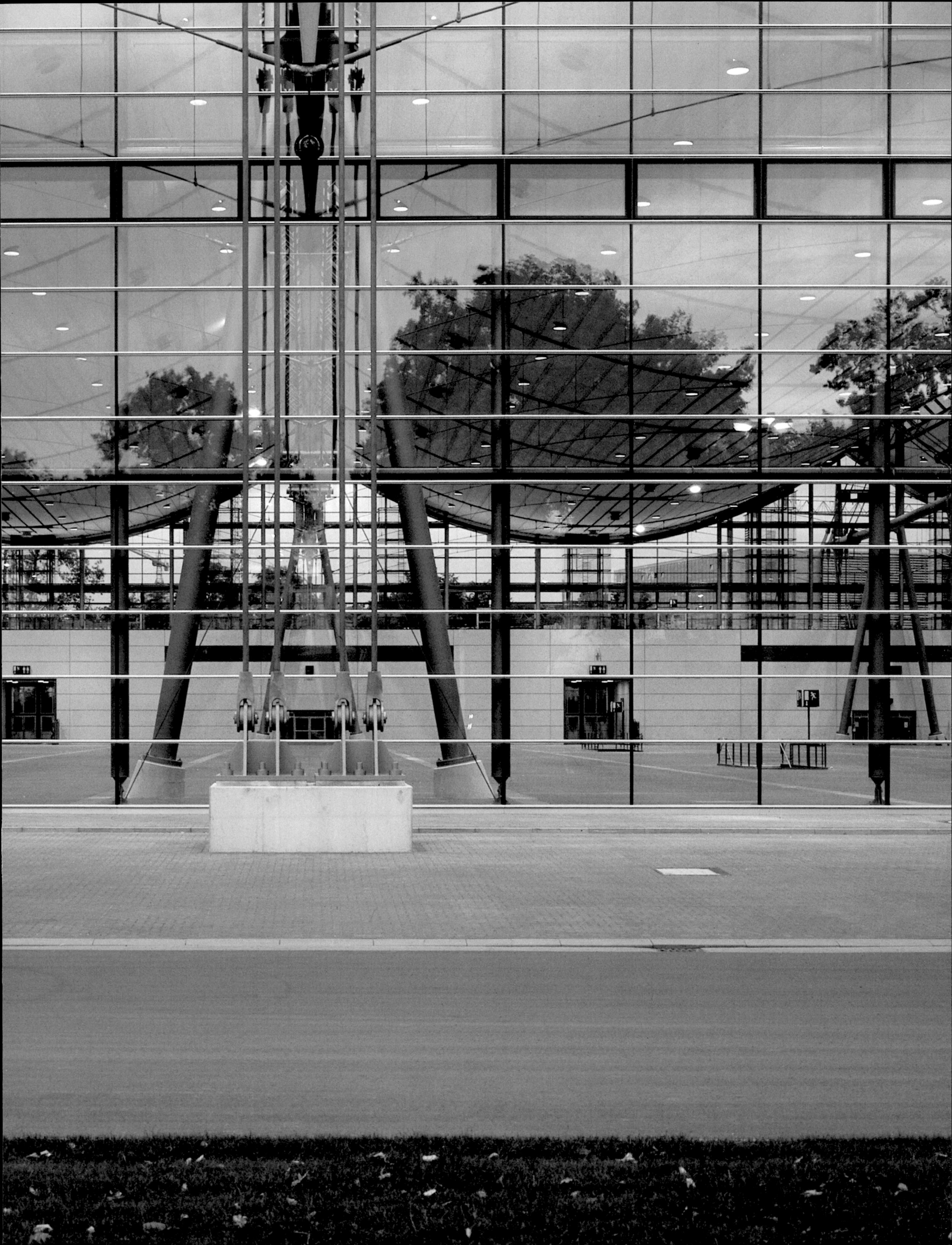

Philips Messestand
Philips Exhibition Stand

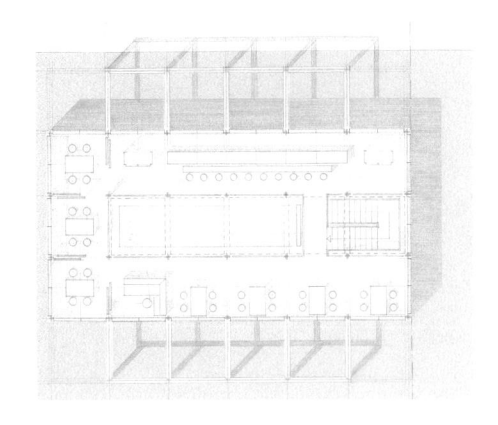

Wettbewerb Competition
1998 – 1. Preis

Entwurf Design
Meinhard von Gerkan mit Wolfgang Haux
und Magdalene Weiß

Bauherr Client
Philips Licht, Hamburg

Bauzeit Construction period
1999

BGF Gross floor area
450 m²

Der Pavillon wird aus einem modularen Bausystem mit wenigen unterschiedlichen Elementen zusammengefügt. Diesem System liegt ein räumliches Rastermaß von 3 m zugrunde. Die Primärstruktur besteht aus einem Pfosten-Riegel-System und wird in Stahlbau gefertigt. Biegesteife Verbindungsknoten sorgen für die notwendige Aussteifung. Die Sekundärstruktur bilden Ausfachungen, die austauschbar sind. Sie können nach Anforderung und geplanter Rauminszenierung aus offenen oder geschlossenen, aus transparenten oder transluzenten, aus selbstleuchtenden oder beleuchteten Elementen bestehen. Als Symbol für die Firma Philips werden die Wände und Raumteiler aus angehäuften Philips-Klarlampen hergestellt, gehalten durch eine Stahl-Rahmen-Konstruktion mit zwei Sicherheits-Glasscheiben. Bei der Präsentation auf der Hannover-Messe 1999 waren in die Wände insgesamt 110.000 Glühlampen eingefüllt.

The pavilion is constructed from a modular system consisting of a few different elements. The elementary system is based on a grid dimension of 3 m in the x-, y- and z-axis. The primary structure consists of a frame system, bend-resistant joints providing the required support. The secondary structure consists of exchangeable infills. According to the spatial design, these infills can be made from open or closed, transparent or translucent, self-illuminating or illuminated elements. As a symbol for the Philips firm, one of the first to develop light bulbs and presently worldwide market leader, walls and separating elements are made from stacked Philips clear bulbs, sandwiched between two safety-glass panes with a steel frame. During the presentation at the Hanover Fair in 1999 the walls were filled with a total of 110,000 light bulbs.

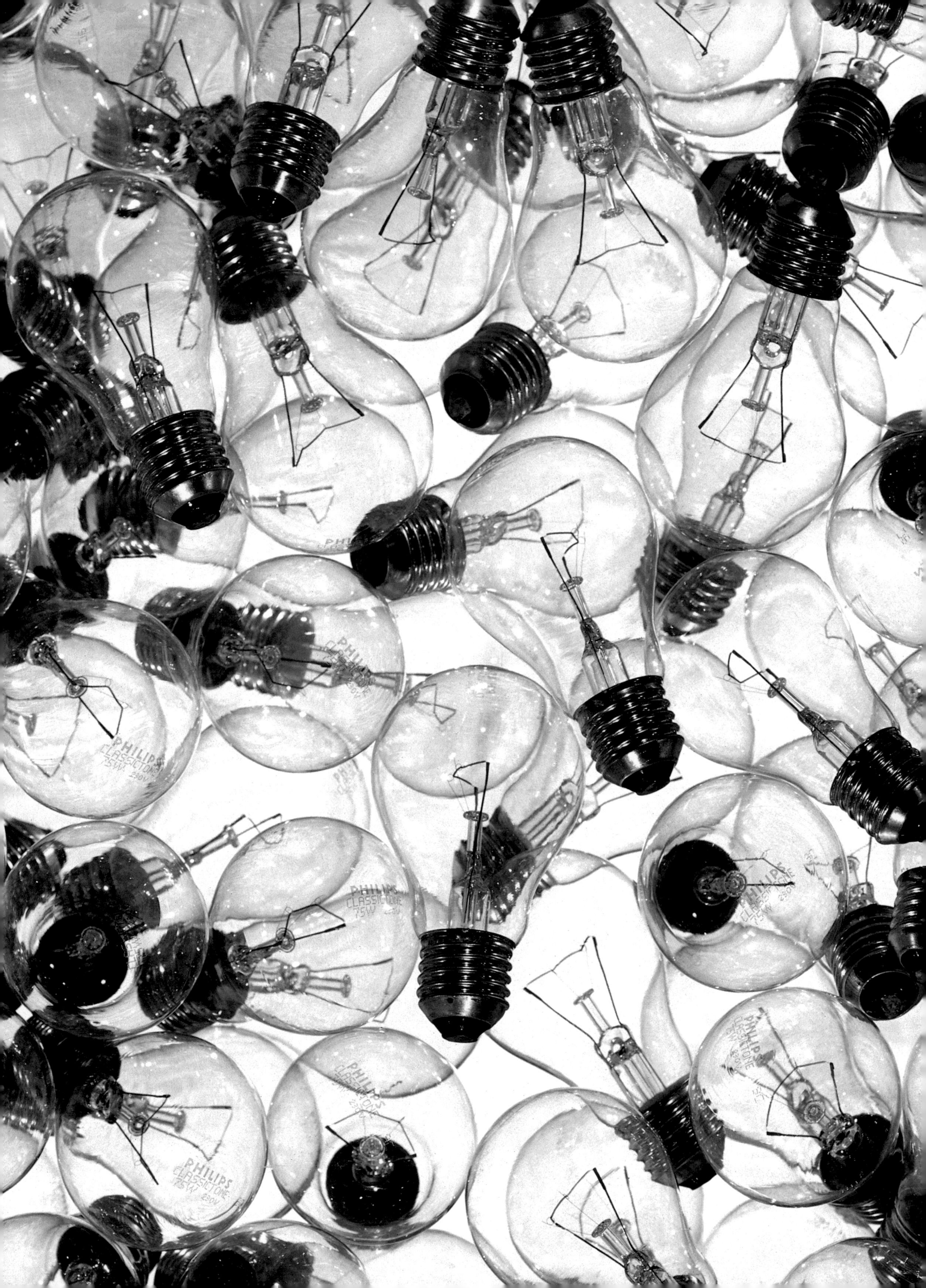
PHILIPS
CLASSICTONE
75W 230V

318

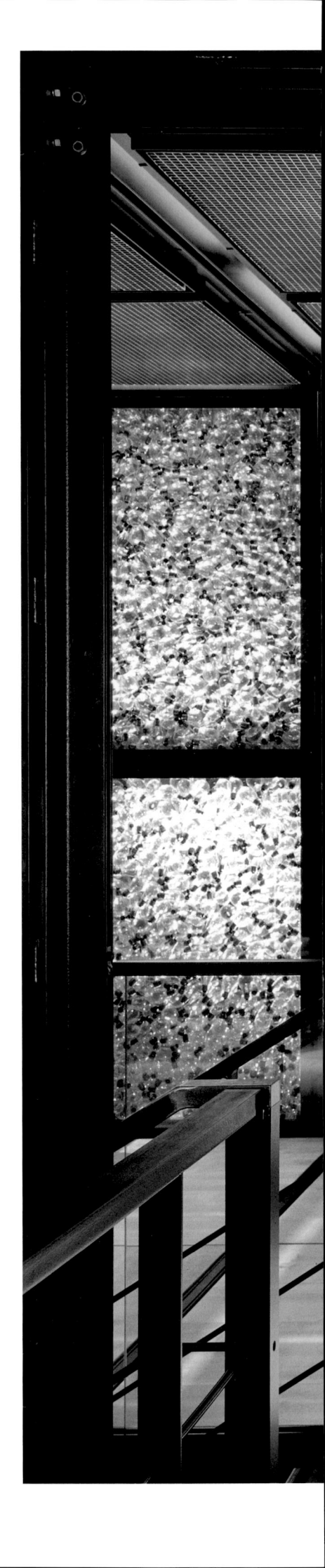

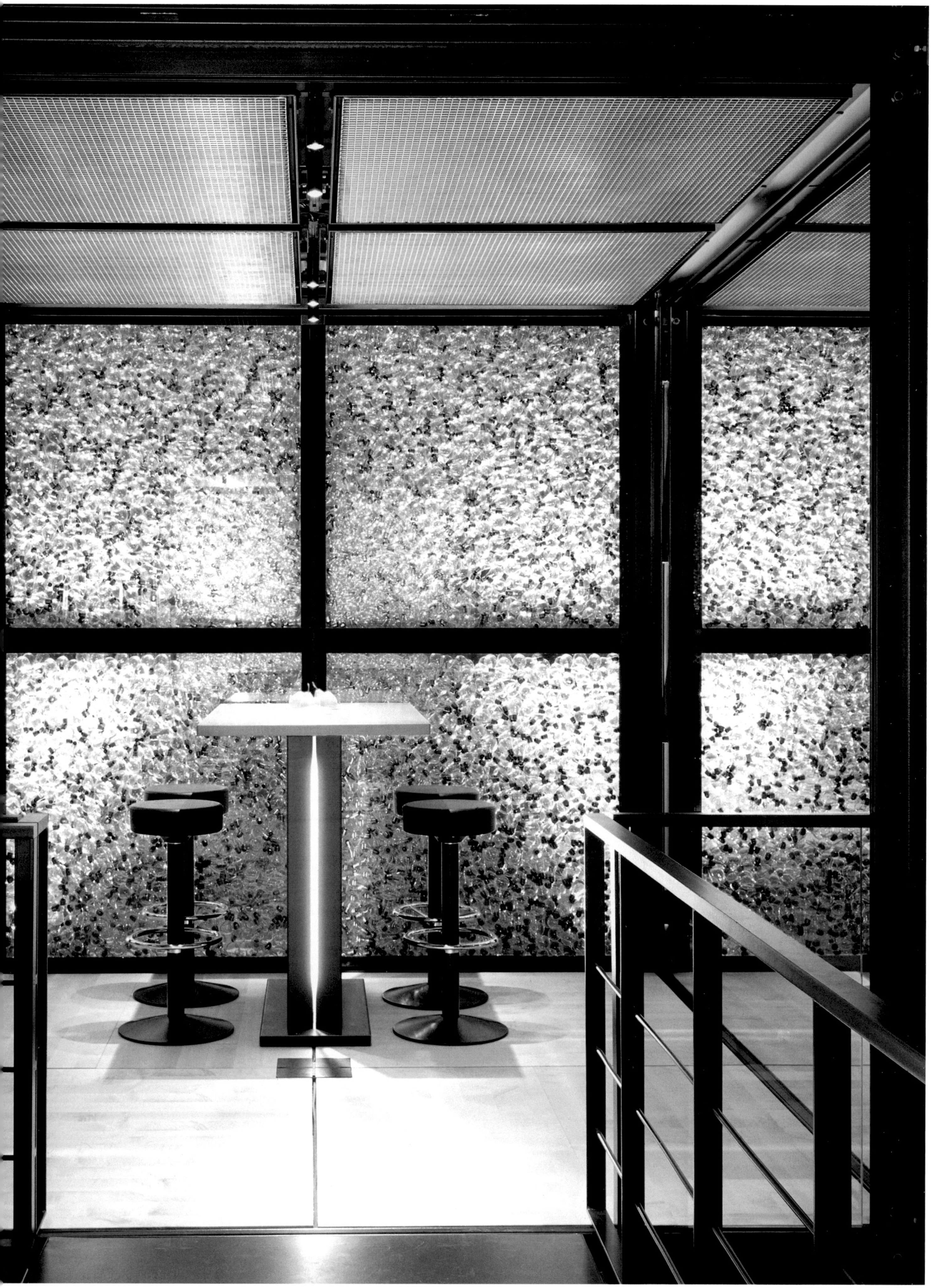

Congress Centrum Neue Weimarhalle
'New Weimar Hall' Congress Centre

Wettbewerb Competition
1997 – 1. Preis

Entwurf Design
Meinhard von Gerkan mit Doris Schäffler
und Stephan Schütz

Partner Partner
Hubert Nienhoff

Bauherr Client
Stadt Weimar

Bauzeit Construction period
1997–1999

BGF Gross floor area
20.000 m²

Der Konzertsaal ist als eigenständiges Element im Gebäude angeordnet. Er lässt sich durch mechanisch verschiebbare Wände im Erd- und Obergeschoss öffnen und schließen: Auf diese Weise entsteht einerseits ein hölzernes Haus im Haus und andererseits ein tageslichtdurchfluteter Veranstaltungssaal, der sich unterschiedlichen Nutzungen nicht nur räumlich-funktional, sondern auch atmosphärisch anpasst. Großzügige Foyerflächen mit Glasfassaden verbinden Außen- und Innenraum miteinander. Das gilt insbesondere für die Gastronomiebereiche, die in den westlichen Seitenarmen angeordnet sind. Die Seitenarme, die das Gebäude symbolisch zum Park hin öffnen, sind der historischen Halle nachempfunden. Ebenso zeichnet der Design die Kubatur der historischen Halle mit geringfügigen Veränderungen nach. Der südliche Hof wird zum Park durch ein Seminargebäude ergänzt, das separat genutzt werden kann.

Inside the building, the shell of the hall itself is an independent, detached element. It can be opened up or closed with mechanical sliding walls on the ground and upper levels. This creates, on the one hand, a wooden house inside the building, and on the other, a naturally illuminated event hall, which is spatially, functionally and atmospherically adjustable to various uses. Generous foyer areas intensify the relationship of interior and exterior through glass façades especially towards the park. This applies in particular to the restaurant areas, located in the western wing. The wings, opening up the building towards the park in a symbolic gesture, are adapted from the historic hall. The design also repeats, with slight variations, the cubic volume of the historic hall. In the park direction, the southern courtyard is complemented by a lecture building, which can be separately used.

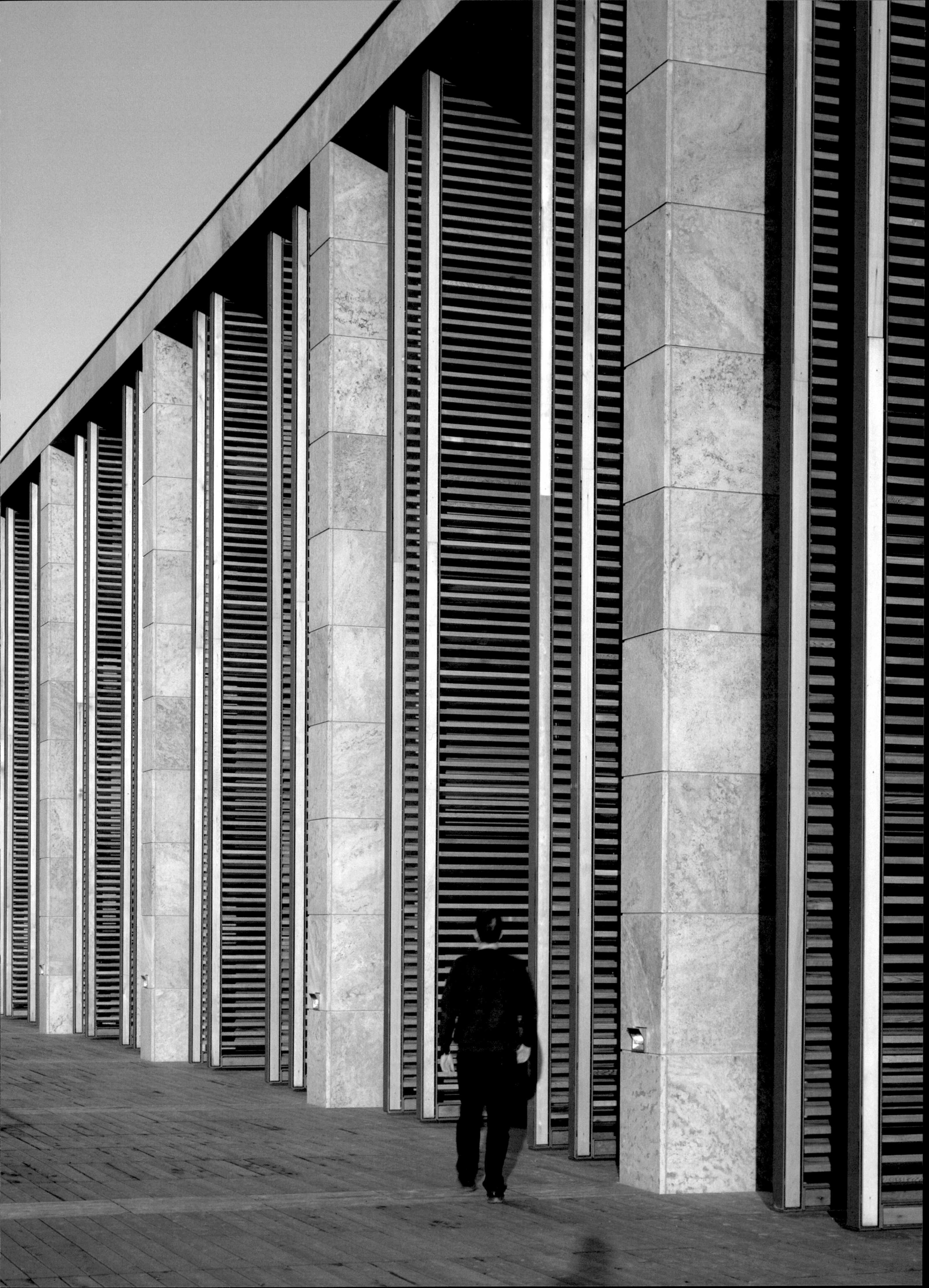

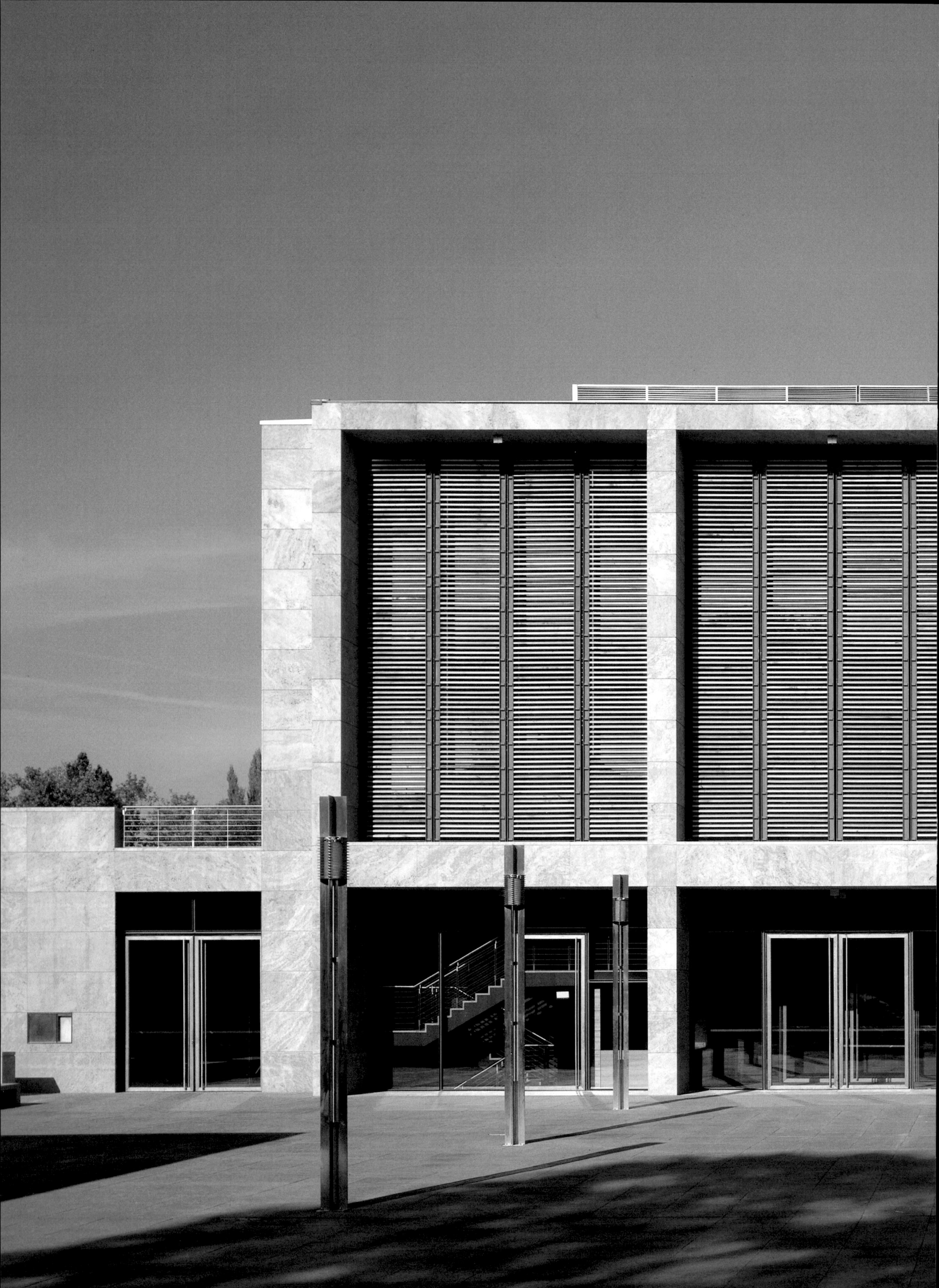

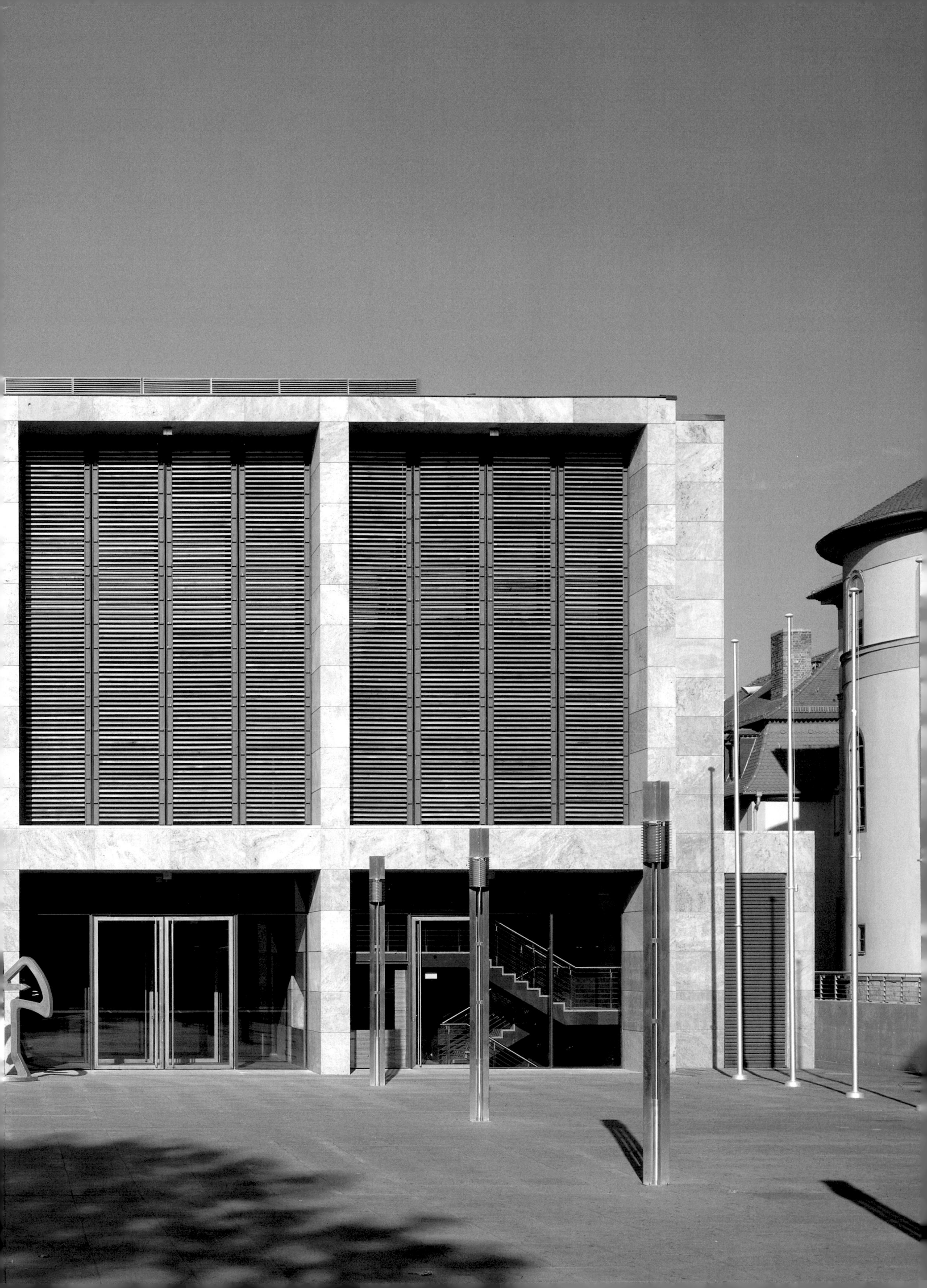

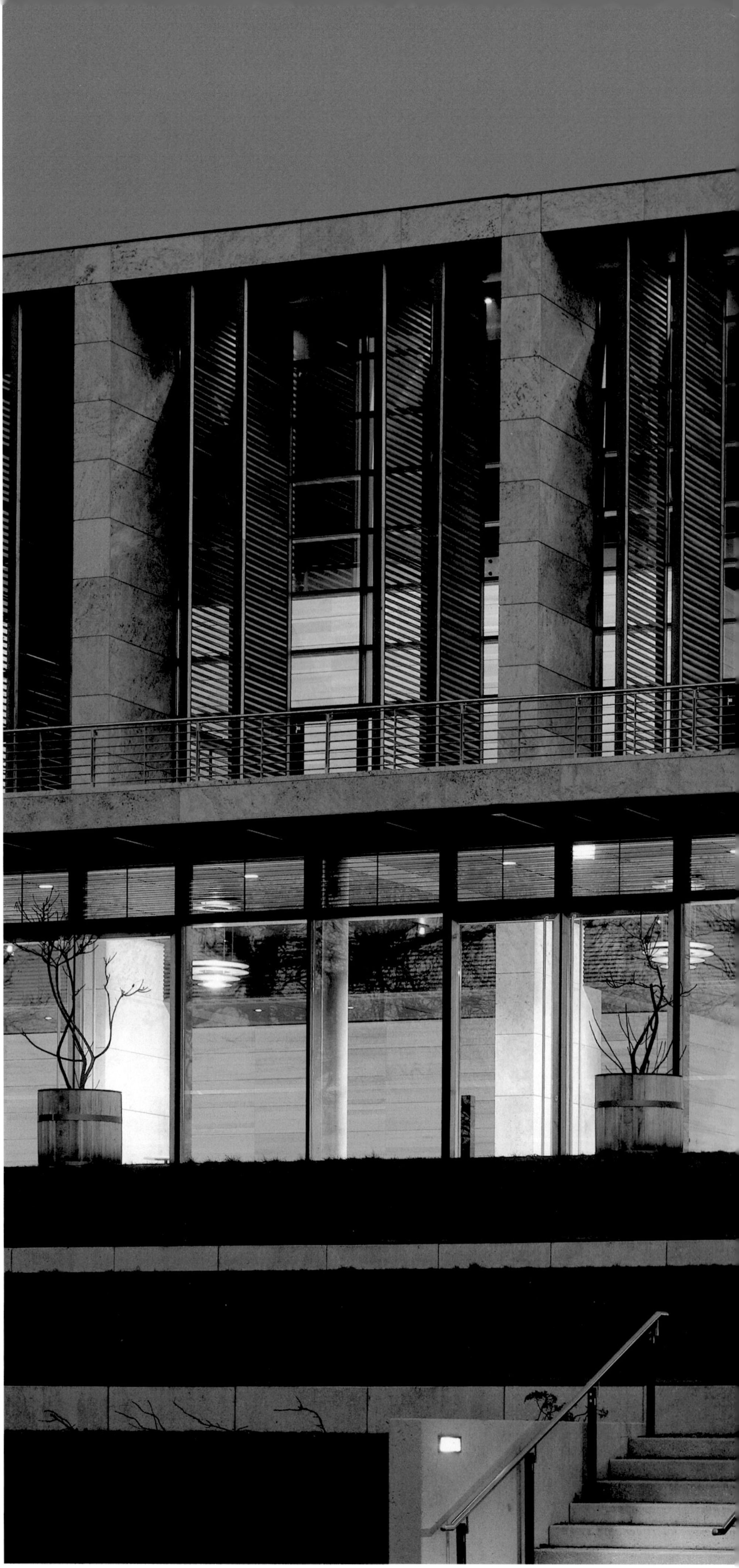

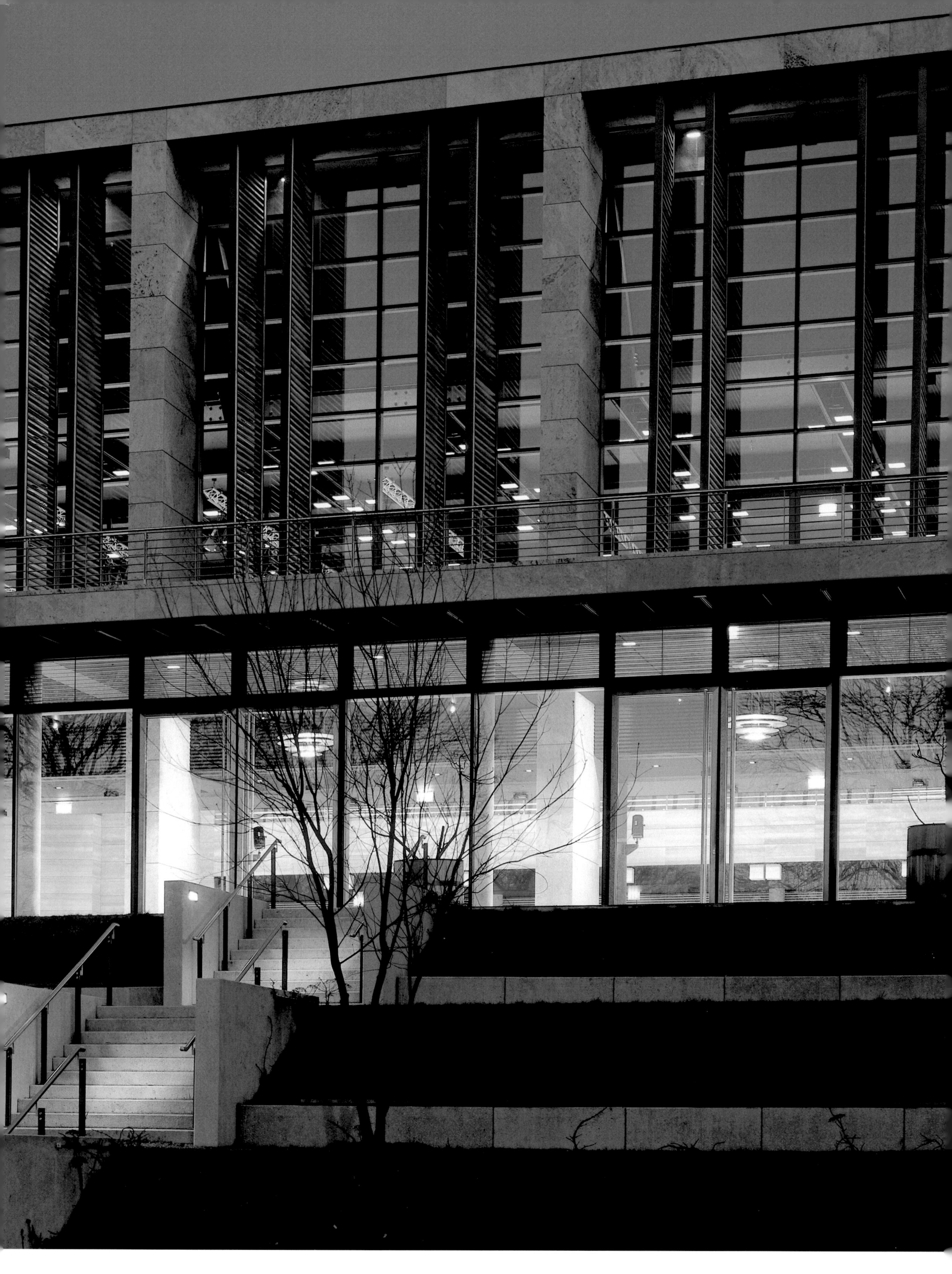

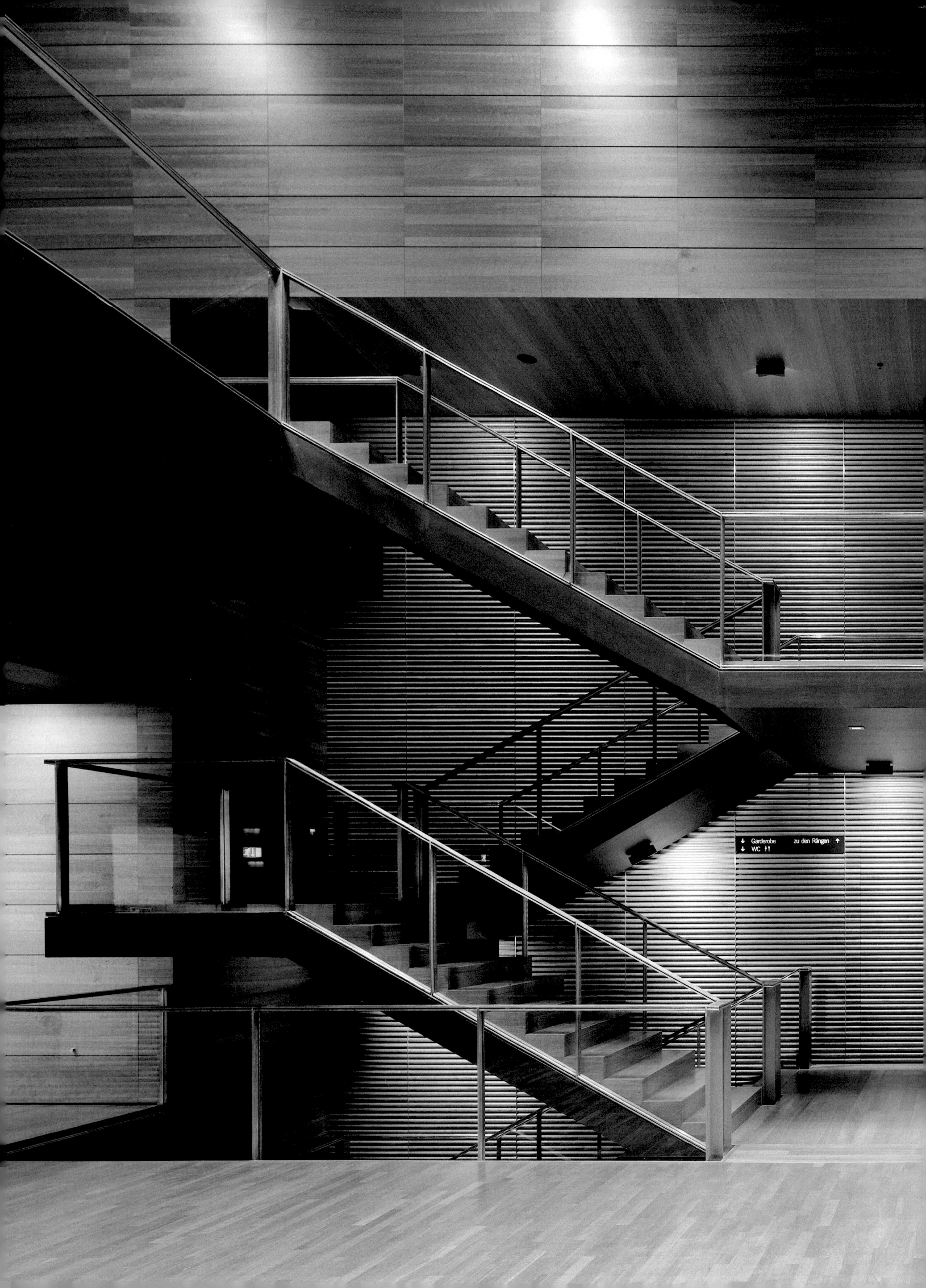
Garderobe
zu den Rängen
WC

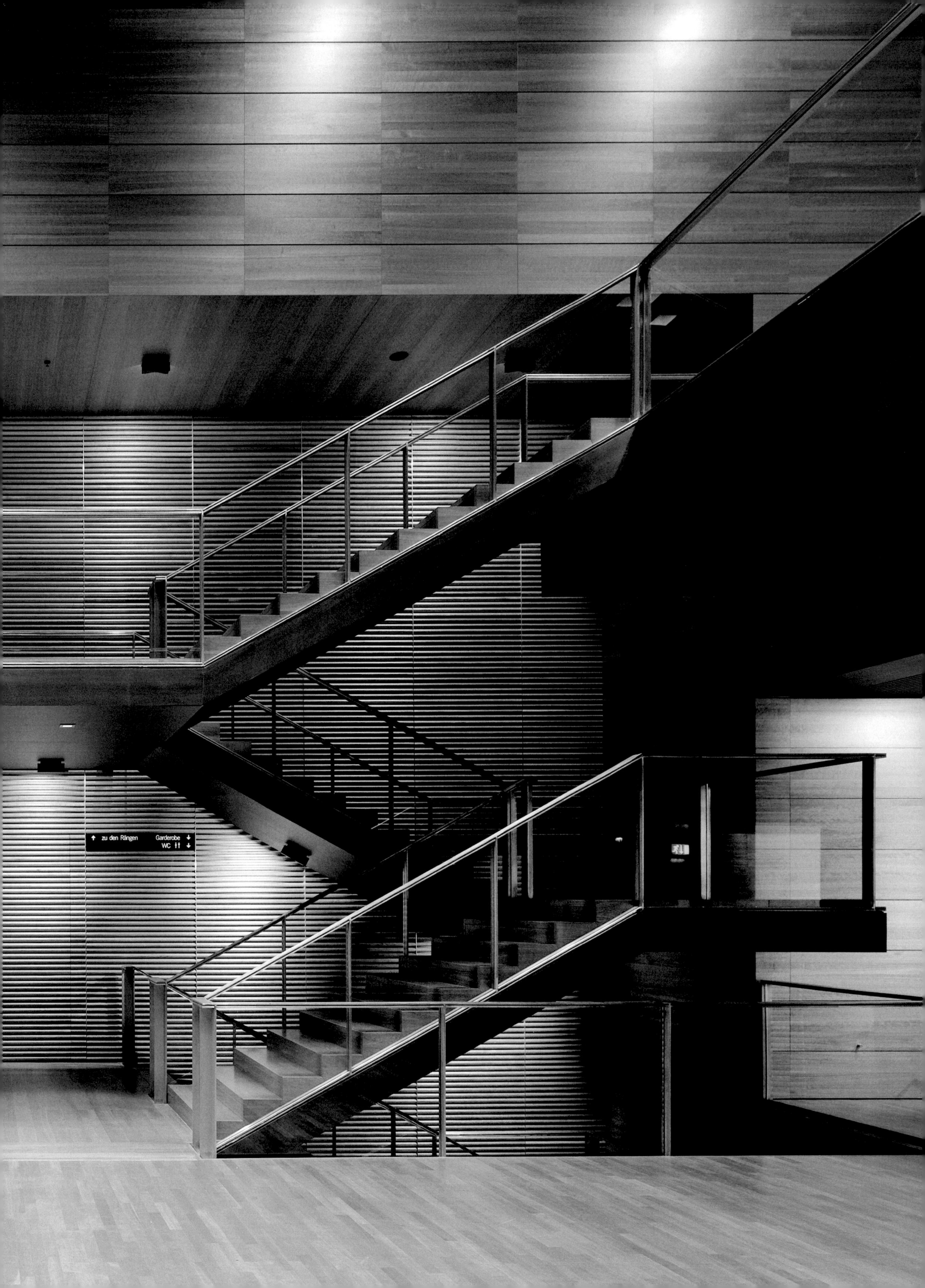
zu den Rängen
Garderobe
WC

Entertainment Center, Hamburg-Wandsbek
Entertainment Centre, Hamburg-Wandsbek

1997

Entwurf Design
Volkwin Marg und Nikolaus Goetze und
SCHILD Architekten + Ingenieure

Bauherr Client
8. Grundstücksverwaltungs AHG Beteiligungs- und
Handelsgesellschaft mbH & Co. KG, Hamburg

Bauzeit Construction period
1998–1999

BGF Gross floor area
17.000 m²

Die Lage an einer Ausfallstraße mit heterogener Bebauung und überwiegend gewerblicher Nutzung erforderte eine klare, großmaßstäbliche und entschiedene Architektur. Der Stellenwert des Vorhabens mit Autohaus einerseits, Kinocenter mit 2.500 Plätzen sowie Gastronomie- und Freizeitbereich andererseits wird durch die Verglasung des an sich einfachen Baukörpers hervorgehoben. Die Fassade des Kinofoyers kragt über einer zweigeschossigen Arkade aus und wird als großflächige, punktgehaltene Planarfassade ausgebildet, die bei Dunkelheit durch eine vom Lichtplaner („Lichtspiel") entwickelte Inszenierung besonders eindrucksvoll wirkt. Der großzügige Raum wird als lichtdurchfluteter, verglaster Wintergarten und Gebäudebalkon verstanden. Als Wahrzeichen dient das verglaste Fahrzeugregal, bei dem über einen automatischen Aufzug Neuwagen auf elf Ebenen präsentiert werden.

The location on an exit road with a heterogeneous building structure and commercial utilization demands a clear, large-scale and decisive architecture. The significance of the project, which contains a car centre as well as a cinema complex with 2,500 seats and gastronomic and leisure facilities, is emphasized by the glazing of the otherwise simple structure. The façade of the cinema foyer cantilevers over a two-storey arcade and is designed as an extensive planar façade with point mountings. When dark, an illumination concept designed by a lighting planner ('Lichtspiel') creates a remarkable impression. The generous space is understood as light-flooded, glazed winter garden and building balcony. The glazed motor-car shelf serves as a symbol; it is accessible via an automatic lift and offers space for the presentation of new cars on eleven levels.

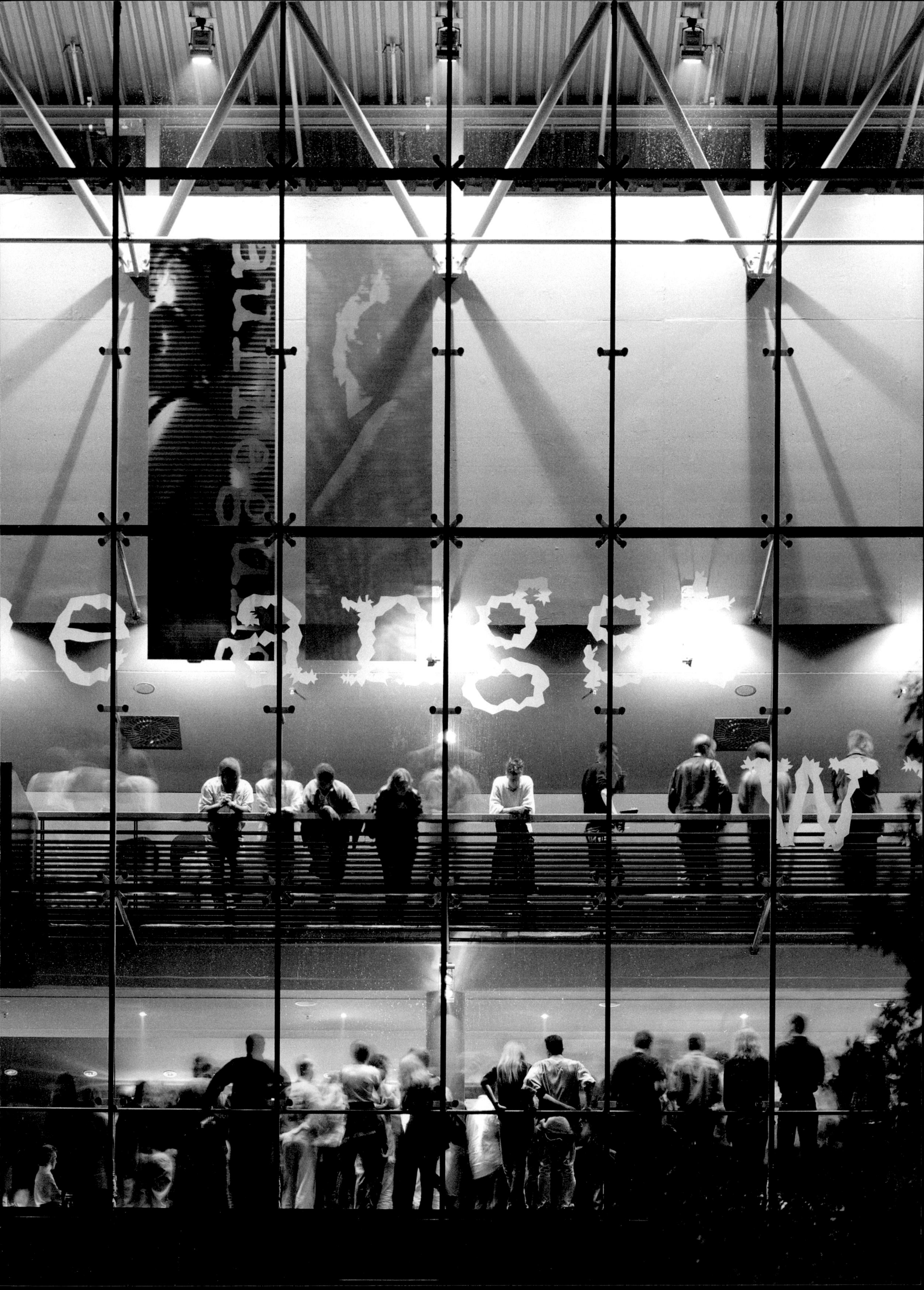

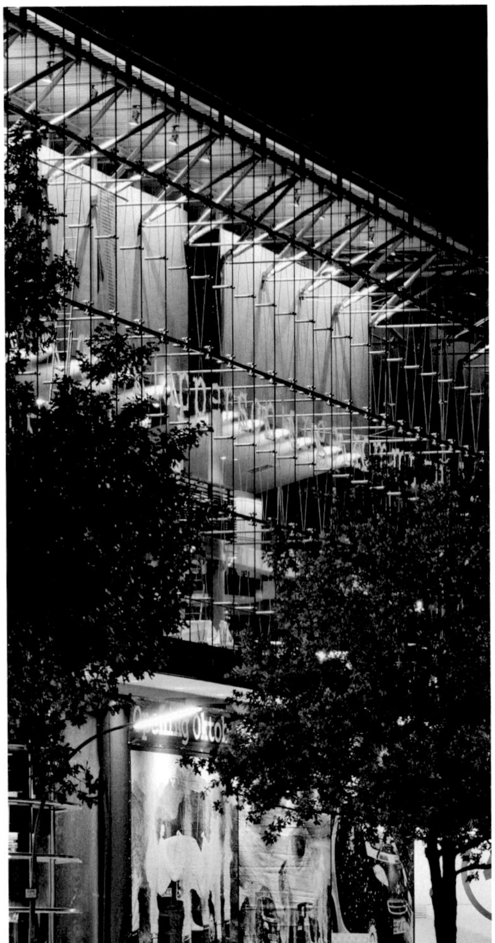

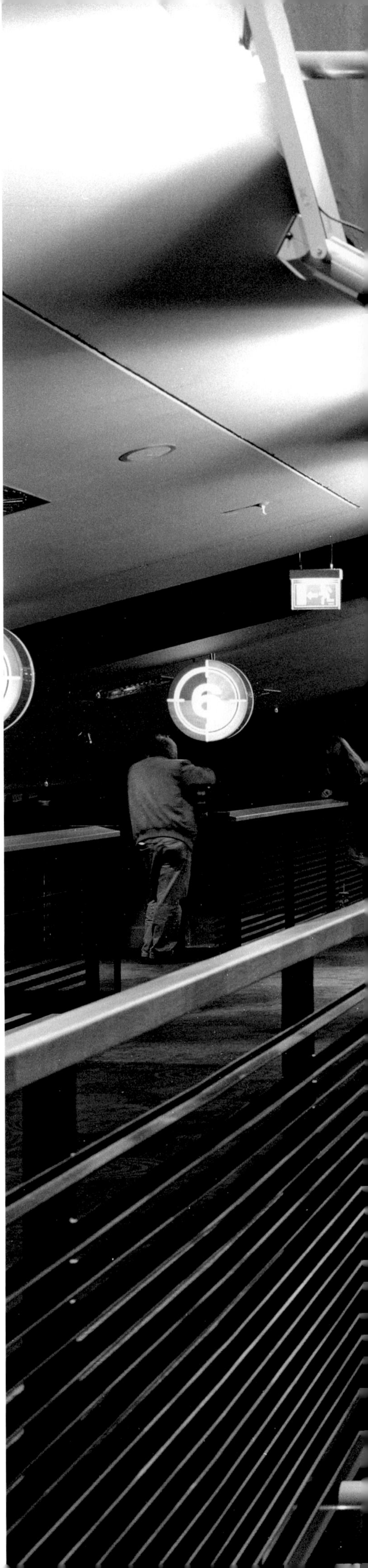

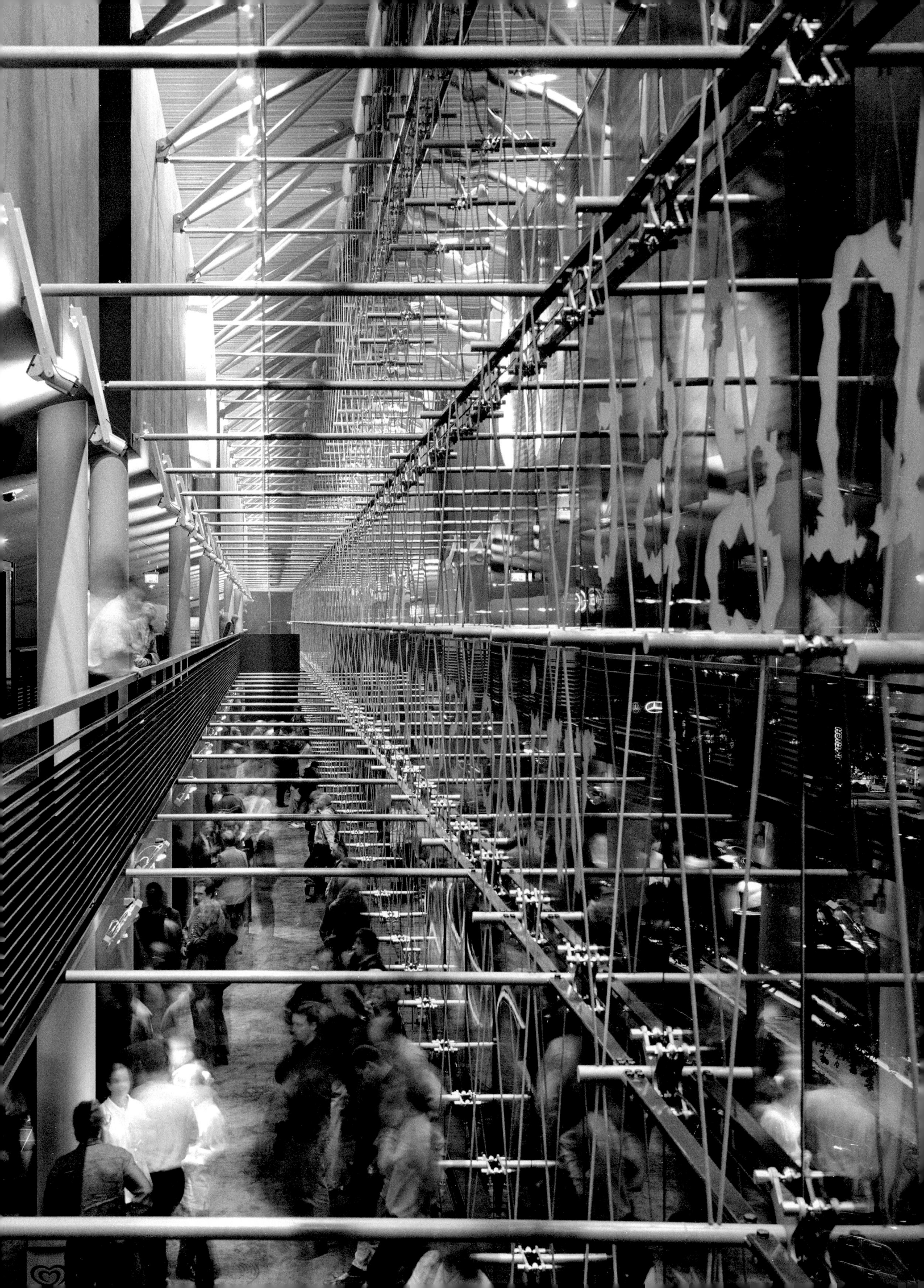

Elbkaihaus, Hamburg
Loft Elbkaihaus, Hamburg

Wettbewerb Competition
1992

Entwurf Design
Volkwin Marg

Partner Partner
Klaus Staratzke

Bauherr Client
GHL III – ein Unternehmen der HHLA-Gruppe

Bauzeit Construction period
1998–1999

BGF Gross floor area
12.300 m²

Das 130 m lange Gebäude, das parallel zum Elbstrom an der Kaimauer liegt, wurde in fünf Häuser gegliedert, die jeweils durch ein Treppenhaus mit einem Aufzug erschlossen werden. Im 1. und 2. Obergeschoss ist über die gesamte Länge der Halle eine Stahl-Glas-Fassade vorgehängt. Die leuchtend rot akzentuierten Wände der Erschließungskerne wirken farblich als edler Kontrast zu den schwarzen Fensterbändern und den dunklen, filigran wirkenden Stahltreppen. Die authentischen Pilzkopf-Säulen, nur mit einer Lasur versehen und in ihrem ursprünglichen Grauton gehalten, erinnern im Gebäude noch an die Konstruktion des Stahlbetonskeletts. Markantes Wahrzeichen des Elbkaihauses sind zwei restaurierte Halbportalkräne. Sie korrespondieren mit den drei weißen Ladebalkonen an der Wasserseite des Elbkaihauses und erinnern an die maritime Tradition des umgebauten Kühlhauses mit Fischauktionshalle.

The 130-m-long building, situated parallel to the Elbe along the quay-wall was divided into five houses, each accessible via a staircase and lift. On the 1st and 2nd floors a steel-glass façade is suspended across the complete length of the hall. The walls of the circulation cores, painted in bright red, act as an elegant contrast to the black window bands and the dark, seemingly lightweight steel staircases. The authentic pillars with column capitals, finished only with a scumble glaze but otherwise left in their original grey tone, refer to the reinforced concrete framework inside the building. A prominent symbol of the Elbkaihaus are two restored semigantry cranes. They correspond to the three white loading balconies on the waterside of the Elbkaihaus and are reminiscent of the maritime tradition of the converted cold store and fish auction hall.

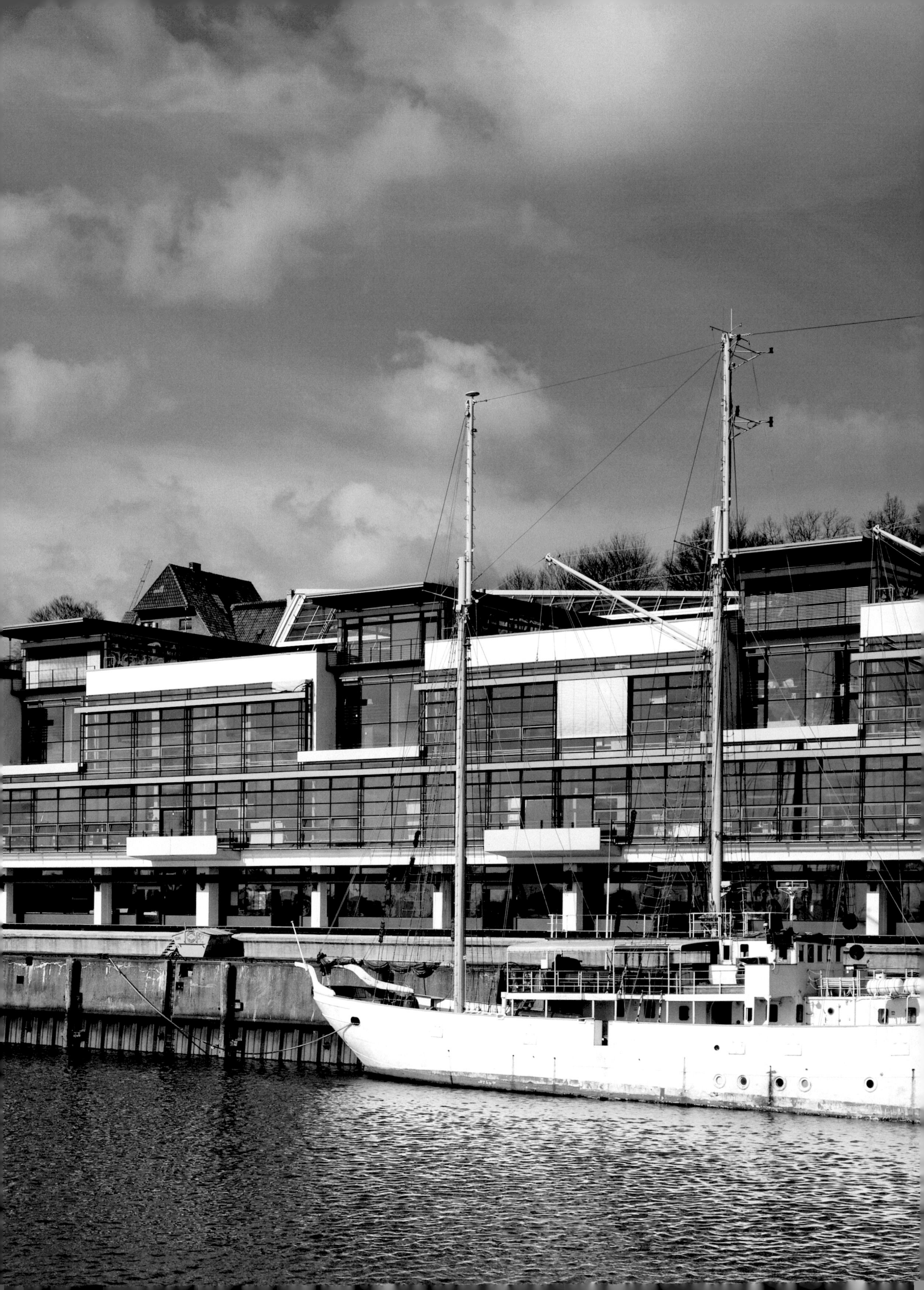

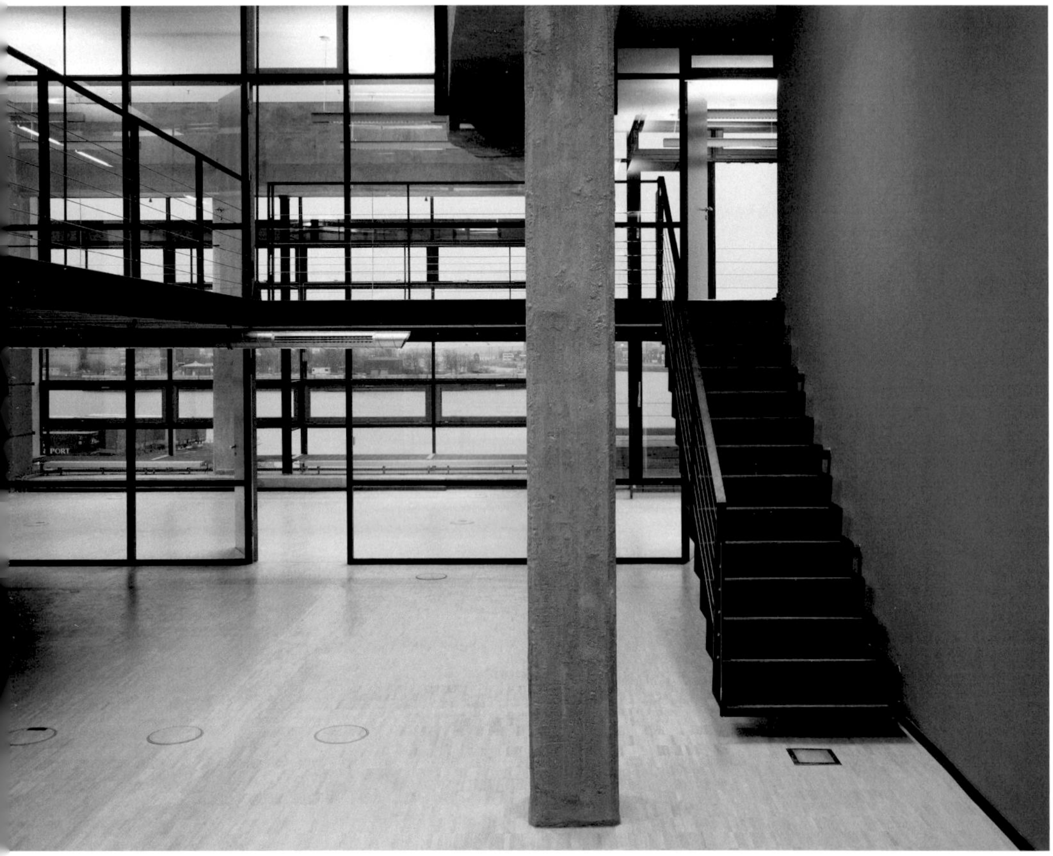

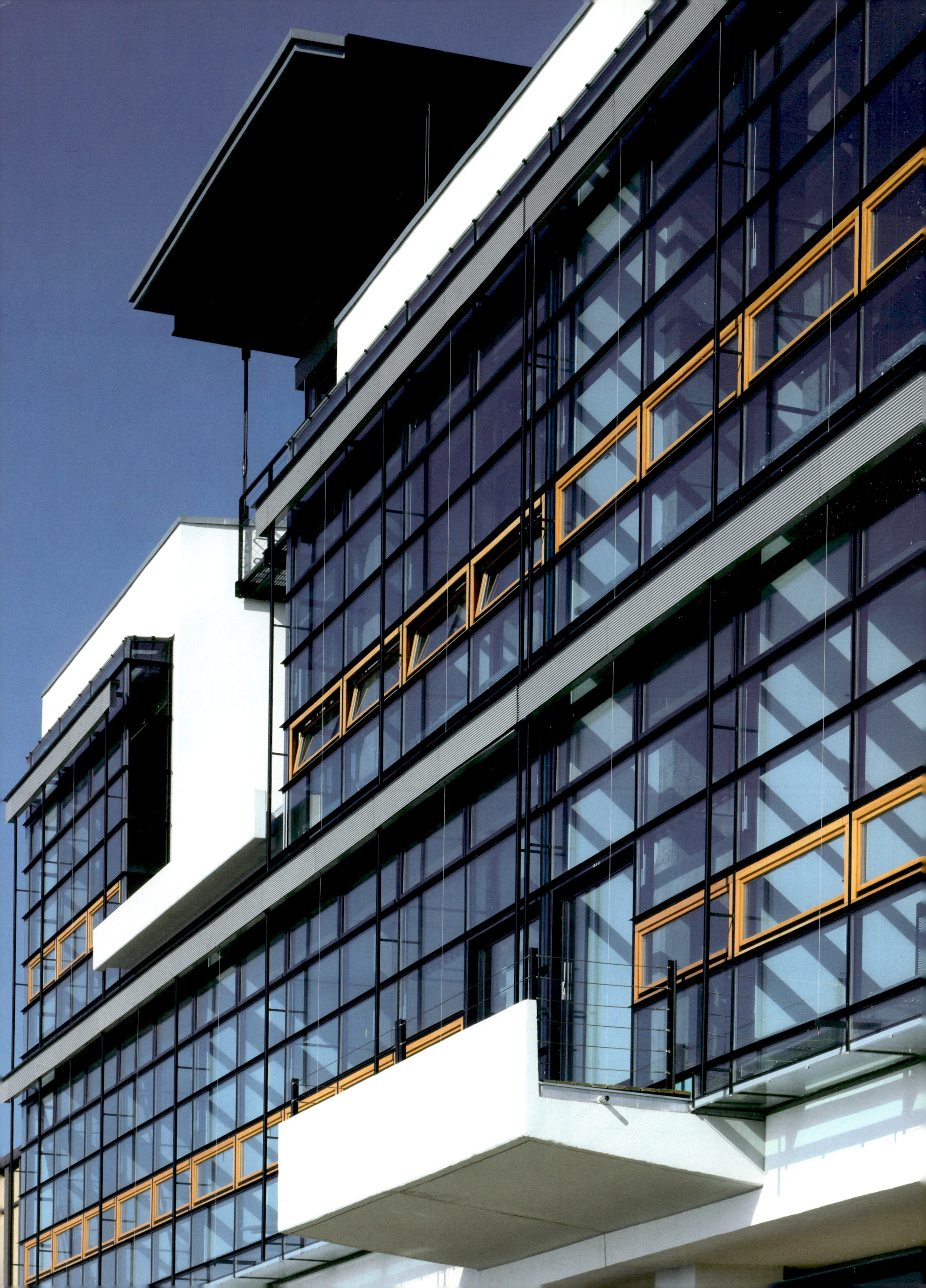

Fassade des Wohnhauses von Gerkan, Elbchaussee, Hamburg
Façade of the von Gerkan Residence, Elbchaussee, Hamburg

1998

Entwurf Design
Meinhard von Gerkan

Bauherr Client
Meinhard von Gerkan

Bauzeit Construction period
1998–1999

Die vorhandene Senkrechtverschalung des Hauses mit weiß lackierten Holzbrettern an der Nord-, West- und Ostseite wurde komplett entfernt und durch eine hinterlüftete Fassadenkonstruktion ersetzt: Auf der vorhandenen Lattung mit dazwischenliegender Wärmedämmung bildet eine schwarzgestrichene, zementgebundene Holzfaserplatte den notwendigen Wetterschutz. Mit Abstand zur Platte prägen senkrecht geschraubte Bretter aus unbehandelter sibirischer Lärche das äußere Erscheinungsbild. Im Querschnitt sind die geschosshohen Bretter rautenförmig gehobelt. Dies hat zur Folge, dass sich je nach Blickrichtung dem Betrachter ein unterschiedliches Erscheinungsbild darstellt. Vor den Fensteröffnungen wurden die Bretter teilweise versetzt angeordnet.

The existing vertical shuttering, made of white, lacquered wooden panels, was completely removed on the north, west and east elevations and replaced by a ventilated façade construction: a black, lacquered, cement-bound fibreboard mounted on the existing lathing with integrated thermal insulation provides the necessary weatherproofing. The external appearance is characterized by untreated panels of Siberian larch, which are vertically fixed with a cavity to the fibreboard. Viewed in cross-section, the storey-high boards are planed in a diamond shape, resulting in a varying appearance depending on the viewer's position. The boards are partially alternated in front of the window openings.

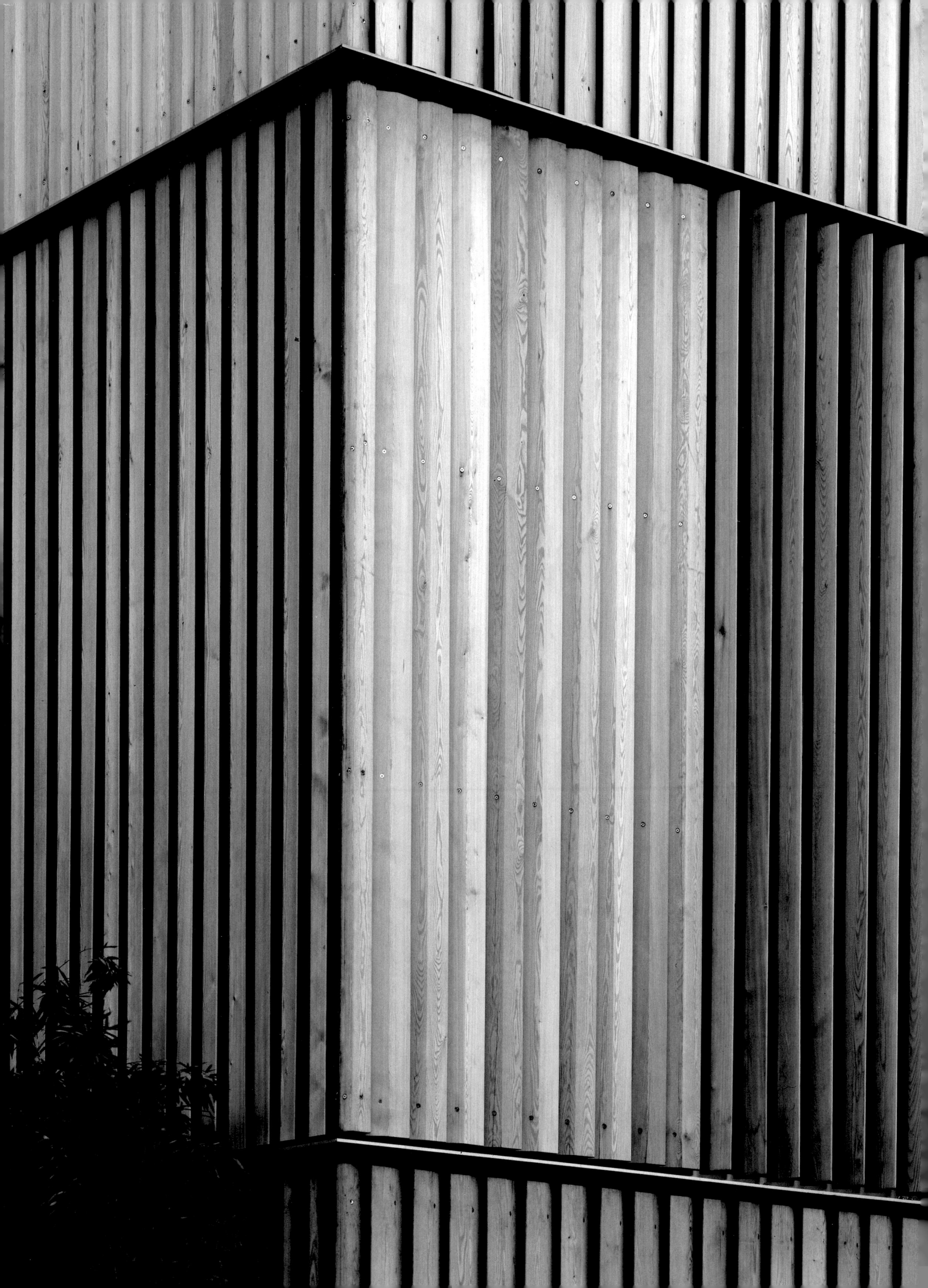

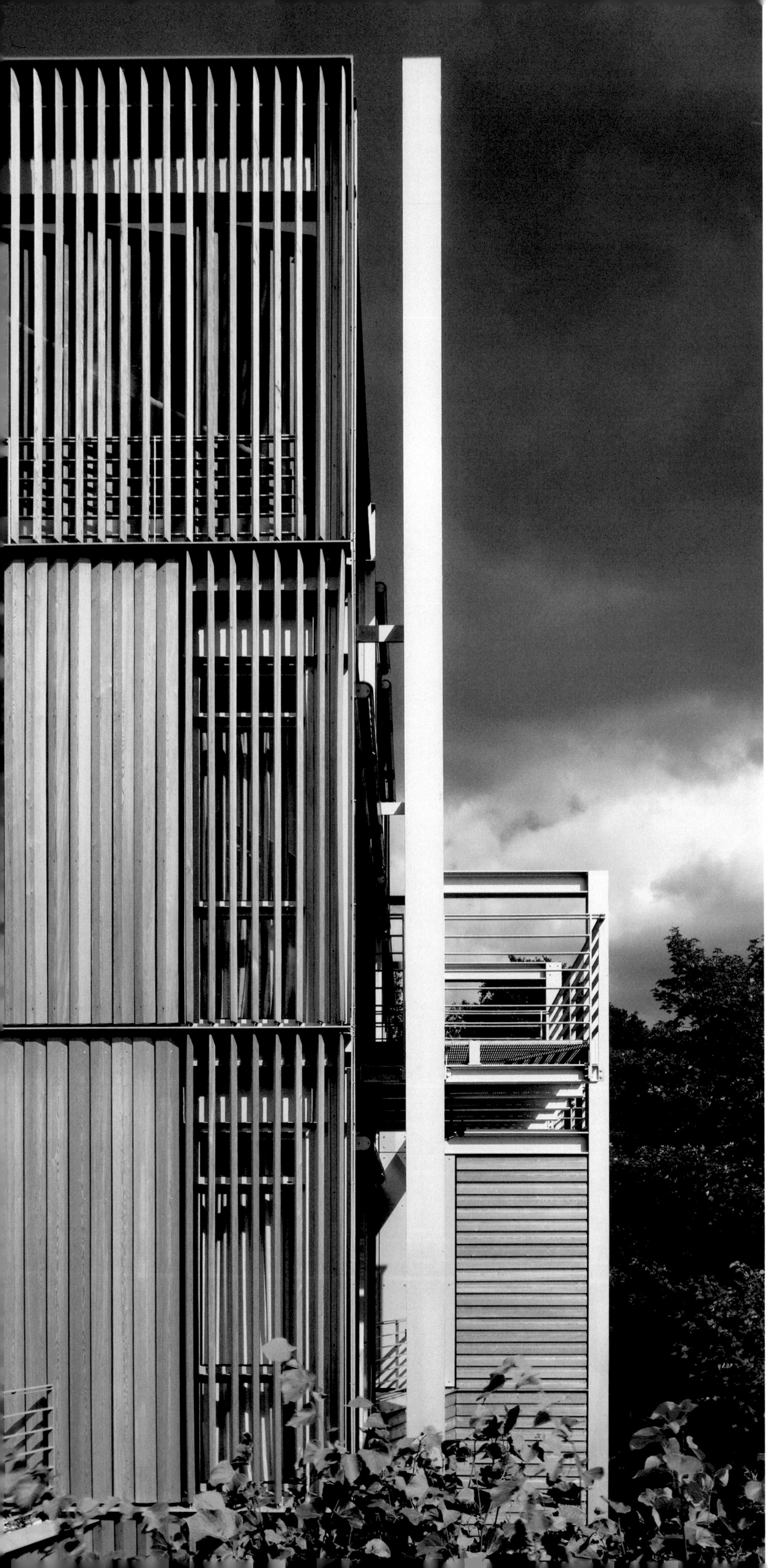

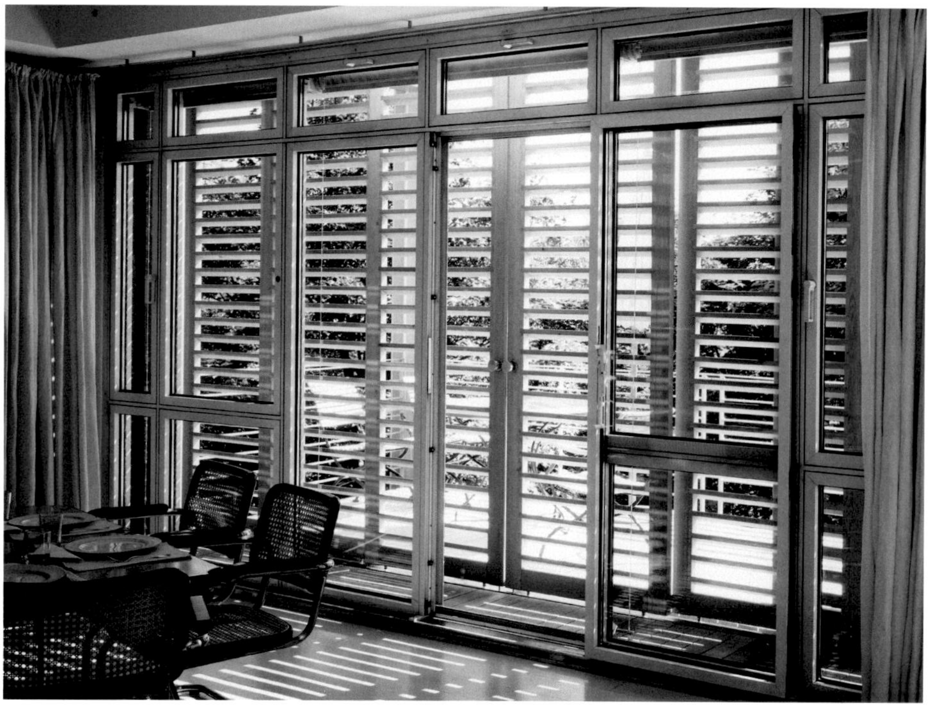

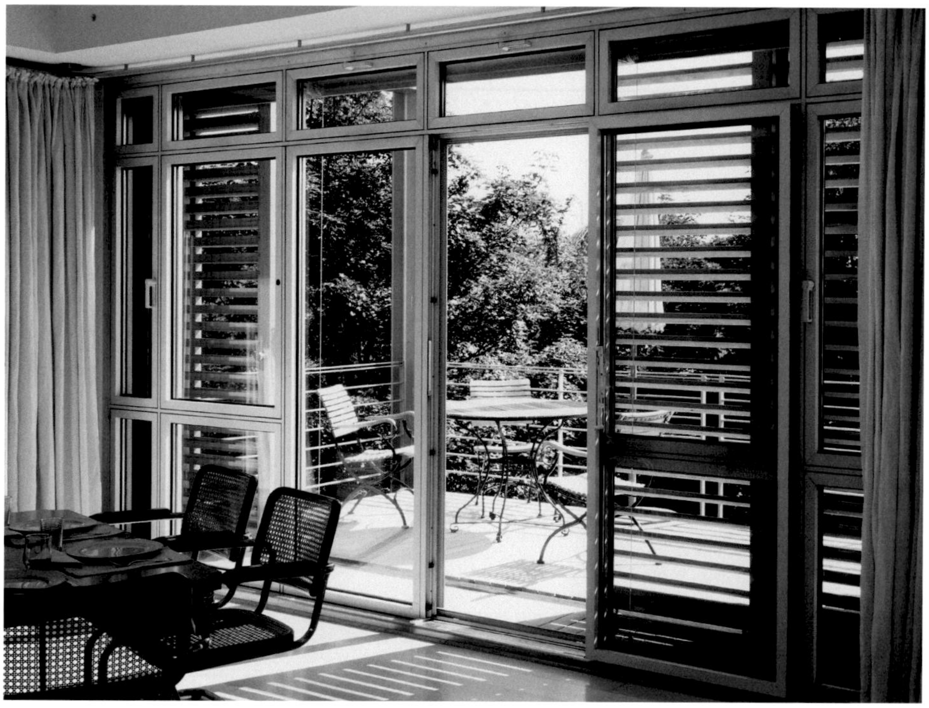

2000

Wohnhaus Alvano, Hamburg-Othmarschen

Das Grundstück für das Haus Alvano entstand aus der Teilung eines Parkgrundstücks. Durch die Situierung des Baukörpers an der östlichen Grenze bleibt der Park in seiner Großzügigkeit so weit wie möglich erhalten. Prägendes Gestaltungsmerkmal des puritanisch anmutenden Hauses sind die Sonnenschutzelemente aus Corteenstahl.

Alvano House, Hamburg-Othmarschen

The site for the Alvano house was created by dividing up a park site. Locating the building at the eastern boundary maintained the park's generous proportions and dimensions to the greatest extent possible, without any confinement caused by a centrally positioned structure. Solar screen elements made of Corten steel give the puritanical-looking house its identity.

Christus-Pavillon auf der Expo 2000, Hannover

Der Pavillon der christlichen Religionen ist ein kontemplatives Gegenstück zum Jahrmarkt der Eitelkeiten mit seinen architektonischen Aufgeregtheiten: strukturell einfach und sinnfällig, reduziert auf wenige Materialien, präzise im Detail, unverwechselbar in der Anmutung und Raumstimmung.

Christ Pavilion at the Expo 2000, Hanover

The Pavilion of Christian religions is a contemplative counterpart to the vanity fair with its architectural highlights: simple and clear in structure, reduced to a few materials, precise in detail, unmistakable in its appearance and spatial atmosphere.

Deutsche Schule Peking, China

Aufgrund des heterogenen Umfeldes entwickelte sich die Idee einer auf sich bezogenen Baukörperdisposition, die das Grundstück über feste Raumkanten in definierte Freiräume teilt. Ein Wechselspiel aus Freiräumen, Abgrenzung und Öffnung entsteht, das die chinesische Bautradition der Gruppierung von Baukörpern aufgreift.

German School, Beijing, China

The concept of a self-orientated building complex, with strong spatial edges dividing the site in clearly defined open spaces, was developed owing to the heterogeneous neighbourhood. An interplay of open spaces, delimitation and openings is created, repeating the Chinese tradition of the grouping of building structures.

Fußgängerbrücken EXPO 2000, Hannover

Zwei externe Straßen queren das Ausstellungsgelände und machten den Bau von vier individuell dimensionierten Fußgängerbrücken notwendig. Das einheitliche, in Breite und Länge variable Tragsystem der Brücken besteht aus einem Spalier von Leucht-Stelen und dazwischengehängten Stegen.

Expo 2000 Pedestrian Bridges, Hanover

The world exhibition (EXPO) site was traversed by two external roads, making necessary the construction of pedestrian bridges at four different locations. The bridges' uniform structural system, variable in lenght and width, consists of an espalier of luminescent stelae, with footbridges suspended in between.

2000

Messehalle 6, Düsseldorf

Im Gegensatz zu den bestehenden, reinen Kunstlichthallen ist die Halle 6 als natürlich belichtete Mehrzweckhalle konzipiert, die je nach Bedarf durch Schließen der „Außenjalousien" vollständig verdunkelt werden kann. Als markanter Solitär bildet sie einen architektonischen Gegenpol zum benachbarten Stadion.

Düsseldorf Exhibition Centre, Hall 6

In contrast to the existing exhibition halls lit entirely by artificial light, Hall 6 was conceived as a naturally-lit, multi-purpose hall. As the need arises, the hall can be completely darkened by means of external louvres. As a distinctive solitary the new hall acts as an architectural counterpart to the neighbouring stadium.

Ausstellungspavillon der TU Braunschweig

An zentraler Stelle im Innenhof der Technischen Universität steht der neue Ausstellungspavillon der „Carolo Wilhelmina". In axialer Zuordnung zum Altbau erfolgt die Haupterschließung über einen Brückensteg vom Treppenpodest des vorhandenen Gebäudes auf die Galerieebene des Pavillons.

Exhibition Pavilion for the Braunschweig Institute of Technology

The new exhibition pavilion for the 'Carolo Wilhelmina' is located centrally in the inner courtyard of the university. In an axial relation to the old building the main access starts across a footbridge from the stair podium of the existing building to the pavilion gallery level.

Bergbauarchiv, Clausthal-Zellerfeld

An den Altbau des Oberbergamtes wurde für den bislang unzureichend gelagerten Schriftfundus zur Technik- und Kulturgeschichte des Harzes ein Archivgebäude angefügt, das aus der Idee eines aufgeschlagenen Buches entstand. Die Holz- und Bleiverkleidung erinnert dabei an den regionalen Abbau des Bleierzes.

Mining Archive, Clausthal-Zellerfeld

The existing building of the mining authority was added to with an archive block, housing the, until then, inadequately stored collection of documents on the technological and cultural history of the Harz Mountains. The design was derived from the idea of an open book. The timber and lead cladding is reminiscent of the regional quarrying of lead ore.

Lenné-Passagen, Frankfurt/Oder

Die bewusst unterschiedliche Baukörpergliederung aus einem rechteckigen Baublock und einer Rotunde spiegelt die Vielfalt des städtischen Organismus. Die überwiegend eingeschossige Arkade verbindet die einzelnen Elemente, eine dreigeschossige Ladenpassage bildet den Fußweg zum Lenné-Park.

Lenné Passage, Frankfurt/Oder

The deliberate composition of different buildings consisting of a rectangular block and a rotunda reflects the variety of the urban fabric. The primarily one-storey arcade links the single elements, whilst a three-storey shopping passage forms the walkway to Lenné Park.

Media City, Leipzig

Die sandfarbenen Ziegelkeramikflächen der Fassaden und inneren Wandverkleidungen wechseln mit Elementen aus Stahl, großzügigen Verglasungen und durchgrünten Freiräumen. Ein Mediengarten dient als gläsernes „Haus im Haus" und bildet das zentrale Foyer des Ensembles aus Verwaltung und Fernsehstudios.

Media Centre, Leipzig

The sand-coloured ceramic brick of the façades and interior wall cladding alternates with steel elements, generously glazed surfaces and landscaped open spaces. The media garden is developed as a glazed 'house inside a house' and forms the central foyer for the ensemble of offices and TV studios.

2000

Kontorhaus am Altmarkt, Dresden

Das Gebäude nimmt die historischen Baufluchten auf, variiert sie jedoch durch plastische Einschnitte, Arkaden und Staffelungen. Die vorgeschriebene Dachkontur wird in Stufen aufgelöst, die mit roten Fassadenplatten verkleidet sind – eine „Ironisierung" der Tradition, die dennoch den Zusammenhang wahrt.

Office Building, Altmarkt, Dresden

The complex continues the historical building lines, simultaneously altering them with three-dimensional niches, arcades and steps. The obligatory sloped roof contour is realized as steps, clad in naturally red façade panels – an 'ironical treatment' tradition, which nonetheless maintains the context.

Marshall-Brücke, Berlin

Das Betontragwerk besteht aus Flächen unterschiedlicher Krümmung, deren untere Ebene auf jeder Seite vier parabelförmige Einschnitte aufweist, sodass der Eindruck eines flachen Tonnen-gewölbes entsteht. Leuchtend rote Lichtstelen markieren die fünfspurige Kanalüberfahrt.

Marshall Bridge, Berlin

The arched structural framework made of concrete consists of two surfaces of different camber, their lower levels having four parabolic cuts on each side. This gives the impression of a flat barrel arch. Bright red luminescent steles mark the five-lane canal crossing in the street space.

Art Kite Museum, Detmold

Charakteristikum der Halle ist die weitgespannte bogenförmige Dachkonstruktion, die sichtbar belassen wurde. Eine Glasfront aus größtenteils transluzentem Glas ersetzt die für den ehemaligen Hubschraubhangar typische breite Front aus Schiebetoren. Das weit auskragende Vordach betont den Eingang.

Art Kite Museum, Detmold

The hall's main feature is a wide-spanned, arched roof structure which remained visible. A glass front of mainly translucent glazing replaces the wide front of sliding gates typical of the former helicopter hangar. A generously projecting roof emphasizes the entrance.

Fachhochschule des Bundes, Schwerin

Der Design schafft durch die Anordnung der Baukörper einen parkartigen, großen Platzraum, auf den sich alle Teile der Anlage beziehen. Die differenzierte Gliederung der Baukörper, ihre mäßige Bauhöhe sowie die vereinheitlichende Typologie geneigter Dächer entspricht dem Maßstab des Ortes und der Umgebung.

Federal College, Schwerin

The design creates a park-like, large square with the allocation of the building masses, which all parts of the complex refer to. The differentiated division of the buildings, their moderate height, as well as the standardized typology of inclined roofs, corresponds to the scale of the location and surroundings.

Umbau des Kesselhauses in der Speicherstadt, Hamburg

Das 1888 in Betrieb genommen Kesselhaus war das erste Hamburger Dampfkraftwerk. In neugotischem Stil gestaltet und mit rotem Backstein gebaut ist es Teil des denkmalgeschützten Ensembles Speicherstadt. Heute, nach dem Umbau, beheimatet es das große Informationszentrum über die Hafencity und ein Café.

Conversion of the Boiler House in the Speicherstadt, Hamburg

The former boiler house – put into operation on 3 March 1888 – was Hamburg's first steam power station. The power station, built in a neo-Gothic style and with red bricks, is part of the overall Speicherstadt ensemble, which is under a preservation order.

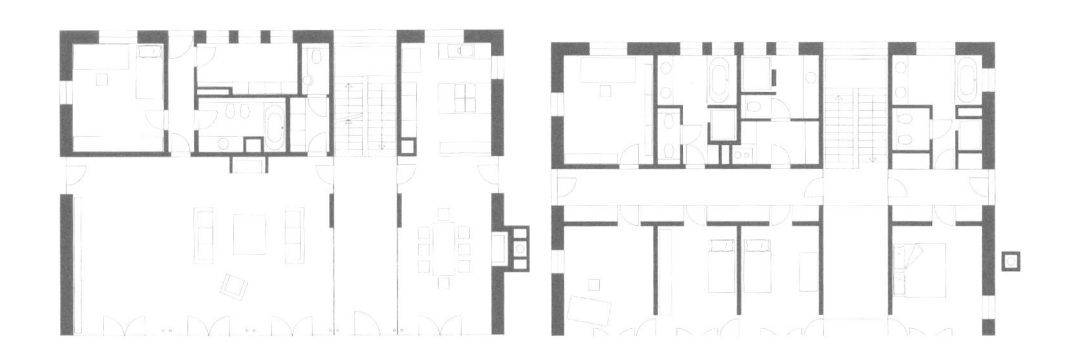

Wohnhaus Alvano, Hamburg-Othmarschen
Alvano House, Hamburg-Othmarschen

1996

Entwurf Design
Meinhard von Gerkan und Nikolaus Goetze

Bauherr Client
Dr. Wolfgang Alvano, Tuki Gräfin Wrangel

Bauzeit Construction period
1999–2000

BGF Gross floor area
400 m²

Das Haus nimmt in seiner Konzeption als zweigeschossiger Solitärbau die Proportionen der angrenzenden Villenbebauung auf und ergänzt seine Umgebung in zurückhaltender Art, ohne sie durch ornamenthafte Eitelkeiten beherrschen zu wollen. Dies wird durch die Materialien unterstrichen: weiß verputzte Porotonwände mit Lochfenstern unterschiedlicher Größe und verschiebbare Sonnenschutzelemente vor den raumhohen Fenstern der Westfassade, bestehend aus einem Geflecht aus Cortenstahlbändern. Diese können abhängig von Sonnenstand und Jahreszeit immer wieder unterschiedlich angeordnet werden. Eine zweigeschossige Eingangshalle, die Raum für die Präsentation von Kunstwerken bietet, verbindet optisch die beiden Wohnebenen. Das Erdgeschoss kann durch Schiebeelemente zu einem großzügigen Raum geöffnet werden. Das erste Obergeschoss bietet aufgrund ähnlich geschnittener Räume, die untereinander verbunden sind, größte Flexibilität.

The Alvano house concept as a two-storey solitaire repeats the proportions of the neighbouring villa development, while complementing its environment in a modest fashion without trying to dominate the neighbourhood with ornamental vanities. This impression is further enhanced by the selected materials such as white plastered Poroton walls with window openings of various sizes and movable shading elements from a netting of Corten steel strips in front of the floor to the ceiling-high windows of the west façade. A two-storey entrance hall visually connects both living levels, simultaneously offering room for the presentation of art pieces. Sliding elements on the ground floor can open up this level into a generous space. On the first level, similarly laid-out rooms, which are interlinked, offer a high degree of flexibility.

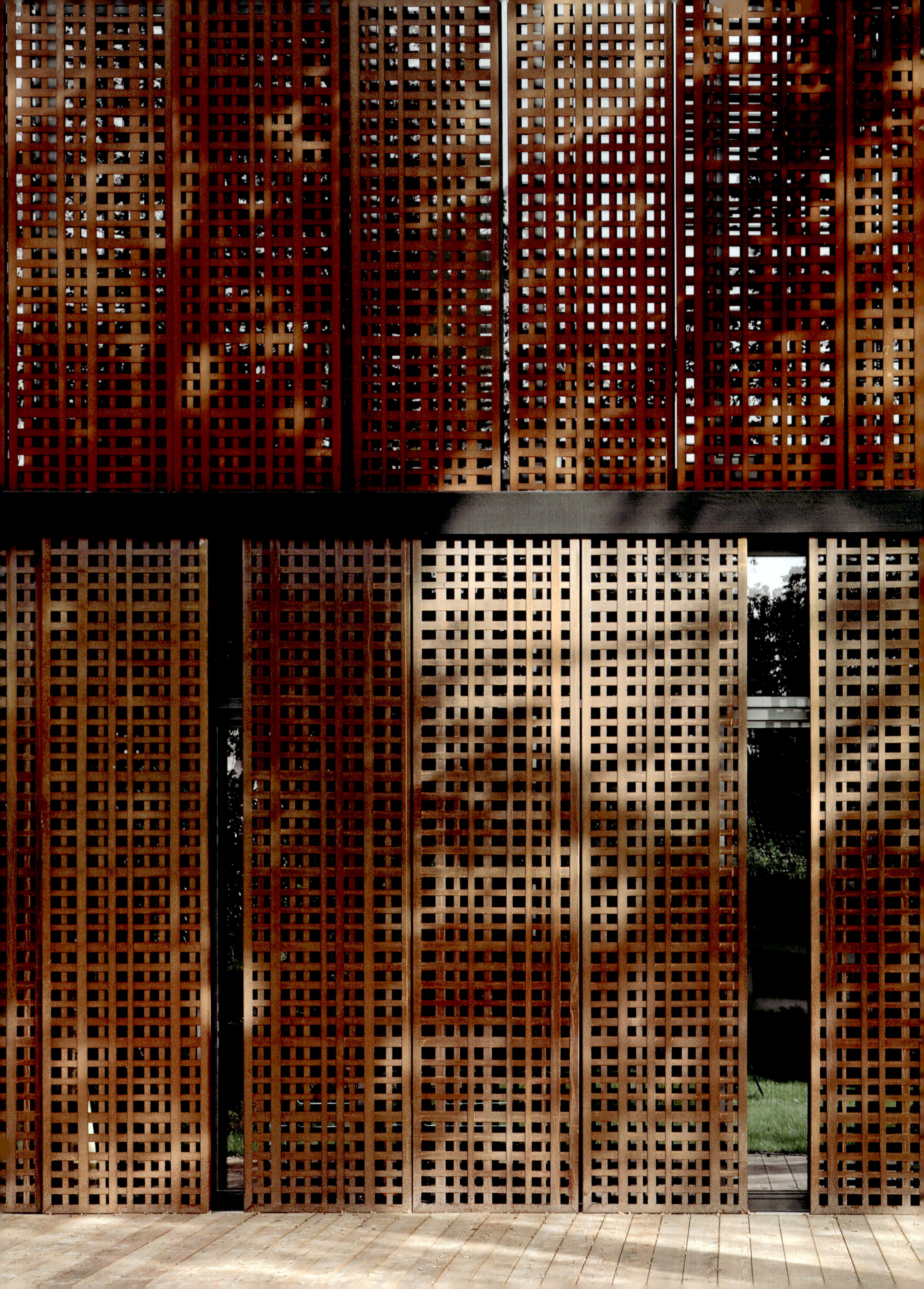

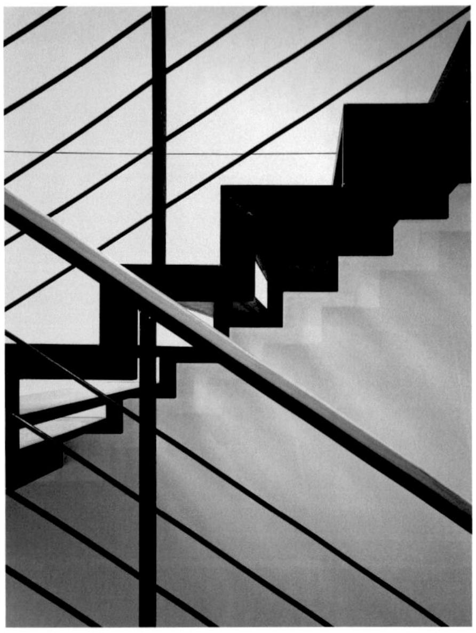

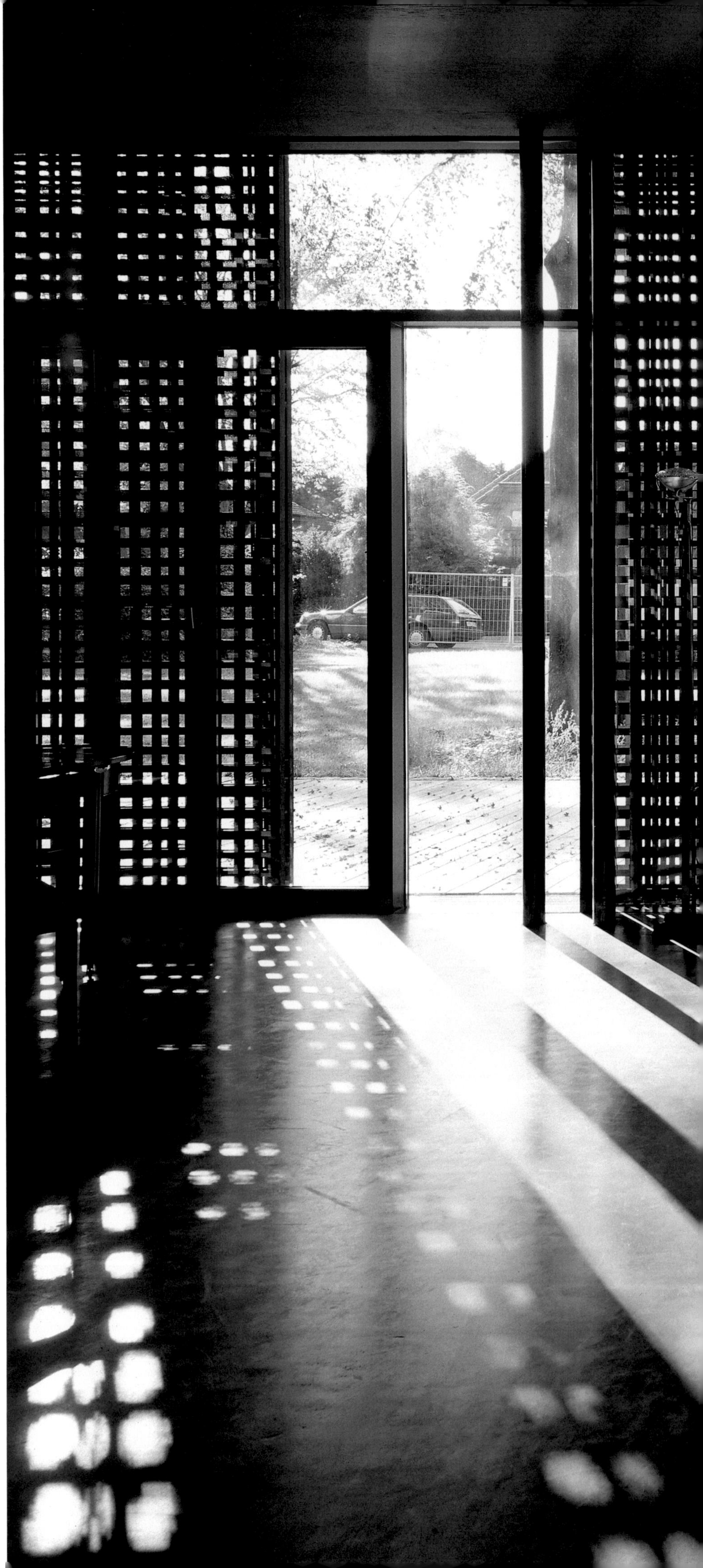

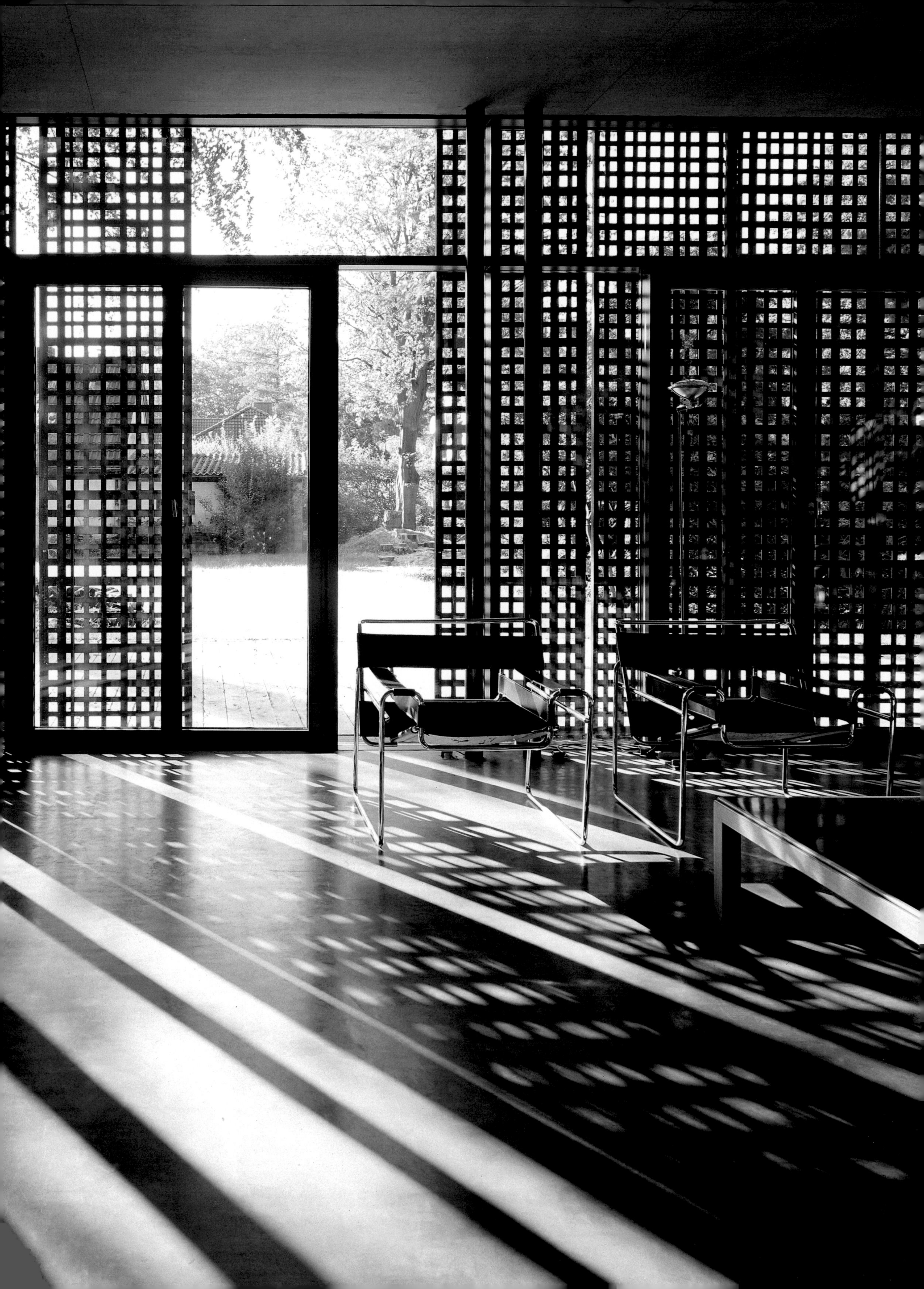

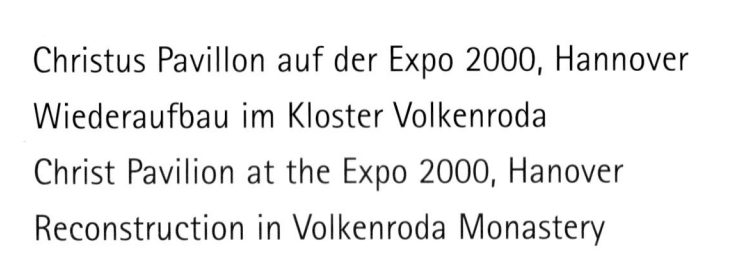

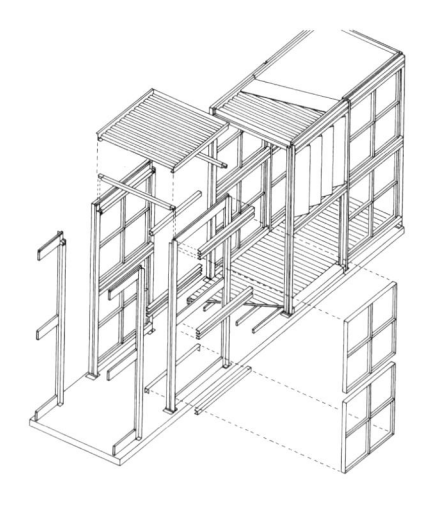

Christus Pavillon auf der Expo 2000, Hannover
Wiederaufbau im Kloster Volkenroda
Christ Pavilion at the Expo 2000, Hanover
Reconstruction in Volkenroda Monastery

Wettbewerb Competition
1990 – 1. Preis

Entwurf Design
Meinhard von Gerkan
und Joachim Zais

Auftraggeber Client
Evangelisches Büro für die Weltausstellung
Expo 2000

Bauzeit Construction period
1999-2000 | 2001

BGF Gross floor area
2.004 m^2

Die Pavillonarchitektur beschränkt sich darauf, das konstruktive Gefüge des modularen Systems mit seinen Details zu zeigen. Ein umlaufender Kreuzgang umgrenzt den Gesamtkomplex und dient zugleich als Wandelhalle und Ausstellungsinszenierung. Im nördlichen Teil umfasst er einen Raum von 21 m x 21 m Grundfläche und 18 m Höhe, dessen Dach von neun schlanken kreuzförmigen Stahlstützen getragen wird. Die Rauminszenierung erfolgt in allen Bereichen mittels Lichtmodulation. Der Christusraum empfängt mittig über den Säulenköpfen Oberlicht, das die Vertikalität der schlanken Säulen betont. Die umhüllende Fläche aus Glas und Marmor bildet eine lichtdurchlässige Schale, deren lebendige Farbigkeit die Raumstimmung erzeugt. Der umlaufende Kreuzgang hat eine zweischalige Glasfassade, deren Zwischenräume mit Materialien verschiedenster Art aus Natur und Technik als Bestandteil einer Gesamtdramaturgie gefüllt sind.

The architecture of the Pavilion is restricted to the clear presentation of the modular construction and its details. The surrounding cloister frames the overall complex and simultaneously functions as an exhibition space. In the north the cloister comprises a voluminous hall 21 m square and 18 m high, with its roof supported by nine slender, cross-formed steel columns. The spatial atmosphere of all areas is created by a modulation of light. The 'Christ Hall' receives light from top lights centrally located above the column heads, emphasizing the vertical quality of the slender columns. The surrounding surfaces of thinly cut marble laminated with glass form a light-transmissive envelope, its lively colours creating a spatial atmosphere. The surrounding cloister is equipped with a double glass façade, the space between filled with materials from nature and technology as part of an overall dramaturgy.

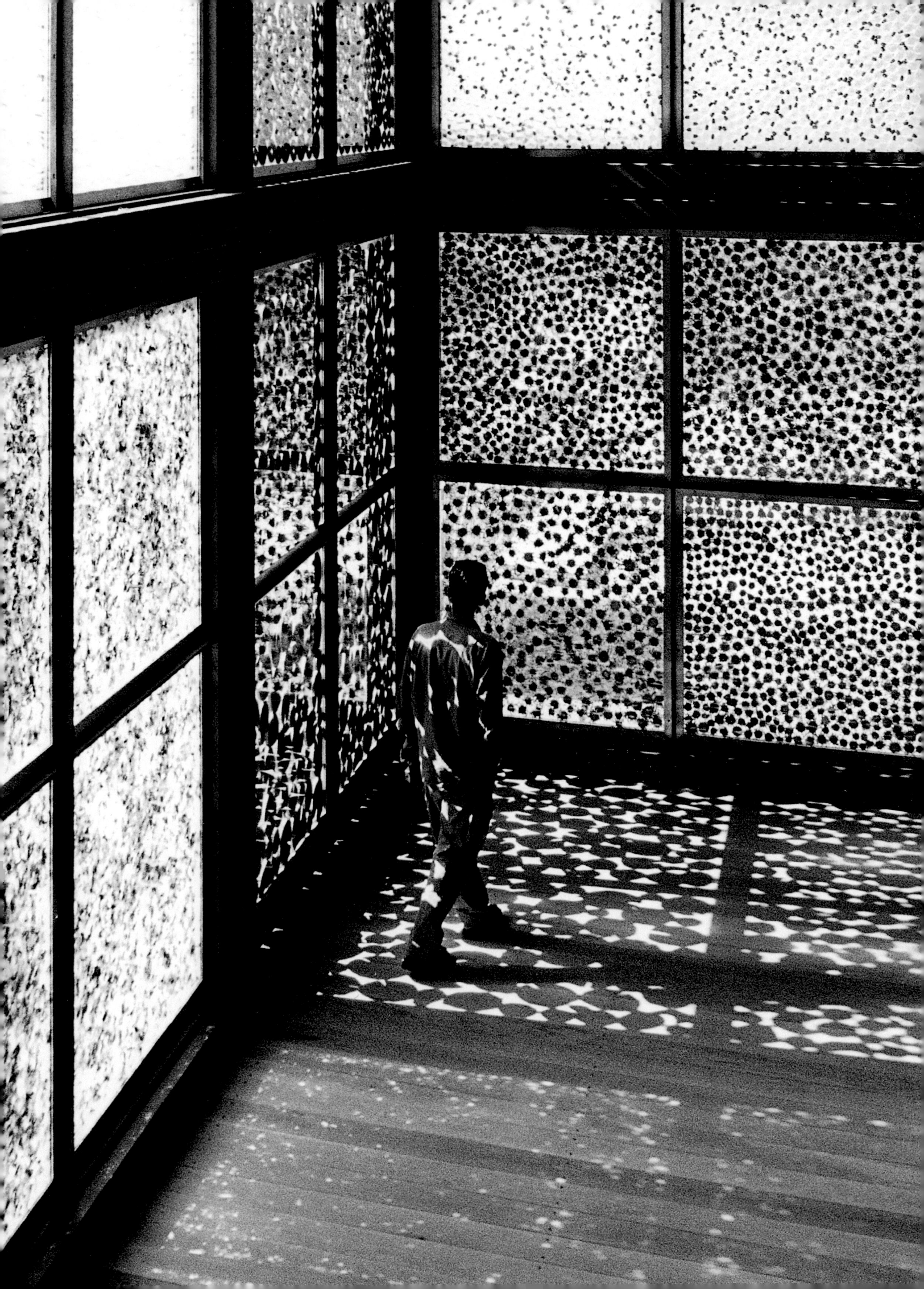

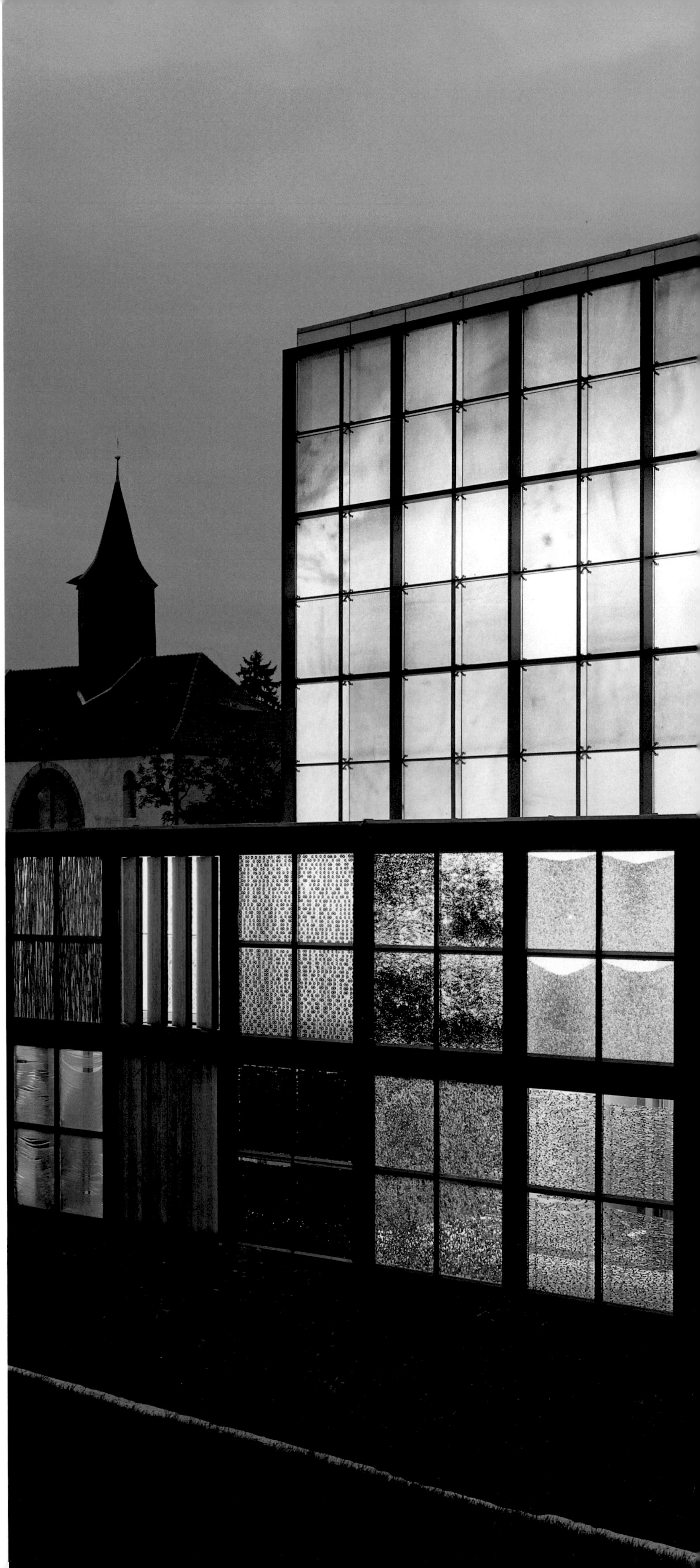

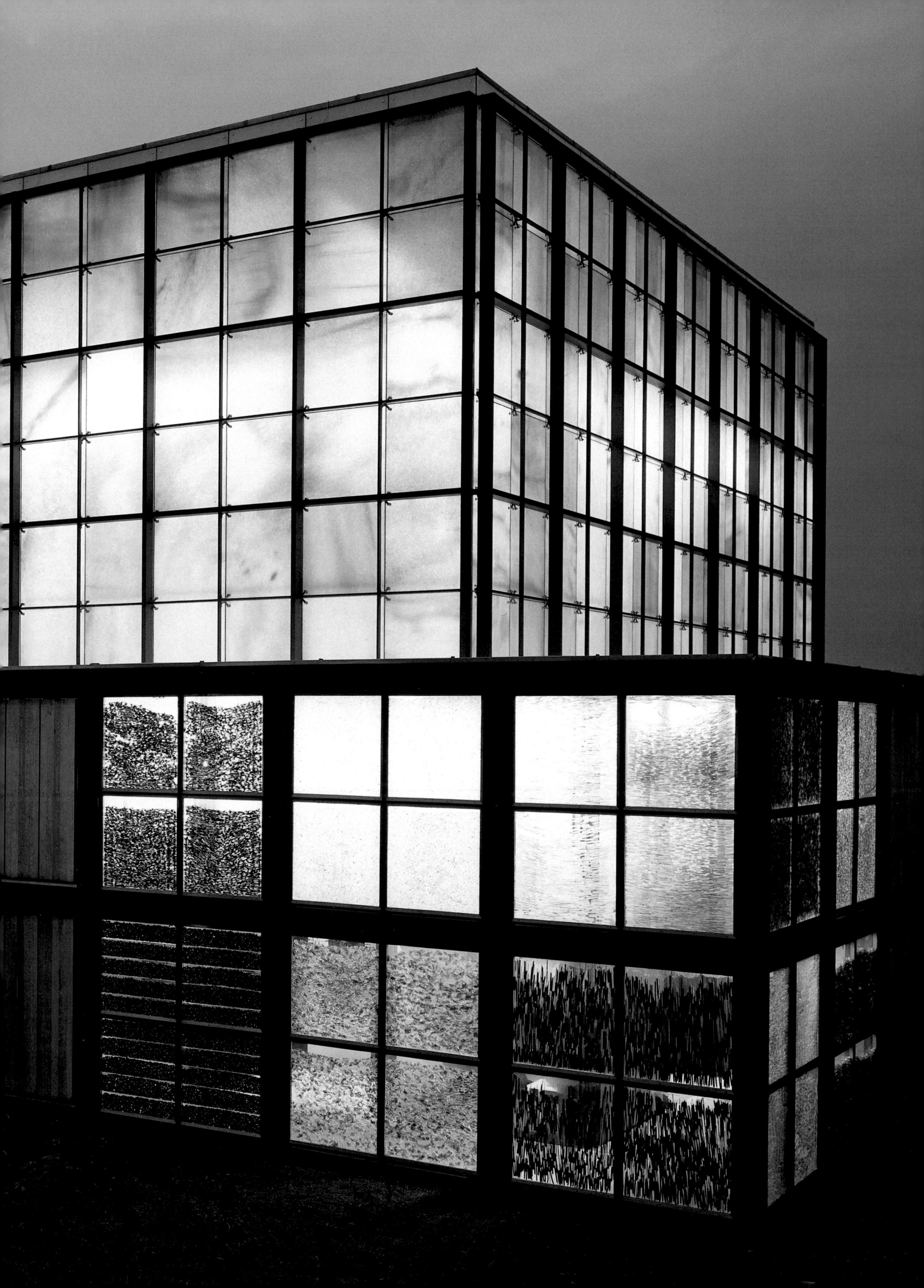

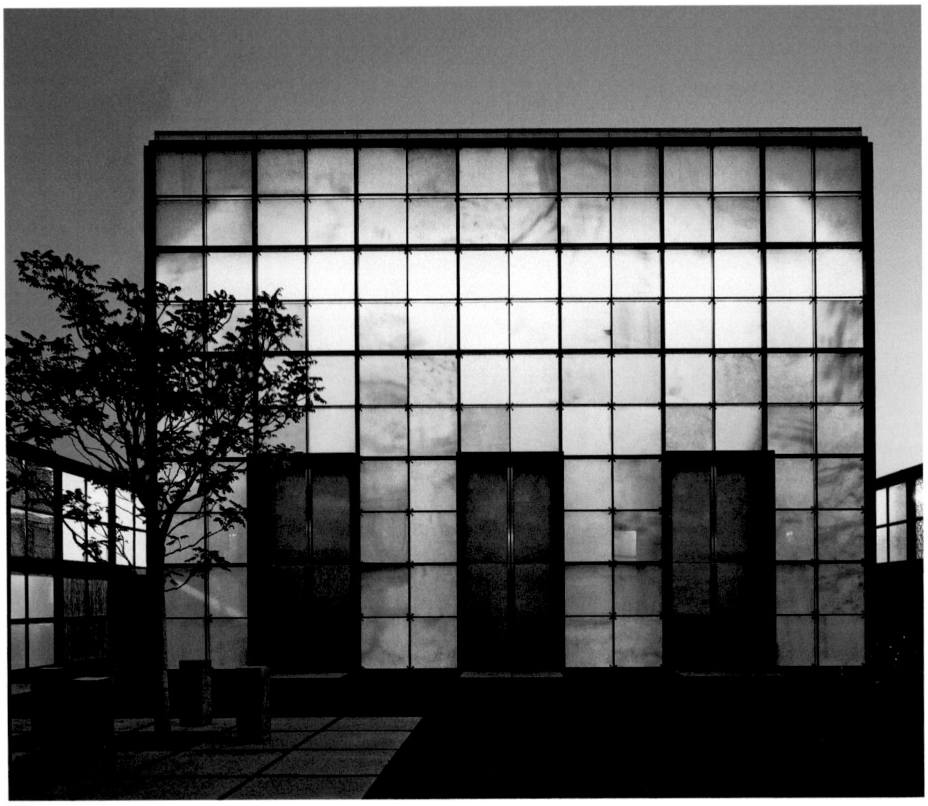

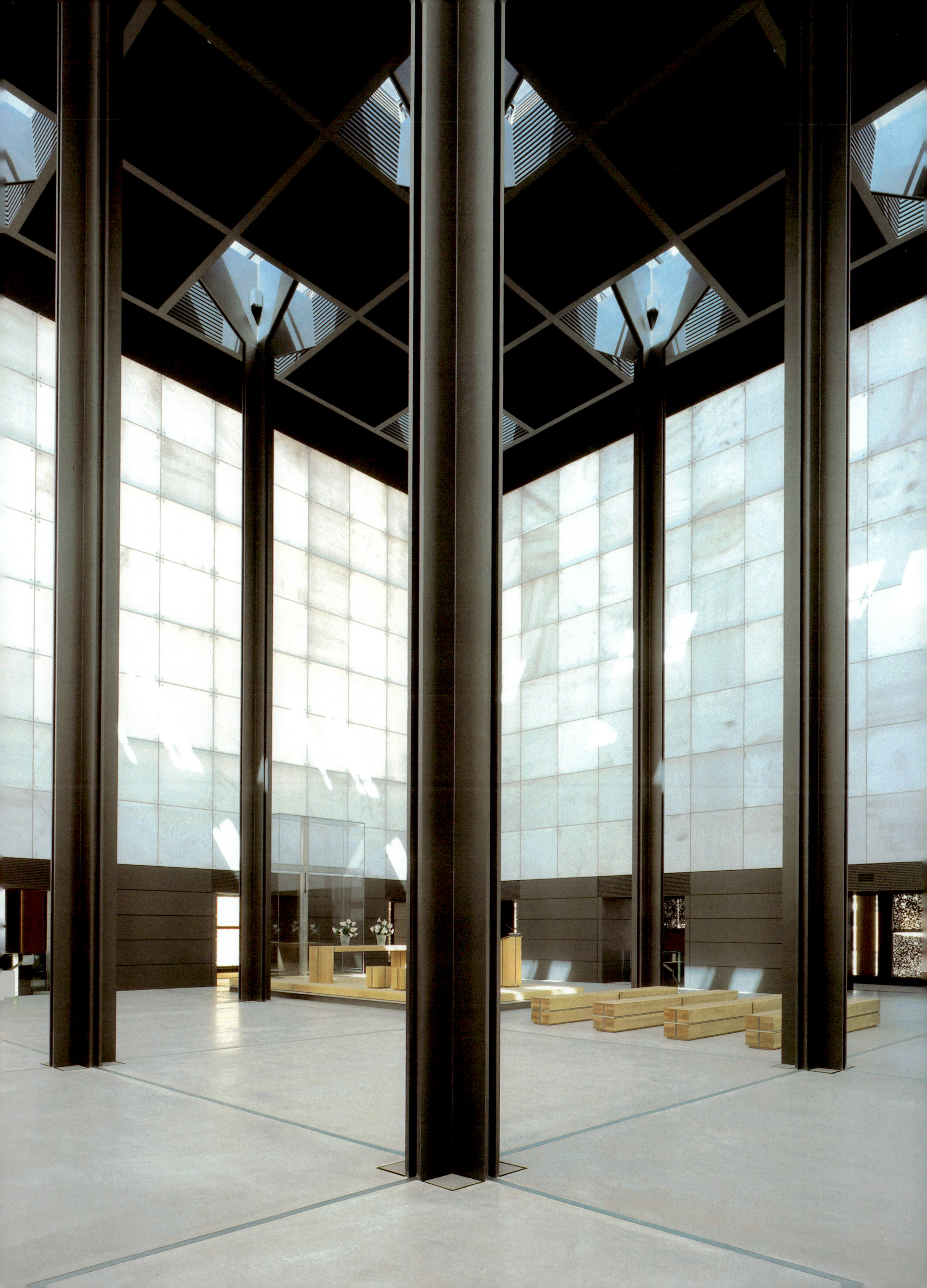

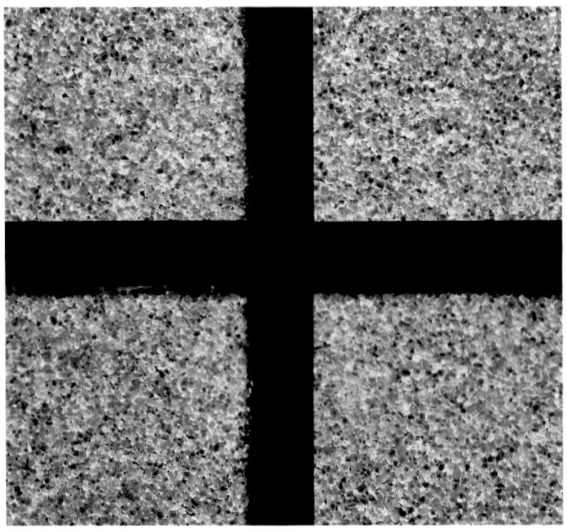

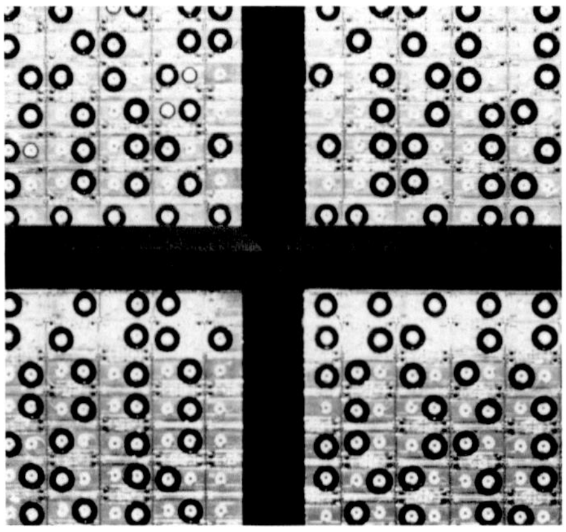

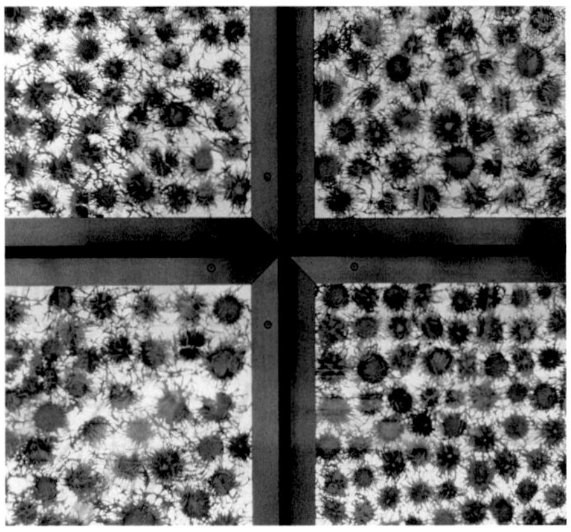

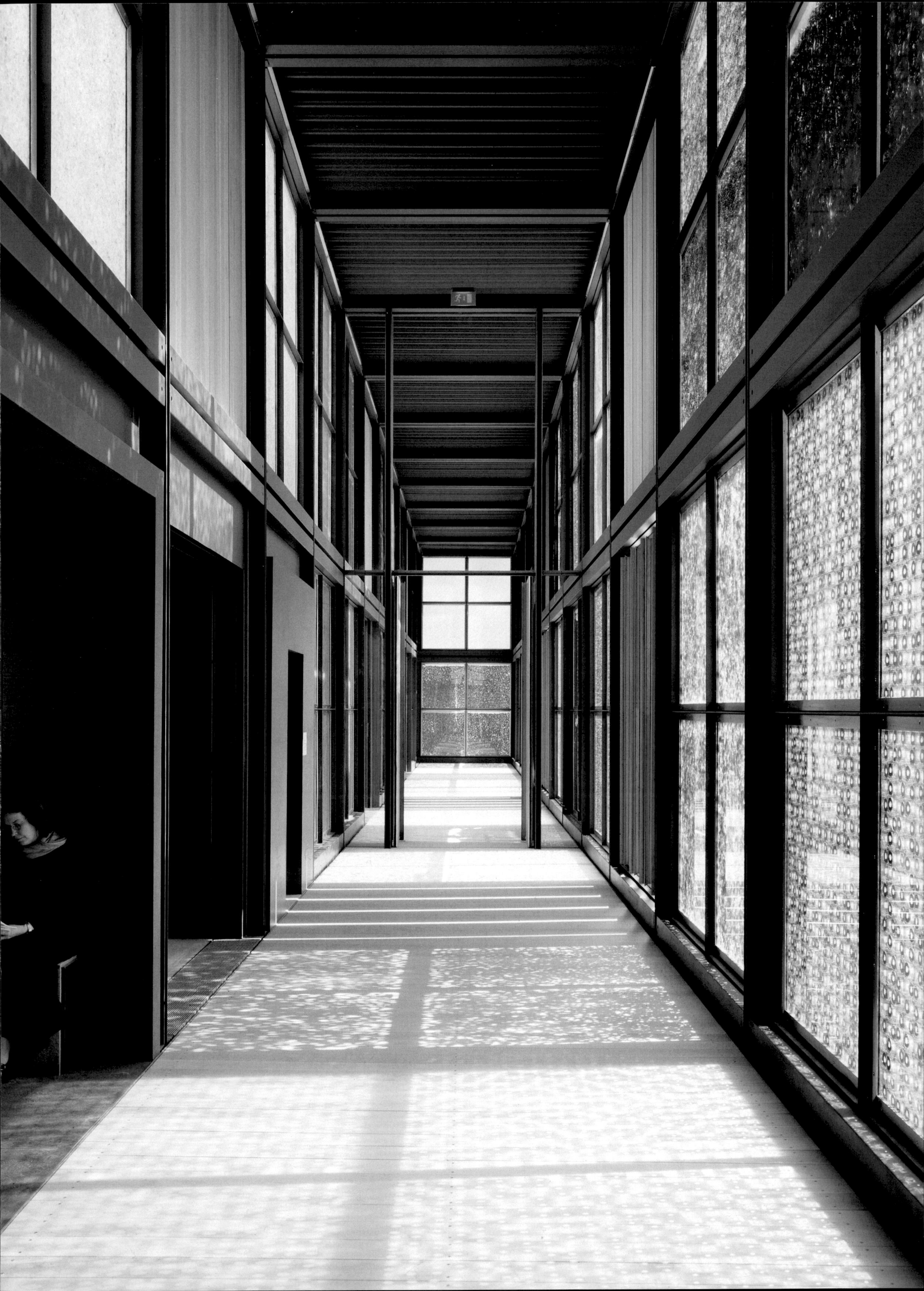

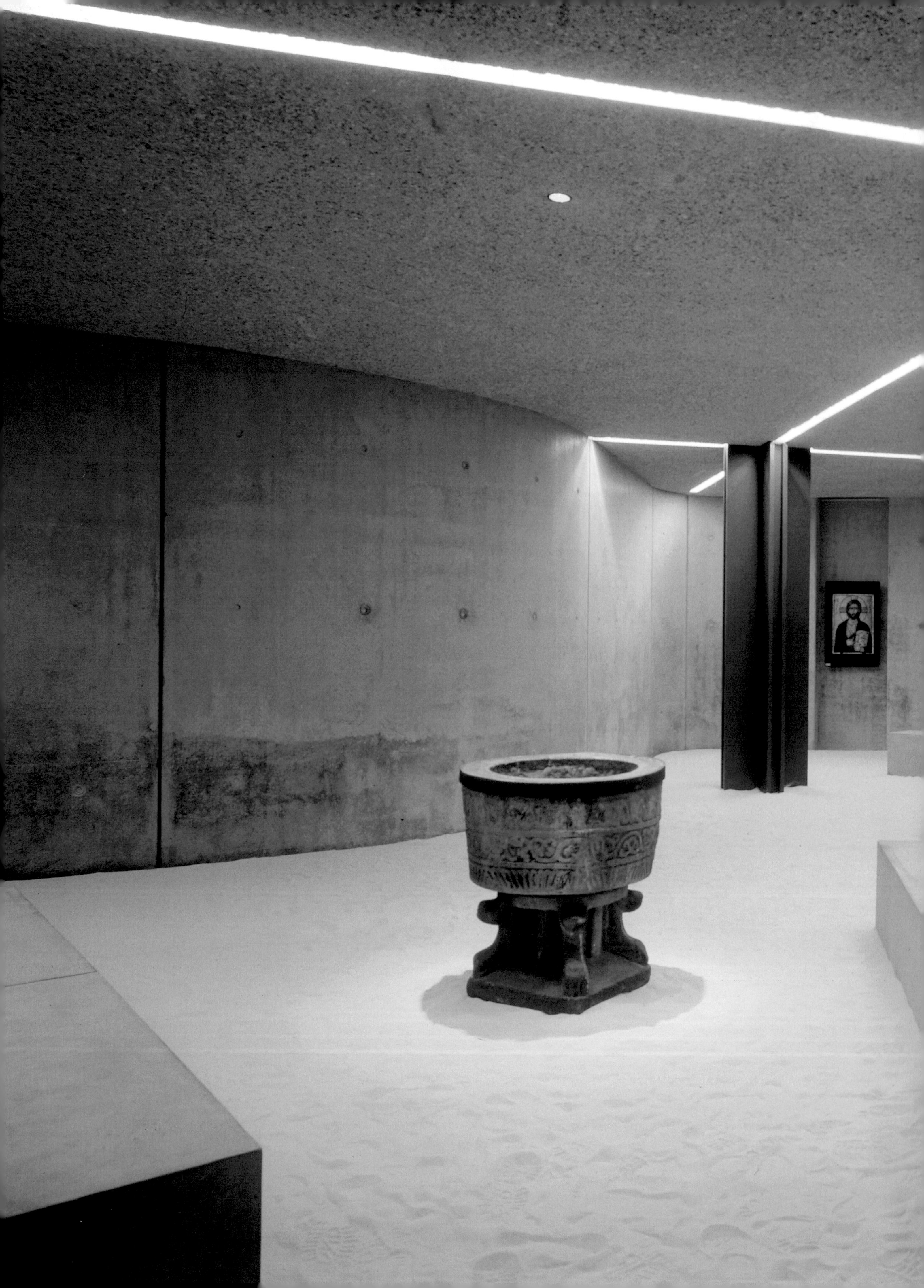

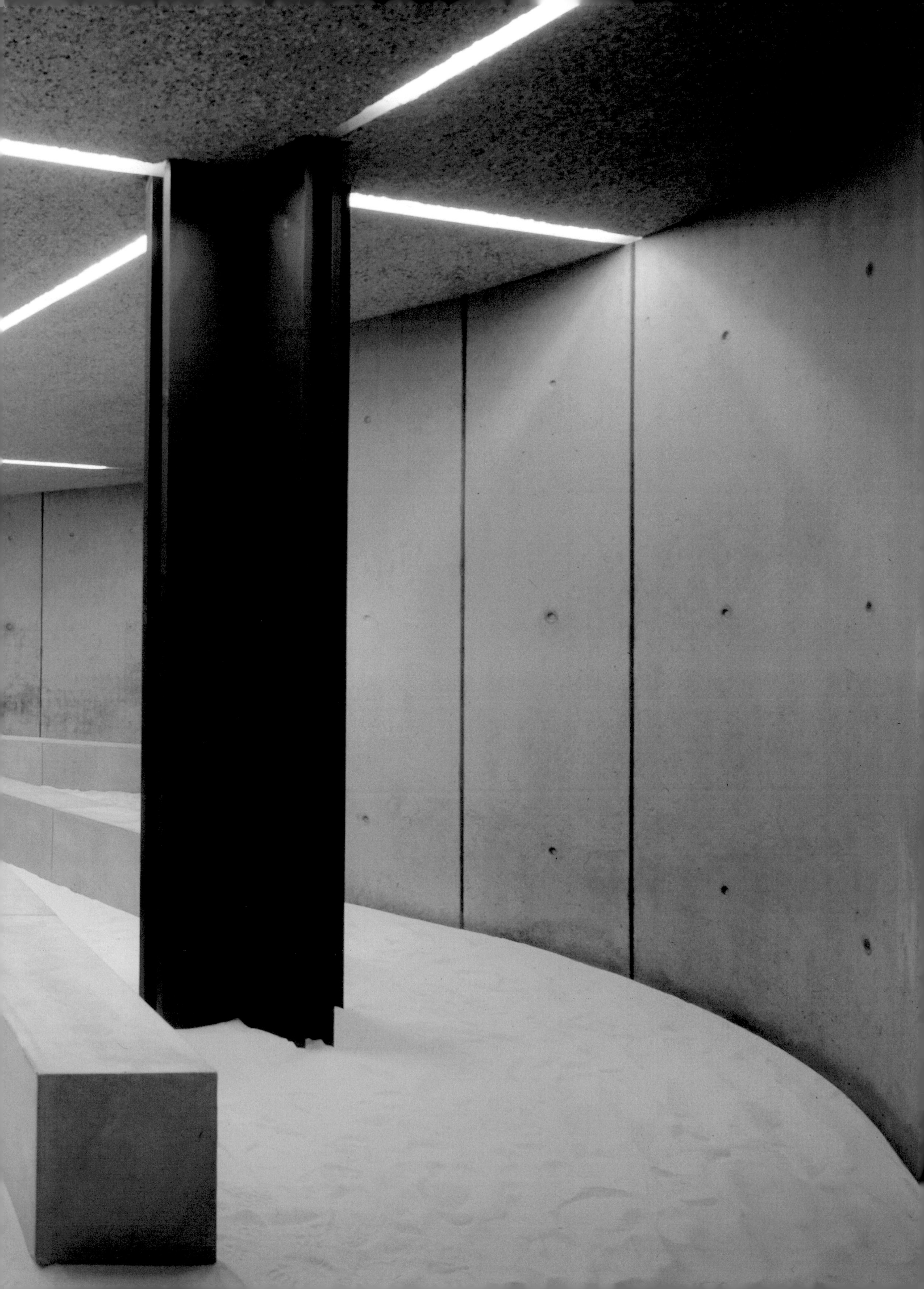

360

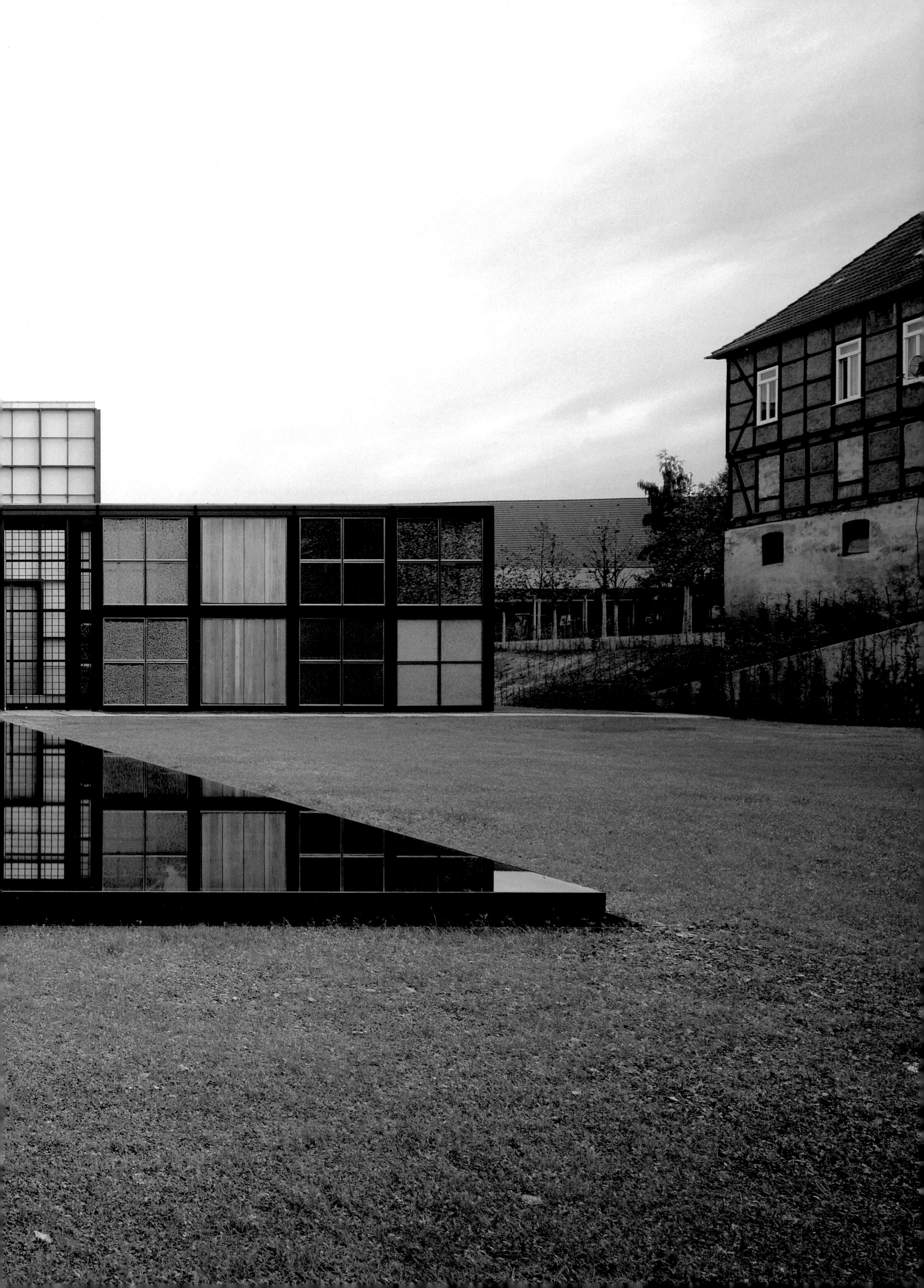

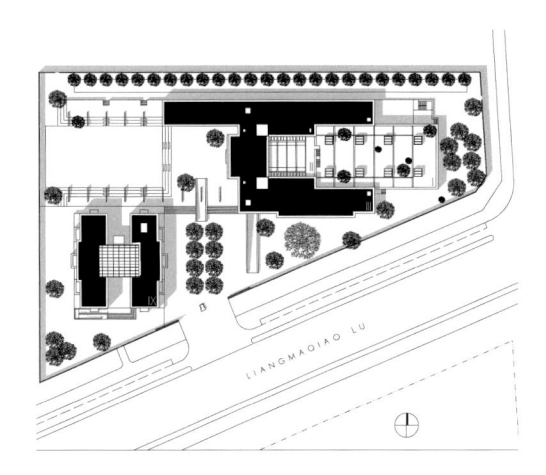

Deutsche Schule und Apartmenhaus, Peking, China
German School and Apartment House, Beijing, China

Wettbewerb Competition
1998 – 1. Preis

Entwurf Design
Meinhard von Gerkan mit Michael Biwer

Partner Partner
Klaus Staratzke

Bauherr Client
Bundesrepublik Deutschland, BBR

Bauzeit Construction period
1999–2000

BGF Gross floor area
Schule: 9.660 m²
Apartments: 9.660 m²

Das Ensemble wird aus einem horizontal geprägten Schulgebäude und einem vertikalen Wohnkomplex gebildet. Beim Schulgebäude flankieren zwei dreigeschossige Riegel die mittlere Schicht der Sondernutzungen. In den Obergeschossen schließen die Klassenflügel begrünte Dachgärten ein, die die Freifläche der Schule erweitern. Über eine offene Glashalle sind die beiden parallel stehenden, neungeschossigen Riegel des Wohngebäudes miteinander verbunden. Gliederung und Materialien für Fassade und Innenräume folgen den Überlegungen für das Schulgebäude. So wird das Farbkonzept der kaiserlichen Farben rot und gelb auch im Wohngebäude fortgesetzt. Vom Schulgebäude mit seiner roten Fassade aus Betonfertigteilen und den roten Bodenbelägen im Innenraum unterscheidet sich das Wohngebäude durch seine gelbe Betonfertigteil-Fassade sowie gelbe Bodenbeläge.

The ensemble is formed by a horizontally emphasized school building and a contrasting vertical residential complex. At the school building, two three-storey building bars flank the central layer with special uses. On the upper levels classroom wings integrate landscaped roof terraces, which enlarge the open space of the school. An open glass hall connects two parallel, nine-storey building bars of the residential building. Division and materials for façade and interior follow the considerations made for the school building. Consequently, the colour concept of the imperial red and yellow colours is repeated in the residential block. The school building, with its red façade from pre-fabricated concrete elements and red floorings in the interior, differs from the residential block with its yellow pre-fabricated concrete façade elements and yellow floorings.

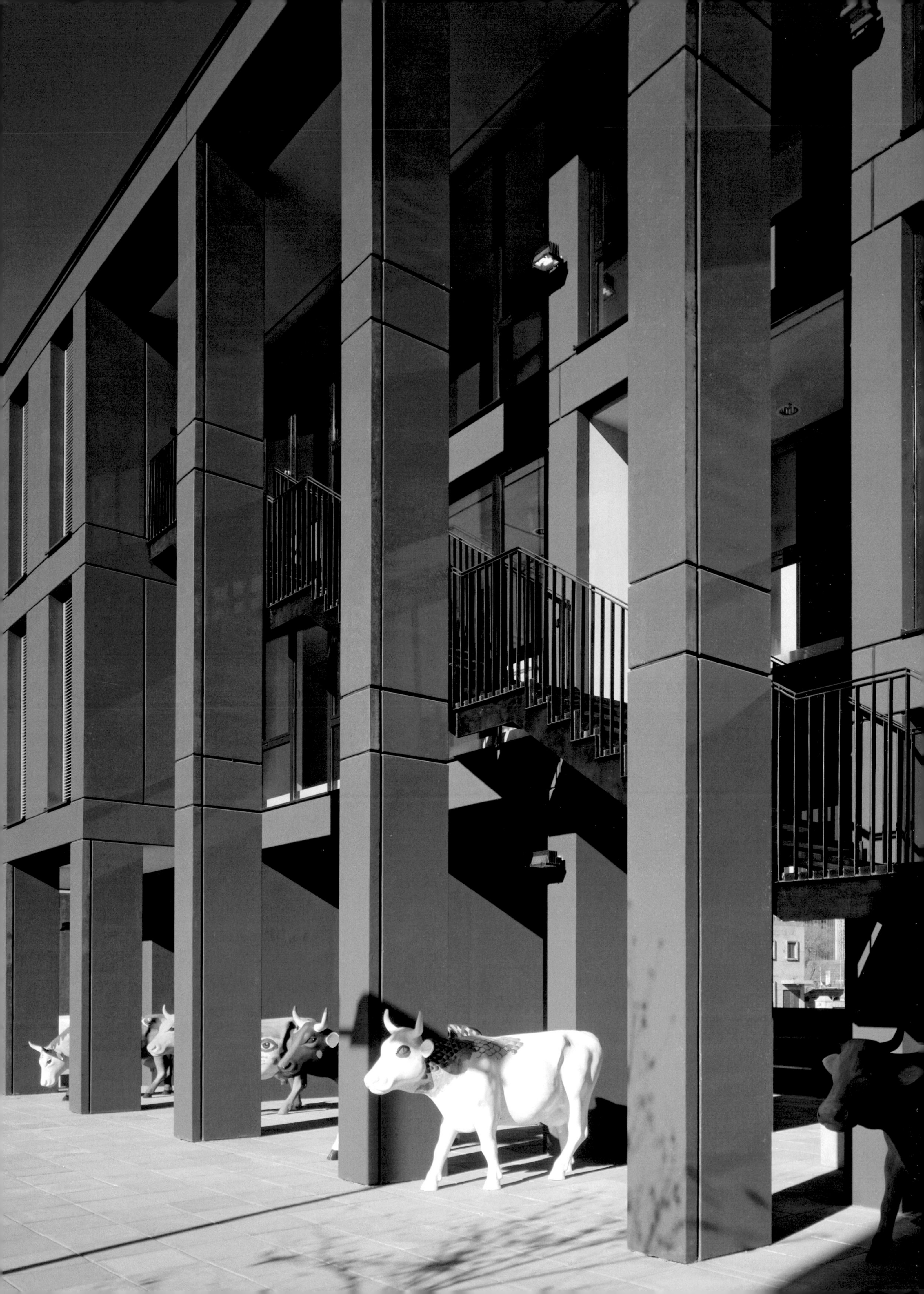

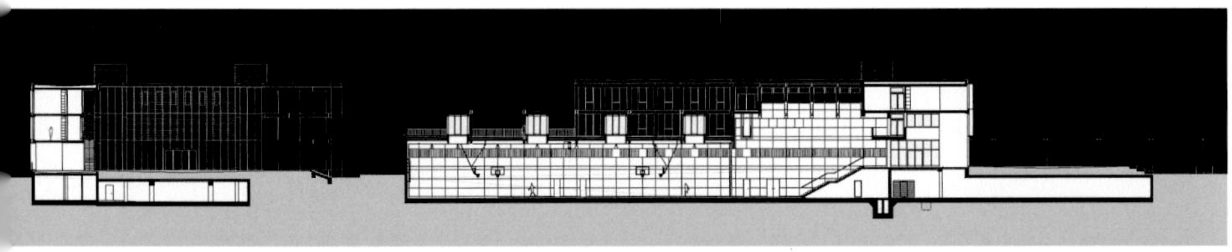

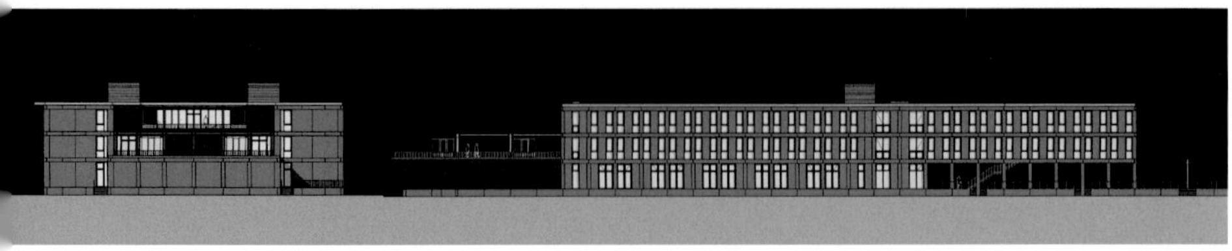

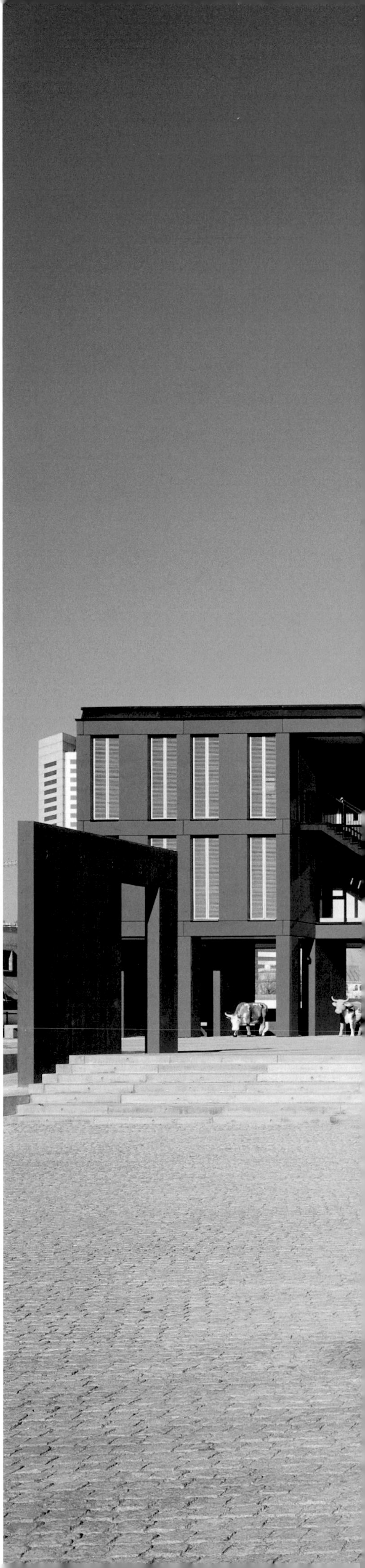

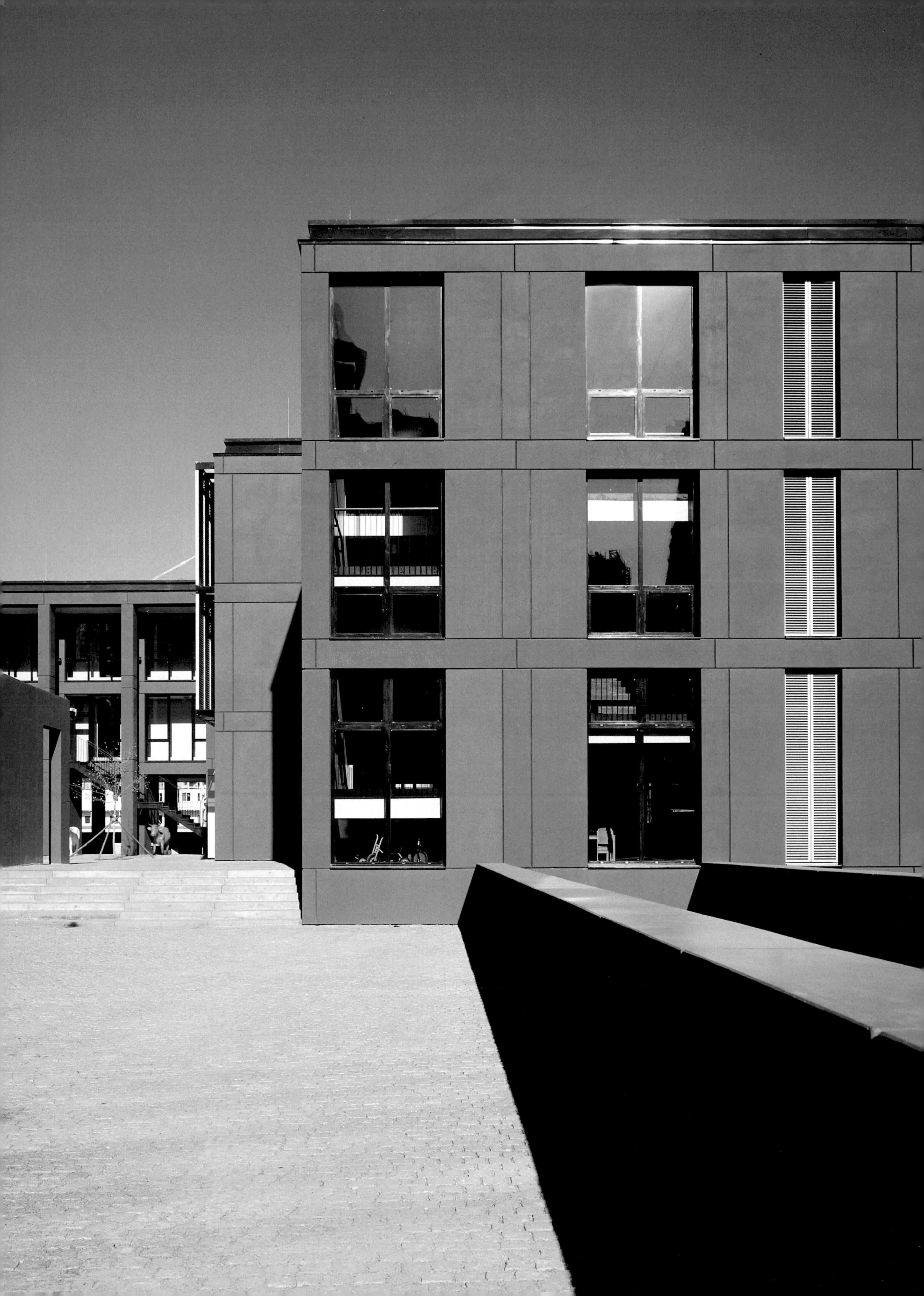

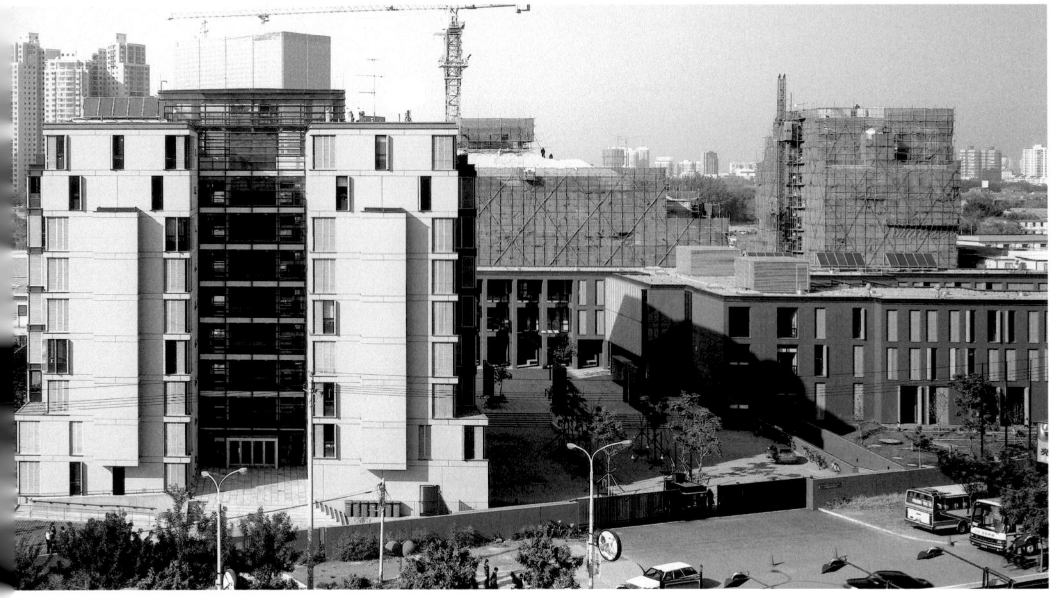

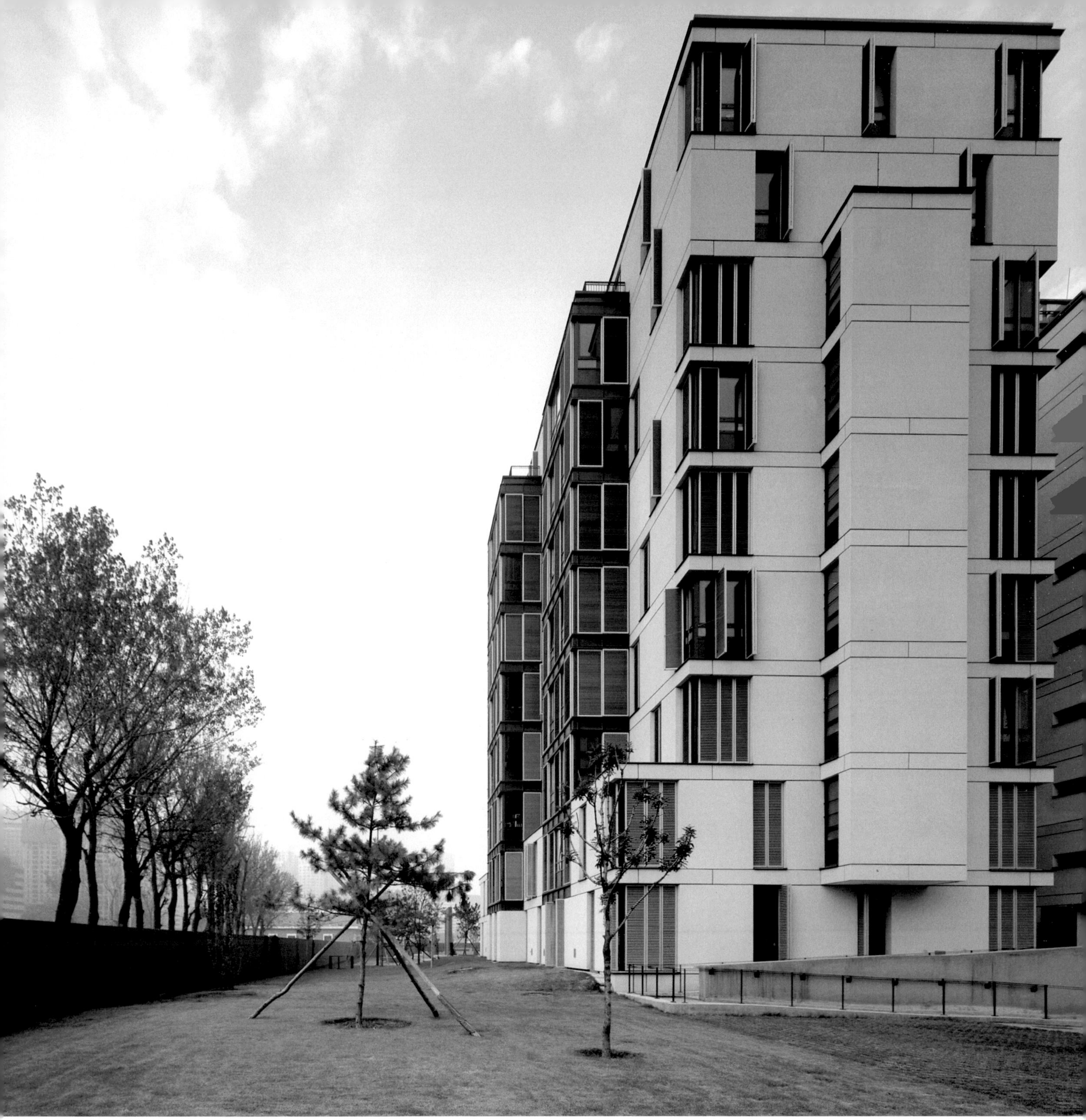

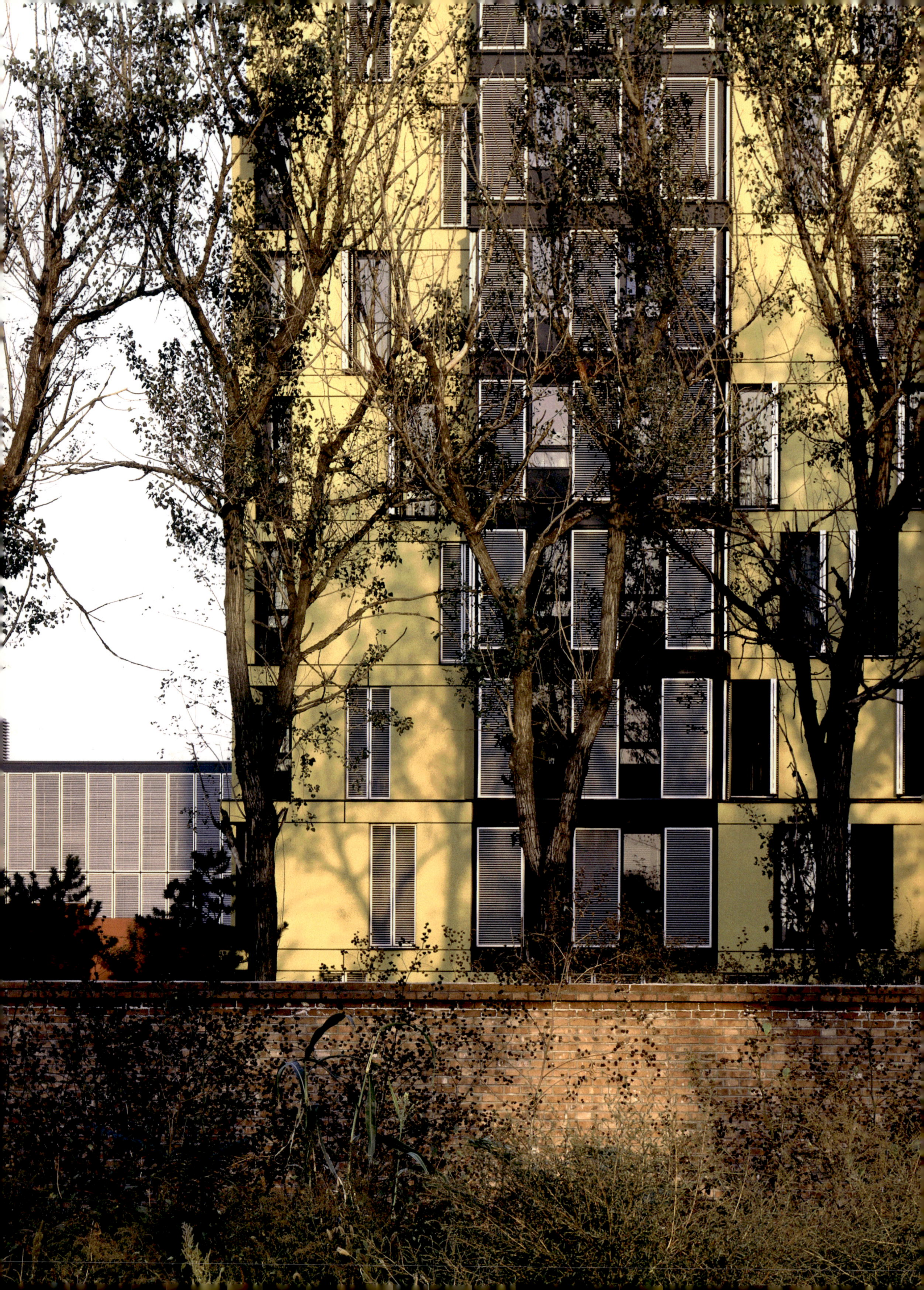

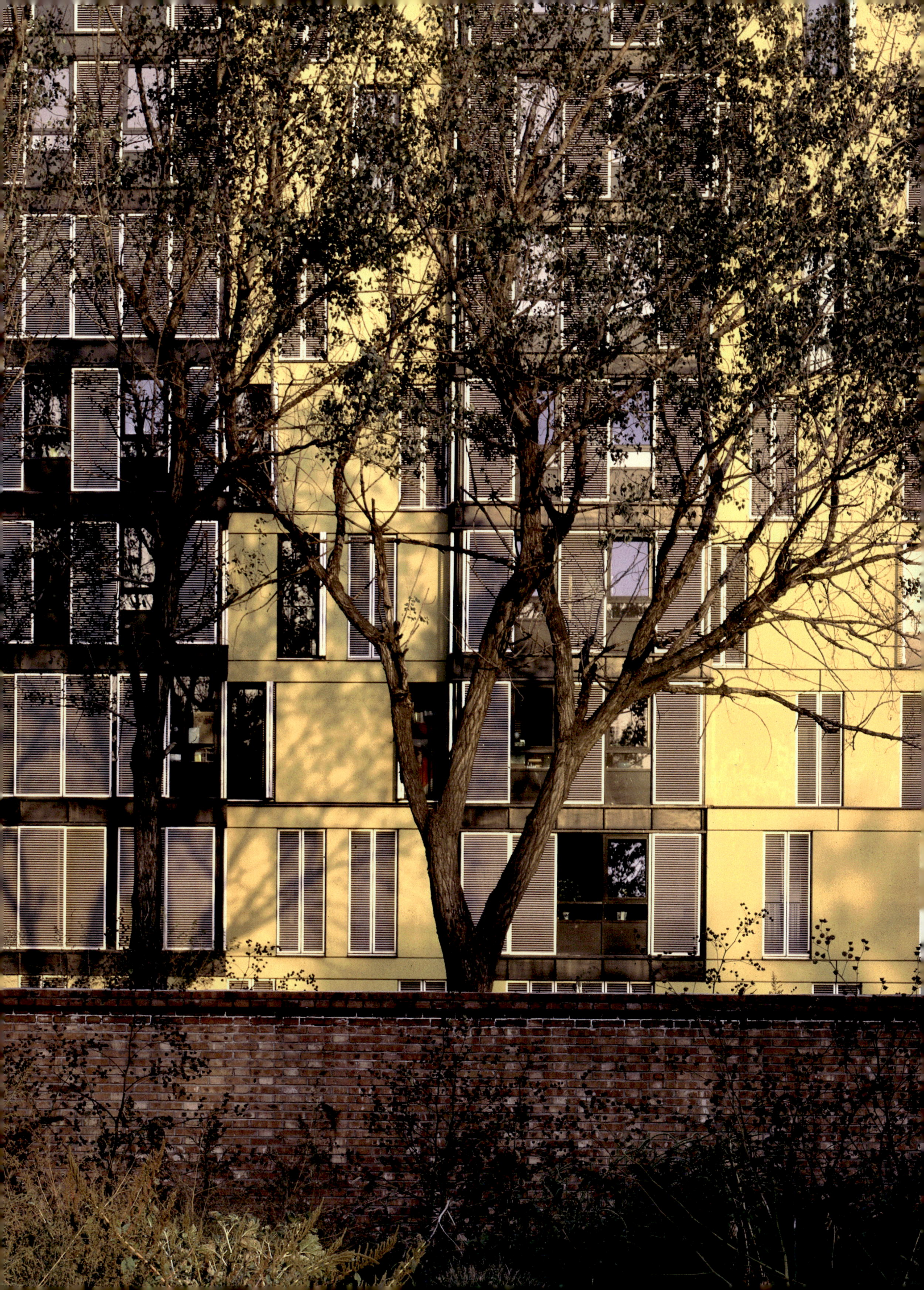

Fußgängerbrücken EXPO 2000, Hannover
Expo 2000 Pedestrian Bridges, Hanover

Wettbewerb Competition
1996 – 1. Preis

Entwurf Design
Volkwin Marg mit Jörg Schlaich

Bauherr Client
EXPO 2000 Hannover GmbH und
Deutsche Messe AG, Hannover

Bauzeit Construction period
1998-2000

Brücke Mitte Central bridge
127,5 m x 30,0 m

Brücke Ost Eastern bridge
90,0 m x 15,0 m

Brücke Nord-Ost North-eastern bridge
142,5 m x 15,0 m

Brücke Süd Southern bridge
90,0 m x 7,5 m

Die Markierung der Ein- und Übergänge benutzt die Metapher des Begrüßungs-Spaliers: Die hohen Stelen, die sich zu ihrer Spitze hin durch einen 1,50 m langen, leuchtenden Glaszylinder „entmaterialisieren", werden wie Mastenwälder durchschritten. Um auf unterschiedliche Situationen flexibel reagieren zu können, sind die Brücken so konstruiert, dass sie die verschiedenen Anforderungen an Länge und Breite, Umbau oder Abbau ohne Veränderung der Gestaltung ermöglichen. Das primäre Tragsystem bilden die Stützen als Teil des Mastenwaldes und die Aufhängungen aus Diagonalen und Ober- und Untergurt. In dieses Tragwerk werden die modularen Füllelemente eingelegt. Die Stützen sind in einem Raster von 7,50 m x 7,50 m auf kegelförmige Fundamentkörper aufgespannt. Trifft dieses Raster auf zu überbrückende Straßen oder Wege, sind die Stützen aufgehängt bzw. in ein abgespanntes Tragwerk eingebunden.

The marking of the entrances and passageways used the metaphor of the welcoming guard of honour: high steles are passed through like forests of masts. Towards their top they seem to dematerialize due to a 1.5-m-long shining glass cylinder. In order to react flexibly to different situations, the bridge construction allows for various demands regarding length and width, conversion or disassembly without change of the overall appearance. The poles as part of the forest of masts and the suspension from diagonals as well as top and bottom flanges form the primary load-bearing system. The modular filling elements are inserted into this load-bearing system. The columns are spanned on conical foundations at a grid of 7.5 m square. If this grid meets roads or paths to be crossed, the columns are suspended or integrated into a guyed structural framework.

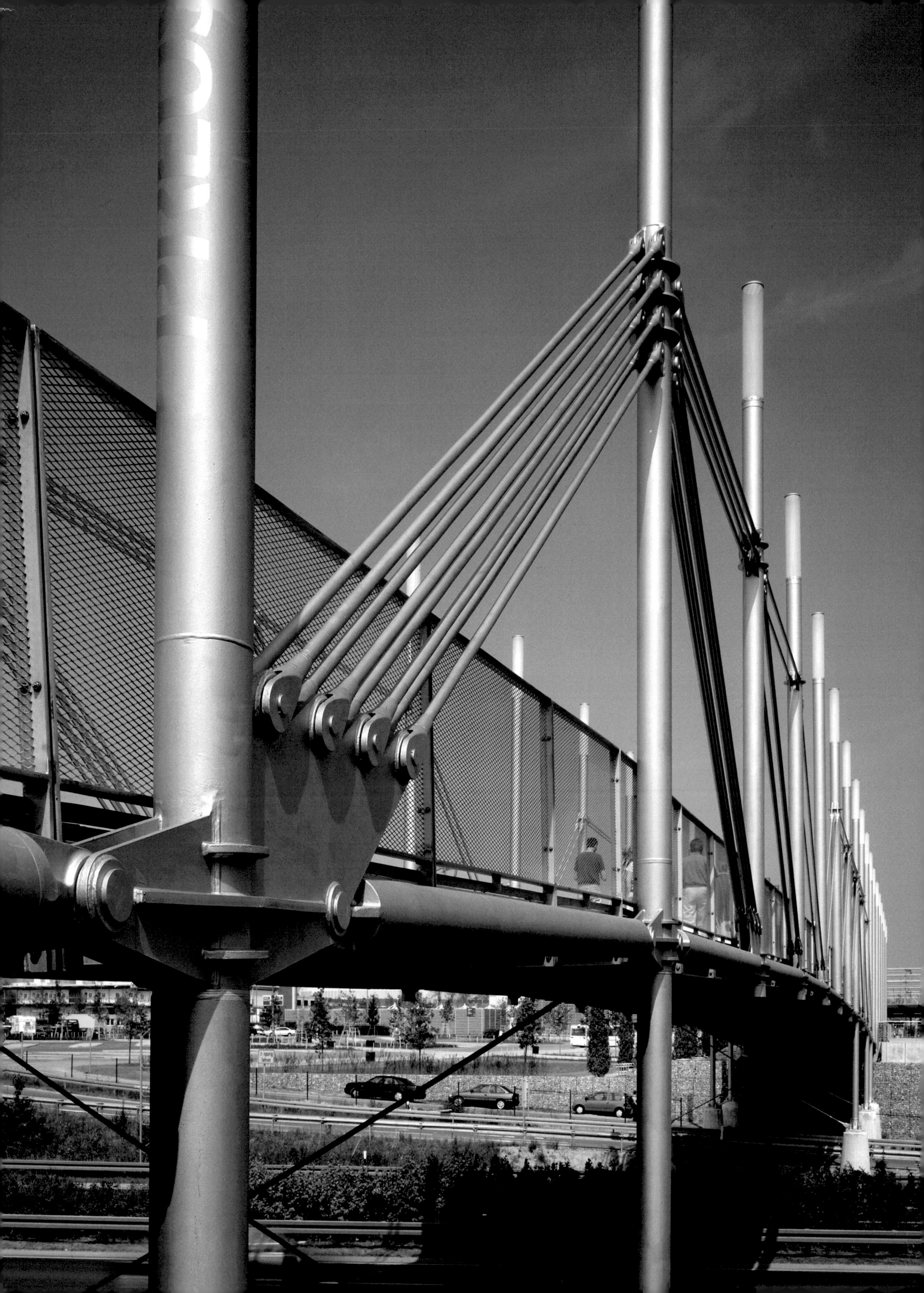

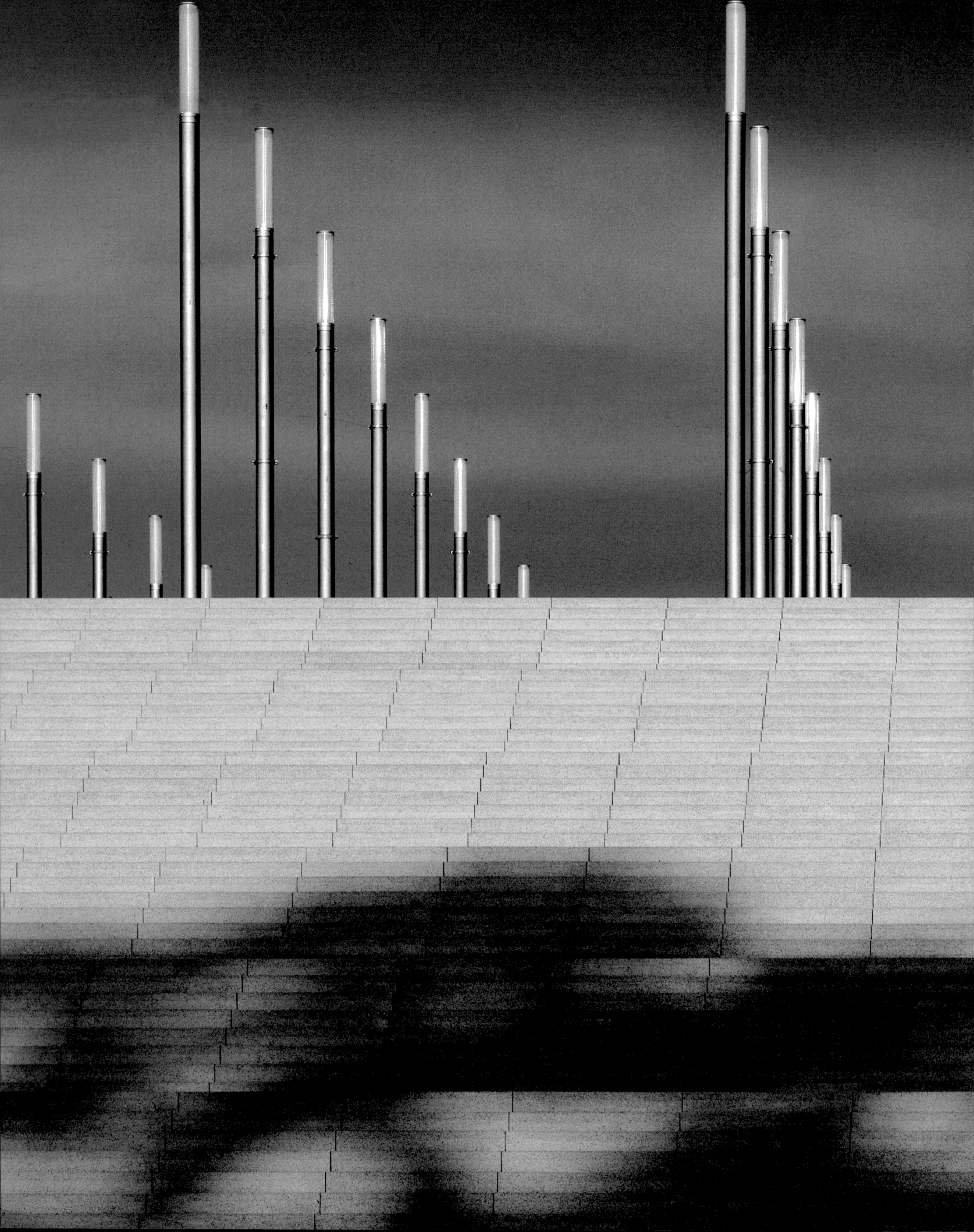

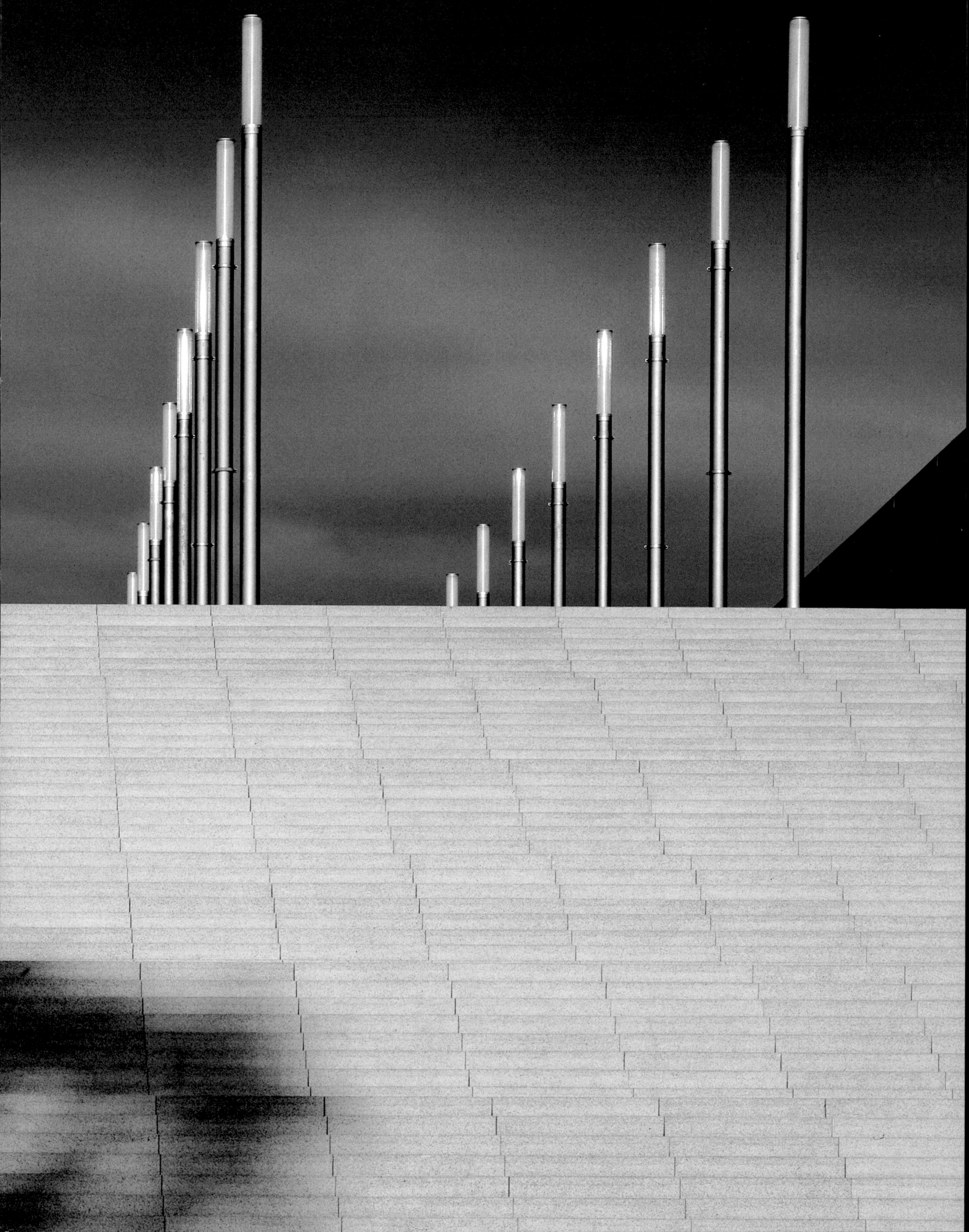

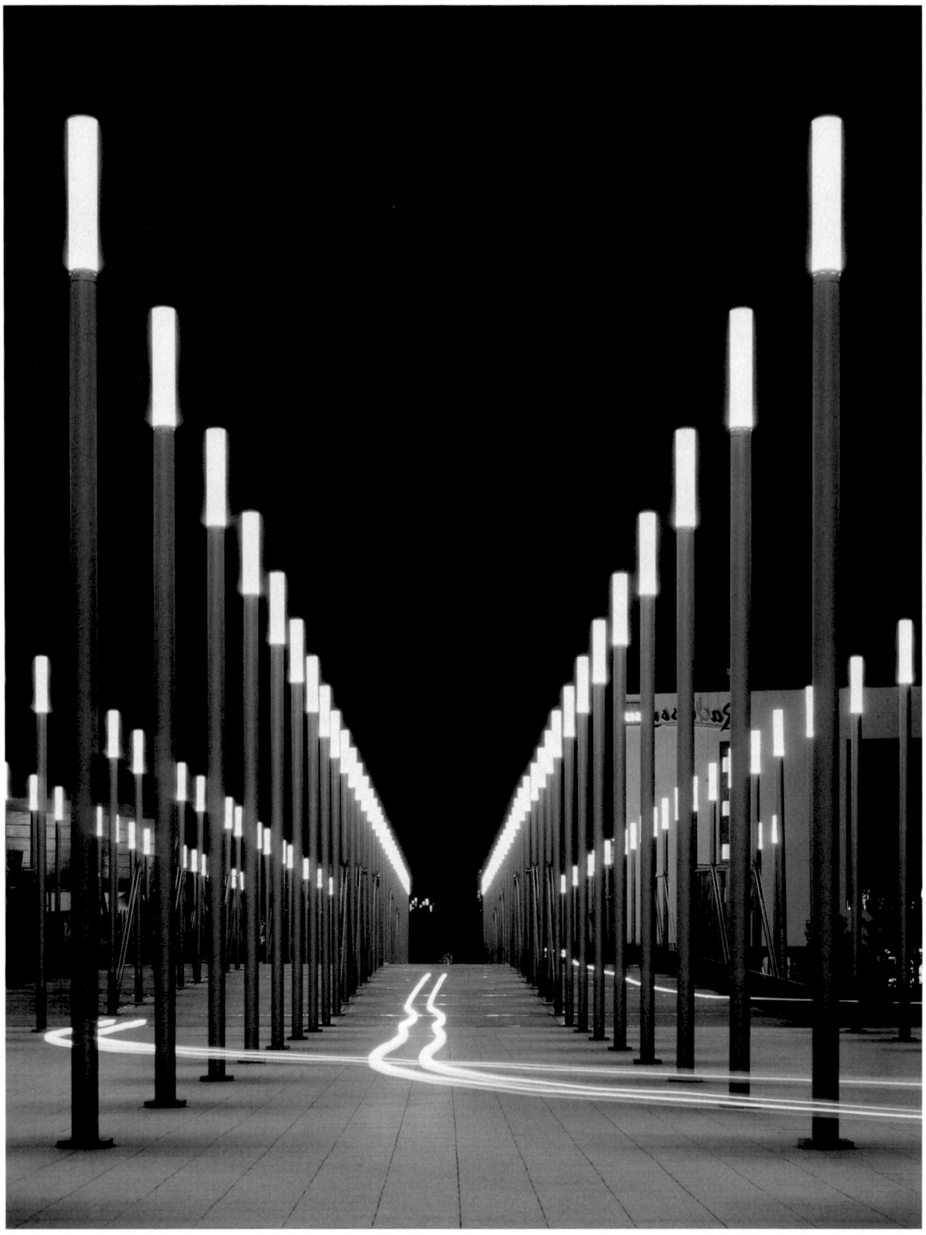

MESSE
GELÄNDE

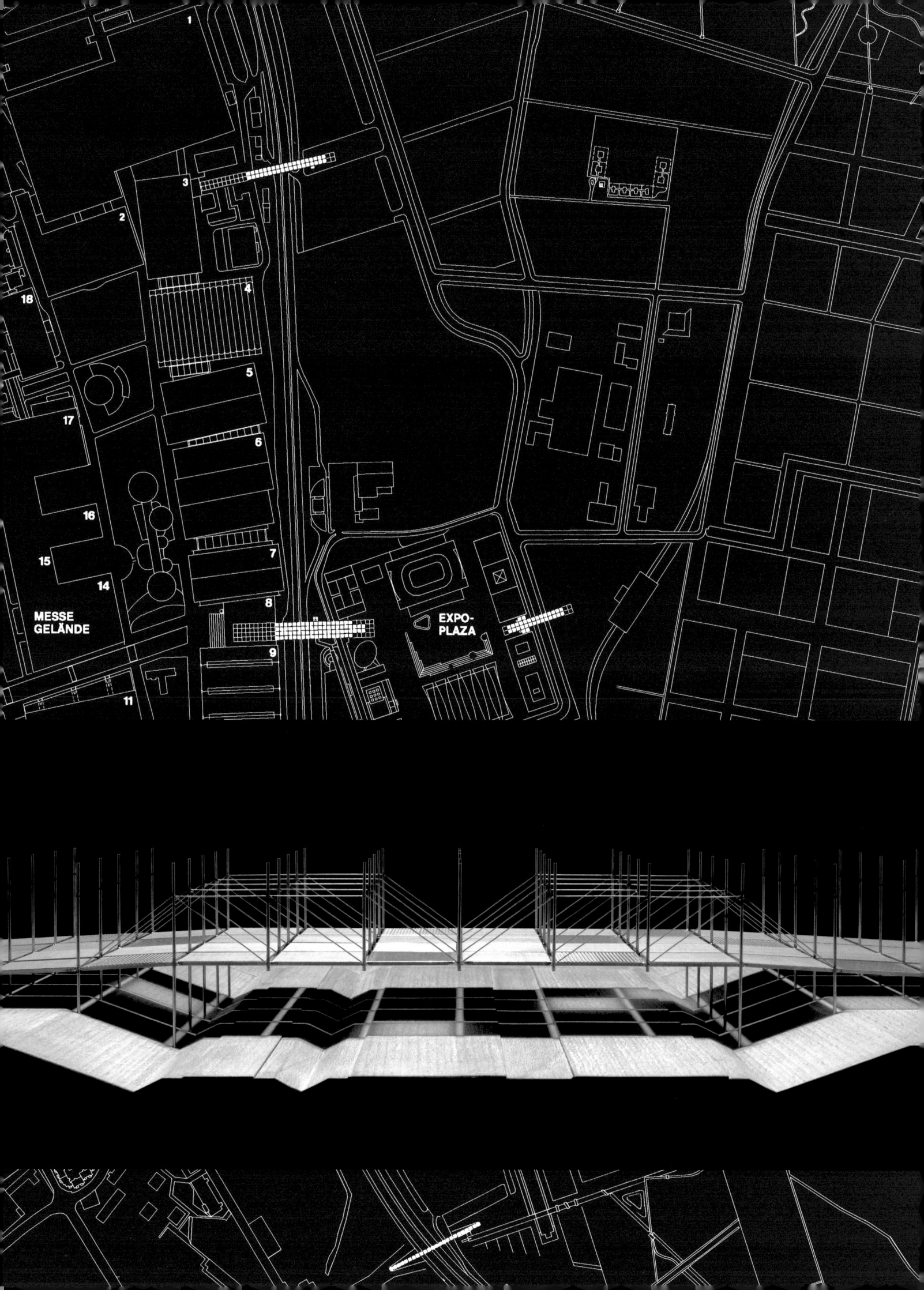

EXPO-
PLAZA

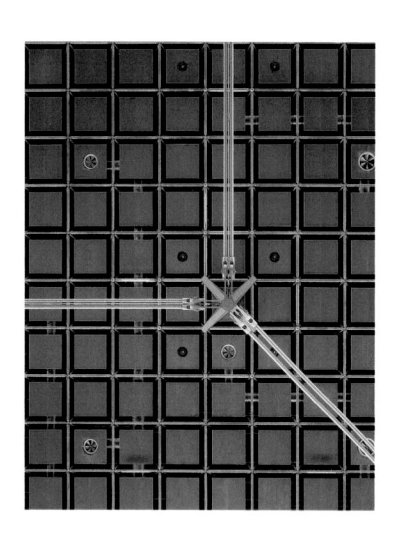

Messe Düsseldorf, Halle 6
Düsseldorf Trade Fair, Hall 6

Wettbewerb Competition
1997 – 1. Preis

Entwurf Design
Volkwin Marg

Bauherr Client
Messe Düsseldorf GmbH

Bauzeit Construction period
1998–2000

BGF Gross floor area
43.500 m²

Die von außen sichtbare Stahlkonstruktion der 160 x 160 m messenden Halle beruht auf vier sich kreuzenden Fachwerk-Kasten-Trägern, die auf vier Stützen liegen. Die überkragenden acht Enden entlasten die 90 Meter überspannenden Mittelträger. Zu diesem Zweck sind sie an ihren Enden durch Pendel-Zugstützen stabilisiert und durch die über dem Dach eingebauten Lüftungszentralen belastet. Im äußeren Bereich schließt das Dach an die Unterkante der Konstruktion, im Kernbereich an die Oberkante an. Daraus ergeben sich die unterschiedlichen Hallenhöhen von 20 und 30 Metern. Der gesamte Hallenraum wird von einem Gebäudering umschlossen, der als umlaufende Flaniergalerie dient und Sanitär- und Lagerräume, Büros und Restaurants aufnimmt. Mobile einschiebbare Tribünen mit ca. 12.000 Sitzplätzen erlauben die multifunktionale Nutzung der Halle 6 für Events jeder Art.

The steel construction of the 160-m² hall, visible from the outside, rests on four crossing box girders which are supported by four columns. The eight cantilevered ends relieve the spine beams spanning 90 metres. To achieve this aim, the ends are stabilized with tensile hinge columns and loaded with the ventilating plants installed on the roof. In the outer area the roof connects to the construction's bottom edge; in the central area to its top edge. This results in varying hall heights of 20 and 30 metres. The total hall space is enclosed by a massive element, which serves as a circulating gallery and houses offices and restaurants, as well as utility rooms such as sanitary and storage rooms. Movable grandstands with approximately 12,000 seats can be erected, allowing for a multipurpose usage of the hall for various events.

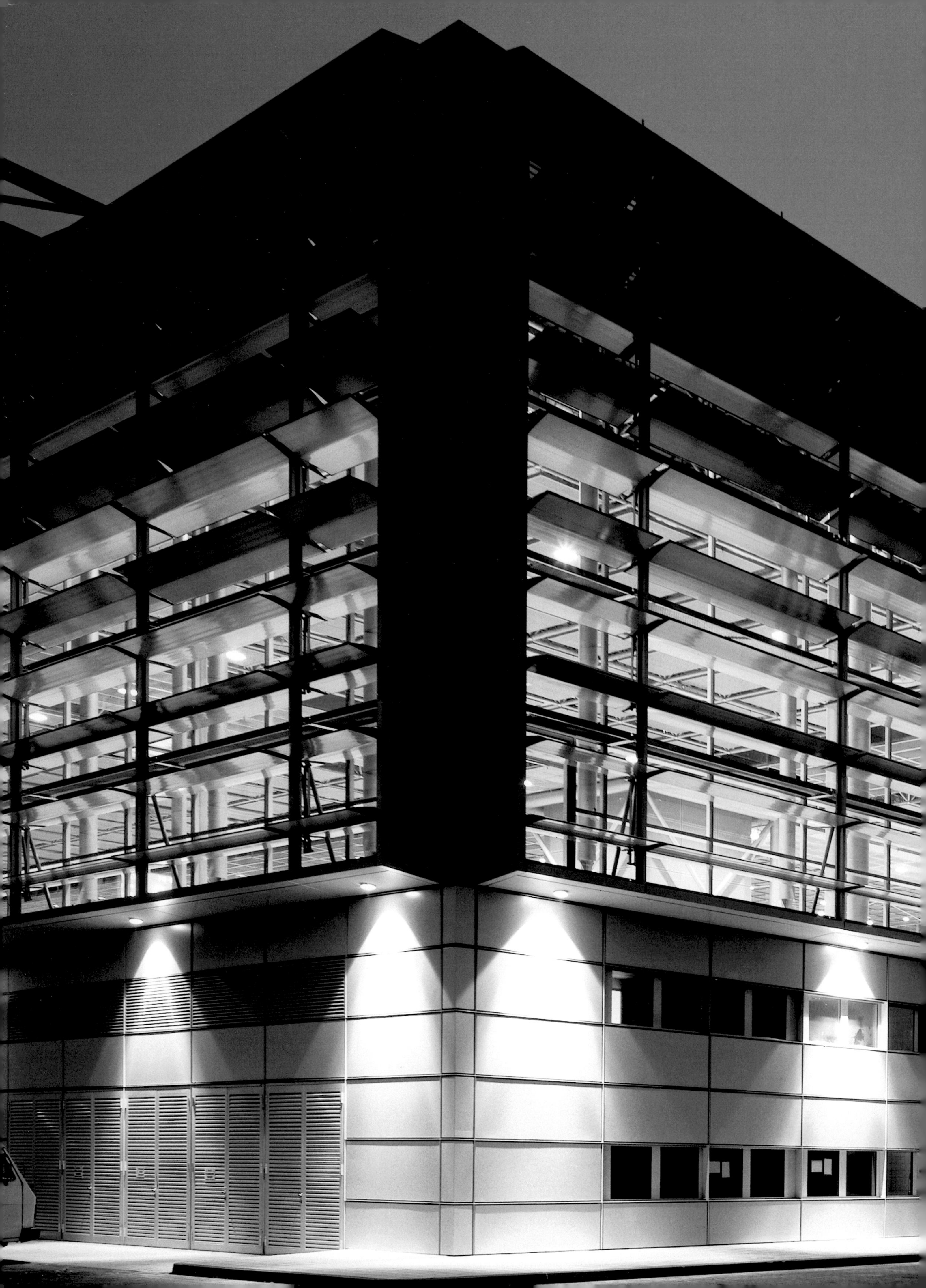

Ausstellungspavillon der TU Braunschweig
Exhibition Pavilion for the Braunschweig Institute of Technology

1999

Entwurf Design
Meinhard von Gerkan
und die Mitarbeiter des Instituts
für Baugestaltung A

Bauherr Client
TU Braunschweig

Bauzeit Construction period
1999–2000

BGF Gross floor area
400 m²

Weite Flügeltüren an der Westfassade des Pavillons öffnen sich zum baumbestandenen Innenhof und beziehen bei Veranstaltungen den Außenraum mit ein. Eine flexible Ausstellungsgestaltung mit 280 m² Hängefläche wird durch mobile 4 m² große Wandsegmente ermöglicht. Die Ausstellungswände können in „Parkpositionen" zusammengeschoben werden. Die architektonische Gestaltung mit einem Galeriegeschoss, die Reduktion auf einfache Materialien (Sichtbeton, Stahl und Glas) mit Geschosshöhen von 3 Metern und 15 x 15 Metern Grundfläche lassen den Pavillon als lichten Kubus wirken. Die zweischalige Fassade aus Glasstegplatten, in die eine transluzente Wärmedämmung eingefügt ist, bedingt den für Ausstellungszwecke geeigneten indirekten Lichteinfall. Das Gebäude verändert sein Gesicht je nach Tageszeit: tagsüber ist es schillernd-reflektierend, nachts ein leuchtender Kubus.

Wide leaf doors on the west façade open up towards the inner courtyard with trees and integrate the outdoor space during events. Mobile wall segments of 4 m² allow for flexible exhibition concepts with a 280-m² hanging area. The exhibition walls can be stored in so-called 'parking positions'. The architectural concept with one gallery level, the reduction to simple materials (fair-faced concrete, steel and glass), storey heights of 3 metres and floor bases of 15 metres square make the pavilion appear as a light cube. The double-skin façade of glass planks with integrated translucent thermal insulation produces the indirect incidence of light suitable for exhibition purposes. The building changes its appearance according to the time of day: during the day it is shimmering and reflecting; at night it is a shining cube.

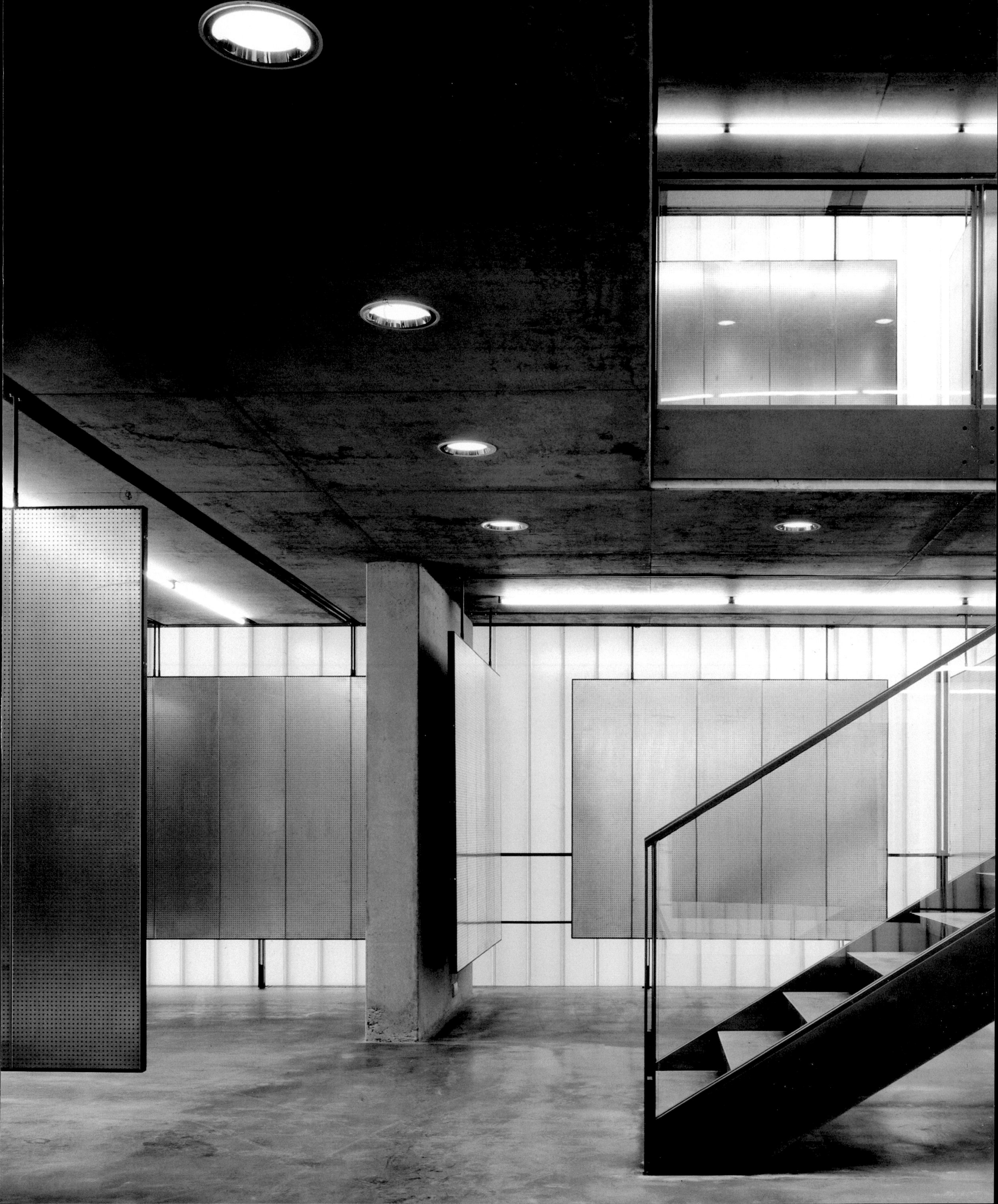

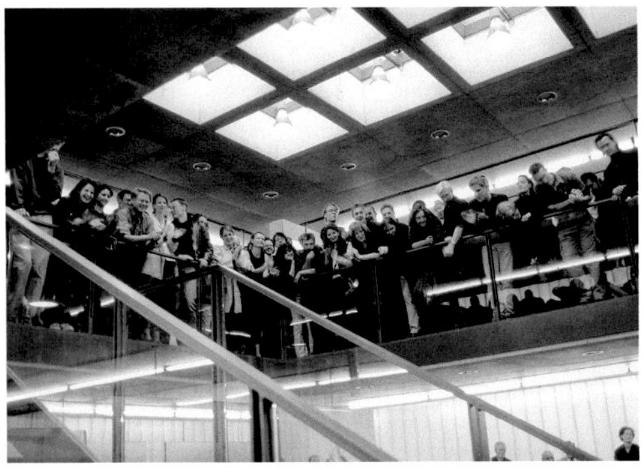

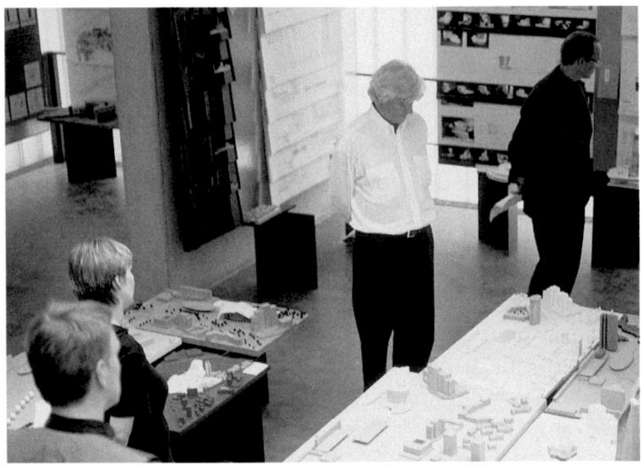

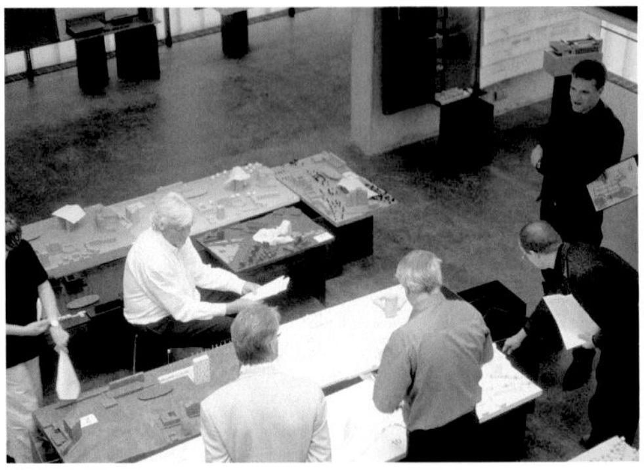

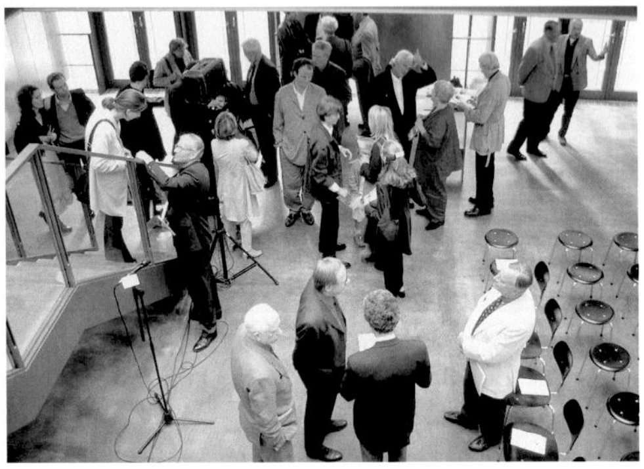

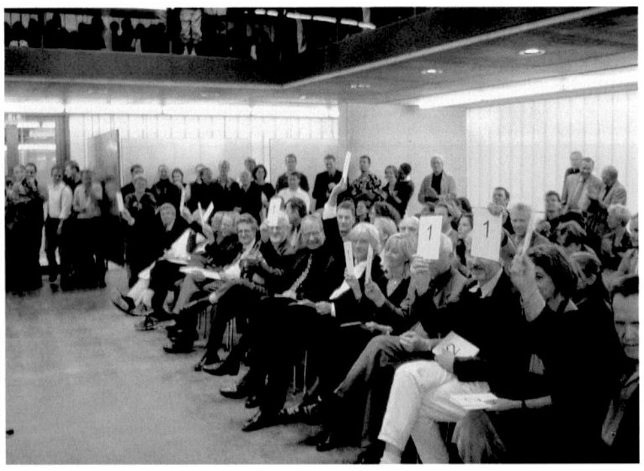

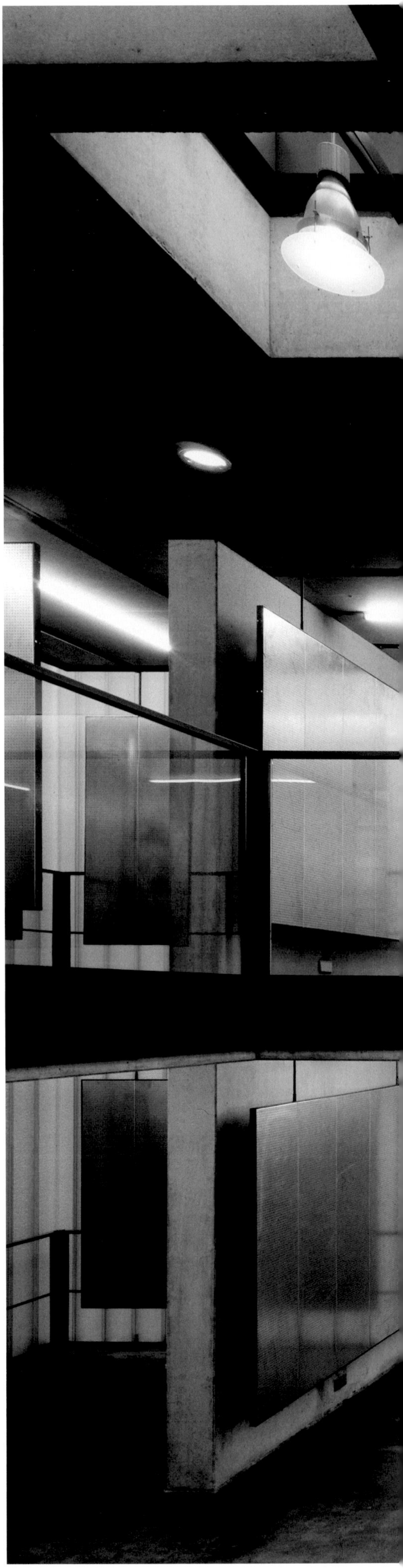

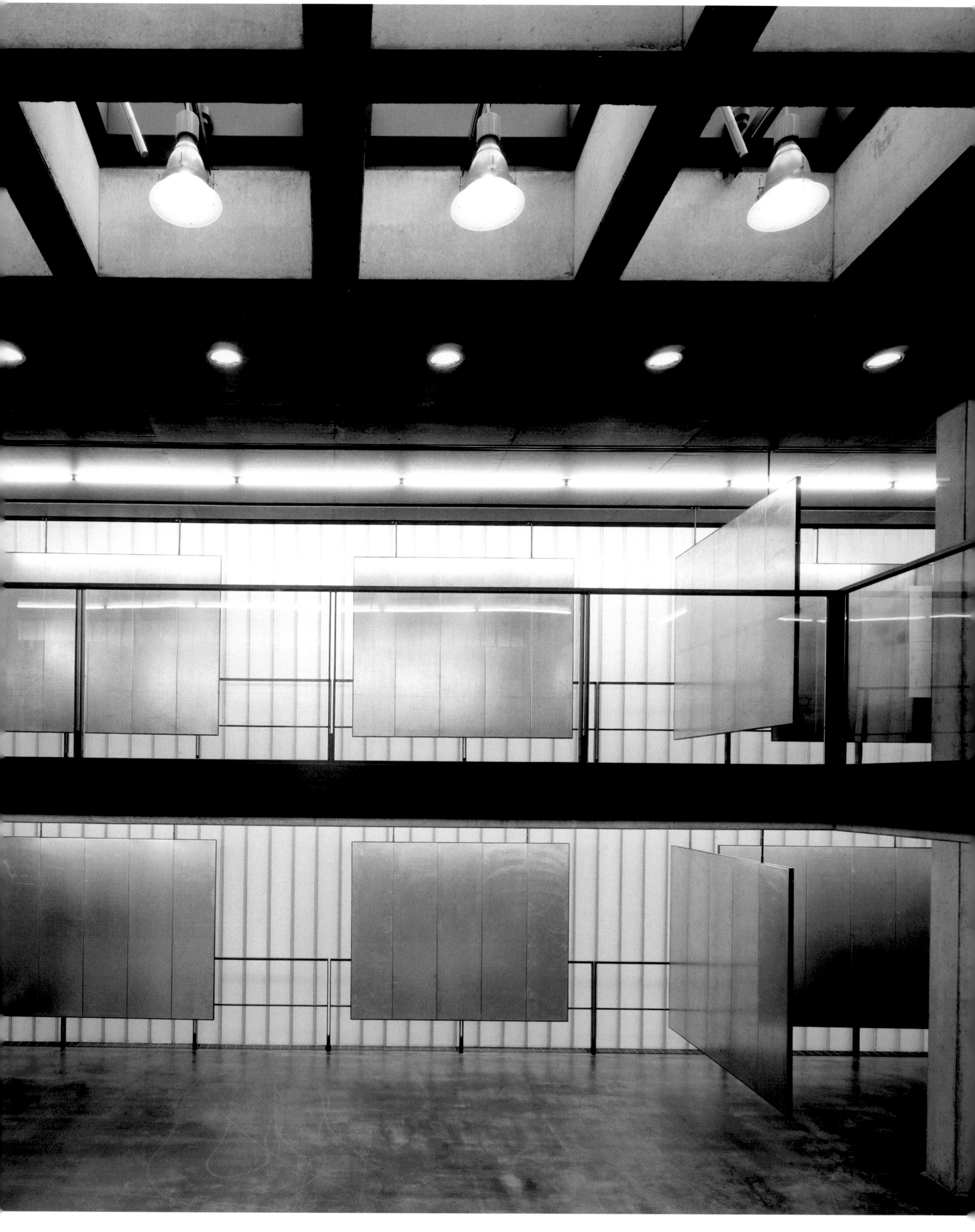

Bergbauarchiv, Clausthal-Zellerfeld
Mining Archive Building, Clausthal-Zellerfeld

1999

Entwurf Design
Meinhard von Gerkan

Partner Partner
Joachim Zais

Objektüberwachung und Beratung Supervision and consultancy
Staatliches Baumanagement Harz

Bauherr Client
Oberbergamt Clausthal-Zellerfeld

Bauzeit Construction period
1999–2000

BGF Gross floor area
843 m^2

Der Idee eines rechtwinklig aufgeschlagenen Buches folgend, nimmt der liegende Buchdeckel des Gebäudes das Foyer auf, das Platz für Ausstellungen und Veranstaltungen bietet. Breite Flügeltüren und eine bis zum Boden reichende Fensterfront lassen Tageslicht in den großzügigen, mit hellem Kirschbaumholz ausgekleideten Veranstaltungsbereich. Über das Treppenhaus gelangt man in die Archivgeschosse, in denen die Dokumente in einer fahrbaren Regalanlage gelagert werden. Dieser Teil des Gebäudes bildet den stehenden Buchdeckel. Er richtet sich als schmale, rechteckige Scheibe auf: 19 Meter in der Höhe und nur 4 Meter in der Breite. Zum Altgebäude des Oberbergamtes hin wurde die Fassade als baulicher Bezug zum umgebenden Harzer Wald mit Lärchenholz verkleidet. Die andere Gebäudeseite wurde als Erinnerung an die Bergbautradition der Stadt mit einer Bleifassade in vertikaler Scharteilung versehen.

Following the idea of a book opened up at a right angle, the book cover lying flat houses the foyer, offering space for exhibitions and events. Wide leaf doors and a floor-to-ceiling high glazed front allow daylight to enter the generous event hall, which is clad in light cherrywood. The archive floors, where the documents are stored in a movable shelving system, are accessed via the staircase. This part of the building forms the upright book cover. It stands up as a narrow rectangular plane: 19 metres high and only four metres wide. The façade is clad in larchwood towards the existing mining authority building as a structural reference to the surrounding Harz Forest. The other flank has a lead façade with vertical division, a reference to the local mining tradition.

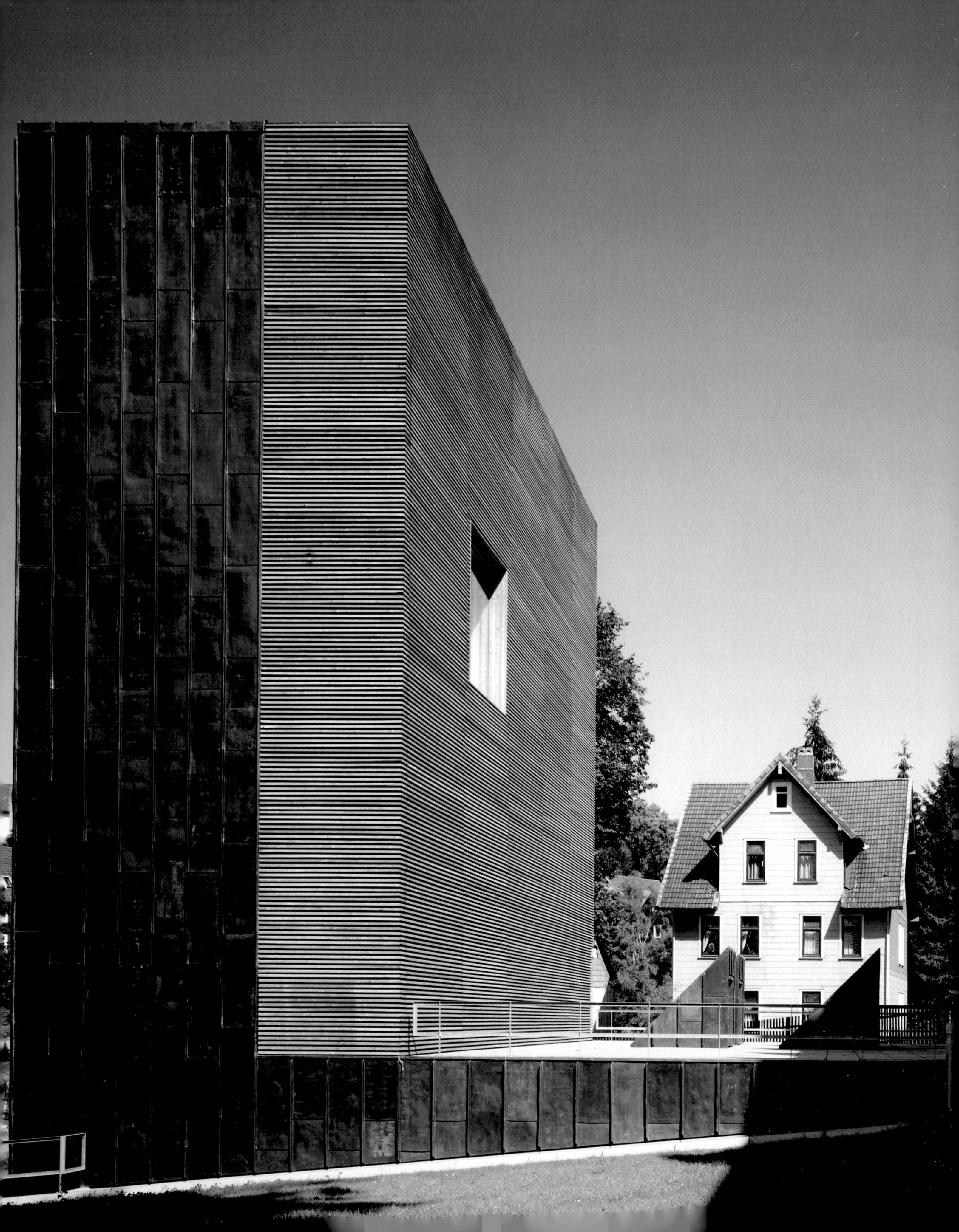

384

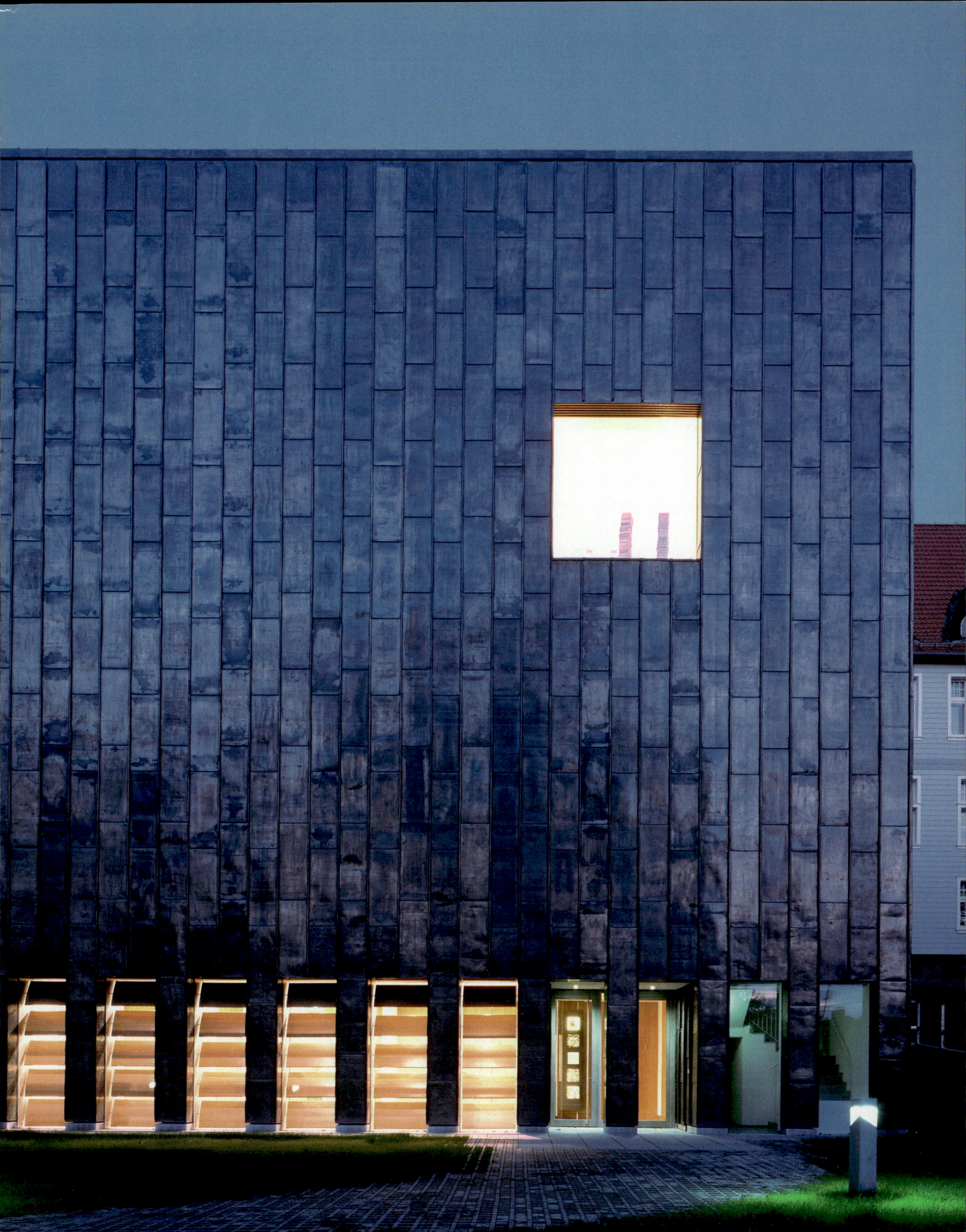

Fachhochschule des Bundes, Schwerin
Federal College, Schwerin

Wettbewerb Competition
1993 – 1. Preis

Entwurf Design
Meinhard von Gerkan

Partner Partner
Klaus Staratzke

Bauherr Client
Bundesanstalt für Arbeit, Nürnberg

Bauzeit Construction period
1998–2000

BGF Gross floor area
Schule: 9.700 m²
Insgesamt: 19.000 m²

Die Wohn- und Freizeitbereiche der Schule sind in freistehenden Langhäusern untergebracht; alle übrigen Teile befinden sich in dem hufeisenförmigen Haupthaus. Die strenge und einfache Baukörperkonfiguration wird durch die Abhängungen der begehbaren horizontalen Verschatter gegliedert und sowohl in der räumlichen Erlebnisqualität wie in der Fassadengestaltung auf diese Weise differenziert. Der große Anteil des regenerierbaren Baustoffes Holz, die Reduzierung des Energieverbrauches durch eine große Speichermasse, konstruktiver Sonnenschutz durch Dachüberstände und außen liegende Verschatter, eine Minimierung der mechanischen Be- und Entlüftung zu Gunsten einer natürlichen Lüftung sowie eine offene Wasserhaltung zur Rückhaltung von Oberflächen- und Stauwasser geben dem Bau die für eine Fachhochschule notwendige Vorbildfunktion für ökologisches Bauen.

The residential and leisure areas are accommodated in detached linear buildings; all remaining parts are located in the horseshoe-shaped main building. The suspension of accessible horizontal shading devices divides the strict and simple building configuration, thereby differentiating the spatial quality as well as the façade design. The extensive use of the renewable building material wood, the reduction of energy consumption with a large storage mass, constructive sun protection via roof overhangs and external shading devices, a minimization of mechanical ventilation in favour of natural ventilation, as well as open dewatering for the retention of surface and backwater all give the building the required examplary role in ecologically sound construction.

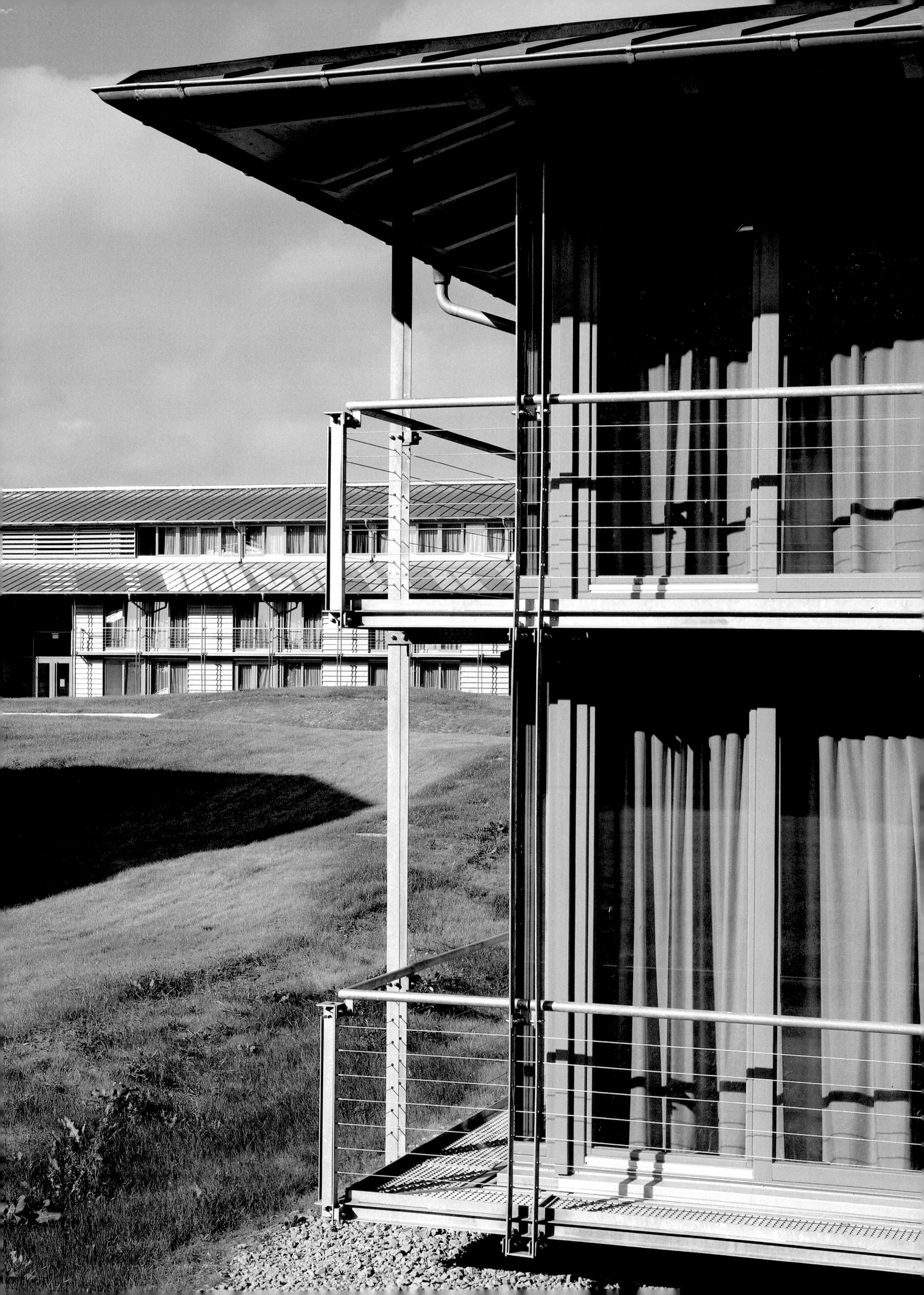

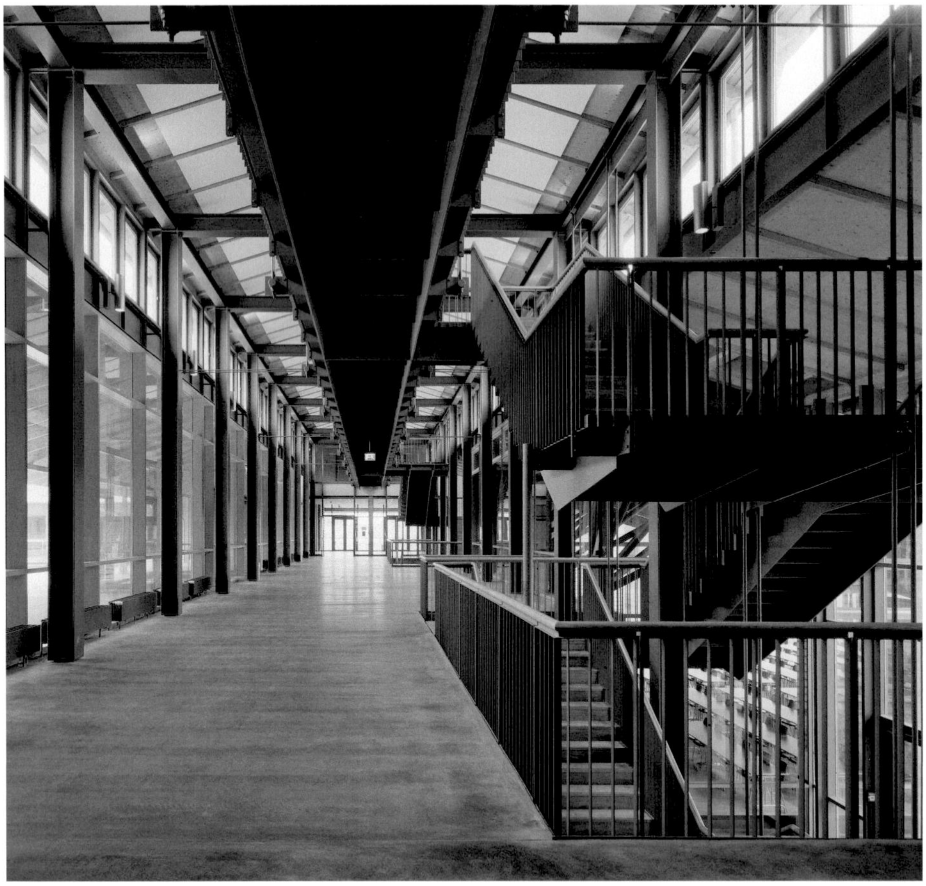

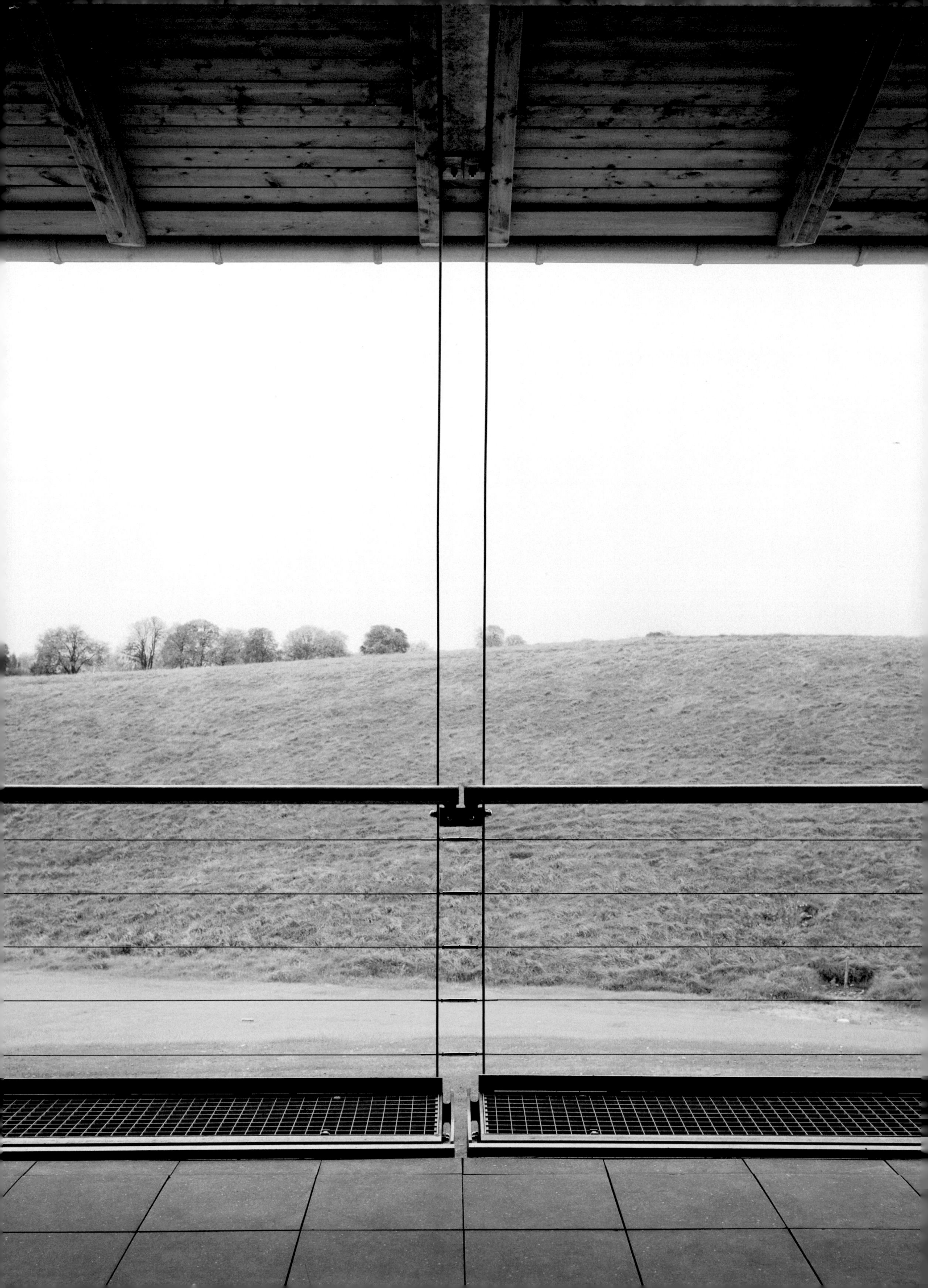

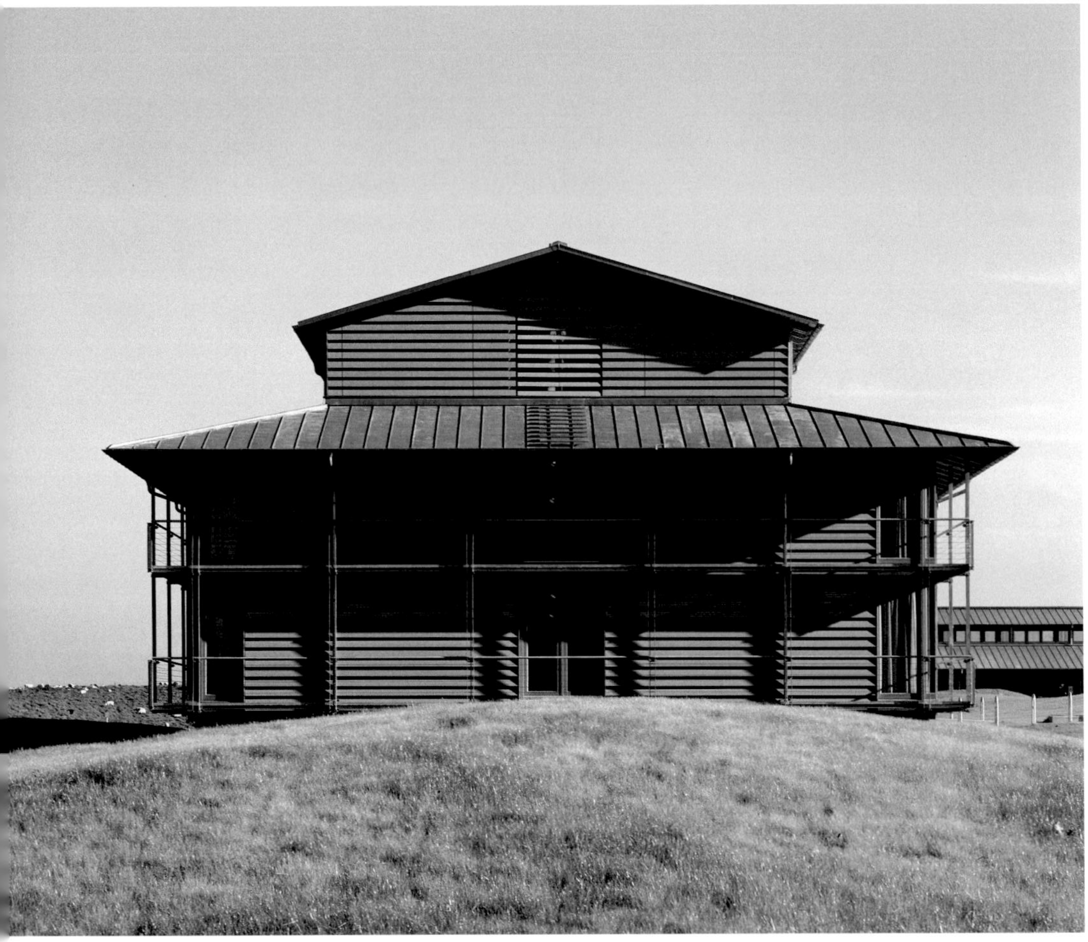

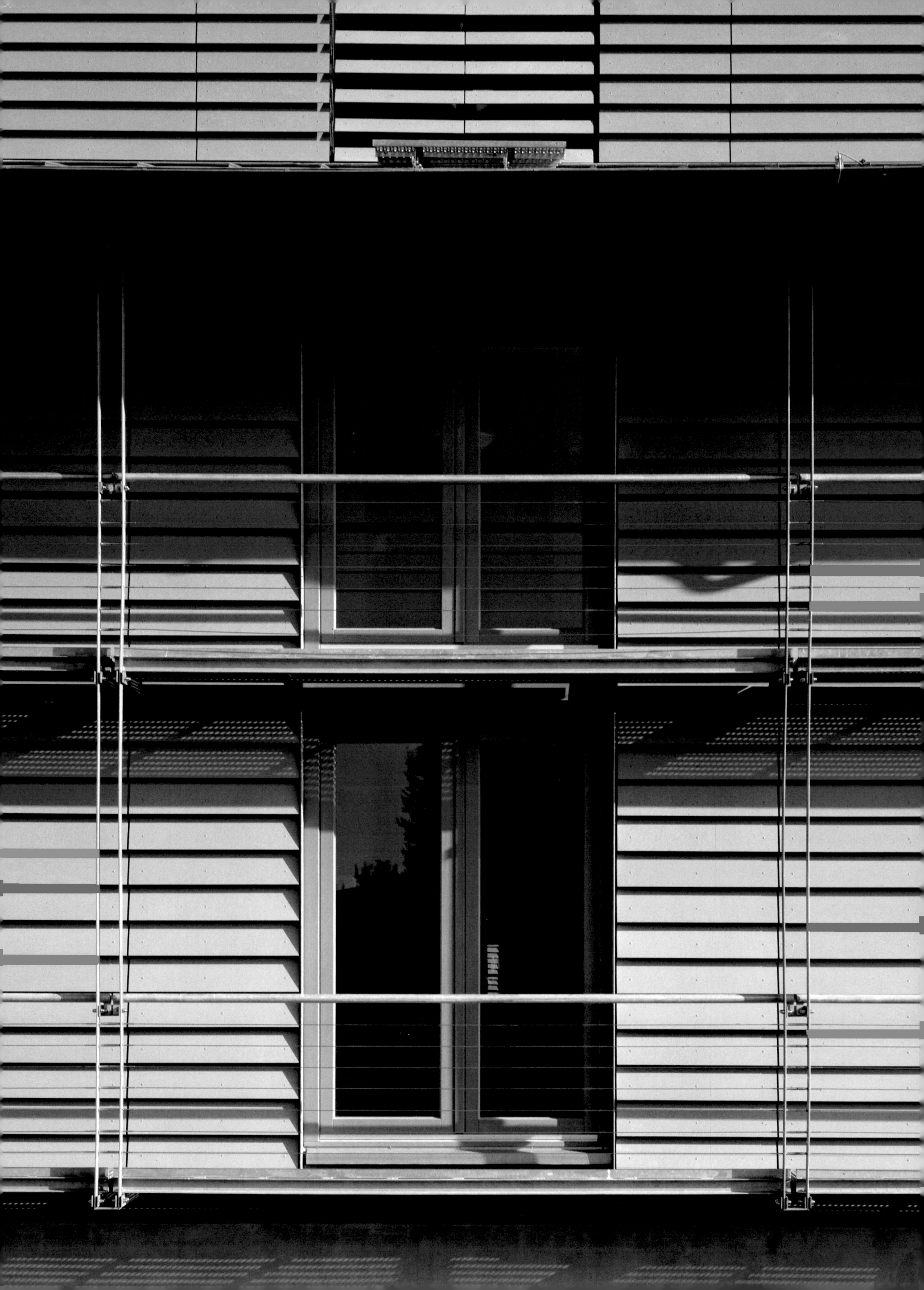

Umbau des Kesselhauses in der Speicherstadt, Hamburg
Conversion of the Boiler House in the Speicherstadt, Hamburg

1999

Entwurf Design
Volkwin Marg und Klaus Staratzke

Bauherr Client
HHLA Hamburg Hafen- und Lagerhaus AG

Bauzeit Construction period
2000

BGF Gross floor area
1.335 m²

Die historische Reminiszenz des Kesselhauses wird durch die abstrahierte Hülle zweier 16 Tonnen schwerer Stahlschornsteine hergestellt. Diese 20 m hohen Konstruktionen vervollständigen die historische Silhouette des Altbaus. Nachts werden sie durch Scheinwerfer in den gemauerten Schornsteinköpfen von innen beleuchtet. Das Erdgeschoss des im Westen gelegenen Gebäudeteils wird als Foyer des Info Centers der HafenCity genutzt. Über eine Brücke durch den Sockel des westlichen Schornsteins gelangt man in die Ausstellungshalle mit Café, in der das Modell der HafenCity ausgestellt ist. Der restaurierte offene Dachstuhl aus einer Stahlbinderkonstruktion mit Holzschalung prägt den lichtdurchfluteten Ausstellungsraum. Im Osten der Halle schließt der hohe Raum des ehemaligen Akkumulatorenhauses an, der mit seiner vertikalen Proportion und dem Blick bis in den Dachstuhl erhalten bleibt.

The historical reference to the boiler house is generated by the abstract envelope of two 16-ton steel chimneys. These 20-m-high structures complete the historical silhouette of the old building. At night they are illuminated with floodlights positioned inside the masonry chimney heads. The ground floor of the western building part is used as the foyer of the HafenCity info centre. A bridge through the socle of the western chimney leads to the exhibition hall with a café, where the Hafen-City model is presented to the public. The restored open roof truss designed as a steel truss structure with wooden boarding characterizes the light-flooded exhibition space. The high room of the former accumulator house adjoins in the east of the hall – its vertical proportions and view into the roof truss preserved.

2001

Villa in Reinbek

Ein Atrium bildet das grüne Zentrum der großzügigen, dreischiffigen Villa. Das verglaste Mittelschiff, das neben Diele und Haupttreppe auch den Wohnraum aufnimmt, wird von zwei holzverkleideten Seitenflügeln mit versetzten Pultdächern flankiert.

Chistus-Pavillon, Volkenroda

Der Bau einer Kirche ist zu einer seltenen Bauaufgabe geworden – eine Kirche auf einer Weltausstellung allemal. Wenn diese Kirche sodann auch noch von dem Rummelplatz der Weltereignisse in die stille Abgeschiedenheit des Klosters Volkenroda wandert, handelt es sich um eine einmalige Begebenheit.

Bahnhofsplatz Koblenz

Ein dreigeschossiges verglastes Gebäude mit geschwungenem Dach teilt den Platz räumlich und funktional in zwei Hälften. Vom Haupteingang des historischen Bahnhofsgebäudes führt ein ebenfalls wellenförmiges Glasdach zum Busbahnhof mit seinen in drei parallelen Reihen angeordneten „Typendächern".

Villa in Reinbek

An atrium forms the centre of the spacious three-nave villa. Two wooden-clad wings with alternated single-pitch roofs flank the glazed central nave, which accommodates the entrance hall and main staircase as well as the sitting room.

Christ Pavilion, Volkenroda

The construction of a church has become a rare building task – especially a church for a world exhibition. When this church is transported from the fairground of world events to the calm seclusion of the Volkenroda Cloister, then this is a unique occasion.

Station Square, Koblenz

A three-storey glazed building with a curved roof divides the square spatially and functionally into two zones. A glass roof, also wave-like leads from the entrance of the historic station building to the bus station with its 'standard roofs', which are positioned in three parallel rows.

Ausstellungshalle für das Xinzhao Residential Area, Peking, China

Der quadratische Pavillon dient zur Präsentation der Apartments im angrenzenden Wohngebiet. Schlanke Stützen gliedern die zurückgesetzte Glasfassade der Halle und tragen eine ausladende Dachkonstruktion. Ein massiver Gebäudewinkel mit Büros schiebt sich rückseitig unter das scheinbar schwebende Dach.

Exhibition Hall for Xinzhao Residential Area, Beijing, China

The square pavilion serves to present the apartments of the adjacent residential area. Slender columns structure the hall's recessed glass façade and support a projecting roof construction. A solid building angle with offices is put on the rear side under the seemingly hovering roof.

Wohnhaus Dr. Manke, Melbeck

Die Vorliebe des Bauherrn für klassizistische Architektur gab den Anstoß für die Interpretation eines klassizistischen Landhauses mit heutigen architektonischen Mitteln. Im Innern des versetzten Pultdachhauses bildet eine etwa 1,50 m breite Mittelzone mit Nebenräumen das „Rückgrat" des Hauses.

Villa Dr. Manke, Melbeck

The client's preference for classical architecture prompted the interpretation of a classical country house through modern architecture. Inside, a 1.50-m-wide central zone with adjoining rooms forms the 'spine' of the pitched-roof house.

Villen Kanzleistraße, Hamburg

Ausgehend von einem Anger wurden Stichwege angelegt, an denen Ensembles aus zwei oder drei durch eingeschossige Bauteile verbundene Einfamilienhäusern entstanden. Den östlichen Abschluss bilden freistehende Häuser mit weißen Putzfassaden und einem mit horizontalen Lamellen verkleideten Staffelgeschoss.

Villas in Kanzleistrasse, Hamburg

Starting out from a meadow, paths were laid out, with ensembles of two or three single houses created along them and connected by one-storey building elements. Detached houses with white plaster façades and a stepped storey clad in wooden lamellas form the eastern termination.

2001

Jakob-Kaiser-Haus, Abgeordnetenbüros des Deutschen Bundestages, Berlin

Die von gmp geplanten Gebäude 4 und 8 bilden den östlichen Abschluss des Jakob-Kaiser-Hauses entlang der Wilhelmstraße. Sie folgen der historischen Typologie der Berliner Blockrandbebauung und erzeugen durch ihre klaren geometrischen Formen einen eindeutig definierten städtischen Raum.

'Jakob-Kaiser-Haus', Parliamentarians' Offices, Berlin

The buildings 4 and 8 planned by gmp form the eastern termination of Jakob-Kaiser-Haus along Wilhelmstrasse. They repeat the historic typology of Berlin's high-density development, their clear geometric forms creating a defined urban space.

Spielbank Bad Steben

Das Auf und Ab des Glückspiels dient als konzeptionelle Metapher, die sich bildlich in Wellenbewegungen der Dachlandschaft umsetzt – sie ist zugleich eine Analogie zur umgebenden Hügellandschaft und dem schmalen Stebenbach. Fünf versetzte Sinuswellen entsprechen der fünfteiligen Gliederung des Bauwerks.

Casino, Bad Steben

The ups and downs of gambling serve as a conceptual metaphor, which is translated in the wave-like formation of the roof landscape. Simultaneously, this is an analogy to the surrounding hilly countryside and the small Steben stream. Five alternated sinus curves correspond to the five-part division of the building.

Ku'damm-Eck, Berlin

Als Großform aus der Durchdringung eines den Grundstücksgrenzen folgenden Sockels und einer Kreisform nimmt der Baukörper die unterschiedlichen Traufhöhen der Nachbarbebauung in fließenden Vor- und Rücksprüngen auf.

Ku'damm-Eck, Berlin

The large-scale building volume is a combination of a form penetrating the socle along the site boundaries and a circular form, which continues the different eaves heights of the neighbouring buildings with flowing projections and recesses.

Tennishalle der Jurmala Residenz, Lettland

Zur Erweiterung der Villa Marta gehört neben dem 1998 fertiggestellten Gästehaus auch eine Tennishalle, deren Fassade mit Sibirischer Lärche verkleidet wurde. Durch die Absenkung des Spielfeldes ließ sich die Traufhöhe so niedrig halten, dass sich die Halle in die Maßstäblichkeit der umgebenden Landhäuser einfügt.

Tennis Hall of the Jurmala Residence, Latvia

Apart from the guest house completed in 1998, the extension to Villa Marta also consists of a tennis hall, its façade being finished with a timber cladding from Siberian larch. The sunken court made it possible to keep the eaves height low enough to allow the hall to blend into the scale of the surrounding country houses.

Apartmenthaus in Riga, Lettland

Die Lage des Grundstücks an der Stadtgrenze des lettischen Seebades Jurmala ermöglicht ein Leben im Grünen. In unmittelbarer Nähe zum Ostseestrand, inmitten von altem Baumbestand wirkt das neue Apartmenthaus wie „eine weiße Perle im Wald".

Apartment House in Riga, Latvia

The site's location on the city boundary of the seaside resort of Jurmala offers residents a life in the country with wonderful views over the surrounding landscape. In di00rect proximity to the beach of the Baltic Sea and located amidst old trees, the apartment house appears like 'a white pearl in the forest'.

Neue Messe Rimini, Italien

Der „Nuova Fiera di Rimini" stehen mit derzeit zwölf Messehallen ca. 80.000 m² Ausstellungs- und 50.000 m² Serviceflächen zur Verfügung. Das architektonische Konzept orientiert sich an der großen Tradition der Emilia Romagna, die die europäische Baugeschichte seit der Antike und der Renaissance geprägt hat.

New Trade Fair, Rimini, Italy

The 'Nuova Fiera di Rimini' with twelve exhibition halls offers approximately 80,000 m² of exhibition and 50,000 m² of service area. The architectural concept is orientated around the Emilia Romagna tradition, which has characterized European architectural history since the Ancient World and the Renaissance.

2001

Swissôtel im Ku'damm-Eck, Berlin

Das Thema der geschwungenen Fassade setzt sich auch im Innenraum des Hotels fort: Geschwungene, mit Holzlamellen verkleidete Wände charakterisieren sowohl das Foyer im Erdgeschoss wie auch die Lobby im dritten Obergeschoss und die Mezzaninebene darüber.

Swissôtel in Ku'damm-Eck, Berlin

The theme of the curved façade is continued in the interior composition of the hotel: curved walls clad in wooden lamellas characterize the foyer as well as the third floor and the mezzanine level above.

Neues Tempodrom, Berlin

Die symbolhafte expressive Dachform ist eine bauliche Interpretation des Phänomens, welches die Identität des Tempodroms in der Vergangenheit prägte – das Erlebnis des Zeltraums. Von 1980 bis 1998 bot das Tempodrom als alternative Kulturinstitution in zwei Zirkuszelten Platz für insgesamt 3.500 Personen.

New Tempodrom, Berlin

The symbolic roof form is a structural interpretation of the phenomenon that has characterized the identity of the Tempodrom in the past – the experience of the tent atmosphere. From 1980 until 1998 the Tempodrom as an unconventional cultural institution provided space for 3,500 people in two big tops.

Landesvertretungen Brandenburg und Mecklenburg-Vorpommern in Berlin

Zwei gleichartige, gegeneinander versetzte Gebäudewinkel repräsentieren die beiden Bundesländer. Ihre Strenge kontrastiert mit der lichten Transparenz der Halle, die sie umschließen. Die turmartige Akzentuierung der Gebäudeecke schafft eine eindeutige Eingangssituation.

State Authority Offices for Brandenburg and Mecklenburg-Vorpommern in Berlin

Two similar building volumes, offset against one another, represent the two federal states. Their severity contrasts with the hall's light transparency, which is surrounded by both building angles. The tower-like accentuation of the corner creates a clearly defined entrance.

Flughafen Paderborn/Lippstadt

Die vorgelagerte Spange, die sowohl als Verteilergang als auch als Wartezone für die abfliegenden Passagiere genutzt wird, verbreitert das bestehende Terminal und kann nach Bedarf erweitert werden. Die filigrane Stahl-Glas-Konstruktion verleiht dem Flughafen ein einheitliches Erscheinungsbild.

Paderborn-Lippstadt Airport Extension

The new connecting building element on the air side functions as a circulation corridor as well as a spacious waiting area for departing passengers while simultaneously deepening the existing terminal. The lightweight glass-steel building construction gives the airport a uniform appearance.

Depesche Hochregallager, Geesthacht

Der grünlich transparente Schimmer der Profilbauglaselemente, die das Gebäude durch ihre Horizontalität niedriger erscheinen lassen, bewirkt eine optische Leichtigkeit. Zusammen mit den dazwischen liegenden, auskragenden Stahlschwertern verleihen sie der Fassade Maßstab und Gliederung.

Depesche High Bay Warehouse, Geesthacht

The greenish, transparent shimmer of the sectional glass elements, their horizontal orientations seemingly reducing the building height, gives rise to a visual lightness. Together with the cantilevered steel swords placed in between, they introduce a scale and structure into the façade.

Alltours Bürogebäude, Duisburg

Der Wechsel von Stahl, Glas und Backstein kennzeichnet die Architektur im Ruhrgebiet. Das Alltours-Gebäude führt die Tradition dieser Bauweise im unmittelbaren städtebaulichen Umfeld fort. Die Wirkung des Neubaus beruht zudem auf der Spiegelung im hochaufgestauten Wasser des Oberhafens.

Alltours Office Building, Duisburg

The alternation of steel, glass and brick characterizes the architecture of the Ruhr Area. The Alltours building repeats this architectural tradition in the immediate urban context. Furthermore, the effect of the new building is based on the reflection in the dammed up water of the Oberhafen.

Villa in Reinbek
Villa in Reinbek

Wettbewerb Competition
1999 – 1. Preis

Entwurf Design
Meinhard von Gerkan

Partner Partner
Nikolaus Goetze

Bauzeit Construction period
2000-2001

BGF Gross floor area
1.680 m²

Wohnfläche Living space
980 m²

Während die Seitenflügel der dreischiffigen Villa mit versetzten Pultdächern und Oberlichtstreifen ausgeführt wurden, besitzt das Mittelschiff ein Satteldach. Im Innenraum des langgestreckten Ensembles ist die Holzkonstruktion der zweigeschossigen Halle mit ihrem offenen Dachstuhl gestaltbestimmendes Element. Ein Wintergarten mit umlaufender Terrasse öffnet das Gebäude zum Mühlenteich auf der Südseite. Hierunter befindet sich im Hanggeschoss ein Hallenbad, das über eine dreiseitige raumhohe Verglasung Tageslicht erhält. Auch im Erd- und Obergeschoss sind alle Fenster raumhoch ausgeführt, Schiebeläden mit Holzlamellen sorgen für die notwendige Verschattung. Die klare, symmetrische Grundrisskonfiguration und der Wechsel von offenen und geschlossenen Räumen schaffen einen differenzierten Raumeindruck mit einer Symbiose aus Weiträumigkeit und Geborgenheit.

Whilst the lateral wings of the three-nave villa are finished with alternated single-pitch roofs and roof lights, the central nave has a saddle roof. The characterizing interior element of the stretched ensemble is the timber construction of the two-storey hall with its open roof truss. A winter garden with a surrounding terrace opens the building towards the pond 'Mühlenteich' on the south side. An indoor swimming pool is located in the sloping storey underneath the winter garden, which receives daylight through floor-to-ceiling glazing on three sides. All windows on the ground and upper floors are also floor-to-ceiling high; sliding shutters with wooden lamellas provide the necessary shading. The clear, symmetrical plan configuration and the alternation of open and closed rooms create a differentiated spatial appearance with a symbiosis of space and comfort.

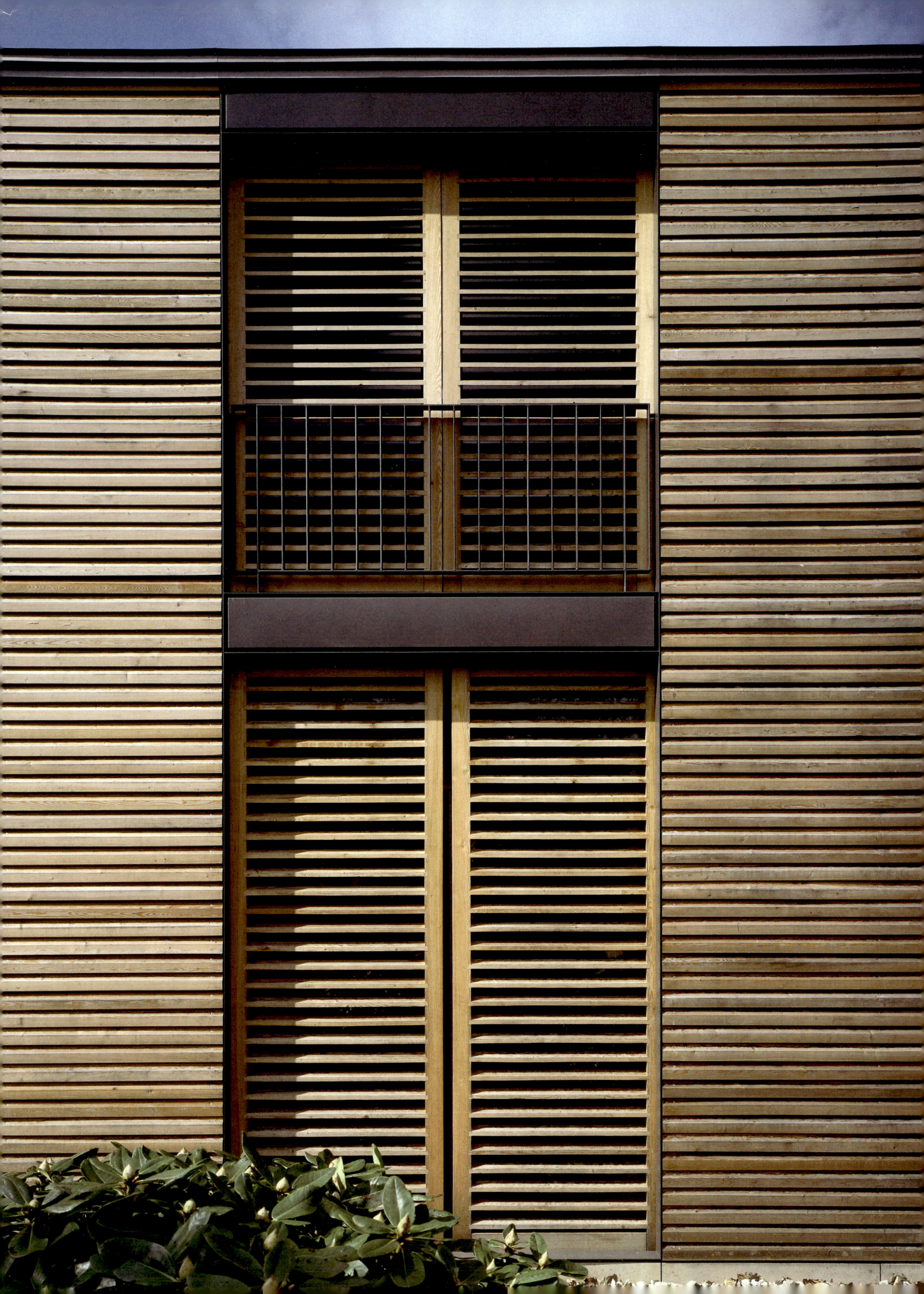

402

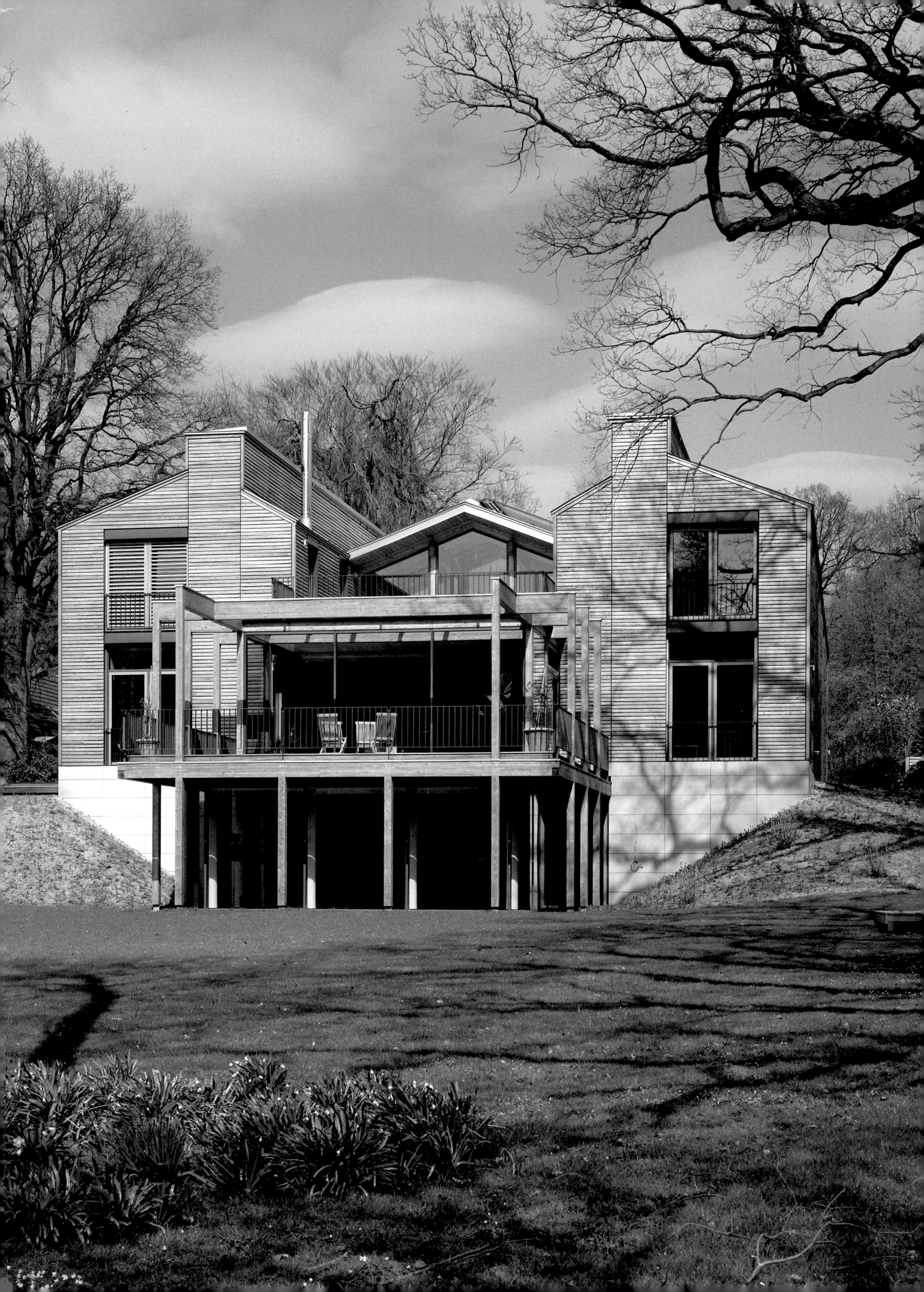

Jakob-Kaiser-Haus, Abgeordnetenbüros des Deutschen Bundestages, Berlin
'Jakob-Kaiser-Haus', Parliamentarians' Offices, Berlin

Wettbewerb Competition
1994

Entwurf Design
Meinhard von Gerkan

Partner Partner
Klaus Staratzke

Bauherr Client
Bundesrepublik Deutschland

Bauzeit Construction period
1997–2001

BGF Gross floor area
38.700 m²

Die Fassaden der Häuser 4 und 8 sind mit Muschelkalk und Zedernholz verkleidet; horizontal klappbare Sonnenschutzelemente sorgen für die Verschattung der Büroräume und sind zusammen mit einem kleinen Austritt – im Sinne eines französischen Balkons – Teil eines Holz-Glas-Kastenelements. Die Proportionen der Fassade basieren auf dem Wechsel von geöffneten Bürobereichen und geschlossenen, ruhigen Wandflächen. Die Besprechungsräume an den Gebäudeecken werden in der Fassade formal durch Loggien mit dahinterliegenden, großflächigen Verglasungen akzentuiert. Der von Haus 3 und 4 U-förmig umschlossene, nördliche Innenhof bildet den stadträumlichen Bezug zur Spree und der Spreepromenade. Die in diesem Bereich ganz in Glas aufgelöste Ost-West-Halle, die das Haus 4 mit dem Nachbargebäude verbindet, durchstößt den Hof und kann durch gebäudehohe, gläserne Drehflügel komplett geöffnet werden.

The façades of buildings 4 and 8 are clad in cedarwood and shell lime; horizontally movable shading devices allow for the shading of the offices. All offices are also equipped with a small balconet similar to a French balcony, which together with the shading devices forms part of a box element of wood and glass. The façade proportions are based on the alternation of open office areas and closed, calm wall surfaces. The conference rooms in the corners of the building are formally accentuated in the façade with loggias and large areas of glass behind. The northern inner courtyard, enclosed by houses 3 and 4, forms the urban spatial relationship to the river Spree and the Spree promenade. The east-west hall, which is completely glazed in this area, connects house 4 with the neighbouring building. It penetrates the courtyard and can be completely opened up with floor-to-roof, glazed revolving leaves.

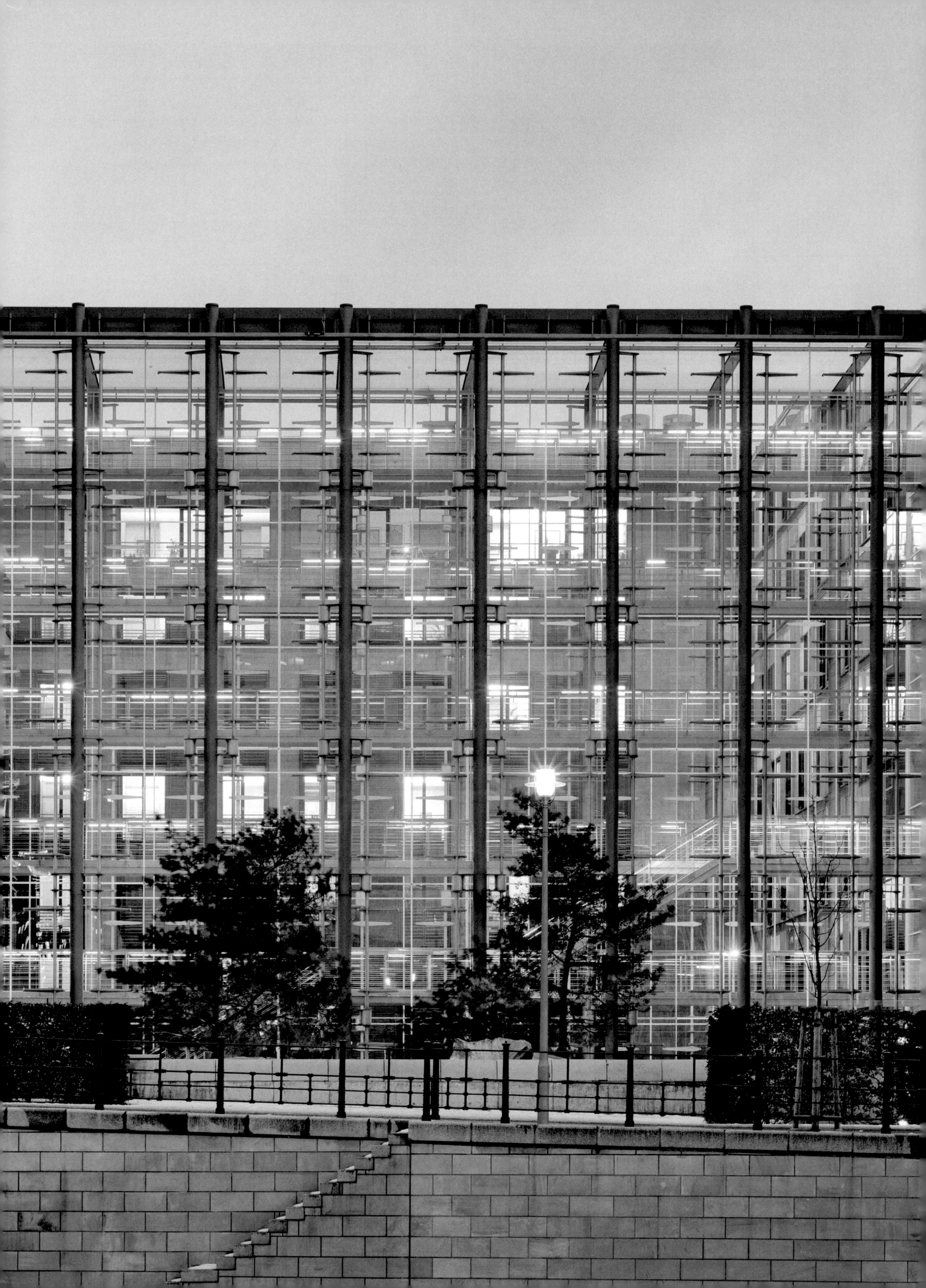

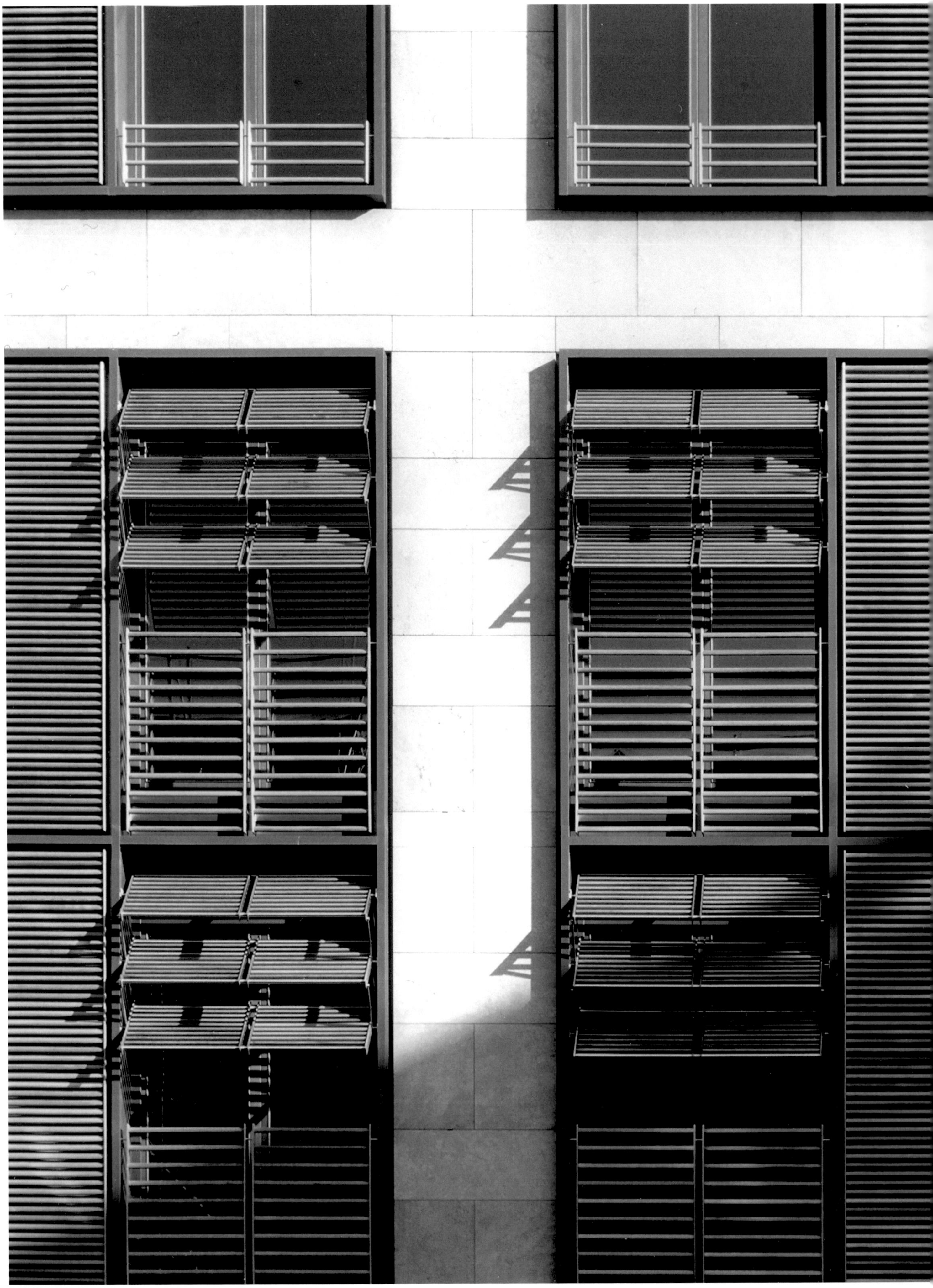

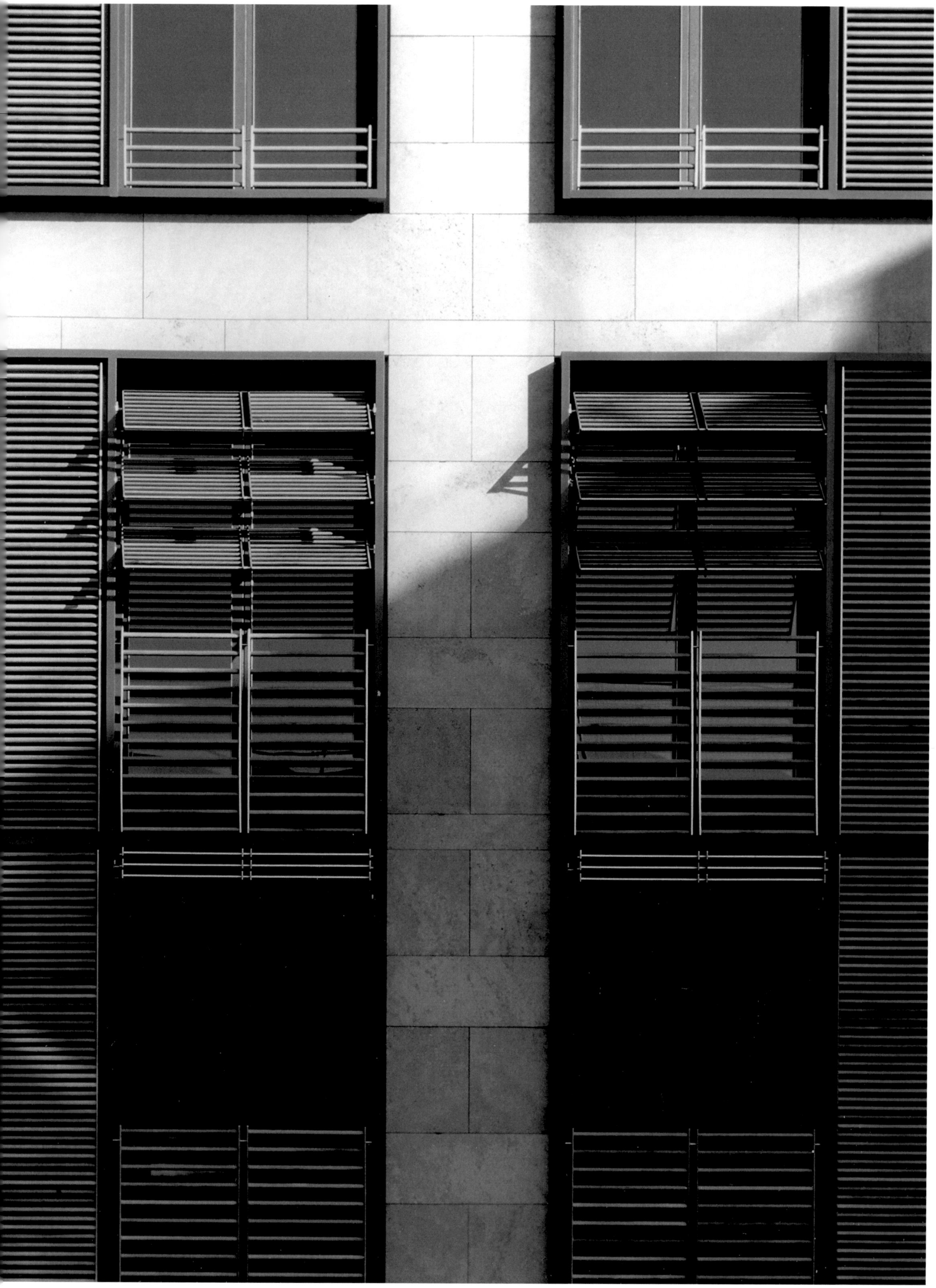

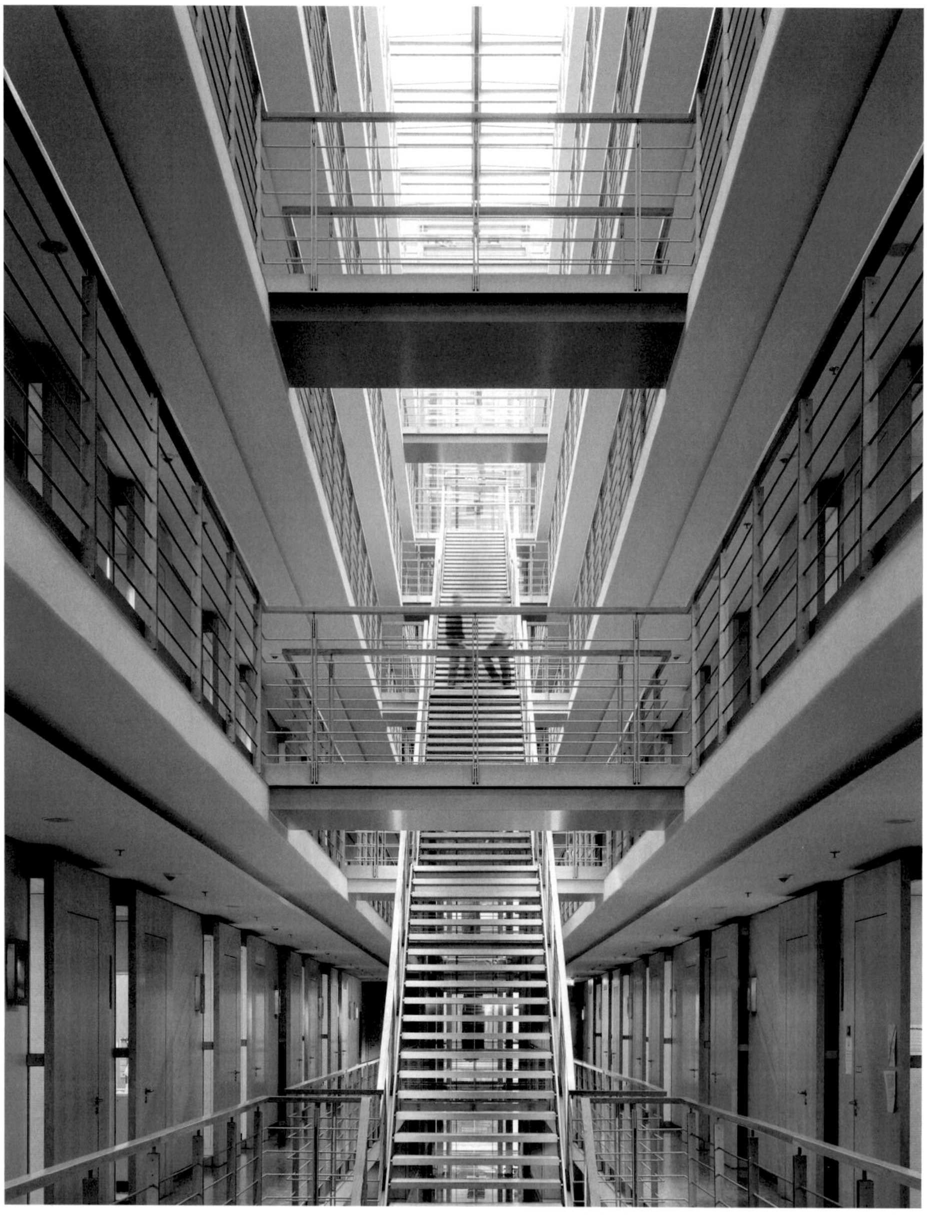

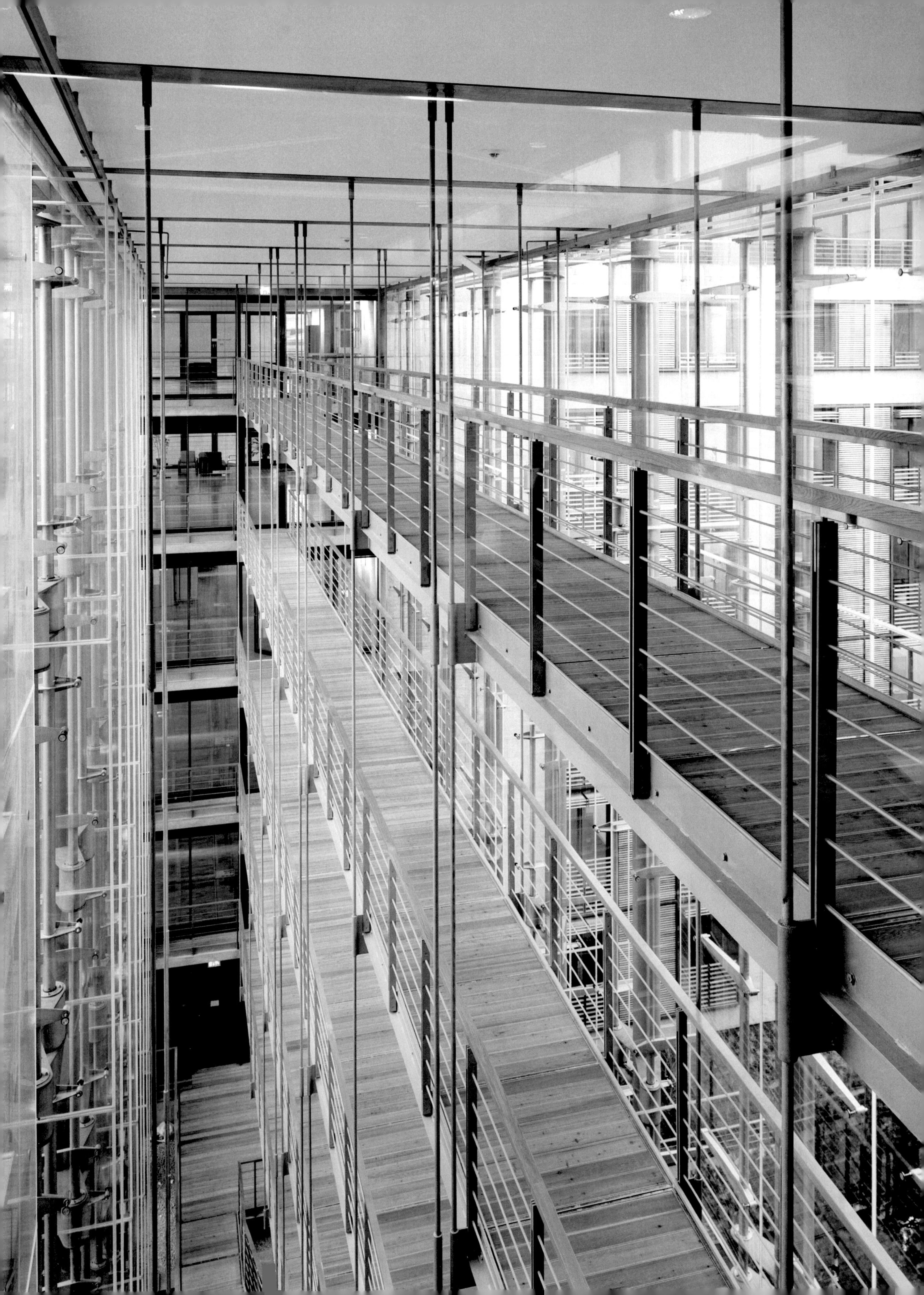

Spielbank Bad Steben
Casino, Bad Steben

Wettbewerb Competition
1997 – 1. Preis

Entwurf Design
Meinhard von Gerkan mit Anja Meding

Partner Partner
Klaus Staratzke

Bauherr Client
Gemeinde Bad Steben

Bauzeit Construction period
1999–2001

BGF Gross floor area
4.200 m²

Eine schwach geneigte Brücke führt als Empfangsgeste von Vorfahrt und Parkplatz über den Stebenbach in die hohe Empfangshalle der Spielbank. Das Wellendach überdeckt weit ausladend den Zuweg. Analog zu den Bändern der Dachwellen gliedern sich die Raumzonen im Innern, so ist jedem der fünf Bänder eine Nutzung zugeordnet. Das breiteste Band in der Gebäudemitte beherbergt, mittig durch die Kasse getrennt, im Norden den Saal für das „Kleine Spiel", im Süden den für das „Große Spiel". Beidseitig dazu wurden im folgenden Band, durch den Tresorraum getrennt, zwei Bars angelagert und zusätzlich auf der südlichen Seite ein Restaurant. Die Außenwände sind mit einer grünschimmernden Glasfassade überzogen. Die Hinterleuchtung der Glasflächen gibt dem Gebäude bei Dunkelheit trotz seiner noblen Zurückhaltung einen sehr selbstbewussten Auftritt.

As a welcoming gesture, a sloped bridge leads from the drive and the car park across the run of the Steben stream into the high entrance hall of the casino. The wave-like roof cantilevers and generously covers the approach. The internal rooms are divided in an analogy to the single sections of the roof waves. A use is assigned to each of the five wave sections. The widest section in the building's centre accommodates the halls for the 'Kleines Spiel' in the north and the 'Grosses Spiel' in the south, both centrally divided by the box office. Adjoining on both sides are two bars in the subsequent sections, divided by a strongroom, and additionally a restaurant to the south. The exterior walls are covered with a green shimmering-green glass façade. The rear lighting of the glass surfaces lends the building a self-confident appearance at night, despite its noble restraint.

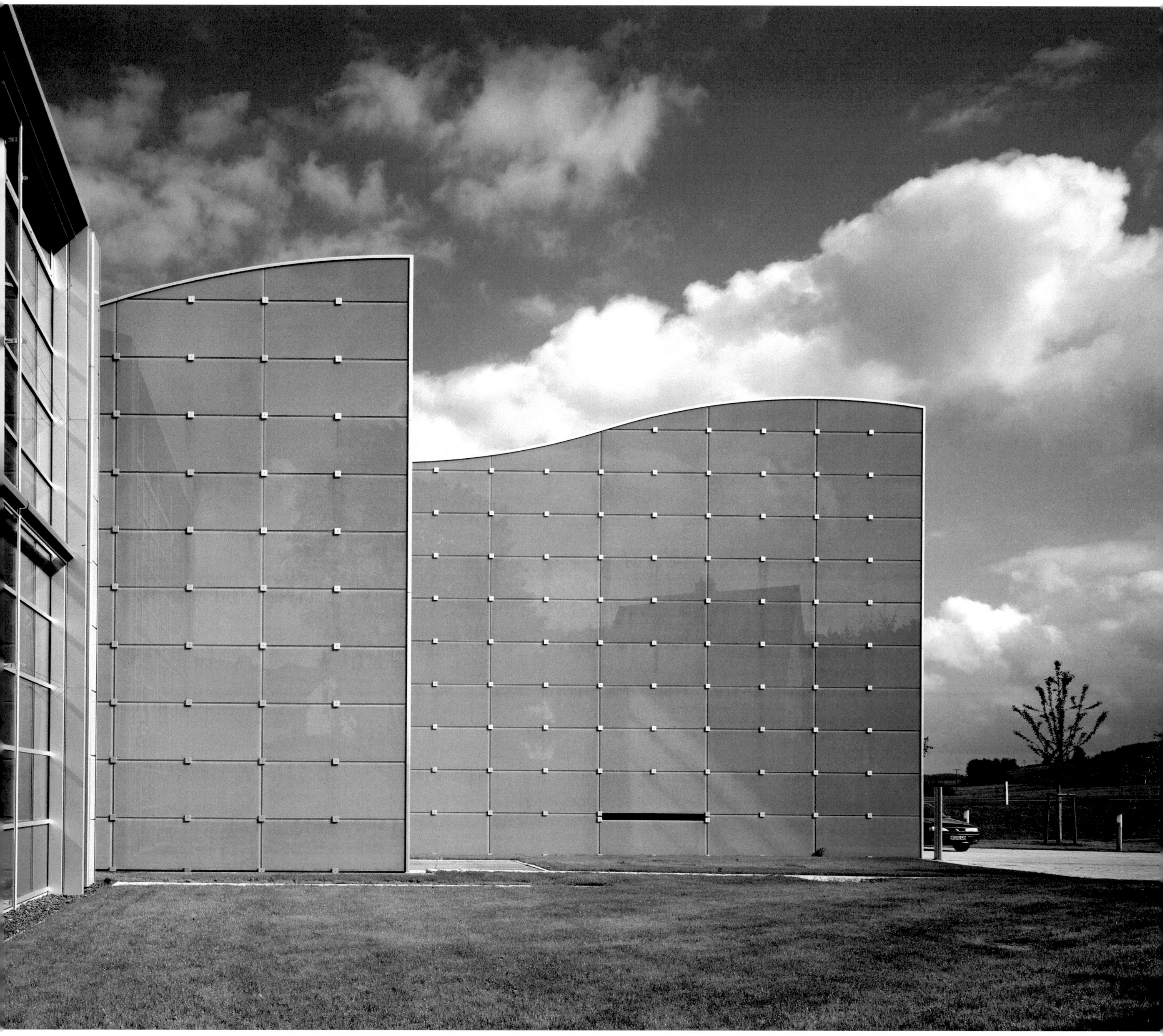

412

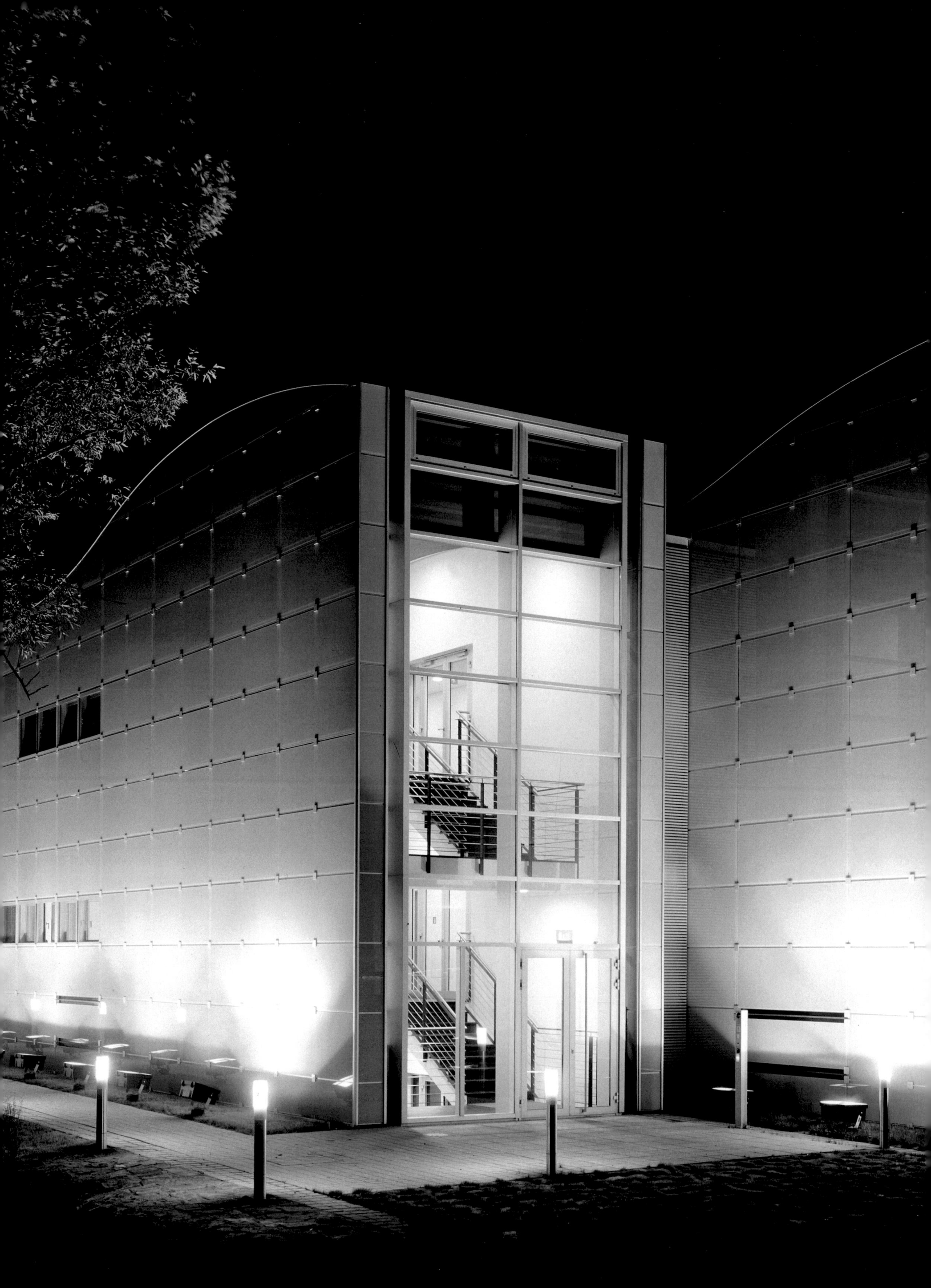

Swissôtel im Ku'damm-Eck, Berlin
Swissôtel in Ku'damm-Eck, Berlin

1999

Entwurf Design
Meinhard von Gerkan

Partner Partner
Nikolaus Goetzke

Bauherr Client
Swissôtel

Bauzeit Construction period
2000-2001

BGF Gross floor area
23.000 m²

Der Eingang des Hotels befindet sich in der Augsburger Straße. Über eine kleine Empfangszone im Erdgeschoss, akzentuiert durch einen viergeschossigen Luftraum mit gläsernen Fahrstühlen, erreichen die Gäste die Lobby im 3. Obergeschoss. Diese verbindet als Verteilerebene spannungsvoll Restaurant- und Konferenzbereiche miteinander. Ausreichende Belichtung erhält der zweigeschossige Lobbybereich über ein verglastes Dach zum Innenhof. Sowohl vom Ballsaal wie auch vom Restaurant genießt man durch die großzügig verglaste Fassade einen freien Blick auf den Kurfürstendamm.
Die 316 Hotelzimmer der Fünf-Sterne-Klasse verteilen sich auf das vierte bis zehnte Obergeschoss. Umlaufende, niedrige Sideboards verbinden alle Einbauten der Zimmer miteinander und beziehen als Fensterbank auch die großen Fensterflächen mit in die Gestaltung des Raumes ein, sodass neben dem warmen Holzton eine durchgängige Horizontalität die Einrichtung der Hotelzimmer bestimmt.

The small reception foyer in Augsburger Strasse – emphasized by a three-storey volume and glass lifts – forms the ground level entrance to the hotel occupying the third to the tenth floors of the building. A glazed roof towards the inner courtyard allows for a sufficient lighting of the two-storey lobby, which connects the gastronomy and conference areas. From the ballroom, as well as from the restaurant, the guests enjoy an open view towards Kurfürstendamm through the generously glazed façade. The 316 rooms of the five-star hotel category are distributed throughout the fourth to tenth floors. Continuous, low sideboards connect all the in-built units inside the rooms, simultaneously integrating the large window areas as a window seat in the design of the hotel rooms. As a result, a continuous horizontal line dominates alongside the warm tone of the wooden interior.

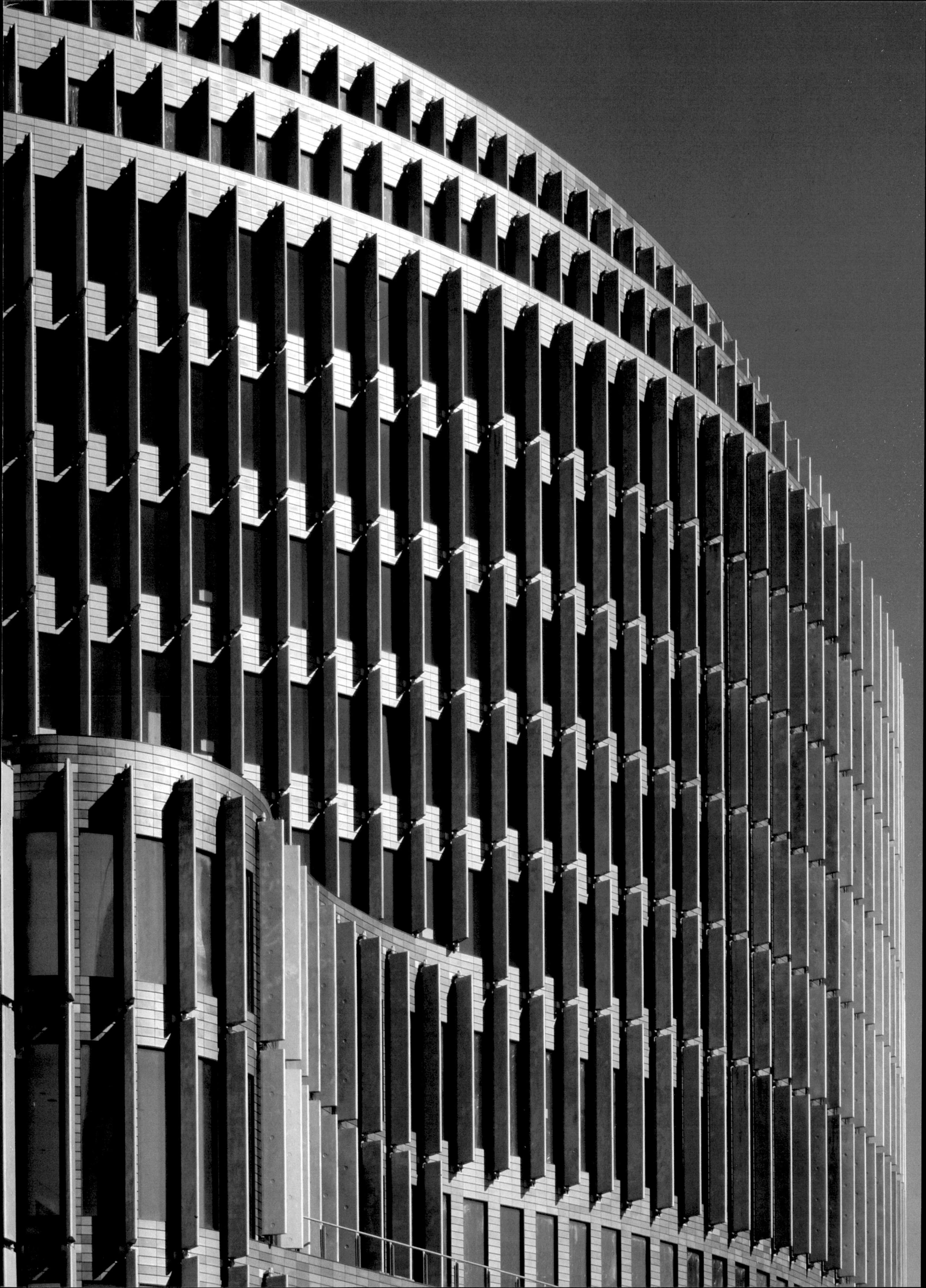

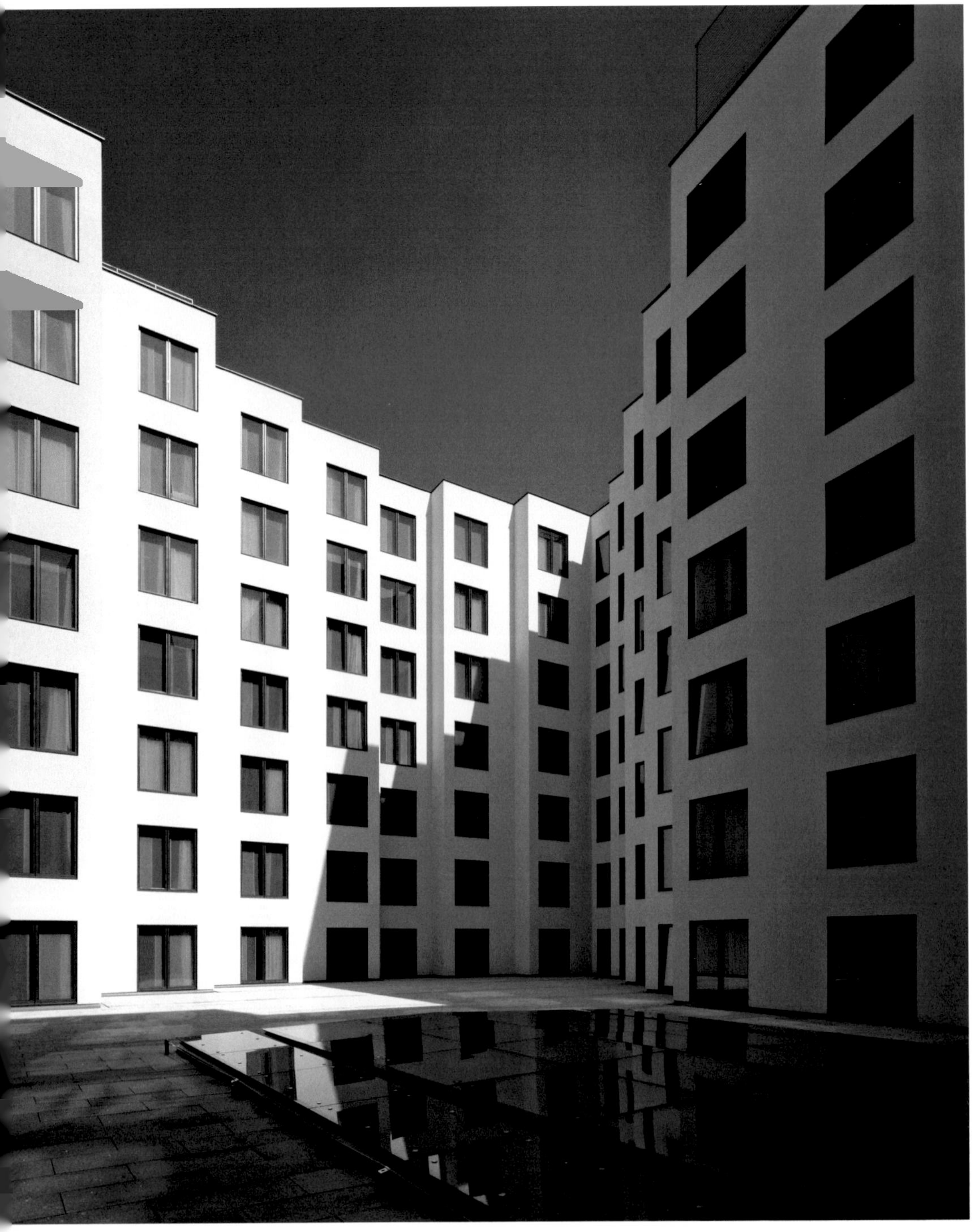

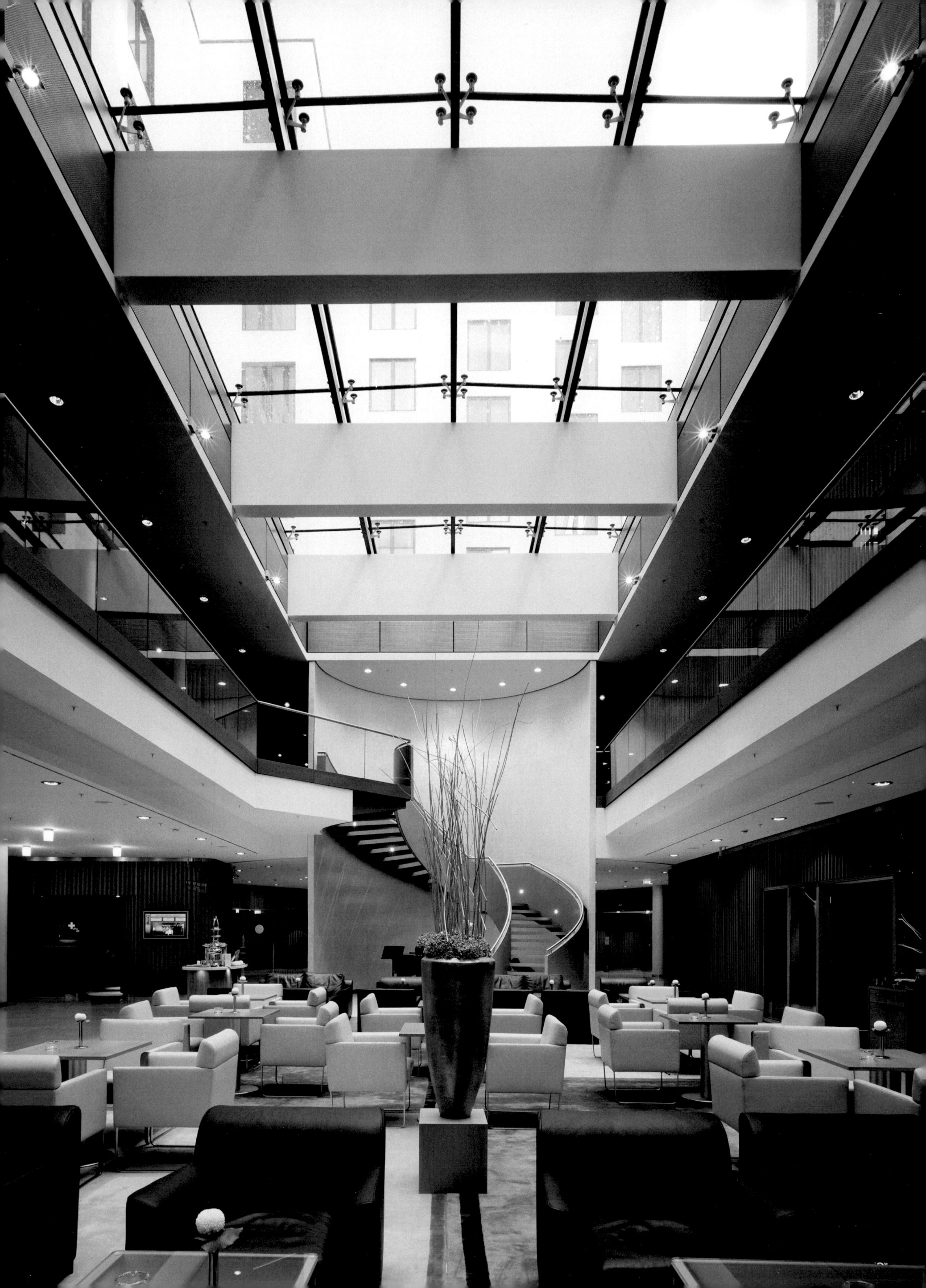

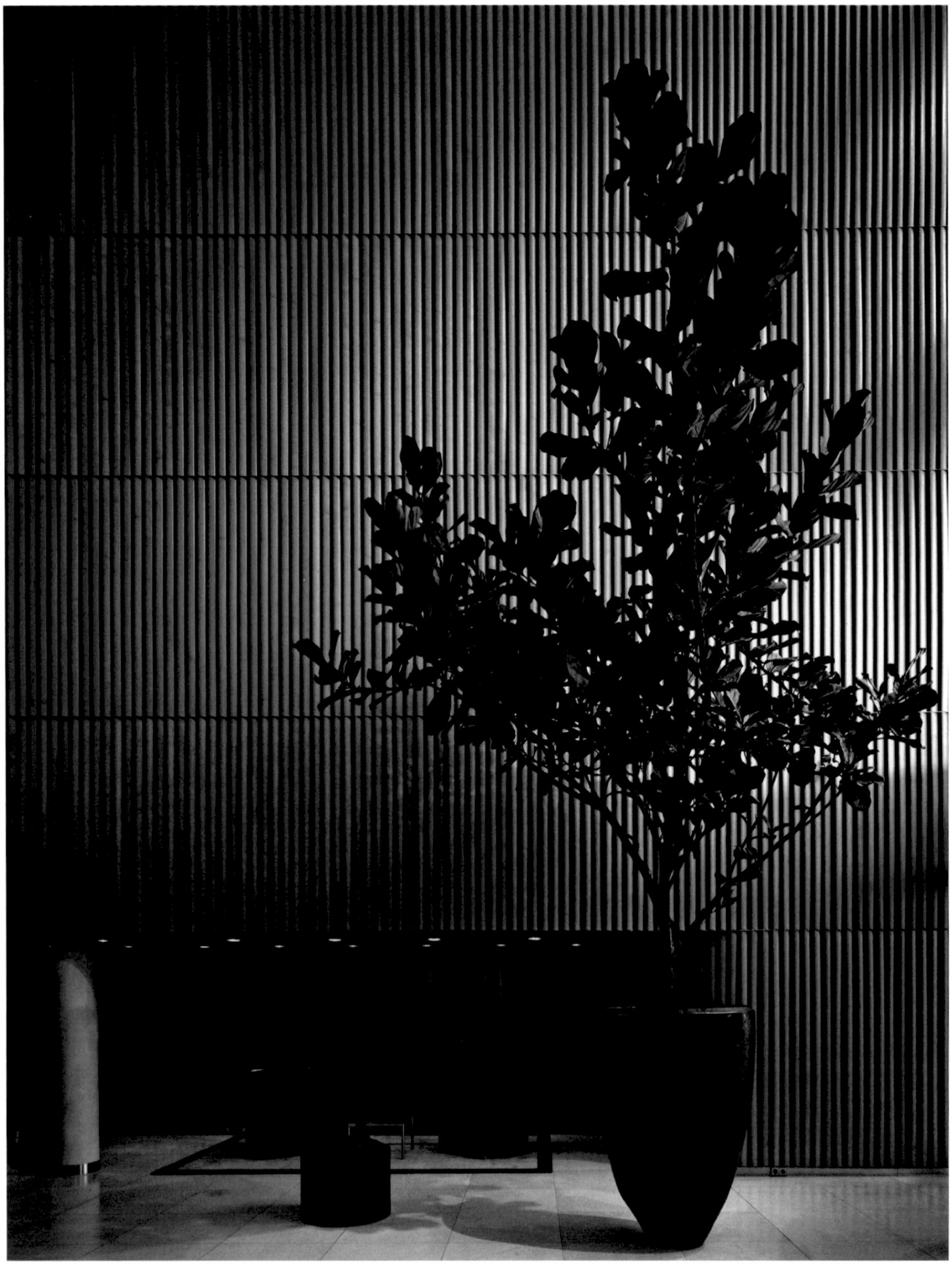

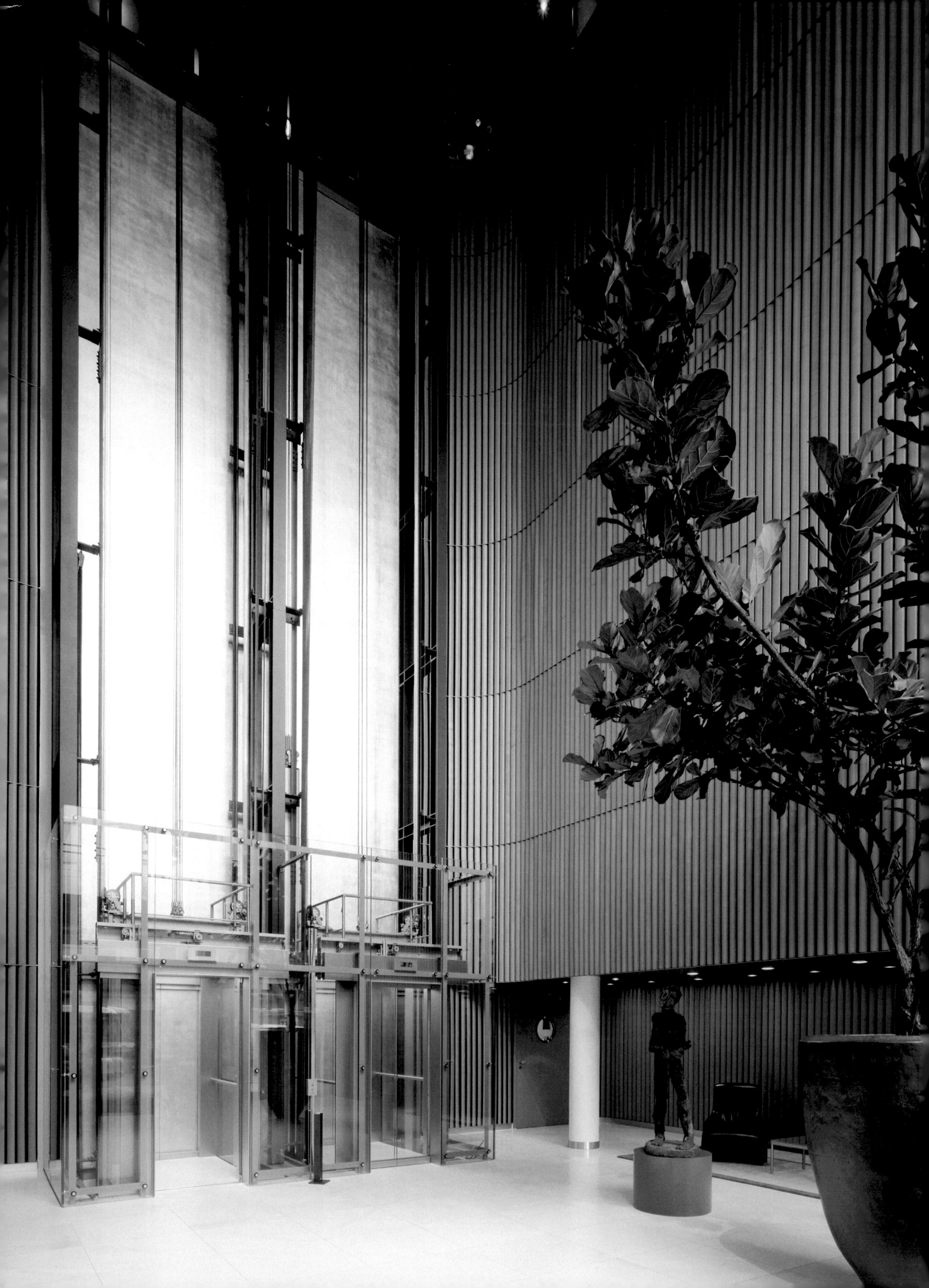

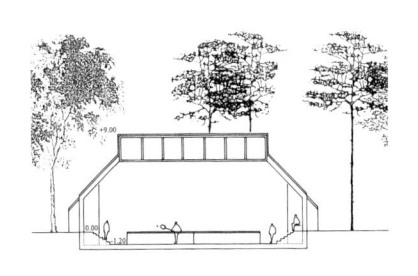

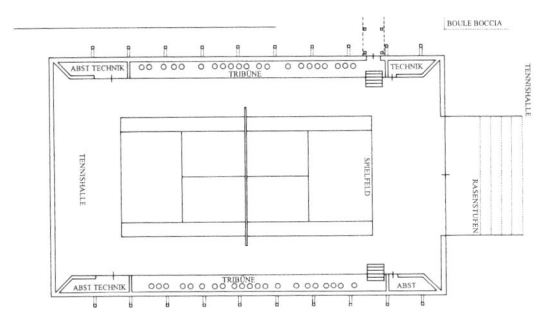

Tennishalle der Jurmala Residenz, Lettland
Tennis Hall of the Jurmala Residence, Latvia

1998

Entwurf Design
Meinhard von Gerkan

Bauherr Client
Familie Krasovicky

Bauzeit Construction period
1999–2001

BGF Gross floor area
814 m²

Die Tennishalle nimmt ebenso wie die anderen Neubauten die Holzbautradition des Ortes mit Mitteln der heutigen Zeit auf. In Anlehnung an die umliegenden Gebäude hat sie Pult- und Walmdächer, die mit Zinkblech eingedeckt sind. Wie das Gästehaus wurde auch die Halle als Holzfachwerkkonstruktion konzipiert. Die Tragkonstruktion besteht aus Brettschichtstützen, die über Zugseile in den Fundamenten rückverankert sind. Auf diesen Kragträgern lagern insgesamt elf Fachwerkträger. Das Spielfeld ist mit einer Sheddachkonstruktion überspannt, die diffuses Nordlicht in die Halle lässt. Im Inneren bestimmt die auberginefarbene Wandverkleidung aus beschichteten Holztafeln den Raumeindruck. Die sichtbare Konstruktion aus heller Sibirischer Lärche strukturiert den Raum. Mit ihrer erhöhten Lage bieten die 90 Sitzplätze entlang der Längsseiten eine optimale Sicht auf das abgesenkte Spielfeld.

The tennis hall, as well as the other new buildings, take reference from the traditional timber construction typical for the area. With reference to the surrounding roof profiles the tennis hall has mono-pitch and hip roofs, which are clad in sheet zinc. Identical to the guest house the hall is also designed as a timber-frame structure. The load-bearing structure consists of columns, which are re-anchored with stay ropes to the foundation. These cantilever beams support a total of eleven truss girders. The court is spanned by a shed roof structure, allowing the diffuse north light to enter the hall. The aubergine wall panelling of coated timber elements defines the interior atmosphere whilst the visible frame construction of light Siberian larch structures the space. On account of their elevated position a total of 90 seats along the longitudinal sides offer an optimal view onto the sunken court.

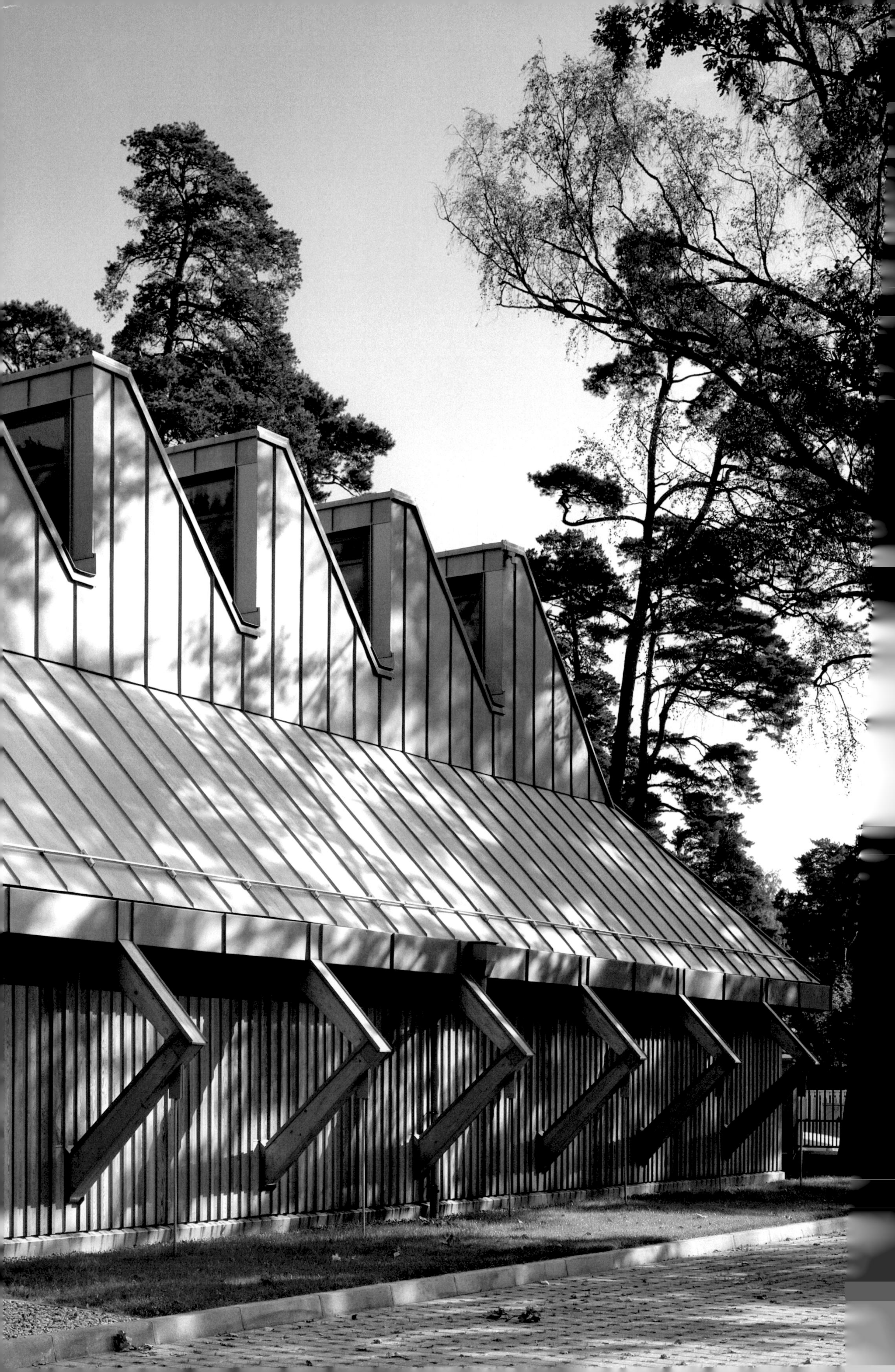

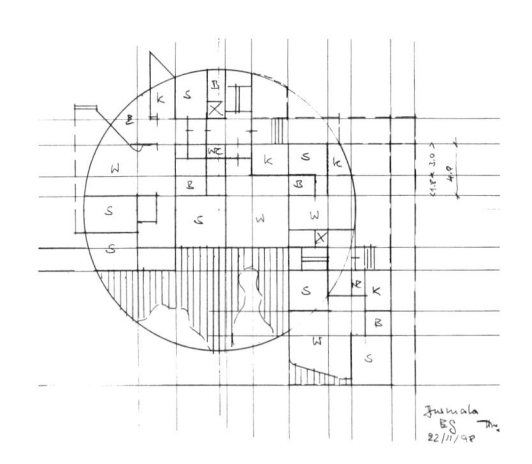

Apartmenthaus in Jurmala, Lettland
Apartment House in Jurmala, Latvia

1998

Entwurf Design
Meinhard von Gerkan

Bauherr Client
Firma Vincents, Riga

Bauzeit Construction period
1999–2001

BGF Gross floor area
2.150 m²
7 Apartments

Die großvolumige, geometrische Plastik thematisiert Innen- und Außenraum, Architektur und Gartenlandschaft zu einer ganzheitlichen Inszenierung. Grenzen zwischen innen und außen verwischen in der Wechselwirkung von Körper und Raum. Wände lösen sich in „Rahmen" auf, der Außenraum dringt in den differenzierten Baukörper in Form von Loggien und Terrassen ein. Die Geometrie des Hauses basiert auf der Überlagerung von Kreisform und orthogonaler Struktur. Die weißen, das Erscheinungsbild des Hauses bestimmenden Putzflächen kontrastieren mit den großformatigen Fensteröffnungen. Luftbalken, Vor- und Rücksprünge sowie Terrassen mit Geländern aus Edelstahl gliedern den Baukörper. Das Haus umfasst sieben Eigentumswohnungen verteilt auf drei Geschosse mit einer Penthousewohnung im Staffelgeschoss. Alle Apartments unterscheiden sich in ihrer Gestaltung und Ausrichtung zur umgebenden Landschaft.

The voluminous geometric sculpture unifies interior and outdoor space, architecture and garden landscape into a comprehensive whole. Boundaries between interior and exterior disappear through the interaction of form and space. Walls dissolve into 'frames'; the exterior space penetrates the differentiated building in the form of loggias and terraces. The building's geometry is based on the layering of the circular form and orthogonal structure. The white plastered surfaces, characterizing the building's appearance, are contrasted with the large window openings. Lattice frames, projections and recesses, as well as terraces with stainless steel balustrades, divide the building. The house comprises seven flats on three levels with a penthouse apartment on the top floor. All apartments differ regarding their design and orientation towards the surrounding landscape.

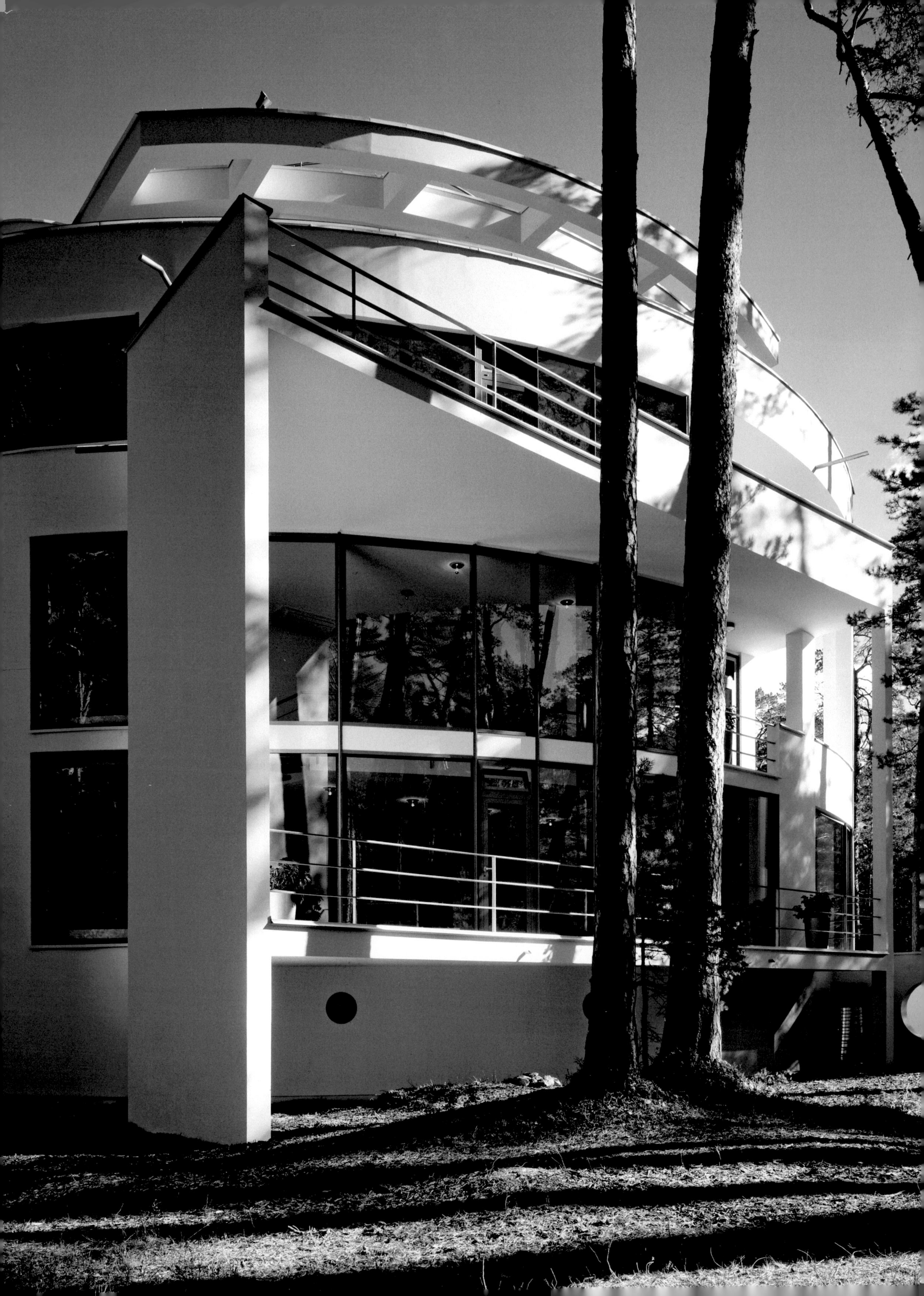

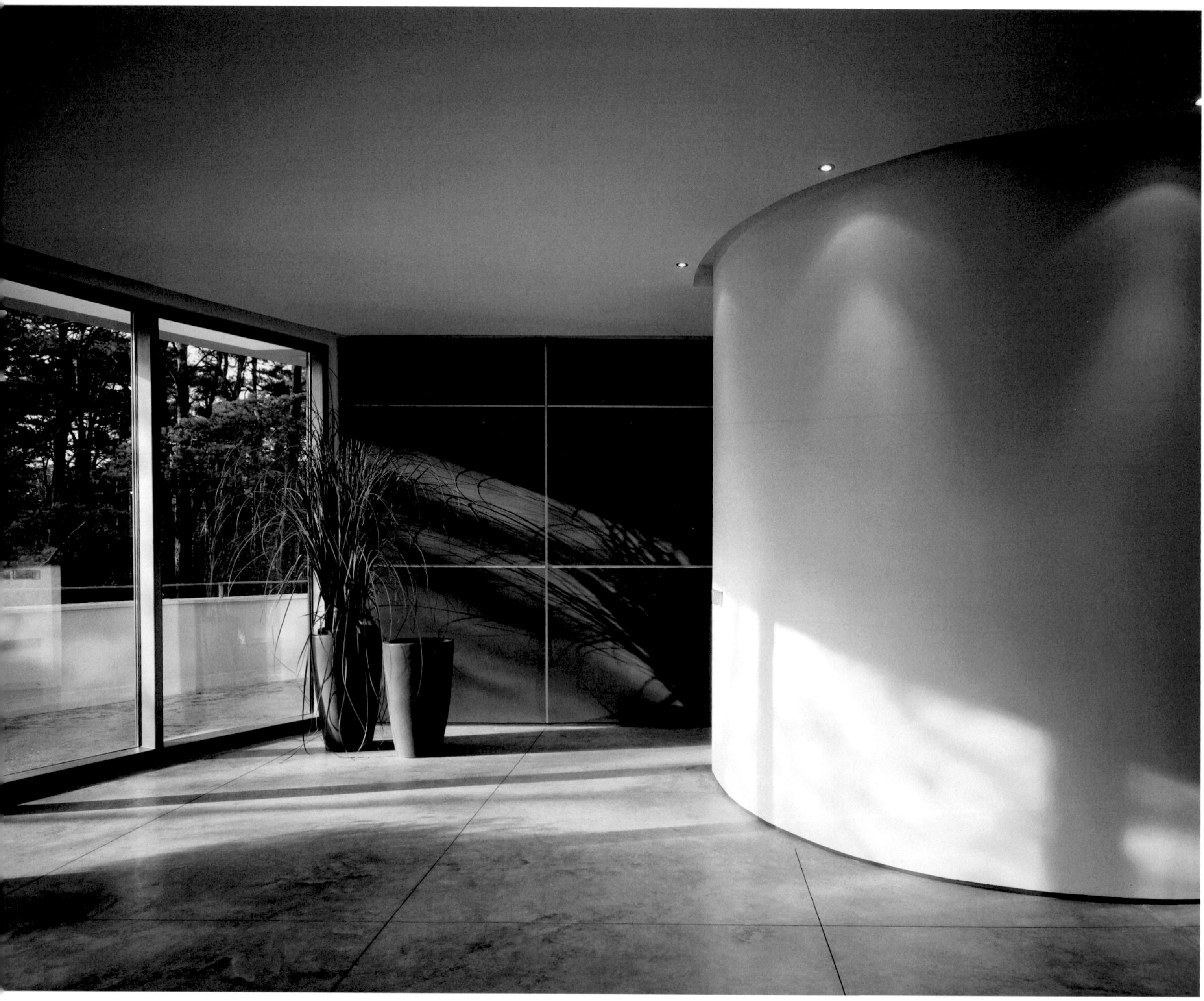

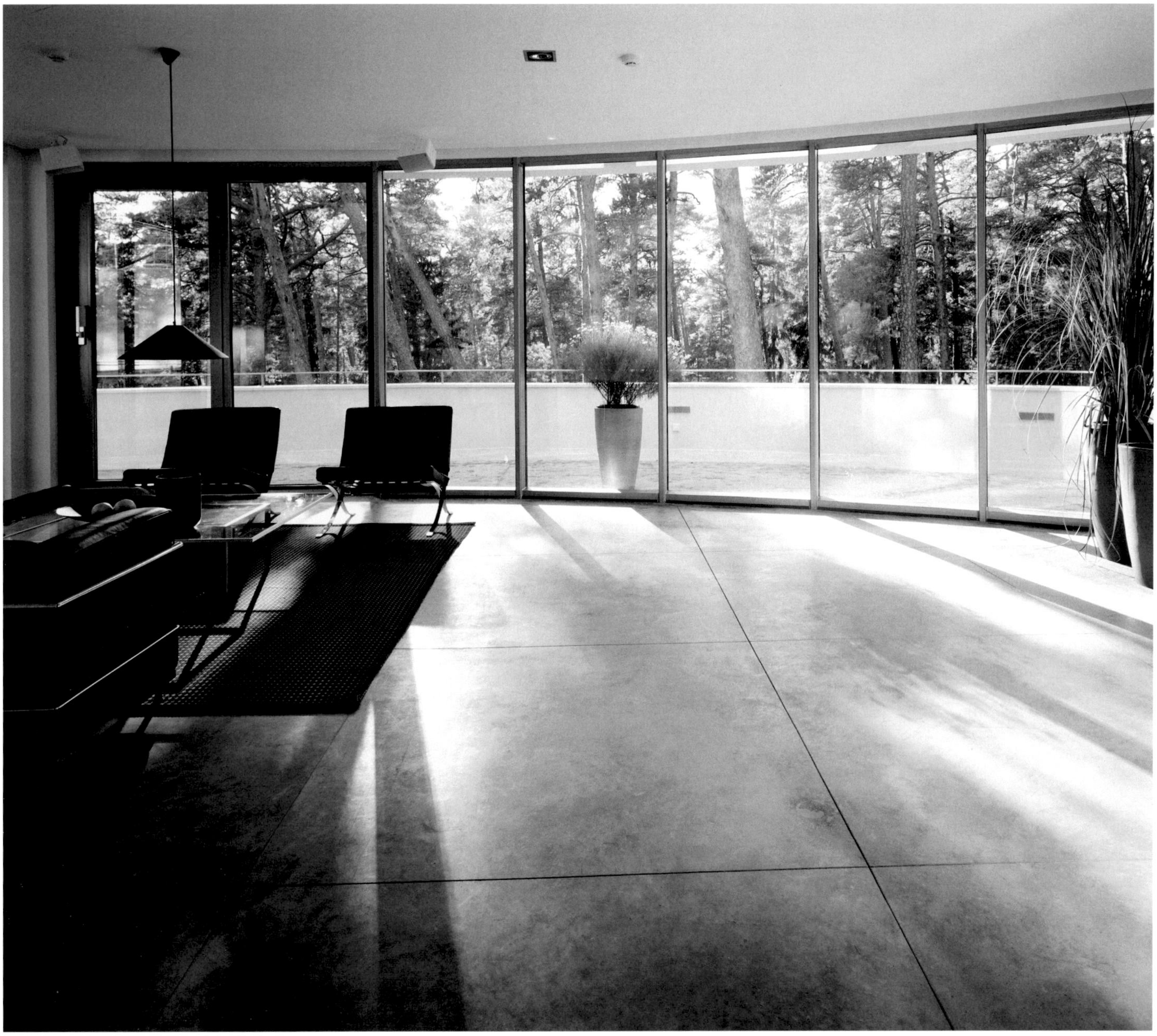

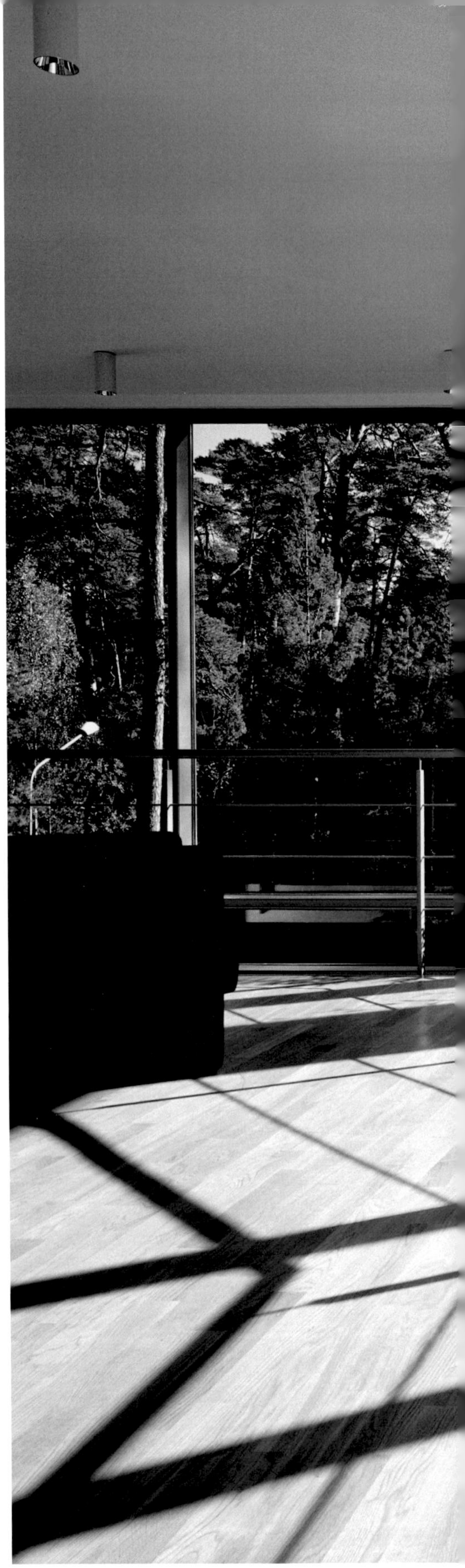

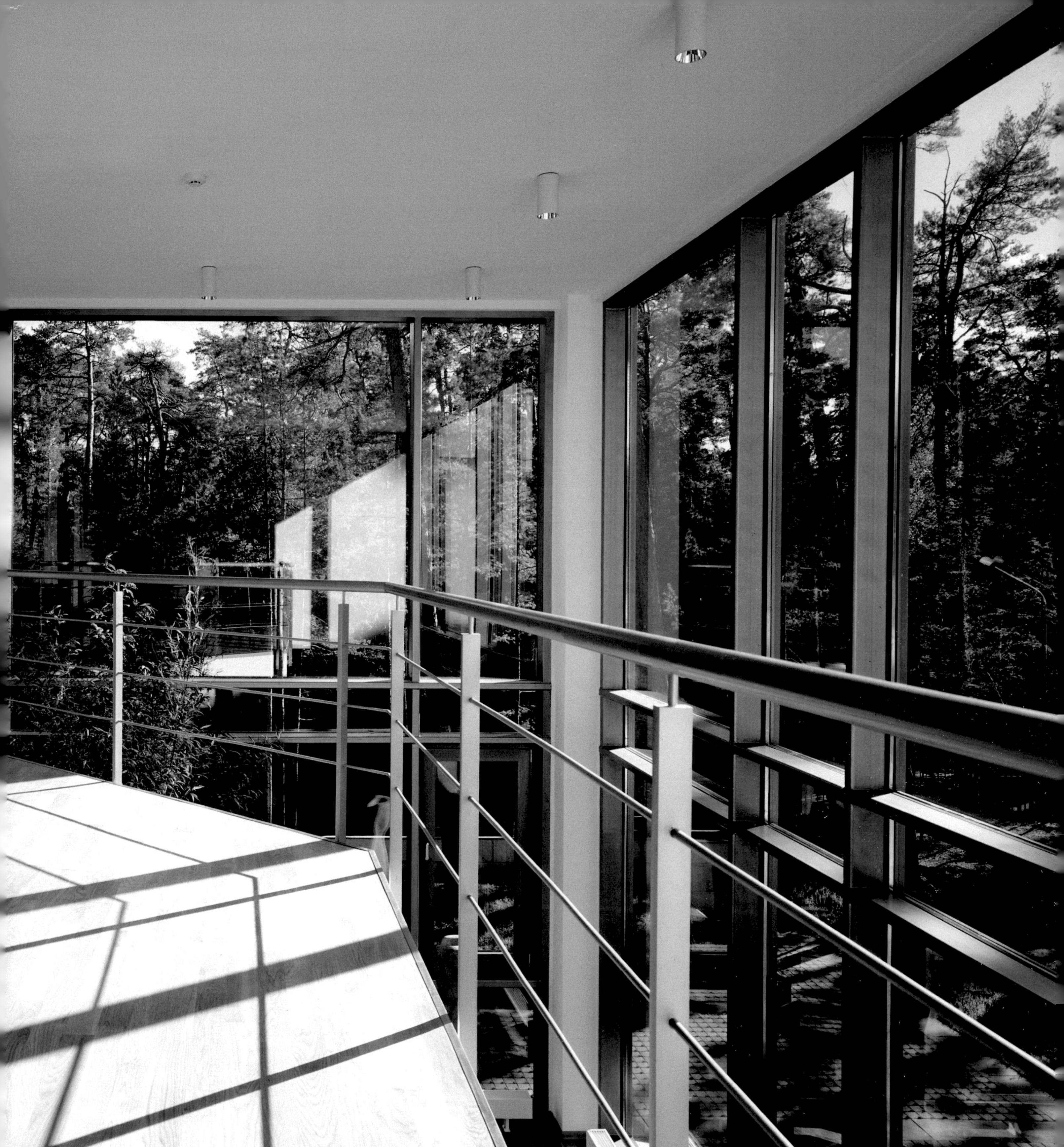

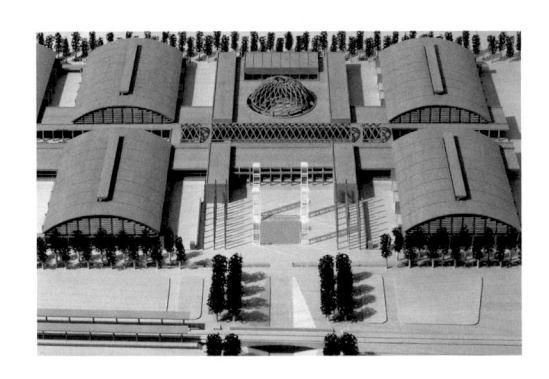

Neue Messe Rimini, Italien
New Trade Fair Complex, Rimini, Italy

Wettbewerb Competition
1997 – 1. Preis

Entwurf Design
Volkwin Marg

Bauherr Client
Ente Autonomo Fiera di Rimini

Bauzeit Construction period
1999–2001

BGF Gross floor area
130.130 m²

Das Gesamtensemble der Messe ist in klassischer Weise axial und perspektivisch gruppiert und zitiert mit den verwendeten Konstruktionen und modernen Materialien die architektonische Traditionen der Region. So ist der Platz vor der zentralen Säulenhalle des Eingangsbereichs mit den Lichttürmen des Tetrapylons weithin sichtbar. Die in Ost-West-Richtung verlaufende Messestraße mit beidseitigen, offenen Kolonnadenfluchten sowie die überdachten Brunnen und treppengesäumten Wasserbecken sind ebenso typisch. Filigrane Fassaden aus Stahl und Glas lassen die Messe licht, weiträumig und transparent erscheinen. Vorbild für die hölzernen Hallendächer, die jeweils eine Fläche von 6.000 m² überspannen, sind die von Friedrich Zollinger in den 1920er Jahren entwickelten hölzernen, netzartigen Dachgewölbe. Neue Techniken im konstruktiven Schicht-Holzbau machen heute jedoch ein vielfaches der damals möglichen Spannweiten baubar.

The trade fair buildings have been grouped in the classical way, that is to say, following axiality and perspective, 'cite' the architectural traditions of the region with modern construction methods and materials. Thus, the square in front of the central columned entrance hall with the illuminated tetrapylon is already visible from quite a distance. The east-west trade fair street, flanked on both sides by open colonnades, and the covered fountains and pools between stairways are also typically classical design elements. Filigree steel-and-glass façades make the exhibition halls appear light, spacious and transparent. The wooden roofs of the halls span an area of 6,000 m² each and are modelled on the web-type wooden vault structures developed in the 1920s by Friedrich Zollinger. Today, however, new technical developments in laminated wood construction make it possible to achieve far larger spans than in Zollinger's time.

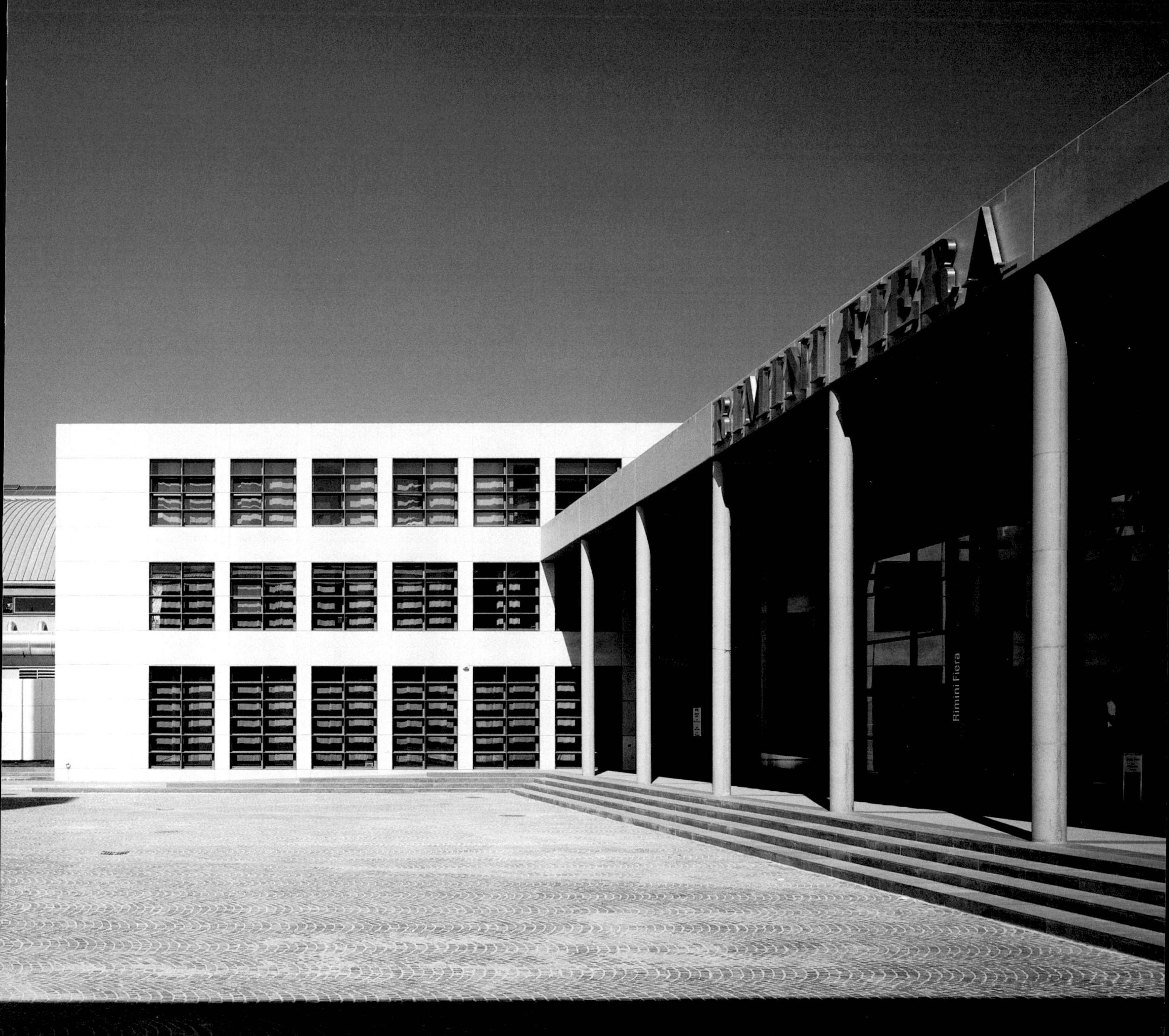
RIMINI FIERA
Rimini Fiera

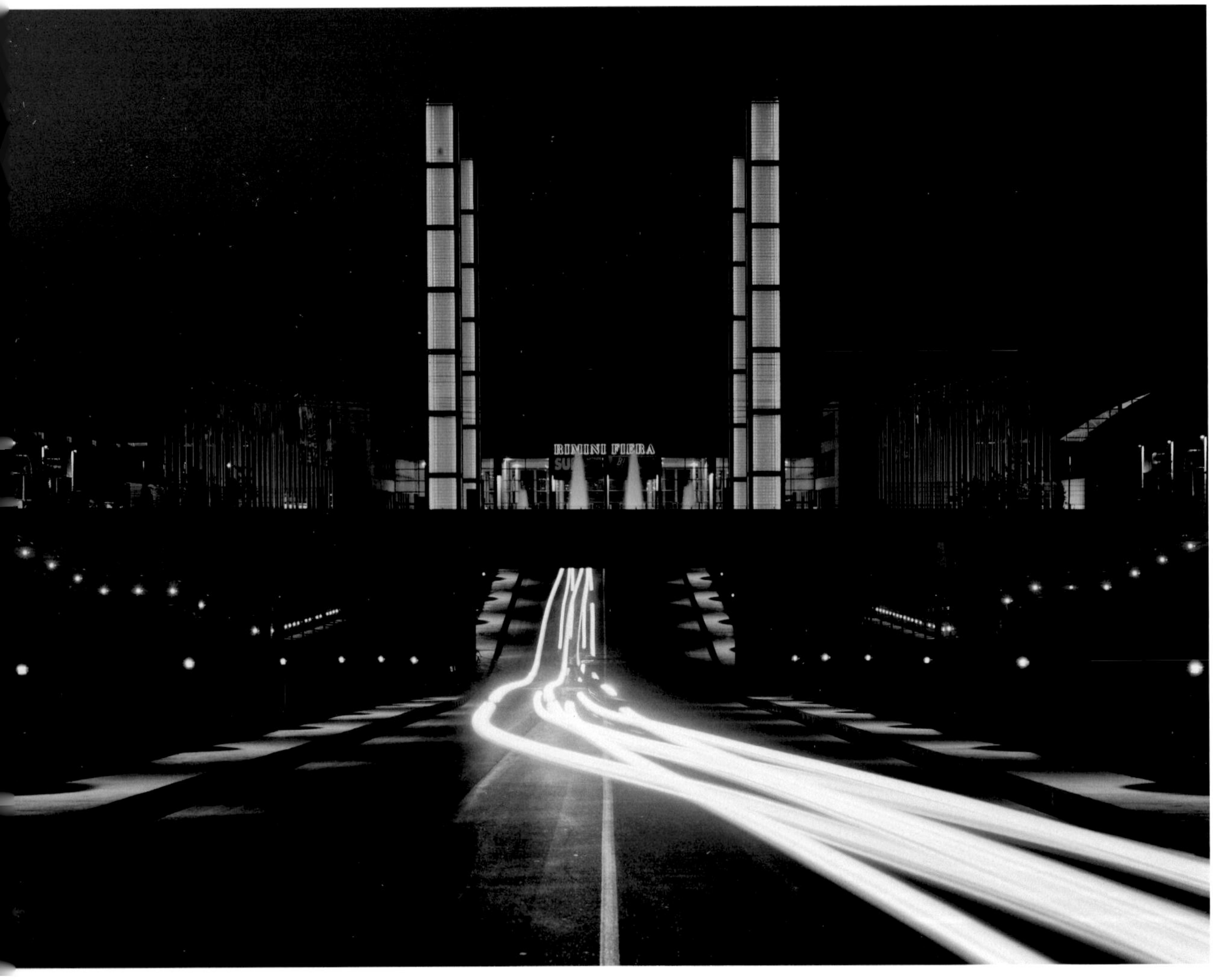
RIMINI FIERA

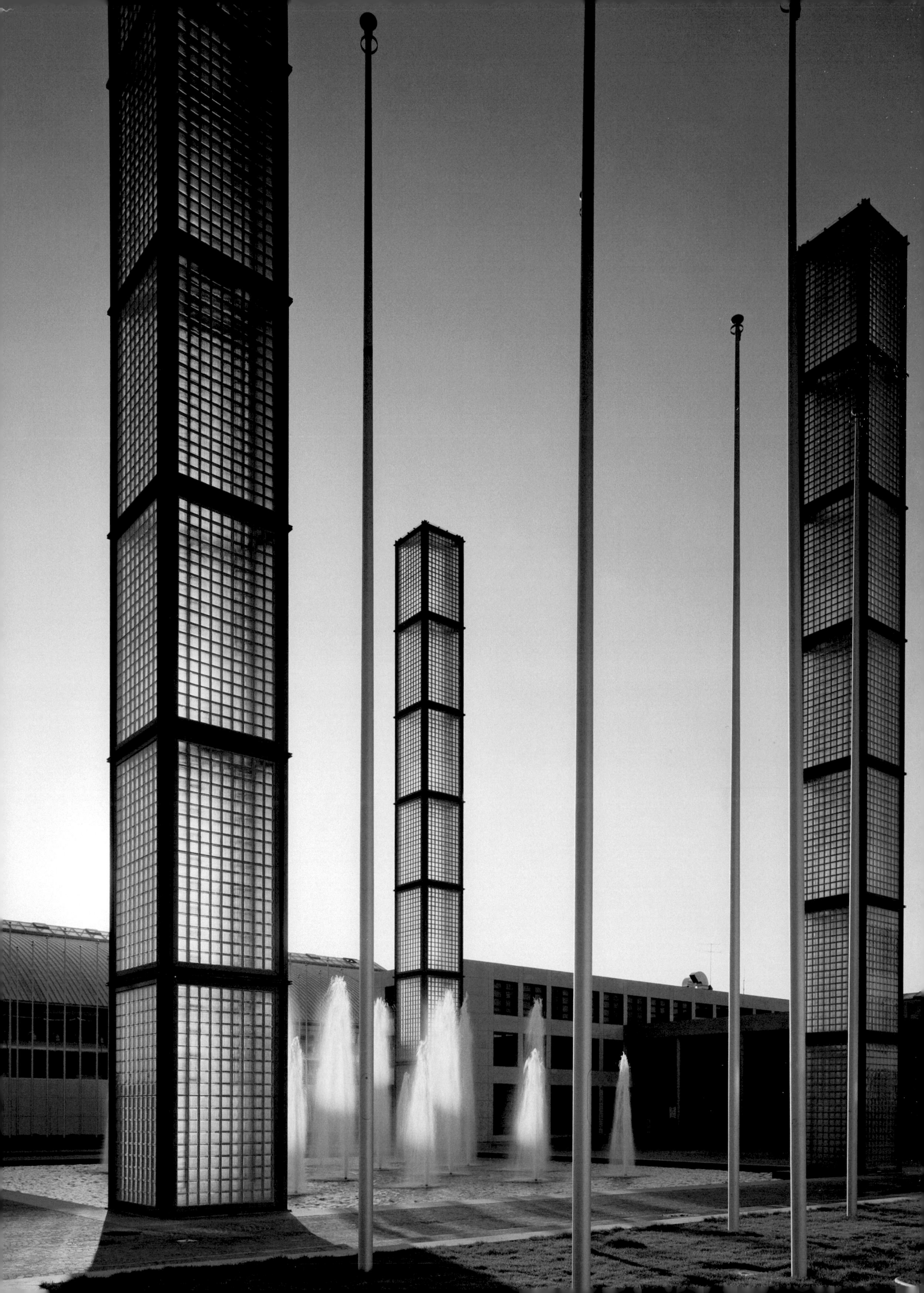

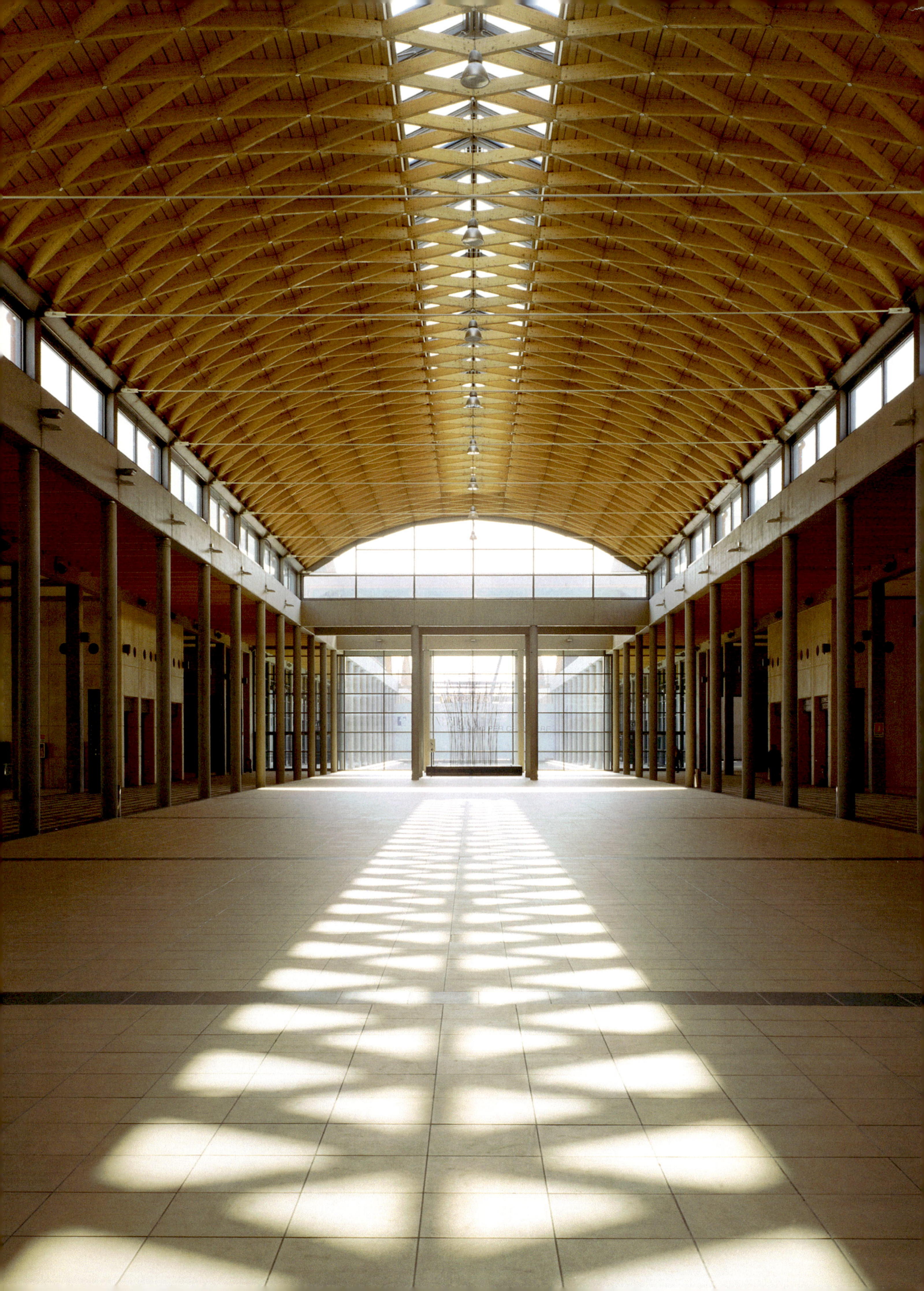

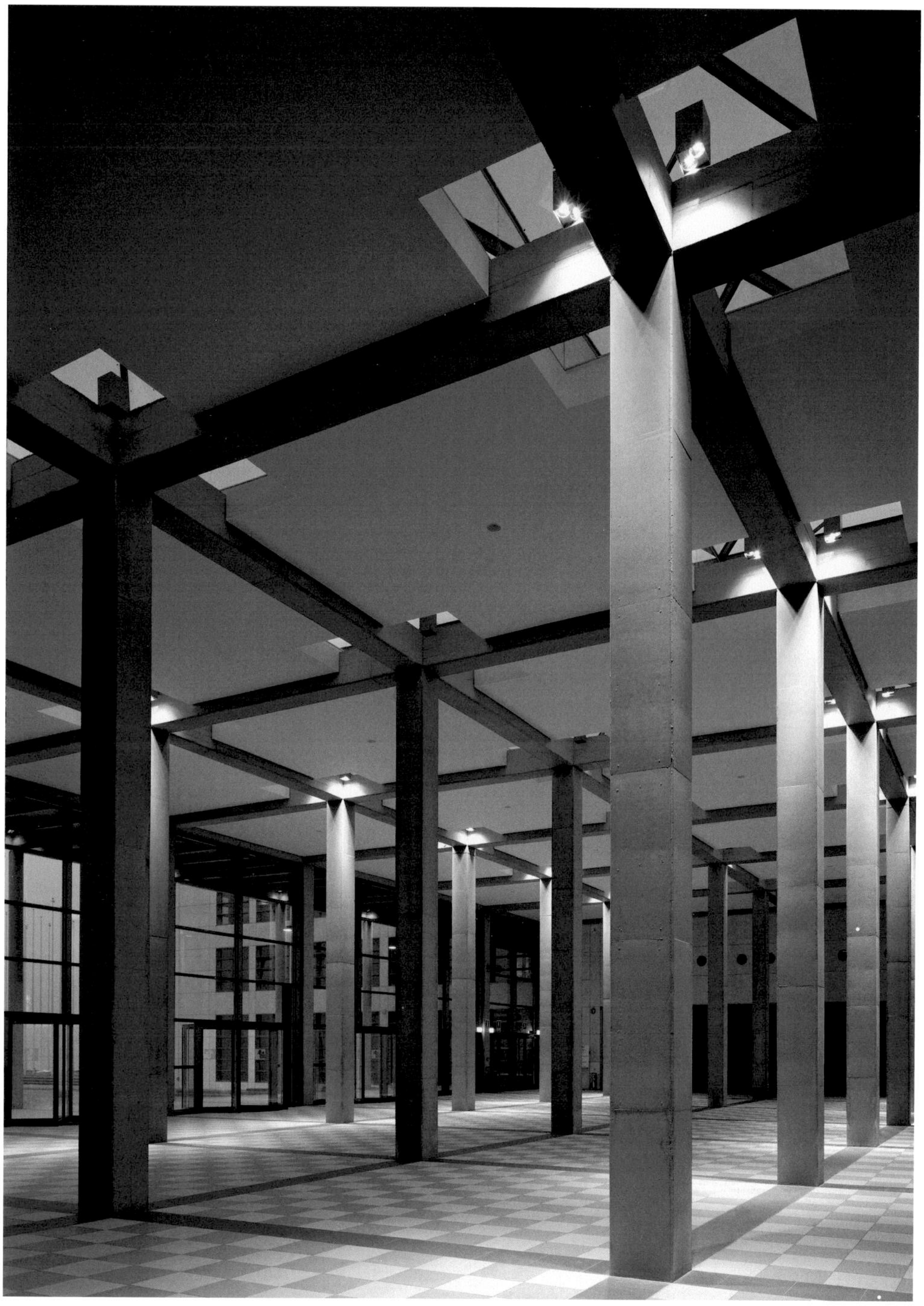

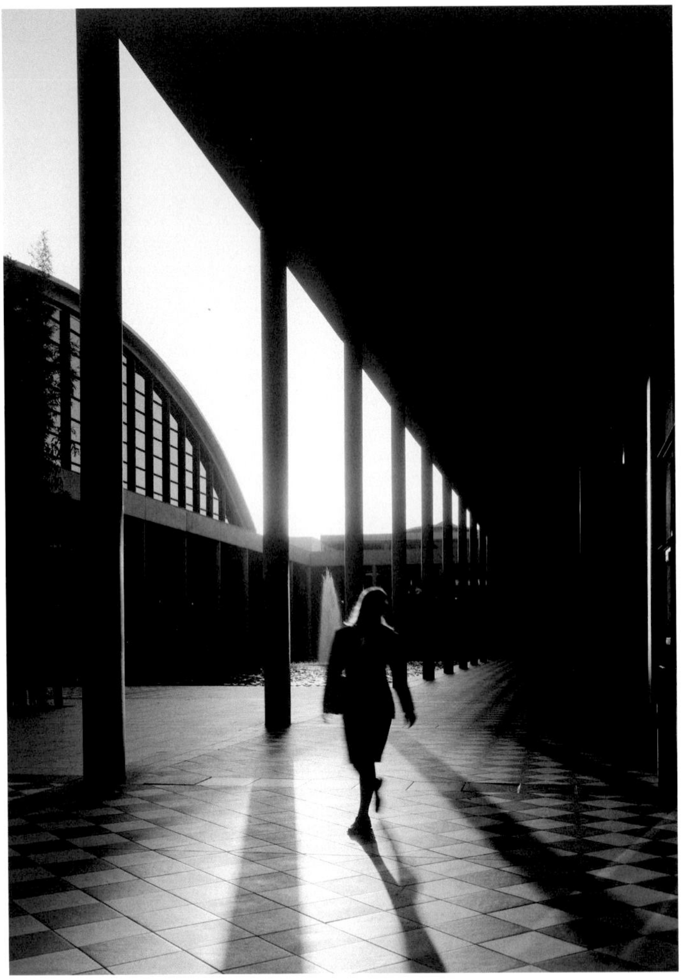

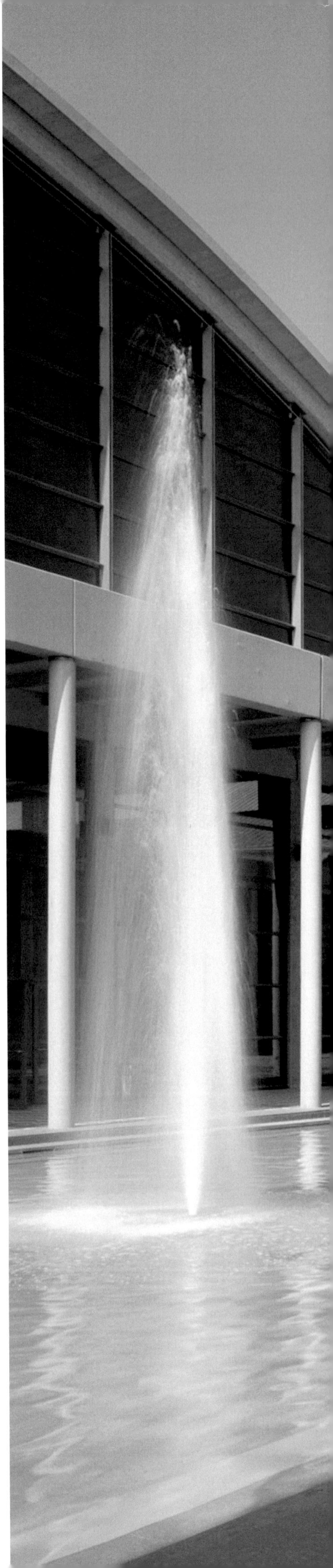

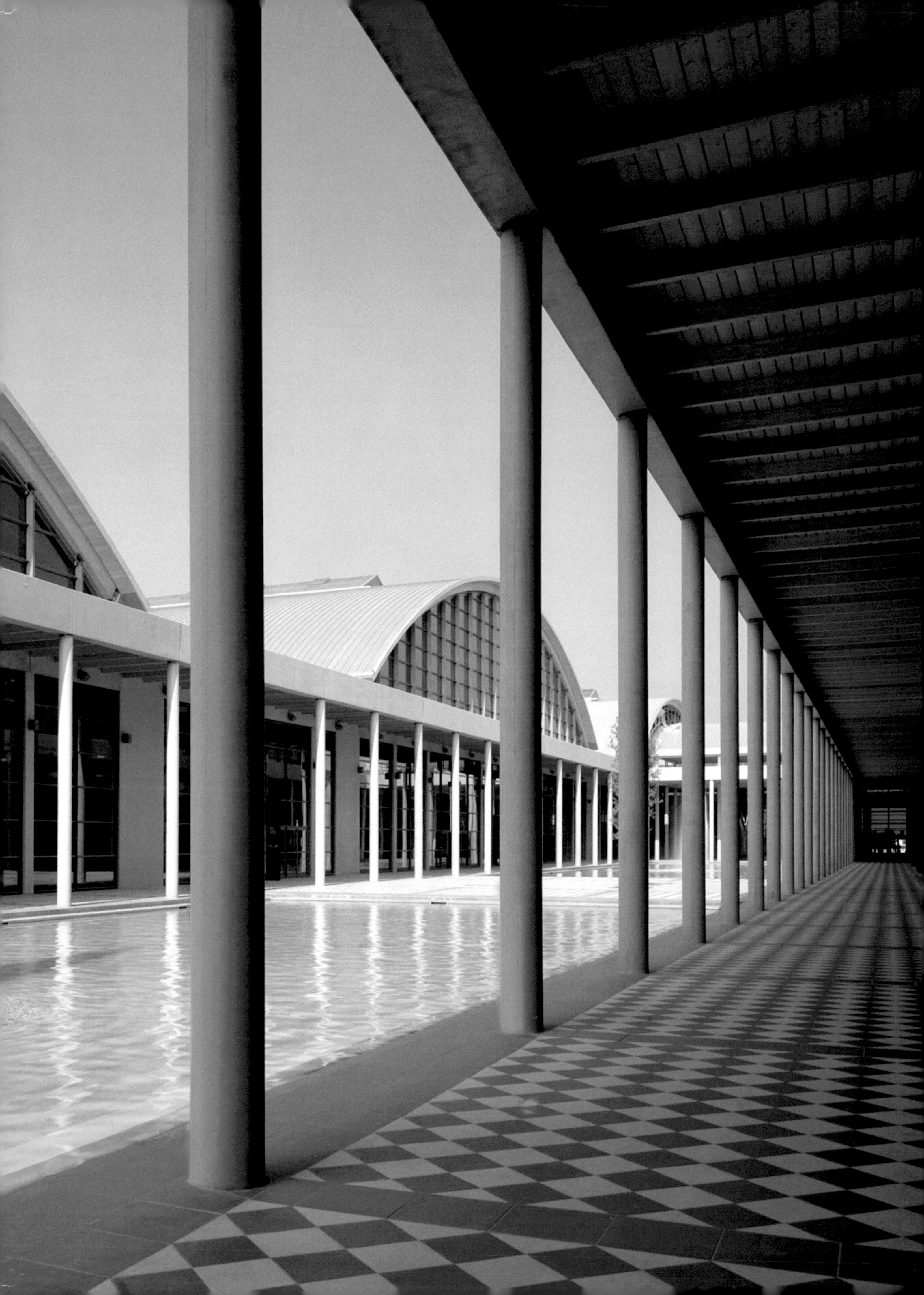

Neues Tempodrom, Berlin
New Tempodrom, Berlin

Gutachten Consultancy
1999 – 1. Preis

Entwurf Design
Meinhard von Gerkan

Partner Partner
Hubert Nienhoff

Bauherr Client
Stiftung Neues Tempodrom

Bauzeit Construction period
1999–2001

BGF Gross floor area
12.400 m²

Den baulichen Höhepunkt des Tempodroms bildet die 37 m hohe zeltähnliche Dachkonstruktion über der Großen Arena, durch deren verglaste Öffnung im Zenit Tageslicht in die Spielstätte fällt. Großflächige Verglasungen in den Fassadenbereichen unterhalb der Dachgrate stellen einen intensiven Bezug zwischen Innen und Außen her. Die Innengestaltung der Großen und der Kleinen Arena entzieht sich bewusst einer eindeutigen Interpretation und Nutzungszuordnung. Die Kleine Arena mit ihren konzentrischen Sitzstufen aus Beton kann sowohl als erweiterter Foyerraum wie auch als intimer Veranstaltungsraum genutzt werden. Dominiert nach außen das spektakuläre Dach die Erscheinung des Tempodroms, sind es im Innenraum die bewusst einfach gehaltenen Materialien. Wände und Decken sind in Sichtbeton ausgeführt, die Böden in geglättetem Gussasphalt. Die Einbauten bestehen aus Betonschaltafeln.

The outstanding structural feature of the New Tempodrom is the 37-m-high tent-like roof construction above the Large Arena, with daylight entering through the glazed opening in its zenith. Large-scale glazings on the façade areas below the roof ridges generate an intensive connection between interior and exterior. The interior finish of the Large and the Small Arena deliberately evades any definite interpretation and functional assignment. The Small Arena with its concentric seating steps of concrete can be used either as an extended foyer or as intimate event hall. Whilst the spectacular roof characterizes the appearance of the Tempodrom towards the outside, the deliberately modest selection of materials defines the interior. Walls and ceilings are finished in fair-faced concrete, the floors with polished poured asphalt. The fixtures consist of concrete formwork panels.

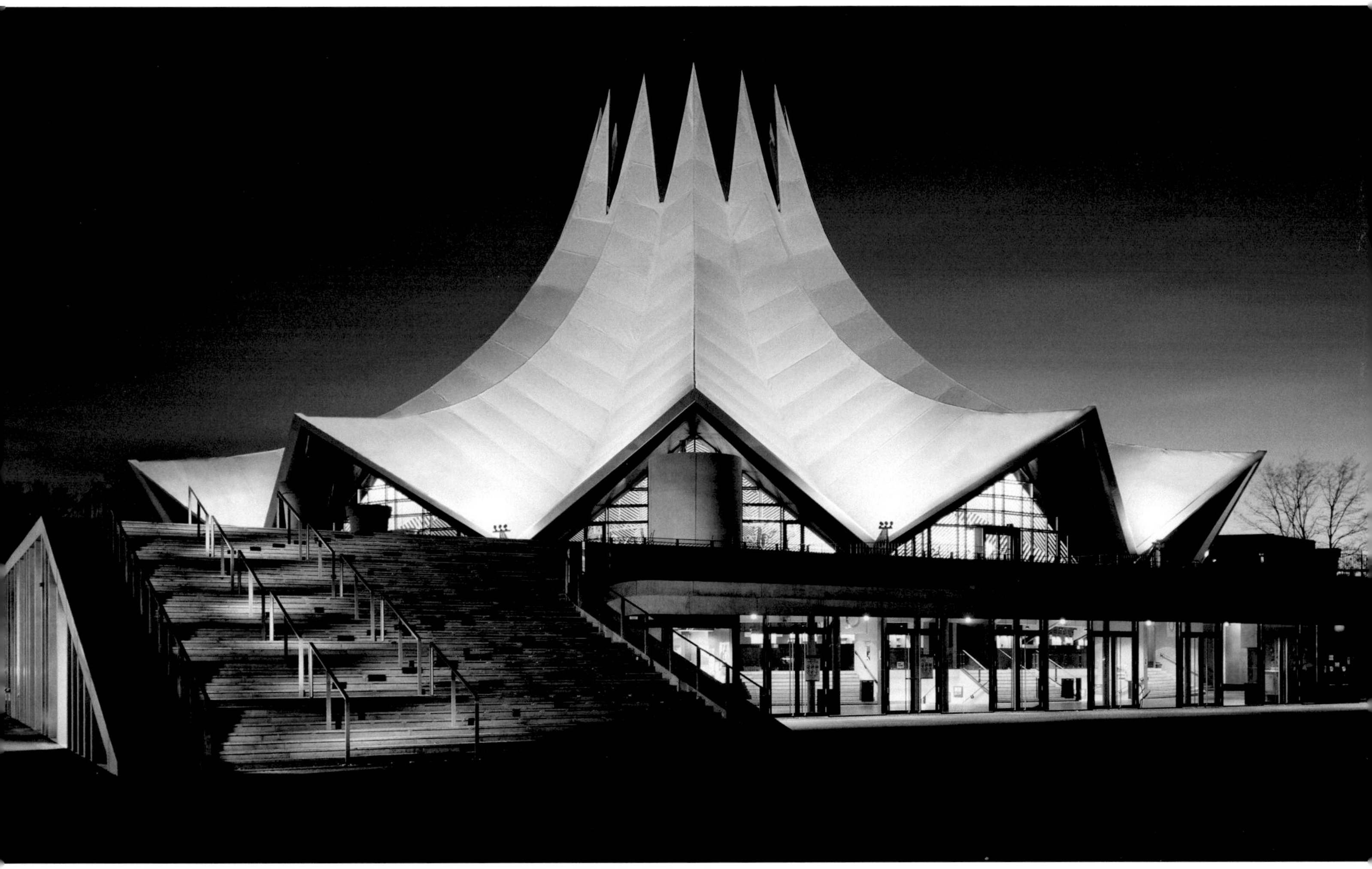

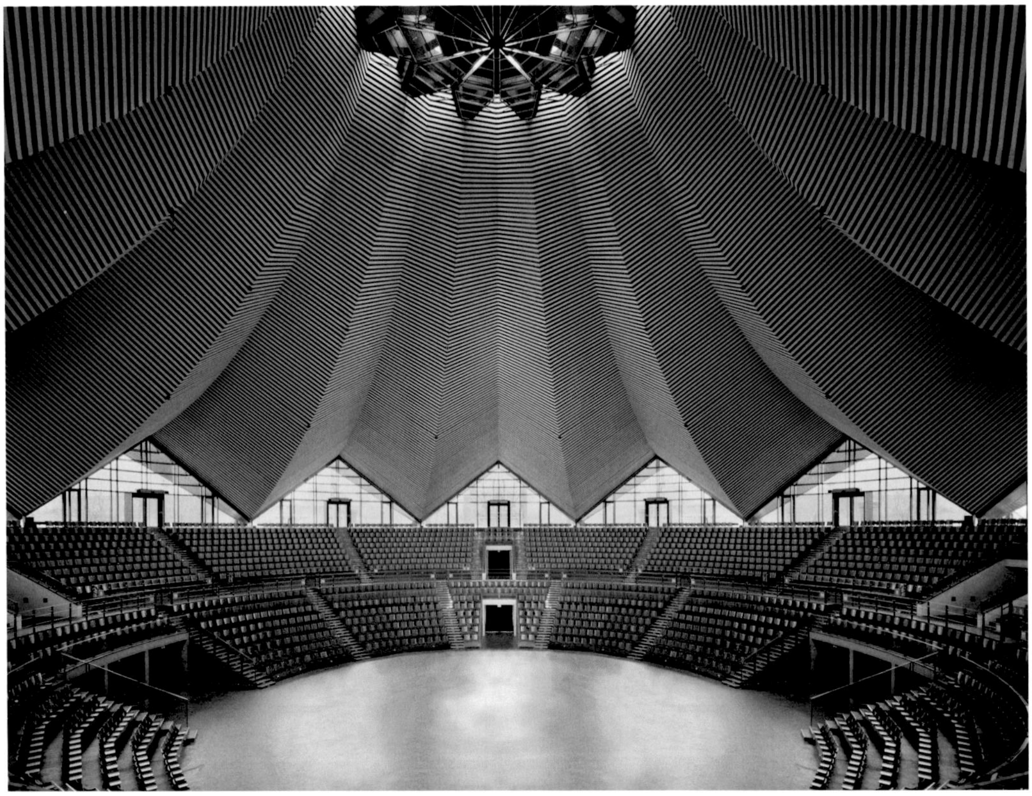

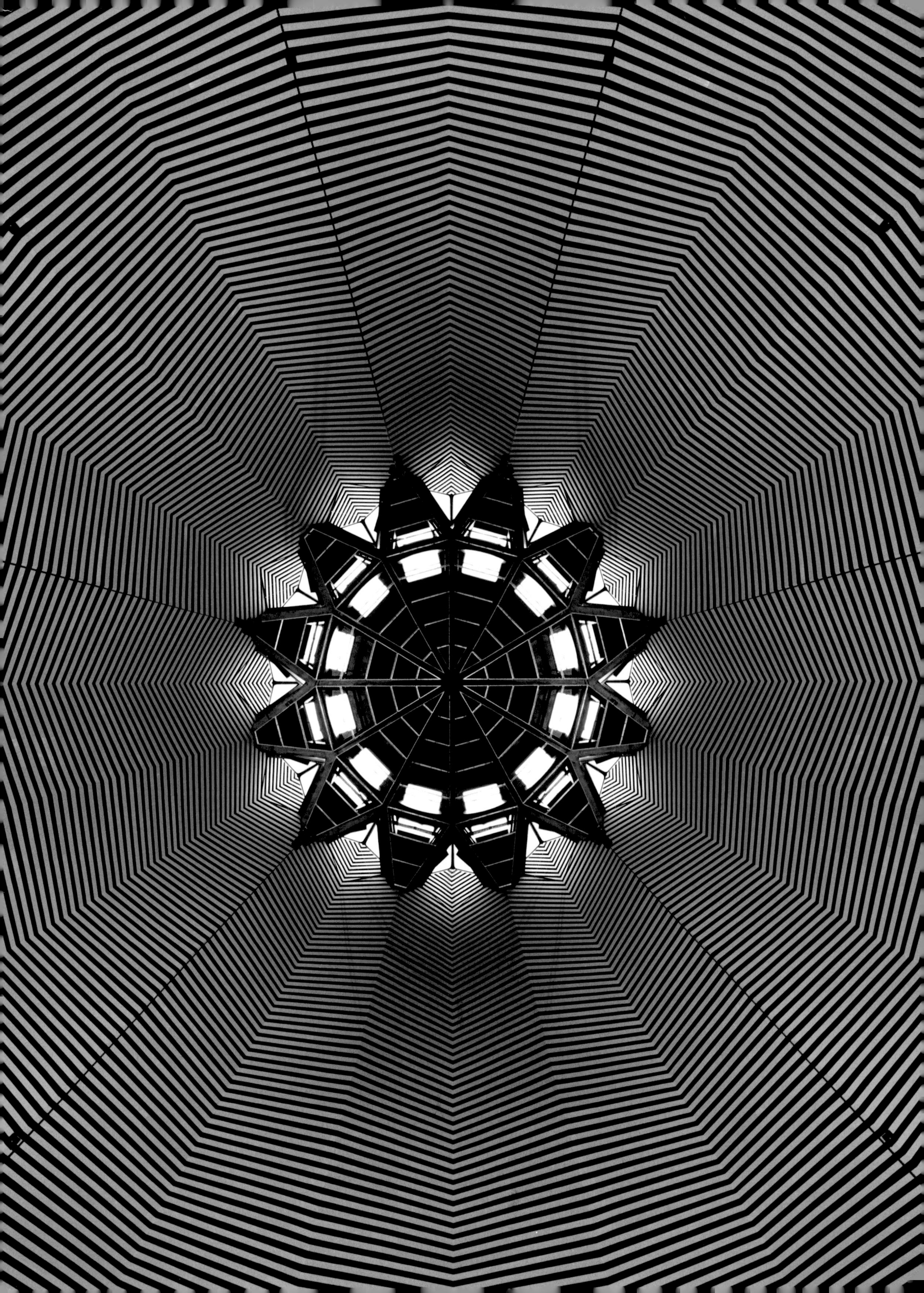

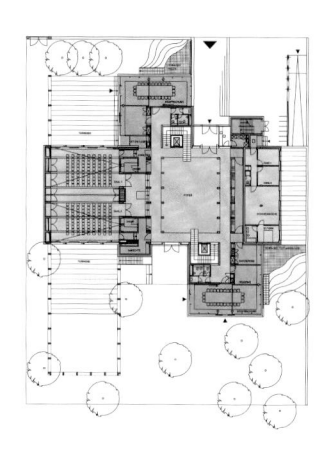

Vertretung der Länder Brandenburg und Mecklenburg-Vorpommern in Berlin
State Authority for Brandenburg and Mecklenburg-Vorpommern in Berlin

Wettbewerb Competition
1998 – 1. Preis

Entwurf Design
Meinhard von Gerkan mit Stephan Rewolle

Partner Partner
Hubert Nienhoff

Bauherr Client
Land Brandenburg, Land Mecklenburg-Vorpommern

Bauzeit Construction period
1999–2001

BGF Gross floor area
4.430 m²

In dem Gebäudetyp einer großen Stadtvilla vereinen sich die Häuser der beiden Landesvertretungen unter einem Dach. Gemeinsame Mitte ist die mehrgeschossige glasüberdeckte Halle, um die sich in radialer Anordnung die Nutzungsbereiche anordnen. Die Vertikalität der Halle steht im bewussten Gegensatz zum Raumcharakter der angrenzenden Veranstaltungsbereiche, die sich an der horizontalen Ausdehnung des Gartens orientieren. Die Reduktion der Material- und Farbwahl auf drei Grundelemente lässt die architektonische Wirkung des reinen Raumes in den Vordergrund treten. Regionalbezüge finden sich sowohl in der Gartengestaltung als auch in den Fassaden. Während die äußere Fassadenschicht aus spaltraumem Schiefer mit einem strengen Raster den brandenburgisch-preußischen Fassadentypus repräsentiert, übernimmt die rückwärtige hölzerne Schicht aus Bootsbaupaneelen den Bezug zu Mecklenburg-Vorpommern mit seinem nordischen Charakter.

Both State Authority Offices are housed together in a building similar to that of a large city villa. A multi-storey atrium hall located under a glass roof forms the central space shared by both authorities, around which the various uses are radially allocated. The hall's vertical emphasis forms a deliberate contrast to the spatial character of the adjoining event areas, which take reference from the horizontal expanse of the garden. The reduction of the material and colour choice to three basic elements emphasizes the architectural quality of the pure space. Regional characteristics are incorporated into the garden as well as into the façades. The clearly organized, external slate envelope of the building is representative of Brandenburg and Prussia, whereas the rear wooden slats made of boat hull panelling is reminiscent of Mecklenburg-Vorpommern with its particular Nordic flair.

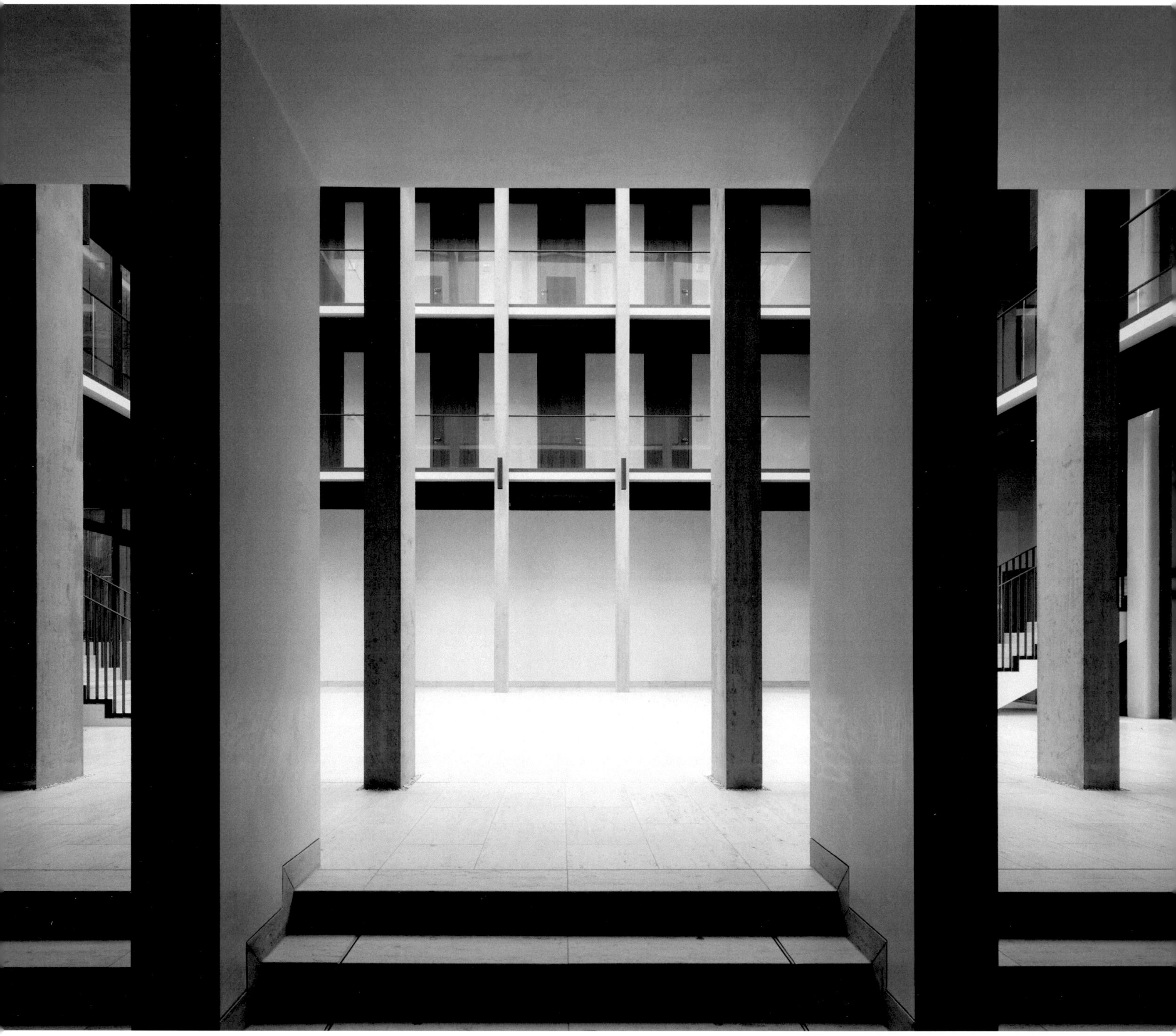

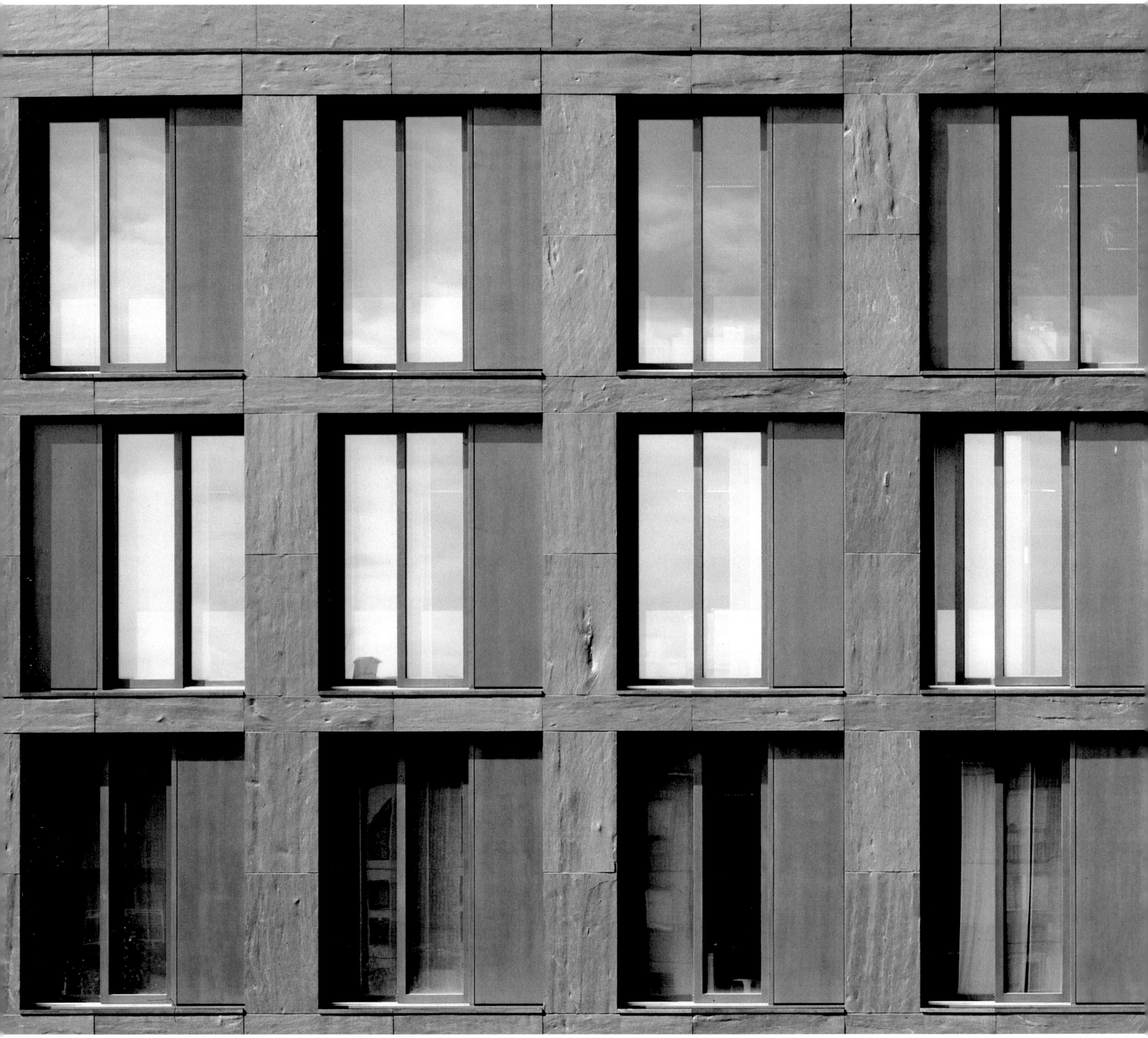

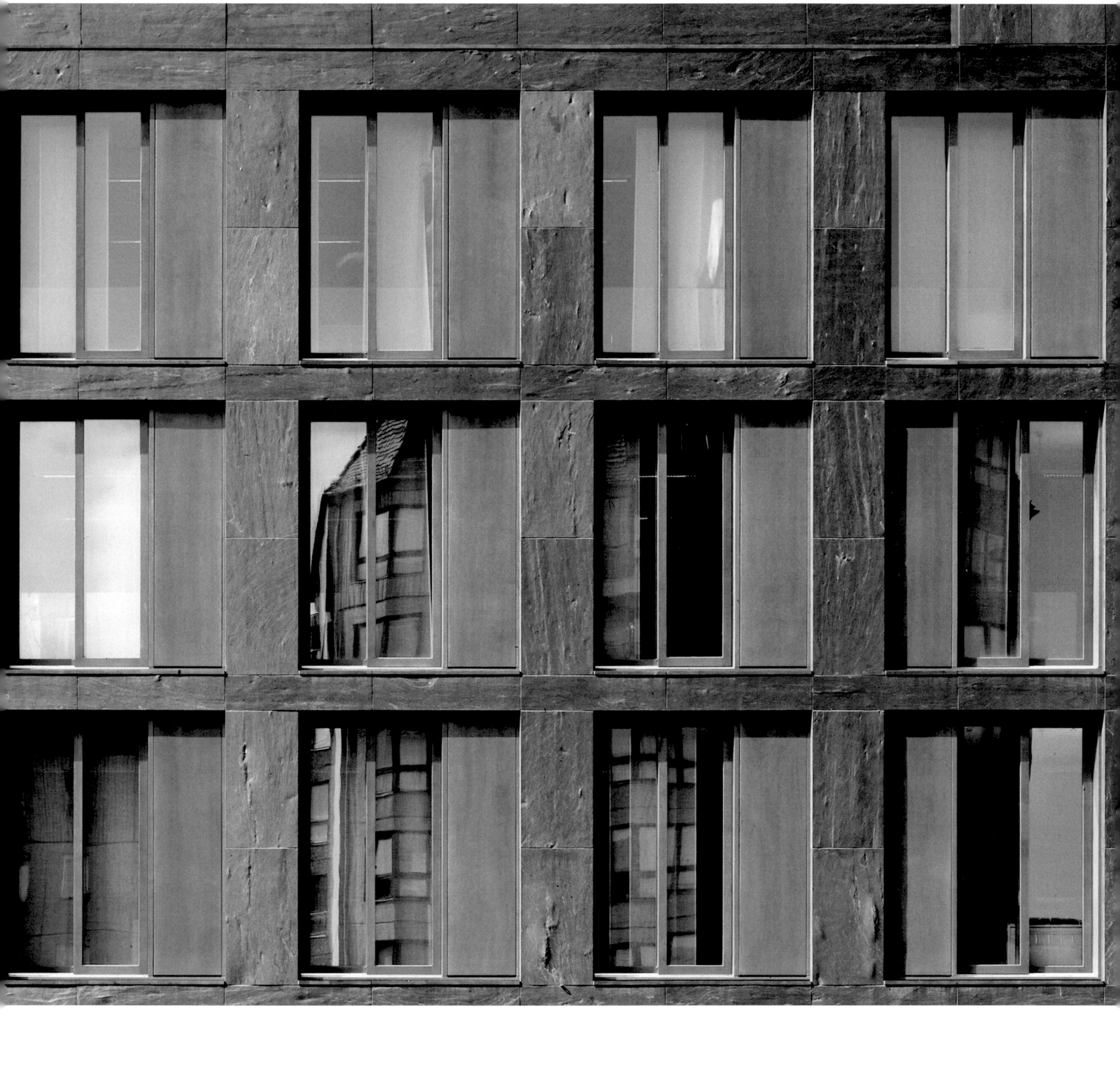

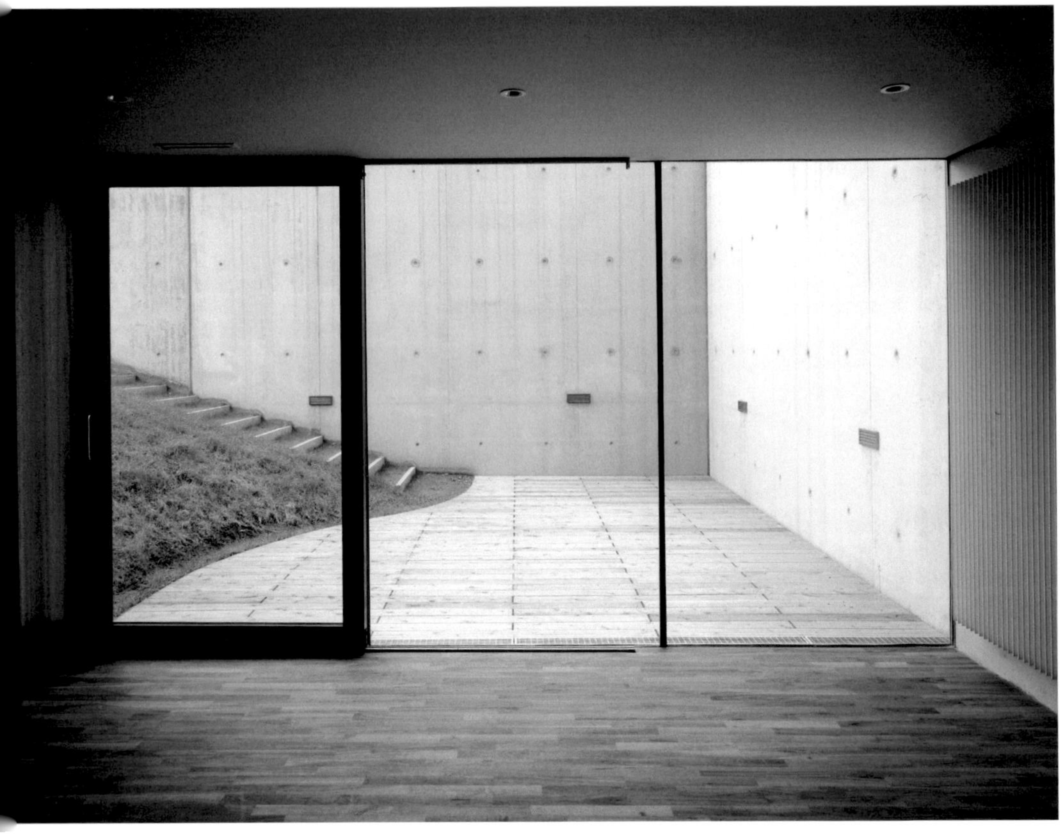

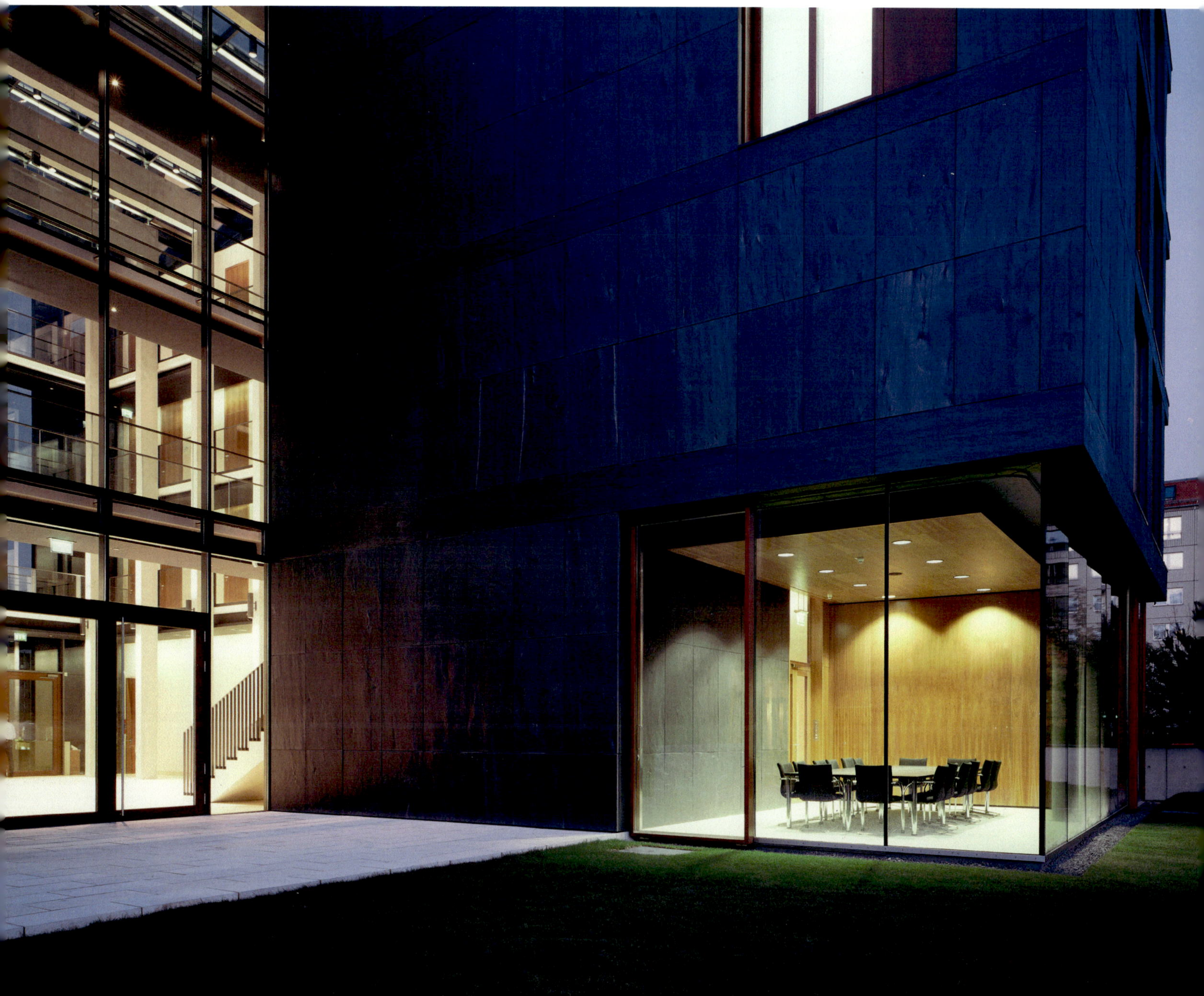

2002

Bodensee-Messe, Friedrichshafen

Hölzerne Tonnengewölbe überspannen in hohem Bogen stützenfrei die 60 Meter breiten Messehallen. Im Zentrum bildet das über ein Glasdach belichtete Aktionszentrum den räumlichen Schwerpunkt des Foyers. Seine 120 Meter lange und 5 Meter hohe Attika ist innen mit dem gemalten Panorama des Bodensees geschmückt.

Bodensee Trade Fair, Friedrichshafen

Wooden barrel vaults span the 60-m-wide halls in a wide arch without columns. In the core, the activity centre, which is daylit via a glass roof above, forms the spatial focus of the foyer. Its 120-m-long and 5-m-high attic is decorated on the inside with a painted panorama of Lake Constance.

Hanse-Messe, Rostock

Die Trag- und Deckenkonstruktionen der Halle und der Pavillon-Rotunde entsprechen als sichtbare Elemente aus Holz, Sichtbeton und Stahl dem übergeordneten Gestaltungskonzept. Die Holzkonstruktion ist als modifiziertes Zollinger-Prinzip in kombinierter Schichtholz- und Stahlbauweise errichtet.

Hanse Trade Fair, Rostock

The load-bearing and roof construction of the hall and the pavilion rotunda correspond to the superior design concept as visible elements of timber, fair-faced concrete and steel. The timber structure is assembled as a modified Zollinger principle with a combined laminated wood and steel method.

Kibbelstegbrücken, Hamburg-Speicherstadt

Mit backsteinverkleideten Bastionen, Kaimauern und Brückenpfeilern, metallisch grauen Bogenkonstruktionen und Geländern in Gestalt von Schiffsrelings fügt sich die 200 m lange, aus drei Brücken bestehende Verbindung zwischen Altstadt und HafenCity wie selbstverständlich in die historische Speicherstadt.

Kibbelsteg Bridges, Hamburg-Speicherstadt

Brick-clad bastions, quayside walls and bridge piers, as well as metallic-grey arch structures and balustrades in the shape of a ship's rail, give the newly-created 200-m-long three-part bridge construction a natural appearance within the context of the historical Speicherstadt and the HafenCity.

Restaurant „Bastion" am Binnenhafen, Hamburg-Speicherstadt

Quadratische Fenster und ein Fensterband rhythmisieren die Ziegelfassade und verstärken den Bastionscharakter des Erdgeschosses. Das Obergeschoss öffnet sich mit einer verglasten horizontal gegliederten Fassade zum Binnenhafen und zur Stadt. Das auskragende Flachdach betont die Länge des Pavillons.

Restaurant 'Bastion' at the Inner Harbour, Hamburg-Speicherstadt

Square windows and a window band introduce a rhythm into the brick façade and emphasize the ground floor's bastion-like character. The upper storey opens up towards the inner harbour and the city with a horizontally structured glass façade. The cantilevered flat roof reinforces the pavilion's length.

2002

Hauptverwaltung der HHLA, Hamburg-Speicherstadt

Ein freitragendes tonnenförmiges Stahl-Glasdach überdeckt den Innenhof des modernisierten Neorenaissancebaus und macht ihn zu einer lichtdurchfluteten Eingangshalle. Die Böden der angrenzenden Speicher wurden durch teilweises Entfernen der Decken miteinander verbunden und großzügiger gestaltet.

HHLA Headquarters, Hamburg-Speicherstadt

A cantilevered, barrel-shaped, steel-glass roof covers the courtyard of the modernized neo-Renaissance building in order to achieve a light-flooded reception hall. In the adjacent warehouses the ceilings were partly removed to allow for a visual link and generate a brighter and airier atmosphere.

Finca „Es Rafalet", Mallorca, Spanien

Ein Neubau mit großer zentraler Halle ergänzt die auf einem Felsvorsprung gelegene Finca. Türen, Fenster, Einbauten, Lampen und Möbel sind aus auberginefarbenen Betoplantafeln gefertigt. Die sichtbaren Holzkonstruktionen aus Robinie harmonieren mit der Stukko-Struktur der Innenwandflächen.

Finca 'Es Rafalet', Majorca, Spain

A new building with a large central hall complements the finca, which is located on a ledge. Doors, windows, built-in units, lamps and furniture are made of aubergine-coloured Betoplan panels. The visible timber structures of locust wood harmonize with the stucco structure of the interior walls.

Speicherblock X, Hamburg-Speicherstadt

Das Kontorgebäude setzt die Zeile der Speicherbauten mit gleicher Bautiefe und Höhe im gestalterischen und stofflichen Kontext fort. Die für die Architektur der Speicherstadt typischen Motive, wie Backsteinfassaden und vertikale Strukturen, werden mit modernen Mitteln interpretiert.

Kundenzentrum des Porsche-Werks Leipzig

Der massive Sichtbetonsockel und der kreiselförmige, mit Metallpaneelen verkleidete Turm bilden eine Landmarke, von der sich die ausgedehnte Gesamtanlage überblicken lässt. Das Gebäude dient als Präsentationsplattform und beherbergt Verwaltung und Werkstatt für den hier gefertigten Geländewagen „Cayenne".

Harburg Arcaden, Hamburg

Die bogenförmige Passage bietet auf drei Ebenen Platz für 65 Geschäfte. Ein als großzügiger Eingang umgestaltetes Jugendstilgebäude und die originalgetreu rekonstruierte Alte Post sind Teile des Ensembles, das durch einen fünfgeschossigen Neubau mit Verkaufsebenen, Büros und einem Parkhaus ergänzt wird.

Warehouse Block X, Hamburg-Speicherstadt

The office building extends the existing row of warehouses with the same building depth and height and the identical design and material context, thus complementing the Speicherstadt ensemble. The architectural expression is orientated at motifs typical of the Speicherstadt, such as brick façades with vertical window formats, and interpreted with modern means.

Customer Centre of the Leipzig Porsche Plant

The massive fair-faced concrete base and the conic tower clad in metal panels form a landmark, from where the extensive complex can be viewed. The building serves as presentation platform housing administration and workshop facilities for the 'Cayenne' cross-country vehicle, which is manufactured here.

Harburg Arcades, Hamburg

The arched arcade offers space for 65 shops on three levels. An Art Nouveau building that has been converted into a spacious entrance and the 'Alte Post', which has been reconstructed true to the original, are part of the ensemble, which is complemented with a new five-storey complex accommodating shopping levels, offices and a multi-storey car park.

2002

Europäisches Patentamt, Umbau Saal 102, München

Die Erweiterung der EU erforderte auch eine Umgestaltung des Saals 102 im Europäischen Patentamt. Die neuen Plätze wurden als innerer, geschlossener Tischkreis dem vorhandenen Rund hinzugefügt und können flexibel auf- und abgebaut werden. Darüber hinaus wurde die technische Ausstattung ergänzt.

European Patent Office, Conversion Hall 102, Munich

The expansion of the European Union consequently demanded the conversion of Hall 102 in the European Patent Office. The new seats were added to the existing circle as an inner, continuous ring of tables; they can be flexibly set up and disassembled. In addition, the technical equipment was complemented.

Wohnbebauung Xinzhao, 1. Bauabschnitt, Peking, China

Das nahezu quadratische Gelände wird durch ein Achsenkreuz in vier große, linear strukturierte Quartiere mit zeilenartigen Gebäuden unterteilt, die eine maximale Anzahl von Nord-Süd orientierten Wohnungen ermöglichen. Die grüne Hauptachse und die kleineren Innenhöfe bieten Freiräume in Wohnungsnähe.

Xinzhao Residential Area, 1st Building Phase, Beijing, China

An axial grid system subdivides the almost square area into four large districts with a linear structure, wherein the rows of buildings allow for a maximum of north-south orientated apartments. The landscaped main axis and the smaller courtyards provide recreation spaces close to the apartments.

Liquidrom im Tempodrom, Berlin

Neben der Großen und der Kleinen Arena bildet das Liquidrom den dritten Veranstaltungsort im Gebäude des Tempodroms. Hauptattraktion ist ein kreisrundes Wasserbecken von 13 m Durchmesser, das von einer kuppelförmigen Betonschale mit einem Oberlicht im Zenit überwölbt wird.

Liquidrom in the Tempodrom, Berlin

Beside the Large Arena and the Small Arena the Liquidrom is the third event hall in the Tempodrom building. The main attraction is a circular water basin 13 m in diameter, which is vaulted with a domed concrete shell incorporating a top light in its zenith.

Finca „Es Rafalet", Mallorca, Spanien
Finca 'Es Rafalet', Majorca, Spain

1999

Entwurf Design
Meinhard von Gerkan

Bauherr Client
Meinhard von Gerkan

Bauzeit Construction period
2000–2001

BGF Bestand Gross floor area: old building
380 m²

BGF Erweiterung Gross floor area: extension
190 m²

Im Norden der Insel Mallorca, in einem abgeschiedenen Tal zwischen Campanet und Pollença, erwarb das Ehepaar von Gerkan eine Finca, die wie ein Adlerhorst an einem Felsvorsprung einen atemberaubenden Blick über die halbe Insel und zur Bucht von Alcudia bietet. Für die sechsköpfige Familie nebst Gästen und für die alljährlichen Partnersitzungen des Büros von Gerkan, Marg und Partner war das an sich großzügige ältere Haus trotzdem zu klein. So entstand im Rahmen der zulässigen Bebauungsgrenzen, die für 500 m² Wohnfläche eine Grundstücksgröße von 15 ha verlangen, eine Ergänzung in Form einer zweiten „Finca". Dachneigung sowie Ziegel der Dacheindeckung waren vorgegeben. Die Außenwände sind geputzt. Alle Holzteile – Türen, Fenster, Läden, Einbauten, Lampen und bewegliche Möbel – sind aus auberginefarbenen Betoplantafeln gefertigt; die innen wie außen sichtbaren Holzkonstruktionen aus Rubinienholz; der Fußboden durchgängig aus Dielen mit Neopren-Fugen wie ein Schiffsdeck. Die Innenwände haben eine Stukko-Struktur. Im Zentrum des Neubaus liegt die 60 m² große Halle mit Blick zum Tal und gegenüber bergseitiger Öffnung zu einem Brunnen.

In the north of Majorca, in a secluded valley between Campanet and Pollença, the von Gerkan couple purchased a finca, which is located on a ledge like an eyrie, offering a breathtaking view over half of the island and towards the Bay of Alcudia. For the family of six plus guests, as well as the yearly partner meeting of the von Gerkan, Marg und Partner practice the spacious older house was still too small. Therefore, an addition in the form of a second 'Finca' was built within the maximum development limits, which demand a site area of 15 hectares for 500 m² of floor area. The roof pitch and roofing tiles were specified. The exterior walls are plastered. All timber components (doors, windows, shutters, built-in units, lamps, and movable pieces of furniture) are made of aubergine-coloured Betoplan panels; the timber structure visible on the inside and outside is made of locust wood. The floor, of continuous floorboards with neoprene joints, is reminiscent of a ship's deck. The interior walls are finished in a stucco structure. A 60-m²-large hall is located in the centre of the new building, offering a view over the valley and towards a fountain on the opposite side facing the mountain.

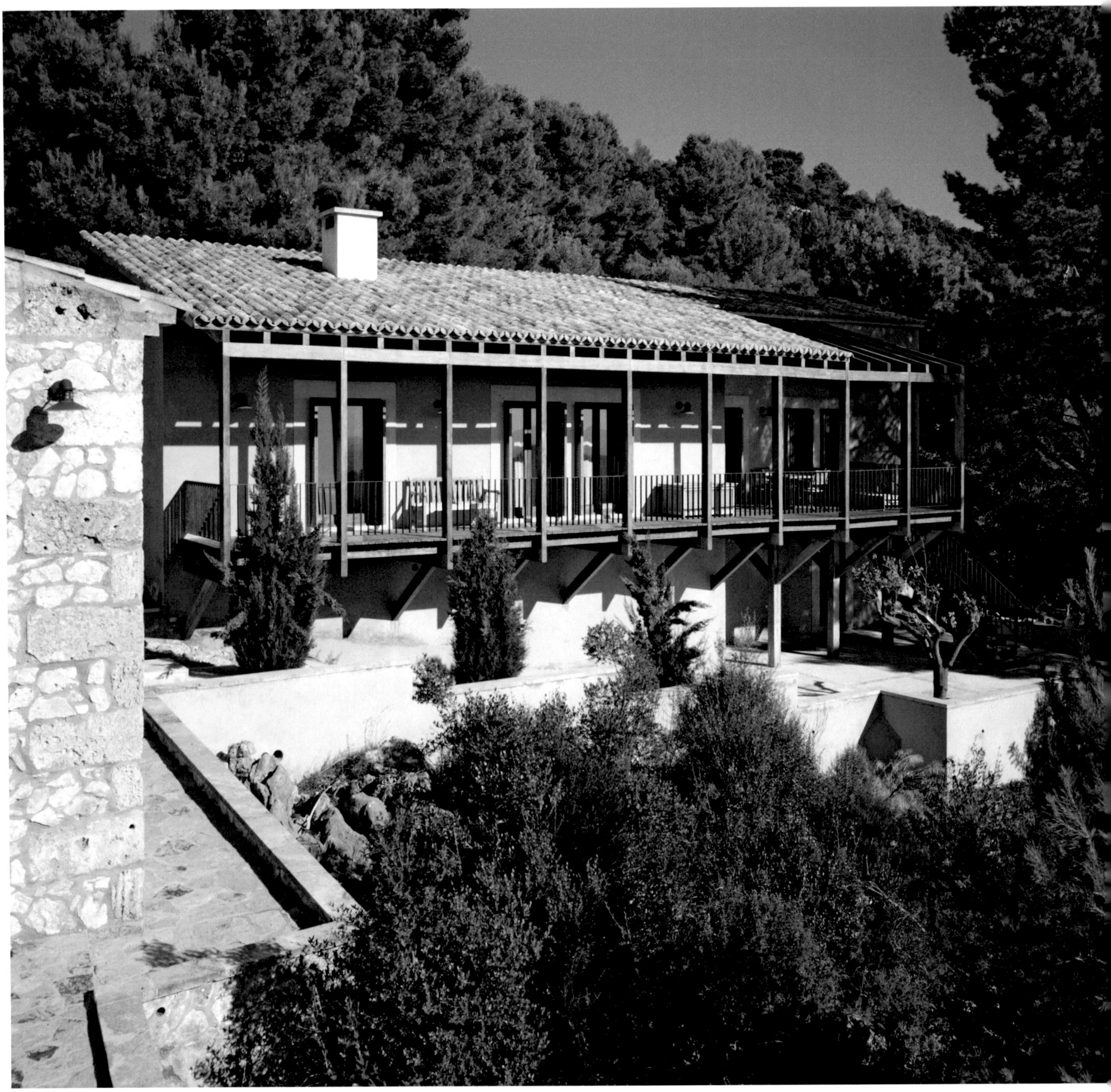

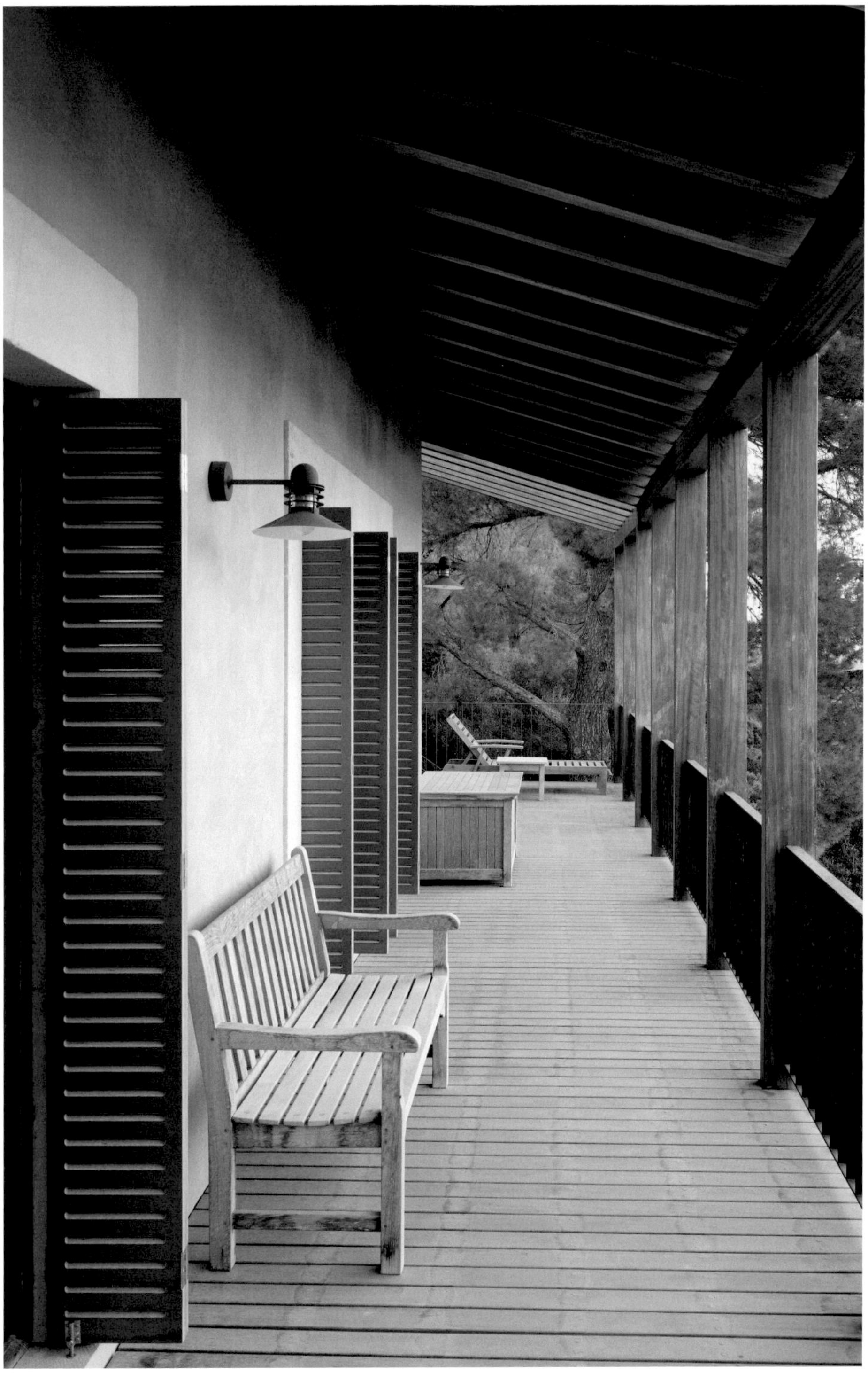

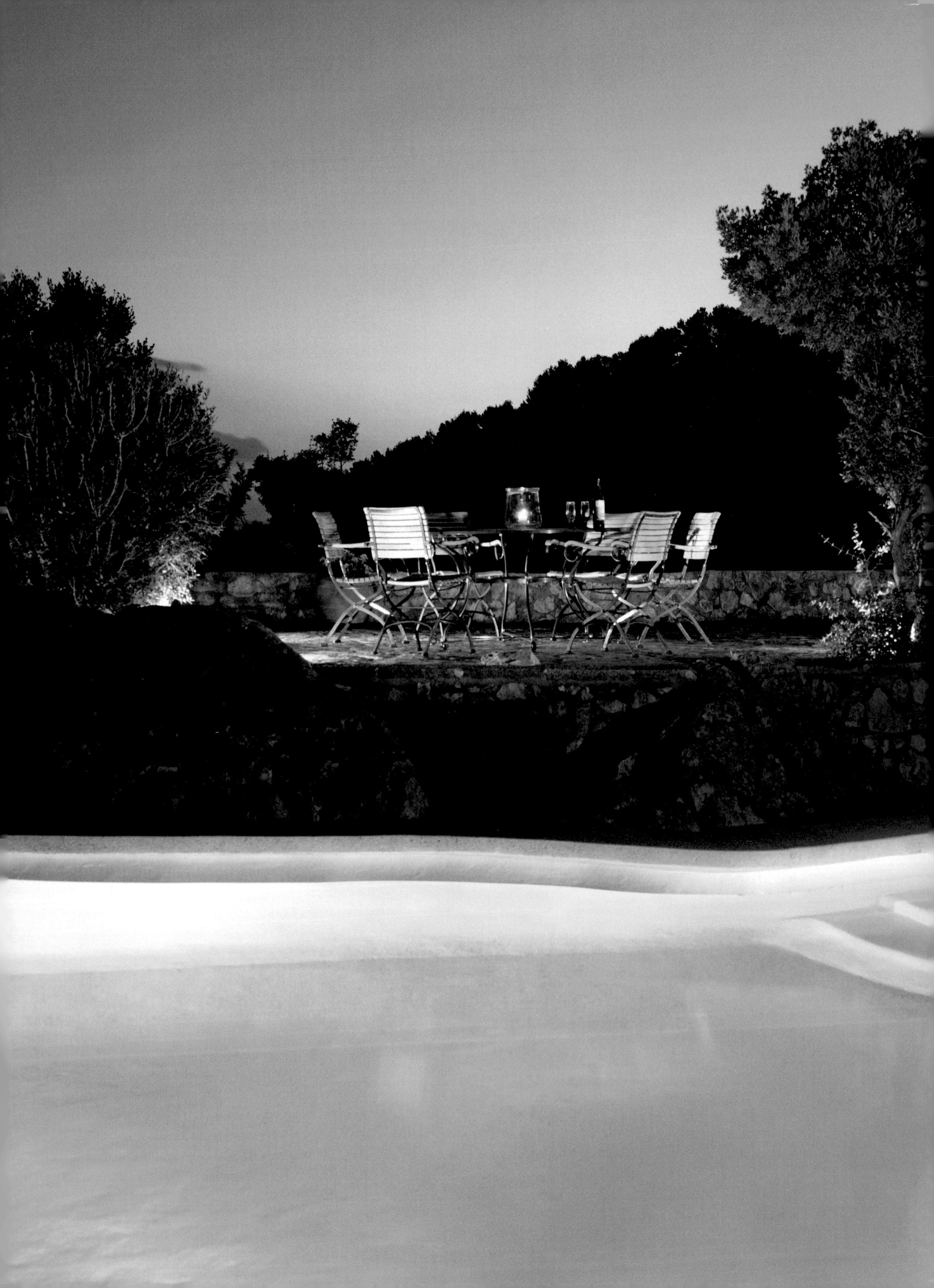

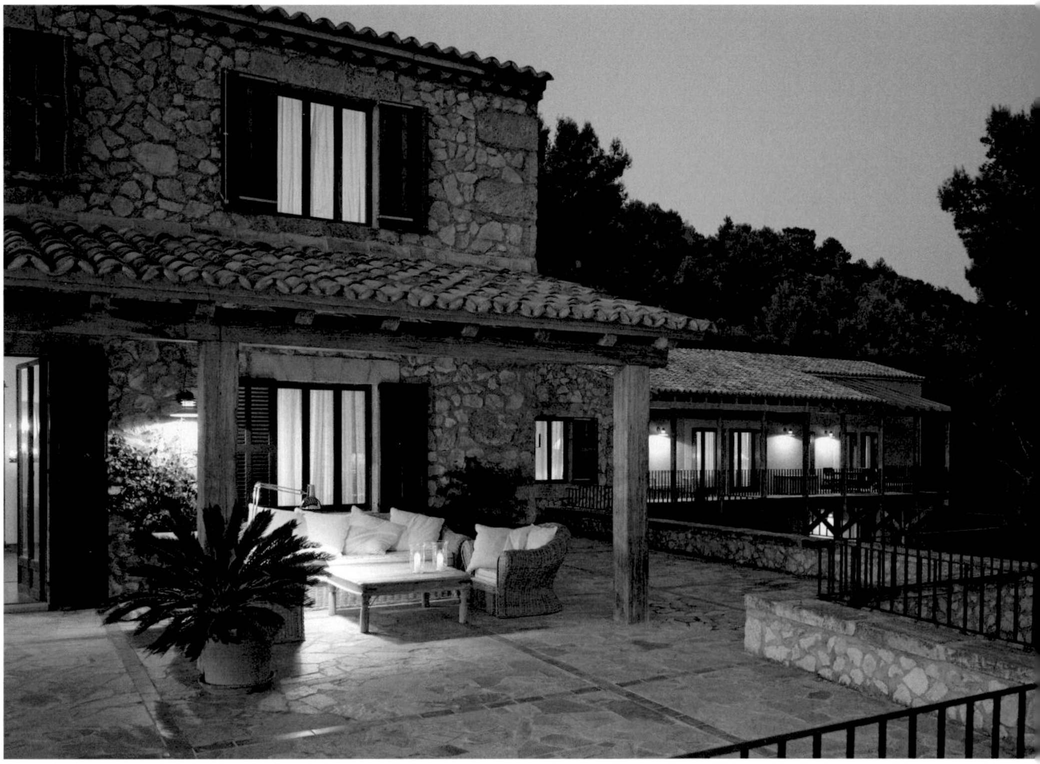

Kundenzentrum des Porsche-Werks Leipzig
Customer Centre of the Leipzig Porsche Plant

Entwurf Design
Volkwin Marg und Hubert Nienhoff

Bauherr Client
Dr. Ing. h.c. Porsche AG

Bauzeit Construction period
2001–2002

BGF Gross floor area
8.780 m²

Sockelgebäude und Turm des Kundenzentrums können unabhängig voneinander genutzt werden: Während auf der unteren Ebene der normale Werkstattbetrieb sowie die Wagenübergabe erfolgt und auf der Außenterrasse eine Sportwagenausstellung gezeigt wird, kann auf der obersten Ebene ein Konzert mit bis zu 500 Besuchern stattfinden. Neben dem kreisförmigen Veranstaltungssaal befinden sich hier ein Gastronomiebereich und eine Ausstellungsgalerie für historische Fahrzeuge. Ein kleines Auditorium im Geschoss darunter ergänzt das Raumangebot. Das Sockelgebäude und der zentrale Kern des Kundenzentrums sind aus Stahlbeton und dienen der Aussteifung des als reiner Stahlbau konzipierten Turms. Auf störende Auskreuzungen innerhalb des Stahltragwerks konnte daher verzichtet werden. Sichtbare Tragelemente im Innenraum sowie die unterschiedliche Fassadenausbildung machen beide Konstruktionsprinzipien erlebbar.

The base building and tower can be used independently: while the regular workshop activities and the handing-over of vehicles proceed on the lower level, and a sports car exhibition is on display on the outdoor terrace, a concert with an audience of up to 500 people can take place on the top level. Apart from the circular event hall this level consists of a gastronomy area and an exhibition gallery for historical vehicles. A small auditorium on the level below complements the spaces provided. The base building and the central core of the Customer Centre were built out of reinforced concrete and serve as stiffening elements to the circular tower, which is designed as a purely steel structure. It was thus possible to do without troublesome braces within the load-bearing steel structure. Visible load-bearing elements in the interior and the different façade formations make it possible to witness both construction principles.

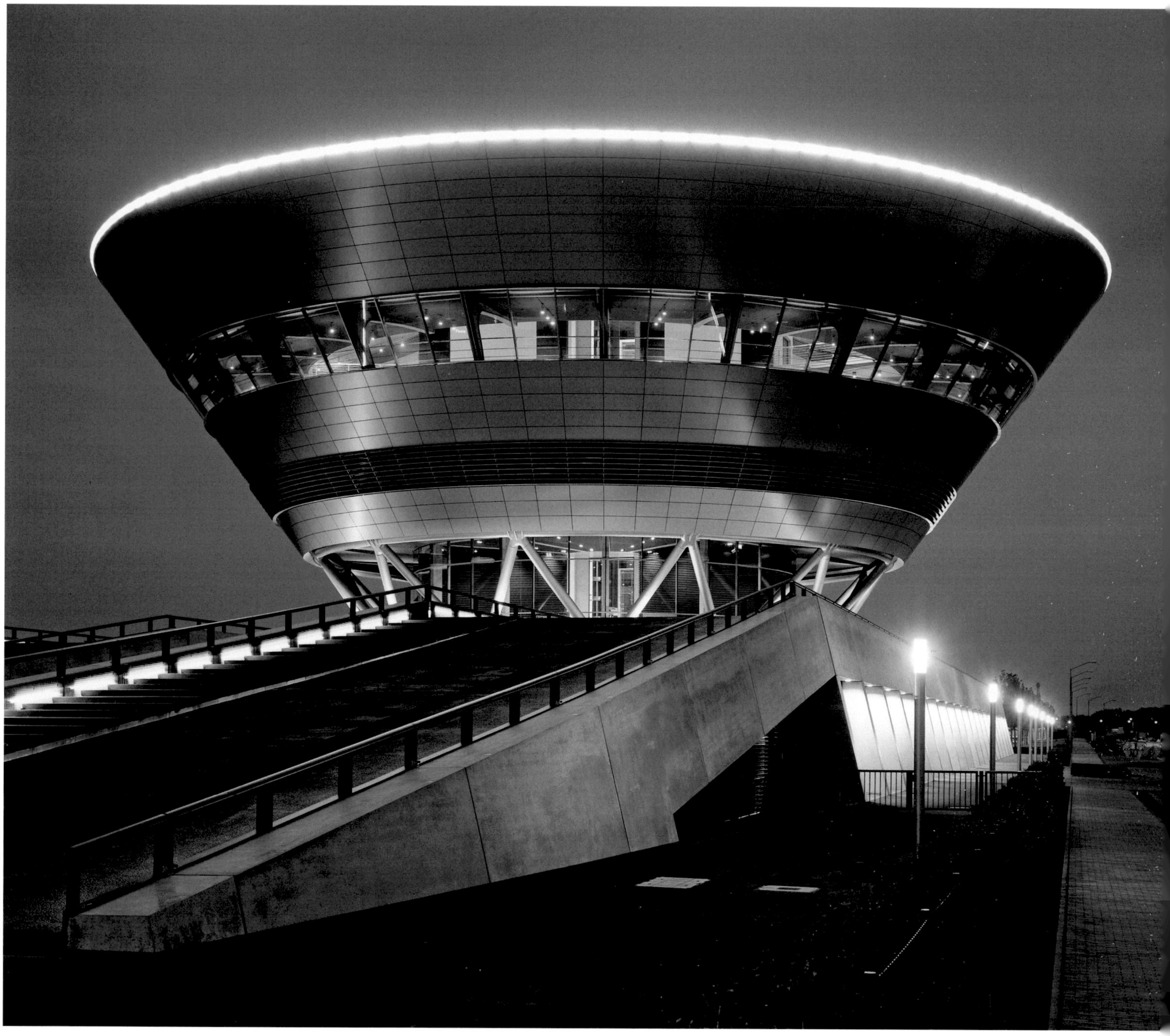

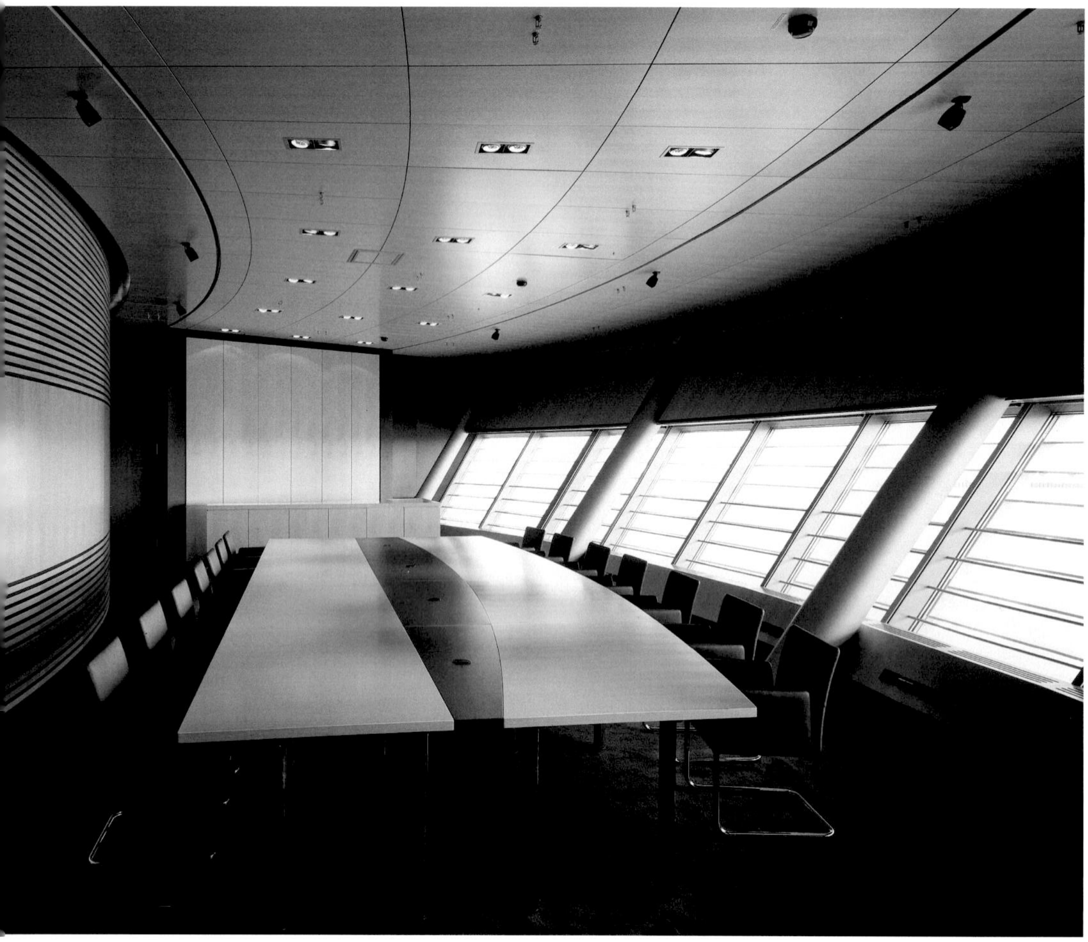

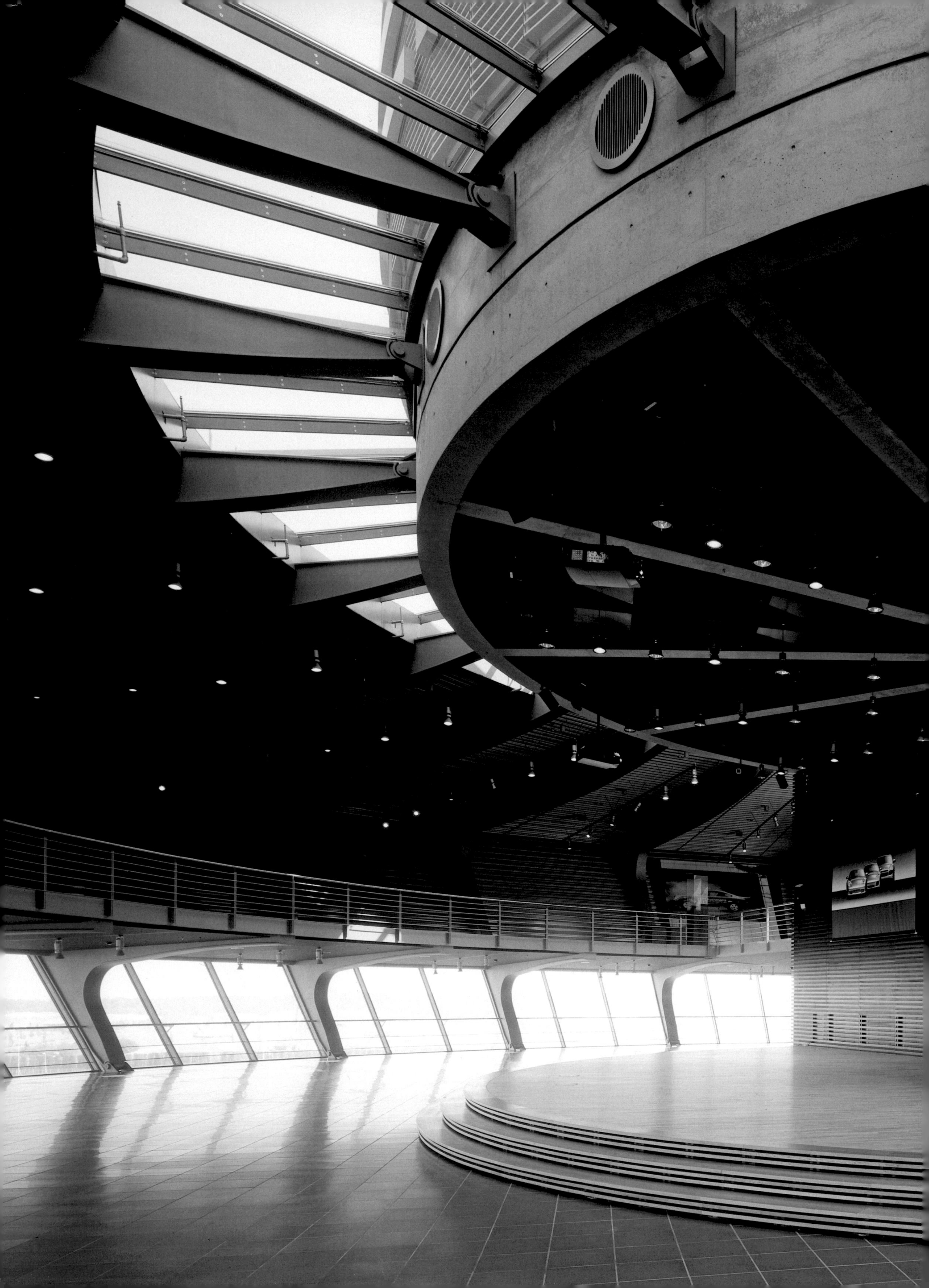

Liquidrom im Tempodrom, Berlin
Liquidrom in the Tempodrom, Berlin

Gutachten Consultancy
1999 – 1. Preis

Entwurf Design
Meinhard von Gerkan

Partner Partner
Hubert Nienhoff

Bauherr Client
Stiftung Neues Tempodrom

Fertigstellung Completion
2002

BGF Gross floor area
1.360 m²

Licht und Klang bestimmen die Atmosphäre des Liquidroms: In dem großen, runden Wasserbecken können bis zu 50 Besucher in körperwarmem Solewasser liegen und über Lichtinstallationen, Unterwasserlautsprecher und vier Klangsäulen ein eindrucksvolles Konzerterlebnis genießen. Neben dem kreisrunden Solebecken ergänzen mehrere Saunen und Dampfbäder, ein nach japanischer Tradition „Onsen" genanntes Heißwasser-Freiluftbecken sowie eine Bar und ein Restaurant das Angebot für die Besucher des Liquidroms. Natürliche Materialien dominieren die Gestaltung der Innenräume und des nach oben offenen Atriums. Die Fußböden und Wände in den Nass- und Badebereichen sind mit einem grünlich-grauen Naturstein verkleidet, in den übrigen Räumen sind die Wände aus veredeltem Sichtbeton. Die Holzwandverkleidungen bestehen aus naturbelassener Rot-Zeder, die Decken sind abgehängt und dunkel beschichtet.

Light and sound define the atmosphere of the Liquidrom: up to 50 visitors can lie back in lukewarm salt water in the large circular water basin can enjoy an impressive concert experience with light installations, underwater loudspeakers and four sound columns. Besides the circular salt-water basin the Liquidrom also consists of several saunas, steam baths, a hot-water open-air basin, which the Japanese call 'Onsen', as well as a bar and a restaurant. Natural materials determine the interior design and the open atrium. The floors and walls in the wet and bathing areas are clad in a greenish-grey natural stone; the walls of all other rooms are finished in refined fair-faced concrete. The wall cladding is of untreated red cedar; the ceilings are suspended and dark coated.

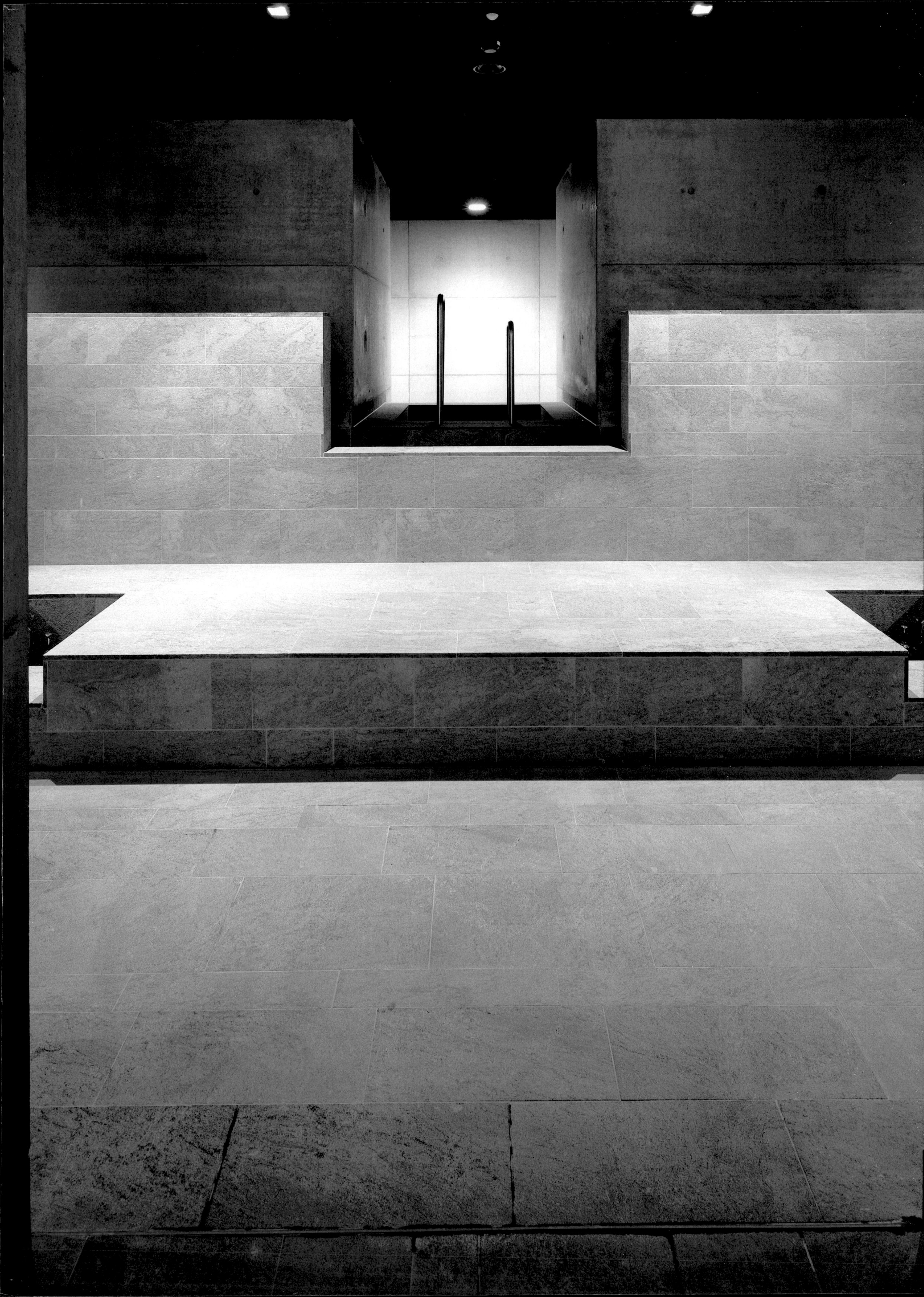

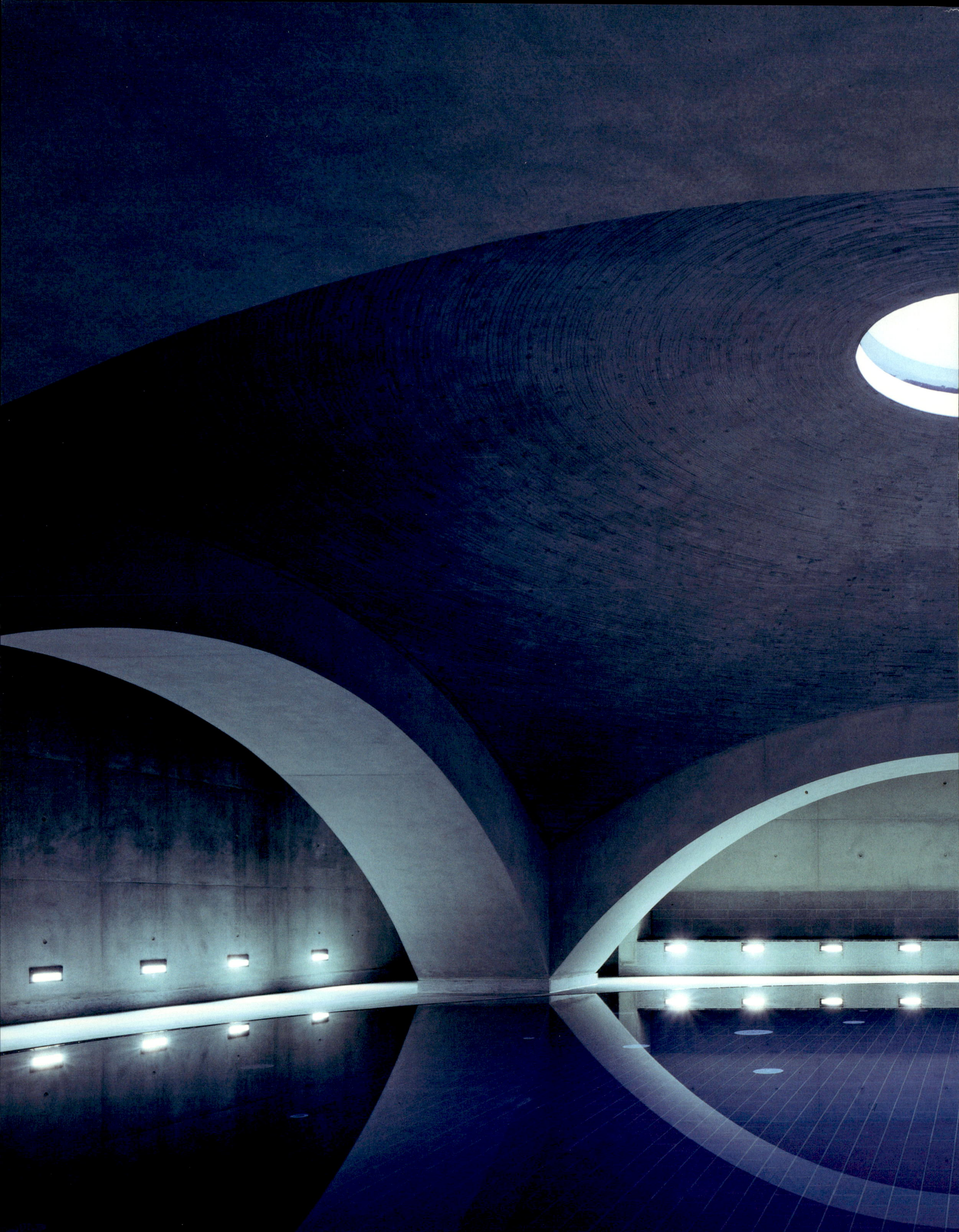

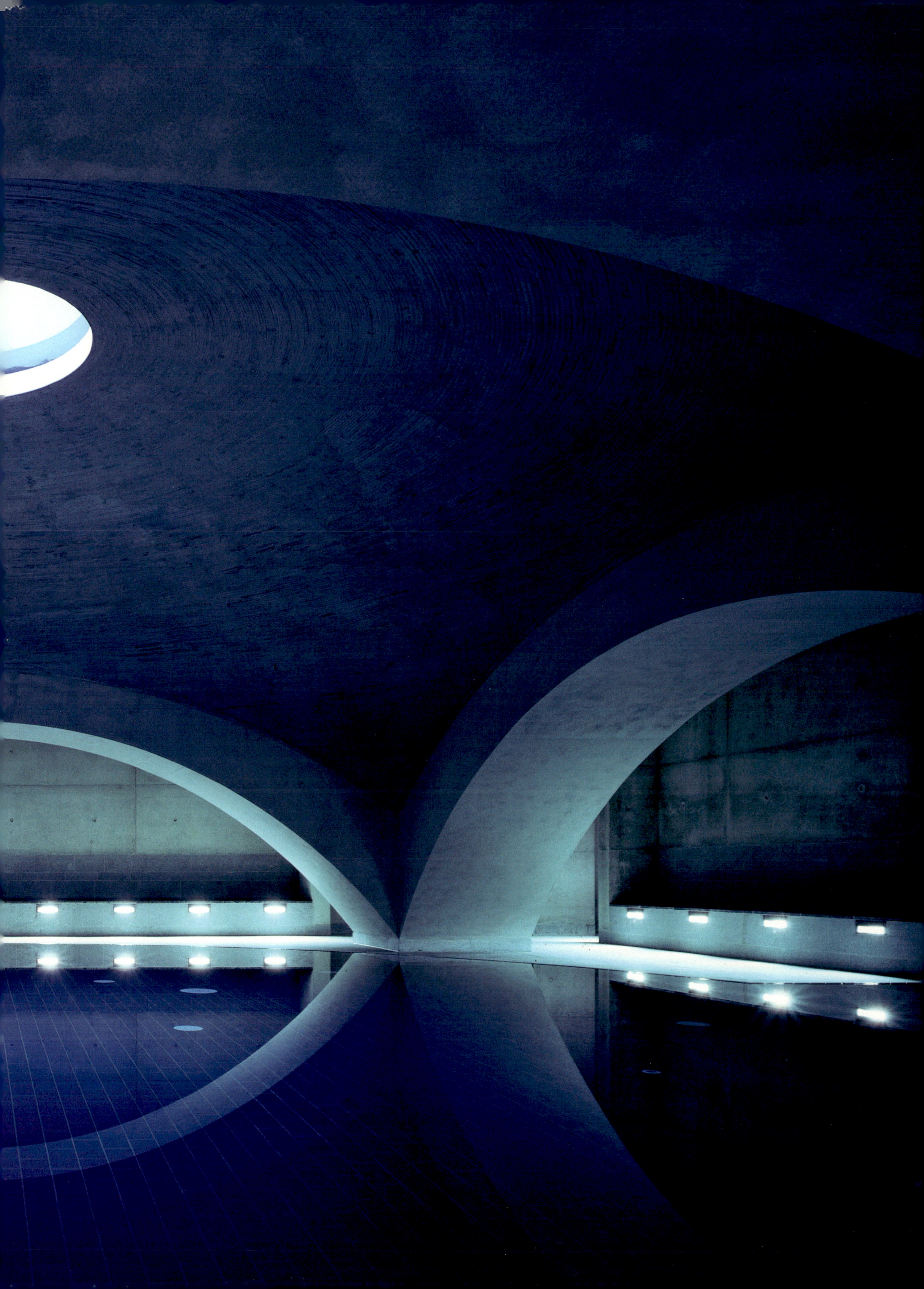

2003

Warnow-Turm der Hanse-Messe Rostock im IGA Park

Das bauliche Ensemble der Hanse-Messe erhält seinen Abschluss und seine unverwechselbare Identität durch einen 62 m hohen filigranen Tensegrity-Turm, der durch seine technische Anmutung und die zunächst verwirrende Anordnung seiner Komponenten, einem System aus Druckstäben und Tragseilen, besticht.

Warnow Tower at the Hanse Trade Fair Rostock in the IGA Park

The ensemble of the trade fair culminates in and gets its unmistakable identity from the 62-m-high filigree 'Tensegrity Tower', which is fascinating because of its technological appearance and the initially bewildering configuration of its components: a system of compression bars and suspension cables.

Airbus A 380-Sektionsbauhalle, Hamburg

Eine Stahlkonstruktion mit außenliegenden Hauptträgern überspannt stützenfrei die 120 m breite und 350 m lange Halle. Großflächige Verglasungen und Aluminiumverkleidungen mit integrierten Fensterbändern gliedern die Fassaden. Im Innern sind an den Längsseiten je drei bügelartige Riegelbauten angeordnet.

Airbus A 380 Major Component Assembly Hall, Hamburg

A steel structure with exterior main girders spans the 120-m-wide and 350-m-long hall without the aid of columns. Large-scale glazing and aluminium claddings with integrated window bands divide the façades. In the interior, three long, bow-like volumes are positioned on each of the longitudinal sides.

Villa Alexandra, Jurmala, Lettland

Die mit Holz verkleidete Villa gliedert sich in fünf parallel angeordnete, unterschiedlich tiefe Gebäudeteile und nimmt so den Maßstab der vorhandenen kleinteiligen Bebauung des lettischen Seebades auf. Die Raumaufteilung im Innern folgt der äußeren Baukörperstruktur mit jeweils unterschiedlichen Nutzungen.

Villa Alexandra, Jurmala, Latvia

The wood-clad villa is divided into five parallel building sections of varying depths, thereby responding to the dimensions of the existing small-scale development of the Latvian seaside resort. The layout of the rooms, each used for a different purpose, is orientated along the external building structure.

2003

Elbkaihaus, Kopfbau West, Hamburg

Der im Westen unmittelbar an das Elbkaihaus angrenzende, 1964 errichtete Kopfbau wurde bis auf das weiterhin zur Fischverarbeitung und Energieversorgung genutzte Erdgeschoss entkernt und um ein Geschoss aufgestockt. Die Obergeschosse des verklinkerten Baus dienen nun als Büroflächen.

Elbkai House, Head Building West, Hamburg

Adjoining the west part of Elbkai House is a second former cold-storage depot. This head building, built in 1964, was cored, apart from the ground floor, which is still used for fish processing and energy supply, and extended by one storey. The upper floors of the clinker construction serve as office space.

Internationales Messe- und Kongresszentrum, Nanning, China

Das Hanggrundstück mit einer Höhendifferenz von 45 m liegt am Rand von Nanning inmitten eines die Stadt umgebenden Grüngürtels. Eine multifunktionale Halle bildet mit ihrem gefalteten Kuppeltragwerk mit einer Gesamthöhe von 70 m und einem Durchmesser von 48 m den Kopf der Messeanlage.

Nanning International Convention & Exhibition Centre, China

The site on a slope with a height difference of 45 m is located on the outskirts of Nanning within the green belt surrounding the city. A multifunctional hall with a folded domical roof, 70 m high and 48 m in diameter, forms the head of the exhibition complex.

Königliche Porzellan-Manufaktur, Berlin

Die Königliche Porzellan-Manufaktur präsentiert sich nach der Sanierung und Neugestaltung ihrer historischen Produktionsstätten wieder am Salzufer in Berlin. Mittelpunkt des neuen städtischen Viertels sind die heute als Ausstellungsraum genutzte Ringofenhalle und das Schlämmereigebäude.

KPM Porcelain Manufacturer, Berlin

After the renovation and reconstruction of its historic production halls, the porcelain company once again presented along the Salzufer in Berlin. The KPM clay-washing building and the annular kiln hall, presently used as an exhibition hall, form the centre of the new urban district.

Stadion der Freundschaft, Cottbus

Ziel dieses mit europäischen Mitteln geförderten Projekts war, mit dem Neubau einer Osttribüne, die 7.300 Zuschauern Platz bietet, das Stadion länderspieltauglich und auch für andere kulturelle Großveranstaltungen nutzbar zu machen.

Stadium of Friendship, Cottbus

The project's objective, which was subsidized with funds from the European Union, was to make the stadium suitable for international matches and big cultural events by building a new east stand capable of accomodating 7,300 spectators.

Villa Alexandra, Jurmala, Lettland
Villa Alexandra, Jurmala, Latvia

2001

Entwurf Design
Meinhard von Gerkan

Bauherr Client
Viktor Krasovicky

Bauzeit Construction period
2002-2003

BGF Gross floor area
700 m²

Große Fensteröffnungen bestimmen die Nord- und Südfassaden der Villa, während die Ost- und Westfassaden nahezu geschlossen bleiben. Die massiven Außenwände sind mit einer horizontalen Holzschalung aus sibirischer Lärche verkleidet und zusätzlich durch vertikale Metallprofileinfassungen gegliedert. Die versetzten Pultdächer erhielten in Anlehnung an die Nachbarhäuser eine Zinkblechdeckung. An der Südseite fasst ein überdachter Laubengang die unterschiedlich weit vorspringenden Gebäudeteile ein und bildet gleichzeitig den Abschluss der vorgelagerten Terrasse, in die ein japanischer Zen-Garten eingelassen ist. Ein ebenfalls nach japanischem Vorbild errichtetes Teehaus scheint über einer rechteckigen Wasserfläche im Garten zu schweben – die offene Holzkonstruktion des Teehauses steht auf einer über dem Wasser auskragenden Betonplatte, deren Auflager dem Betrachter verborgen bleiben.

Large window openings define the villa's north and south façades, whilst the east and west façades remain almost closed. The massive exterior walls are horizontally clad in Siberian larch and additionally structured by vertical metal profiles. A response to the neighbouring houses is the staggered profile of mono-pitched roofs with a sheet zinc cladding. On the south side a covered walkway frames the building sections, which protrude to a varying extent, simultaneously forming the termination of the terrace with its sunken Japanese Zen garden. A teahouse, also built according to the Japanese model, seems to hover above a rectangular water area located in the garden – the open timber structure of the teahouse is supported by a concrete platform cantilevering above the water, its foundations concealed from the viewer.

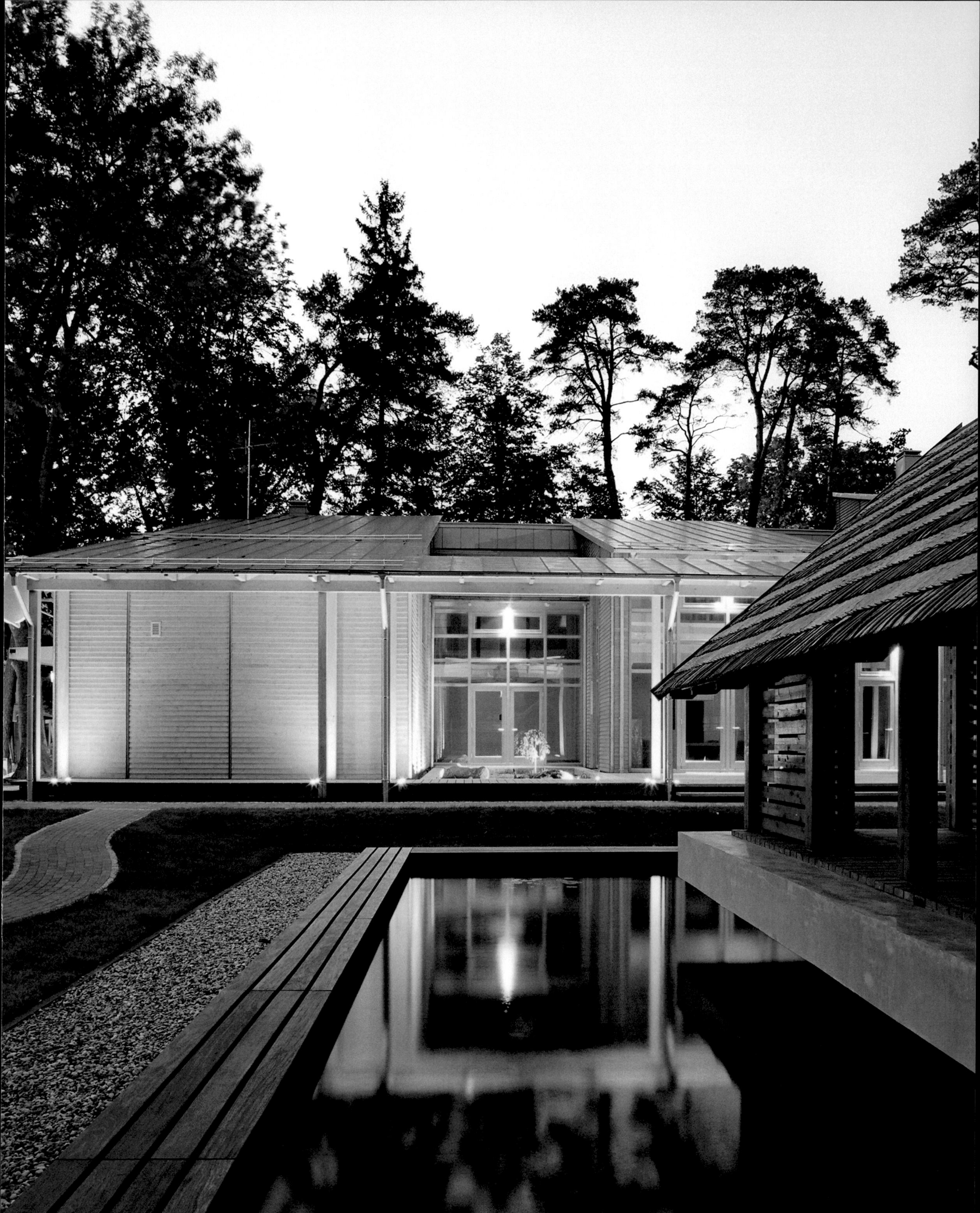

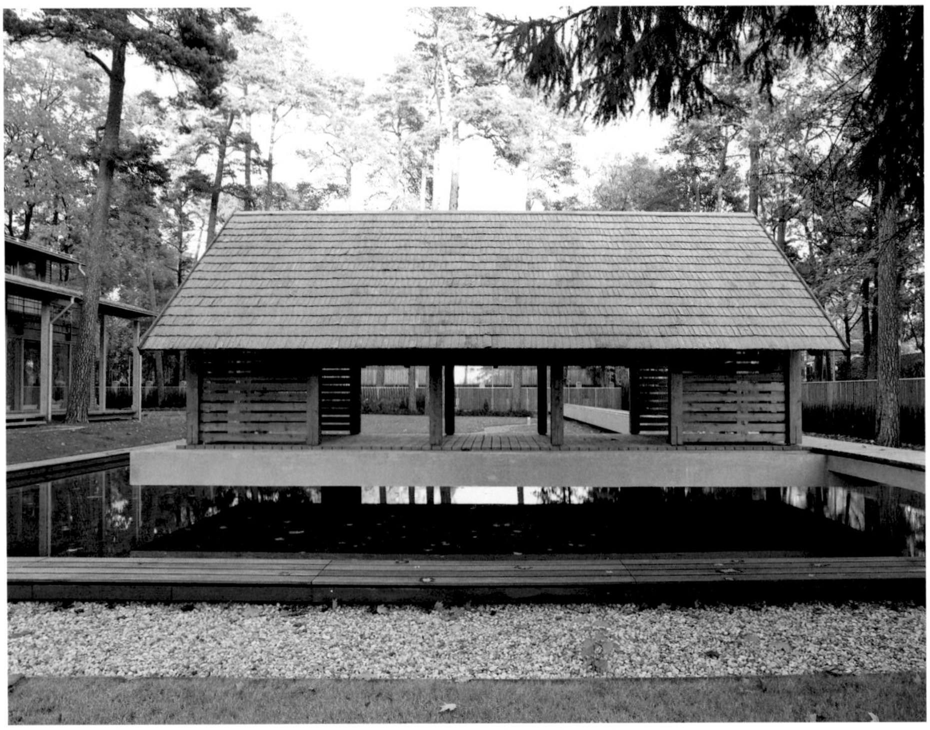

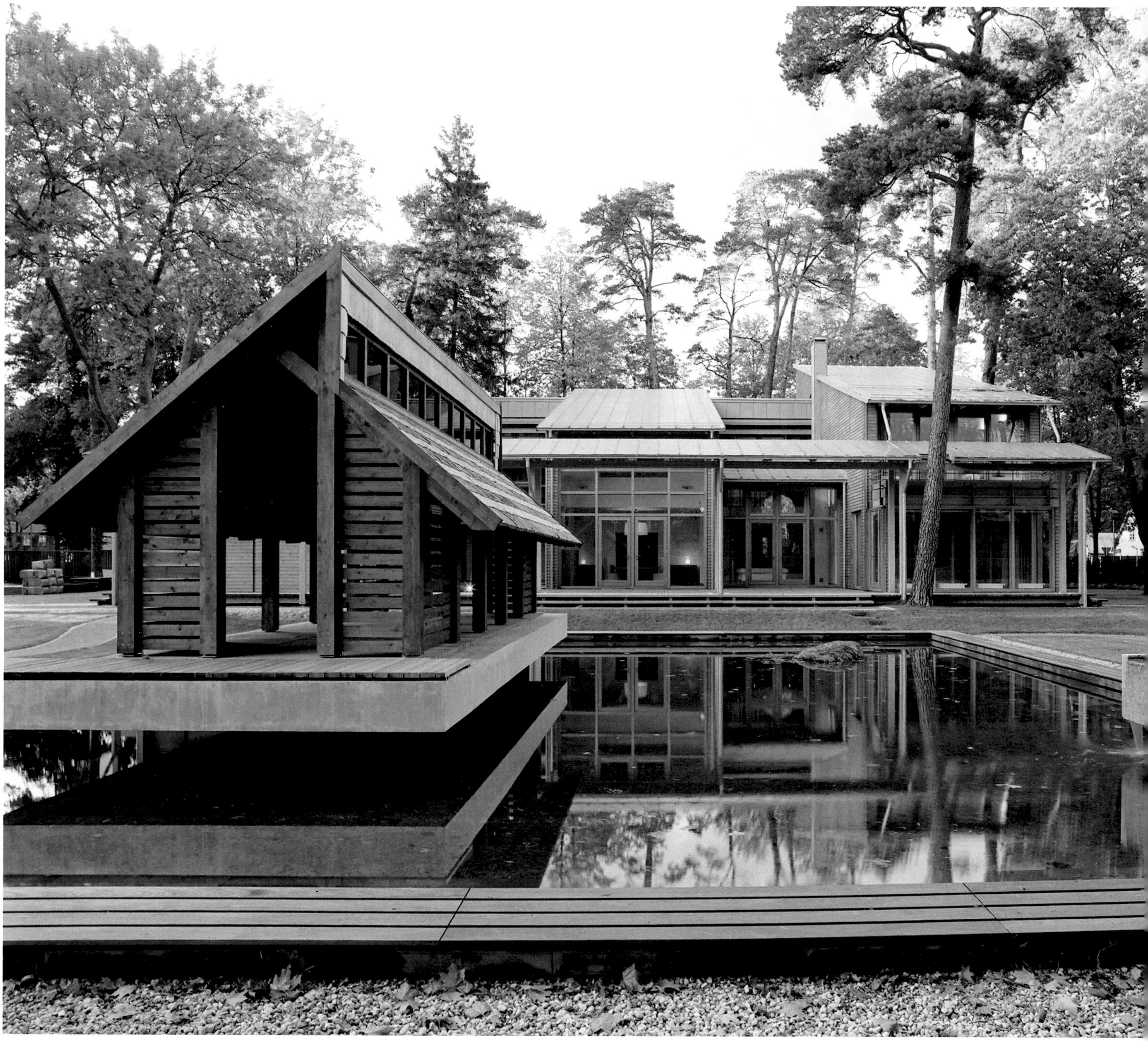

Internationales Messe- und Kongresszentrum, Nanning, China
Nanning International Convention & Exhibition Centre, China

Wettbewerb Competition
1999 – 1. Preis

Entwurf Design
Meinhard von Gerkan und Nikolaus Goetze

Bauherr Client
Nanning International Convention & Exhibition Co., Ltd.

Bauzeit Construction period
1999–2003 | 2005

BGF Gross floor area
130.000 m²

Die multifunktionale, kreisrunde Halle ragt als Landmarke über die Silhouette der Stadt hinaus. Ihre Dachkonstruktion besteht aus einem filigranen Stahltragwerk, das beidseitig mit einer transluzenten Membran bespannt ist, die in der Nacht diffuses Licht nach außen scheinen und die „Dachkrone" über Nanning erstrahlen lässt. Die Ausstellungshallen schließen an die separat nutzbare Rotunde an und werden zu beiden Seiten eines zweigeschossigen Foyers erschlossen. Die neun Hallen des ersten Bauabschnitts verfügen über jeweils zwei Ausstellungsebenen und können zu Gruppen zusammengeschlossen werden. Ein Natursteinsockel bildet das optische Fundament; während der Veranstaltungen kann er als Freiterrasse und Ausstellungsfläche genutzt werden. Stahlbetonstützen erstrecken sich über die volle Höhe der Hallen und tragen das durch die Kerne rhythmisch gegliederte, signifikante Dach.

A multifunctional circular hall rises like a landmark above the city skyline. The roof construction was conceived as a filigree, load-bearing steel structure, which is covered on both sides with a translucent membrane. This allows a diffuse light to shine out of the hall at night with the 'roof crown' radiating above Nanning. The exhibition halls adjoining the rotunda, which can be used separately, are accessible from both sides of a two-storey foyer. All nine halls built during the first construction phase consist of two exhibition levels each and can be interlinked as groups. A natural stone plinth forms the visual foundation; during events it can be used as an open-air terrace and exhibition area. Reinforced concrete columns stretch across the complete height of the halls and support the impressive, rhythmically structured roof.

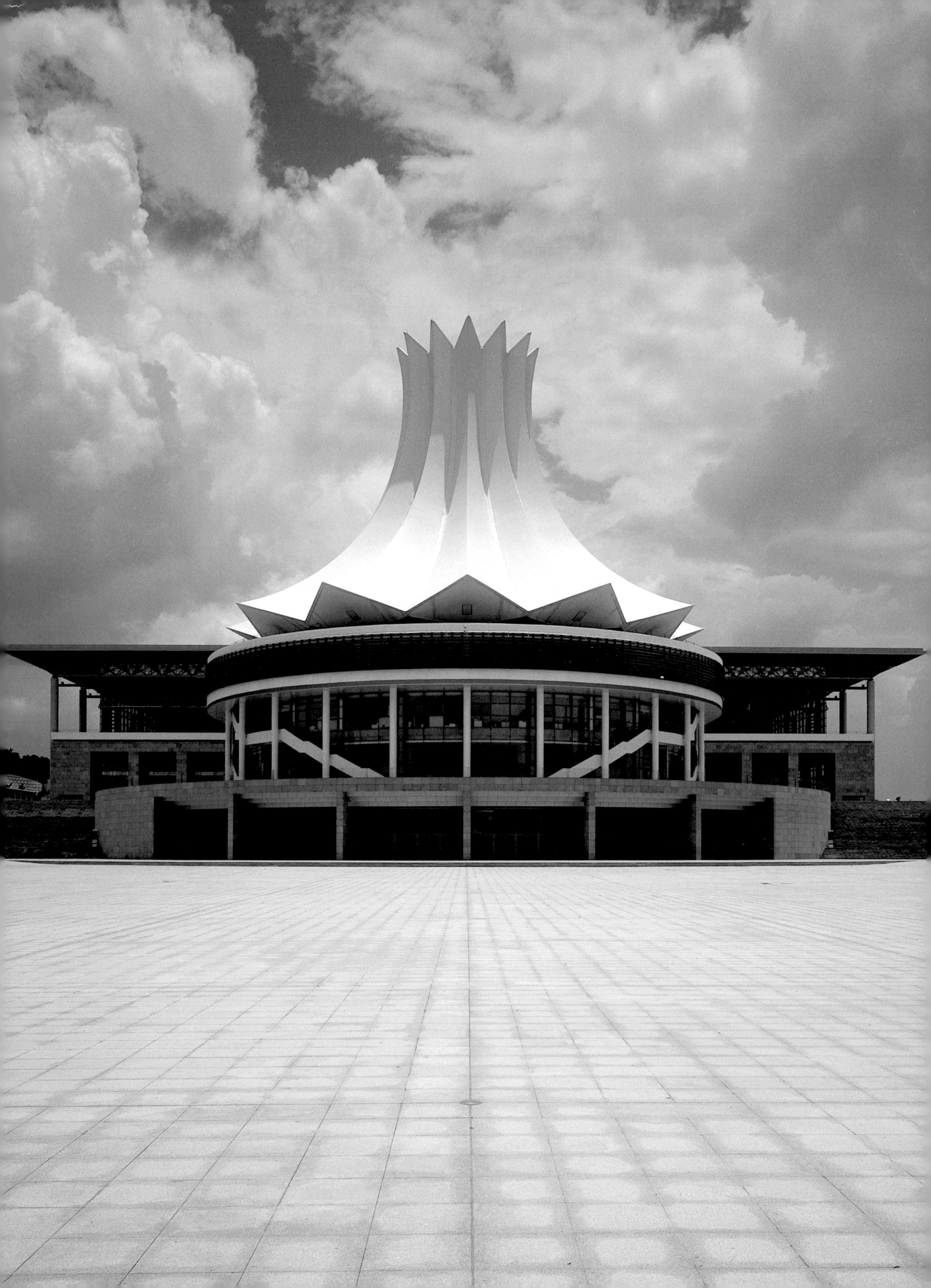

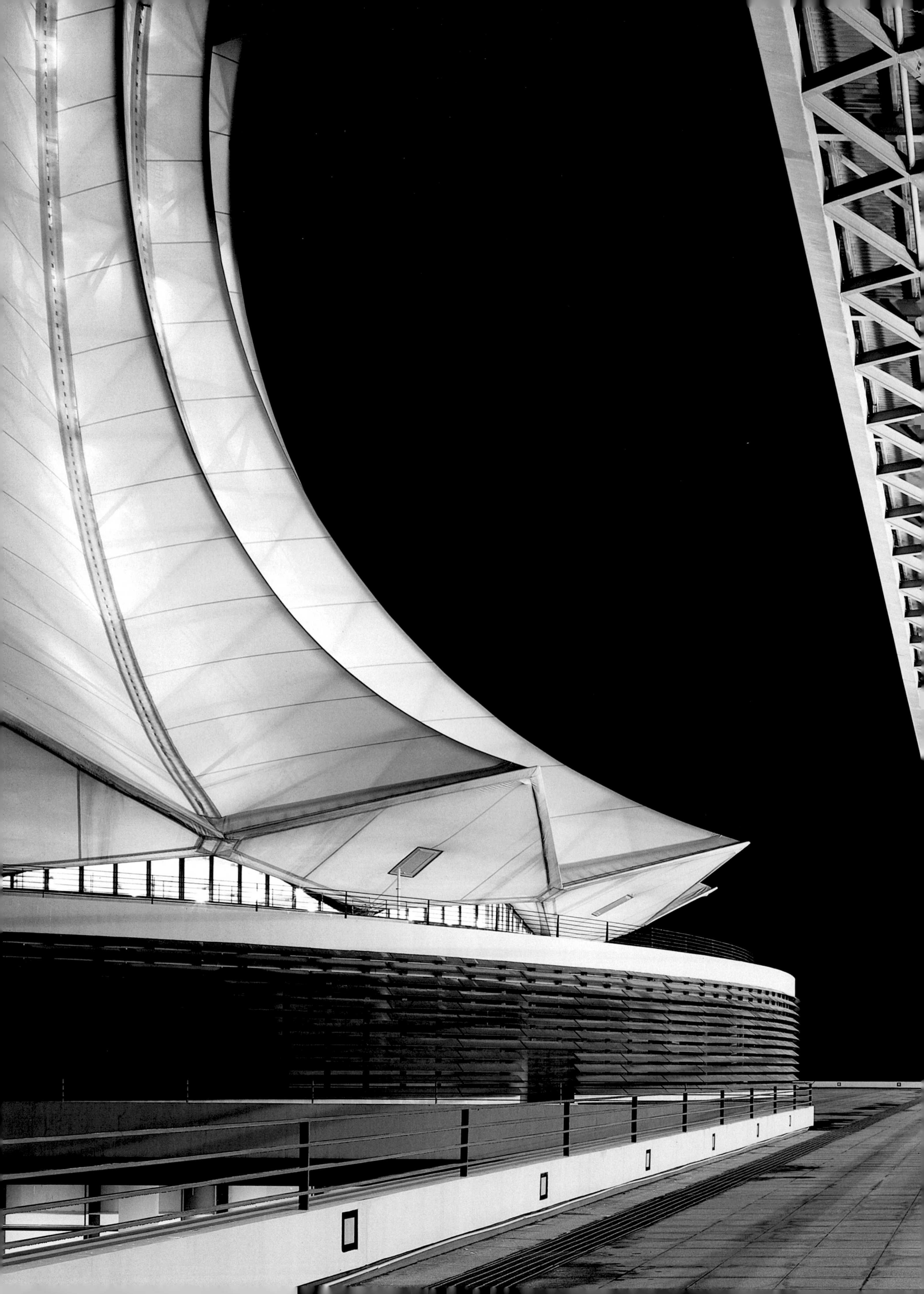

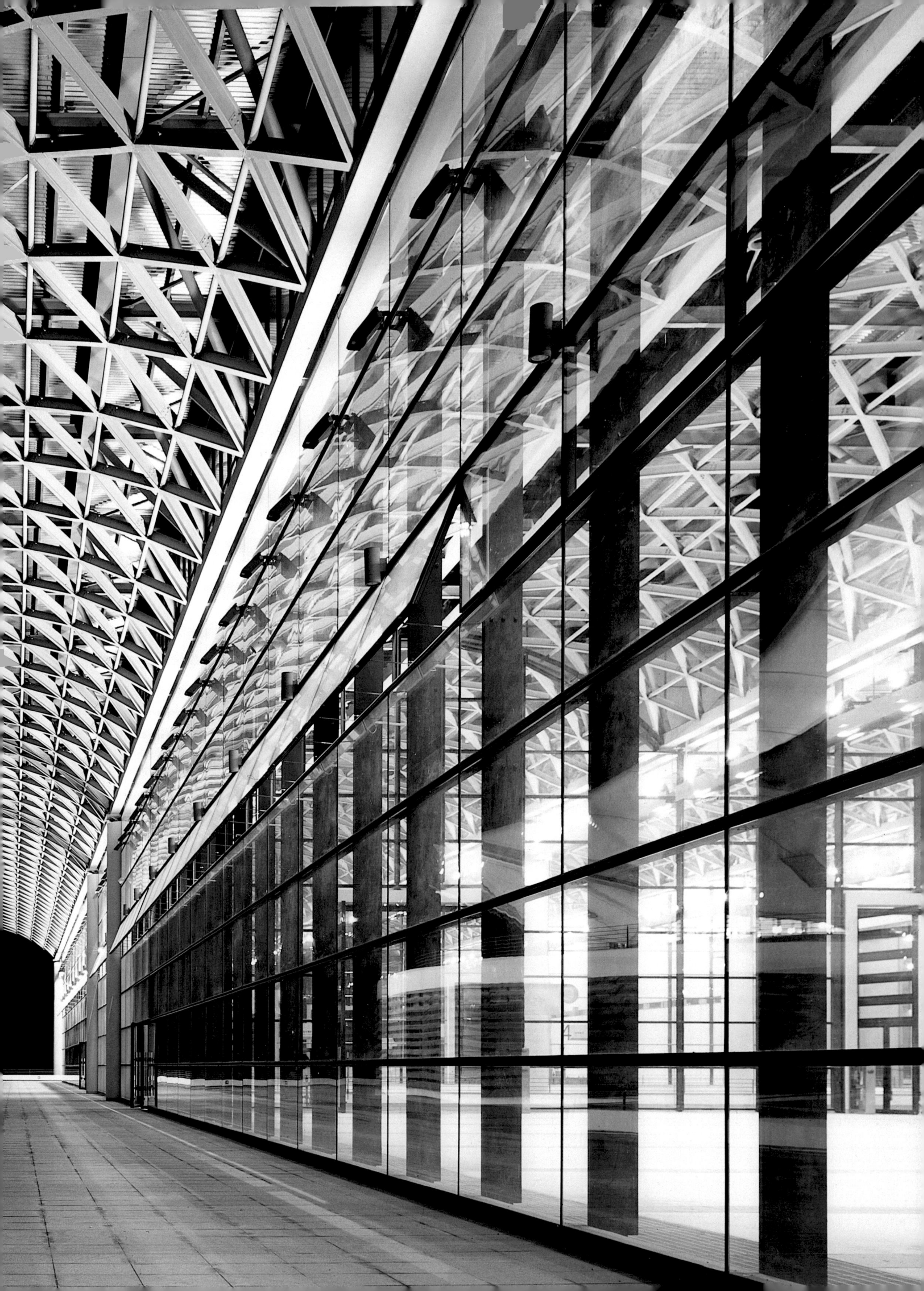

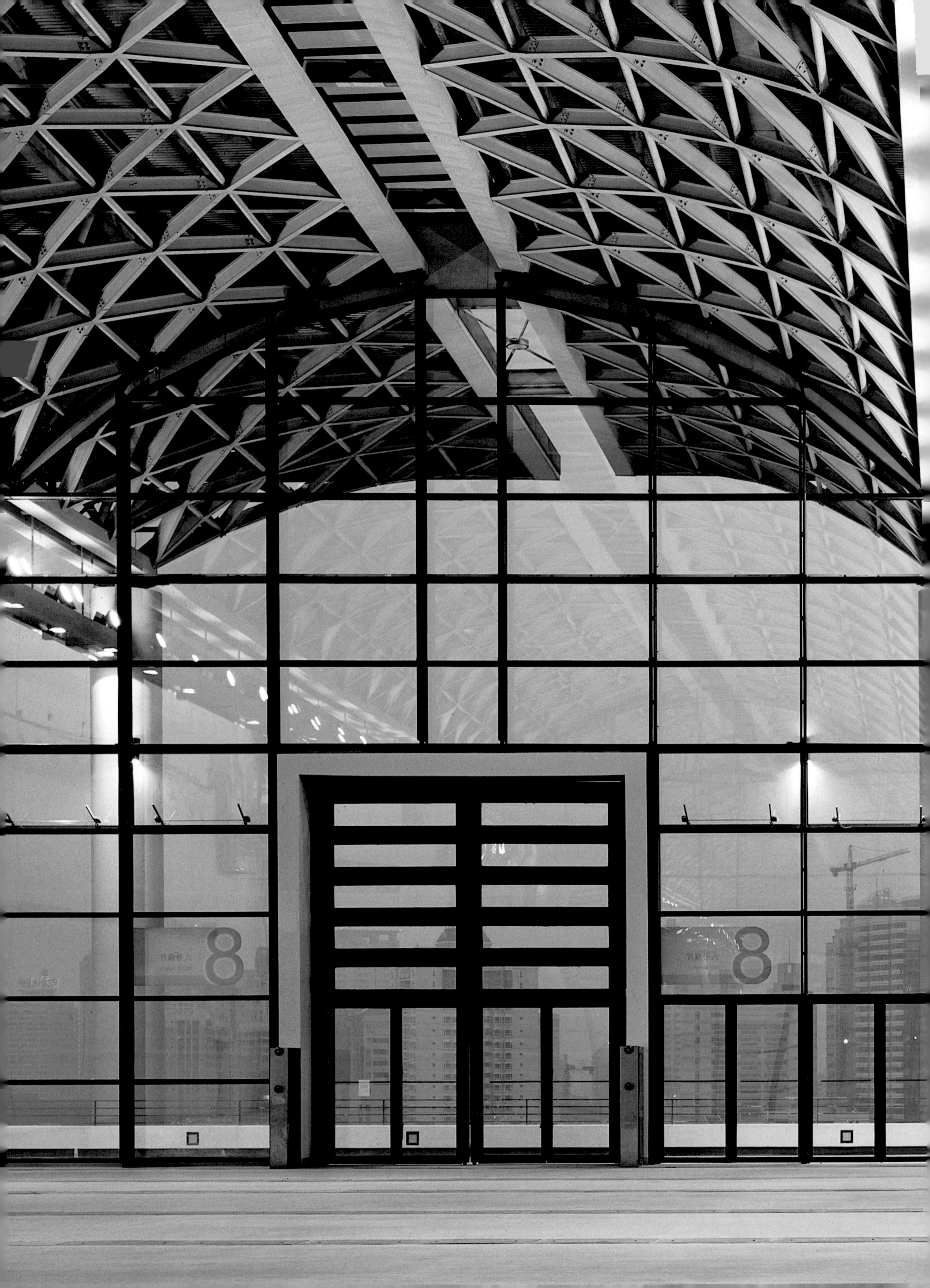
8
8

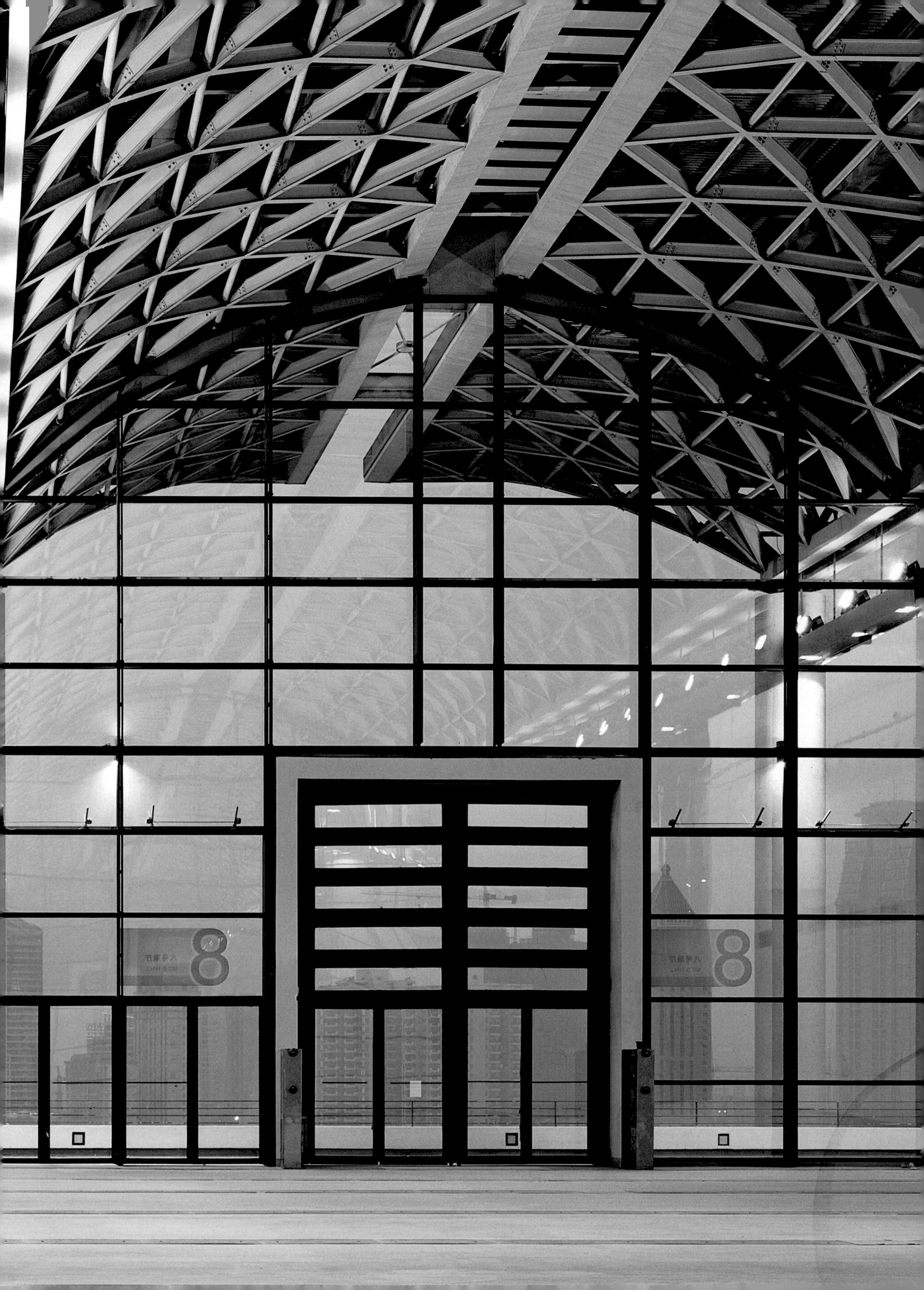
8
8

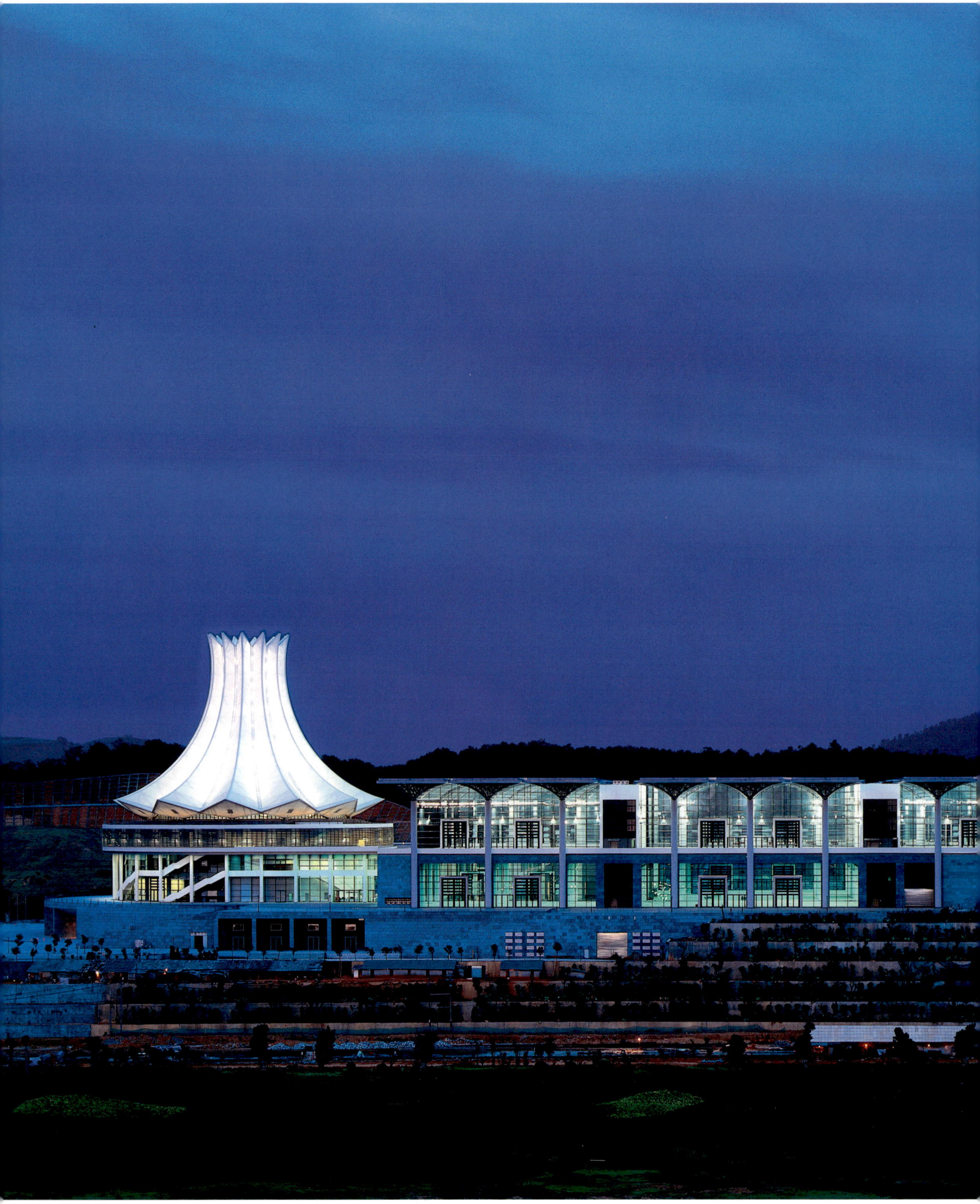

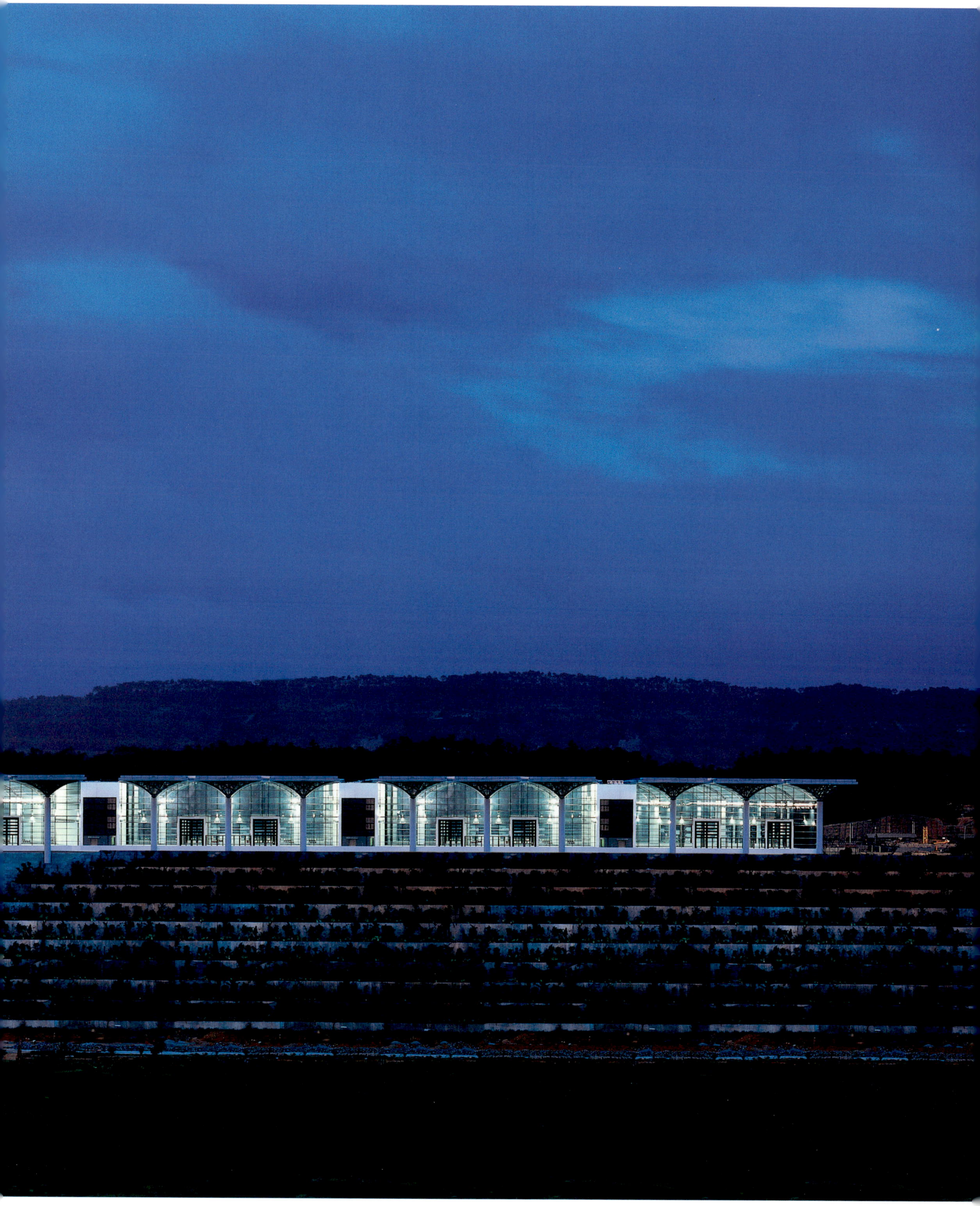

Königliche Porzellan-Manufaktur, Berlin
KPM Porcelain Manufacturer, Berlin

2001

Entwurf Design
Meinhard von Gerkan mit Doris Schäffler
und Kristian Uthe-Spencker

Partner Partner
Hubert Nienhoff

Bauherr Client
GSG Gewerbesiedlungsgesellschaft mbH

Bauzeit Construction period
2002–2003

BGF Gross floor area: annular kiln hall
1.600 m^2

BGF Gross floor area: clay-washing building
2.900 m^2

Ein durchgängiges gestalterisches Konzept, das Architektur, Ausstellungspräsentation, Lichtführung und grafisches Erscheinungsbild umfasst, verbindet die denkmalgeschützten Altbauten, den zentralen Hof und den Weg in das Quartier hinein zu einer Einheit. Eine Freitreppe über die gesamte Front der Ringofenhalle betont deren übergeordnete Bedeutung als Verkaufs- und Ausstellungsgebäude. Der Innenraum wird dominiert von den Öfen, deren obere Ebene über Stahltreppen und Galerien zugänglich ist. Alle neu hinzugefügten Elemente wurden bewusst zurückhaltend gestaltet und orientieren sich an der industriellen Vergangenheit des Gebäudes, dessen Ambiente aus Stahl, Ziegeln und rauen Putzflächen einen deutlichen Gegensatz zu dem feinen, weißen Porzellan bildet. Die Aufstockung des Schlämmereigebäudes nimmt Rhythmus, Proportion und Material des Bestands auf, die neuen Elemente sind jedoch im Detail deutlich ablesbar.

An integral design concept, which comprises architecture, exhibition presentation, lighting design and graphic appearance, unifies the historic buildings, which are under a preservation order, the central courtyard and the path into the quarter. A flight of front stairs stretching across the entire front of the kiln hall emphasizes its higher priority as a sales and exhibition building. The interior is dominated by the kilns, which are accessible on their upper level via steel stairs and galleries. All newly-added elements were deliberately characterized by a modest design and respect the industrial history of the complex, whose ambience is defined by steel, brick and rough plaster surfaces, thus forming a strong contrast to the delicate, white porcelain. The addition of one storey to the clay-washing building takes reference from the existing rhythm, proportion and material; in detail, however, the new elements are clearly detectable.

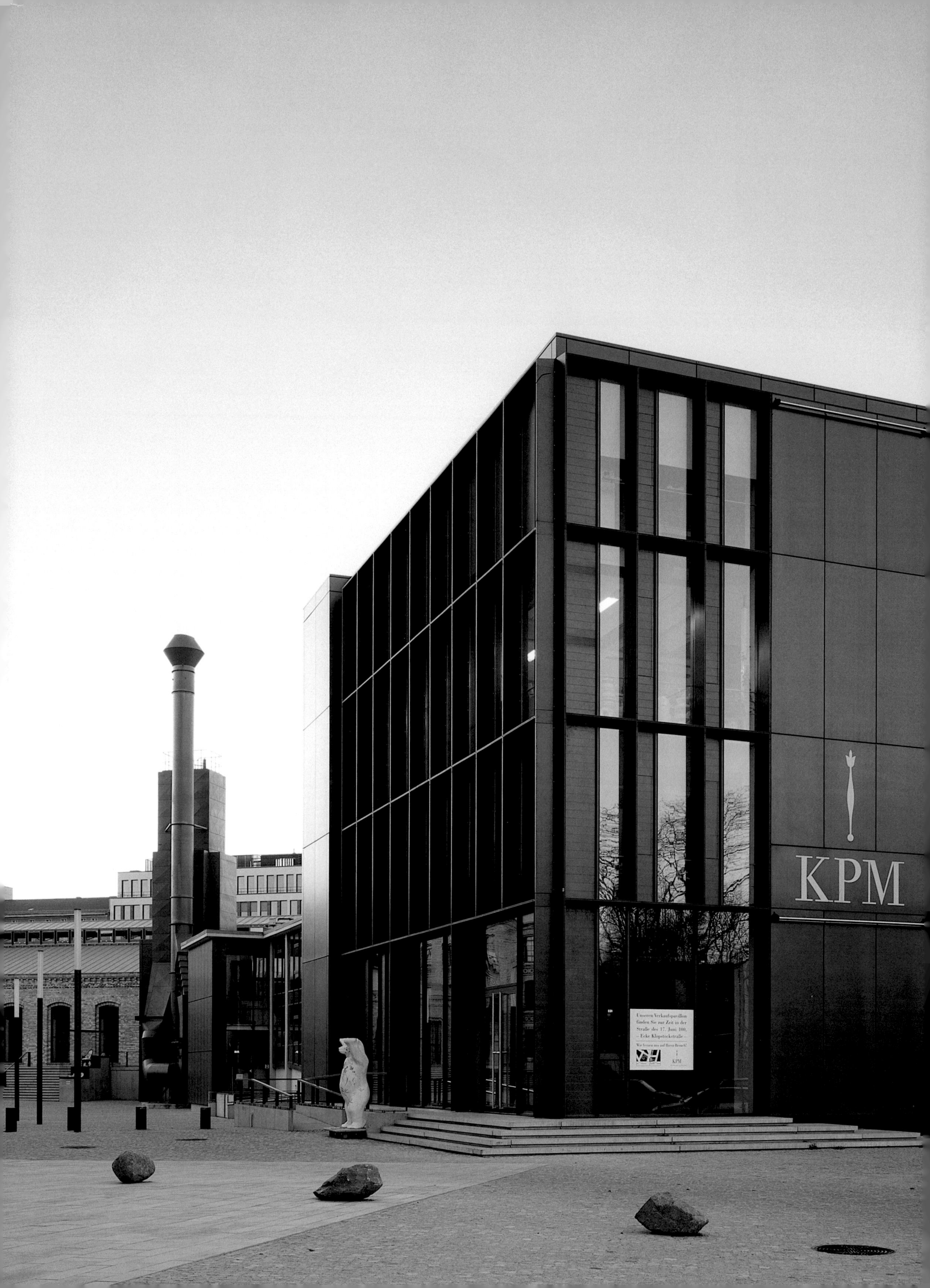
KPM

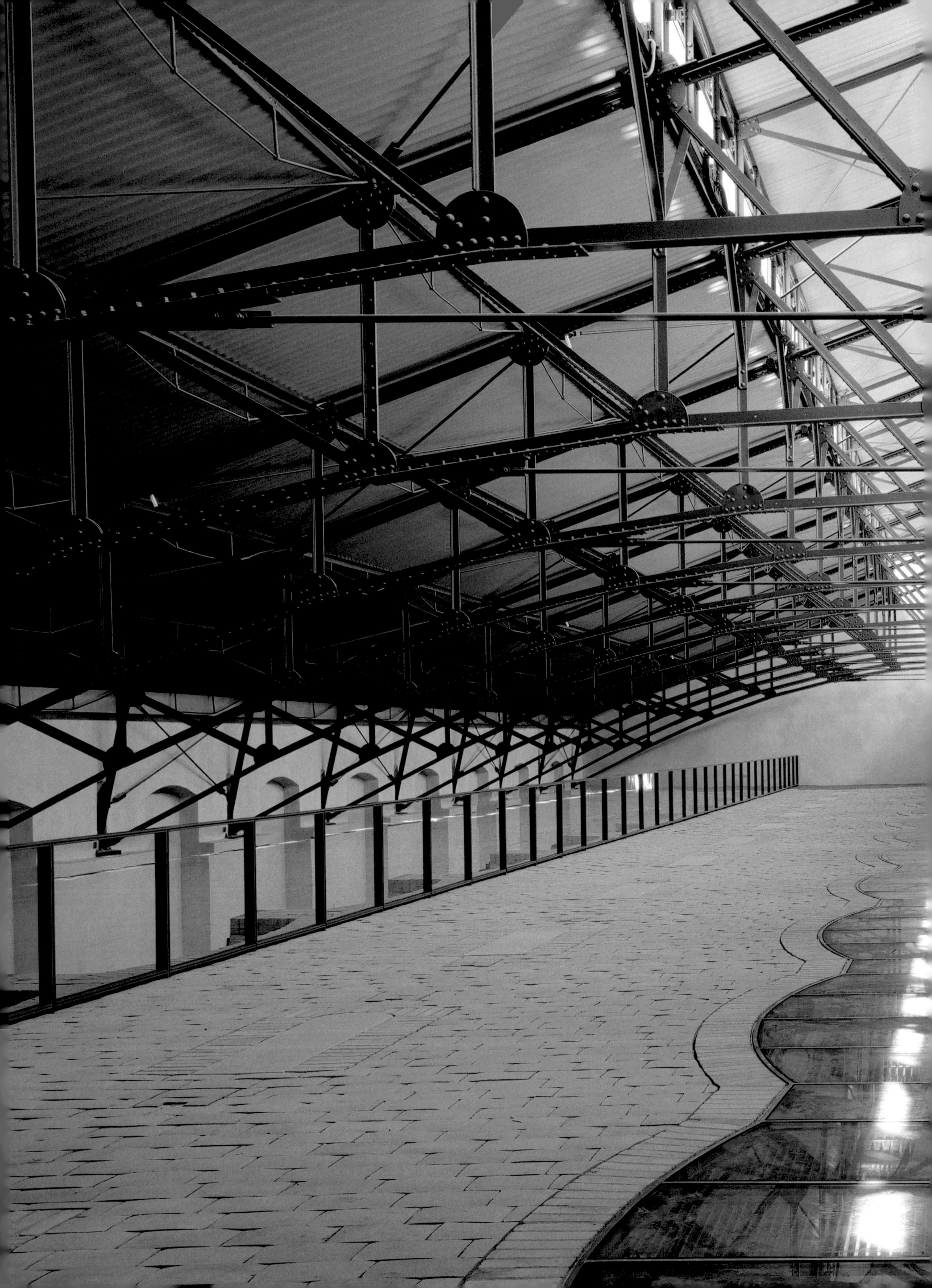

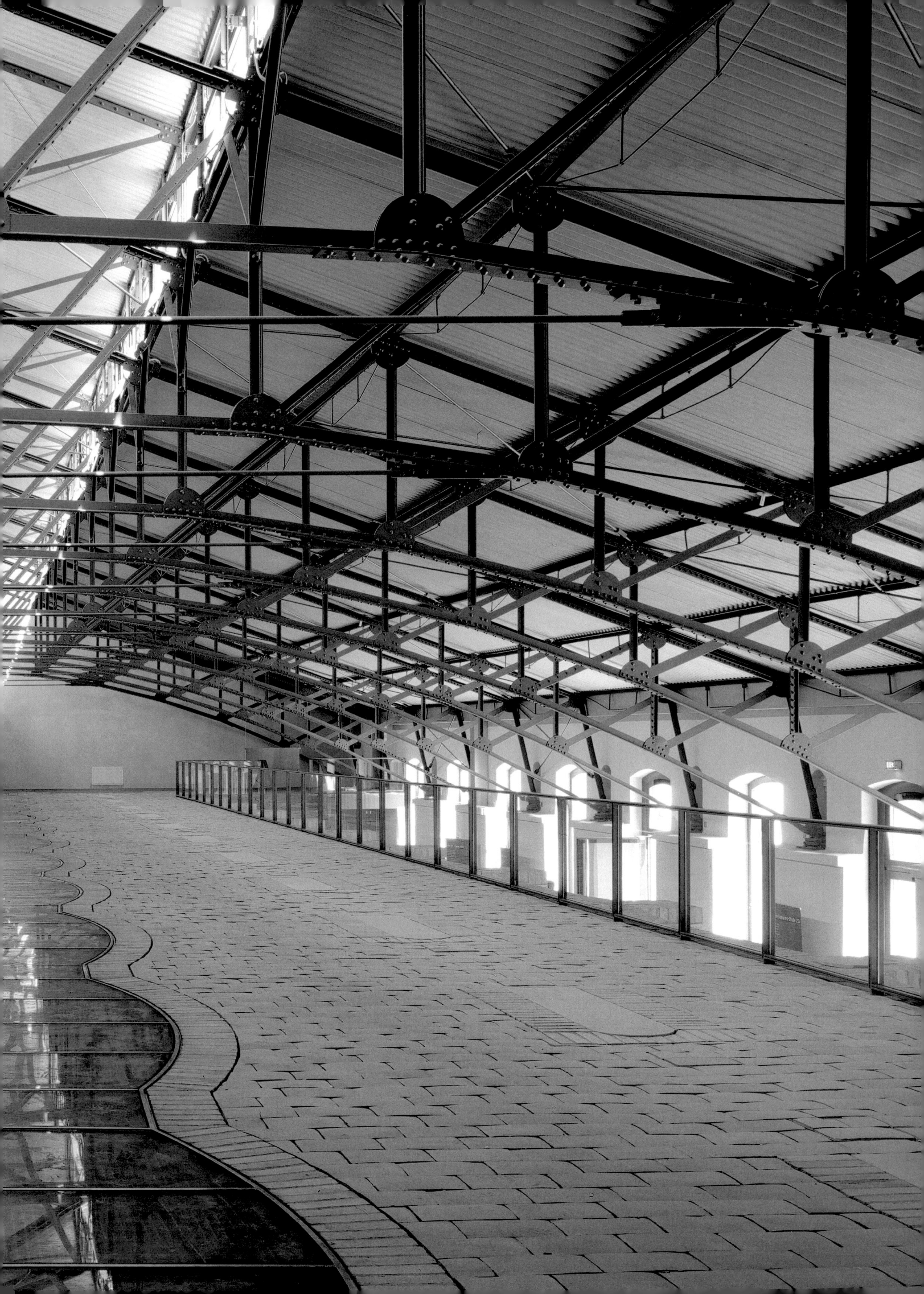

Stadion der Freundschaft, Cottbus
Stadium of Friendship, Cottbus

Wettbewerb Competition
2001 – 1. Preis

Entwurf Design
Volkwin Marg

Bauherr Client
Stadt Cottbus

Bauzeit Construction period
2002–2003

BGF Gross floor area
8.100 m²

Der Neubau der Osttribüne als Pendant zur bestehenden Westtribüne des in den 1930er-Jahren errichteten Stadions greift die räumlichen Qualitäten der umgebenden Parklandschaft auf und wahrt den Charakter der Anlage als „Stadion im Landschaftsraum". Auf den angrenzenden Eliaspark wird durch eine differenzierte Gliederung der Baumasse Rücksicht genommen. Der untere Bereich der Tribüne ist als monolithischer Betonkörper mit großen Öffnungen ausgebildet, in die die Eingänge mit den Kassen als Metallkuben eingestellt sind. Dazwischen zeigen großflächige, bedruckte Glaselemente als Fassadenverkleidung die Bewegungssequenz eines Läufers. Das Motiv wurde so gestaltet, dass es sich erst aus größerem Abstand zu einem Bild fügt, aus der Nähe aber als abstraktes Muster wahrgenommen wird. Eine scheinbar schwebende, abgespannte stählerne Dachkonstruktion bildet den oberen Abschluss des Tribünenbauwerks.

The newly-built east stand, designed as a counterpart to the existing west stand of the stadium constructed in the 1930s, adopted the spatial qualities of the surrounding park landscape and maintains the facility's character of a 'stadium within the landscape'. The differentiated division of the building mass respects the adjoining 'Eliaspark'. The lower area of the stands was laid out like a monolithic concrete volume with large openings, into which the entrances and ticket offices were inserted as metal cubes. Large, printed, glass elements used as façade lining depict the motion of runners. The motif was designed in such a way that it can be perceived as an image only when viewed from a distance, whilst appearing as an abstract pattern when viewed close-up. A guyed steel roof construction forms the seemingly hovering termination of the stand structure.

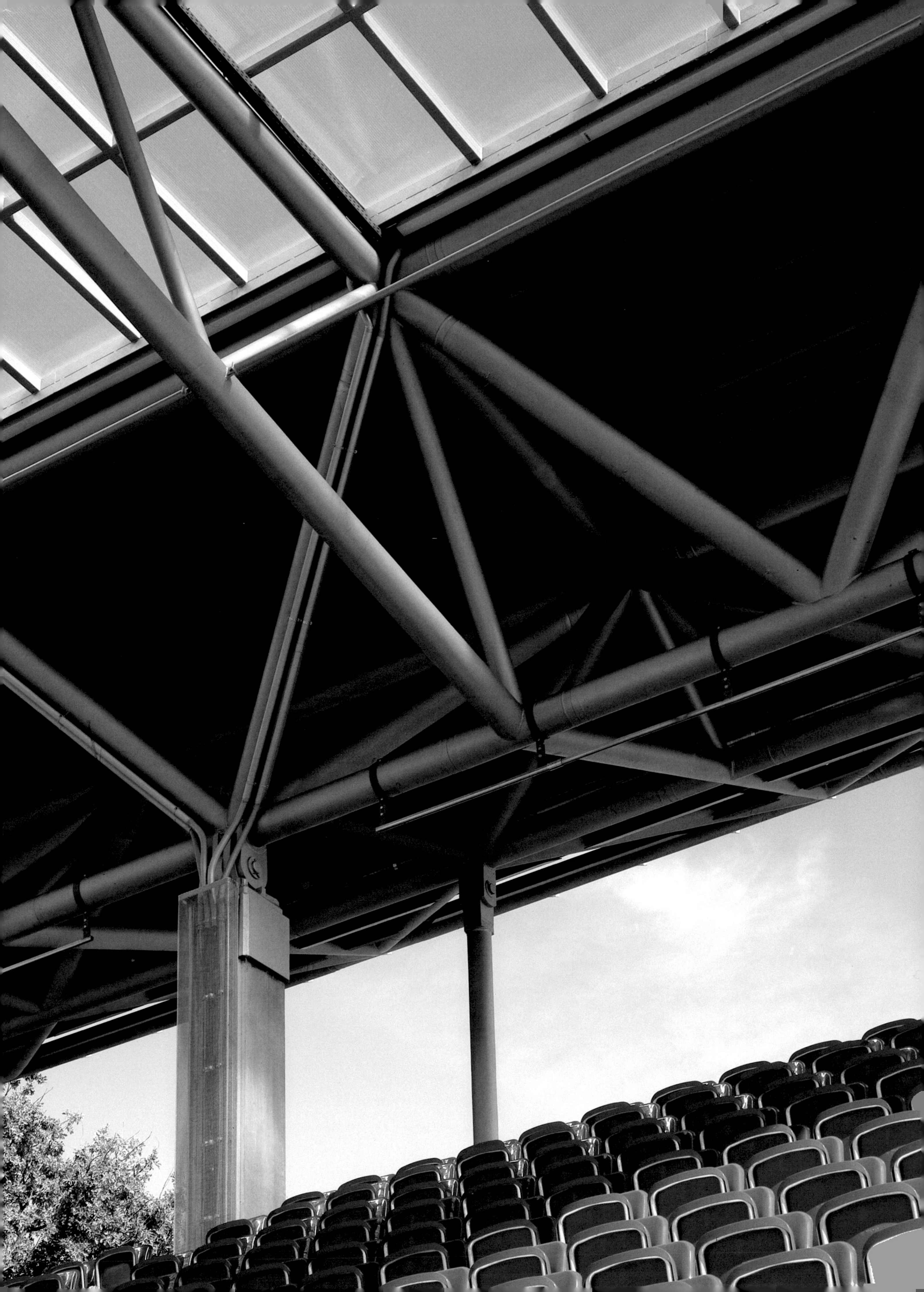

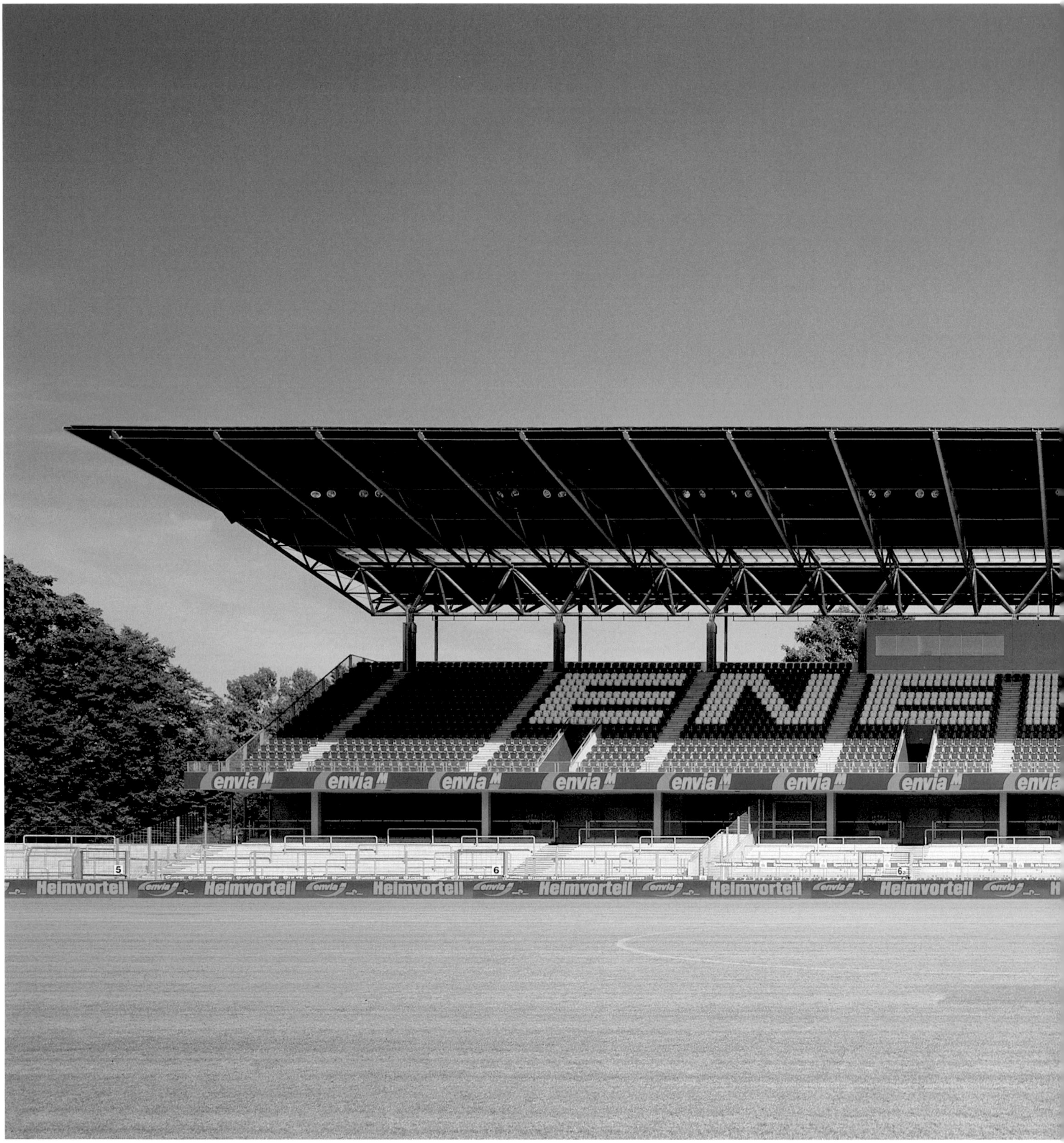
envia
Heimvorteil

envia
envia
envia
envia
envia
envia
envia
envia
Heimvorteil
Heimvorteil
Heimvorteil
Heimvorteil
Heimvorteil
Heimvorteil

2004

Hauptbahnhof Kiel – Renovierung und Neugestaltung

Neben der wiederhergestellten zentralen Halle mit dem Haupteingang und der Stahl-Glas-Querhalle mit dem Kaiserportal als neuem Direktzugang zu Fördedampfern, Oslo-Fähre und Hörnbrücke wertet insbesondere die städtebauliche Neugestaltung des Vorplatzes den vormals kriegsbeschädigten Kopfbahnhof auf.

Kiel Central Station – Reconstruction and Redesign

Apart from the reconstructed central hall with the main entrance and the transverse glass-and-steel concourse with the Emperors Gate as direct access to inlet steamers, Oslo Ferry and Hörn Bridge particularly the urban redesign of the forecourt increases the quality of the once war-damaged station.

Messebahnhof Rimini, Italien

Charakteristisches Element des Bahnhofs, der sich in Materialität und Farbgebung an der Architektur der Messe orientiert, ist das circa 100 m lange, leicht geschwungene, stählerne Bahnsteigdach. Die Serviceräume des Bahnhofs befinden sich im Untergeschoss, so dass der Blick auf die Messe frei bleibt.

Railway Station of the New Rimini Trade Fair, Italy

The approx. 100-m-long slightly curved steel platform roof characterizes the station, which takes up from the exhibition centre's architecture regarding its material and colour scheme. The service rooms are located in the basement, thus allowing unrestricted views towards the exhibition centre.

Frischemarkt Frankfurt

Eine Markt- und eine Lagerhalle sowie zwei Verwaltungsgebäude bilden das Frischezentrum für Obst und Gemüse. Filigrane Stahlkonstruktionen auf tragenden Betonstützen dienen als Vordächer und Überdachungen. Den Eingang akzentuiert eine 32 m hohe, beleuchtete Stele aus vier schlanken, weißen Betonsäulen.

Frankfurt Fruit and Vegetable Market

The fruit and vegetable market consists of a market, a warehouse and two administration buildings. Filigree steel structures on load-bearing concrete columns function as projecting canopies and roofs. A 32-m-high, illuminated stele constructed from four slender, white concrete columns accentuates the entrance.

Flughafen Stuttgart, Terminal 3

Die für den 1991 realisierten Terminal 1 so charakteristischen Gestaltungsmerkmale, wie die Baumstützen des Tragwerks und der zum Vorfeld orientierte deichartige Gebäuderiegel, wurden bei der Erweiterung fortgeführt. Um die Baumstruktur beibehalten zu können, wurde das Dach jedoch in Sheds aufgelöst.

Stuttgart Airport, Terminal 3

The characteristic design features of Terminal 1, built in 1991, such as the tree props of the load-bearing structure and the dike-like building bar orientated towards the apron, were continued throughout the extension. The roof was, however, dissolved into sheds, in order to maintain the tree structure.

Flughafen „Raffaello Sanzio", Ancona-Falconara, Italien

Weit spannende Dachbinder aus Stahl überbrücken stützenfrei die Abfertigungshallen, in denen Abflug und Ankunft zur besseren Orientierung konsequent voneinander getrennt wurden. Zweigeschossige, als schlichte Kuben ausgebildete Funktionsboxen sind als Einzelbaukörper in die Terminals eingestellt.

'Raffaello Sanzio' Airport, Ancona-Falconara, Italy

The terminal halls are column-free and bridged by wide-span, steel roof trusses and the consistent separation of departures and arrivals into one terminal hall each makes for easier orientation. Two-storey simple cubic function boxes are located inside the terminal halls as detached structures.

RheinEnergieStadion, Köln

Vier beleuchtete Stahltürme, von denen die Tribünendächer abgehängt sind, kennzeichnen das neue Stadion. Anstelle des ehemaligen Marathontores erlaubt nun das „Stadion-Fenster" unterhalb der von einem offenen Stahlbetongerüst getragenen Tribünen den eintretenden Besuchern einen Blick in das Stadionrund.

RheinEnergie Football Stadium, Cologne

Four illuminated steel towers carrying the suspended stand roofs characterize the new stadium. Instead of the former marathon gate, the 'stadium window' underneath the stands, which are supported by an open concrete framework, now offers the visitors a first view across the entire stadium interior.

2004

Olympiastadion, Berlin
Umbau und Überdachung

Das von Werner March für die Olympischen Spiele 1936 als Gesamtkunstwerk gestaltete Gelände bleibt als städtebauliches Denkmal erhalten. Das neue Tribünendach wird nicht zum Ring geschlossen, sondern bleibt zum Marathontor offen und tritt nach außen nur als horizontale Linie oberhalb der Attika in Erscheinung.

Olympic Stadium, Berlin
Conversion and Roofing

The master plan proposed by Werner March in 1936 remains under urban historic preservation. The new roof structure is not a closed ring but open-ended towards the Marathon Gate, and is only minimally visible, like a low horizontal line, above the parapet of the stadium.

Xinzhao Wohnbebauung, 2. Bauabschnitt, Peking, China

Die turmartigen, versetzt angeordneten Wohnhochhäuser des zweiten Bauabschnitts betonen die geschwungene südliche Kante der die vier Quartiere von Westen nach Osten durchziehenden Parklandschaft und bilden einen Kontrast zu den rechtwinkligen, geschlossenen Strukturen der Quartiersblöcke.

Xinzhao Residential Area, 2nd Building Phase, Beijing, China

The staggered, tower-like high-rise blocks of the second building phase emphasize the curved southern edge of the park landscape, which runs through the four districts from west to east. The towers form a contrast to the rectangular, closed structures of the district blocks.

Große Parkrotunde am Flughafen Hamburg

Das zehngeschossige, zylindrische Parkhaus mit insgesamt 2.115 Plätzen hat einen Durchmesser von 92 m bei einer Höhe von 29 m. Eine vorgehängte Teilfassade aus verzinkten Gitterrosten variiert die Ansicht; einseitig verglaste Brücken verbinden die Parkebenen mit dem vorgelagerten Haupttreppenhaus.

Large Car Park Rotunda at Hamburg Airport

The new cylindrical Car Park Rotunda with a total of 2,115 places on ten levels has a diameter of 92 m and a height of 29 m. Its transparent and air-permeable façade from galvanized steel grating animates the elevation. The main staircase is positioned in front of the façade and connected to the parking levels via bridges, which are glazed on one side.

Wohnhaus Luserke, Hamburg

Drei parallel zur Straße verlaufende Gebäuderiegel zeichnen das zweigeschossige Wohnhaus aus. Gläserne Fugen, in denen sich die Flure befinden, trennen die massiv eingefassten Baukörper voneinander, deren zurückgesetzte Glasfassaden nach Süden transparent und nach Norden weiß emailliert sind.

Luserke House, Hamburg

Three building bars positioned parallel to the road characterize the two-storey residential building. Glazed joints, which accommodate the corridors, separate the massively framed structures from each other. Their recessed glass façades are transparent towards the south and finished in a white enamelling towards the north.

Institut für Physikalische Chemie, Aachen

Die beiden zweibündigen Baukörper sind um einen Gartenhof angelegt, der zum Hörsaal im Untergeschoss kaskadenartig abfällt. Die tragende Konstruktion aus Betonfertigteilstützen und -riegeln bildet auch die sichtbare Fassade, in der die Eingangshalle und die Treppenhäuser als gläserne Fugen wirken.

Institute for Physical Chemistry, Aachen

Both buildings with a two-corridor layout are designed around a garden courtyard, which descends cascade-like towards the auditorium in the basement. The load-bearing structure of pre-cast concrete columns and horizontal members also forms the visible façade, in which the entrance hall and the staircases appear as glazed joints.

Messe- und Kongresszentrum Shenzhen, China

Mit einer Gesamtfläche von rund 256.000 m² gilt die Messe Shenzhen als eines der größten Infrastrukturprojekte Südchinas. Ihre Lage inmitten der Stadt forderte einerseits urbane Kompaktheit, andererseits steht der horizontale Baukörper als Alleinstellungsmerkmal im Kontrast zur vertikalen Stadtstruktur.

Shenzhen Convention and Exhibition Centre, China

The Shenzhen Exhibition and Convention Centre is regarded as one of South China's biggest infrastructure projects. Its central location within the city demands an urban compactness, whilst the horizontal building volume simultaneously forms a unique landmark that contrasts with the vertical urban structure.

RheinEnergieStadion, Köln
RheinEnergie Football Stadium, Cologne

Wettbewerb Competition
2001 – 1. Preis

Entwurf Design
Volkwin Marg

Bauherr Client
Kölner Sportstätten GmbH

Bauzeit Construction period
2001–2004

Sitzplätze Seats
46.200

Die Eindeutigkeit und die klare Linie in der rechtwinkligen Geometrie des Stadionneubaus werden in Grund- und Aufriss durchgehalten und durch die Materialwahl und Konstruktionsweise betont: Beleuchtete, 60 m hohe Stahltürme tragen ein leichtes Tribünendach mit einer äußeren Metall- und einer inneren Glaseindeckung, die das Wachstum des Rasens gewährleistet. Um stützenfreie Tribünen ohne Sichtbehinderung für die Zuschauer zu ermöglichen, sind die Einzeldächer entlang ihrer Mittellinie nach dem Prinzip einer klassischen Hängebrücke aufgehängt: Jeweils zwei parallele Hängeseile tragen die vertikalen Dachlasten zu den Masten am Dachende, die wiederum nach außen abgespannt sind. Durch auskreuzende Zugstangen wird die gesamte Dachfläche zu einer zusammenhängenden Scheibe, so dass jedes der vier Einzeldächer für sich alleine standsicher ist und durch weitere Dächer ergänzt werden kann.

The clear design of the new stadium's right-angled geometry is maintained in plan and elevation and emphasized by the choice of materials as well as the structural system: illuminated, 60-m-high steel towers support a lightweight stand roof with an exterior metal and an interior glass roof, ensuring that the grass grows. In order to realize column-free stands with unrestricted views for the spectators, the individual roofs are suspended along their central line. The suspension system was designed like a traditional suspended bridge: two parallel suspension ropes transfer the vertical roof loads through to the masts at the roof's end, which, in turn, are guyed towards the outside. The entire roof surface was designed as one connected plate held in place by tension members. Each of the four roofs is separately stable and can be added to with other single roofs.

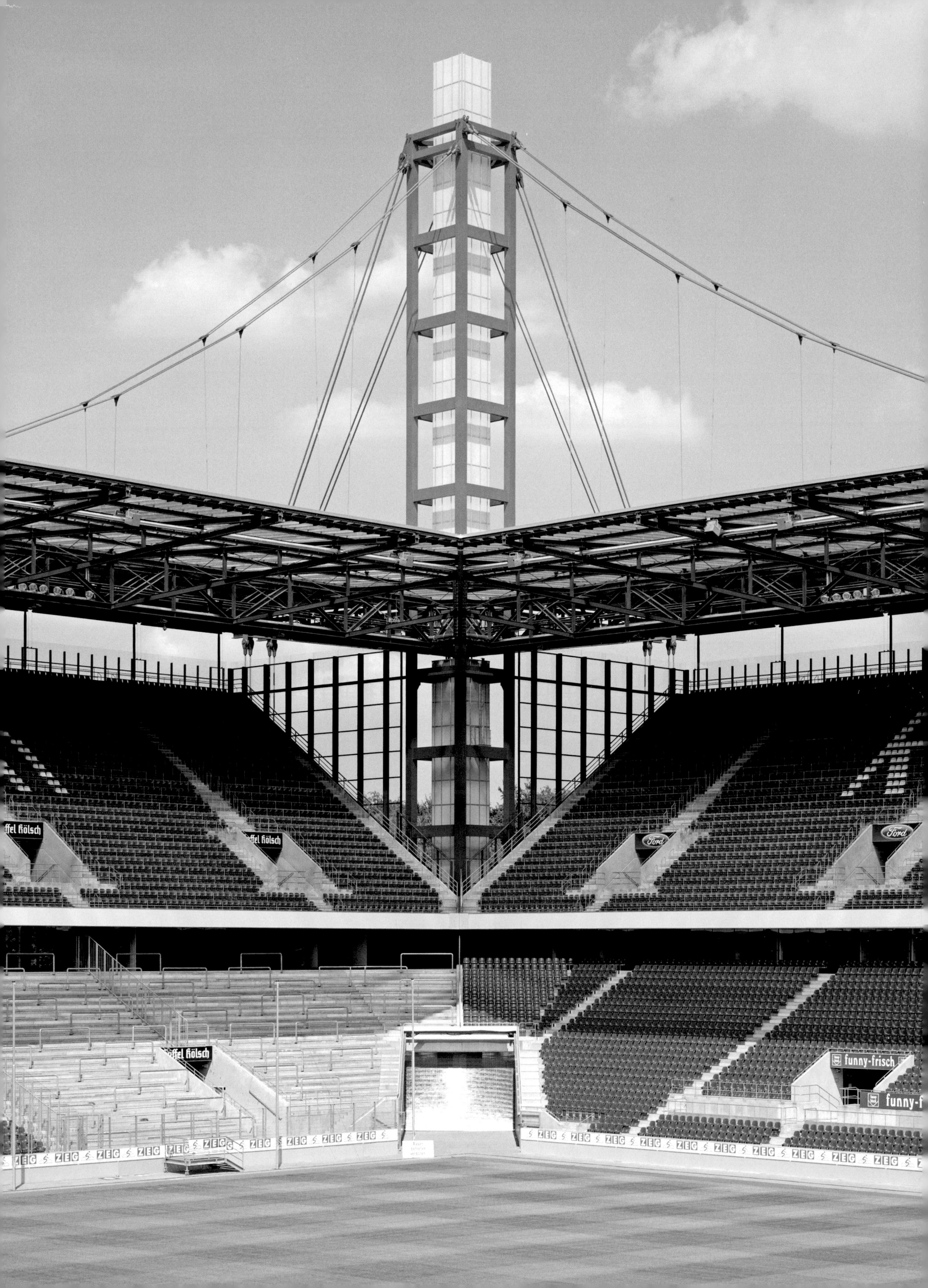
Ford
funny-frisch
ZEG

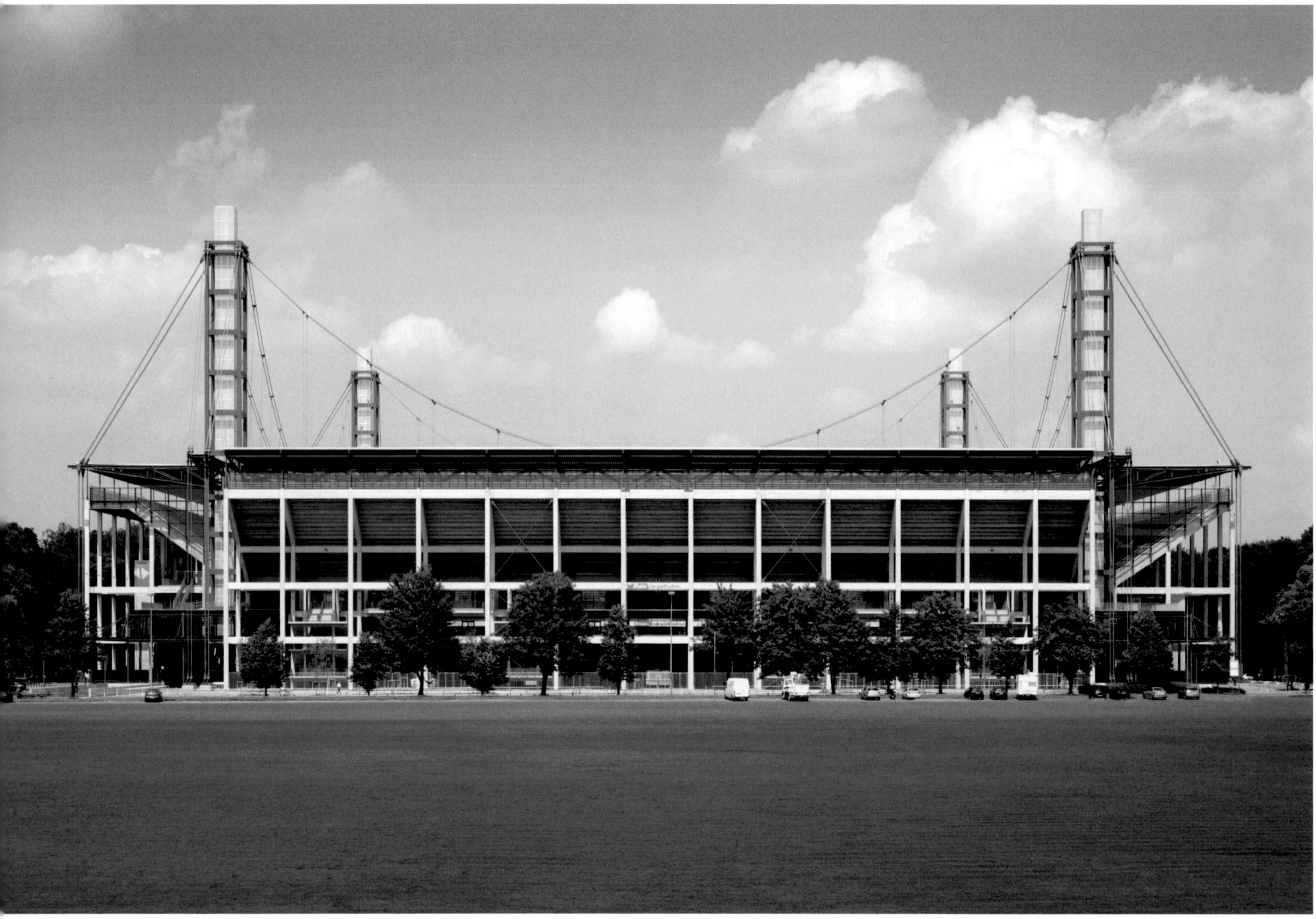

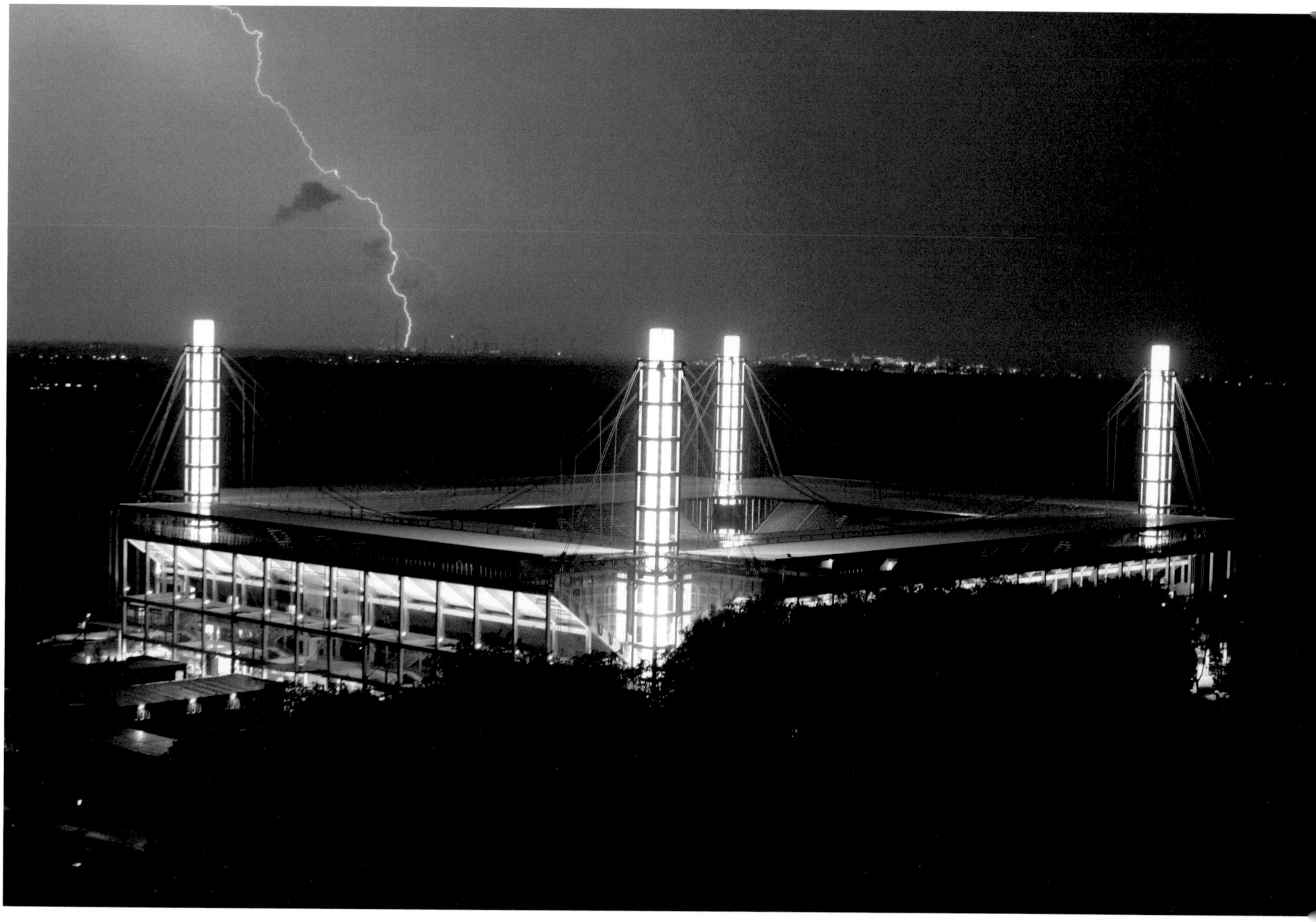

Olympiastadion Berlin, Umbau und Überdachung
Olympic Stadium, Berlin, Conversion and Roofing

Wettbewerb Competition
1998 – 1. Preis

Entwurf Design
Volkwin Marg und Hubert Nienhoff

Bauherr Client
Land Berlin, vertreten durch die
Senatsverwaltung für Stadtentwicklung

Bauzeit Construction period
2000–2004

Sitzplätze Seats
ca. 76.000

Das Modernisierungskonzept unterstützt die Qualitäten des Altbaus und ordnet sich ihm unter, so dass die äußere Anmutung des Stadions erhalten bleibt. Alle notwendigen Neubauten sind daher unterirdisch, außerhalb des Stadions untergebracht. Die neue Tribünenüberdachung setzt sich durch ihre feingliedrige Konstruktion und die Materialwahl der Oberflächen bewusst von der massiven Tektonik des historischen Stadionbaus ab. Die leichte Kragarmkonstruktion mit einer Membran als oberer und unterer Dachhaut gleicht im Querschnitt einem Flugzeugflügel. Ihre Spannweite beträgt umlaufend ca. 68 m. 20 sehr schlanke Baumstützen tragen im Bereich der Oberringtribüne das Stahlrohrfachwerk, das als Haupttragstruktur durch die transluzente Membran hindurch erkennbar bleibt. Die als „Ring of Fire" inszenierte Spielfeldbeleuchtung und die Stadionbeschallung sind in den inneren Dachrand integriert.

The modernization concept reinforced the quality of the existing structure and was subordinate to it, the stadium's external appearance making it possible to maintain. All necessary new structures were therefore located underground and outside the stadium. The delicate structure and the selected surface materials deliberately contrast the new grandstand roof against the solid tectonics of the historic stadium. The light, cantilevered structure with a membrane as upper and lower roof skin resembles an aerofoil in section. The circumferential span is approximately 68 m. In the area of the upper tier stands, 20 very slender tree-shaped columns support the tubular steel framework, which remains visible through the translucent membrane as the primary load-bearing structure. The illumination of the playing field, which is stage-managed as a 'Ring of Fire', and the stadium's sound system are integrated into the inner roof edge.

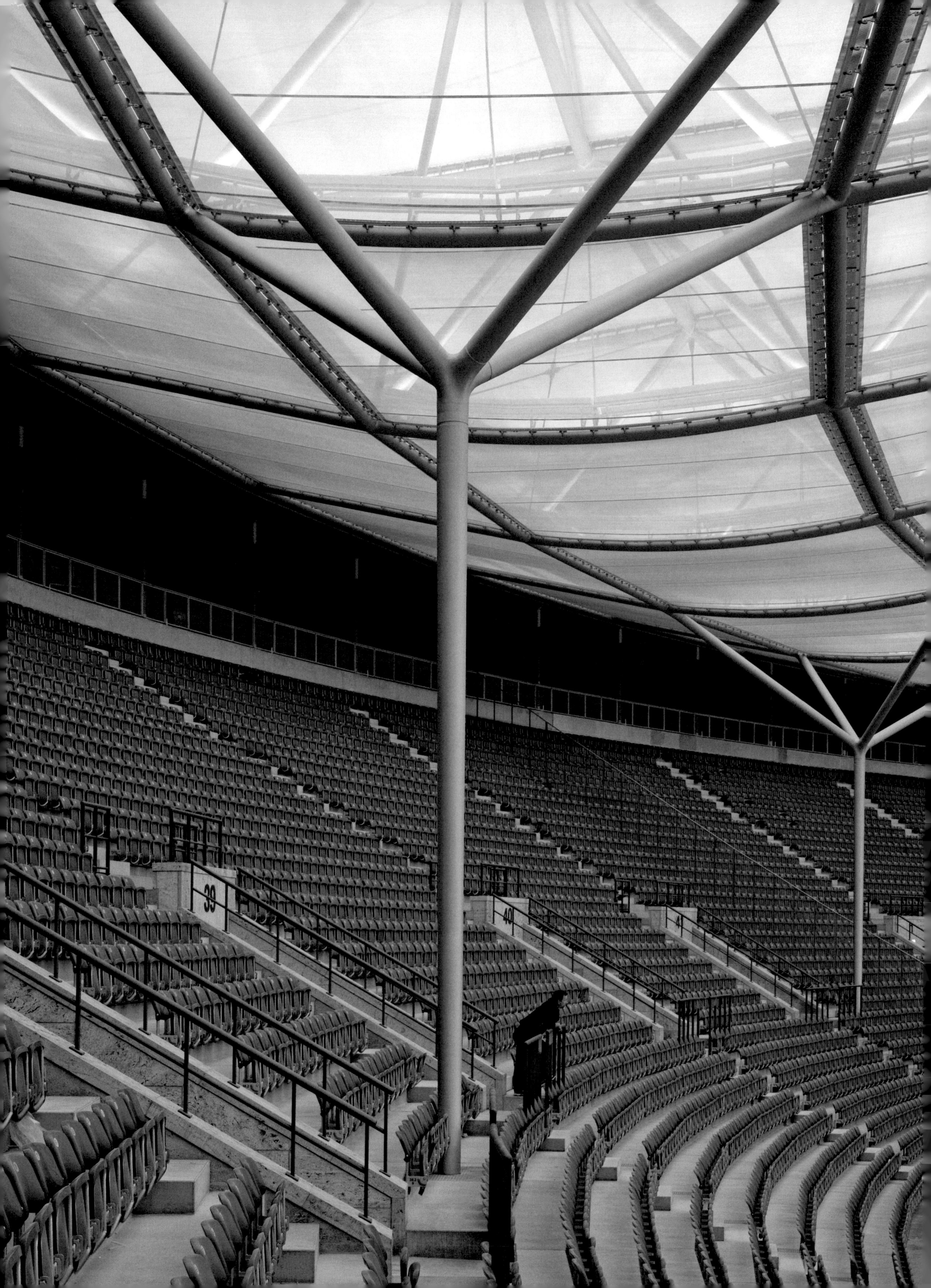
39
40

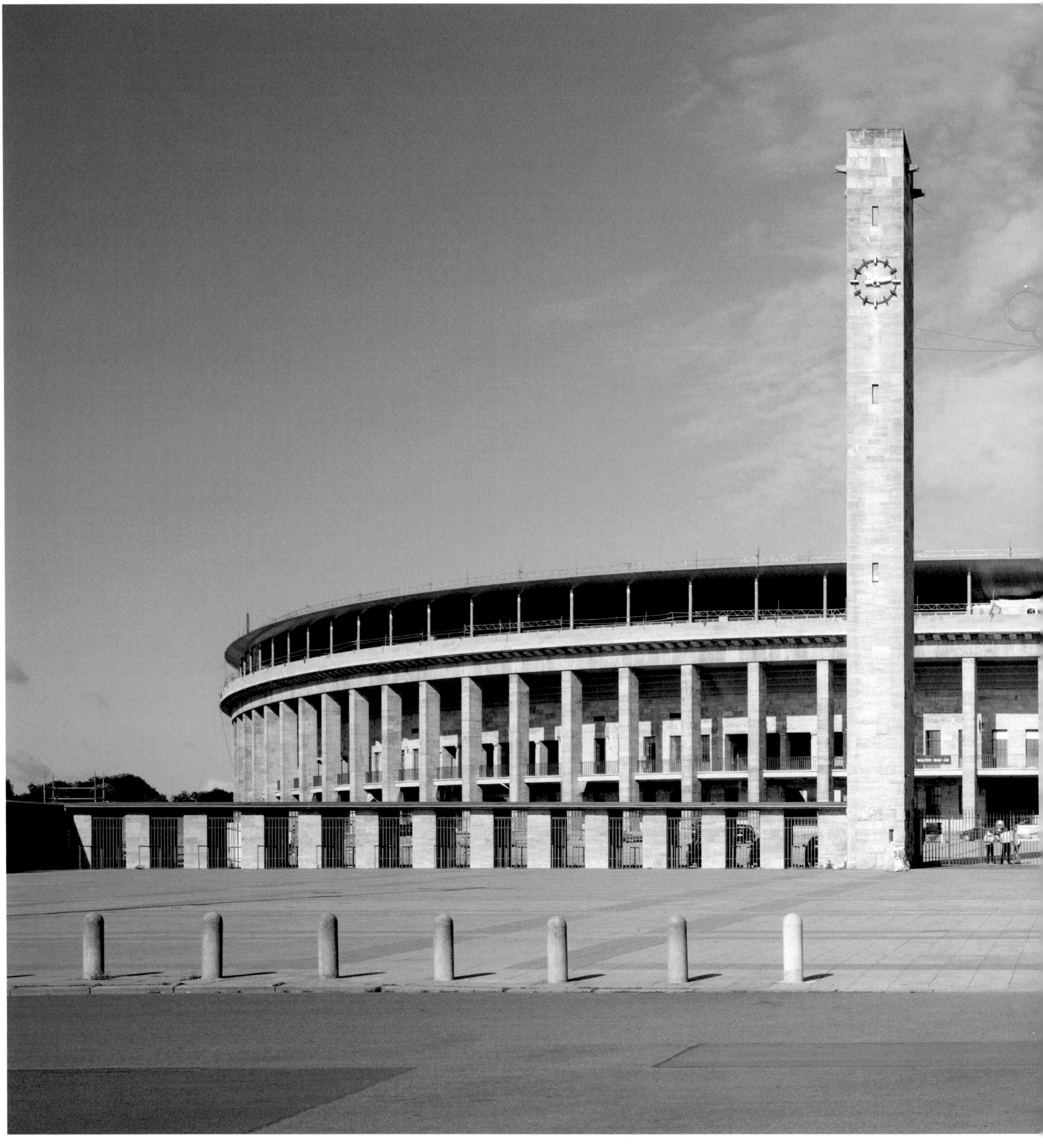

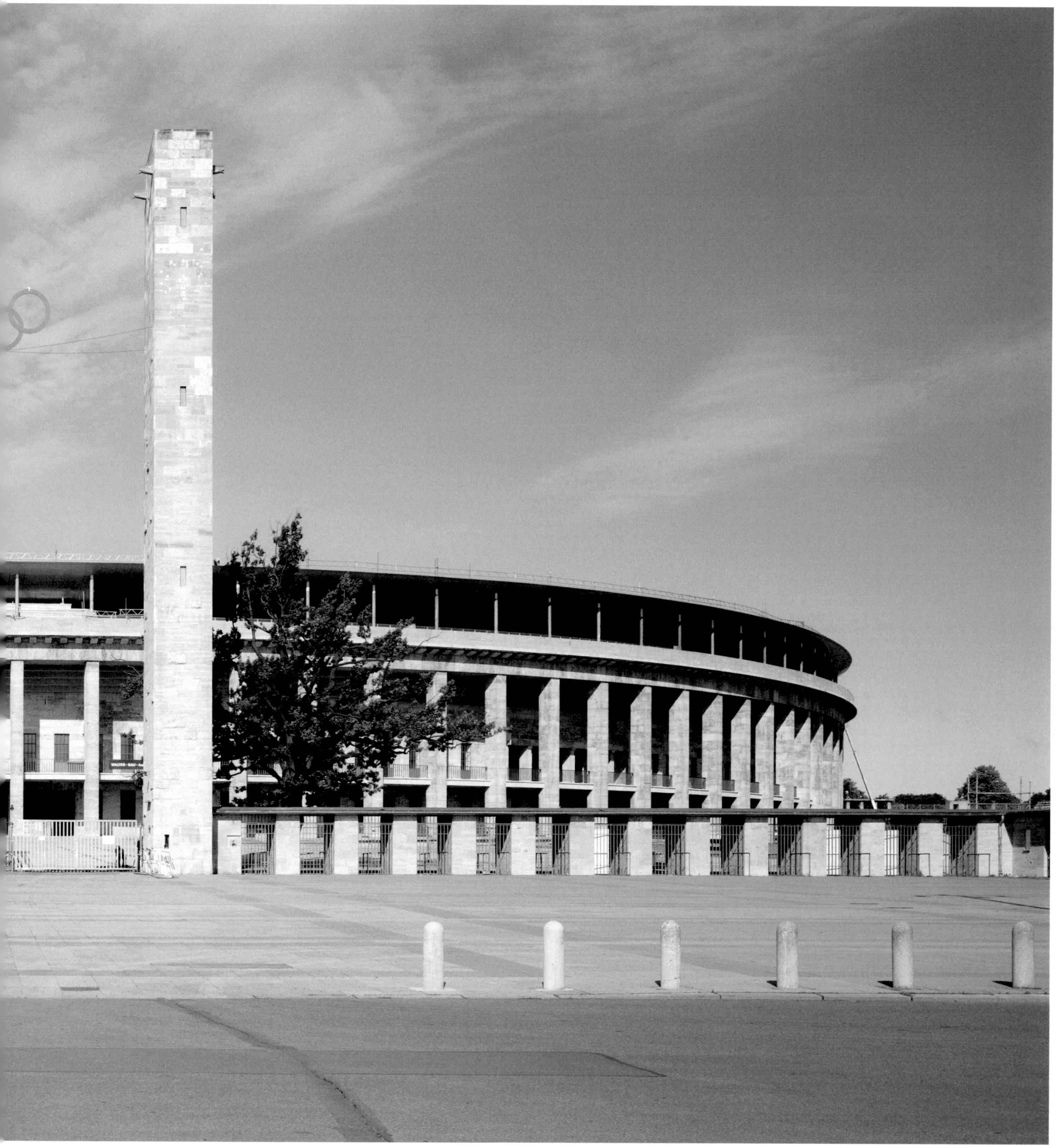

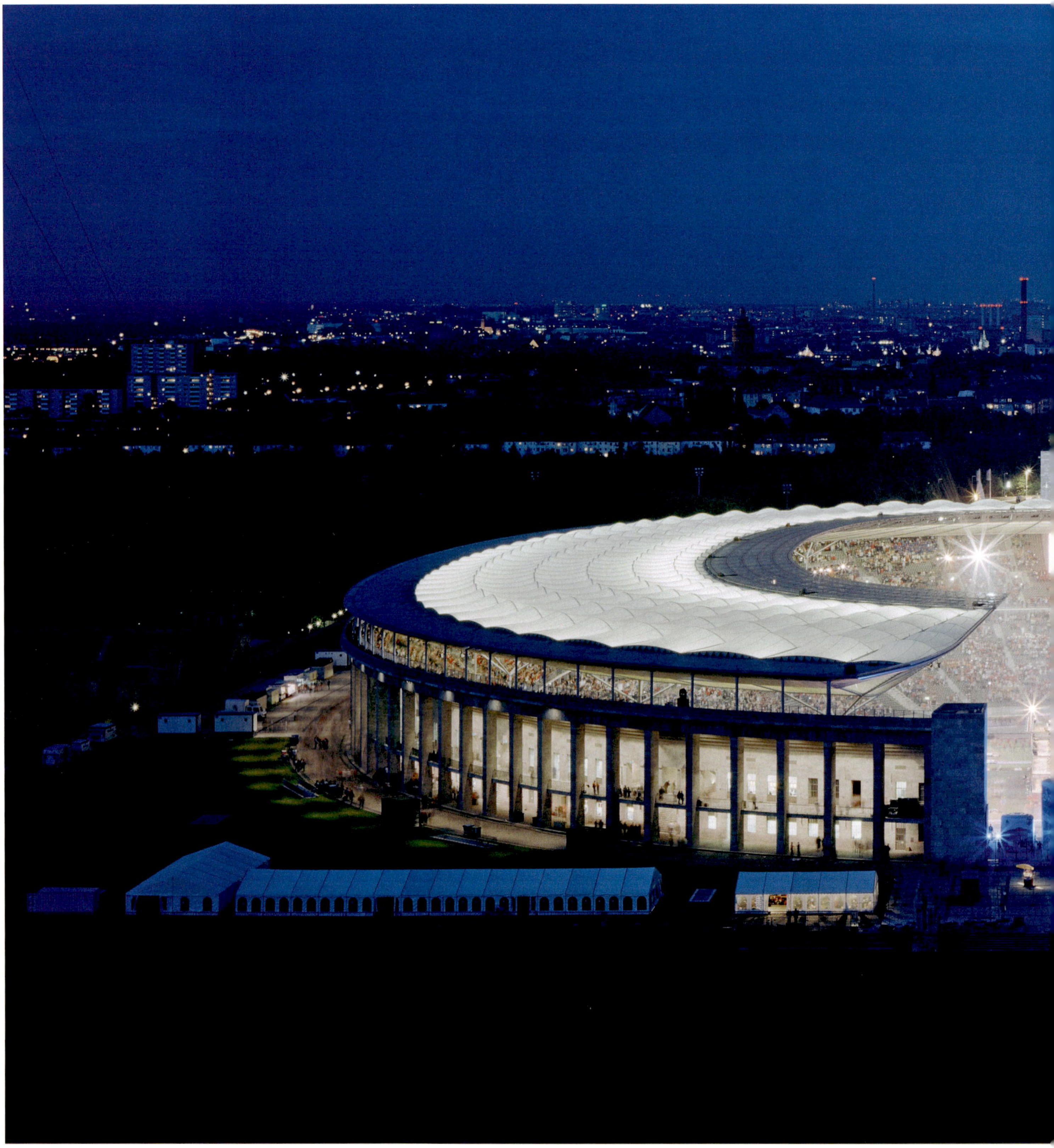

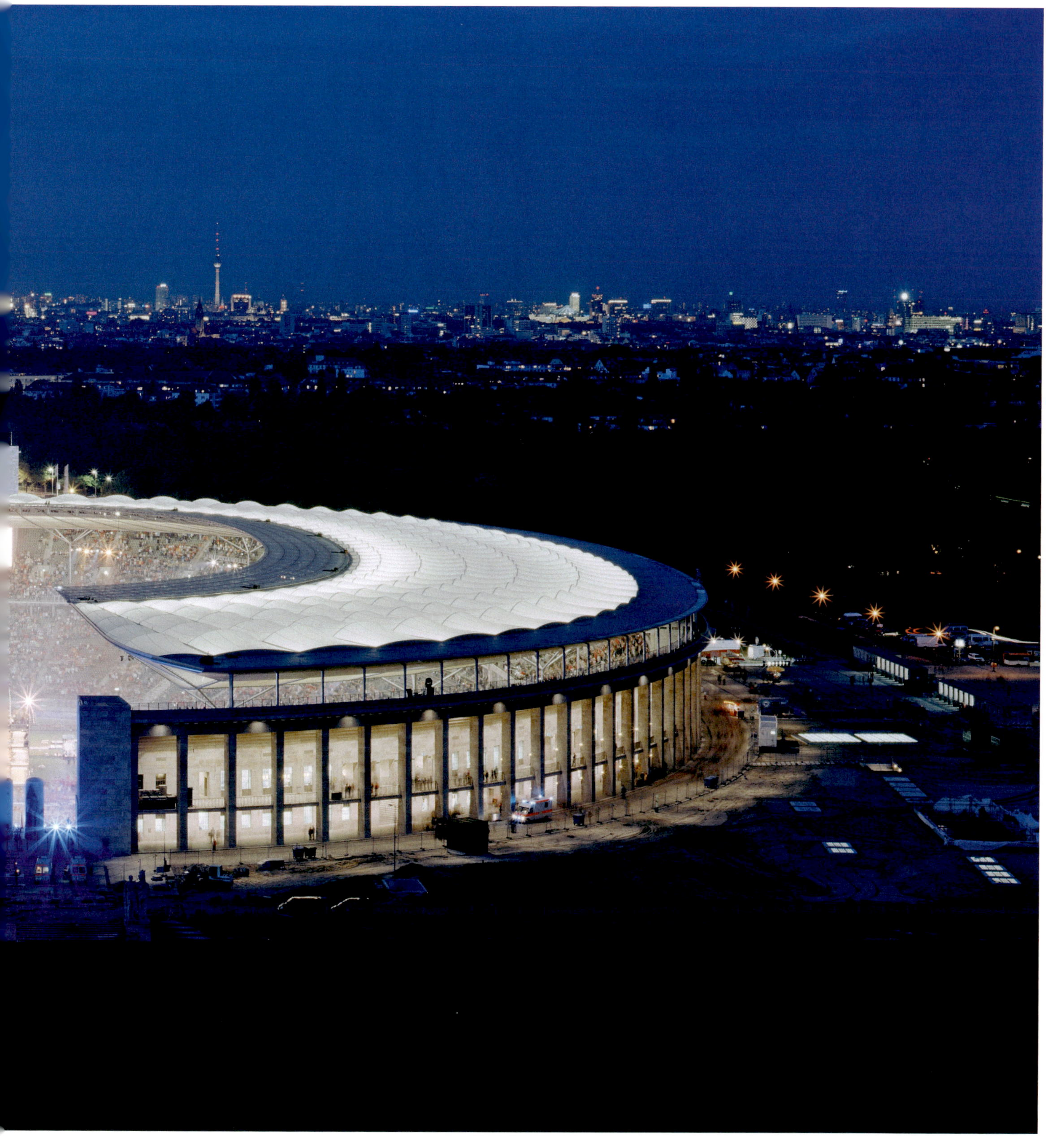

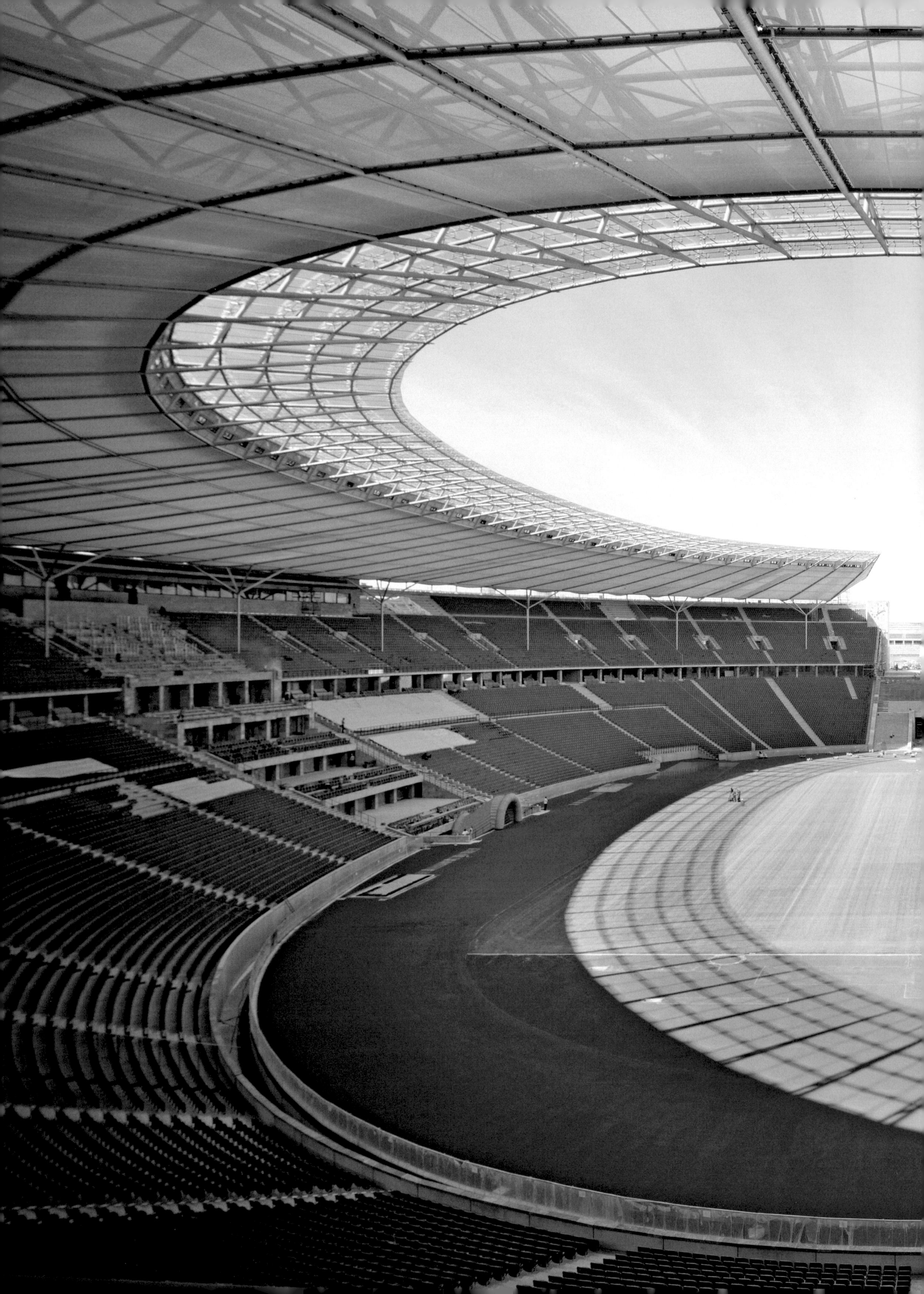

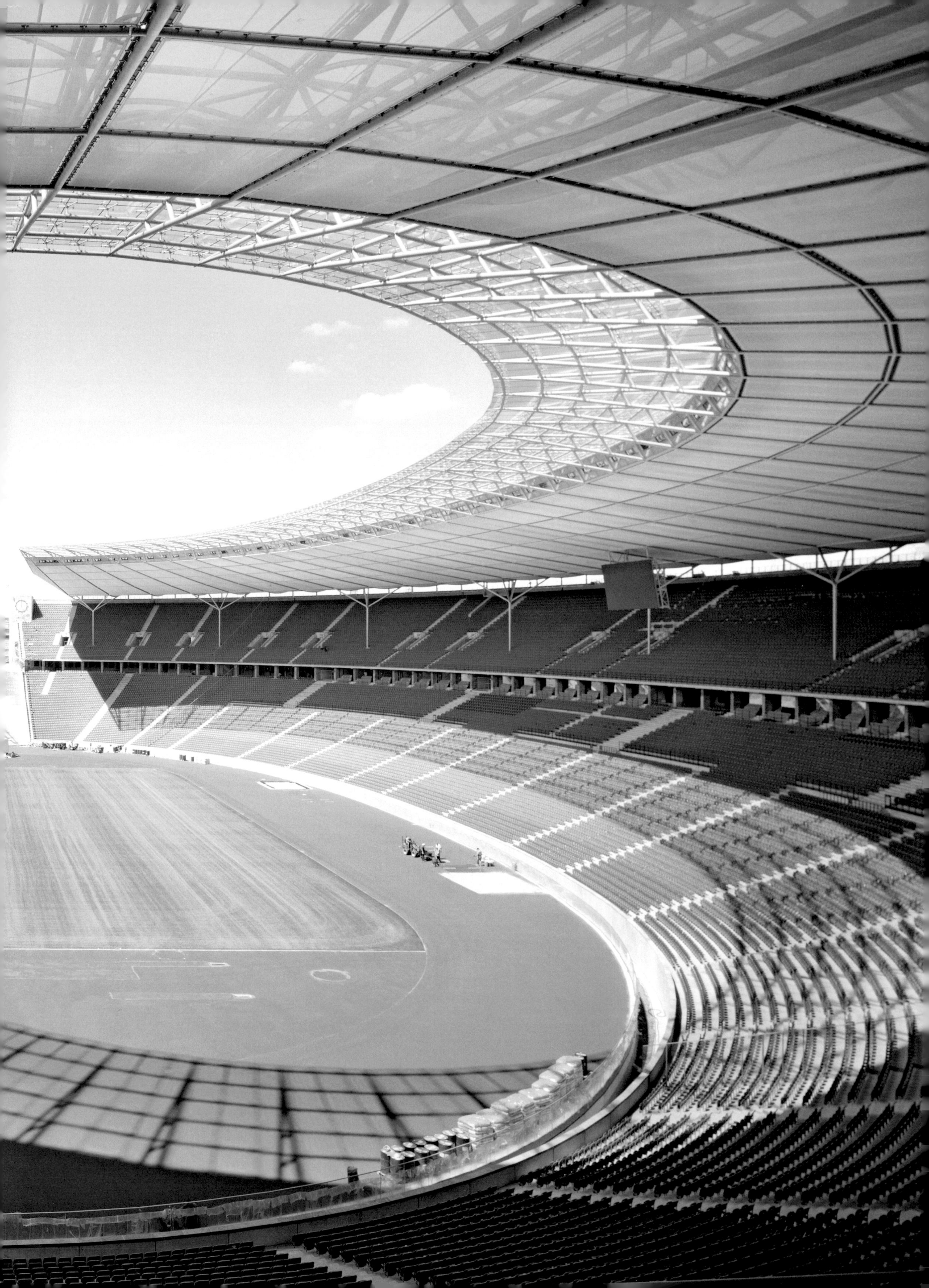

Flughafen Stuttgart, Terminal 3
Stuttgart Airport, Terminal 3

Wettbewerb Competition
1998 – 1. Preis

Entwurf Design
Meinhard von Gerkan mit Klaus Lenz

Bauherr Client
Flughafen Stuttgart GmbH

Bauzeit Construction period
2000–2004

BGF Gross floor area
57.000 m²

Insgesamt 18 Stahlbäume tragen das abgetreppte Dach des Terminals 3, dessen im Vergleich zum Terminal 1 geringere Bauhöhe bei gleicher Dachneigung eine Auflösung in einzelne Shedflächen notwendig machte. Ein aus dem Gebäude „herausgeschobener" Baukörper sorgt für ein größeres Flächenangebot auf der Vorfeldseite. Er ist räumlich mit dem prägnanten Riegel des Hauptgebäudes verbunden, löst sich jedoch optisch durch Glasoberlichter von diesem. Sämtliche flughafenspezifische und betriebliche Abläufe orientieren sich am Bestand bzw. wurden aufgrund von Erfahrungen aus dem laufenden Betrieb des Terminals 1 optimiert. Die Ankunftshalle verbindet landseitig als Mall über 260 m die Terminals 1 und 3. Die einfache und sinnfällige Anordnung der Erschließungselemente und Lufträume, die vertikale Blickbeziehungen erlaubt, ermöglicht die schnelle Orientierung im neuen „Terminal der Übersichtlichkeit".

A total of 18 steel trees support the stepped roof of Terminal 3. The dissolving into single shed areas was necessary due to the identical roof incline but reduced building height compared to Terminal 1. A structural element projecting from the building bar provides an increased floor area on the apron side. Spatially, it is connected to the precise main bar building, but is visually separated by glass top lights. All airport-specific and operational procedures are orientated on the existing organization or were optimized according to the experience gained from the running operation in Terminal 1. On the landside, the arrival hall connects Terminal 1 and 3 by way of a mall over a distance of 260 m. The simple and obvious positioning of the access elements and voids, which allow vertical visual links, guarantee immediate orientation in the new 'Terminal of Clarity'.

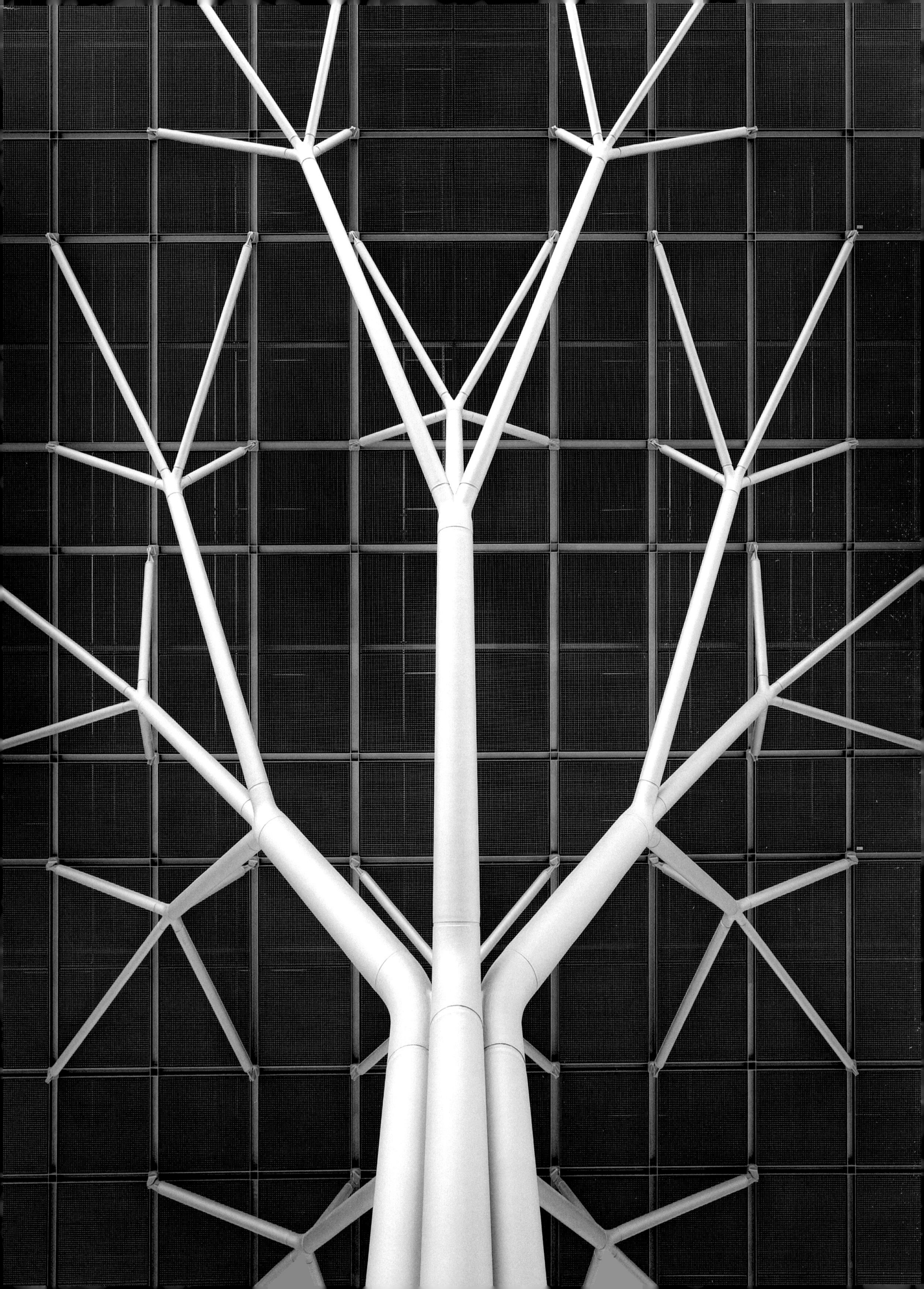

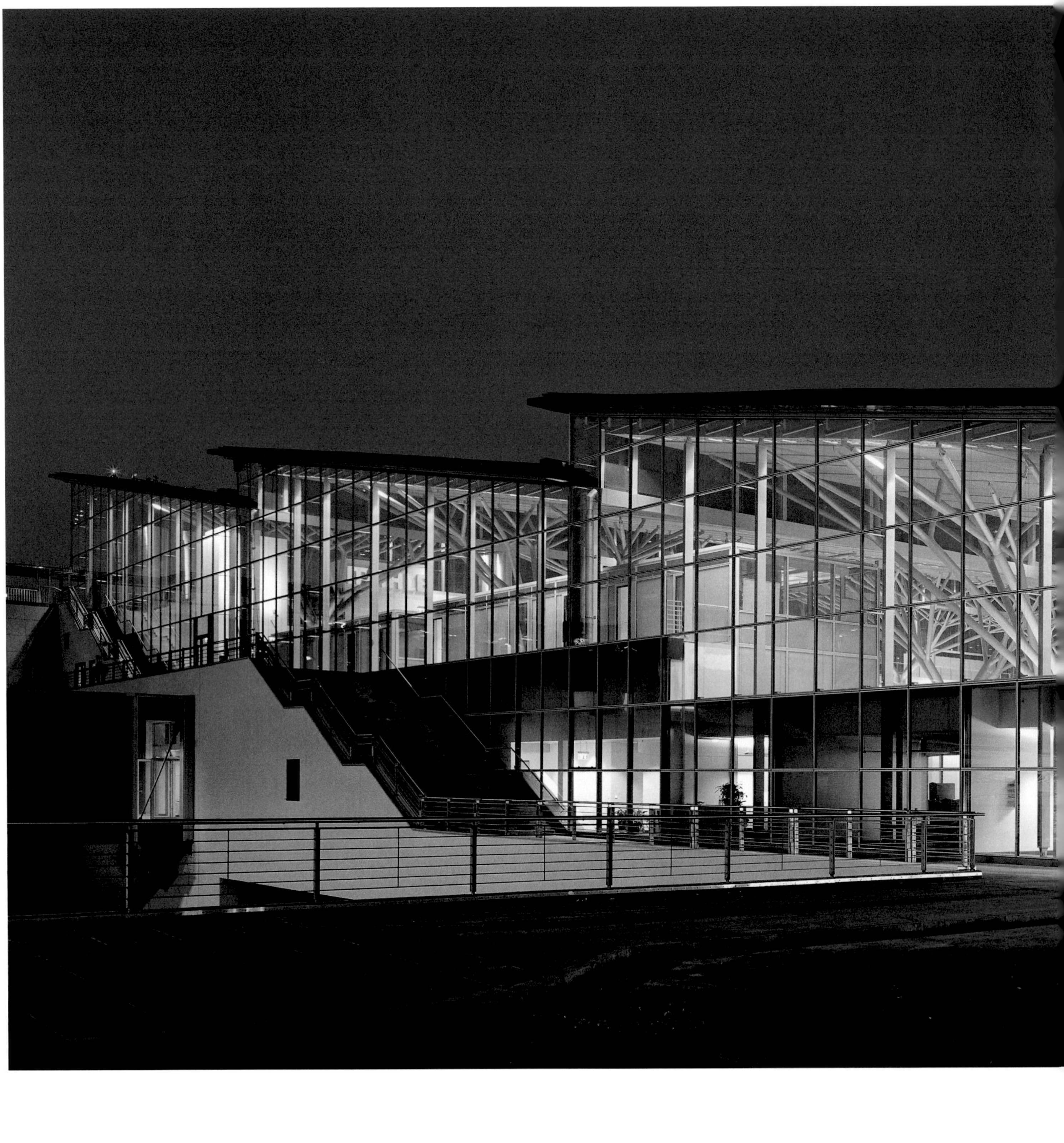

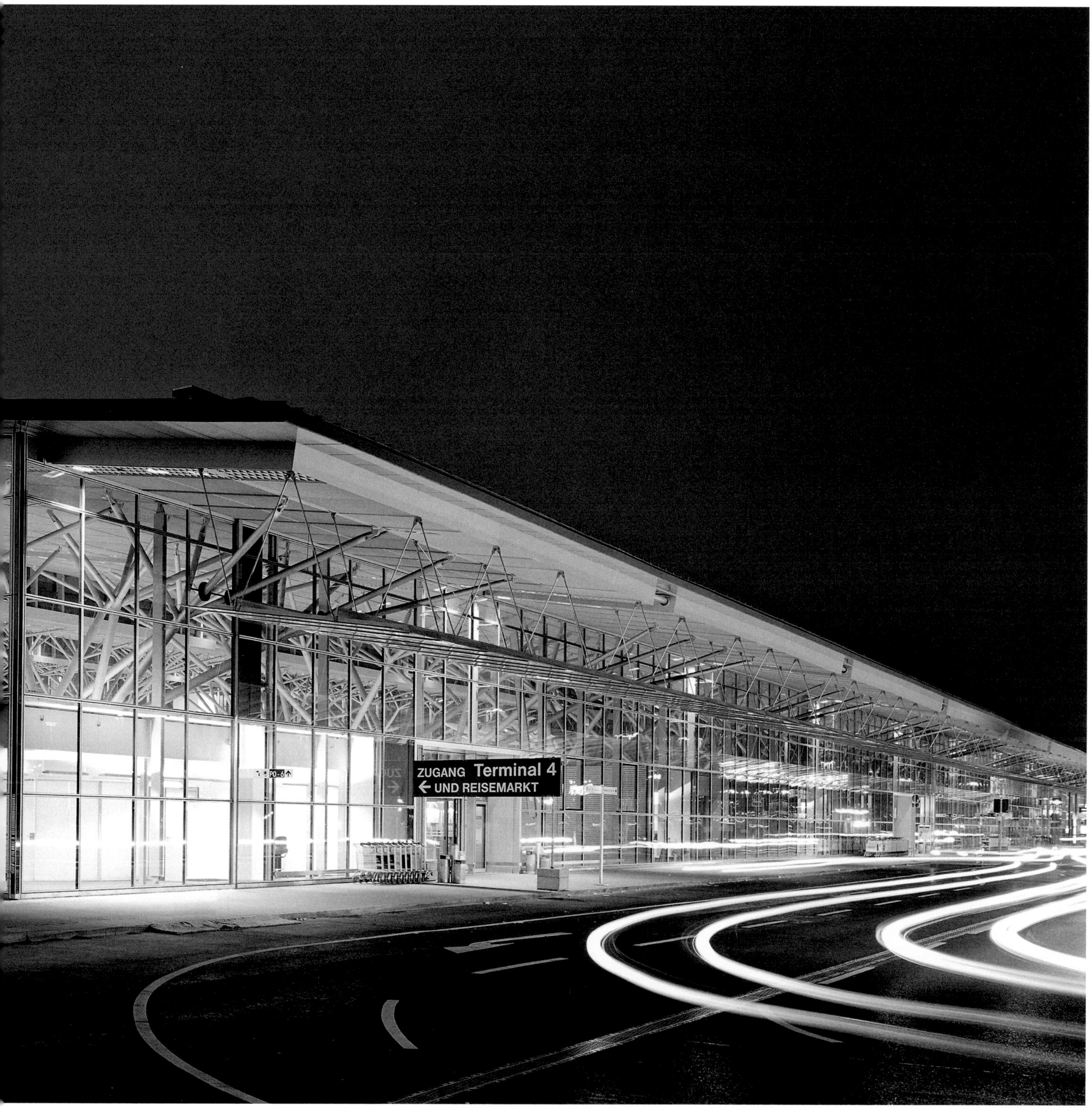
ZUGANG Terminal 4
← UND REISEMARKT

Wohnhaus Luserke, Hamburg
Luserke House, Hamburg

Entwurf Design
Meinhard von Gerkan und Nikolaus Goetze

Bauherr Client
Joachim Luserke

Bauzeit Construction period
2003-2004

BGF Gross floor area
1.000 m²

Das parkähnliche Grundstück an der Elbchaussee fällt zur Elbe hin ab und setzt den im Stil eines englischen Landschaftsparks gestalteten, angrenzenden Jenischpark außenräumlich bis zur Elbe fort. Im Norden verläuft das modellierte Gelände ebenerdig zur Elbchaussee, im Süden folgt der Garten dem natürlichen Elbhang. Hinterlüftete, weiß emaillierte Glastafeln, die durch tief eingeschnittene, raumhohe, schlanke Öffnungsflügel gegliedert sind, bilden die Nordfassade der Villa. Vor der transparenten Aluminium-Glaskonstruktion der Südfassade können in verschiedenen Ebenen Verschatter aus Holzlamellen bewegt werden, so dass sich die Transparenz, je nach Wetterlage, ändert. Im Gegensatz zu dem kühlen Äußeren wurden in den Wohnräumen bewusst warme Oberflächen, wie Eichenparkett und Holzeinbauten eingesetzt. Im Untergeschoss befindet sich ein Schwimmbad mit angrenzendem Fitness- und Saunabereich.

The park-like site on the Elbchaussee declines towards the river Elbe and is a continuation of the adjoining Jenisch Park, which was designed in typical English landscaping tradition. In the north the modelled ground runs at ground level with the Elbchaussee; in the south the garden follows the natural slope towards the river. Ventilated, white-enamelled glass plates, divided by slender, deeply carved, floor-to-ceiling leaves, form the villa's north façade. Shading devices made of wooden lamellas can be moved in various levels in front of the transparent aluminium-glass structure of the south façade; the transparency therefore changes according to the weather conditions. In contrast to the cool exterior, the living spaces were deliberately designed with warm surfaces, such as oak parquet and timber built-in units. A swimming pool with adjoining fitness and sauna area is located in the basement.

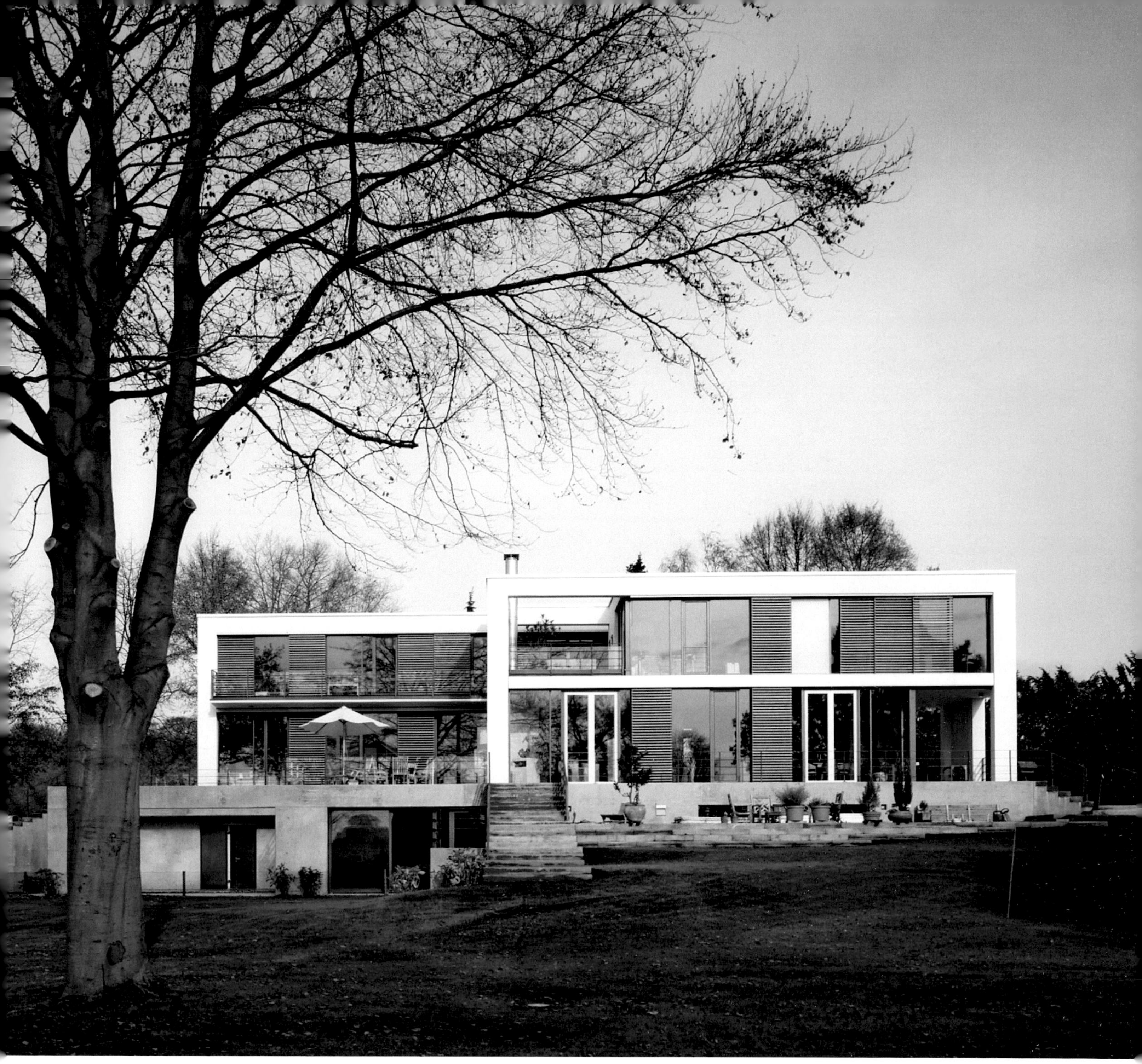

Messe- und Kongresszentrum Shenzhen, China
Shenzhen Convention and Exhibition Centre, China

Wettbewerb Competition
2001 - 1. Preis

Entwurf Design
Volkwin Marg und Marc Ziemons

Partner Partner
Nikolaus Goetze

Bauherr Client
Shenzhen Convention & Exhibition Center

Bauzeit Construction period
2002-2004

BGF Gross floor area
256.000 m²

Die gesamte Ausstellungsfläche befindet sich auf einer Ebene, so dass ein geeignetes Tragwerk gefunden werden musste, das einerseits die riesigen Ausstellungshallen stützenfrei überspannt und das darüber „schwebende" Kongresszentrum trägt, während es sich andererseits in den städtebaulichen Kontext einfügt. Entlang der Mittelachse der Hallen sind in Abständen von 30 m große stählerne A-förmige Bock-Konstruktionen angeordnet. Sie ragen fast 60 m in die Höhe und stemmen das Kongressgebäude um mehr als 15 m über die eigentliche Hallenkonstruktion. Die ebenfalls in der Mittelachse gelegene Eingangs- und Besucherplattform auf einer Höhe von 7,50 m über dem Ausstellungs- und Straßenniveau erlaubt die separate Erschließung einzelner Hallen oder zusammengefasster Hallenkomplexe. Die Besucher können von hier aus das Ausstellungsgeschehen überblicken und sich leicht orientieren.

The entire exhibition area is located on one level. This required a suitable structural framework which would, on the one hand, span the huge exhibition hall without columns and support the convention centre 'hovering' above, whilst, on the other hand, blending into the urban context. Along the hall's central axis, large A-shaped steel trestle structures are positioned at 30 m intervals. They rise to a height of almost 60 m and raise the convention building by more than 15 m above the actual hall structure. The entrance and visitor platform, which is also positioned in the central axis at 7.50 m above the exhibition and street level, provides separate accesses to single halls or joined hall complexes. From this location visitors can get an overview of the exhibition activities and easily find their way around.

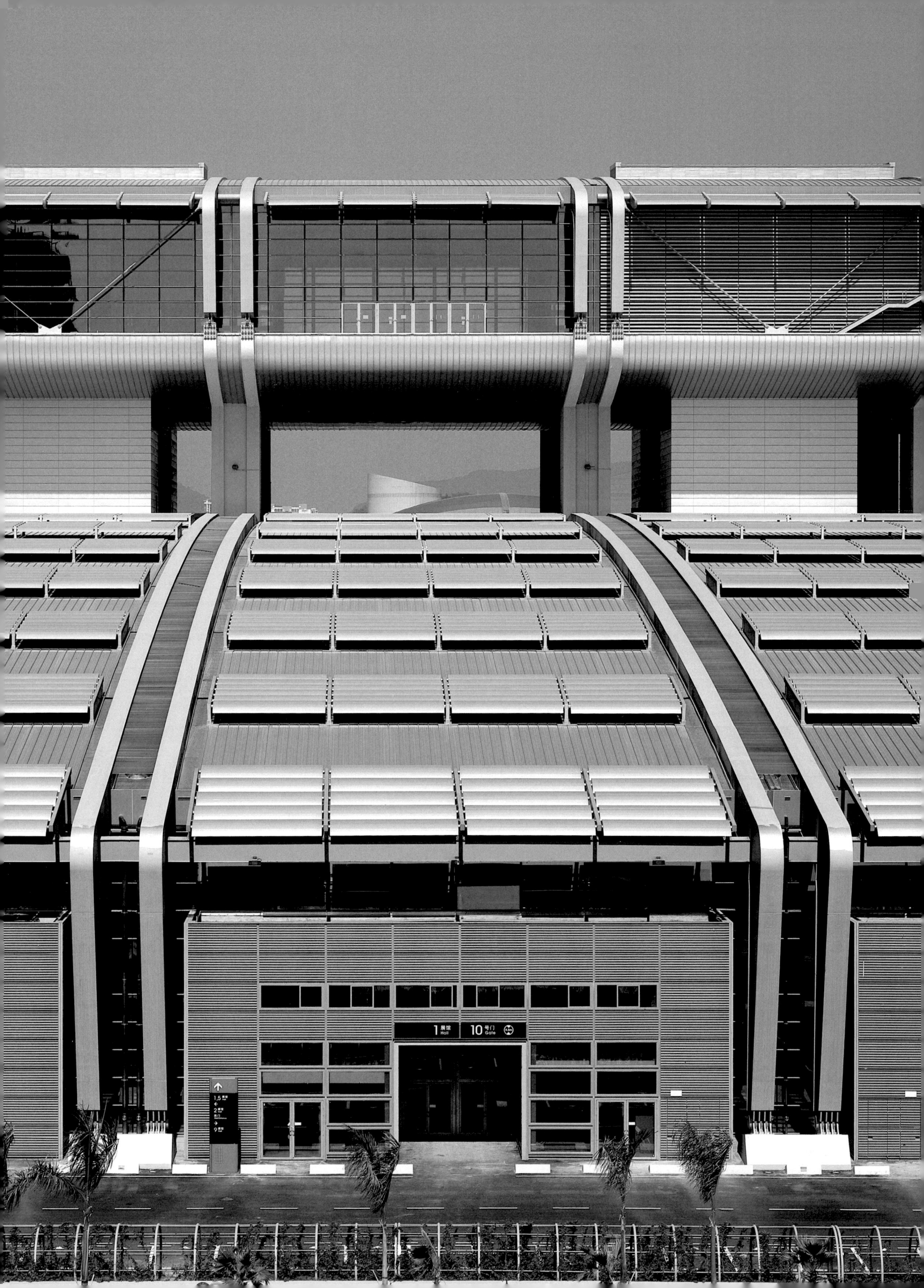
1 展馆 Hall
10 号门 Gate
4.5m

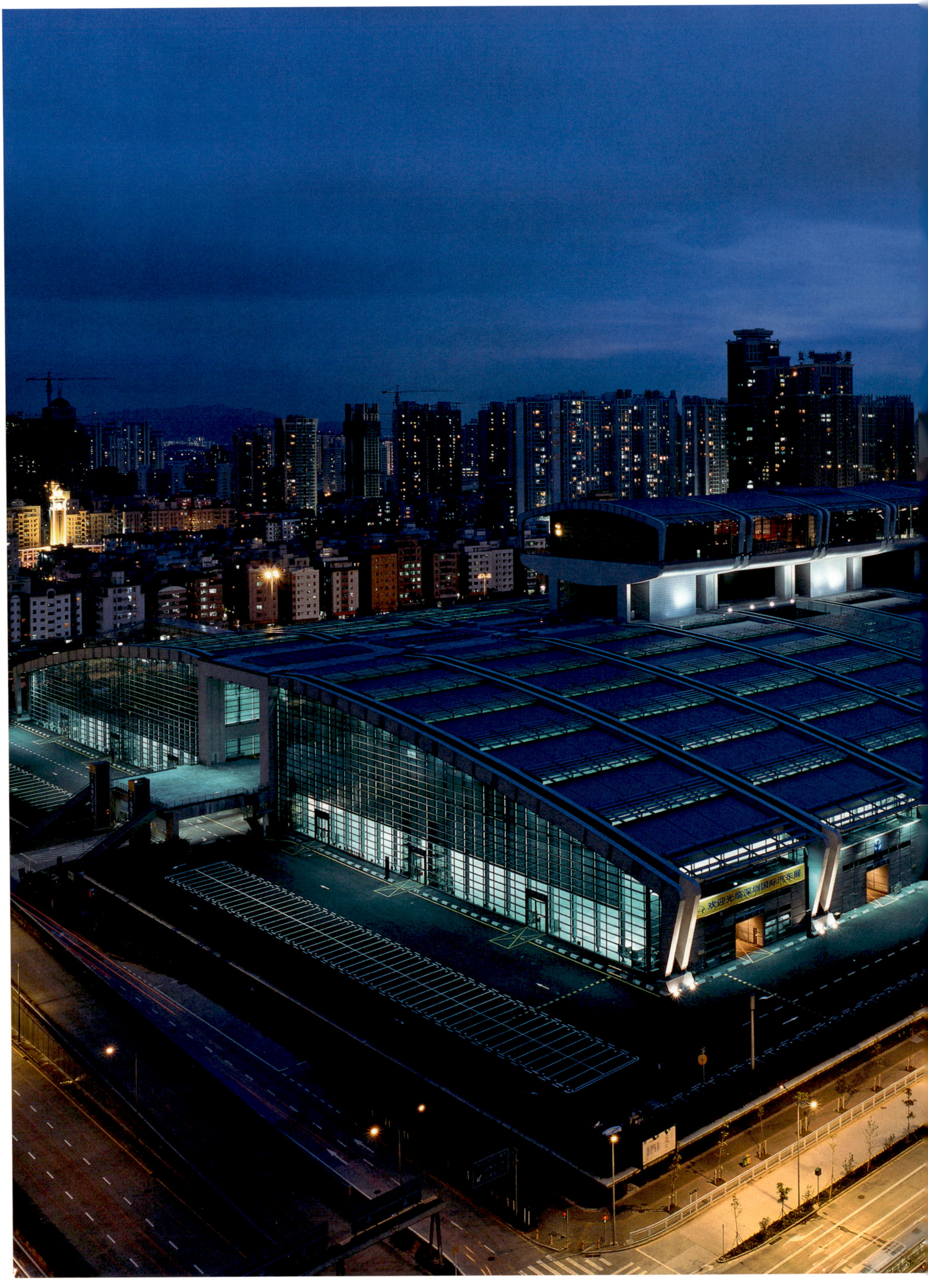

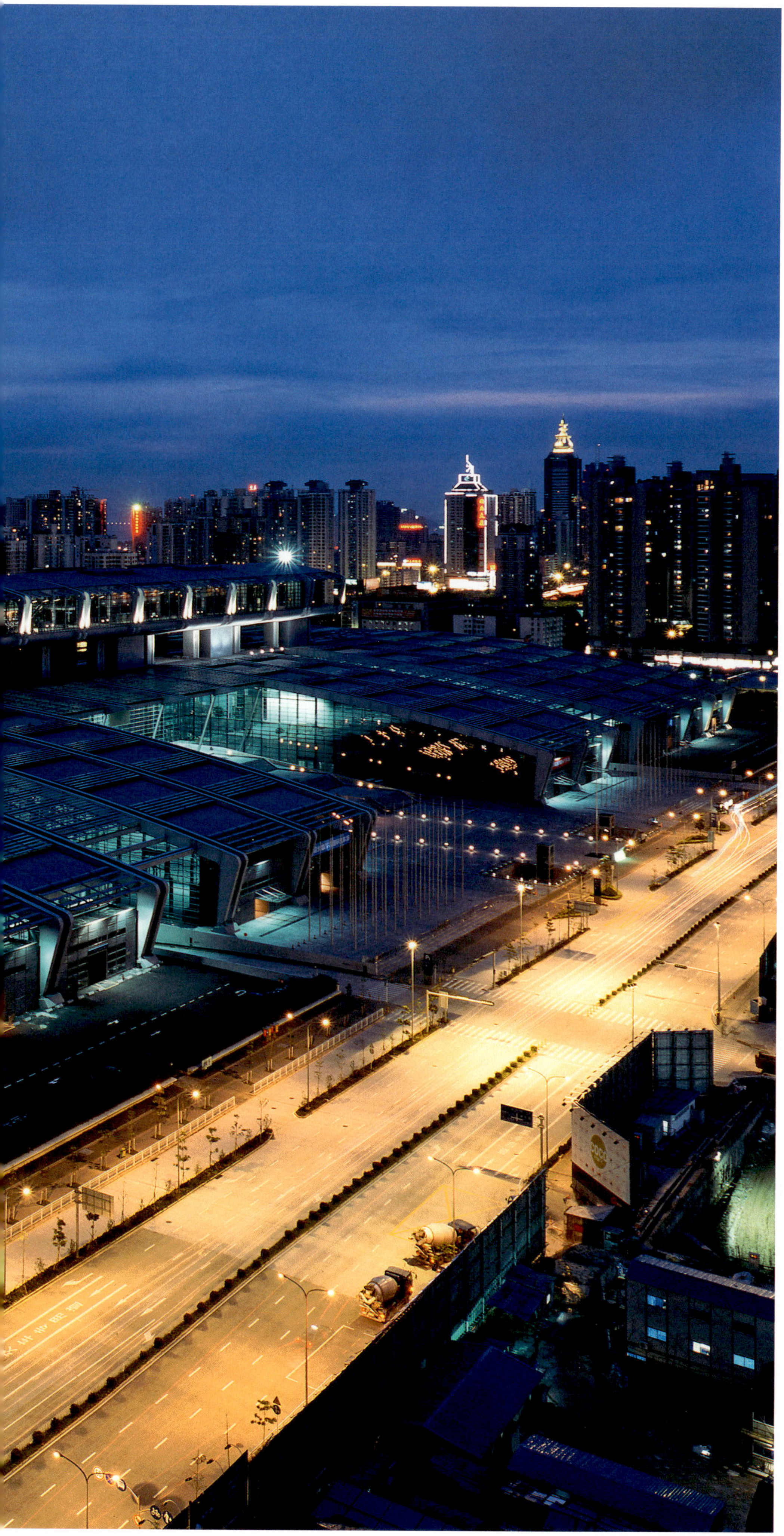

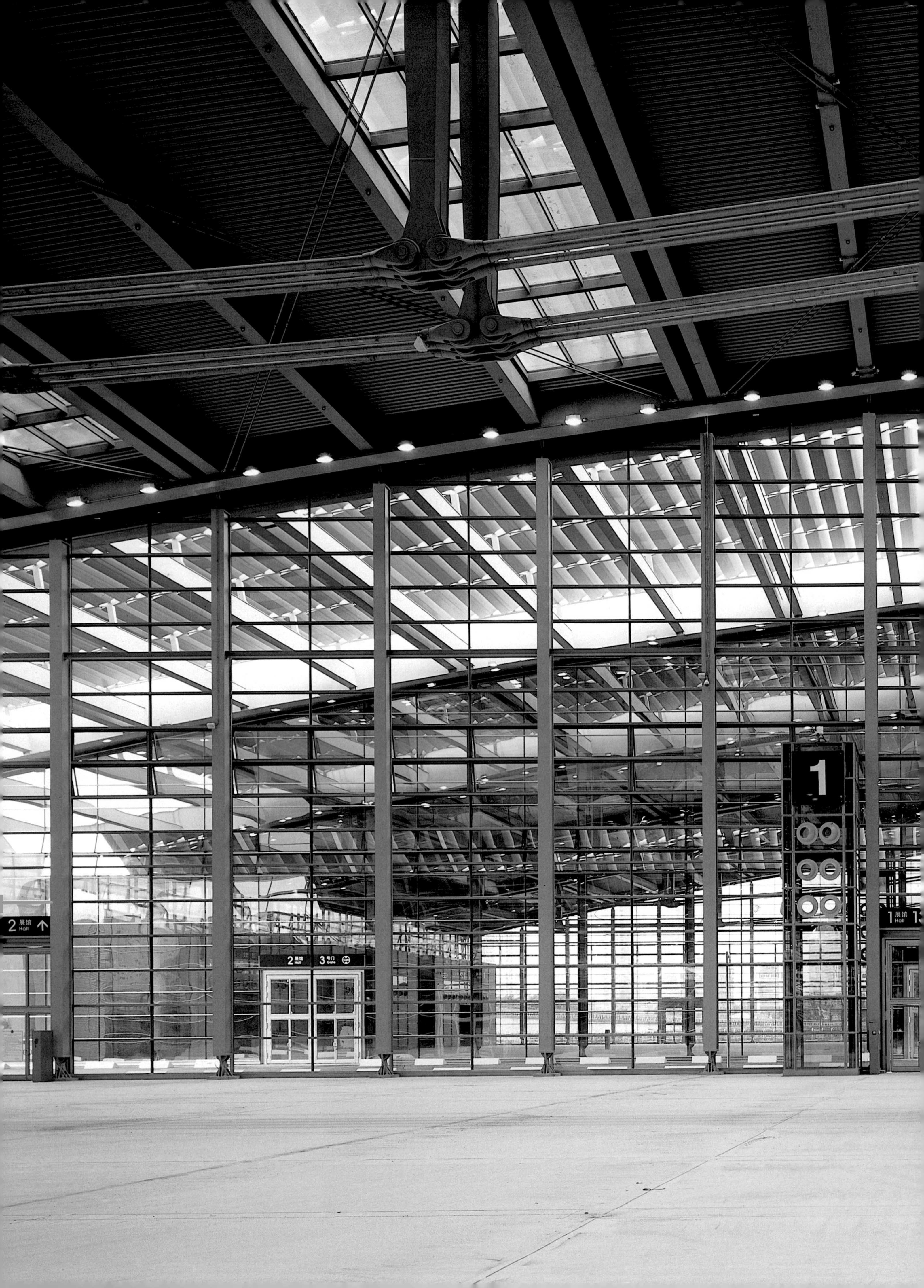
2 展馆 Hall
1

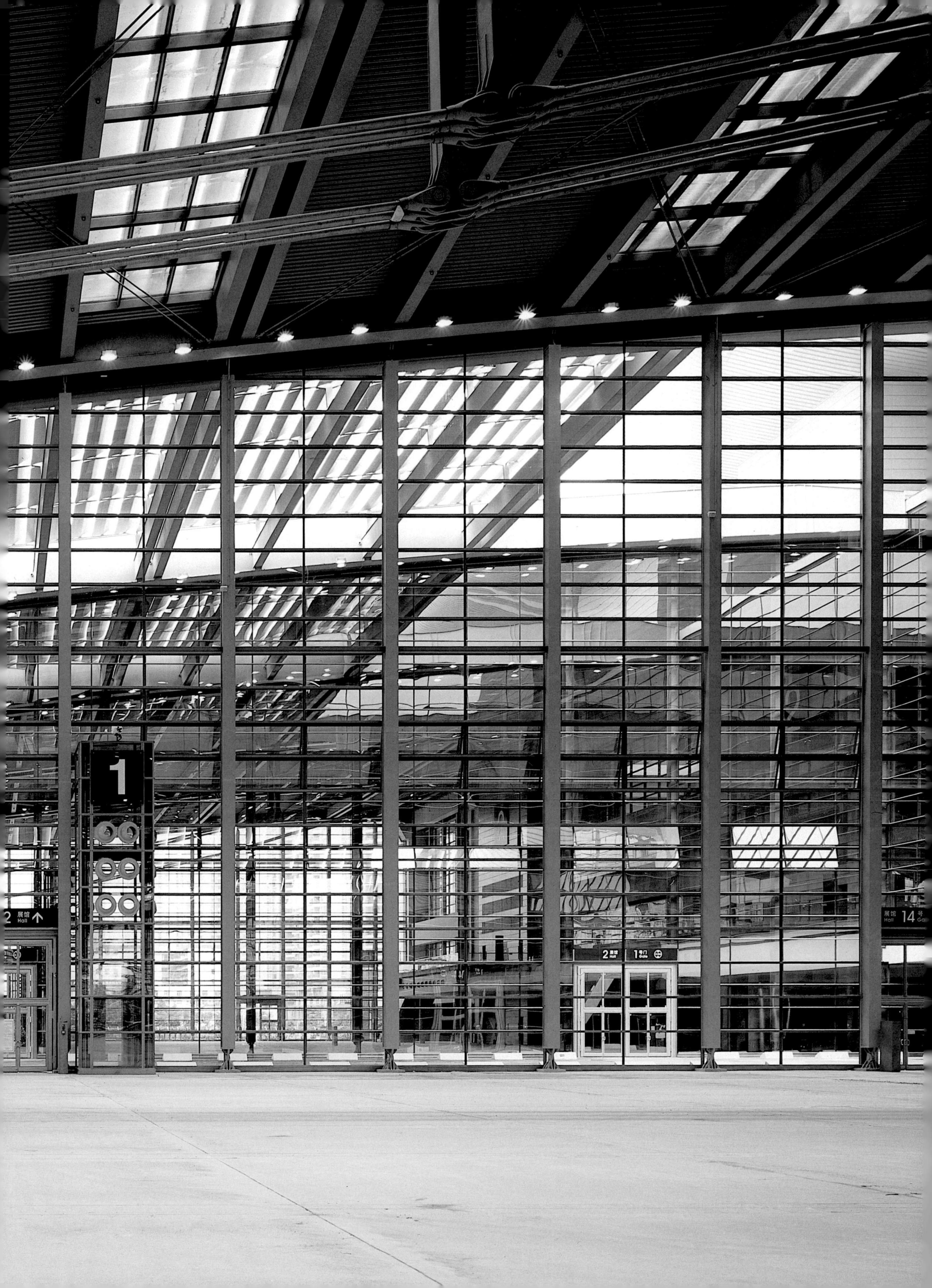
1

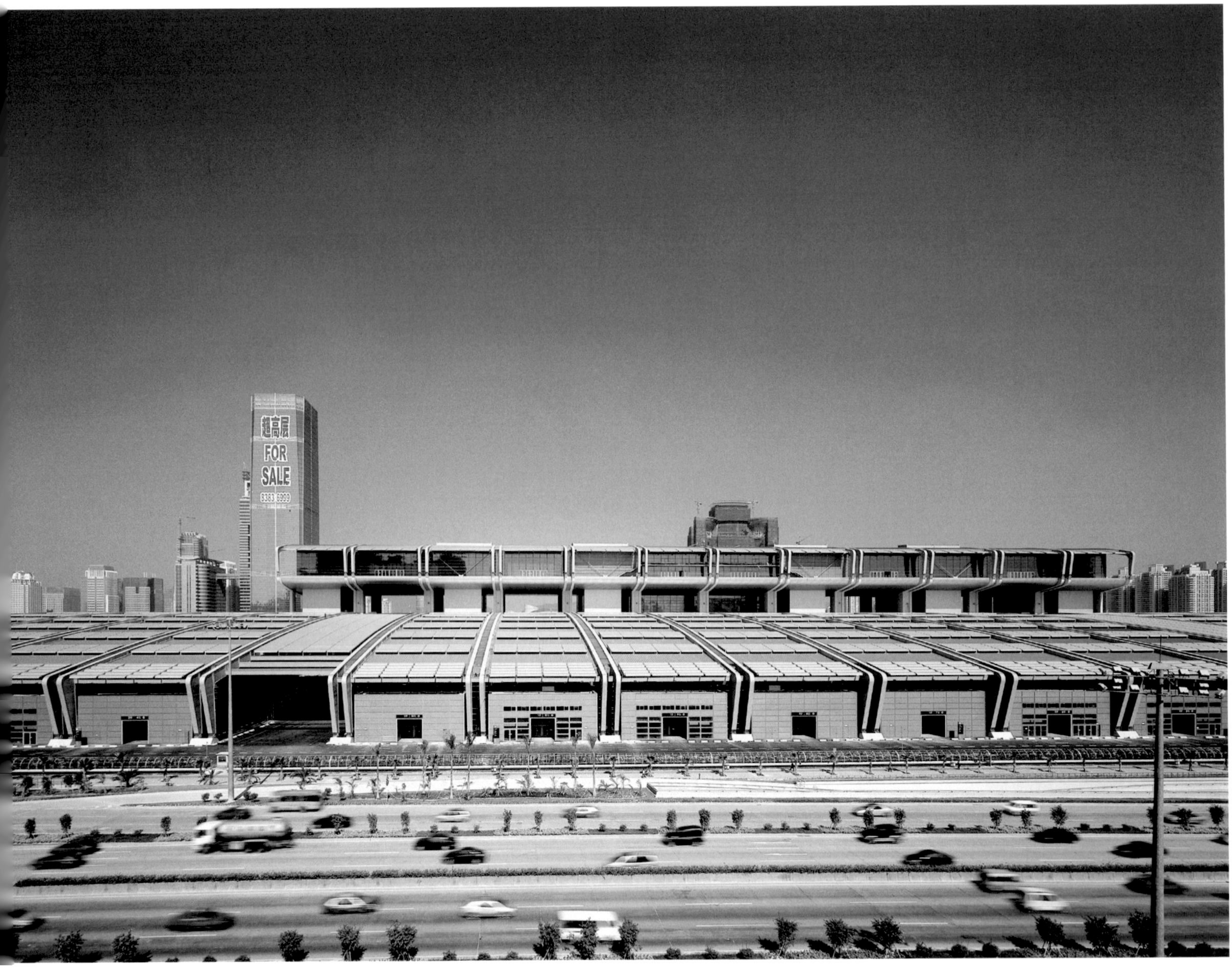
超高层
FOR
SALE
8383 6999

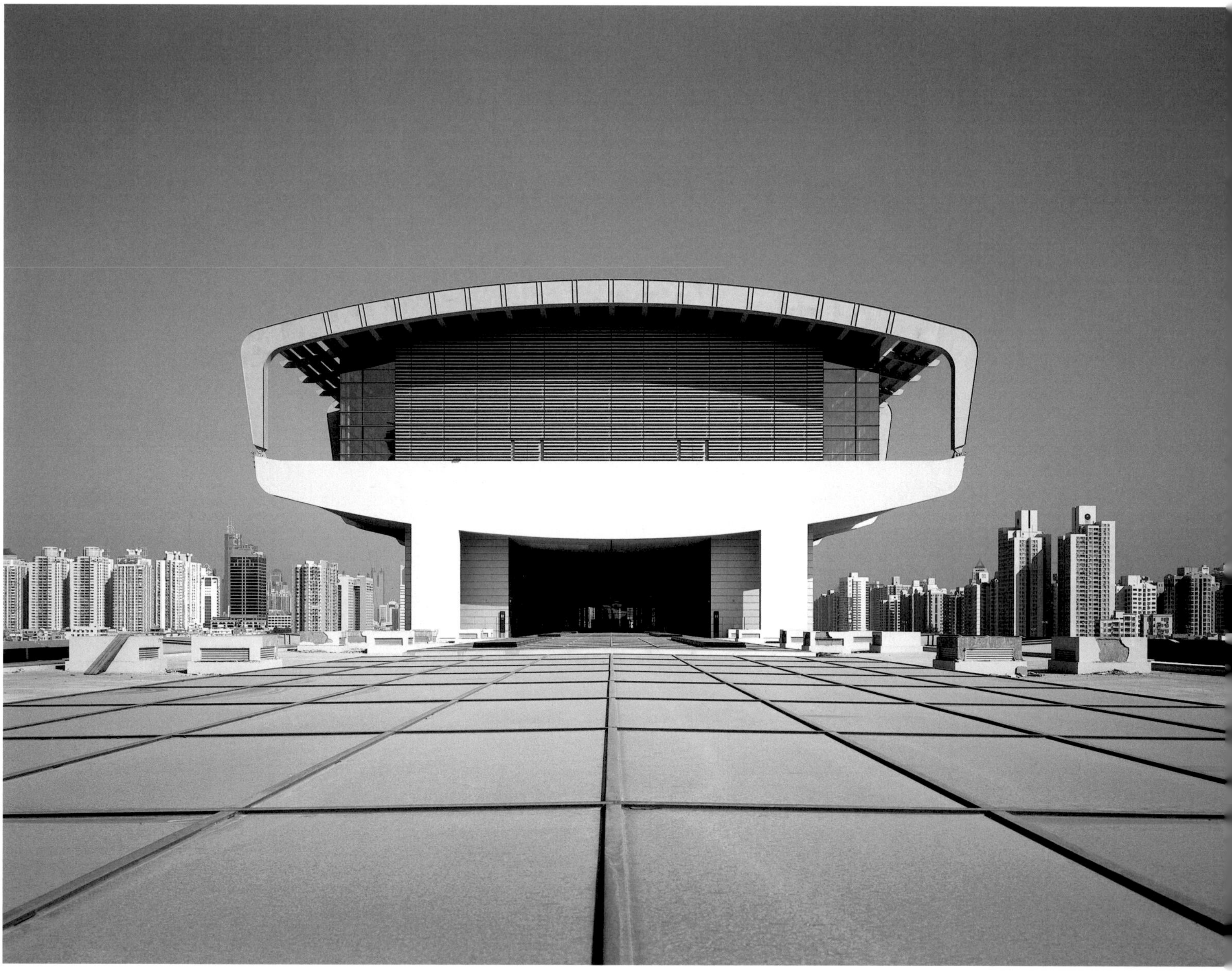

2005

Development Central Building, Guangzhou, China

Das Bürohochhaus ist in drei vertikale Scheiben gegliedert. Im Kontrast zu dem gläsernen, 149 m hohen Mittelteil prägt eine Rasterstruktur die niedrigeren Seitenflügel: Jeweils zwei Geschosse werden in großen „Fensteröffnungen" zusammengefasst, in denen senkrechte Verschatter dem Sonnenstand folgen.

Development Central Building, Guangzhou, China

The office tower block is divided into three vertical slabs. The glazed, 149-m-high central piece is contrasted with the grid structure of the lower lateral wings: two storeys each are combined as large 'window openings', in which vertical shading elements follow the position of the sun.

Fußgängerbrücke über den Ryck, Greifswald

Die einfache Schwenkbrücke aus Stahl und Holz setzt mit ihrem hohen Mast und zwei schräg aussteifenden Spieren eine weithin sichtbare und nachts angestrahlte Peilmarke. Sie wird auf einer Länge von 10,6 m von Hand mittels Absperrketten und Handkurbel, Zahnrad und Verriegelung des Auflagers geöffnet.

Pedestrian Bridge across the Ryck, Greifswald

With its high pylon and two slanted bracing spars the simple turntable bridge made of steel and timber forms a 'direction finder', visible from afar and spot-lit at night. The 10.6-m-long turntable section is opened manually using chain cordons, crank handles, cog wheel and fixing of the bearing.

Vogelbeobachtungsstation auf dem Graswarder in Heiligenhafen

Die Holzkonstruktion ordnet sich als filigrane Skulptur – einem stilisierten sitzenden Vogel gleich – in das Vogelschutzgebiet ein. Eine zweiläufige Treppe erschließt den 15 m hohen mit Diagonalverbänden ausgesteiften Turm, dessen verglaste Aussichtskanzel auch größeren Besuchergruppen Platz bietet.

Bird-Watching Tower, Graswarder in Heiligenhafen

The timber structure blends into the bird sanctuary as a filigree sculpture resembling a stylized sitting bird. The 15-meter-high tower, stiffened by diagonal braces, is accessible via a platform stair. The glazed viewing pulpit offers space even for larger groups of visitors.

Airbus A380 Ausstattungsmontagehalle, Hamburg

An die Halle mit vier aneinandergereihten, stützenfreien Montageplätzen schließt im Süden – „durchstoßen" vom Bug des Airbus – ein Verwaltungsbau an. Auf dem Hallendach sorgen vier so genannte Heckhutzen für die notwendige Höhe. Die 370 m lange verglaste Nordfassade öffnet sich in ganzer Länge zur Elbe.

Airbus A380 Interior Equipment Assembly Hall, Hamburg

To the south, a solid administration building – 'penetrated' by the nose of the Airbus – follows the hall with its four column-free assembly spaces. Four so-called tail scoops on the hall's roof provide the necessary height. The entire length of the 370-m-long glazed north façade opens up towards the Elbe River.

Flughafen Hamburg, Terminal 1

Terminal 1 und 3 (in Bau) setzen die gestalterische Linie des Terminals 2 fort, der als tageslichtdurchflutete Halle ein großes räumliches Kontinuum unter einem analog einer Flugzeugtragfläche geschwungenen Dach bildet. Ein vorgelagerter Pier verbindet als Rückgrat die Terminals miteinander.

Hamburg Airport, Terminal 1

Terminal 1 and Terminal 3 (under construction) continue the design scheme of Terminal 2, which, as a daylight-flooded hall, forms a generous spatial continuum underneath a roof whose curvature follows the curve of an aeroplane wing. A pier positioned in front interlinks the terminals like a spine.

Commerzbankarena, Frankfurt am Main

Um das Stadion innerhalb kurzer Zeit überdachen zu können, wurde es mit einer Membran ausgestattet, die zusammengefaltet in der Mitte eines Seiltragwerks geparkt wird. Der zylindrische Hüllkörper, der die zusammengelegte Membran schützt, öffnet und schließt sich beim Ausfahren des Daches wie eine Blüte.

Commerzbankarena, Frankfurt am Main

In order to cover the stadium as quickly as possible, a membrane construction was fitted which, when 'parked', is folded together in the centre of a tensile cable structure. The cylindrical drum protects the folded-up membrane and opens and closes like a blossom whenever the roof is extended.

2005

Fachmarktzentrum II, Göttingen

Zwei dreieckige, eingeschossige Baukörper bilden als stadträumliche Fortsetzung des existierenden Fachmarktzentrums eine klare Raumkante. Wie beim Bestand verbindet ein Kolonnadenvordach die unterschiedlich großen Gebäude. Verglaste Eingänge und Schaufenster unterbrechen die horizontal gegliederte Metallfassade.

Trade Market Centre II, Göttingen

Two triangular buildings of one storey each form a clear spatial edge as the urban extension of the existing trade market centre. Analogue to the existing situation a colonnade canopy connects the different sized buildings. Glazed entrances and shop windows break up the horizontally structured metal façade.

Allianz Bürogebäude, Taunusanlage, Frankfurt am Main

Eine kammartige Bebauung bildet den Rahmen der aus Neu- und Altbauten bestehenden Taunusanlage. Mit sechs Vollgeschossen und einem Staffelgeschoss orientieren sich die mit römischem Travertin verkleidet Neubauten am Bestand. Die Erschließung erfolgt über eine weiträumige Piazza.

Allianz Office Building, Taunusanlage, Frankfurt/Main

A comb-like development combining new and old buildings forms the framework of the Taunusanlage project. The new seven-storey buildings, clad in Roman travertine, take reference from the existing buildings. A spacious piazza serves as access point.

Lingang Service Center, bei Shanghai, China

Um eine Plaza gruppieren sich ein Verwaltungs- und ein Bankgebäude sowie – zum westlich gelegenen Kanal orientiert – ein Viersternehotel, ein Apartmenthaus und ein Veranstaltungsgebäude. Verkleidet mit hellem Naturstein und bestehend aus je zwei ineinander geschobenen Kuben unterschiedlicher Höhe bilden sie das administrative Zentrum des neuen Stadtteils.

Lingang Service Centre, near Shanghai, China

Grouped around a plaza are an administration building, a bank and – orientated towards the canal situated to the west – a 4-star hotel, an apartment block and an events complex. Clad in a light-coloured, natural stone the ensemble consists of two telescoped cubes of different height and forms the administrative centre of the new district.

Erweiterung des Sheraton Hotels, Ankara, Türkei

Neben dem 1991 von gmp erbauten Hotel entstand in direkter Verbindung ein Kongress- und Kulturzentrum mit einem sechsgeschossigen Aparthotel. Mit dunkel eloxierten Glasfassaden, Sonnenschutzelementen aus Metall und weißen Sichtbetonstützen fügen sich die Neubauten harmonisch in die Gesamtanlage ein.

Extension of the Sheraton Hotel, Ankara, Turkey

A congress and cultural centre with a six-storey Aparthotel was built with a direct connection right next to the hotel that gmp constructed in 1991. With its dark anodized glass façades, metal shading elements and white fair-faced columns the new building harmoniously integrates into the overall ensemble.

Museum Shanghai-Pudong, China

Das Museum dokumentiert und archiviert die Geschichte und Entwicklung des neuen Stadtbezirks Pudong und informiert die Öffentlichkeit zudem auf modernen, multifunktionalen und offenen Ausstellungsflächen mit einer ständigen Ausstellung und Sonderausstellungen zu ausgewählten Themen der Stadtgeschichte.

Shanghai-Pudong Museum, China

The Museum documents and archives the history and development of the new district of Pudong. Modern, multifunctional and open exhibition spaces are developed to inform the public with a permanent exhibition and special exhibitions about selected aspects of the city's history.

Laboratorium für Werkzeugmaschinen und Betriebslehre der RWTH Aachen

Um die Maschinenhalle gruppieren sich U-förmig alle Räume. Sie werden von der Halle bzw. von offenen Galerien erschlossen. Die Hallenfassade ist verglast, ansonsten wechseln ziegelrote Keramikelemente mit geschosshohen Fenstern. Stählerne Fluchtbalkone führen zu vier vorgelagerten Treppenhaustürmen.

Laboratory of Machine Tools and Production Engineering at RWTH Aachen

All rooms are grouped in a U-shaped formation around the machine hall and are accessible from the hall or open galleries. The hall façade is glazed, otherwise brick-red ceramic elements alternate with floor-to-ceiling windows. Steel escape balconies lead to four staircase towers positioned in front.

Guangzhou Development Central Building, China
Guangzhou Development Central Building, China

Wettbewerb Competition
2001 – 1. Preis

Entwurf Design
Meinhard von Gerkan

Partner Partner
Nikolaus Goetze

Bauherr Client
Guangzhou Developing New City Investment Co., Ltd.

Bauzeit Construction period
2002–2005

BGF Gross floor area
78.600 m²

Höhe Height
150 m

Die vertikale Dreiteilung und die Gliederung der Fassaden unterscheidet das GDCB deutlich von den umgebenden Hochhäusern. Typologisch betrachtet haben die Seitenteile eine massive, mit Naturstein verkleidete Fassade, die jedoch so aufgelöst wurde, dass nur noch Stützen und Querbalken vorhanden sind, die ein stark plastisches, quadratisches Raster bilden. In jeder der zweigeschossigen Öffnungen stehen drei vertikale, drehbar gelagerte Verschattungselemente aus Lochblech. Dem Lauf der Sonne folgend werden die Lamellen zentral gesteuert, können aber auch individuell eingestellt werden, so dass das GDCB ständig sein äußeres Erscheinungsbild verändert, je nach Sonnenstand und den Bedürfnissen der Mieter. Im Innenraum ist es vor allem die Wandverkleidung des zentralen Kerns mit jadegrünem Strukturglas, die neben den übrigen hochwertigen Materialien die Exklusivität des Gebäudes ausmacht.

The vertical trisection and the division of the façade clearly differentiates the GDCB from the surrounding tower blocks. Considered typologically, the side elements have a solid, stone-clad façade, which has, however, been reduced to such an extent that only columns and cross-beams are left, forming a strongly plastic, square grid. Three vertical, pivoted shading elements made of perforated sheet metal stand in each of the two-storey openings. The lamellas are centrally controlled to follow the course of the sun, but can be individually adjusted; consequently, the GDCB constantly changes its exterior appearance according to the sun's position and the requirements of its occupants. In the interior, the building's exclusivity is defined by the high-quality materials and especially the wall cladding of the central core with its jade-green, textured glass.

发展中心

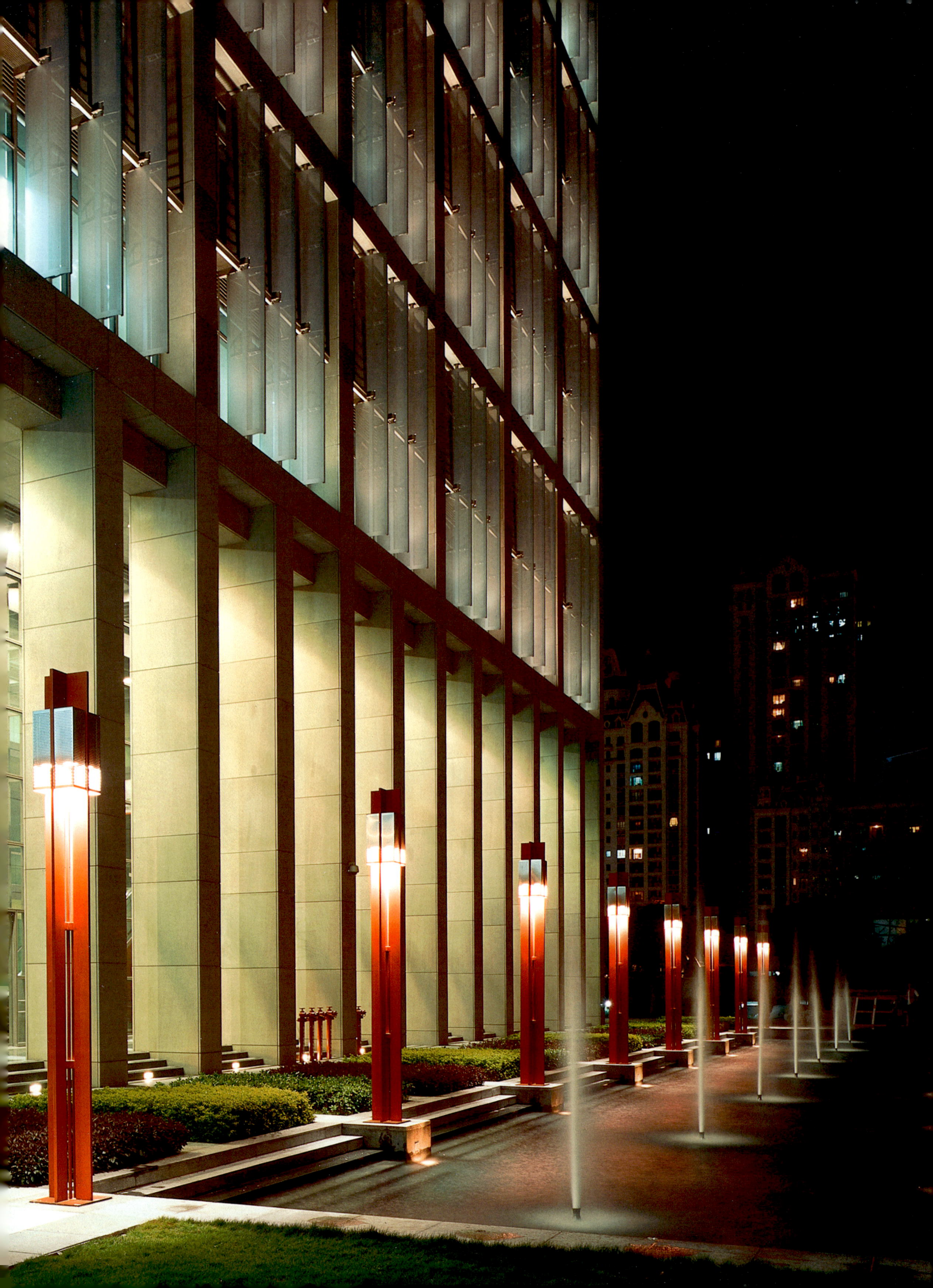

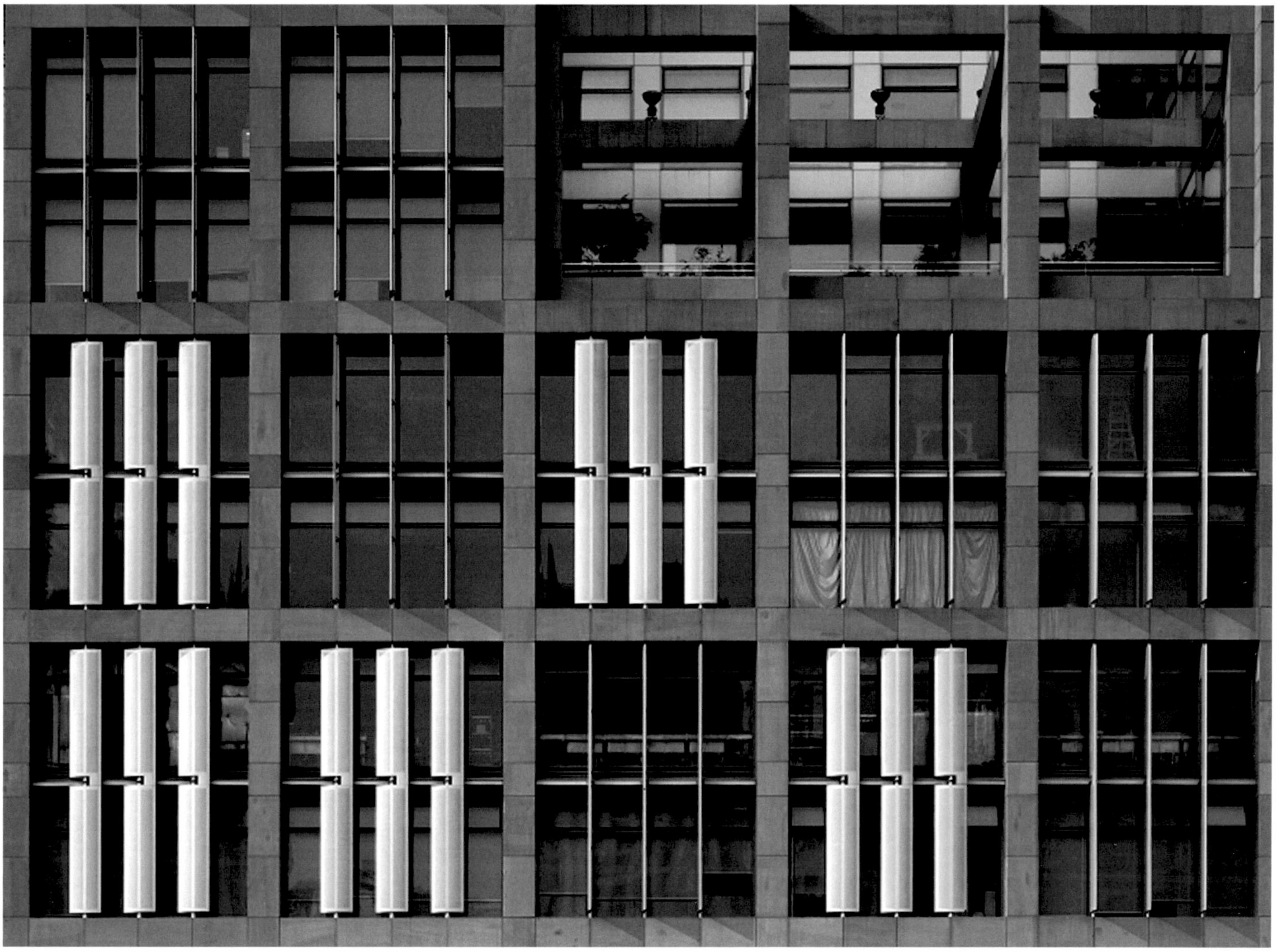

Commerzbankarena, Frankfurt am Main
Commerzbank Arena, Frankfurt am Main

Wettbewerb Competition
2000 – 1. Preis

Entwurf Design
Volkwin Marg

Partner Partner
Hubert Nienhoff

Bauherr Client
Waldstadion Frankfurt am Main
Gesellschaft für Projektentwicklung mbH

Bauzeit Construction period
2002-2005

Sitzplätze Seats
48.000

Der Umbau des Waldstadions anlässlich der WM 2006 zu einem reinen Fußballstadion greift die räumlichen Qualitäten des Sportfeldes im Stadtwald als Gesamtensemble auf: Die Neuorientierung zur Festwiese mit einer großzügigen Öffnung des Foyers steht im spannungsreichen Kontrast zur landschaftlichen Einbindung in die vorhandene Topographie. Hohe Medientürme, die weit über die Tribünenoberkante hinausragen, akzentuieren die Hauptschließungsachse. Der Oberrang setzt sich durch seine markante Schalenform vom Unterrang ab und findet seinen Abschluss in dem schmalen Band der äußeren Dachansicht. Das nach dem Prinzip eines Speichenrades konstruierte Stahlseil-Membrandach mit Spannweiten bis zu 240 m gewährleistet trotz der vollständigen Tribünenüberdachung das einwandfreie Wachstum des Rasens. Mittig über dem Spielfeld ist am Zentralknoten der Radialseile ein Videowürfel befestigt, der die Innendachmembran aufnimmt.

The renovation of the 'Waldstadion' into purely a football stadium in preparation for the 2006 World Cup addressed the spatial qualities of the sports field in the municipal forest as an overall ensemble: the novel orientation to the fairgrounds with a spacious foyer opening represented an exciting contrast to the landscape-oriented integration into the existing topography. Tall media towers, which extend far beyond the stands' upper edge, accentuate the main access axis. The upper stand circle is distinguished from the lower one by its striking bowl-shaped form and is concluded in the narrow band of the exterior roof elevation. Constructed along the lines of a spoke wheel, the steel cable membrane roof spans up to 240 m. Although the stands are completely roofed over, ideal conditions exist for the grass to grow. Located centrally above the pitch, a multimedia cube housing the inner roof membrane is suspended from the central knot of the radial cables.

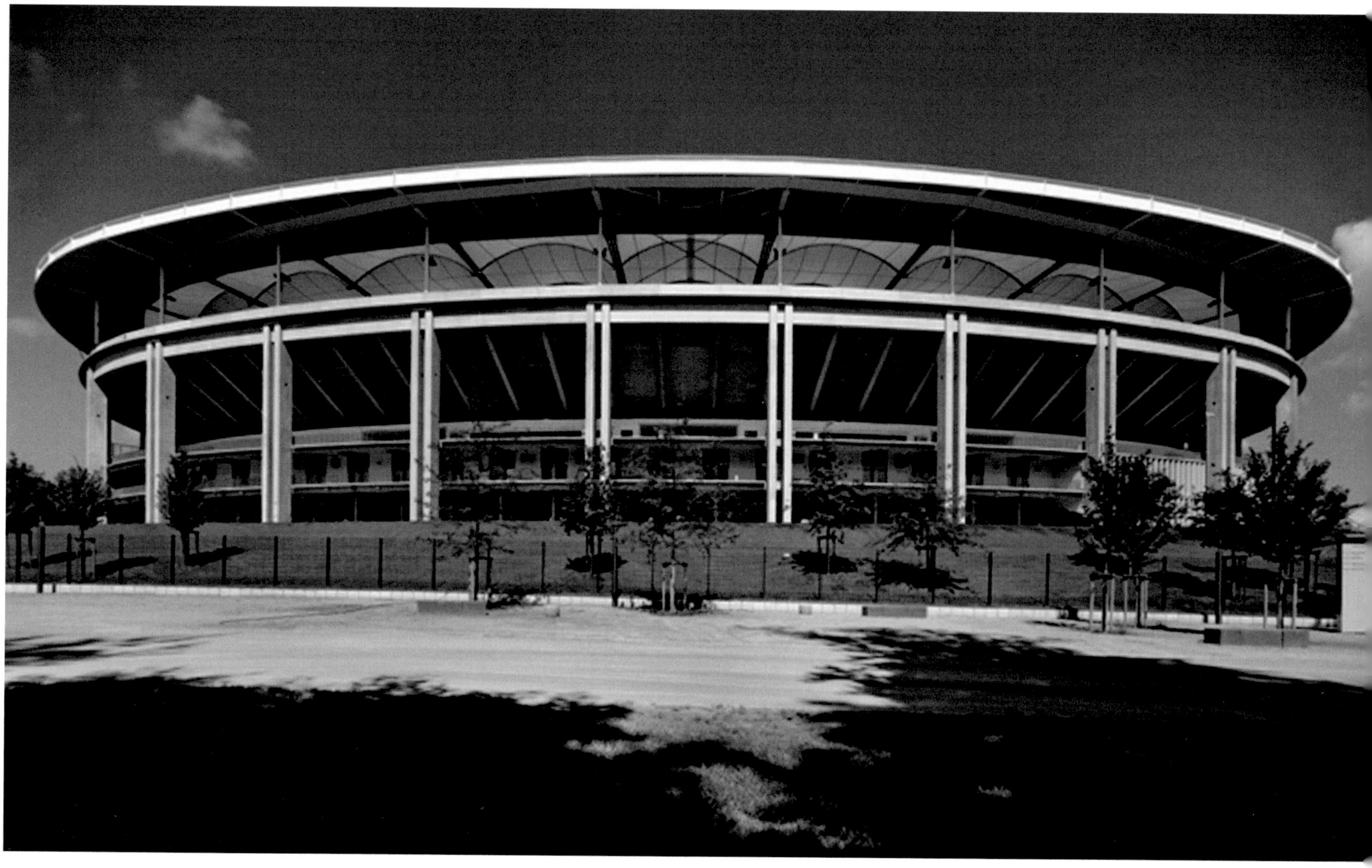

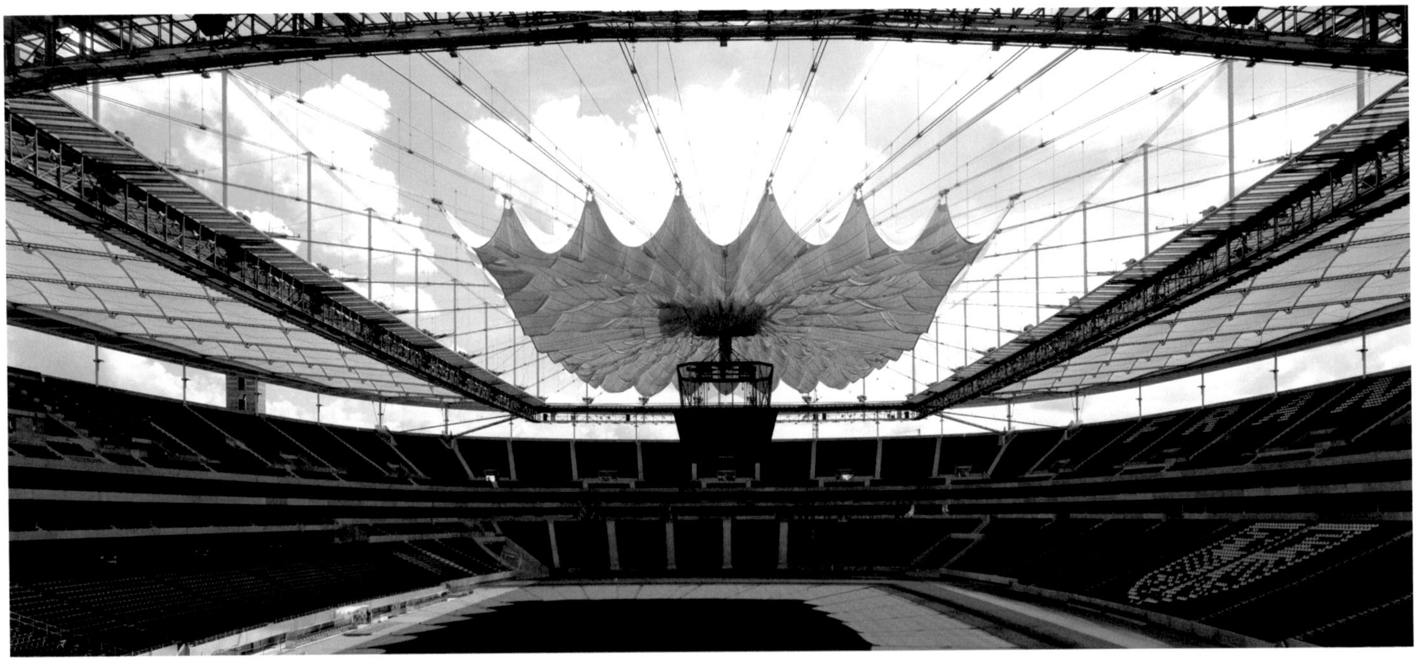

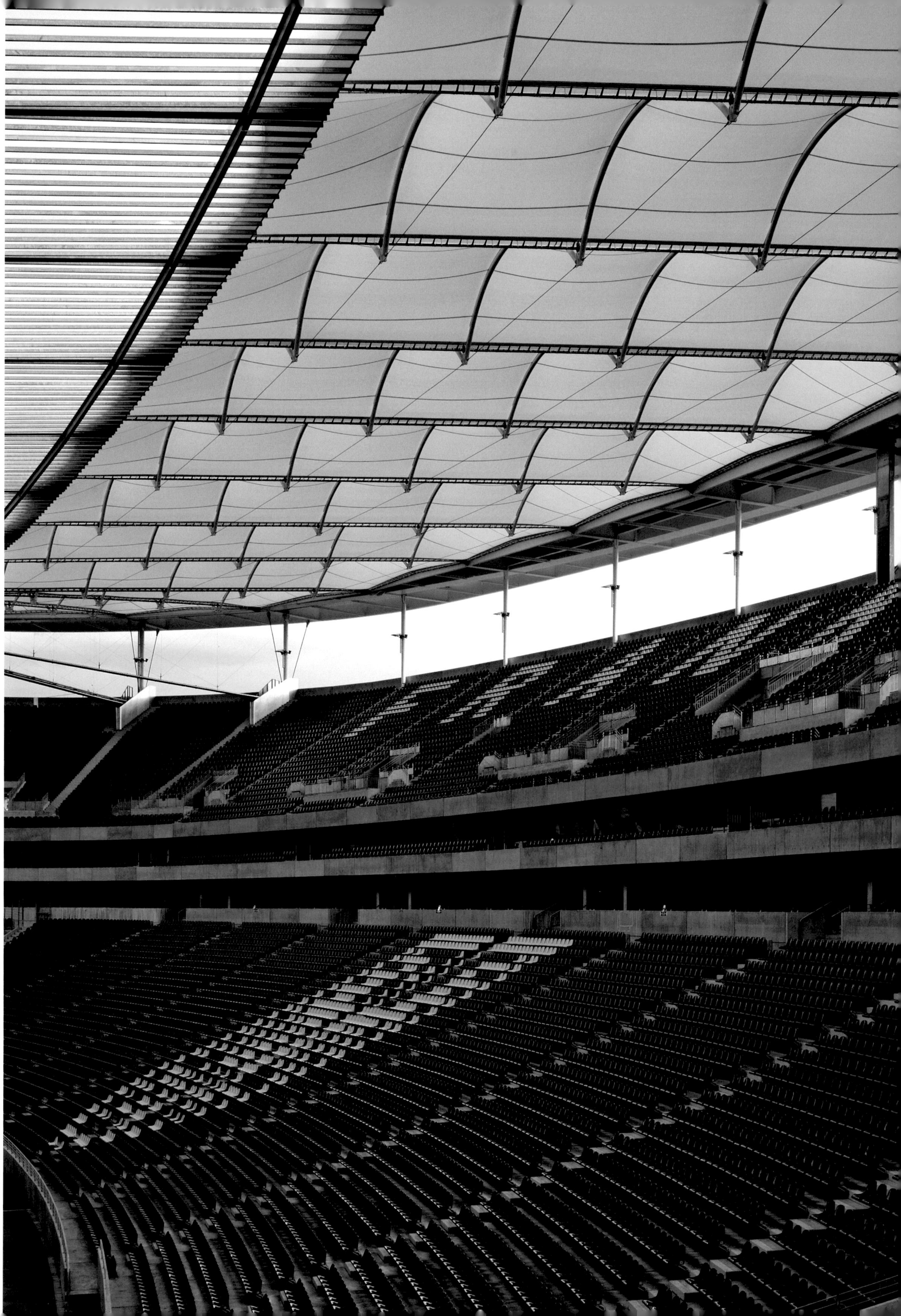

Museum Shanghai-Pudong, China
Shanghai-Pudong Museum, China

Wettbewerb Competition
2002 – 1. Preis

Entwurf Design
Meinhard von Gerkan

Partner Partner
Nikolaus Goetze

Bauherr Client
City of Shanghai, New District Pudong

Bauzeit Construction period
2003-2005

BGF Gross floor area
41.000 m²

Die Gebäudekomposition besteht aus drei Elementen: dem quadratischen Hauptgebäude, einem deutlich breiteren, 4 m hohen Sockel mit umlaufenden Treppen, der die Archive beherbergt, und einem Verwaltungsriegel. Zwei parallele Ebenen bilden die Fassade des oberen, geschlossenen Teils des Hauptgebäudes, wobei die äußere aus Glas besteht und die innere aus raumhohen, geschlossenen Paneelen. Diese sind entlang ihrer Längsachse drehbar und können – entsprechend den Anforderungen des Ausstellungskonzeptes – geschlossen oder geöffnet werden, sodass Sichtbeziehungen von innen nach außen und umgekehrt entstehen. Die transparente Glashaut ist mit aufgerasterten Bildern aus dem Bestand des Archivs bedruckt, die aus der Entfernung gesehen wiederum ein Großbild ergeben. An exponierten Stellen werden auf semi-transparentem Glas mittels im Fassadenzwischenraum angeordneter Projektoren Bilder, Filme oder Text projiziert.

Three elements form the building complex: the square-shaped main building; a much broader, 4-m-high base with surrounding stairs, which accommodates the archives; and an administration tract. Two parallel façade-layers form the façade of the upper, closed part of the main building. The outer layer consists of glass and the inner one of room-high, closed wall panels. These elements can be rotated along their longitudinal axis and can be opened or closed, according to the requirements of the exhibition concept, so that views from the inside to the outside and vice versa are created. The transparent glass skin displays material from the archive in small patterned pictures, which form a big picture when seen from a distance. In some exposed spaces, images, movies or texts are projected onto semi-transparent glass by video projectors mounted between the two façade layers.

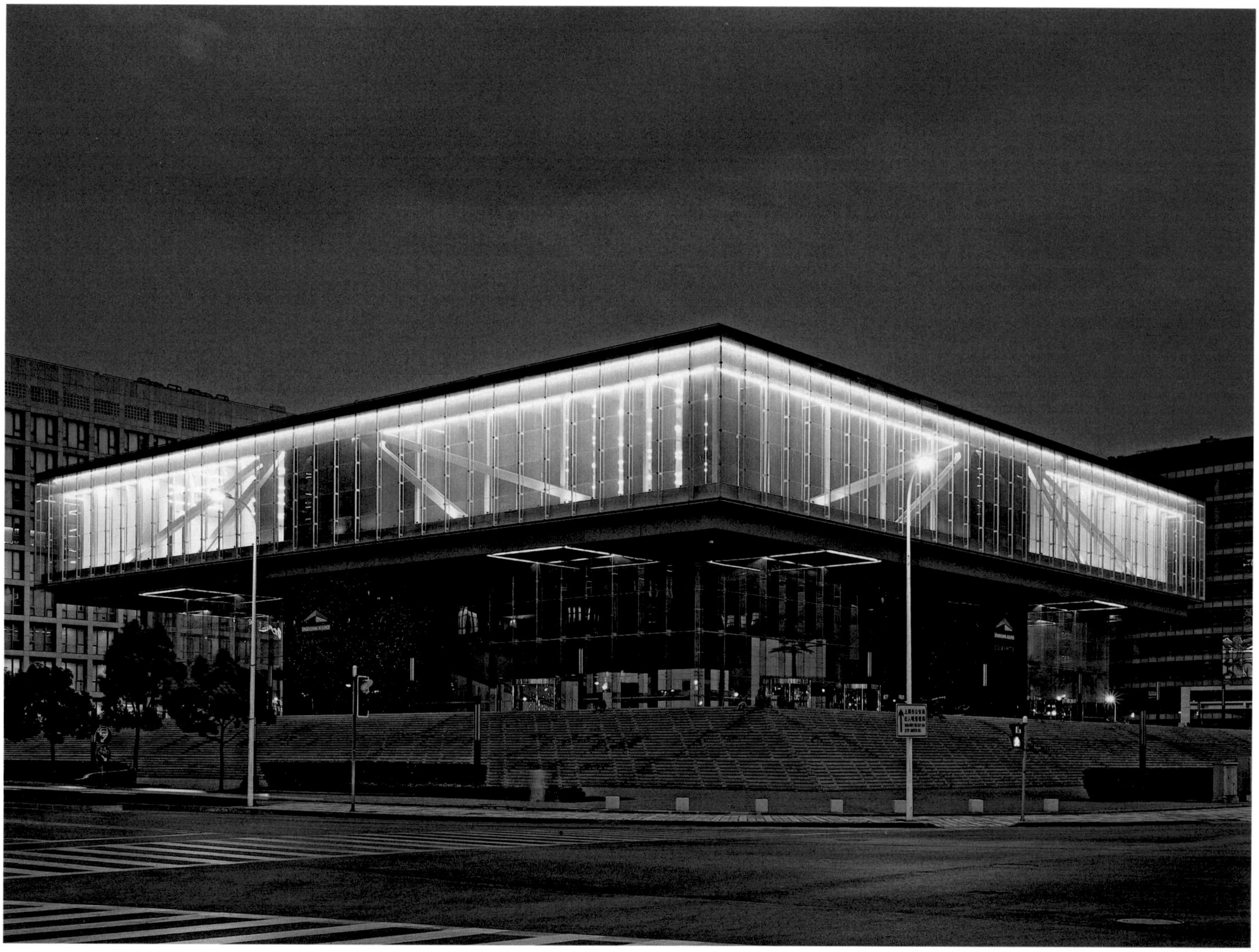

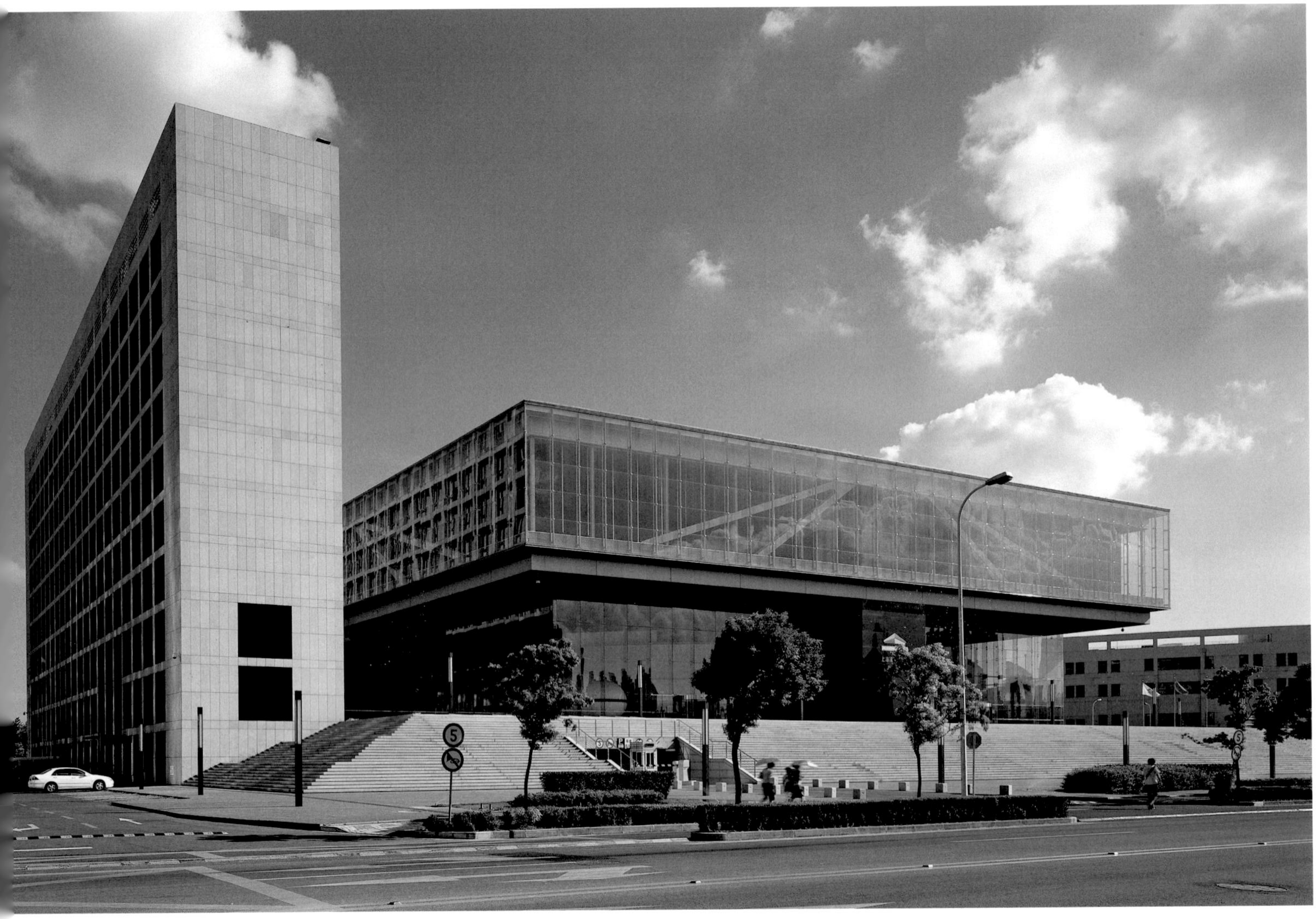

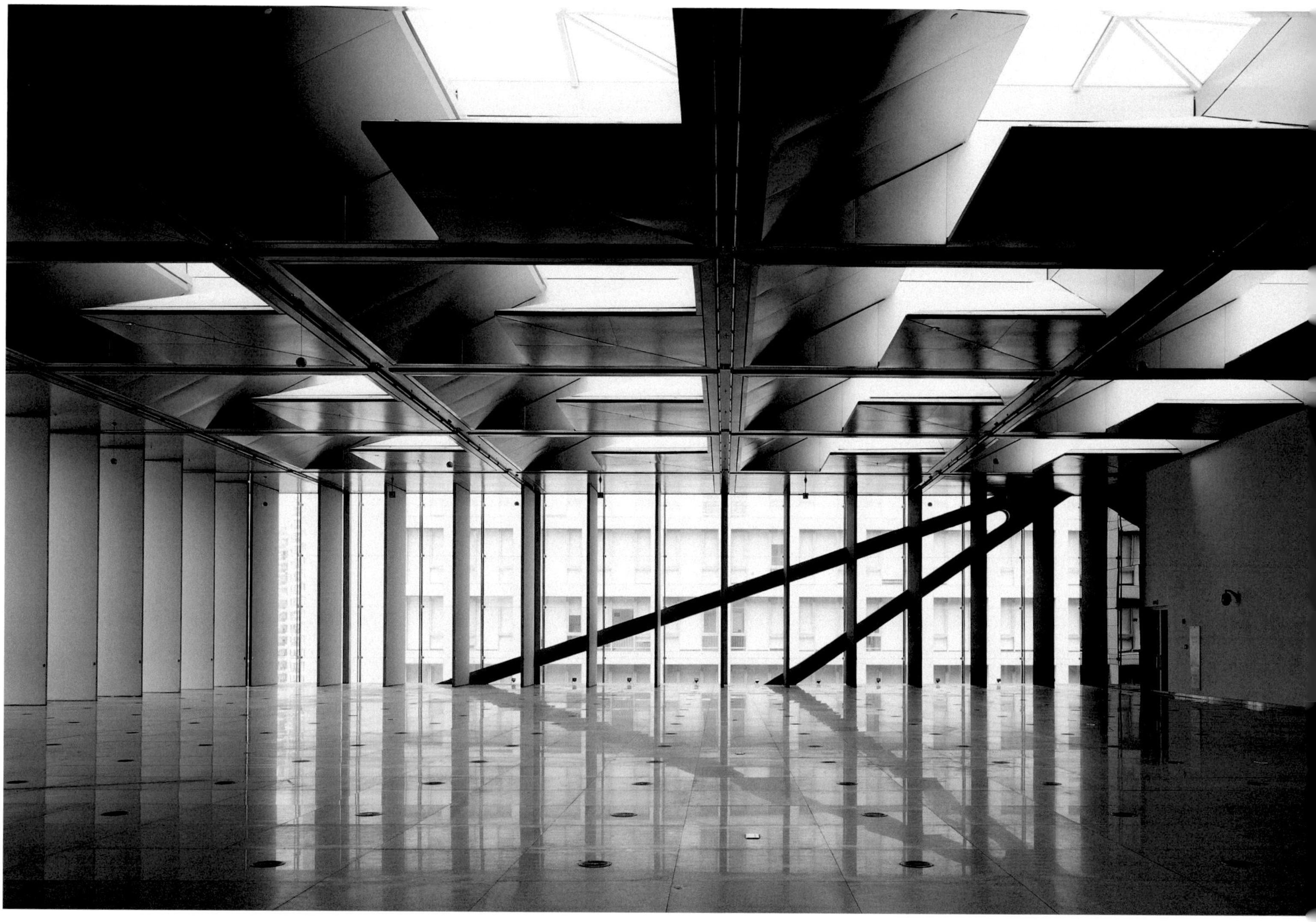

2006

Abbe-Zentrum, Jena-Beutenberg

Zwischen zwei geschwungenen Gebäudescheiben, die eine Analogie zu den gekrümmten Flächen in der Forschung von Abbe und Zeiss darstellen, entfaltet sich eine dynamische Mittelzone mit Foyer, Hörsaal und Mensa, die in der Gestaltung der terrassierten Außenanlagen ihre geometrische Fortsetzung findet.

Abbe Centre, Jena-Beutenberg

A dynamic central zone with foyer, auditorium and canteen unfolds between two curved building slabs, which represent an analogy to the bent surfaces in the research conducted by E. Abbe and C. Zeiss. This centre is geometrically continued with the design of the terraced outdoor facilities.

CYTS Plaza, Peking, China

Eine Passage teilt das Gebäude über die Gesamthöhe von 75 m und verbindet, einem Stadttor gleich, die historische Kaiserstadt mit dem neuen Central Business District. Zwei Atrien dienen als Foyers und definieren zwei L-förmige Gebäudehälften, die sich mit ihrem großmaßstäblichen Fassadenraster deutlich von der Umgebung abheben.

CYTS Plaza, Beijing, China

A passage divides the building up to a height of 75 m and connects, much like a city gate, the historic Forbidden City with the new Central Business District. Two atria serve as foyers and define two L-shaped building halves that clearly stand out from their surroundings with their large-scale façade grid.

Zhongguancun Kulturzentrum, Peking, China

Umlaufende Bänder aus Glas umfassen das Gebäude in einer fließenden Bewegung. Im Bereich der Innenhöfe springen sie, dem trapezförmigen Grundriss folgend, zurück und verleihen dem Baukörper Plastizität. Demgegenüber kennzeichnet die bewusste Modellierung der Glasbänder die Eingänge.

Zhongguancun Cultural Centre, Beijing, China

Surrounding glass strips enclose the building in a flowing movement. In response to the inner courtyards the façade possesses curvilinear setbacks, which follow the trapezoidal plan and present great plasticity. At the same time the deliberate modelling of the glass strips characterizes the entrances.

Dixingju Bürogebäude, Peking, China

Eine Glashalle bildet das Zentrum des aus einem einzelnen Bürogebäude im Westen und vier windmühlenartig angeordneten Baukörpern im Osten bestehenden Ensembles. Auf drei Seiten des Grundstücks umgeben horizontale Lamellen den Komplex. Sie bieten optimalen Sonnenschutz und formen zudem individuelle Höfe.

Dixingju Office Building, Beijing, China

A glass hall is the centre of the ensemble consisting of a single office building to the west and four office volumes in a windmill-like structure to the east. On three sides of the site horizontal louvres surround the complex, providing ideal sun protection and, furthermore, creating individual courtyards.

2006

Nationales Konferenzzentrum, Hanoi, Vietnam

Konferenzzentrum, Hotel und Museum sind eingebettet in eine Parklandschaft mit symbolischen Bezügen zur vietnamesischen Kultur und Tradition. Das expressive wellenförmige Dach des Komplexes schwingt sich über dem Kongresssaal zu seiner größten Höhe auf und formuliert so eine unverwechselbare Landmarke.

National Conference Centre, Hanoi, Vietnam

Conference centre, hotel and museum are embedded in a park landscape, which integrates symbolic references to Vietnamese culture and traditions. The expressive, undulating roof of the complex rises up to its greatest height above the congress hall, thus creating a distinctive landmark.

„Beijing Château", Peking, China

Das luxuriöse Apartmenthochhaus liegt inmitten des Pekinger Zentrums. Seine fließenden Grundrissformen ermöglichen 80 individuelle Wohnungstypen mit mehreren Terrassen und großen Lufträumen. Die attraktiven Apartments sind geschossübergreifend als Maisonettewohnungen ausgeführt.

'Beijing Château', Beijing, China

The luxurious apartment tower block is located in Beijing's city centre. Its ground-plan shapes allow for the design of 80 individual apartment types with several terraces and large spaces. The attractive apartments are laid out as maisonettes stretching over two storeys.

Gong Yuan Building, Hanzhou, China

Zwischen zwei natursteinverkleideten Hochhausgruppen mit markanten, dreigeteilten Türmen im Norden und Süden des Grundstücks erstreckt sich ein im Westen und Osten von hohen Kolonnaden gesäumter, grüner Innenhof. Das viergeschossige Pressezentrum durchdringt als gläserne Rotunde die östliche Kolonnadenreihe.

Gong Yuan Building, Hanzhou, China

Two groups of high-rise buildings clad in natural stone, each with striking triple towers, occupy the north and south of the site, while a green courtyard bordered on the east and west by colonnades stretches between them. The four-level press centre in the form of a glass rotunda penetrates the eastern colonnade.

Ausstellung Langemarckhalle, Olympiastadion Berlin

Die Halle im ersten Obergeschoss wird mit großformatigen Scheiben rahmenlos mit Abstand zur Substanz verglast. Die Ausstellungsarchitektur ist einfach und robust mit Aluminiumstelen und -bänken gestaltet. In der Eingangshalle dient ein transparenter Kubus als Museumsshop.

Langemarckhalle Exhibition, Berlin Olympic Stadium

The hall on the first floor is glazed with frameless, large-scale panes and with a gap between the glass and the building structure. The exhibition architecture is characterized by a plain and robust design with aluminium steles and benches. In the entrance hall a transparent cube functions as museum shop.

Kapelle im Olympiastadion Berlin

Die ökumenische Kapelle ist ein schlichter Raum tief unten im Stadion auf gewachsenem Boden. Hier können sich – umgeben von einer elliptischen Wand und vielsprachigen Bibeltexten auf goldenem Grund – bis zu 50 Personen versammeln. Hinter dem Altar ist in der Textur deutlich sichtbar ein Kreuz frei gelassen.

Chapel in the Berlin Olympic Stadium

The ecumenical chapel is a plain space deep down in the stadium on genuine ground. Up to 50 people can gather here, surrounded by elliptical walls and multilingual bible passages on a golden background. Behind the altar a crucifix has been left blank and is clearly visible in the surface texture.

Berlin Hauptbahnhof

Die Nord-Süd-Trasse des Kreuzungsbahnhofs verläuft 15 m unter der Erde, die von einem Glasdach überspannte Ost-West-Linie 25 m darüber. Zwei Brückengebäude markieren den unterirdischen Verlauf im Stadtraum. Die Eingangshalle dazwischen und die Ost-West-Halle kreuzen sich in Form einer gläsernen Vierung.

Berlin Central Station

The north-south line of the railway station runs 15 m underground; the east-west line with its glass-covered roof runs 25 metres above it. Two bridge buildings follow the course of the underground line in the cityscape. A glazed crossing is created at the intersection point with the east-west hall.

Gong Yuan Building, Hangzhou, China
Gong Yuan Building, Hangzhou, China

2003

Entwurf Design
Meinhard von Gerkan

Partner Partner
Nikolaus Goetze

Bauherr Client
Hangzhou Nice Source United Real Estate Co., Ltd.

Bauzeit Construction period
2003–2006

BGF Gross floor area
123.000 m²

Das Gong Yuan Building bietet dem gegenüberliegenden Sportzentrum ein repräsentatives Entree. Zwischen den beiden markanten 75 m hohen Drillingstürmen erstreckt sich ein auf den Längsseiten von hohen Kolonnaden gesäumter Park, zu dem großzügige Stufen hinaufführen. Die Nord- und Südfassaden der Hochhäuser sind mit hellen Naturstein-Lisenen und zurückliegenden horizontalen Sonnenschutzlamellen aus Metall stark strukturiert. Die massiven seitlichen Wandscheiben sind flächig gestaltet und mit hellgrauem Naturstein verkleidet. Viergeschossige Sockelgebäude, deren natursteinverkleidete Längsfassaden als Fortsetzung der Kolonnadenstruktur vertikal gegliedert sind, flankieren die Hochhäuser. Die viergeschossige Rotunde des Pressezentrums präsentiert sich dagegen – entsprechend ihrem öffentlichen Charakter – mit einer filigranen Stahl-Glas-Fassade und horizontalen Sonnenschutzlamellen.

The Gong Yuan Building provides a prestigious entree for the sports centre located opposite. A park, lined by high colonnades on the longitudinal sides and approached by broad steps, stretches between the two striking, 75-m-high triple towers. The north and south façades of the tower blocks are strongly structured with pilaster strips of light-coloured, natural stone and recessed horizontal shading lamellas made of metal. The solid, lateral shear walls are clad in light-grey stone. Four-storey socle buildings flank the towers; as a continuation of the colonnade structure their stone-clad longitudinal façade is vertically divided. The four-storey rotunda of the press centre is, on the contrary, defined by a filigree steel-glass façade (corresponding to the public character) and horizontal shading.

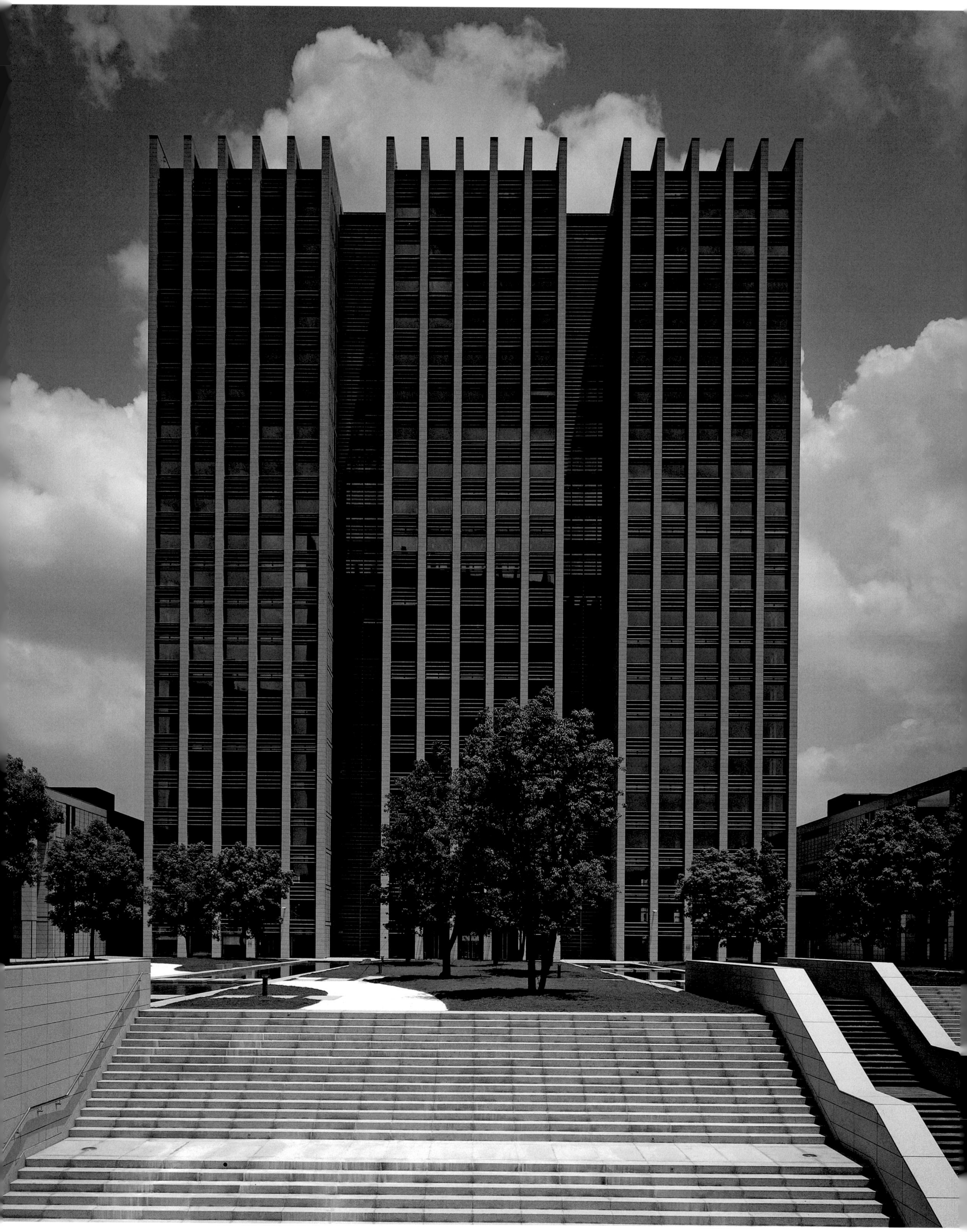

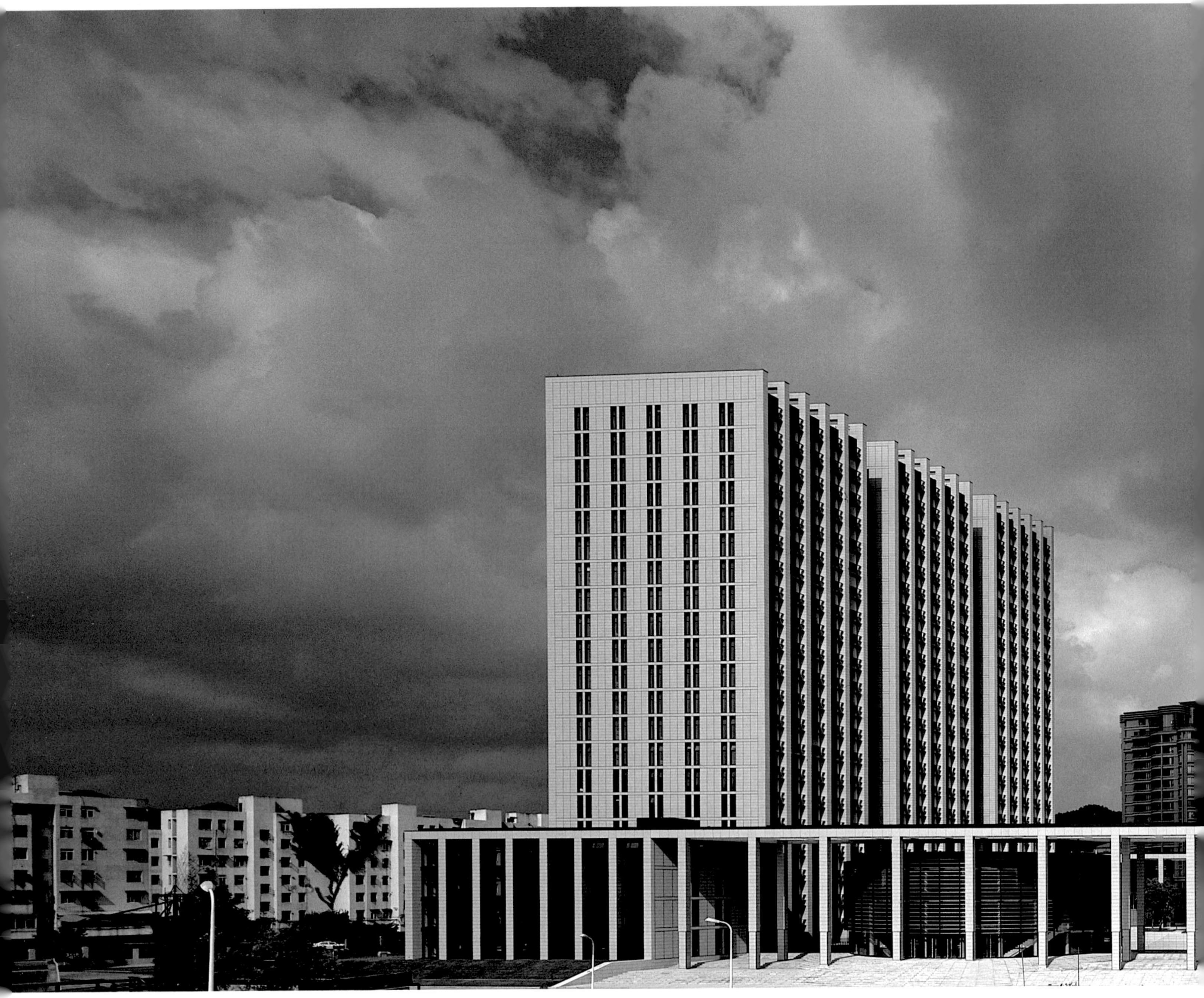

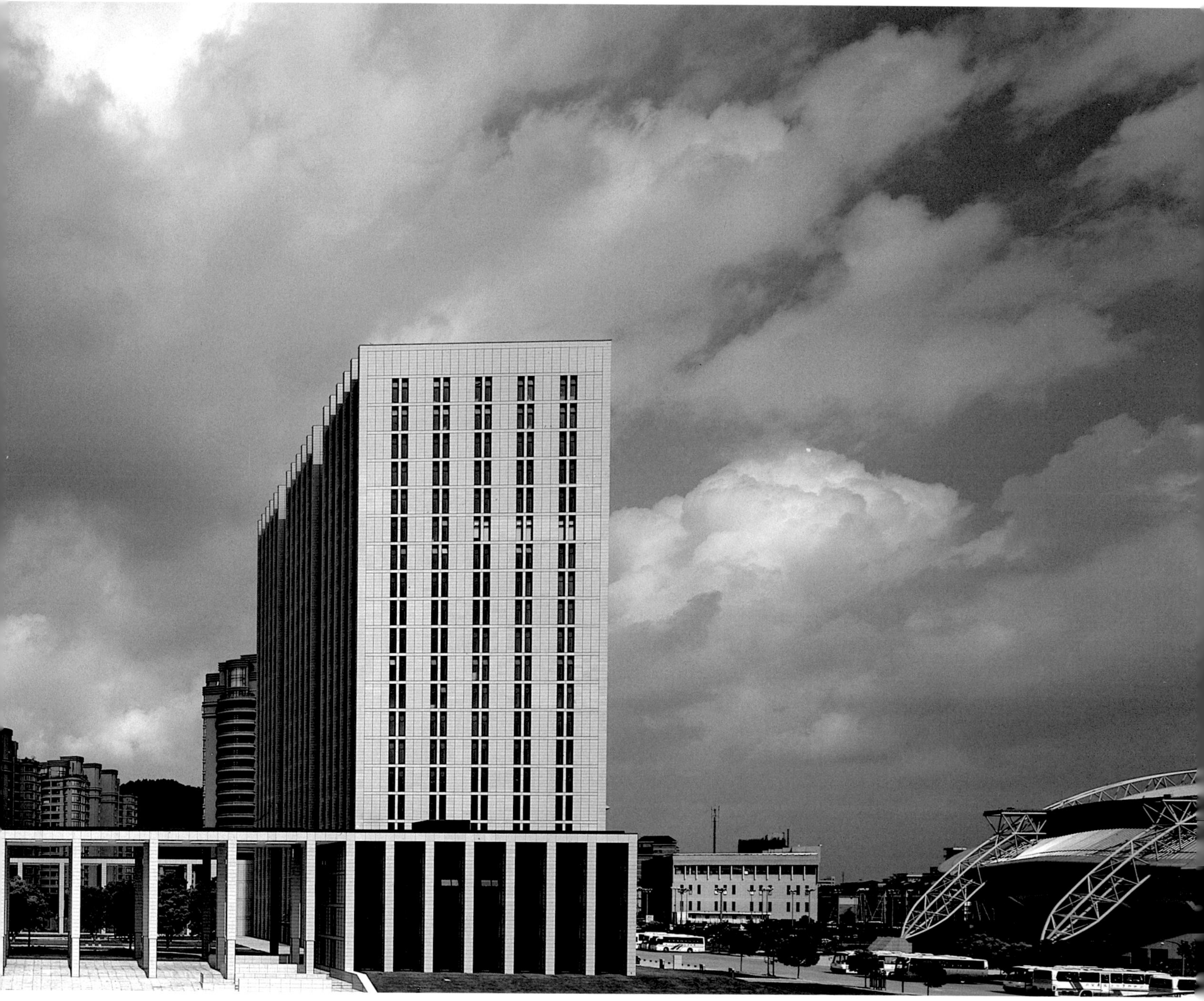

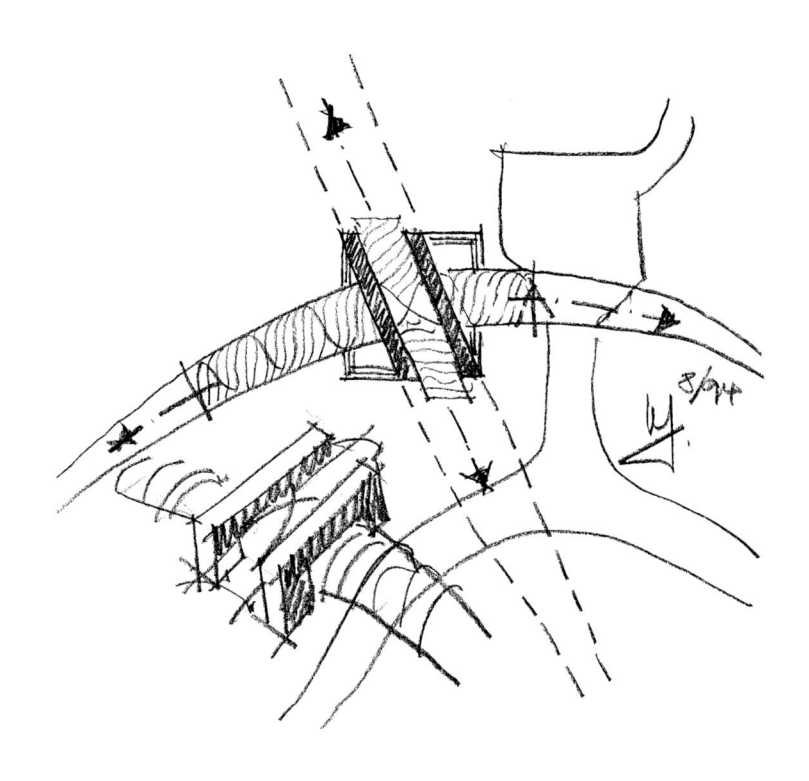

Berlin Hauptbahnhof
Berlin Central Station

Wettbewerb Competition
1993 – 1. Rang

Entwurf Design
Meinhard von Gerkan und Jürgen Hillmer

Bauherr Client
Deutsche Bahn AG

Bauzeit Construction period
1996–2006

BGF Gross floor area
175.000 m²

Das zentrale Entwurfsprinzip des Kreuzungsbahnhofs ist die markante Betonung des Gleisverlaufs im städtischen Raum. Große filigrane Glasdächer über den Bahnsteigen der Ost-West-Linie sowie zwei überbückende Bürogebäude oberhalb der unterirdischen Nord-Süd-Trasse setzen dies mit architektonischen Mitteln um. Im Zentrum des auf einem Gebäudesockel ruhenden Bahnhofskreuzes verfügen alle Decken über große Öffnungen, die Tageslicht bis auf die Bahnsteigebenen tief unter der Erde lassen und eine gute räumliche Übersicht und klare Orientierung gewährleisten. Das 321 m lange Glasdach der Ost-West-Halle ist als Gitterschalennetz aus nahezu quadratischen, mit Seilen ausgekreuzten Netzmaschen konstruiert. Im Süden ist die Dachfläche mit Photovoltaikmodulen belegt. Auf Wunsch des Bauherrn wurde das Dach um 110 m verkürzt, so dass der Bahnhof in seiner jetzigen Form ein Torso bleiben wird.

The central design principle of the station is the prominent emphasis of the existing railway tracks in the urban context. Large filigree glass roofs over the platforms of the east-west track, as well as two bridging office buildings above the underground north-south track, translate this principle with architectural means. In the centre of the station cross, which rests on a building socle, all ceilings are equipped with large openings, allowing daylight to penetrate as far as the underground platform levels, simultaneously ensuring a clear spatial orientation. The 321-m-long glass roof of the east-west hall is constructed like as a lattice shell of almost square net elements varying in dimension and stiffened with steel ropes. To the south the roof surface is covered with photovoltaic modules. At the request of the client the roof was shortened by 110 m. If it is left in its current form the station will remain a torso.

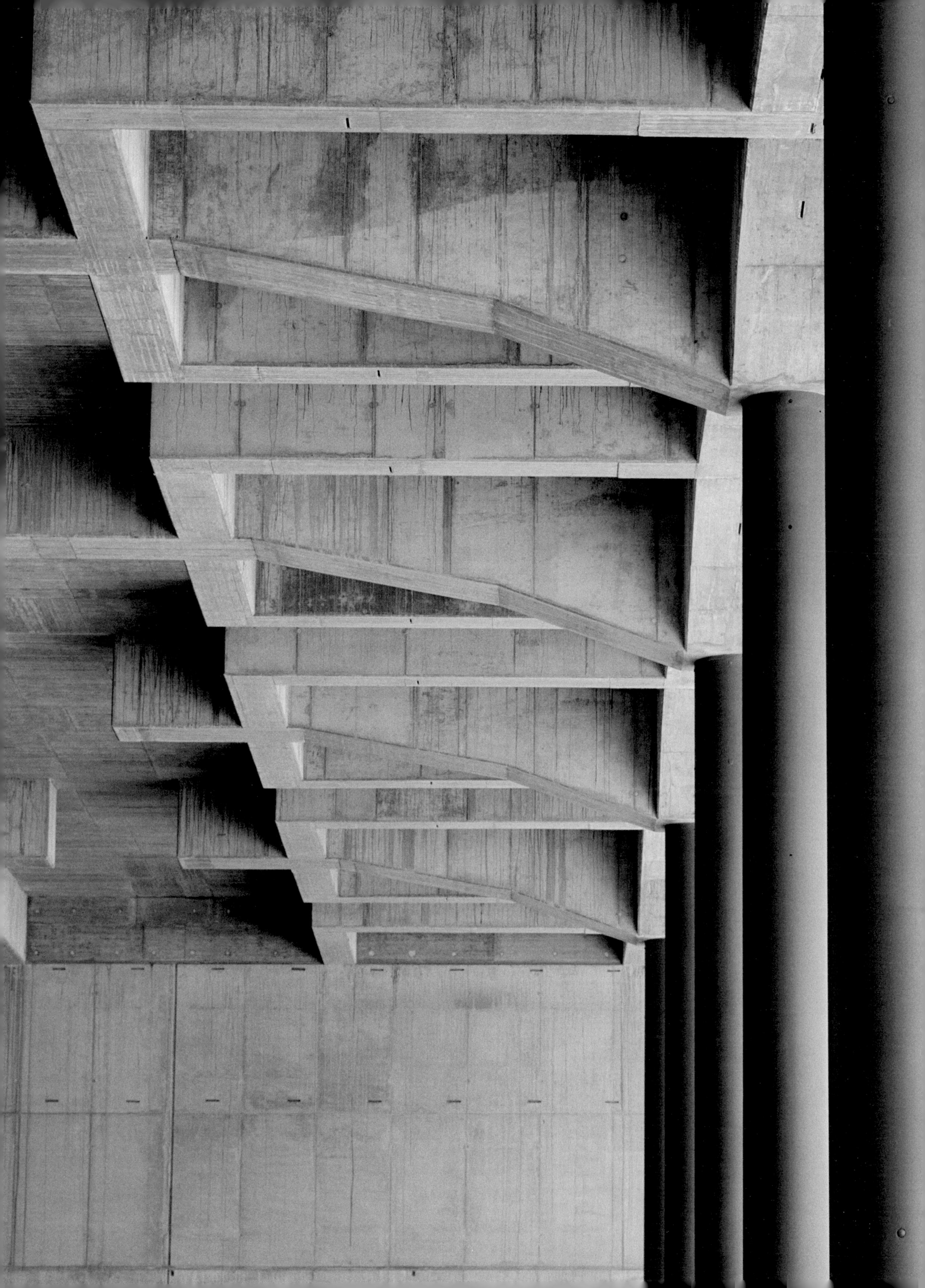

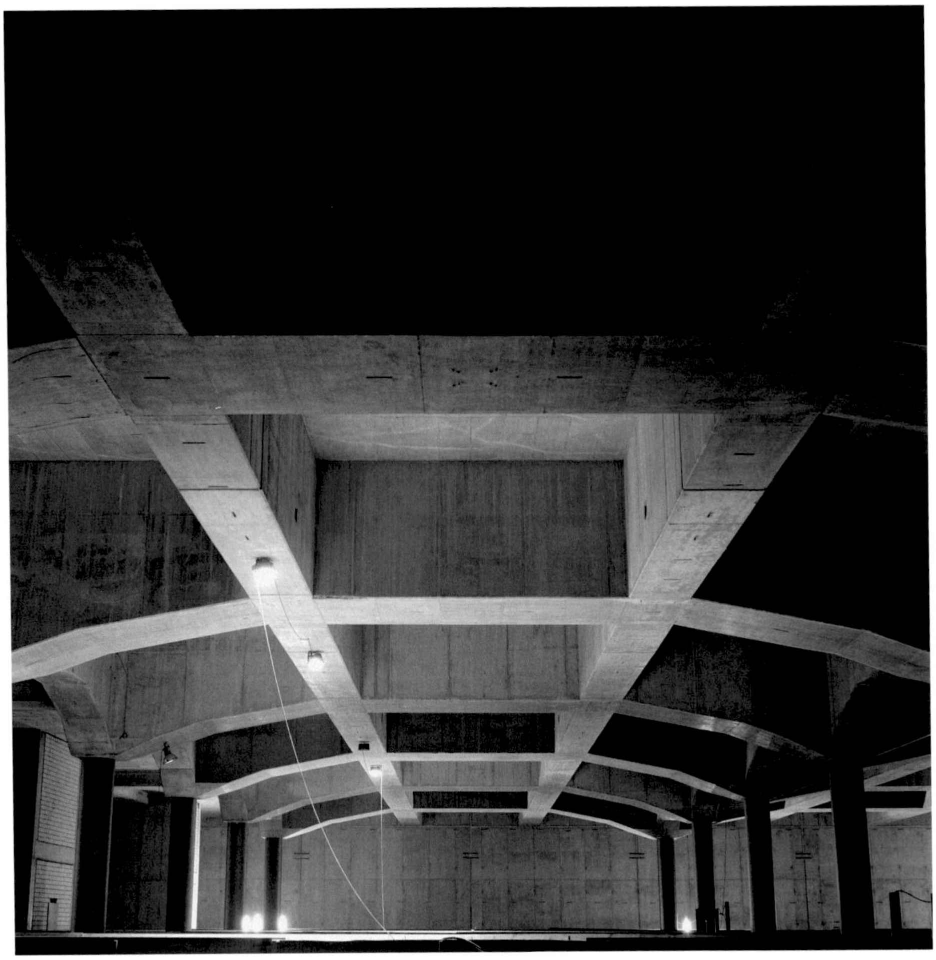

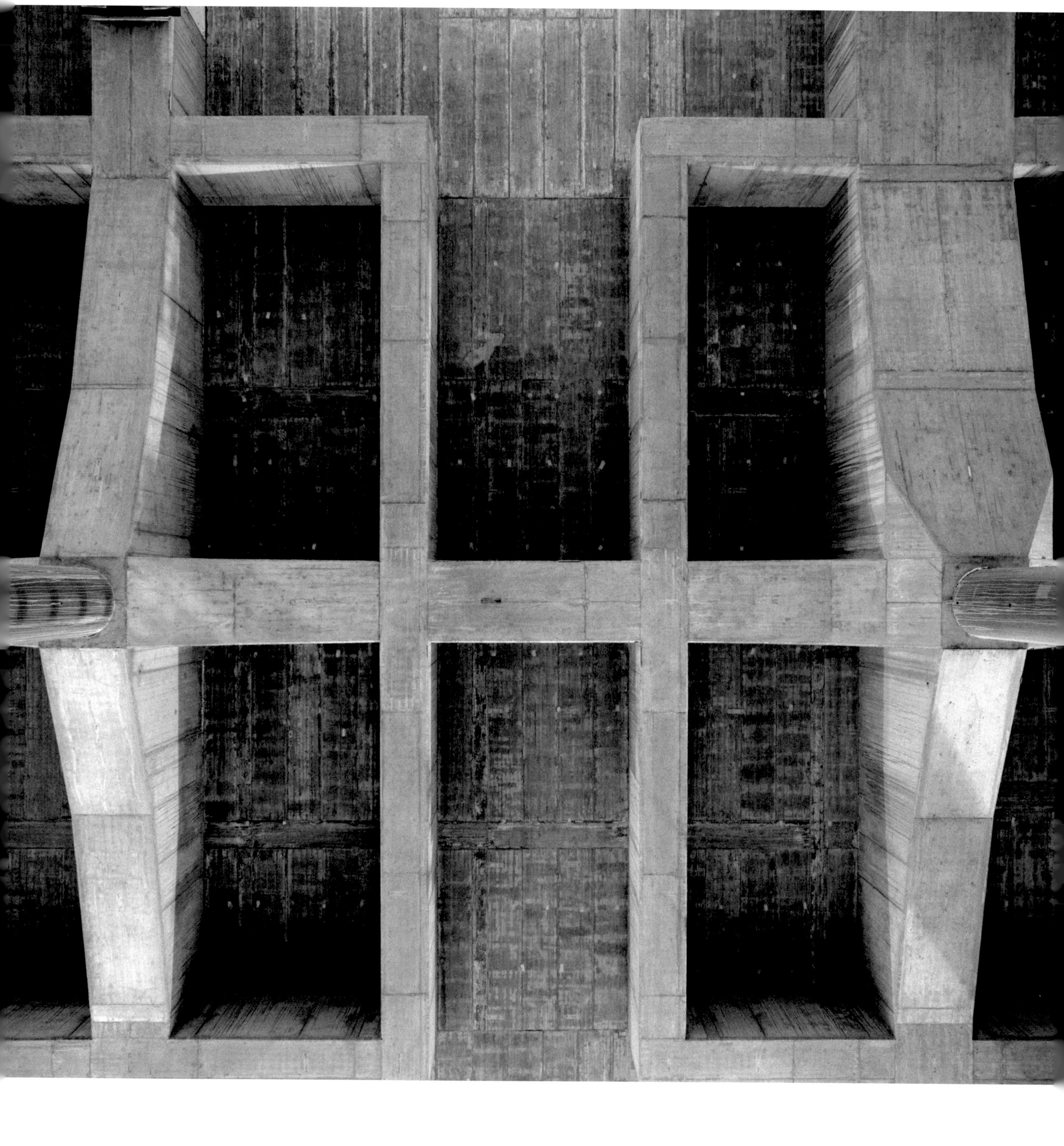

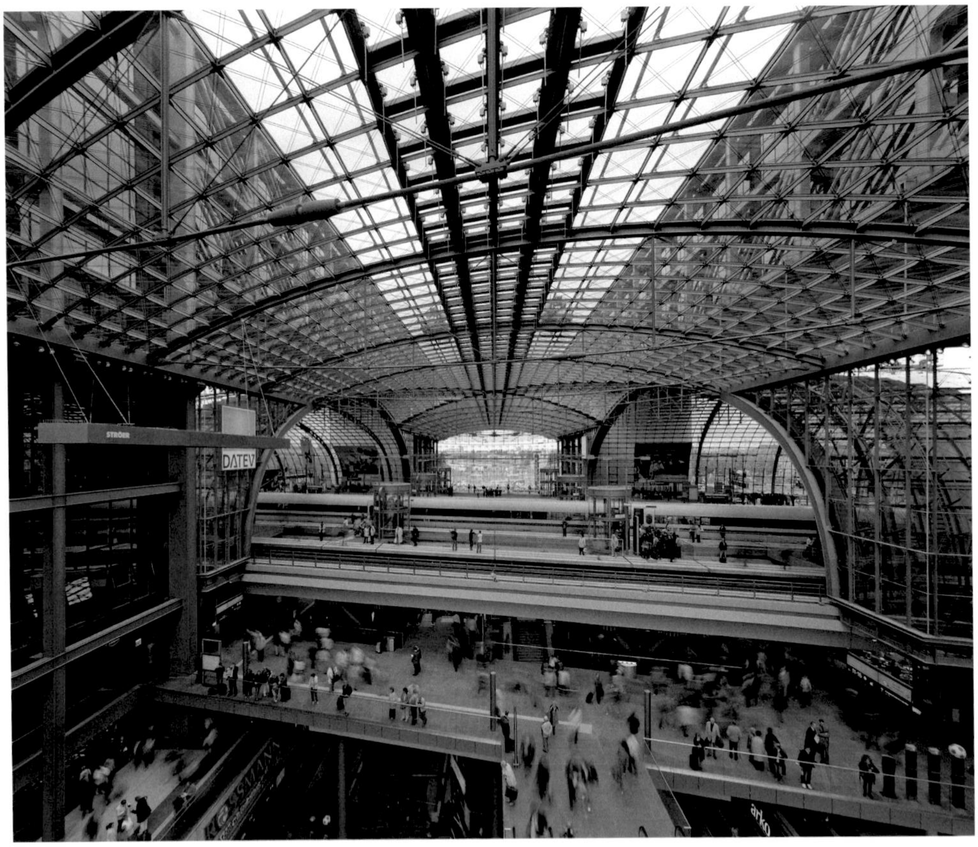
DATEV

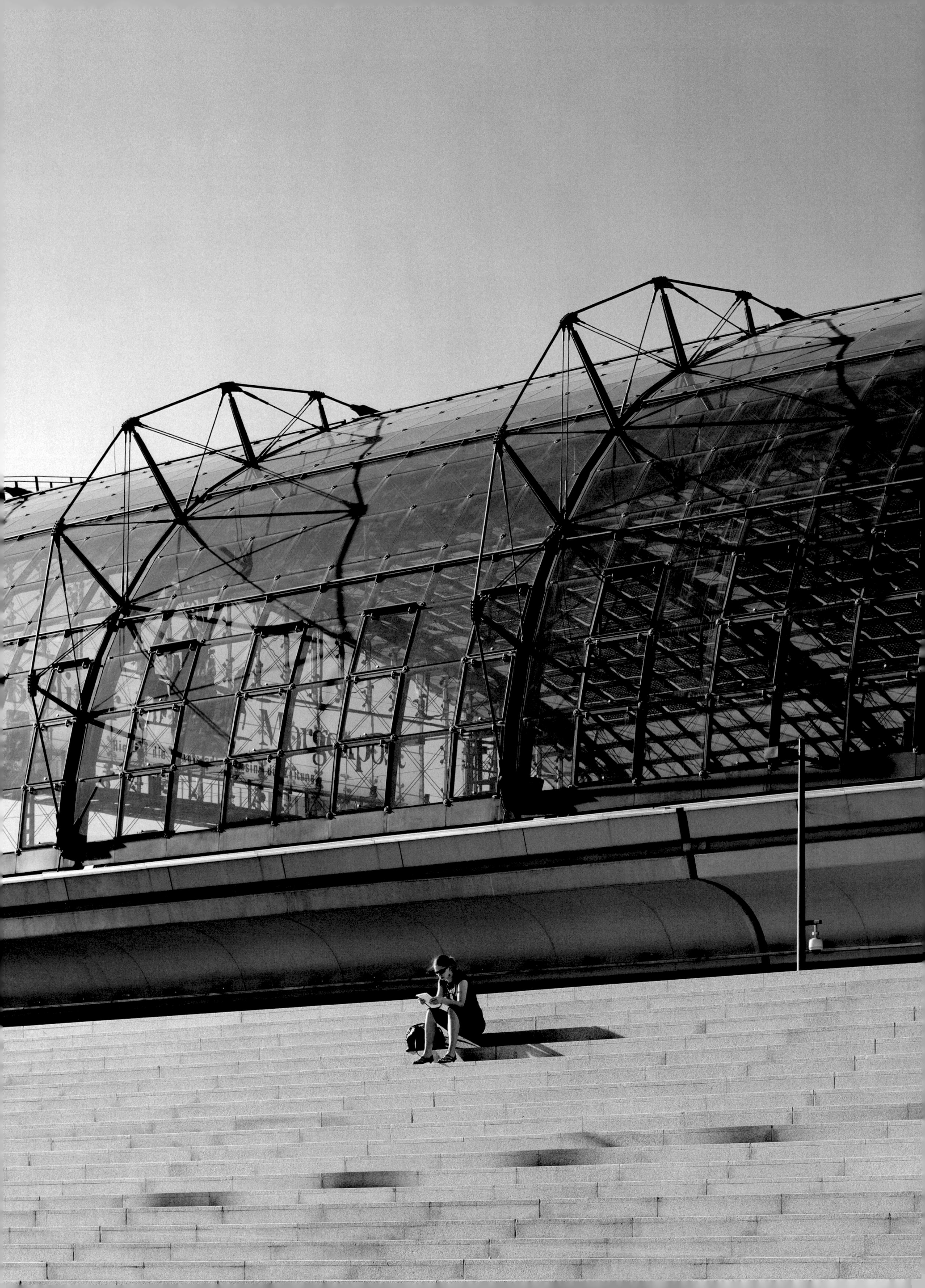

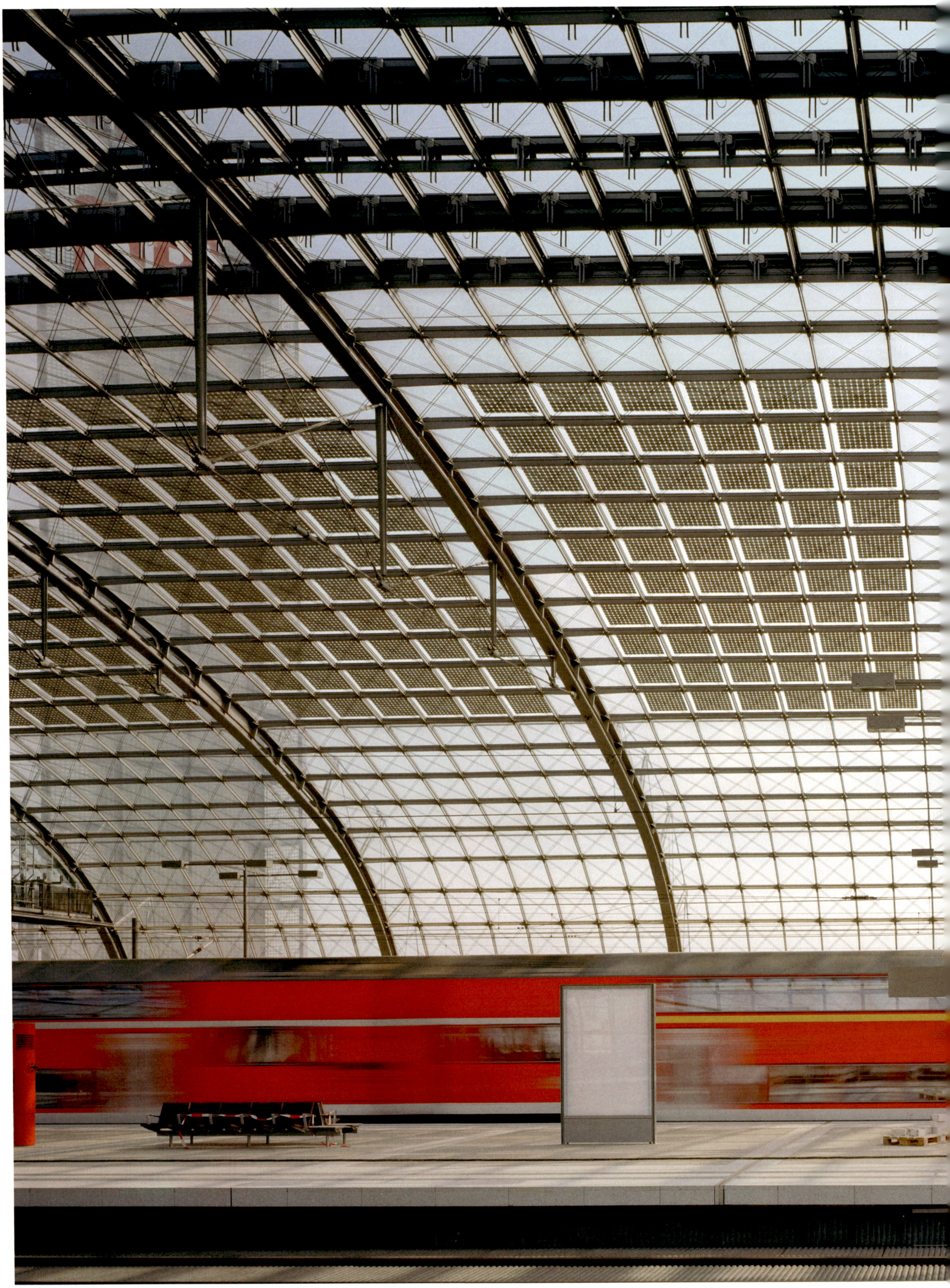

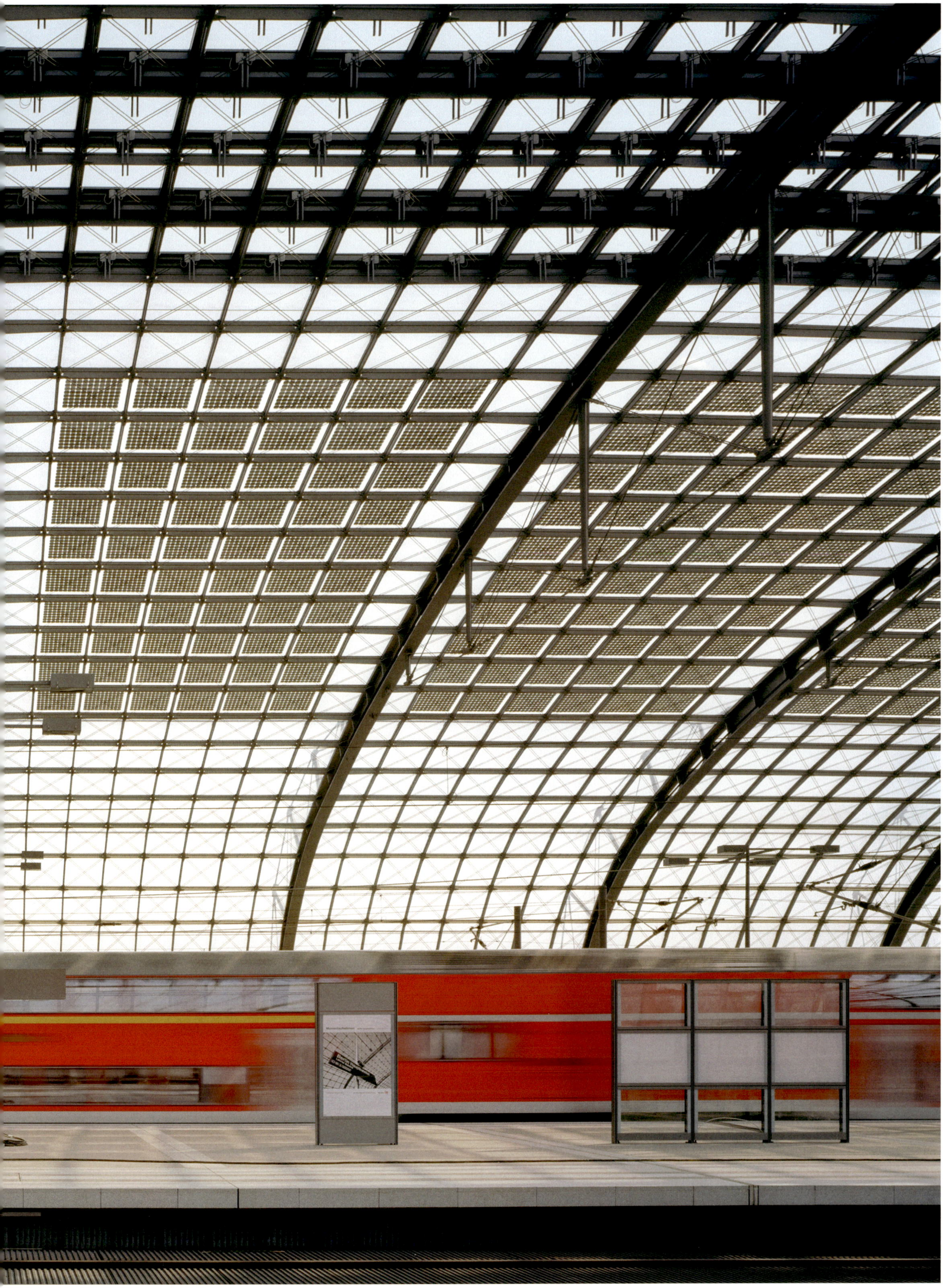

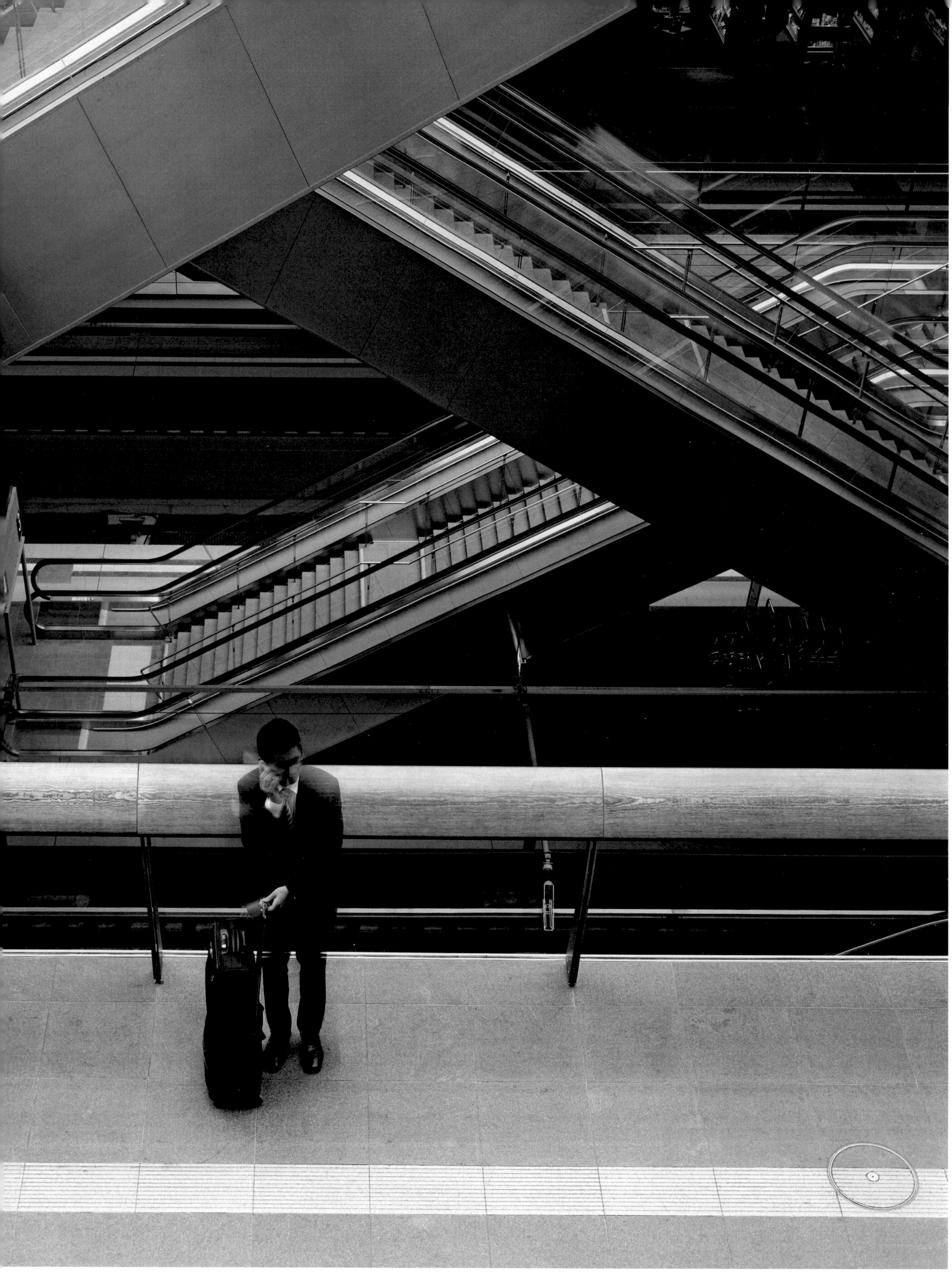

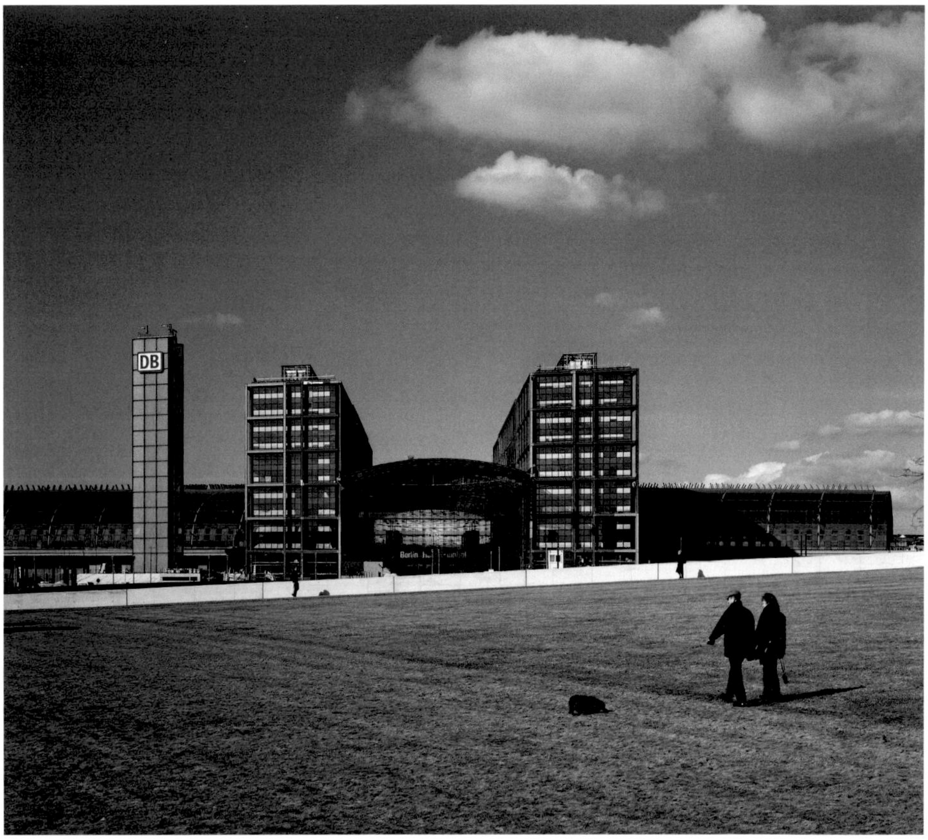
DB

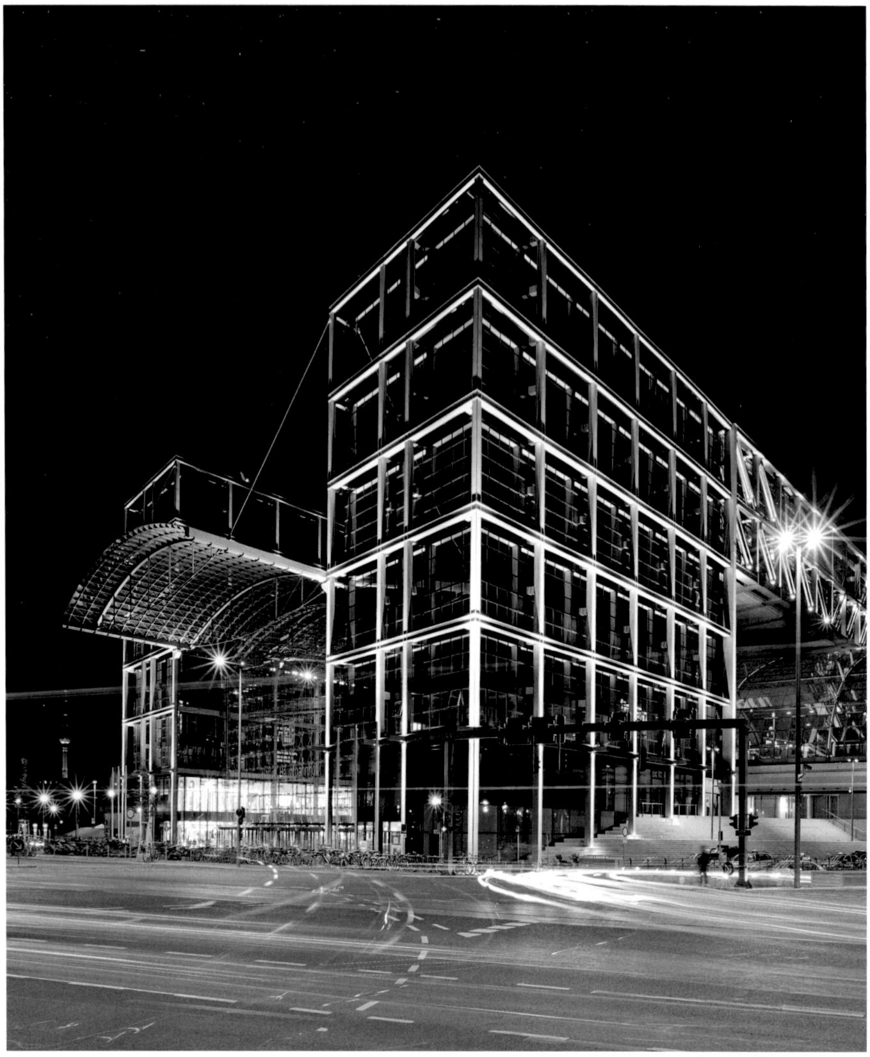

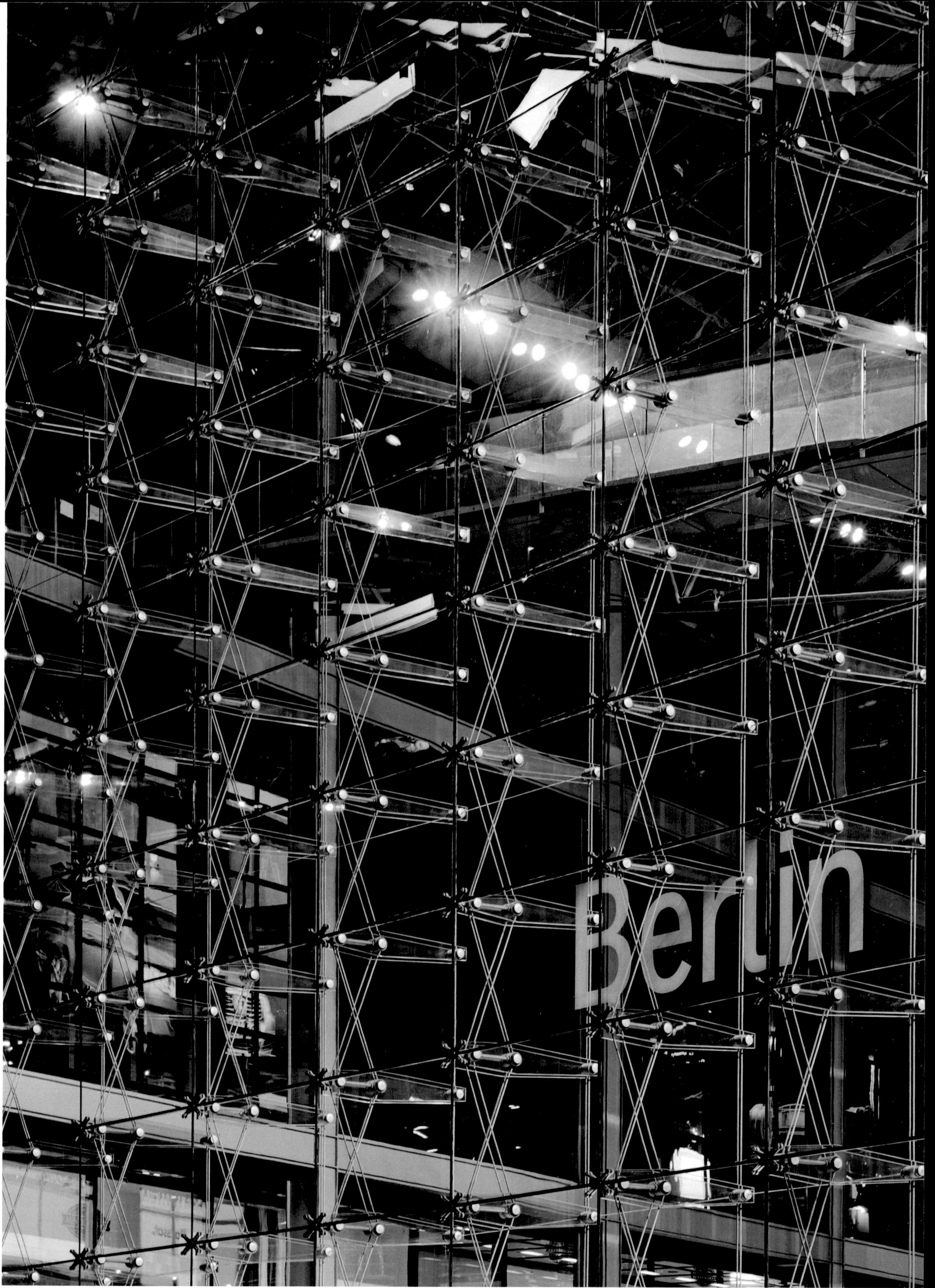
Berlin

Ausblick
Outlook

Marriott Hotel, Binjiang Plaza, Ningbo, China

Zwei gebogene, in der Mitte durch den gläsernen Erschließungskern verbundene Scheiben bilden die Grundstruktur des x-förmigen Büro- und Hotelhochhauses. Der jadegrünen Glaskeramikfassade sind horizontale Lamellen vorgelagert, die der Fassade Plastizität verleihen und einen wirksamen Sonnenschutz bieten.

Marriott Hotel, Binjiang Plaza, Ningbo, China

Two curved slabs connected in the centre via the glazed access core form the basic structure of the x-shaped office and hotel tower. In front of the jade-coloured façade made of glass ceramics, horizontal lamellae give plasticity to the façade and create an effective sunscreen.

Century Lotus Sportpark, Foshan, China

Das kreisrunde Stadion inmitten eines ringförmigen Wasserbeckens überragt als „Lotusblüte" den Sportpark mit Schwimmhalle. Die Speichenradkonstruktion des Tribünendachs mit der gefalteten weißen Membrandeckung misst 350 m im Durchmesser. Über dem Spielfeld lässt sich das Dach öffnen und schließen.

Century Lotus Sports Park, Foshan, China

Surrounded by a ring-like water basin, the circular stadium dominates the sports park with the swimming hall like a 'lotus blossom'. The spokes-wheel construction of the stand roof with the folded, white, membrane covering measures 350 m in diameter. Above the field the roof can be opened and closed.

Tourismus Center, Hangzhou, China

Die 27-geschossige Hochhausskulptur mit zwei in Höhe und Breite gestaffelten, über eine Glasfuge verbundenen Baukörpern dominiert das natursteinverkleidete Gebäudeensemble. Der neungeschossigen offenen Einkaufspassage ist ein großer Platz vorgelagert, von dem Treppen hinab in den Fährterminal führen.

Tourism Centre, Hangzhou, China

The 27-storey high-rise sculpture, consisting of two structures which are staggered in height and width and are connected via a glass joint, dominates the building ensemble clad in natural stone. From the large plaza in front of the 9-storey open mall stairs lead down to the ferry terminal.

Wohnen am Philosophenweg, Innenhafen Duisburg

Der Wechsel verglaster und geschlossener Loggien führt zu einer mäanderförmigen Gliederung der Fassaden, die in Anlehnung an die Bausubstanz des Industriehafens mit Ziegeln bzw. Klinkerplatten verkleidet sind. Weit auskragende Flugdächer bilden den signifikanten Abschluss der Staffelgeschosse.

Residential Buildings, Philosophenweg, Duisburg Inner Harbour

The interchange of glazed and closed loggias creates a meandering façade structure, which, in reference to the building fabric of the industrial harbour, are clad in bricks or clinker slabs. Widely-projecting shed roofs form the significant top of the staggered levels.

Polizeipräsidium Bonn

Der Solitär inmitten einer Parkanlage ist als leuchtend roter Bau mit rhythmischen Lochfassaden gestaltet. Weiße Stahlstrukturen kennzeichnen den Eingang und die gläserne Magistrale, die entlang der drei Höfe für kurze Wege sorgt und alle Abteilungen horizontal und vertikal verbindet.

Police Headquarters, Bonn

The solitaire in the midst of a park was designed as a vivid red building with rhythmically perforated façades. White steel structures mark the entrance and the glazed thoroughfare, which guarantees short distances along the three courtyards and connects all departments horizontally and vertically.

Christliche Kirche Peking, Haidin District

Die geschwungene Form der homogenen Gebäudehülle unterscheidet die Kirche von den umliegenden kommerziell genutzten Bauten. Durch den Wechsel von Öffnungen und geschlossenen Flächen verleiht das markante Stabwerk der Fassade dem Innenraum eine besondere, der sakralen Nutzung angemessene Lichtstimmung.

Beijing Christian Church, Haidin District

The curved form of the homogeneous building envelope distinguishes the church from the surrounding commercially used buildings. With its interplay of openings and solid areas, the façade's striking framework generates a special interior lighting atmosphere that is appropriate to the building's religious purpose.

Herzzentrum der Uniklinik Köln

Verglasungen und Holzpaneele gliedern die Natursteinfassade des H-förmigen Neubaus, dessen gläserne gebäudehohe Eingangshalle als Zentrum und Verteiler dient und somit auch das Hotel im Staffelgeschoss erschließt. Ein Innenhof im zweiten Obergeschoss ist als intimer Garten für die Patienten angelegt.

Centre for Cardiac Medicine, University Hospital, Cologne

Glazing and wooden panels structure the natural-stone façade of the H-shaped building. The glazed, building-high entrance hall serves as centre and circulation point and thus also provides access to the hotel on the top level. A courtyard on the second floor is laid out for the patients like a garden with an intimate atmosphere.

China Telecom, Häuser 12 und 13, Shanghai

Die quadratischen Gebäude nehmen technische Einrichtungen des digitalen Transfers sowie Büros auf. Ihre Fassaden bestehen oberhalb der Sockelzone aus einer vor die Außenwand gehängten gläsernen Haut, die, von hinten beleuchtet, mit abstrahierten technischen Schaltkreisen und Netzwerken bedruckt ist.

China Telecom, Buildings 12 and 13, Shanghai

The square buildings accommodate technical facilities for digital transfers as well as offices. Above the plinth zone their façades consist of a glass skin which is suspended in front of the exterior wall. Illuminated from behind it is printed upon with abstract technical circuits and networks.

Forschungsgebäude auf dem UKE-Campus, Hamburg

Der H-förmige Grundriss mit zentraler Erschließung ermöglicht eine optimale Anordnung der Büros und Labors entlang der Längsseiten und der gemeinschaftlich genutzten Flächen in der Gebäudemitte. Ein gepflasterter Hof dient als Vorplatz, während ein begrünter mit Sitzstufen zum Verweilen einlädt.

Research Building, Hamburg University Hospital

The H-shaped plan with central circulation allows for an optimal organization of offices and laboratories along the longitudinal sides and the commonly used areas in the centre of the building. A paved courtyard serves as a forecourt, whereas a landscaped one with steps invites one to sit down and linger.

Twin Towers, Dalian, China

Mittige Rücksprünge, die durch großflächige Verglasungen zu Wintergärten werden, kennzeichnen die beiden über 280 m hohen, im Grundriss rechteckigen Türme. Die zentralen gläsernen „Skylobbys" fassen jeweils acht Geschosse zusammen und bieten auch in den oberen Etagen großzügige Hallen und Foyers.

Twin Towers, Dalian, China

Both towers are more than 280 m high and based on rectangular floor plans. They are characterized by central recesses, which become conservatories thanks to their extensive glazing. These 'sky lobbies' span the height of eight floors each and allow for spacious halls and foyers also on the upper floors.

Internationales Bildungszentrum Hui Jia, Peking, China

Das Gebäude besteht aus sieben parallelen horizontal und vertikal gestaffelten Scheiben, die der Straße im Süden folgen. Auf der Nordseite schließen großzügige Terrassen an die Klassenzimmer und öffentlichen Veranstaltungsräume an. Eine öffentliche Bibliothek ergänzt das Bildungszentrum.

Hui Jia International Education Centre, Beijing, China

The building consists of seven parallel stripes, which are horizontally and vertically stepped back, following the line of the street to the south. On the north side, wide terraces adjoin the classrooms and public function rooms. A public library complements the eduction centre.

Internationales Messe- und Kongresszentrum Xi' an, China

Sieben identische Messehallen schließen wechselseitig an eine zentrale Passage mit begrünten Innenhöfen an, die als funktionales Rückgrat der Anlage auch die bereits vorhandene Halle anbindet. Galerien mit Besprechungsräumen bieten einen Überblick über die ebenerdigen Ausstellungsflächen der Hallen.

Xi' an International Conference and Exhibition Centre, China

Seven identical exhibition halls are arranged on both sides of a central mall with green inner courtyards. As a functional spine, the exhibition mall also links the existing hall to the complex. Galleries with meeting rooms offer a view of the halls' exhibition areas at ground level.

Wanda Plaza, Peking, China

Vertikale Türme entwickeln sich aus den horizontalen Sockeln der beiden mit hellem Naturstein verkleideten Gebäudeskulpturen. Mit den ausragenden oberen Geschossen der Türme, den Staffelgeschossen und den vertikalen Einschnitten entsteht eine markante Einheit im heterogenen Stadtgefüge.

Wanda Plaza, Beijing, China

Vertical towers develop from the horizontal socles of the two building sculptures clad in light-coloured natural stone. The projecting floors of the towers, the recessed top levels of the socles and the vertical recesses form a striking unity in the heterogeneous urban fabric.

Anhang
Appendix

Meinhard von Gerkan
Prof. Dr. h. c. mult. Dipl.-Ing. Architekt BDA

geboren am 3. Januar 1935 in Riga/Lettland.

1964	Diplom an der TU Carolo-Wilhelmina zu Braunschweig.
seit 1965	Freiberuflicher Architekt, zusammen mit Volkwin Marg. Mehr als 230 fertig gestellte Bauten. Mehr als 400 Preise in nationalen und internationalen Wettbewerben zusammen mit Volkwin Marg, darunter mehr als 200 erste Preise. Zahlreiche Preise für vorbildliche Bauten. Zahlreiche Veröffentlichungen im In- und Ausland. Zahlreiche Preisrichter- und Gutachtertätigkeit.
1972	Berufung in die Freie Akademie der Künste in Hamburg.
1974	Berufung an die TU Carolo-Wilhelmina zu Braunschweig als ordentlicher Professor/Lehrstuhl A für Entwerfen. Institutsleiter des Instituts für Baugestaltung A.
1982	Berufung in das Kuratorium der Jürgen-Ponto-Stiftung, Frankfurt.
1988	Gastprofessor an der Nihon Universität, Tokio/Japan.
1993	Gastprofessor an der Universität von Pretoria/Südafrika.
1995	American Institute of Architects, Honorary Fellow, USA. Ehrenauszeichnung der Mexikanischen Architektenkammer.
2000	Verleihung des Fritz-Schumacher-Preises der Alfred Töpfer Stiftung F.V.S.
2002	Außerordentliches Mitglied der Berlin-Brandenburgischen Akademie der Wissenschaften.
2002	Verleihung des Rumänischen Staatspreises.
2002	Verleihung der Ehrendoktorwürde durch den Fachbereich Evangelische Theologie an der Philipps-Universität Marburg.
2003	Konvent-Präsidiumsmitglied der Bundesstiftung Baukultur, Berlin.
2004	Verleihung der Plakette der Freien Akademie der Künste Hamburg.
2005	Großer Preis des Bundes Deutscher Architekten.
2005	Verleihung der Ehrendoktorwürde für Entwerfen durch die Chung Yuan Christian University in Chung Li/Taiwan.

born on January 3rd, 1935 in Riga/Latvia.

1964	Diploma in Architecture at the University Carolo-Wilhelmina at Braunschweig.
since 1965	Freelance architect together with Volkwin Marg. More than 230 completed buildings. More than 400 national and international competition awards together with Volkwin Marg, incl. more than 200 1st prizes. Numerous awards for outstanding buildings. Numerous publications in Germany and abroad. Considerable involvement in competition juries and feasibility studies.
1972	Appointment to the Free Academy of Arts, Hamburg.
1974	Appointment to the University Carolo-Wilhelmina at Braunschweig as professor/chair A for design. Director of the Institute for Architectural Design A.
1982	Appointment to the board of the Jürgen-Ponto-Foundation, Frankfurt.
1988	Guest professor at the Nihon University, Tokyo/Japan.
1993	Guest professor at the University of Pretoria/South Africa.
1995	American Institute of Architects, Honorary Fellow, USA.
1995	Honoured by the Mexican Architectural Society.
2000	Recipient of the Fritz Schumacher Award.
2002	Honorary Member of the Berlin-Brandenburg Academy of Sciences.
2002	Recipient of the Romanian National Award.
2002	Recipient of the Honorary Degree of Doctor conferred by the Faculty of Protestant Theology at the Philipps-University, Marburg.
2003	Member of Convent Chairmanship of the 'Bundesstiftung Baukultur', Berlin.
2004	Recipient of the 'Plakette' of Freie Akademie der Künste (Free Academy of Arts), Hamburg.
2005	Grand Award of the Association of German Architects (BDA).
2005	Recipient of the Honorary Degree of Doctor of Design conferred by the Christian University in Chung li/Taiwan.

Volkwin Marg
Prof. Dipl.-Ing. Architekt BDA

geboren am 15. Oktober 1936 in Königsberg/Ostpreußen, aufgewachsen in Danzig.

1964	Diplom-Examen an der TU Braunschweig.
seit 1965	Freiberuflicher Architekt mit Meinhard von Gerkan. Mehr als 230 fertig gestellte Bauten. Mehr als 400 Preise in nationalen und internationalen Wettbewerben zusammen mit Meinhard von Gerkan, darunter mehr als 200 erste Preise. Zahlreiche Preise für vorbildliche Bauten. Zahlreiche Veröffentlichungen und Vorträge im In- und Ausland zu Architektur, Städtebau und Kulturpolitik. Zahlreiche Preisrichter- und Gutachtertätigkeit.
1972	Berufung in die Freie Akademie der Künste in Hamburg.
1974	Berufung in die Deutsche Akademie für Städtebau und Landesplanung.
1975–1979	Vizepräsident des Bundes Deutscher Architekten BDA.
1979–1983	Präsident des BDA.
1986	Berufung an die RWTH Aachen, Fakultät Architektur, Lehrstuhl für Stadtbereichsplanung und Werklehre.
1996	Verleihung des Fritz-Schumacher-Preises der Alfred Töpfer Stiftung F.V.S.
2004	Verleihung der Plakette der Freien Akademie der Künste Hamburg.
2005	Großer Preis des Bundes Deutscher Architekten.
2006	Großer DAI Preis für Baukultur.

born on October 15th, 1936 in Königsberg/East Prussia, childhood in Danzig.

1964	Diploma in Architecture at the University Carolo-Wilhelmina at Braunschweig.
since 1965	Freelance architect together with Meinhard von Gerkan. More than 230 completed buildings. More than 400 national and international competition awards together with Meinhard von Gerkan, incl. more than 200 1st prizes. Numerous awards for outstanding buildings. Numerous publications and lectures in Germany and abroad on architecture, urban planning and cultural politics. Considerable involvement in competition juries and feasibility studies.
1972	Appointment to Freie Akademie der Künste (Free Academy of Arts), Hamburg.
1974	Appointment to German Academy for Urban and Environmental Planning.
1975–1979	Vice President of the Association of German Architects (BDA).
1979–1983	President of the Association of German Architects (BDA).
1986	Appointment to the Chair of Town Planning, Aachen University of Technology.
1996	Recipient of the Fritz Schumacher Award by the Alfred Töpfer Stiftung F.V.S.
2004	Recipient of the 'Plakette' of Freie Akademie der Künste (Free Academy of Arts), Hamburg.
2005	Grand Award of the Association of German Architects (BDA).
2006	Grand DAI (German Architects and Engineers Association) Award for Building Culture.

Hubert Nienhoff
Dipl.-Ing. Architekt

geboren am 4. August 1959 in Kirchhellen/Westfalen.

1985	Diplom-Examen an der RWTH Aachen.
1985–	
1987	Mitarbeit im Büro für Architektur und Stadtbereichsplanung Christoph Mäckler, Frankfurt/Main.
1987–	
1988	Auslandsaufenthalt in den USA, städtebauliche Studien.
1988–	
1991	Assistent an der RWTH Aachen, Lehrstuhl für Stadtbereichsplanung und Werklehre, Prof. Volkwin Marg.
1988	Mitarbeit im Büro von Gerkan, Marg und Partner, Aachen.
seit	
1993	Partner im Büro von Gerkan, Marg und Partner.

born on August 4th, 1959 in Kirchhellen/Westfalen.

1985	Diploma in architecture at the Aachen University RWTH.
1985–	
1987	Collaboration with Christoph Mäckler, Frankfurt/Main.
1987–	
1988	Foreign visit to USA with urban studies.
1988–	
1991	Assistant lecturer at the Aachen University RWTH, Chair for Town Planning, Prof. Volkwin Marg.
1988	Collaboration with von Gerkan, Marg und Partner, Aachen.
since	
1993	Partner of von Gerkan, Marg und Partner.

Nikolaus Goetze
Dipl.-Ing. Architekt

geboren am 25. September 1959 in Kempen.

1980	Architekturstudium an der RWTH Aachen.
1985–	
1986	Meisterklasse Prof. W. Holzbauer, Hochschule für angewandte Kunst, Wien.
1987	Diplom an der RWTH Aachen. Mitarbeit im Büro von Gerkan, Marg und Partner, Hamburg.
1994	Assoziierter Partner im Büro von Gerkan, Marg und Partner.
seit	
1998	Partner im Büro von Gerkan, Marg und Partner.

born on September 25th, 1959 in Kempen.

1980	Architectural education at Aachen University RWTH.
1985–	
1986	Master Class Prof. W. Holzbauer, University of Applied Arts, Vienna.
1987	Diploma in architecture at the Aachen University RWTH. Collaboration with von Gerkan, Marg and Partner.
1994	Associate Partner of von Gerkan, Marg und Partner.
since	
1998	Partner of von Gerkan, Marg und Partner.

Jürgen Hillmer
Dipl.-Ing. Architekt

geboren am 26. Dezember 1959 in Mönchengladbach.

1980	Architekturstudium an der TU Carolo-Wilhelmina in Braunschweig.
1988	Diplom.
1988–1992	Mitarbeit im Büro von Gerkan, Marg und Partner, Hamburg.
1992–1995	freiberuflicher Architekt in Haltern, Nordrhein-Westfalen.
1994	Assoziierter Partner im Büro von Gerkan, Marg und Partner.
seit 1998	Partner im Büro von Gerkan, Marg und Partner.

born on December 26th, 1959 in Mönchengladbach.

1980	Architectural education at the Carolo-Wilhelmina in Braunschweig.
1988	Diploma in architecture.
1988–1992	Collaboration with von Gerkan, Marg und Partner, Hamburg.
1992–1995	Freelance architect in Haltern, North Rhine-Westphalia.
1994	Associate Partner of von Gerkan, Marg und Partner.
since 1998	Partner of von Gerkan, Marg und Partner.

Stephan Schütz
Dipl.-Ing. Architekt BDA

geboren am 17. Februar 1966 in Duisburg.

1994	Diplom an der TU Braunschweig.
1994	Mitarbeit im Büro von Gerkan, Marg und Partner, Berlin.
2000–2004	Büroleitung im Büro von Gerkan, Marg und Partner, Peking, zusammen mit Wei Wu.
2004	Assoziierter Partner im Büro von Gerkan, Marg und Partner.
seit 2006	Partner im Büro von Gerkan, Marg und Partner.

born 17th February 1966 in Duisburg.

Diploma at the TU Braunschweig.

1994	Collaboration with von Gerkan, Marg und Partner.
2000–2004	Head of office von Gerkan, Marg und Partner, Beijing, together with Wei Wu.
2004	Associate Partner of von Gerkan, Marg und Partner.
since 2006	Partner of von Gerkan, Marg und Partner.

Wolfgang Haux
Dipl.-Ing. Architekt BDA

geboren am 13. August 1947 in Hamburg.

1969	Architekturstudium an der Hochschule für Bildende Künste.
1975	Diplom-Examen.
1976	Mitarbeit im Architekturbüro Prof. Dieter Hoor, Steinhorst.
1978	Mitarbeit im Büro von Gerkan, Marg und Partner, Hamburg.
seit 1994	Assoziierter Partner im Büro von Gerkan, Marg und Partner.

born on August 13th, 1947 in Hamburg.

1969	Architectural education at University of Fine Arts.
1975	Diploma in architecture.
1976	Collaboration with architectural practice Prof. Dieter Hoor, Steinhorst.
1978	Collaboration with von Gerkan, Marg und Partner, Hamburg.
since 1994	Associate Partner of von Gerkan, Marg und Partner.

Wei Wu
Dipl. Arch. ETH

geboren am 8. März 1971 in Lanzhou/Gansu, China.

1992	Bachelor of Technology (Architecture) am Chongqing Architecture and Engineering Institute in Chongqing, China.
1992–1994	Architekt am Gansu Institute of Architectural Design.
1994–1995	Studium der Deutschen Sprache in Freiburg (CH) und Zürich.
1995–1997	Architekturstudium an der Eidgenössischen Technischen Hochschule (ETH) in Zürich.
1997–2000	Mitarbeit im Büro Skyline Architecture und in der Firma SwissGerman Consulting in Zürich.
2000	Diplom an der ETH Zürich am Lehrstuhl Prof. Mario Campi.
2000–2001	Freier Mitarbeiter im Büro von Gerkan, Marg und Partner, Hamburg.
2001	Mitarbeit im Büro von Gerkan, Marg und Partner, Chefrepräsentant des gmp-Büros in Peking.
seit 2004	Assoziierter Partner im Büro von Gerkan, Marg und Partner.

born on 8 March 1971 in Lanzhou/Gansu, China.

1992	Bachelor of Technology (Architecture) at Chongqing Architecture and Engineering Institute in Chongqing, China.
1992–1994	Architect at Gansu Institute of Architectural Design.
1994–1995	German studies in Freiburg and Zurich, Switzerland.
1995–1997	Architectural study at ETH Zurich, Switzerland.
1997–2000	Work with Skyline Architecture and SwissGerman Consulting in Zurich, Switzerland.
2000	Diploma at ETH Zurich at Chair Prof. Mario Campi.
2000–2001	Free lance work with von Gerkan, Marg und Partner.
since 2001	Collaboration with von Gerkan, Marg und Partner, Chief representative of gmp office in Beijing.
since 2004	Associate Partner of von Gerkan, Marg und Partner.

Büroprofil
The Practice

Die 1965 von Meinhard von Gerkan und Volkwin Marg gegründete Architektensozietät besteht mittlerweile aus sechs weiteren Partnern. Mit über 300 Mitarbeitern, die sich auf acht Büros verteilen, ist gmp im In- und Ausland aktiv.

gmp gehört zu den wenigen Büros mit einer generalistischen Position, die sich für ein Projekt von seiner entwurflichen Idee und deren Realisierung bis hin zum Interieurdesign verantwortlich fühlt.

Meinhard von Gerkan, Volkwin Marg und ihre Partner haben in den vergangenen 40 Jahren in nahezu allen großen Städten der Bundesrepublik geplant und gebaut. Ihre Projekte reichen von Einfamilienhäusern, Hotels, Museen, Theatern und Konzerthallen, Bürogebäuden, Handelszentren und Krankenhäusern bis hin zu Forschungs-, Sport- und Bildungseinrichtungen sowie Verkehrsbauten, Gewerbebauten und Masterplanungen.

Bekannt wurde gmp vor allem durch seine Flughafen-Architektur: 1975 wurde Berlin-Tegel als Drive-In-Airport eröffnet. Dieser innovative Entwurf ist für die Abflug- und Ankunftebenen der Flughäfen Stuttgart und Hamburg weiterentwickelt worden. Weltweite Beachtung finden nicht nur ihre Projekte wie die Neue Messe Leipzig, die Messe Rimini oder der Christus Pavillon für die EXPO 2000, sondern auch ihre Entwürfe, z. B. für die Restrukturierung und Überdachung des Olympiastadions in Berlin, das RheinEnergie-Stadion in Köln oder für den im Jahr 2006 fertig gestellten Berliner Hauptbahnhof. Bei nationalen und internationalen Wettbewerben errang gmp über 400 Preise, darunter mehr als 200 erste Preise sowie zahlreiche Auszeichnungen für beispielhafte Architektur. Mehr als 230 Bauten sind bis heute realisiert.

In China sind unter anderem die Messe- und Kongresszentren in Nanning und Shenzhen sowie das Museum in Shanghai-Pudong, das Zhongguancun Kulturzentrum in Peking und der Sportpark in Foshan realisiert. Weitere Projekte befinden sich in Bau und in Planung, darunter die Oper in Chongqing, das Chinesische Nationalmuseum in Peking sowie das Siemens Center in Shanghai.

Mit ihren städtebaulichen Studien für „Stuttgart 21", „Frankfurt 21" und „Bukarest 2000" sowie einer Vielzahl städtebaulicher Projekte in China, darunter die Planung von Lingang New City, haben von Gerkan, Marg und Partner ihre Kompetenz auch auf diesem Gebiet unter Beweis gestellt.

Zurzeit engagiert sich gmp mit Projekten außerhalb Deutschlands unter anderem in China, Vietnam – wo das Nationale Kongress-Zentrum fertig gestellt wurde –, Russland, Italien, Spanien, der Türkei, Luxemburg und mit bereits sechs realisierten Projekten in Lettland.

The architectural practice von Gerkan, Marg und Partner was founded by Meinhard von Gerkan and Volkwin Marg in 1965. Since its inception it has grown to include six additional partners and more than 300 employees in eight offices in Germany and abroad.

gmp is one of the few practices with a generalist position, which takes responsibility for a project from the design idea and its realisation right through to the interior design.

In the past forty years Meinhard von Gerkan, Volkwin Marg and their partners have planned and constructed buildings in most major German cities. They have designed small scale homes, hotels, museums, theatres and concert halls, office buildings, commercial centres and hospitals as well as research, educational and sports facilities, buildings for transportation, trade and industry buildings and master plans.

gmp became internationally known as a team of airport architects when, in 1975, the Berlin-Tegel building with its drive-in airplane terminal for 'stacked parking' was established. This innovative design has been further developed to transform the departure and arrival halls at Stuttgart and Hamburg airports.

They are internationally recognized not only for their projects like the New Trade Fair in Leipzig, the Rimini Exhibition Centre or the Christ Pavilion for the EXPO 2000, but also for their designs. Key examples are the designs for the reconstruction and roofing of the Olympic Stadium in Berlin, the RheinEnergie Stadium in Cologne or Berlin Central Station, which was completed in 2006. gmp has succeeded in winning more than 400 prizes in national and international competitions, among them more than 200 first prizes and a large number of awards for exemplary architecture. More than 230 buildings have been constructed by gmp worldwide.

Amongst others, the exhibition and congress centres in Nanning and Shenzhen, the Shanghai-Pudong museum, the Zhongguancun Cultural Centre in Beijing as well as the Foshan Sports Park have been realized in China. Numerous projects are under construction or in the planning stage, for example the Chongqing Opera House, the Chinese National Museum in Beijing and the Siemens Centre in Shanghai.

Von Gerkan, Marg und Partner have demonstrated town-planning competence with their visionary proposals for the urban master plan of Bucharest/Romania, the projects 'Stuttgart 21' and 'Frankfurt 21' for the Deutsche Bahn as well as many urban projects in China, including the planning of Lingang New City.

Aside from Germany, gmp is currently also involved in projects in China, Vietnam – where the National Congress Centre was built –, in Russia, Italy, Spain, Turkey, Luxemburg and Latvia with six realized projects, to name a few.

„Angemessene und akzeptable Antworten und Lösungen auf die Probleme der Umweltgestaltung zu finden, setzt voraus, zum Dialog bereit zu sein und seinen eigenen Standpunkt auch auf veränderte Bedingungen einzustellen. Die Entscheidung, was und wie gebaut wird, trifft die Gesellschaft mit ihren komplizierten politischen und wirtschaftlichen Mechanismen. Wir Architekten haben nicht nur die Verpflichtung, wir haben die Verantwortung, uns diesem Dialog zu stellen und mit innerer Überzeugung am Gespräch teilzunehmen."

'The development of appropriate and acceptable answers and solutions for problems demands an openness for dialogue and the adaptation of one's standpoint to changing conditions. Society and its complex political and economic mechanisms decide what is being built in what fashion. We architects have not only the obligation, but the responsibility to lay ourselves open to this dialogue and take part in the discussions with a firm conviction.'

Meinhard von Gerkan

gmp Philosophie
gmp Philosophy

Unser Ideal ist es, die Dinge so einfach zu gestalten, dass sie inhaltlich und zeitlich Bestand haben. Formale Zurückhaltung und Materialeinheitlichkeit liegen in diesem Bekenntnis begründet, weil für uns Sinnfälligkeit ein kategorischer Imperativ ist. Wir wollen ein Haus lediglich selbstverständlich gestalten, es zur Hülle für die Vielfalt des menschlichen Daseins möglichst dauerhaft ausbilden. Expressionistische Formen, die nur der künstlerischen Willkür entspringen, ohne Bezug zur Nutzung, Konstruktion und Gebrauchstüchtigkeit, versuchen wir durch kritische Distanz zu aktuellen Architekturerscheinungen zu meiden. Von den Medien wird diese tradierte Einfachheit zur „neuen" Einfachheit umetikettiert. Der auf die Spitze getriebene Purismus, der sich in den Zeichnungen durch Informationsverweigerung und in den Bauten durch eine allzu herbe Kargheit ausdrückt, bleibt uns jedoch fremd. Wir meinen eine Reduktion, die auf Plausibilität und Selbstverständlichkeit bezogen ist und vermeintliche Stilbrüche, die durch Aufgabenstellung und Standort provoziert werden, integrieren muss. Für die Konzeption von Gebäuden und Interieurdesign gelten die Positionen des dialogischen Entwerfens als Leitlinie unserer Architekturauffassung:

_ **Einfachheit**
Suche in deinen Entwürfen nach der sinnfälligsten Lösung. Erstrebe vom Einfachen das Beste.

_ **Vielfalt und Einheit**
Schaffe die Einheit in der Vielfalt. Erzeuge die Vielfalt in der Einheit.

_ **Unverwechselbarkeit**
Entwickle eine Identität des Entwurfs aus dem Spezifischen der Situation und der Aufgabe.

_ **Strukturelle Ordnung**
Gib den Entwürfen eine strukturelle Ordnung. Organisiere die Funktionen zu klaren Bauformen.

Our ideal is to design in such a reduced form, that the results endure content and time. Formal restriction and uniformity of materials contribute to this standpoint because we understand obviousness as a categorical imperative. We want to design a house simply as a statement, to form it as a durable cover for the variety of human existence. With a critical distance from recent architectural expressions, we try to avoid expressionist forms which are only derived from artistic caprice, without reference to use, construction and functionality. The media renames this traditional simplicity as 'new' simplicity. This purism carried to extremes, expressed as a denial of information in drawings and as severely barren buildings, remains alien to us. We want a reduction which is based on plausibility and self-evidence and has to integrate supposed stylistic inconsistencies provoked by building task and site.

For the conception of buildings and interiors the positions of dialogical design are relevant as the guidelines of our architectural understanding:

_ **Simplicity**
Search for the clearest solution for your design. Strive for the best of simplicity.

_ **Variety and uniformity**
Create uniformity within variety. Create variety within uniformity.

_ **Distinctiveness**
Develop an identity of the design from the specific conditions of location and task.

_ **Structural order**
Render a structural order to the design. Organize functions as clear building forms.

Auszeichnungen
Distinctions

Über 400 Wettbewerbspreise insgesamt seit 1964, davon mehr als 200 erste Preise

Auswahl

- Bukarest 2000, Rumänien
- Expo 2000 Plaza, Hannover
- Flughäfen Berlin-Tegel, München II, Moskau, Algier, Hamburg
- Nationalbibliothek, Teheran, Iran
- Hochschule für Bildende Künste, Hamburg
- Verlagshaus Gruner & Jahr, Hamburg
- Deutsche Schule in Peking, China
- Neue Messe Leipzig
- Flughafen Berlin Brandenburg International
- Berlin Hauptbahnhof
- Hörsaalzentrum, Techn. Universität Chemnitz
- Christus-Pavillon, Expo 2000, Hannover
- Mediencenter Leipzig
- Olympiastadion Berlin, Restrukturierung
- Internationales Messe- und Kongresszentrum Nanning, China
- Messe- und Kongresszentrum Shenzhen, China
- Lingang New City, China
- Pionierschule Ingolstadt
- Museum in Shanghai-Pudong, China
- Parlamentsgebäude und Konferenzzentrum Hanoi, Vietnam
- Chinesisches Nationalmuseum, Peking

Über 120 Auszeichnungen für gute Architektur

Auswahl

- BDA-Preise
- Deutscher Architekturpreis
- Deutscher Stahlbaupreis
- Balthasar-Neumann-Preis
- Bauwerk des Jahres
- Mies-van-der-Rohe-Preis
- FIAIBCI Prix d'Excellence
- Peter-Joseph-Krahe-Preis
- USITT Architectural Honor Awards
- red dot Award
- Lichtarchitekturpreis
- Renault Traffic Design Award

More than 400 competition awards since 1964, incl. 200 first prizes

Selection

- Bucharest 2000, Romania
- Expo 2000 Plaza, Hanover
- Airports Berlin-Tegel, Munich II, Moscow, Algiers, Hamburg
- National Library, Teheran, Iran
- Academy of Fine Arts, Hamburg
- Gruner & Jahr Publishing House, Hamburg
- German School in Beijing, China
- New Trade Fair, Leipzig
- Berlin Brandenburg International Airport
- Lecture Theatre Centre, Chemnitz Technical University
- Berlin Central Station
- Christ Pavilion, Expo 2000, Hanover
- Media City, Leipzig
- Reconstruction of the Olympic Stadium, Berlin
- Nanning International Conference & Exhibition Center, China
- Shenzhen Convention and Exhibition Center, China
- Lingang New City, China
- Sapper School, Ingolstadt
- Museum in Shanghai-Pudong, China
- National Assembly House and Conference Hall, Hanoi, Vietnam
- Chinese National Museum, Beijing

More than 120 awards for outstanding architecture

Selection

- BDA-Preise
- Deutscher Architekturpreis
- Deutscher Stahlbaupreis
- Balthasar-Neumann-Preis
- Bauwerk des Jahres
- Mies-van-der-Rohe-Preis
- FIAIBCI Prix d'Excellence
- Peter-Joseph-Krahe-Preis
- USITT Architectural Honor Award
- red dot award
- Lichtarchitekturpreis
- Renault Traffic Design Award

Publikationen
Publications

Auswahl
Selection

1994 **Architektur im Dialog**
Verlag Ernst und Sohn Berlin

1997 **Architecture for Transportation – Architektur für den Verkehr**
Birkhäuser Verlag
Basel, Boston, Berlin

1997 **Neue Messe Leipzig – New Trade Fair Leipzig**
Birkhäuser Verlag
Basel, Boston, Berlin

1997 **The Architecture of von Gerkan, Marg + Partners**
Prestel Verlag München, New York

2000 **Modell/Virtuell – Analoge und digitale Medien in der Architektur**
Verlag Ernst und Sohn Berlin

2002 **VOL 2**
gmp - von Gerkan, Marg und Partner
Erlebnisräume – Spaces Design + Construction
awf-Verlag Heidelberg

2002 von Gerkan, Marg und Partner
La Nuova Fiera di Rimini/ The Rimini Trade Fair
Federico Motta Editore Milano

2003 **Architecture 2000–2001**
von Gerkan, Marg und Partner
Birkhäuser Verlag
Basel, Boston, Berlin

2004 von Gerkan, Marg und Partner
Architecture 1966–2001
9 Miniaturbände im Schuber
9 miniature volumes in a slipcase
Birkhäuser Verlag
Basel, Boston, Berlin

2005 **Ideale Stadt – Reale Projekte Ideal City – Real Projects**
Architekten von Gerkan, Marg und Partner in China
Hatje Cantz Verlag Ostfildern

2005 **Architecture 2001–2003**
von Gerkan, Marg und Partner
Birkhäuser Verlag
Basel, Boston, Berlin

2005 **VOL 3**
gmp – von Gerkan, Marg und Partner
Berliner Bauten und Projekte 1965–2005
Buildings and Projects in Berlin 1965–2005

2006 **Stadien und Arenen Stadia and Arenas**
von Gerkan, Marg und Partner
Hatje Cantz Verlag Ostfildern

2006 **VOL 4**
gmp – von Gerkan, Marg und Partner
Private Houses
Jovis Verlag Berlin

2007 **VOL 5**
gmp – von Gerkan, Marg und Partner
Möbel Furniture
Jovis Verlag Berlin

seit 1965 mehr als zweitausend Publikationen in in- und ausländischen Büchern, Jahrbüchern, Fachzeitschriften sowie Tageszeitungen über Bauten und Entwürfe von von Gerkan, Marg und Partner.

since 1965 – more than two-thousand publications in German and international books, annuals, technical journals and newspapers featuring the buildings and concepts of von Gerkan, Marg und Partner.

Bildnachweis
Picture Credits

Dieter Ameling 351

Gerhard Aumer 185-2, 187-3, 188, 192, 208, 254, 255-1, 256-3, 262, 280, 293-1, 298, 300, 320, 360, 410

Hans Bach 285, 289, 296-3

Gert von Bassewitz 33-3, 161

Bau Bild Berlin/Stefan Falk 257-1, 257-2, 291, 297-1

Sanderine Biermann 220/221

Blende 45/Nipp 283

Felix Borkenau 447-2

Ulrike & Andreas Braun 256-1

Marcus Bredt 38-3, 46, 47, 48, 49, 50, 51, 53, 55, 56, 57, 59, 405, 482, 502/503, 539-3, 548, 549, 550/551, 552, 553, 554, 555

Hans-Christoph Brinkschmidt 112 o., 115

Richard Bryant 128, 129, 134-3, 135-3, 137-2, 147, 151

Burg/Schuh 95-2, 229-3

Busam + Richter 217-1, 218, 219

Francesco Castanga 491-2

Ebba Dangschat 484/485

Wilfried Dechau 564

Dorfmüller + Kröger 490-1

Guna Eglite 467-3, 471, 472, 473

Hans-Georg Esch 185-1, 222

Bernt Federau 33-1, 64, 65-1, 65-3, 67, 69, 72, 78-2, 79-3, 80-2

Klaus Frahm 113, 116, 117, 136-3, 156, 157-1, 158, 160, 163, 164/165, 167, 170, 171-1, 171-2, 172, 173-1, 173-2, 175, 178, 179, 180/181, 182, 183, 185-3, 186, 187-1, 187-2, 189, 191, 193, 194/195, 196, 197, 198, 199, 201, 202, 203, 204, 205, 207, 209, 210/211, 212, 213, 214/215, 216, 225-2, 225-3, 226-1, 227-1, 227-2, 229-1, 229-2, 236, 341-3, 237, 240/241, 243, 244, 245, 251, 253, 256-2, 258, 259, 260/261, 275, 276, 277, 278, 279, 281, 282, 299, 332, 333, 340, 341-1, 343-1, 343-2, 345-2, 345-3, 347, 348, 349, 354, 358/359, 371, 374, 387, 388, 389, 390, 391, 393, 394-1, 394-3, 395-3, 396-2, 397, 398-1, 399-2, 401, 402, 403, 411, 412, 413, 416, 417, 418, 419, 421, 423, 424, 425, 427, 429, 430, 431, 432, 433, 434, 435, 447-3, 449-3, 469-3, 487, 488/489, 493-1, 511

Franz Sill GmbH 344-2

Christian Gahl 398-2, 398-3, 415, 436, 437, 438, 439, 441, 443/443, 444, 445, 451-3, 462, 463, 464/465, 469-2, 514/515, 525, 526, 527, 533, 534, 535, 539-2

Wolf-Dieter Gericke 148/149, 150, 157-3, 168, 169, 173-3, 269, 270/271, 451-1

gmp Archiv 33-2, 35, 37-1, 37-3, 38-1, 38-6, 41-2, 41-3, 63, 65-2, 71, 75, 78-1, 78-3, 79-1, 79-2, 81-1, 81-3, 85, 87-3, 89-2, 89-3, 100-3, 157-2, 171-3, 242, 342-2, 356-2, 356-3, 370, 380, 451-2, 490-2, 497, 520-1, 522-2, 523-2, 537-3, 538-1, 538-2, 539-1, 557-1, 557-2, 557-3, 558-1, 559-3, 560, 561, 568-2

Reinhard Görner 232

Götz Werkfoto 39-2

Bernadette Grimmenstein 177, 449-1

Hapag Lloyd 217-3

Heinrich Heidersberger 37-2, 43, 61-2

Oliver Heissner 296-1, 492-3, 521-2

Jochen Helle 396-3, 399-3, 414

Franz Heller 345-1

Jörg Hempel 493-2, 523-3, 558-2

A. K. Holstein 565

Roland Horn 545, 546, 547

Gert Kähler 10, 11, 12, 13, 14, 15, 16, 17, 18, 19, 20, 21, 22, 23, 24, 25, 26, 27, 28, 29, 30

Bertram Kober 217-2, 223

Tim Kölln 567-2

Waltraud Krase 70-1

Hans-Joachim Krumnow 520-2

Landesbildstelle Berlin 38-2, 45

Heiner Leiska 80-1, 81-2, 83, 86, 87-1, 87-2, 89-1, 91, 93, 94, 95-1, 95-3, 96, 97, 98, 99, 100-1, 100-2, 101, 103, 104, 105, 106, 107-1, 107-3, 109, 110/111, 112 u., 119, 121, 123, 124, 125, 127, 130, 131, 134-1, 136-1, 137-3, 143, 144, 145, 146, 153, 154/155, 257-3, 293-3, 295-1, 295-2, 307, 308, 310, 314, 315, 317, 318, 319, 328, 329, 330, 331, 372/373, 375, 399-1, 428, 447-1, 448-2, 452, 453, 454, 455, 456, 457, 467-2, 492-1, 495, 496, 499, 500/501, 504/505, 520-3, 521-1, 521-3, 523-1, 529, 530, 531, 559-2, 559-3

Luftbild Laubner 268

Stefan Marquardt 490-3

Ben McMillan 537-1, 537-2

MERO 286/287, 467-1

Arved Messmer 396-1, 406/407, 408, 409

Sigrid Neubert 70-2

Klemens Ortmeyer 139, 140/141, 378, 379, 381

Michael Pfisterer 536

Uwe Rau 39-1, 88

Dominik Reipka 395-2

Hans-Christian Schink/PUNCTUM 225-1, 226-3, 227-3, 228, 230, 231, 233, 234, 235, 246, 247, 248, 249, 255-2, 255-3, 263, 264/265, 266, 267, 273, 288, 295-3, 296-2, 309, 312/313, 321, 322/323, 324/325, 326/327, 343-3, 344-1, 459, 460, 461

Jürgen Schmidt 73, 226-2, 239, 293-2, 297-2, 297-3, 301, 302/303, 304/305, 311, 334, 335, 336, 337, 338, 339, 342-1, 352/253, 355, 356-1, 357, 361, 376, 383, 384, 385, 394-2, 446, 448-1, 468, 491-1, 491-3, 507, 508/509, 522-1

Uwe Schossig 449-2

Ute-Karen Seggelke 566, 567-1, 568-1

Jan Siefke 366, 367, 368/369, 395-1, 469-1, 475, 476/477, 478/479, 480/481, 492-2, 493-3, 513, 516/517, 518, 519, 522-3, 538-3, 541, 542/543

Frank Springer 132/133

Wilfried Täubner 40-1, 40-2, 41-1, 60, 61-2, 61-3

Tuyen Tran-Viet 284

Vincents 274

Ingrid Voth-Amslinger 77

Andreas Wiese 377

Michael Wortmann 107-2, 134-2, 135-1, 135-2, 136-2, 137-1

Chaoying Yang 341-2, 363, 365

Trotz intensiver Recherche ist es nicht gelungen, sämtliche Rechteinhaber ausfindig zu machen. Zur Klärung bitten wir, sich mit dem Herausgeber in Verbindung zu setzen.